THE REGIONAL AND TRANSREGIONAL IN ROMANESQUE EUROPE

The Regional and Transregional in Romanesque Europe considers the historiography and usefulness of regional categories and in so doing explores the strength, durability, mutability, and geographical scope of regional and transregional phenomena in the Romanesque period.

This book addresses the complex question of the significance of regions in the creation of Romanesque, particularly in relation to transregional and pan-European artistic styles and approaches. The categorization of Romanesque by region was a cornerstone of 19th- and 20th-century scholarship, albeit one vulnerable to the application of anachronistic concepts of regional identity. Individual chapters explore the generation and reception of forms, the conditions that give rise to the development of transregional styles and the agencies that cut across territorial boundaries. There are studies of regional styles in Aquitaine, Castile, Sicily, Hungary, and Scandinavia; workshops in Worms and the Welsh Marches; the transregional nature of liturgical furnishings; the cultural geography of the new monastic orders; metalworking in Hildesheim and the valley of the Meuse; and the links which connect Piemonte with Conques.

The Regional and Transregional in Romanesque Europe offers a new vision of regions in the creation of Romanesque relevant to archaeologists, art historians, and historians alike.

John McNeill teaches at Oxford University's Department of Continuing Education and is Honorary Secretary of the British Archaeological Association, for whom he has edited and contributed to volumes on Anjou, King's Lynn and the Fens, the medieval cloister, and English medieval chantries. He was instrumental in establishing the BAA's International Romanesque Conference Series and has a particular interest in the design of medieval monastic precincts.

Richard Plant has taught at a number of institutions and worked for many years at Christie's Education in London, where he was deputy academic director. His research interests lie in the buildings of the Anglo-Norman realm and the Holy Roman Empire, in particular in architectural iconography. He is Publicity Officer for the British Archaeological Association, and in addition to this volume has co-edited *Romanesque and the Past* (2013), *Romanesque Patrons and Processes* (2018), and *Romanesque Saints, Shrines and Pilgrimage* (2020).

THE REGIONAL AND TRANSREGIONAL IN ROMANESQUE EUROPE

Edited by
John McNeill and Richard Plant

BRITISH ARCHAEOLOGICAL ASSOCIATION
2021

LONDON AND NEW YORK

First published 2021
by Routledge
4 Park Square, Milton Park, Abingdon, Oxon OX14 4RN

and by Routledge
605 Third Avenue, New York, NY 10158

Routledge is an imprint of the Taylor & Francis Group, an informa business

British Library Cataloguing-in-Publication Data
A catalogue record for this book is available from the British Library

Library of Congress Cataloging-in-Publication Data
Names: McNeill, John, 1957– editor. | Plant, Richard, 1962– editor. | British Archaeological Association. Biennial International Romanesque Conference (5th : 2018 : Université de Poitiers)
Title: The regional and transregional in Romanesque Europe / edited by John McNeill and Richard Plant.
Description: Abingdon, Oxon ; New York, NY : Routledge, 2021. | Includes bibliographical references and index.
Identifiers: LCCN 2021028727 (print) | LCCN 2021028728 (ebook) | ISBN 9780367755270 (hardback) | ISBN 9780367752552 (paperback) | ISBN 9781003162827 (ebook)
Subjects: LCSH: Architecture, Romanesque. | Art, Romanesque. | Cultural geography—Europe—History—To 1500. | Civilization, Medieval—Historiography.
Classification: LCC NA390 .R44 2021 (print) | LCC NA390 (ebook) | DDC 709.02/16—dc23
LC record available at https://lccn.loc.gov/2021028727
LC ebook record available at https://lccn.loc.gov/2021028728

ISBN: 9780367755270 (hbk)
ISBN: 9780367752552 (pbk)
ISBN: 9781003162827 (ebk)

DOI: 10.4324/9781003162827

Typeset in Times New Roman
by Apex CoVantage, LLC

CONTENTS

NOTES ON CONTRIBUTORS

Claude Andrault-Schmitt is Professor Emerita of Medieval Art History at the *Centre d'études supérieures de civilisation médiévale* (University of Poitiers). She works on monastic architecture of the 12th and 13th centuries, as well as the early Gothic architecture of Aquitaine and the Loire Valley. She has written or directed monographs on Notre-Dame-la-Grande at Poitiers, the Cathedral of Tours, canonial life and culture at St-Yrieix, the abbey of Solignac and, above all, on Poitiers Cathedral. Besides more synthetic papers for various journals, Claude has published a number of short monographs for the Société française d'archéologie in its annual *Congrès archéologique*. She is currently co-director of an archaeological programme for the ducal palace in Poitiers. Claude is also president of the *Societé des Antiquaires de l'Ouest* and edits its journal.

Marcello Angheben is Lecturer in Medieval Art History at the University of Poitiers and a member of the *Centre d'études supérieures de civilisation médiévale*. His research centres on imagery between the 11th and 14th centuries, particularly as it is found in sculpture, wall-painting, stained glass, metalwork and manuscript illumination, with a particular interest in the iconography of the Last Judgement and Apocalypse. He has published widely on Romanesque sculpture and wall-painting in France, among which publications are *Les chapiteaux romans de Bourgogne: thèmes et programmes* (2003), *D'un jugement à l'autre: La représentation du jugement immédiat dans le jugements derniers françaises 1100–1250* (2013), and *Les portails romans de Bourgogne* (2020). He is currently completing an interdisciplinary study of the paintings in the nave of Saint-Savin-sur-Gartempe, as part of a research project which was preceded by a colloquium on representations of the Old Testament between the 4th and 12th centuries, which was published as *Les stratégies de la narration dans la peinture médiévale* (2020). He is also currently working on the functions of images attached to altars in France, Italy, and Spain between the 11th and 14th centuries in terms of the Eucharist, devotion, and patronage.

Tancredi Bella is Professor of Medieval Art History at the University of Catania. Since 2012, he has been a member of the Centre d'Études Supérieures de Civilisation Médiévale (CÉSCM) at the University of Poitiers. He completed his PhD research at the Faculty of Architecture of the University of Catania in 2009. In the three-year period 2017–19 he was external professor in History of Medieval Architecture at the Catholic University of Milan. His studies focus on Norman architecture in Sicily and the historical-artistic and monumental remains of the medieval settlements of the Holy Land in eastern Sicily. He also deals with Lombard Romanesque architecture as well as the historiography of medieval art in the 19th century. On these topics he has published essays and articles in both Italian and international journals. He has published two books; *S. Andrea a Piazza Armerina, priorato dell'Ordine del Santo Sepolcro. Vicende costruttive, cicli pittorici e spazio liturgico* (2012); *La Basilica di S. Ambrogio a Milano. L'opera Inedita di Fernand de Dartein* (2013). He is currently preparing another book for publication on the medieval configuration of the Norman cathedral of Catania (2021).

Sheila Bonde is the Christopher Chan and Michelle Ma Professor of the History of Art at Brown University. Her research combines architectural history, archival research, archaeology, and social anthropological approaches to the medieval built and non-built environment. Professor Bonde's published work includes the book *Fortress-Church: Architecture, Religion and Conflict in Twelfth-Century Languedoc*, the co-edited volume *Re-Presenting the Past*, and a special digital issue of *Speculum* devoted to Digital Medieval Studies. With Clark Maines, she has co-directed excavations at six monastic sites, and co-authored numerous publications on the Augustinian abbey of Saint-Jean-des-Vignes in Soissons, including *Saint-Jean-des-Vignes: Approaches to Its Architecture, Archaeology and History*, and *Saint-Jean-des-Vignes, Soissons*.

Philip Bovey read History at Peterhouse, Cambridge, where he was a Scholar. He spent most of his working life as a UK Civil Servant, reaching the relatively high level of Under-Secretary at an early age. At that level he would normally have spent his time on management, but his lack of conformity and failure to support management initiatives (and probably lack of ability in that respect) meant that he progressed no further. However, the result was that he was given non-mainstream projects involving extensive research and analysis such as areas of 'old' law (for example, corporate law), often dating back to the Middle Ages, which the Government were seeking to modernise (or the EU to harmonise), with a view to understanding what it was important to keep and what could be changed or dispensed with. Following his retirement, he has applied these skills in research into a long-term interest in the depiction of (mainly) Romanesque architecture, seeking to analyse how the portrayal, particularly in printed photographic books, affects our perception of the subject matter. As part of that research, he was awarded the Associateship of the Royal Photographic Society for a submission of large-format (10″×8″) photographs of Burgundian Romanesque churches.

Jordi Camps i Sòria is Chief Curator of the Medieval Department of the Museu Nacional d'Art de Catalunya (MNAC, Barcelona). He has been Associate Professor at the Universitat de Barcelona and at the Universitat Autònoma de Barcelona. His research is focused on sculpture in Catalonia between the 11th and 13th centuries, such as the cloisters at Ripoll, Solsona, Tarragona, the Cabestany Master, Majesties, and Descent from the Cross groups, etc. Part of his work is also concerned with museography and museology, in relation to the collections of Romanesque art at MNAC, especially in terms of mural painting. He has curated several exhibitions: *Obras Maestras del Románico. Esculturas del Valle de Boí*, coordinated with the musée national du Moyen Âge in Paris, in collaboration with Xavier Dectot (Paris, Barcelona, 2004–5) and *El Románico y el Mediterráneo. Cataluña, Toulouse, Pisa. 1120–80*, with Manuel Castiñeiras (MNAC 2008). He is the scientific coordinator, along with Manuel Castiñeiras, of the *Enciclopedia del Románico en Cataluña*.

Manuel Castiñeiras is Full Professor of the History of Medieval Art at the Universitat Autònoma de Barcelona (UAB), where he was Head of the Department of Art and Musicology between 2014 and 2017. Previously he was Chief Curator of the Romanesque Collections at the *Museu Nacional d'Art de Catalunya* (MNAC, Barcelona) (2005–10) and Associate Professor in the University of Santiago de Compostela (Spain) (1997–2005). His research focuses on Romanesque art and medieval panel painting. He has also worked widely on medieval pilgrimage and the question of artistic exchange in the Mediterranean between the 11th and 15th centuries. As a result of his Samuel H. Kress Senior Fellowship at the Center for Advanced Study in the Visual Arts–National Gallery of Art, in Washington, D.C. in 2017–18, he is preparing a book: *Latin Perceptions of the Byzantine East: Art and Identity in Flux during the Catalan Expansion across the Late Medieval Mediterranean* (Rome, forthcoming 2021).

Gaetano Curzi is Professor in Medieval Art History at the University of Chieti–Pescara. He took a degree (1991), a post-lauream certificate (1994), and a PhD (1999) at the University of Rome *La Sapienza*, and was awarded scholarships to work in London, Munich, and Chieti. Between 1990 and 1999, he was on the staff of the *Enciclopedia dell' Arte Medievale*, and from 1999 to 2002, he worked at the Museo Nazionale di Capodimonte in Naples. Between 2002 and 2021, he was first a Full Researcher and then Associate Professor in Medieval Art History at the University of Chieti–Pescara and the University of Siena. He has published books and papers on Medieval Rome, Wooden Sculpture, the Military Orders, Angevin Apulia, and Giotto.

Eric Fernie is retired from having been Director of the Courtauld Institute of Art. His area of research is medieval architecture, particularly in the earlier centuries and the Romanesque period. He has specialised in the study of architectural iconography and proportions, and in metrology. His books include *The Architecture of the Anglo-Saxons* (1983), *An Architectural History of Norwich Cathedral* (1993), *Art History and Its Methods* (1995), *The Architecture of Norman England* (2000), and *Romanesque Architecture: The First Style of the European Age* (2014).

Cecily Hennessy is the Academic Director of Christie's Education, London. Previously, she was the Programme Director for the Art and Collecting: Antiquity to Renaissance MA. She received her PhD from the Courtauld Institute in 2001 and subsequently worked at the Courtauld as Head of Short Courses and Adult Learning before joining Christie's Education in 2006. She has published on the imagery of children, adolescence, and the family in Byzantium, on middle and late Byzantine manuscripts, and on the topography, architecture, and paintings of Constantinople, Ravenna, and Jerusalem. Her current research focuses on the interrelation of Byzantine and western art. In addition to many articles, she has published a book *Images of Children in Byzantium* (2008) and two guidebooks, *Painting in Cappadocia: A Guide to the Sites and Byzantine Church Decoration* (2013) and *Early Christian and Medieval Rome: A Guide to the Art and Architecture* (2017).

Wilfried E. Keil studied film and TV business administration in Dortmund, and Art History, Philosophy and Classical Archaeology in Munich before receiving his PhD in 2011 at the Ruprecht-Karls-University Heidelberg with a thesis on Romanesque beast-columns, published as *Romanische Bestiensäulen* (Berlin 2018). He has participated in several research initiatives concerned with building archaeology (e.g. Worms Cathedral), inventory, and excavations at the Institute for European Art History at Heidelberg University. From July 2011 to June 2019, he was a postdoctoral researcher concerned with script and character as part of a major project entitled Material Text Cultures. Materiality and Presence of Writing in Non-Typographic Societies. In October 2019, he was Visiting Researcher at the Department d'Art i Musicologia of the Universitat Autònoma de Barcelona, and in 2020 he habilitated at the University of Heidelberg with a thesis on the presence and restricted presence of inscriptions in medieval architecture and sculpture (publication in preparation), subsequently being appointed a Privatdozent at the Universtiy of Heidelberg. From April to June 2021 he was a Paul Mellon Centre Rome Fellow at the British School of Rome working on early photographs of Rome by Robert Macpherson. His research interests are Medieval Architecture and Sculpture, Renaissance Sculpture, Animal Iconography, Inscriptions, Photography and Film. He has written a number of scholarly articles and co-edited three books.

Gerhard Lutz is the Robert P. Bergman Curator of Medieval Art at the Cleveland Museum of Art. He was Curator and Associate Director at the Dom-Museum Hildesheim from 2009 until 2020. He has taught at the Technische Universität Dresden (2001–2008), the Institute of Fine Arts–New York University (2013) and the University of Bern (2018/19); he is an Associate Member of the Board of Directors of the International Center of Medieval Art, New York (2019–22) and a co-founder of the biennial conference series *Forum Medieval Art*. His publications are concerned with medieval sculpture and metalwork: he is co-editor of *1000 Jahre St. Michael in Hildesheim* (2012), *Medieval Treasures from Hildesheim* (2013), and *Christ on the Cross: The Boston Crucifix and the Rise of Monumental Wood Sculpture, 970–1200* (2020).

Aleuna Macarenko is a PhD candidate in Art History and Archaeology at the University of Liège (Belgium). Her doctoral thesis is dedicated to the study of illuminated manuscripts belonging to the 12th-century Mosan group of 'Floreffe-Averbode' codices. Her approach combines studies of style and iconography, with consideration of the materials and techniques used in the making of these manuscripts. Her first monograph, focused on the *Averbode Gospels* (Liège, University Library, MS. 363), was published in 2020.

Clark Maines is Professor Emeritus of Art History and Archaeology and Kenan Professor of the Humanities at Wesleyan University. His research focuses on the material and textual history of monasticism and on early modern iconoclasm. Professor Maines's published work includes two books on the Augustinian abbey of Saint-Jean-des-Vignes, another on the Benedictine priory of Saint-Loup-de-Naud. He has also co-edited a volume on monastic customaries and another on the concept of the palimpsest in architecture. His articles have appeared in the *Congrès archéologique, Bulletin monumental, Speculum*, and *Gesta*, for which he also served as editor for three years.

John McNeill teaches at Oxford University's Department of Continuing Education and is Honorary Secretary of the British Archaeological Association, for whom he has edited and contributed to volumes on Anjou, King's Lynn and the Fens, the medieval cloister, and English medieval chantries. He was instrumental in establishing the BAA's International Romanesque Conference Series and has a particular interest in the design of medieval monastic precincts.

Julia Perratore is Assistant Curator in the Department of Medieval Art and The Cloisters at The Metropolitan Museum of Art in New York, where she specializes in western medieval sculpture from 1100 to 1500. She completed her PhD in the History of Art at the University of Pennsylvania in 2012, with a dissertation on the architectural sculpture of Santa María de Uncastillo. Her current research focuses on the impact of interfaith interaction on the arts of medieval Iberia and throughout the western Mediterranean region.

Richard Plant has taught at a number of institutions and worked for many years at Christie's Education in London, where he was deputy academic director. His research interests lie in the buildings of the Anglo-Norman realm and the Holy Roman Empire, in particular in architectural iconography. He is Publicity Officer for the British Archaeological Association, and in addition to this volume, has co-edited *Romanesque and the Past* (2013), *Romanesque Patrons and Processes* (2018), and *Romanesque Saints, Shrines and Pilgrimage* (2020).

John Sheffer is a GIS Analyst for Nobis Engineering. He took his BA in Earth and Environmental Sciences and in Archaeology at Wesleyan University and his Master's in Archaeology and GIS at the University of Edinburgh. His academic work has focused on identifying quarries, construction energetics, and using GIS to build predictive archaeological models. In addition to his work on the quarries used to build Tiron, he is working on a chapter in a volume on the Charterhouse of Bourgfontaine for which he has also identified the quarries.

Béla Zsolt Szakács lectures in Art History at the Pázmány Péter Catholic University in Budapest, as well as for the Department of Medieval Studies at the Central European University. He is particularly interested in Romanesque architecture in Central Europe, Christian iconography, and the history of monument protection. He is editor and co-author of an overview of photographic collections in East Central Europe (*Guide to Visual Resources of Medieval East Central Europe*, Budapest 2002) and published a monograph on the iconography of the 14th-centrury Hungarian Angevin Legendary (Budapest 2006, in English as *The Visual World of the Hungarian Angevin Legendary*, Budapest 2016). He is involved in various ongoing projects that concern the medieval heritage of East Central Europe and has recently edited a manual of liturgical art entitled *Ars Sacra* (Budapest 2019).

Elizabeth Valdez del Álamo is Professor Emerita of Art History at Montclair State University and was a University Distinguished Professor. Her publications centre on mourning, memory, monasticism, and the affective role of architecture, primarily in the Iberian Peninsula. Publications on cloisters include *Palace of the Mind: The Cloister of Silos and Spanish Sculpture of the Twelfth Century* (Brepols 2012), and 'Le cloître, lieu de résonances de la vie monastique' (Cuxa 2015). Her current research is on art in Castile during the reign of Alfonso VIII and Leonor Plantagenet (1158–1204), including published articles on 'The Marriage of Castile and England as Seen in the Bible of Burgos' (Princeton 2017) and 'Leonor Plantagenet: Reina y Mecenas' (Madrid 2017).

Michele Luigi Vescovi is Senior Lecturer in Medieval Art, Architecture, and History in the School of History and Heritage at the University of Lincoln. His research focuses on the geography of art, monastic networks, and the interaction between liturgical performance and monumental portals. His work has appeared in international journals, such as *Arte Medievale, Bulletin Monumental*, and *Gesta*, as well as in many edited volumes and in a monograph (*Monferrato Medievale*, 2012). His current research project explores how the invisible presence of the bodies of saints was made visibly manifest through architecture and images.

Tomasz Węcławowicz is an architect and art historian. He has published widely on aspects of medieval art and architecture, and his research combines the methodologies of art history and cultural anthropology. He is a Professor at the Andrzej Frycz Modrzewski Krakow University and is attached to the Department for Comparative Studies of Civilisations at the Jagiellonian University in Krakow. He is a member of the History of Art Committee at the Polish Academy of Arts and Sciences and of the History of Architecture and Conservation Division of the Committee on Architecture and Urban Planning of the Polish Academy of Science. He is also a supervisor of the Division of Sacral Art at the Polish Theological Society and a built heritage consultant to the Polish Minister of Culture and National Heritage.

Benjamin Zweig is currently the Digital Projects Coordinator at the National Gallery of Art, Washington, D.C. A digital humanist and medievalist, he was awarded his PhD in the History of Art at Boston University with a dissertation on images of suicide in medieval art. He was previously the Robert H. Smith Postdoctoral Research Associate for Digital Art History at the Center for Advanced Study in the Visual Arts (CASVA). He has published numerous articles on both digital and medieval art history. His research broadly explores the intersection of image making and intellectual history from late antiquity through to early gothic, with a particular interest in the art and architecture of medieval Scandinavia and the Baltic, as well as on topics such as the impact of technology on iconographic studies and the intersection of machine vision learning and art history. He has been the recipient of awards from Boston University, the Kress Foundation, the Society for the Advancement of Scandinavian Study, and the Fulbright program.

PREFACE

The categorisation of Romanesque by region was a cornerstone of 19th- and 20th-century scholarship, albeit one which has always been vulnerable to the application of anachronistic concepts of geography or regional identity. At its worst, this led to the privileging of certain regions over others in ways which created models for perceived chronologies of Romanesque, divorced from historical evidence or support, or narratives of isolation and exceptionalism were constructed for regions or polities that were neither isolated nor exceptional. The question of the significance of regions in the creation of Romanesque art has also been eclipsed by theoretical or object-centred approaches over the last half century. But the question remains, particularly in relation to transregional and pan-European artistic styles and approaches. Hence, our decision to devote the fifth in the BAA's biennial Romanesque conference series to *The Regional and Transregional in Romanesque Europe*.

The result is a volume which considers the extent to which regional styles and preferences were important in the material culture of the 11th and 12th centuries. How might we describe the cultural geography of the Latin West between *c.* 1000 and *c.* 1230. In an attempt to identify at least some potentially useful perspectives, our initial call for papers asked for considerations of the strength, durability, mutability, and geographical scope of regional styles, reviews of whether or how artistic regions are aligned with political regions, and the extent to which 'regional' forms are related to or countered by portability. Does portability make a difference, enhancing the potential for artistic exchange? What are the conditions that give rise to the development of transregional styles? Is identification by 'gens' rather than locality significant, particularly in areas where political change is effected through conquest? Are regional styles ever extinguished, and if so, how and why? Is it appropriate to talk of centres and peripheries? Are materials – marble, brick, bronze – the dissemination, enshrinement and celebration of saints (particularly episcopal saints) – the emergence of civic patronage – the adoption of myths and legends – the assumption of imported motifs – important in affirming regional identity? How effective are the agencies that cut across territorial boundaries?

Not all these appeals were answered, but these were the premises from which we hoped the conference would take shape, helped by what we saw as the immense promise of Poitiers as a forum for the various themes. The papers that were finally delivered were highly varied in subject and approach, touching on Scandinavia, Britain, Poland, Hungary, France, Spain, Italy, and Germany, while ranging across media to include discussions of liturgical practice, patronage, workshop organisation, transmission, monastic filiation and identity, and technology. This geographical variety was also reflected in the 106 people who attended the conference, and made their way to Poitiers from the UK, Spain, Italy, France, Belgium, Germany, Hungary, Poland, Norway, Finland, Greece, Brazil, Canada, and the United States, twelve of them postgraduate students to whom the British Archaeological Association awarded scholarships covering the cost of the conference, visits, and accommodation. The discussion did not end with the final conference dinner. As most scholars had travelled considerable distances to attend the conference, there were two additional days of visits on 7–8 April, enabling the majority of those who attended the conference to spend further time together and to visit a variety of Romanesque monuments at Nouaillé-Maupertuis, Montmorillon, Saint-Savin-sur-Gartempe, Chauvigny, and Poitiers itself.

For their help in making the conference possible and furthering its progress, we would like to thank Centre d'études supérieurs de civilisation médiévale in Poitiers, and in particular Martin Aurell, Cécile Voyer, Marcello Angheben, and Claude Andrault-Schmitt, who were wonderfully supportive at all stages of the conference. The CESCM generously agreed to host the conference, while Marcello Angheben co-convened the event. We would also like to thank Cécile le Bourdennec, who was generosity personified in allowing the conference to visit the Musée Sainte-Croix in Poitiers after hours and hold a reception there, and the Mayor and Municipality of Poitiers, who allowed the conference to hold a dinner in the magnificent salle d'honneur of the Hôtel de Ville. The Thursday and Friday visits were enlivened with site presentations by Claude Andrault-Schmitt, John McNeill, Manuel Castiñeiras, Marcello Angheben, Emily Guerry, Alexandra Gajewski, Richard Plant, Cécile Voyer, and Eric Sparhubert, to all of whom we acknowledge our debt. Grateful thanks are also due to the Conference team and steering group, namely Marcello Angheben, Claude Andrault-Schmitt, Manuel Castiñeiras, Rosa Bacile, John McNeill, Richard Plant, Cécile Voyer, and, above all, Ann Hignell, who acted as conference secretary and remained unflappable and superbly effective throughout. The conference coincided with a strike by SNCF workers and a student barricade of the Humanities and Social Sciences faculty at Poitiers University. Overcoming the problems thrown up by both demanded a measure of resourcefulness and self-sacrifice – qualities embodied by Ann Hignell and Richard Plant. The Association owes both its profound thanks.

Finally, bringing out a set of conference transactions always seems to take longer than it should, and in the course of steering the volume towards publication, the editors have incurred innumerable debts. Grateful thanks are due to Tony Carr for his preparedness to provide an index for this volume, and the magisterial clarity he has again brought to the task, and to the copy and production editors at Routledge. However, much the greatest debt is owed to John Osborn, for without his interest, patience, and keen generosity, there would be no International Conference series. The editors, the British Archaeological Association, and the wider world of Romanesque scholarship owe him a great deal.

John McNeill and Richard Plant

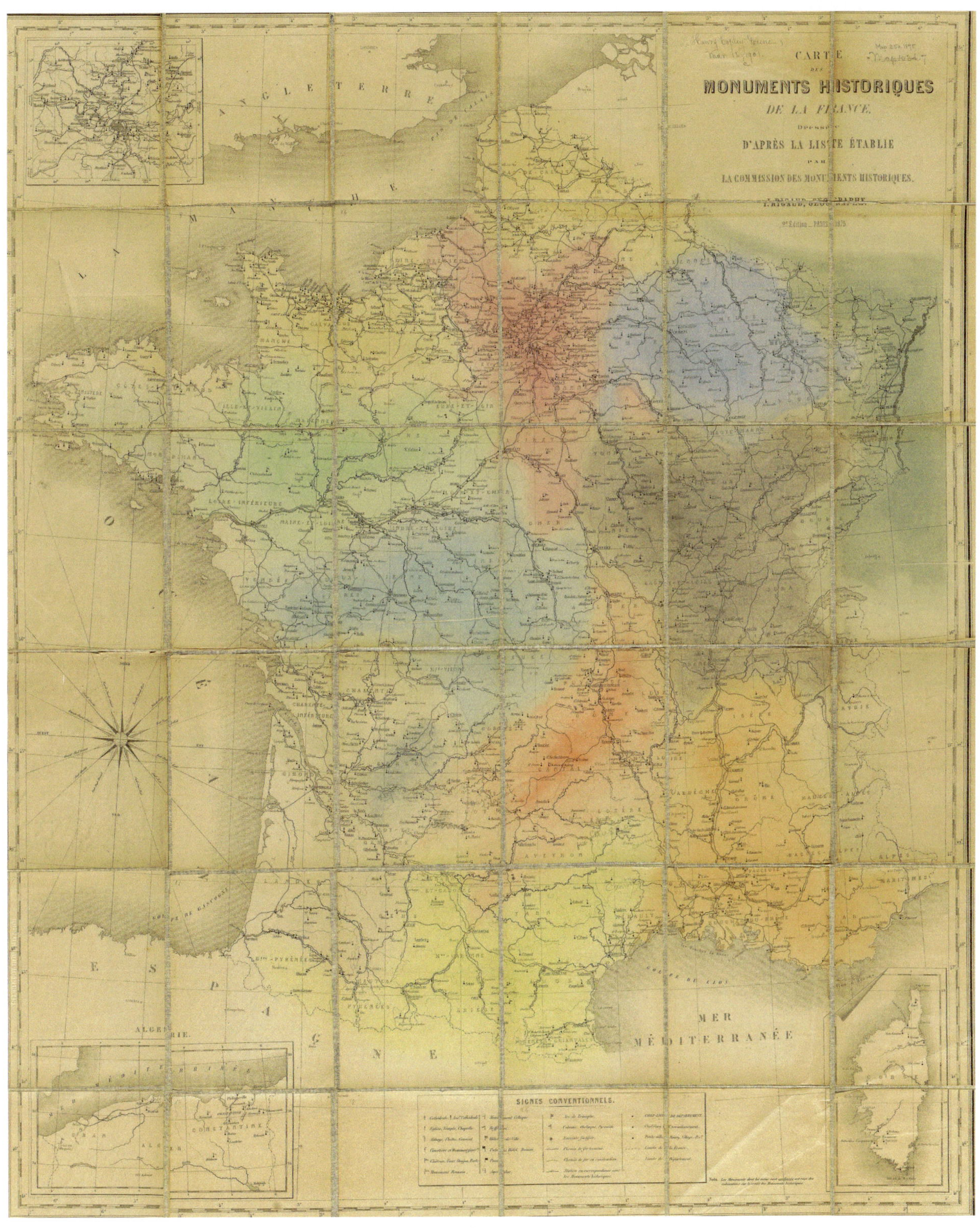

PLATE I *Art schools in French territory during the first half of the 12th century: an official document (1875) (Map reproduced courtesy of the Norman B. Leventhal Map & Education Center at the Boston Public Library)*

Plate II (TOP) *Dom Angelico Surchamp OSB, at a reception given on 2 April 2012 to mark his appointment as Chevalier de la Légion d'honneur (Philip Bovey)*

Plate II (BOTTOM) *Saint-Jouin-de-Marnes: west front (Marcello Angheben)*

PLATE III (TOP) *Santiago de Compostela: digital reconstruction of the high altar of Diego Gelmírez for the exhibiton, Compostela and Europe. The Story of Diego Gelmírez (2010). (Tomás Guerrero–Magneto Studio and Manuel Castiñeiras)*

PLATE III (BOTTOM) *Bari, San Nicola: ciborium (1105–23) (John McNeill)*

PLATE IV *Hildesheim Cathedral: Baptismal Font, Wilbrand of Oldenburg in the Dedication Scene, c. 1226 (Dommuseum Hildesheim, M. Zimmermann)*

PLATE V *Hildesheim, Dommuseum: aquamanile in the form of a senmurv, Hildesheim, second quarter of 12th century, inv.-no. 2016–1 (Dommuseum, Florian Monheim)*

Plate VI *Stavelot Altar (Bruxelles, Musées royaux d'Art et d'Histoire, inv. 1590) (© MRAH-KMKG, Brussels)*

Plate VII (TOP) *Saint Matthew (Troyes, Trésor de la Cathédrale, inv. 012) (© DRAC Grand-Est, Boulangé-Geffroy, Troyes Classified as Monument historique on the 1894/09/15)*

Plate VII (BOTTOM) *Balfour ciborium (London, Victoria and Albert Museum, inv. M.1:1, 2–1981) © Victoria and Albert Museum, London)*

PLATE VIII (TOP) *Winchester Cathedral: Holy Sepulchre Chapel, Lamentation/Entombment, lower register east wall (© Cecily Hennessy)*

PLATE VIII (BOTTOM) *Winchester Cathedral: Holy Sepulchre Chapel, Marys at the Tomb, lower register east wall (© Cecily Hennessy)*

PLATE IX *Oxford: Bodleian Libraries, MS Gr. th. f. 1, fol. 4r (© Bodleian Libraries, University of Oxford)*

Plate X *Lamentation and Anointing, Marys at the Tomb, Ingeborg Psalter (Chantilly, Musée Condé, MS 9, fol. 28v): (Cliché CNRS – IRHT © Bibliothèque du château de Chantilly)*

PLATE XI *Cavagnolo: Santa Fede, portal (Michele Luigi Vescovi)*

PLATE XII (TOP) *Tiron: Romanesque church, view from the north (Bonde and Maines)*

PLATE XII (BOTTOM) *Wachock: Cistercian Abbey, chapter-house (J. Kopka)*

Plate XIII (TOP) *Catania Cathedral: aerial view from east (Tancredi Bella)*

Plate XIII (BOTTOM) *Catania Cathedral: view of the apses from the mullioned window of the north transept (Tancredi Bella)*

Plate XIV *Worms Cathedral: eastern façade (Wilfried E. Keil)*

PLATE XV *Kilpeck: St Mary, South Portal (John McNeill)*

Plate XVI (TOP) *Saint-Mandé-sur-Brédoire: south portal (Luke Purser)*

Plate XVI (BOTTOM) *Leyre: San Salvador, west portal archivolts (John McNeill)*

PLATE XVII *San Miguel de Uncastillo: south portal (Museum of Fine Arts, Boston. Museum purchase with funds from the Francis Bartlett Donation of 1912, 28.32) (Photograph © 2021 Museum of Fine Arts, Boston)*

PLATE XVIII *Crucifixion Sant Joan de Caselles (Andorra), Crucifixion: stucco relief (Majestat typology) (Jordi Camps)*

PLATE XIX *Sant Miqueu de Vielha (Val d'Aran): Christ from Mijaran (vestige of a Descent from the Cross)*

PLATE XX *Crucifix from 1147, detail (Museu Nacional d'Art de Catalunya) (Jordi Camps)*

Plate XXI *Virgin from Ger, Cerdanya, Museu Nacional d'Art de Catalunya: (© Museu Nacional d'Art de Catalunya) (Photographers: Calveras, Mèrida, Sagristà)*

PLATE XXII *Celano, Museo d'Arte Sacra della Marsica: wooden door from San Pietro at Alba Fucens (Archivio DILASS)*

Plate XXIII *Canosa, Mausoleum of Bohemond: detail of bronze door (Gaetano Curzi)*

Plate XXIV (TOP) *Homoróddaróc/Drăuşeni/Draas: view from north-east (Béla Zsolt Szakács)*

Plate XXIV (BOTTOM) *Lébény, Benedictine Abbey: decoration of the south portal (Béla Zsolt Szakács)*

Plate XXV (TOP) *Lund Cathedral: view from north-east (Francois Polito/Wikimedia Commons)*

Plate XXV (BOTTOM) *Lund Cathedral: crypt (Benjamin Zweig)*

PLATE XXVI (TOP) *Stavanger Cathedral: nave looking east (Arkeologisk Museum, Universitetet i Stavanger)*

PLATE XXVI (BOTTOM) *Vä, Sant Mary: chancel arch and wall-paintings of donors (Jonas Dahlin)*

PLATE XXVII *The Bible of Burgos: Story of Adam and Eve (Genesis 2–4), c. 1175–80. (Biblioteca Pública Provincial de Burgos, BP m-173, f. 12r (olim MS 846). By permission of the Biblioteca Pública Provincial de Burgos)*

PLATE XXVIII (TOP) *Cardeña Beatus: Seven Angels Hold the Cups of the Seven Last Plagues; The Hymn of the Lamb (Revelation 15³), fol. 132r, c. 1180. (New York, Metropolitan Museum of Art, 1991.232.14a)*

PLATE XXVIII (BOTTOM) *León, Museo San Isidoro de León: Leonor Plantagenet, embroidered stole and maniple, silk with gold thread (Therese Martin)*

THE EPISTEMOLOGICAL, POLITICAL, AND PRACTICAL ISSUES AFFECTING REGIONAL CATEGORIES IN FRENCH ROMANESQUE ARCHITECTURE

Claude Andrault-Schmitt

Categorisation according to region is one of the cornerstones of French Romanesque historiography. The following paper examines the historical and political circumstances of the birth of this concept in the first half of the 19th century. At that time, when Paris-based French scholars wrote to their provincial correspondents, their initial aim was to develop a simple typology in order to create the first lists of protected monuments. However, some also wished to build a true 'science' on the back of this, one which would enable them to classify architectural groupings according to their vaults, arches, abutments, and other means of articulation. Thus was born a theory of regional styles, albeit one created in the ideological (and conservative) context of the development of folklore. It is important to grasp the implications of the attractive and popular mental landscape compounded by the 'Romanesque schools'. This last became so influential that certain specific features of Romanesque churches considered to be paragons of a regional style are, in fact, the consequence of 19th-century 'restoration' and are better considered as examples of the architecture of a Romanesque Revival.

Both the theme of this volume and the localisation of the conference on which it was based in Poitiers beg a number of questions, not least those concerned with language and epistemology. First, every historian of art is eventually made aware that the word 'Romanesque' puzzles translators. Some translate the French *roman* into 'Roman', while others translate the English 'Romanesque' into the French *romanesque* (fictional) or *roman* (a novel). The first mistake is interesting because it suggests that Romanesque has Mediterranean roots – a topic of much discussion in the first BAA Romanesque Conference. The second mistranslation invites me to use this paper to develop a sort of 'Romanesque novel', in French *le roman du roman*. Now, more than ever, it seems appropriate to join the celebrations of the University of Poitiers in honour of Michel Foucault (1926–1984), who was born in Poitiers and was buried nearby. In his book *The Order of Things: An Archaeology of the Human Sciences* (1966), Foucault argued that 'conditions of possibility' in each and every historical period explain what is acceptable in scientific discourse.[1] These conditions form the concept of *episteme*, which in turn enables me to outline an 'archaeology' of regional Romanesque as a typology.[2]

AN ARCHAEOLOGY OF REGIONAL ROMANESQUE AS A TYPOLOGY

From Enlightenment to the 20th century

We owe a great deal to the Enlightenment. Categorisation as a scientific tool was developed during the Enlightenment, more specifically by the Swedish 'botanist prince', Carl Linnaeus (aka Carl von Linné, 1707–78), the man who also coined the term *Homo sapiens*. The categories developed by Linnaeus in his *System naturae* gave birth to the Latin binominal nomenclature of animals, plants, and minerals. The Linnaean system is artificial and purely descriptive, and very much still in use today throughout the world. However, botanists have no illusions as to the real value of this nomenclature: they do not consider the terms immutable but simply regard them as convenient labels.

It is noteworthy that the Linnaean system is based on morphological features. The criteria according to which French Romanesque art were classified were morphological too: aisles, proportions, buttresses, vaulting types, towers seem to have similar functions to such categories as roots, sepals, number of petals, pistils, and stamen.[3] The best 19th-century experts, whose purposes were

  DOI: 10.4324/9781003162827-1

pedagogical and didactic, perfectly understood the practical usefulness of morphological features. Unfortunately, others reified these features and did so as if these categories reflected the reality of biological, anthropological, and eventually territorial entities. This last division, which supposes spatial or topographical boundaries, profoundly affected the French approach to the history of Romanesque Art. Moreover, because the concept enabled authors to draw clear maps, it soon became very popular. I should add that mapping became a prolific and commercially profitable trend among editors. The maps of French Romanesque schools created by Auguste Brutails at the beginning of the 20th century[4] (Figures 1.1 and 1.2) were still being published as recently as 2015.[5]

Among scholars, the golden age of regional categorisation was between *c.* 1880 and the 1960s, though the concept was not universally endorsed before the end of the 19th century.[6] In the decades before the 1870s, we should pay tribute to the philosophical culture and Hegelian conception of art pioneered by Prosper Mérimée, the famous General Inspector of Historical Monuments.[7] Mérimée expressed disdain at the 'buffoon essays' of provincial savants, and with his delightful sense of humour, he mocked the local patriotism of the city of Toulouse: 'If it is proved by the restorers that Toulouse was a [Visigothic] capital, that Clovis and Charlemagne were rascals while Alaric and Vaifre were heroes, then the City of Toulouse would give a lot of money to restore the church'.[8]

Regional categorisation was thus inherited relatively late and might be considered the result of an unnatural wedding between the Norman, Arcisse de Caumont, the great 'agitator for the French province', and 'decentralisation Crusaders', Republican and progressive experts such as Jules Quicherat. It is interesting to analyse, or to unravel, this wedding between Royalists and Jacobins, one favoured by the patriotic feelings consecutive to the 1870 defeat and also to the First World War. Viollet-le-Duc's evolution before and after 1870 is relevant to this.

The key role of Arcisse de Caumont

As is well known, Arcisse de Caumont was influenced by English Antiquaries, as well as by 18th-century figures such as Lamarck and Linnaeus. We know that he met Georges Cuvier. He was a founder of the *Société linnéenne du Calvados* in 1823, when he was just twenty years old, as well being a member of the Royal Swedish Academy, the director of the French Provincial Institute, and founder of the *Société française d'Archéologie*, among many other academic or self-proclaimed titles.[9] In his famous *Cours d'antiquités monumentales*, he wrote:

> There is no science if isolated observations are not coordinated, nor fertilised by induction; they must be joined together so as to constitute several *corps de doctrine*.[10]

His first attempt at categorisation consisted of aligning stylistic denominations with geological eras. With great success, Romanesque styles were thus chronologically distinguished: 'primary' or 'primordial', 'secondary', 'tertiary' or 'transitional'. In 1825, he conceived of the development of art as a type of strange tree, with the roots at the top. This took into account what he considered to be foreign influences. Branches then provided some sort of respiratory chlorophyll to the main current, but they were very small.[11] After this, his 'Monumental statistics' were published and provided with maps. As early as 1831, he formulated the notion of 'Stylistic geography'.[12] He invented a 'Poitevin School', the only 'school' other than 'Norman' that he admitted, essentially because he confined his studies to western France (he conceded he knew nothing about eastern France). Fifteen years later, after endless travels across France, he upheld the concept of 'the monumental region'.[13] The mapping of Romanesque France fitted his conception of provincial identities (Figure 1.3). Above all, the drawings substantiated his theory about the influence of the natural world on human activity because they suggested there was an underlying parallel with geological maps.

The influence of de Caumont was profound, given his central role at the head of the *Société française d'archéologie*. There were exchanges of questionnaires between, on the one hand, national experts from Paris and, on the other, local scholars who generally behaved with modesty and humility in their role as corresponding partners. Much gratitude was expressed toward 'the great agitator, the dizzying whirlwind' who organised the SFA's meetings.[14] By the 1850s, Arcisse de Caumont required a preliminary 'programme' for each decentralised conference (constituting something like school homework). This programme was made up of questions which inquired after the 'features which differed' and probed 'the dominating architectural style of the country'. De Caumont also spoke of 'architectural families'. In 1864, he wished to build 'an applied archaeology, that is to say, the application of the principles of classification in each country where the Company was sitting'. In 1865, he spoke of Romanesque 'schools'. After his death, as a *fait accompli*, an interesting item was expressed in the 'programme', which by now had been published in the opening pages of the conference proceedings:

> No 7. Pay attention to the main religious monuments of the region. Say if they form a special school or if they must be associated with another school prevailing in neighbouring provinces.[15]

Is the notion of Romanesque schools due to Jules Quicherat?

Considering its debts to the Enlightenment, some scholars talk of a 'natural history' of medieval style (de Caumont as Linnaeus) and an 'historical biology' of medieval style (Quicherat as Cuvier).[16]

Jules Quicherat (1814–82) came from the French meritocracy; he was a remarkable historian and, above all, a teacher.[17] In 1847 he inaugurated a course of archaeological lectures at the École des Chartes. Two years later, he

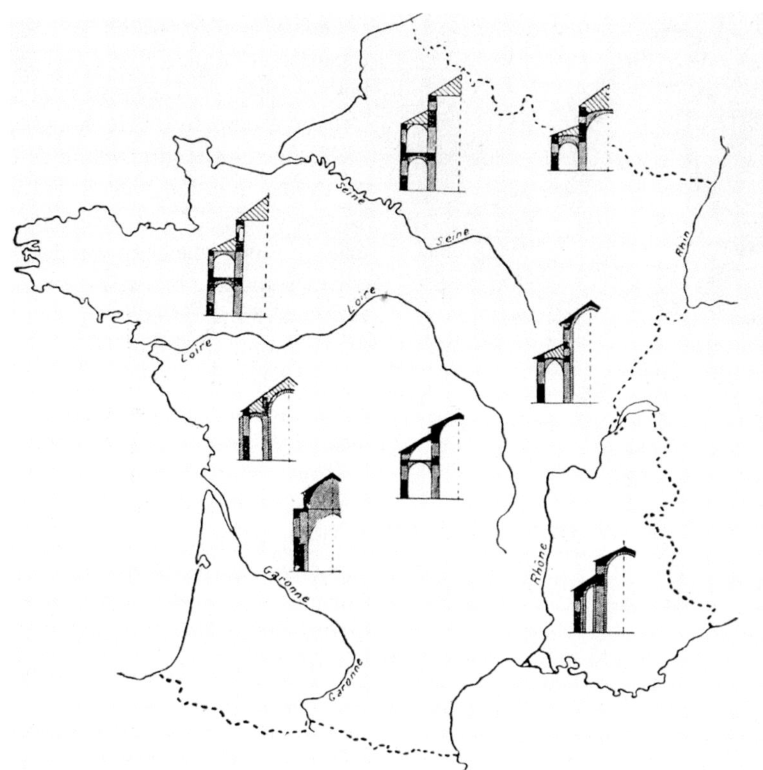

FIGURE 1.1

Romanesque map published in 1918 (J.-A. Brutails, Pour comprendre les monuments de la France)

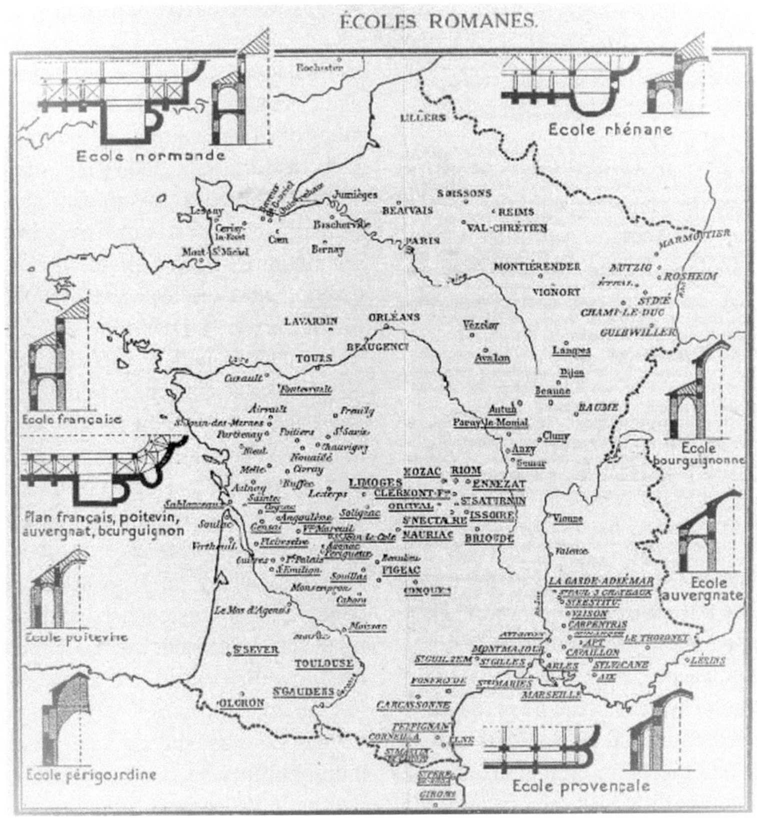

FIGURE 1.2

Romanesque map published in 1918 (J.-A. Brutails, Pour comprendre les monuments de la France*)*

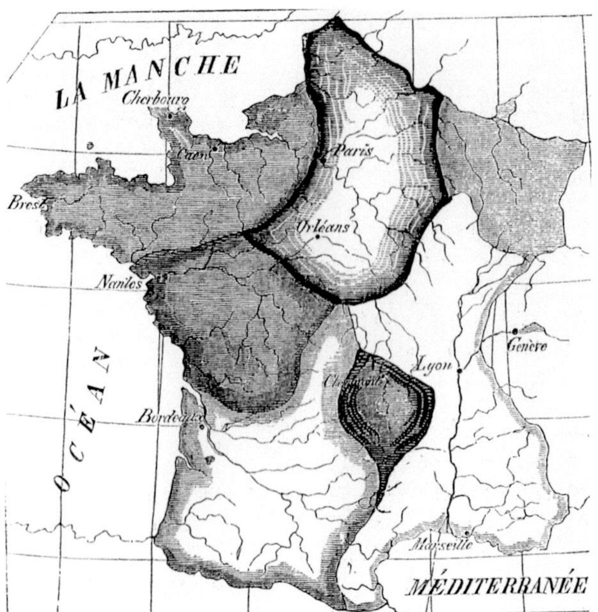

FIGURE 1.3

Map in the fifth edition of Arcisse de Caumont, Abécédaire ou rudiment d'archéologie *(Architecture religieuse (1867), 292)*

became the first permanent holder of the chair of archaeology, a post created so as to distinguish the subject from aesthetic teaching. Quicherat published very few papers, and unfortunately for posterity, many of his arguments were only ever sketched out with a piece of chalk in the classroom. His *Mélanges d'archéologie et d'Histoire* were posthumously published by Robert de Lasteyrie (1886). It is now difficult to understand how his students and successors extended and interpreted his theories.

However, in 1851, Quicherat mocked the notion of 'mural Flora', that is to say the characterisation of architecture by ornamental detail.[18] According to him, a scientific approach cannot be based upon style, 'which is ornamentation'; it should be based on conformation, 'which is the nave vaulting'. This deserves to be raised to the first rank.

> [H]ere [the addition of vaults to the basilica] is the first draft of the Romanesque church and the coarse embryo from which were soon developed limbs which were added and which responded to the conformation of the body.[19]

As such, Quicherat proposed that the notion of style should be replaced by the notion of conformation. The vaulting system would be upheld as a unique criterion. Quicherat believed in human progress; a sort of whiggism led him to favour vaults because what he perceived as a continuous improvement in stone vaulting indicated technical progress and therefore human progress. He claimed that 'buildings before 1100 are imprinted with imperfection and are tentative'. This perception crystallised into a lasting and common prejudice, one which became fundamental to Viollet-le-Duc's thesis as well.

Quicherat also mocked 'archaeologists who are lost in a parochial attitude'.[20] As early as 1852, he denounced both Arcisse de Caumont's chronological system and 'artistic geography'.[21] He thought artistic geography was insufficiently scientific, while de Caumont's chronological system was too narrow and too rigid to include all known examples and incapable of incorporating new data. In short, Quicherat wanted something akin to Mendeleev's periodic table. His concern was that the history of art should be raised to the rank of a Positivist science. So he proposed four 'classes' of Romanesque church, distinguished according to their nave vaulting. This, he argued, was a major evolutionary feature. Within three of these four 'classes', he separated 'species' and/or 'families' according to secondary features, which he illustrated with short monographs. Quicherat's groups were not regional. In one, for example, we find Saint-Junien (Limousin), Arles (Provence), Saintes (Saintonge), and Cunault (Anjou). He recognised regional diversity and several Romanesque schools, but for Quicherat these stemmed from major building sites and not from the land like country wines.

Thus it is unfair to attribute regional Romanesque schools to Quicherat. All the more so given that his classification was anything but monolithic. However, we must concede that his system remained insufficiently heuristic to become popular.

A consensus-based mapping

In this same year, 1852, and in a periodical with a limited circulation, Viollet-le-Duc published a series of three maps of France: a map of the 'styles during the 11th and 12th centuries', a geological map, and a feudal map.[22] Given his intellectual opposition to taxonomy, this series of maps may seem surprising, but his interest in Gothic architecture partly explains this decision. In the accompanying text, Viollet wrote that before the birth of 'a centralised art' (i.e. the Gothic style) and before an historical movement in which 'the clerical aristocracy and Royalty provoked the almost complete fusion of all styles', approaches to building mostly depended on the nature of the stone. The three maps were intended to demonstrate this thesis: 'comparing these three maps, one can observe that the stylistic regions are closer to geological regions than to political regions'.

Twenty years later, in 1875, in a sensitive patriotic context, a consensus-based map of Romanesque regional types was released by the Commission for Historical Monuments. Considered as the supreme expert, Viollet-le-Duc then proposed several 'schools'; he asked for twelve colours and several 'semi colours' to indicate mutual influences (Colour Plate I). Both the national and international context, and the purpose of this map are very interesting.[23] Viollet-le-Duc wished to respond to a German map which 'was wrong, especially concerning France'. Viollet-le-Duc's map was entitled 'Art schools in actual French territory during the first half of the 12th century' and was intended to act as a type of legal framework to help local scholars answer the questionnaires sent out by the *Société française d'Archéologie* or by the State department of *Beaux-Arts*. The Historical Monuments Commission also decided to send this map to Philadelphia for the Centennial Exhibition (1876) and to publish it with thirteen colours as an appendix to the long report from E. Du Sommerard on the Universal Exhibition in Vienna of 1873.[24] Nicely arranged and vaguely delineated, the colours have no boundaries to separate the artistic regions they represent. But Sommerard's book also included monographic chapters, a departmental inventory, and, above all, a list of 'schools' which were strictly surrounded by boundaries thanks to cities and rivers:

> *de l'Ile-de-France, champenoise, bourguignonne, rhénane, du Poitou, de la Saintonge, du Périgord, auvergnate, languedocienne, provençale, picarde, normande, angevine.*

Two years later, Anthyme Saint-Paul demanded that consideration of 'the distribution of organic elements within the building' was paramount, suggesting there was a link between architectonic forms and functions as inspired by the example of physiology.[25] Following Quicherat, references to physiology were added to geological, botanical, and linguistic descriptors. This type of systematic grouping betrayed its Enlightenment roots, in the sense that it created closed systems. Romanesque art became 'a sort of historical *fait accompli*' while in reality the term is no more than an artificial label and a convenient fiction.[26]

THE DOWNWARD SLIDE OF REGIONAL CATEGORISATION

Political backgrounds

There is no doubt that we now consider 'artistic geography' to be a 'poisoned landscape', to quote Patrick Geary, speaking of the nationalist interpretations of earlier times.[27]

Romanesque architecture is not the only field affected by regional categorisation. A similar ideological context explains the sorting of various things. I will propose some trivial analogies in order to better understand the problems raised by this regional categorisation. One example is that maps of regional types of cattle flourished at the end of the 19th century (till now). But their distinctive features were not natural; they are the result of selective breeding. At the same time as the non-natural selection of the cattle was promoted, regional costumes were distinguished by more and more readily identifiable characters. In Brittany, for example, the famous Bigouden headdresses became taller and taller, so as to sharpen their regional identity.[28] Other regional costumes were also fossilised at the end of the 19th century, but the Breton analogy is perhaps all the more meaningful because Brittany is a blank area in maps of Romanesque art.

A few years after the publications of the liberal and progressive Michelet, Mérimée, Quicherat, Viollet-le-Duc and others, the cultural context changed. Opposition to centralisation was increasing in France and contributed to the reinforcement of the regionalist trend. At the beginning of the 20th century, certain troublesome features were added to the concept of artistic geography: the notions of 'racial genius and tradition'.[29]

Louis Courajod, a sculpture expert who was a student of Quicherat, abominated the word 'Romanesque' because of its Roman roots. He called for the 'meticulous analysis of a Romanesque church from the point of view of its different ethnic components'. He invited his colleagues 'to consider the respective dispositions of the ethnographic features'.[30] At the same time he used botanical metaphors which he took from philologists:

> The natural and savage plant is growing, pure and without cross-breeding, from the national ground and from the savage sap [. . .]; it is not, among the growing plants, the Roman seed which won.[31]

This dangerous and problematic argument about purity allows me to insist on a consideration of its political background. There developed a sort of collusion between patriotic feeling and faith in regional characterisation. The patriotic offensive is revealed in 1917 by the polemical book in which Emile Mâle reacted to the burning of Reims cathedral by German bombs.[32] At the core of an analysis of German Romanesque art, Mâle included six pages (100–06) in praise of seven French Romanesque schools. By embedding the Romanesque schools theory within the text, he wanted to demonstrate that German medieval architects had discovered or invented nothing. He pointed to 'creative powerlessness' beyond the Rhine and juxtaposed French Romanesque diversity to 'German monotony'.

Words and frontiers: Picrocholine battles[33]

In erudite circles in France, the concept of Romanesque schools led to Picrocholine wars of words, which in retrospect seem as absurd as the debates in *Bouvard and Pécuchet*. Experts fought passionate battles over the number and the boundaries of the schools.

De Caumont defined seven Romanesque schools as early as 1850. Subsequently, Auguste Choisy proposed the same number of schools but asserted this was arrived at on a 'rational basis, not from regional or fictional features'.[34] At the same time, and paradoxically, his map charted the diffusion of regional *savoir-faire* (Figure 1.4). Anthyme Saint-Paul chose to define six 'groups' and fifteen 'schools' and fought to distinguish a Limousine school from a Poitevine school.[35] Lefevre-Pontalis counted nine schools.[36]

Let us now return to the map produced in 1875 (Colour Plate I). As previously stated, this was based on the work of Eugène Viollet-le-Duc, which he submitted to validation with great courtesy and humility. His

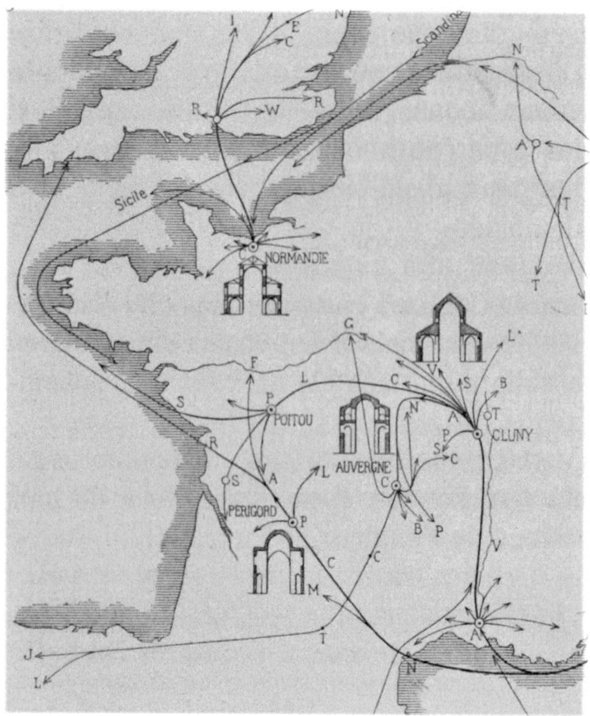

FIGURE 1.4

Map published in A. Choisy, Histoire de l'architecture, *II (Paris 1899), 240*

colleagues then made requests for changes that I roughly translate here:

> M. Abadie proposes the Saintonge school should be extended further to Agen.
> M. Viollet-le-Duc approves the Saintonge and Périgord schools, which he considers together as a family, not a race. He adds that some locations have been influenced by several different schools.
> M. de Lasteyrie says that the term 'manifest boundaries' sounds too absolute.
> M. Quicherat wishes to add a school for the French Rhineland, and to note the existence of mutual influence between the French Pyrenees and Spain.[37]

First, we must remember that the word 'race' had not at this point acquired the same heavy connotations it carries today, despite the ambiguity introduced by the commonly held notion of the existence of 'bastard styles'. Second, it seems that Viollet-le-Duc was embarrassed by regional categorisations, as he thought these did not rely on political areas but on geological features and intermixing influences. I wonder whether he felt compelled to act as he did to reconcile opposing ideologies, as Quicherat did.

These quarrels finally invaded public space in the first quarter of the 20th century, at a time when a number of papers with telling and absurd titles were published:

> The Touraine as the cradle of the Romanesque churches of South-Western France (1913).[38]

> To which school may the church of Beaulieu be assigned? (1914)[39]

> The Romanesque school of Périgord does not exist (1923).[40]

Major epistemological failures

Where is history in these debates? Even when they were talented historians, only a few of the French 19th-century experts really examined the historical background to establish their rigid or bastard groups and their guidelines, and they used a vague dating model based on stylistic arguments. Their approach concealed a lack of real historical method, despite the attempt to assimilate Romanesque schools into feudal territories and the inclusion of a few naive words about the difficulty of travel (I used to say that mules do not need motorways).[41] The lack of historical rigour in the writing of regional art-historical monographs is a paradox if we observe that it was at this same time that many manuscripts and documentary sources were discovered and published with critical rigour – sometimes even by these same scholars. Quicherat, for example, was a good palaeographer.

Analyses of Angoulême Cathedral illustrate the problematic consequences of the hold exercised by the theory of Romanesque schools on French scholarship. Because experts knew that the building belonged to the school of domed churches (called the 'School of Périgord'), they favoured the nave and did not consider the transepts, which they supposed similar to others within this stylistic family. Thus Edouard Corroyer claimed that only one transept tower was ever built at Angoulême. Amazingly, he appears not to have noticed the three domes over the transept, instead describing two barrel vaults and an inauthentic central dome.[42] A historical enquiry would have demonstrated a cultural as much as a formal relationship with Cluny, and this relationship, in turn, would have emphasised the level of Angoulême's ambition.[43] This, however, would have nourished the thesis that Romanesque architecture was susceptible to international trends – the very thesis which the Jacobins, Quicherat, and Viollet-le-Duc wished to curb.

In this particular case, categorisation according to type – the search for the typical – prevailed over Angoulême's historical singularity. Indeed, theories of regional divisions are always likely to conceal the exceptional. To illustrate this last point I would invoke a sample of the rare Romanesque clerestories in northern Aquitaine that I covered in an earlier BAA Romanesque volume.[44] The morphological features of the churches of La Chaize-le-Vicomte in Vendée, Chinon in Touraine, and Chambon-sur-Voueize in the Limousin are at variance with the so-called 'Poitevin elevation'. They are basilican when the Poitevin elevation is either single storey or consists of a 'vaults upon arches' arrangement. They shouldn't exist inside a system of Romanesque architectural schools.

I must confess that when I started teaching, I warned my students against monographs on Romanesque buildings into the 1970s. For more than a century, the historical specificities of each building seemed not to have stimulated scholars. Fortunately, this has now changed, thanks to the influence of more rigorous ways of thinking in the 1960s connected to the *sciences sociales*. This brings one back to Michel Foucault. According to Foucault, 'History', generally speaking, does not exist, except in so far as it provides methods and conceptual tools for the History of Philosophy, History of Literature, History of Science, History of Art, etc.[45] So, to resume the critical analysis and bring with it a certain amount of self-criticism, I am convinced that regional classifications correlate with the current tendency to highlight mutual influences and the search for 'artistic roads'. The concept of artistic pathways is interesting because mutual inspiration is a reasonable explanation for the appearance of similar features. However, I do wonder if 'roads' are not simply a substitute for 'schools'. This currently fashionable way of thinking, which again underestimates artistic creativity and 'the human factor', is not itself innocent of the weight of historiography.

THE HEAVY CONSEQUENCES OF THE CONCEPT OF SCHOOLS IN THE THEORY AND PRACTICE OF RESTORATION

In spite of the intellectual revolution of the 1960s, the concern for regional style persists in contemporary texts or coffee table books, where it produces both picturesque and apparent didacticism. But the most significant and continuous consequences of this bias are the principles underlying the restoration of buildings.[46]

The connection between regionalisation and restoration

Notwithstanding his misleading appraisal of Angoulême Cathedral, the architect Edouard Corroyer (1835–1904) became sceptical of Romanesque schools in the later stages of his career, after 1888. Despite the respect he entertains for his famous predecessors and his espousal of the primacy of stone vaulting, Corroyer classified churches according to their plans and articulation.[47] Thus Vignory and Saint-Genou are not churches which belong to the Champagne and Berry but are recollections of Roman basilicas. Issoire, Orcival, and Notre-Dame-du-Port at Clermont did not stem from the school of Auvergne but were all built by the same architect and team of masons and must be interpreted in relation to Saint-Hilaire and Notre-Dame-la-Grande in Poitiers. And Saint-Sernin at Toulouse has been influenced from the Auvergne. Corroyer used the word 'school' but only incidentally. At the same time, he was cautious about restoration: 'with what great vehemence, French and foreign scholars point out the consequences of the last offending restorations'.[48] He denounced the obsession with stylistic unity as well as the 'obliteration of all traces of the history of the buildings': two pitfalls connected to the regionalist conception of medieval architecture, as we shall see.

A few famous cases

Among the most heavily restored buildings we have inherited, the rotunda of Neuvy-Saint-Sépulchre (Indre) in Berry is telling as an index of different trends in restoration. Above all, we can observe the opposition between the generations of Viollet-le-Duc on the one hand and on the other that of architects active at the beginning of the 20th century. In 1399, a vault collapse made it necessary to repair the rotunda.[49] A huge overhead roof probably dated from these repairs. Working in the middle of the 19th century, Viollet-le-Duc wisely assumed that the upper storeys were partly inauthentic and decided to build a terracotta dome to replace a wooden structure (1845–50). He also introduced a clerestory, so that the building became more significant in a universal sense, reminding us that ancient mausolea could be identified by a *tambour* of windows (Figure 1.5). But seventy years later, Albert Mayeux replaced Viollet's upper superstructure with a new concrete dome. He also decided to regionalise the church with two picturesque features: first, in 1923, he added a ridiculous bell cote which he called '*un campanile romano-byzantin*'; second, in 1936, he added a tiled roof with a steep slope, '*à la berrichonne*' (Figure 1.6).

The famous case of Saint-Sernin in Toulouse demonstrates the persistence of a regional interpretative framework until the end of the 20th century, when the open attic storey known as the '*les mirandes*' was built (Figure 1.7). The '*mirandes*' were not a Romanesque feature and had been removed by Viollet-le-Duc. Although their reinstatement was supported by good archaeological arguments – among which the need for a de-restoration was prominent – the re-restoration was essentially a regional proclamation.

These cases are striking because they have affected buildings which are aligned with international types. But small Romanesque churches could be still more affected by the strong positions of the restorers, both because they are severely over-restored, as is the case of Saint-Nectaire in the Auvergne and because it is highly unlikely they will be returned to a state it is known they once enjoyed. Notre-Dame-la-Grande at Poitiers has never been re-established with separate roofs over its nave and aisles because a roof which unifies both the central nave with the aisles is supposed to be characteristic of the Poitevin type. However, I will close with a different example, an altogether less well-known Romanesque building.

The church of Saint-Désiré and the trend towards 'Auvergnatisation'

The church of Saint-Désiré is situated in the Bourbonnais, a geographically marginal area between the Auvergne, Berry, and Burgundy. Above all, the Bourbonnais borders

FIGURE 1.5

Neuvy-Saint-Sépulchre: church after restoration by Viollet-le-Duc (Commission des Monuments historiques)

on the Auvergne, and in terms of 19th- and 20th-century historiography, the Auvergne is supposedly the best French province for Romanesque architecture:

> A very complete and advanced art, more advanced than the Poitevin school. (Viollet-le-Duc)[50]

> The Auvergne is the last entrenchment of Ancient art, the impregnable fortress of pagan culture, the Valkyrie who has first rejected Siegfried. (Courajod)[51]

> The static balance is here resolved with perfection, giving a model; but what would be the logic without the charm? (Mâle)[52]

FIGURE 1.6

Neuvy-Saint-Sépulchre (Jean-Pierre Andrault)

> The Auvergne school is without doubt one of the most powerful in France. (Brutails)[53]

I am personally convinced that the primacy given to the Romanesque architecture of the Auvergne is due to a combination of Vercingetorix (as a Gallic revenge) and its geographical position in the heart of the hexagon. We see it at the very centre of the Romanesque maps, depicted in the manner of a little mandorla or a type of belly button (Figure 1.3). Romanesque churches are here presented as if they rose like a Celtic spirit from the volcano, free from Roman influence as well as from anything Byzantine or German. It is not therefore surprising if the Romanesque art of the Auvergne overshadowed Romanesque art in Berry, Bourbonnais, and far beyond.

As elsewhere, the restorers would have looked upon the church of Saint-Désiré quite differently, had they considered its history. The church was founded as a priory of the Sacra di San Michele (Piemonte), far from its famous Alpine motherhouse.[54] The church was thus built as part of an international network which would have favoured cultural and artistic exchange.

What survives is very interesting. The crypt dates to the early 11th century, while the main spaces were built before 1128. However, by 1884–86 (Figure 1.8), the building was in poor repair, so the restorer, Georges Darcy, was called on to strengthen the structure. But Darcy also rewrote the exterior shape of the building, adding a series of stepped

FIGURE 1.7

Toulouse: Saint-Sernin (Claude Andrault-Schmitt)

gables, so as to create a *massif barlong*, or Auvergnat transept (Figure 1.9). He knew and evidently applied Emile Mâle's paean of praise to Auvergat Romanesque: 'The most beautiful architectural crescendo that ever existed. Developing inside like a theorem, the Auvergnat Romanesque church ends outside as an ode'.[55]

Darcy also used a particular quarry to provide ashlar with contrasting colours and raised the crossing. He ordered large numbers of sculpted corbels to form new cornices. He also divided the two intermediate apses, erasing the originally sloping ground made of beaten earth, and adding stairs to connect each of their two storeys. The restoration of the nave had to wait, and the nave anyway puzzled Darcy. It was built with neither transverse arches nor stone vaulting, contrary to the transept, and was later than the east end. Nonetheless, Darcy added windows, buttresses, barrel vaults, and transverse arches to impose a Romanesque rhythm across the four bays. In so doing, he has deprived us of the building's medieval archaeology. Finally, he invented a western tower to replace a 16th-century asymmetrical structure. He even wanted to cover the church with Volvic stone tiles but had to renounce this last nod in the direction of the Auvergne. Thus in the restoration of Saint-Désiré, three different but compatible contemporary trends were applied: regionalisation (in this case colonisation), purity, and readability.

CONCLUSION

Regional features do exist in Romanesque buildings, even if much of what appears to be regional is the result of emulation, specific technical skills, and the use of local tools and local stones. But it is important to note that the historical memory embedded in buildings as they appear now is also permeated by the concept of *les écoles romanes*. Above all, that was the concept which inspired restorers and consequently distorted the monumental medieval landscape.

Moreover, the concept of regional schools tended to emphasise structural features. Were structural features decisive for the medieval faithful? Is not the implicit hierarchy which puts structure and volume above detail an anachronism? I am tempted to postulate that impressiveness (the exterior shape) on the one hand and detailing (stone cutting, mouldings, sculptural enrichment), on the other hand, were more important in the 12th century than 'conformation' or vaulting. But this, my own anachronism, opens another field of investigation it would not be appropriate to explore here.

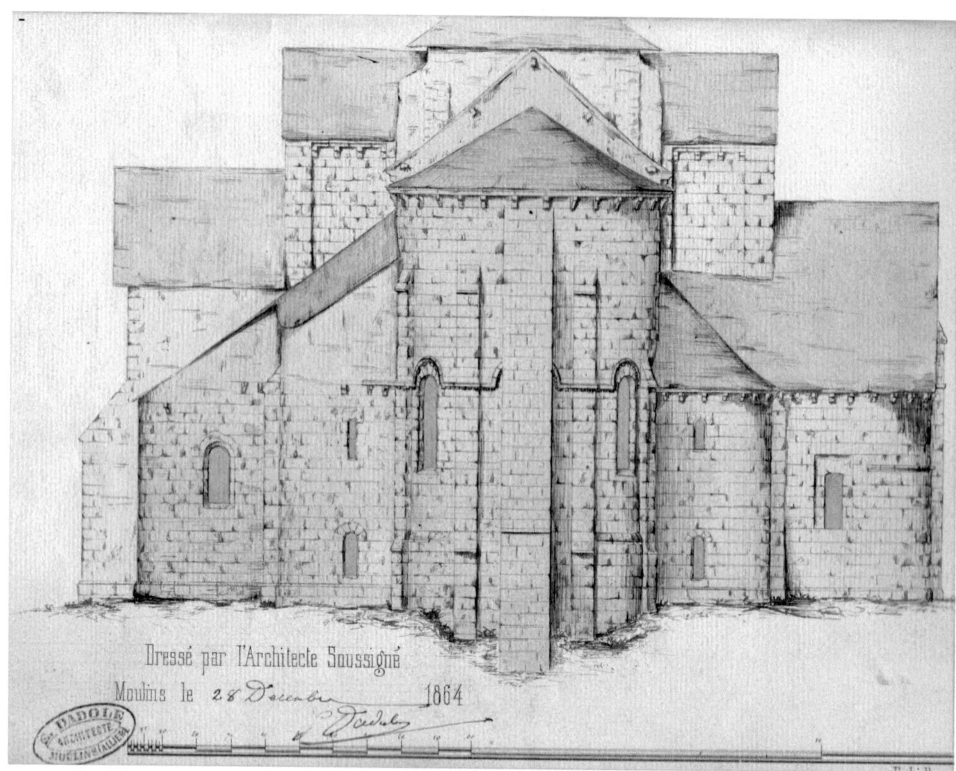

FIGURE 1.8

Saint-Désiré in 1864 (Archives de restauration, Médiathèque du Patrimoine)

FIGURE 1.9

Saint-Désiré (Jean-Pierre Andrault)

NOTES

[1] M. Foucault, *Les mots et les choses* (Paris 1966). The book was immediately translated into English as *The Order of Things*.

[2] I first broached this subject ten years ago. See C. Andrault-Schmitt, 'L'identité régionale des églises romanes: une théorie appliquée (xixe–xxe s.)', *L'art régional, entre mythe et réalité, Les Cahiers du GERHICO*, 8 (Poitiers 2005), 15–31; Eadem, 'Orgueil et préjugés: le Limousin et l'invention artistique au Moyen Age (xie–xiiie siècles)', in *Le Limousin, pays et identités. Enquêtes d'histoire de l'Antiquité au xxie siècle*, eds. J. Tricard and P. Grandcoing (Limoges 2006), 175–210. For a complete epistemological survey, see the remarkable book by J. Nayrolles, *L'invention de l'art roman à l'époque moderne (xviiie–xixe siècles)* (Rennes 2005).

[3] For a non-French interpretation, see G. Stamp, 'In Search of the Byzantine: George Gilbert Scott's Diary of an Architectural Tour in France in 1862', *Architectural History*, 46 (2003), 189–228. Stamp points to a debt to the anatomist Georges Cuvier (192).

[4] J.-A. Brutails, *Pour comprendre les monuments de la France. Notions pratiques d'archéologie à l'usage des touristes* (Paris 1918), 164. It is important to note that his *Précis d'archéologie du Moyen Age* (1908) was published without any maps but that he added a map in the third edition. The map of the 1936 edition was reproduced from 'La géographie monumentale de la France aux époques romane et gothique', *Le Moyen Age. Revue d'histoire et de philologie* (1923), 1–31. However, in J.-A. Brutails, *L'archéologie du Moyen Age et ses méthodes. Études critiques* (Paris 1900), Brutails had denounced the parallel between a building and a plant. Many of his comments remain relevant.

[5] J.-A. Brutails, *Pour comprendre les monuments de France*, ed. Gérard Montfort (Paris 1991), was repackaged as a 'Scholars choice' edition in 2015.

[6] E. Lambert partly accepted this notion in the middle of the 20th century. E. Lambert, 'Introduction à l'étude de la géographie artistique de la France médiévale', *L'information géographique* (1954), 10–12.

[7] Nayrolles, *L'invention de l'art roman* (as n. 2), 124–34. See also, P. Mérimée, *Essai sur l'architecture religieuse du Moyen Age, particulièrement en France* (1837).

[8] F. Bercé, ed., *Lettres de Mérimée à Ludovic Vitet* (Paris 1998), 157.

[9] V. Juhel éd., *Arcisse de Caumont (1801–1873), érudit normand et fondateur de l'archéologie française*, actes du colloque tenu à Caen en 2001 (Caen 2004).

[10] A. de Caumont, *Cours d'antiquités monumentales, professé à Caen en 1830. Histoire de l'art dans l'ouest de la France*, vol. 4 (Paris 1831), 37.

[11] Published in *Cours d'antiquités monumentale* (as n. 10), *Atlas*, 4, fig. LXII.

[12] Ibid., 189–91.

[13] *Bulletin monumental*, 12 (1846), 157.

[14] The words are those of A. de Longuemar concerning the preparation of the Limoges Conference: *Limoges et le congrès scientifique en 1859. Extrait du Journal de la Vienne* (Poitiers 1859), 10.

[15] For example, the *Congrès archéologique de 1890 tenu à Brive* (1891), 2.

[16] Nayrolles, *L'invention de l'art roman* (as n. 2), 166–71.

[17] Quicherat was a labourer's son who won a grant and became a student in 1835 at the Ecole des Chartes. R. de Lasteyrie, *Jules Quicherat. Sa vie et ses travaux* (Paris 1883).

[18] J. Quicherat, 'De l'architecture romane', *Revue archéologique*, 8 (1851), 145–58.

[19] *Mélanges d'archéologie et d'Histoire. Archéologie du Moyen Age. Mémoires et fragments réunis par R. de Lasteyrie* (Paris 1886), 430.

[20] Ibid., 30.

[21] J. Quicherat, 'De l'architecture romane. II. Classification des espèces', *Revue archéologique*, 8 (1852), 525–40.

[22] *Revue générale de l'architecture et des travaux publics* (1852), pl. 15, 16, 17.

[23] *Commission historique*, official report, 9 avril and 8 juin 1875: Online edition, éd. J.-D. Pariset: http://elec.enc.sorbonne.fr/monumentshistoriques/Annees/1875.html.

[24] *Carte des monuments historiques de la France d'après la liste établie par la Commission* (Paris 1875); *Exposition universelle de Vienne en 1873. Section française. Les monuments historiques de France à l'exposition de Vienne* (Paris 1876), Annexe IV, 392–95. Sommerard was the general Commissioner for France at Universal Exhibitions, and he inserted texts from Viollet-le-Duc and others. He proposed to use credits provided for the Vienna Exhibition to pay for printing the map.

[25] Anthyme Saint-Paul, 'Les écoles d'architecture romane', from the *Annuaire de l'archéologue français*, 1 (1877), 52–65 and 93–112. At the same time, Saint-Paul selected many features which are not morphological.

[26] To quote, among many others, a recent remark by Tadgh O'Keeffe: 'Romanesque [is treated] as a sort of historical *fait accompli* rather than as a construct invented two hundred years ago'. T. O'Keefe, *Archaeology and the Pan-European Romanesque* (London 2007), 51.

[27] P. Geary, 'Différence ethnique et nationalisme au xixe siècle: un paysage empoisonné', in *Quand les nations refont l'histoire* (Paris 2004), 35. See also P. Geary and G. Klaniczay, eds., *Manufacturing Middle Ages: Entangled History of Medievalism in Nineteenth-Century Europe* (Brill 2013).

[28] Quicherat's remarkable and well-illustrated *History of Costume in France* (Paris 1875) was not established on regional divisions because it ended with the Revolution.

[29] Brutails, 'La géographie monumentale' (as n. 4), 27.

[30] A. Marignan, *Un historien de l'art français. Louis Courajod. I. Les temps francs* (Paris 1899), 119.

[31] Lectures published in *Bulletin Monumental* (1891–92), 54. Courajod also wrote: 'We are all barbarians'.

[32] E. Mâle, *L'Art allemand et l'Art français du Moyen âge* (Paris 1917). The first part concerns '*L'Art allemand'*; a second and shorter part concerns 'German vandalism' and Reims cathedral.

[33] Picrochole is a character in 'Gargantua and Pantagruel' by François Rabelais, who started a stupid and entirely pointless war against the father of Gargantua.

[34] A. Choisy, *Histoire de l'architecture*, vol. 2 (Paris 1899), 240–45. This book was the Bible in architecture schools until the 1970s.

[35] Anthyme Saint-Paul, *Histoire monumentale de la France* (Paris 1883), 111. See also Anthyme Saint-Paul, 'Les écoles d'architecture romane', in *Annuaire de l'Archéologue français* (1877), 106, where he deplored this situation. 'The Limousine school is generally erased from maps'.

[36] F. Deshoulières, *La théorie d'Eugène Lefèvre-Pontalis sur les écoles romanes* (Paris 1925).

[37] *Commission historique*, official report, 9 avril and 8 juin 1875 (see n. 19).

[38] G. Plat, 'La Touraine, berceau des écoles romanes du sud-ouest', *Bulletin Monumental*, 77 (1913), 347–78.

[39] Lefèvre-Pontalis, 'A quelle école faut-il rattacher l'église de Beaulieu (Corrèze)? *Bulletin Monumental*, 78 (1914), 58–87.

[40] Lefèvre-Pontalis, 'L'école du Périgord n'existe pas', *Bulletin Monumental*, 82 (1923), 7–35.

[41] 'We know the reasons for this diversity: the fragmentation of feudal France into provinces which became withdrawn into themselves, the great difficulty of travelling': J.-A. Brutails, *Précis d'archéologie*, 3rd ed. (Paris 1936), 100. See also *Mélanges d'archéologie et d'histoire. Archéologie du Moyen Age. Mémoires et fragments réunis par R. de Lasteyrie* (Paris 1886), 451–54.

[42] E. Corroyer, *L'architecture romane* (Paris 1888), 279. The author was unaware of the southern tower, which was the tallest but which fell down in the 16th century. On Corroyer, see section 'The connection between regionalisation and restoration'.

[43] C. Andrault-Schmitt, 'D'Angoulême à Poitiers, la voûte en majesté pour l'évêque (1110–1167)', *Cahiers de Saint-Michel de Cuxa*, 44 (2013), 39–53; Eadem, 'A Western Interpretation of an Oriental Scheme: The Domed Churches in Romanesque Aquitaine', in *Romanesque and the Mediterranean. Points of Contacts Across the Latin,*

Greek and Islamic Worlds c. 1000–c. 1250, eds. R. M. Bacile and J. McNeill (Leeds 2015), 225–40.

[44] Claude Andrault-Schmitt, 'Archaism or Singularity? The Nave Clerestory in Romanesque Architecture Between the Loire and Dordogne', in *Romanesque and the Past*, eds. John McNeill and Richard Plant (London 2013), 95–108.

[45] Nevertheless, historians of art, of philosophy . . . should be properly resentful. While they admit and apply mutual concepts and methods, French historians (meaning 'pure' historians or 'historians strictly speaking') preserve their primacy.

[46] Concerning the political specificities of restoration and the link between the need for classification and restoration practice, for a non-French point of view, see Stamp, 'In Search of the Byzantine' (as n. 3).

[47] Corroyer, *L'architecture romane* (as n. 42), passim.

[48] 'Etudes sur l'archéologie à propos du salon d'architecture de 1890', *L'architecture*, 20 (1890), 21, 24 mai. An International Conference assembled by the Minister of Commerce and Industry to prepare the International Exhibition in 1889 expressed the view that 'as regards reparations, architects henceforth should limit themselves to what is necessary to strengthen the buildings'. Once more we note the importance of the International Exhibitions. 'Strengthen' is Corroyer's master word. He attributes malpractice to the architects who hold sway over the archaeologists (though he concedes that some restorations in Germany and England were even worse!).

[49] S. Bryant, 'La collégiale Saint-Etienne de Neuvy-Saint-Sépulchre (Indre). Une étude de la rotonde et de la nef', *Revue archéologique du Centre*, 43 (2004), 171–207.

[50] E. Viollet-le-Duc, *Dictionnaire raisonné de l'architecture française*, Tome V (Paris 1861), 162.

[51] H. Lemonnier et H. Michel, *Leçons professées à l'Ecole du Louvre (1887–1896)* (Paris 1899), I, 525.

[52] Mâle, *L'Art allemand et l'Art français* (as n. 32), 101.

[53] Brutails, 'La géographie monumentale' (as n. 4), 3.

[54] C. Andrault-Schmitt, 'L'église de Saint-Désiré', *Congrès archéologique du Bourbonnais* (Paris 1991), 339–51.

[55] Mâle, *L'Art allemand et l'Art français* (as n. 32), 101.

The Regional and Transregional in Romanesque Europe (2021), 13–18

HANS KUBACH'S TREATMENT OF REGIONS IN THE STUDY OF ROMANESQUE ARCHITECTURE

Eric Fernie

One of the exceptions to the overall tendency to categorize the Romanesque by regions is to be found in the work of Hans Kubach. Using his Architektur der Romanik *of 1974, the paper examines and assesses his preference for the* Kunstlandschaft *in the explanation of groups and variations and his concomitant rejection of the role of both ecclesiastical and secular units. This means that master masons are the chief and in some cases the only category of people determining the design of the buildings. His approach is particularly clearly demonstrated in chapter 3, that dealing with church buildings of the years between c. 1070 and c. 1150. In the case of the pilgrimage, Kubach rejects the grouping of five churches associated with that of Santiago, on the grounds that there are churches of the same type which are not on the pilgrimage routes. This argument is also assessed.*

As the outline of the conference says, 'The categorization of Romanesque by region was a cornerstone of 20th-century scholarship'. There were of course exceptions to this overall tendency, one of which is provided by Hans Kubach. He does this particularly with regard to the significance of the organisations of church and state in explanations of similarities and differences between church buildings. I disagree strongly, to the point of criticism, with Kubach's view of the insignificance of such units, so, before I go any further I want to make it clear that (that point aside) I have the greatest respect for Kubach's scholarship, especially for his masterly and detailed analyses of hundreds if not thousands of buildings. His publication on Speyer cathedral, with Walter Haas, shows him as one of the world's greatest architectural historians in the collecting, organising and presenting of the data relevant to the building. It is a model of its kind.

Kubach's rejection of ecclesiastical and political units is well attested in a number of his publications, such as the volume with Albert Verbeek accompanying their gazetteer of churches in the Rhine-Meuse area, but I have selected his *Architektur der Romanik* of 1974 for this study because it deals with the style as a whole.[1] What follows is divided into three parts, concerning, respectively, the book's introduction, its third chapter, and its discussion of the Santiago pilgrimage.

THE INTRODUCTION TO *ARCHITEKTUR DER ROMANIK*

Here are three quotations from the introduction, taken from the English edition of 1988.[2] The introduction is brief, so they are prominent. In the section headed 'Organisation of Bishoprics and Parishes', he says: 'It is all too easy to conclude that such distribution of ecclesiastical authority and such legal interdependence must have determined certain important architectural variations, but this can seldom be demonstrated and has all too often led to erroneous conclusions'. In that on 'Monastic Orders': 'The influence of such [that is, monastic] reforms on church architecture has been the object of much study and debate but seems often to have been unduly overrated.' And in the section on 'State and Nation':

> The innumerable small territorial states may be compared to the multitude of art centres which likewise were often sharply demarcated from each other. Yet those centres were by no means geographically identical with the territories, and, furthermore, display interrelationships on a higher level which have no parallel whatsoever with any ecclesiastical or civil entities to be found on the map.[3]

The first and second quotations, those which deal with bishoprics, parishes, and the monastic orders, leave open a possibility that some buildings or aspects of them might be explained by social units, but the third one makes it clear how small that possibility is, not least because, despite the paragraph being about the state, it concludes with a resounding statement which includes the church as well. Further, there is in that final statement the (if anything more significant) reference to the connections between the art centres existing at a higher level than any church or state boundaries on a map. The original German *übergeordente* appears to be accurately translated as 'higher', more accurately than in either the Italian or French translations. The Italian has *sopraregionale*,

  DOI: 10.4324/9781003162827-2

which suggests that the art centres existed on a larger scale than the political units. The French has *sans rapport*, again avoiding the implication of superiority present in the German and English versions.[4] However one translates *übergeordente*, the statement is none the less clear: that the buildings are seldom explained by the political or social units.

CHAPTER THREE

There are six chapters in the book, four on Romanesque church architecture covering its pre-, early, high, and late phases, a very brief fifth one on domestic and military architecture, and a sixth on subjects such as construction and iconography, restricted to churches. Chapter 3, on the high or middle phase, from *c.* 1070 to *c.* 1150, can therefore be considered the core of the volume. Three aspects of the chapter particularly bring out Kubach's approach, concerning (1) the mention of states, (2) the sections into which the text is divided, and (3) the illustrations.

On the first point, the pre- and early Romanesque chapters do acknowledge the importance of states (the Carolingian and Ottonian dynasties as well as the Salians and Speyer) in the formation of contemporary taste, and the late chapter stresses the connection between the new Gothic style and the French monarchy.[5] Hence it is noticeable that chapter 3 makes no reference to the Empire, France, or patrons, and references to other political units are only to locate the buildings. Only two political events are mentioned, the Norman conquests of England and Apulia, and those very much in passing.[6] It is significant that there are no maps in the book.

On the second point, the chapter is divided into sections on the vaulted basilica, the flat-ceilinged basilica, and mature forms in south-western Europe.[7] All three sections are therefore based on elements in the buildings and the groups they make up, forming what Kubach calls the *Kunstlandschaft*, or art landscape. There is no doubt that the buildings in question do form groups based on these elements, and it is necessary to identify and understand them. In addition, many aspects of the buildings were the concern of the masons, who were the ones who knew how to build a barrel vault, for example, and, perhaps more important, how to keep it standing. The *Kunstlandschaft* is an essential part of explanations of the style and a worthy hypothesis. But here the master mason has been proposed as the main and almost sole driver of architectural variety and change, not only in construction but in all respects. This omits what is perhaps the single most important other factor, namely, how the buildings were paid for, and by whom, that is, the patrons, both secular and ecclesiastical, and the role which competition would often have played in their choices. Kubach does mention the importance of patrons and how they could be involved in the designs of churches, but he does so only in chapter six, that on themes, and he does not apply it here.[8] It is as if the designing of churches inhabited a sphere in which considerations such as patronage did not apply and objects were not affected by politics, ideologies, economics, or indeed motives of any sort other than those of the masons. The section on south-western Europe makes the point in a different way, by mentioning a geographical area. Kubach says that 'south-western Europe' refers to buildings in southern France and northern Spain. Thus the label is used because it is a neutral geographical description free of cultural associations, an architectural grouping which ignores the relevance of the political entities of the area. In consequence one might ask what role the cultural power of the Duchy of Aquitaine or the French kingdom played in the decisions of master masons and of the patrons who employed them. Was it, for instance, pure chance or the cheapest quote that caused Bishop Peláez of Santiago to appoint French master masons to build his cathedral?

The third point is the way the chapter is illustrated, concerning which there is a single extraordinary fact, that, while all the illustrations have figure numbers, they are not referred to in the text. This practice could perform a useful function, namely showing what the buildings have in common across the area claimed for the use of the style, without concentrating on individual structures. Kubach's study would again form an instructive part of a book on Romanesque architecture, but the disjunction between text and image weakens the possibility of making specific connections between the buildings and their contexts.[9]

THE SANTIAGO PILGRIMAGE GROUP

Kubach also comments on one other subject where social forces are in play, that is, the phenomenon of the pilgrimage, in particular that to Santiago. Five churches, at Tours, Limoges, Conques, and Toulouse on the routes across France and that at Santiago itself, have been claimed as forming a group and explained by their association with the Santiago pilgrimage, as first proposed by Kenneth Conant (Figure 2.1).[10] This is one of the biggest issues in the historiography of Romanesque architecture because opinion is so evenly divided.

Taking first whether they form a group, those who disagree include Raymond Oursel, Alan Borg, Kubach, Thomas Lyman, Quitterie Cazes, and Isidro Bango. Those who accept them as a group include Serafín Moralejo, Annie Shaver-Crandell, Paula Gerson, John Williams, Henrik Karge, James D'Emilio, José Luis Senra, Manuel Castiñeiras, and Claude Andrault-Schmitt.[11] I agree with those who see the buildings as forming a group, but it has to be acknowledged that those against raise important arguments, such as, for example, the significance of changes of plan between phases in some of the buildings.

On the second question, whether the group can be explained by the Santiago pilgrimage, Andrault-Schmitt makes a powerful and completely convincing case against the concept. This she does chiefly with reference to the *Guide*, where equal prominence is given to St Eutrope at Saintes, St Hilaire at Poitiers, and St-Gilles-du-Gard, and

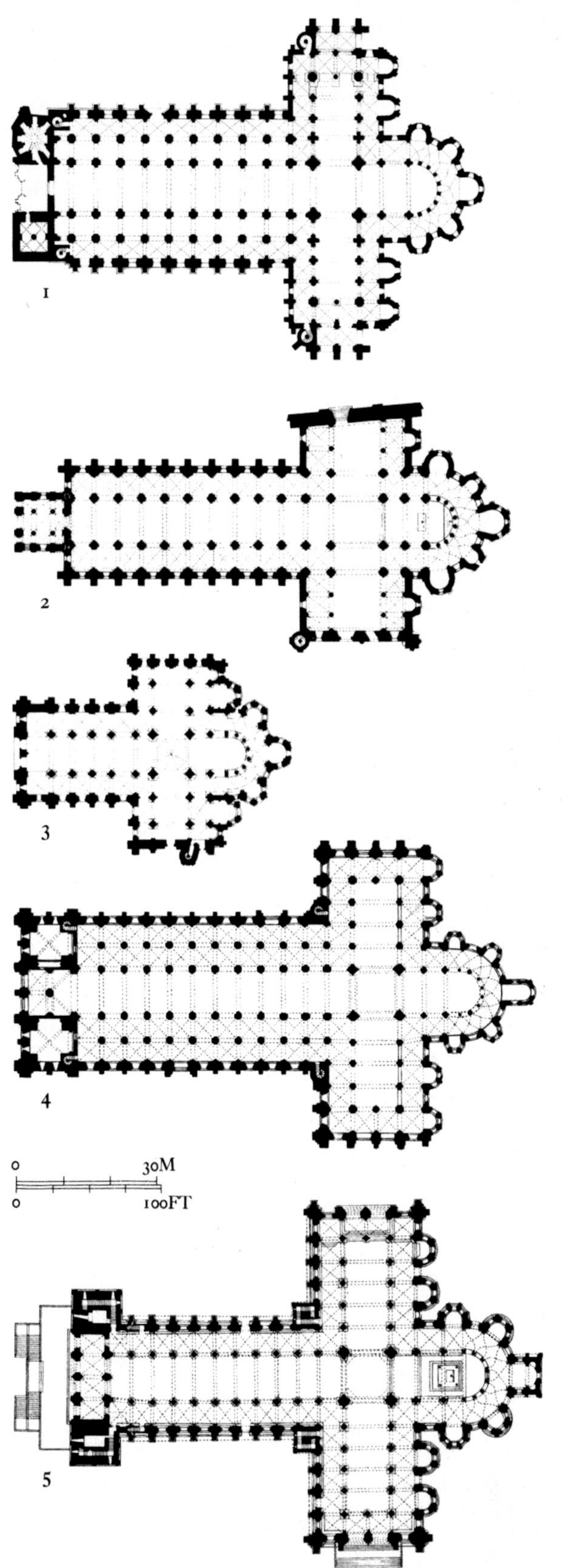

FIGURE 2.1

Plans of the five 'Santiago group' churches, at Tours (Indre-et-Loire), Limoges (Haute-Vienne), Conques (Aveyron), Toulouse (Haute-Garonne), and Santiago (Galicia) (Conant, 1974, Figure 113) there is not even a mention of St Martial at Limoges.[12] One of the results of this conclusion must be that the location of one church on each route and one at the goal is the result of coincidence, but then there are few things as common as coincidences.

These aspects need not, however, concern us further here, as the matter in hand is Kubach's argument for denying that there is a group, where I think that his wish to reject social explanations has led him to ignore both the physical evidence and logic. I accept the five as a group chiefly for the following reason: that these buildings all share five features (except for one at St Martial) and that they are the only ones which do so. Table 2.1 sets out those features, restricted to the five which were in play in the 1960s and 1970s when Kubach was writing his book: an ambulatory with radiating chapels, transept arms with aisles on all three free sides, galleries, no clerestory (except in the apse), and barrel vaults.

Kubach's reason for rejecting them as a group is that there are what he describes as churches of the Santiago type off the pilgrimage routes, such as those at Coimbra in Portugal, Marcilhac near Cahors, Orense near Santiago, and Alet in Brittany.[13] Yet these buildings, to an almost embarrassing degree, do not exhibit the five elements of the churches of the Santiago group, as indicated by Table 2.2.

Of Kubach's four examples, Coimbra is the closest, with three of the features (Figure 2.2), Marcilhac has only galleries in common with the five buildings, and Orense and Alet appear to have none (Figure 2.3).

TABLE 2.1

Five churches of the Santiago group indicating the presence or absence of the five elements

	Ambulatory and radiating chapels	*Transept with three aisles to each arm*	*Gallery*	*No clerestory, except in the apse*	*Barrel vault*
Conques	x	x	x	x	x
Limoges	x		x	x	x
Toulouse	x	x	x	x	x
Santiago	x	x	x	x	x
Tours	x	x	x	x	x

TABLE 2.2

Five elements shared by the churches of the Santiago group, illustrating their presence or absence in the four buildings cited by Kubach

	Ambulatory and radiating chapels	*Transept with three aisles to each arm*	*Gallery*	*No clerestory, except in the apse*	*Barrel vault*
Coimbra			x	x	x
Marcilhac			x		
Orense					
Alet					

CONCLUSION

Kubach does invoke one social factor, in the introduction, where he notes that the extent of Romanesque buildings, from Ireland to central Europe and from Scandinavia to the Italian islands, was 'a territory that constituted nothing less than the domain of the Roman Church in the Middle Ages'.[14] But, if the Latin Church was as important as this for the whole style, marking its maximum extent, something for which ecclesiastics must have been in some way responsible, it is difficult to see how those churchmen could not be relevant to at least some of the variations within the area of the style. In addition, the boundary between the Latin and Orthodox churches

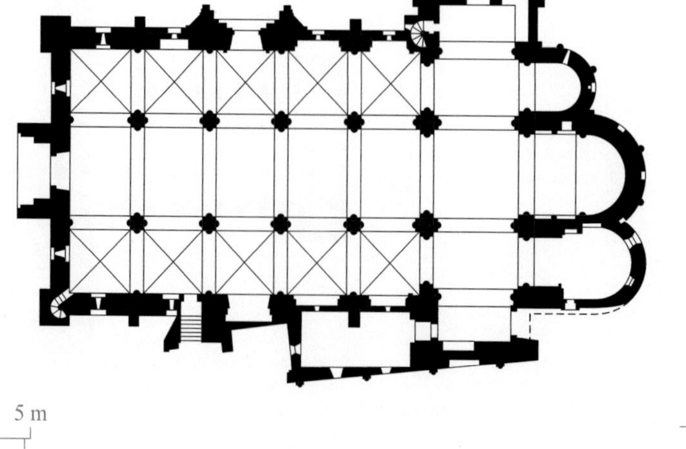

FIGURE 2.2

Coimbra (Coimbra), Old Cathedral: plan

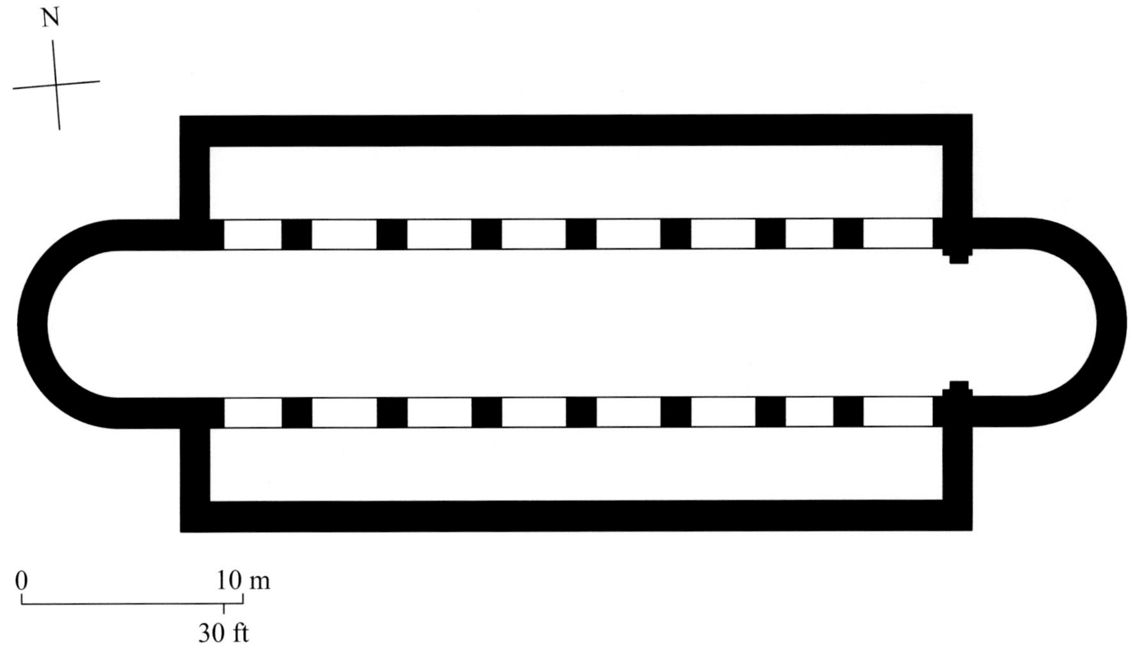

FIGURE 2.3

Alet (Ille-et-Vilaine, Brittany): ruined church, plan

is largely a boundary between secular units, which must also therefore play a part in the extent and definition of the style.[15] The point is that more than one factor needs to be explored in order to explain the buildings.

ACKNOWLEDGEMENTS

I would like to record my thanks to Richard Plant and Andreas Puth for their generous help with this paper.

NOTES

1 H. Kubach, *Architektur der Romanik* (Stuttgart 1974). An Italian translation was published in 1972 (*Architettura romanica*, Milan), an English translation in 1975 (*Romanesque Architecture*, New York), and a French one in 1981 (*Architecture romane*, Paris). A second, abbreviated edition of the German text was published in 1986 (*Romanik*, Stuttgart). A second, also abbreviated, English edition was published in 1988 (*Romanesque Architecture*, London). For some reviews of the 1975 edition, see E. G. Carlson, *Art Bulletin*, 59/2 (1977), 269–71, K. J. Conant, *Journal of the Society of Architectural Historians*, 36/1 (1977), 44, and P. Kidson, *Times Literary Supplement*, 18 March 1977, 323. I have used the 1988 edition for the English quotations. On the Rhine-Meuse: Hans Erich Kubach and Albert Verbeek, *Romanische Baukunst an Rhein und Maas: katalog der vorromanischen und romanischen Denkmäler,* four volumes, Deutsche Verlag für Kunstwissenschaft (Berlin 1976–88) Each chapter has a concluding section on the subject, and chapter 6 is devoted to it.

2 Kubach, *Romanik*, 1974 (as n. 1), 11–12; Kubach, *Romanesque*, 1988 (as n. 1), 9–10.

3 There is an error in the 1988 English translation of the third quote: in the German, Italian and French texts there is no mention of the states being 'small'. (For these texts see note 4.)

4 Kubach, *Romanik*, 1974 (as n. 1), 12: '*Den zahlreichen Territorien entsprechen die Kunstlandschaften, die sich oft sehr deutlich gegeneinder abgrenzen. Sie fallen aber keineswegs geographisch mit den Territorien zusammen, und vor allem zeigen sie übergeordnete Zusammenhänge, zu denen es auf der Landkarte weder im Bereich der Kirche noch des Staates Parallelen gibt*'. Kubach, *romanica*, 1972 (as n. 1), 12: '*Ai numerosi territori correspondono i paesaggi artistici, che spesso si distinguono l'uno dall'altro; ma essi non coincidono geograficamente con quei territori, e sopratutto presentano connessioni sopraregionali, per le quali non ci sono paralleli sulla carta geografica nell'ambito della Chiesa ne in quello dello Stato*'. Kubach, *romane*, 1981 (as note 1), 12: '*au morcellement regional correspond bien une topologie de l'art révéllant des cloisonnement et des blocages. Mais le decoupage artistique ne correspond pas à celui des anciennes provinces: de plus il met en evidence des similitudes sans rapport avec la repartition des dioceses, pas plus qu'avec celle des territories politiques en formation*'.

5 Kubach, *Romanik*, 1974 (as n. 1), 110–14, 244–5; Kubach, *Romanesque*, 1988 (as n. 1), 64, 130–31.

6 Kubach, *Romanik*, 1974 (as n. 1), 148, 192; Kubach, *Romanesque*, 1988 (as n. 1), 85 and 108.

7 Kubach, *Romanik*, 1974 (as n. 1), first section, 147–72; second section, 172–98; third section, 199–241. 'Mature' is '*hochromanische*' in the German text.

8 Kubach, *Romanesque*, 1988 (as n. 1), 380–81 and 192–93.

9 This could be the result of a policy on the part of Electa, publishers of the first edition, that authors should not refer to illustrations. Yet whatever the explanation for the lack of references to illustrations, it fits with the other aspects of Kubach's approach.

10 K. J. Conant, *Carolingian and Romanesque Architecture 800 to 1200*, 3rd ed. (Harmondsworth 1974), 156–75.

11 For clear summaries of the question, see J. Williams, 'The Basilica in Compostela and the Way of Pilgrimage', in *Compostela and Europe: The Story of Diego Gelmírez*, ed. Manuel Castiñeiras (Santiago de Compostela and Milan 2010), 110–21; H. Karge, 'The European Architecture of Church Reform in Galicia. The Romanesque Cathedral of Santiago de Compostela', in *Culture and Society in Medieval Galicia. A Cultural Crossroads at the Edge of Europe*,

ed. and trans. James D'Emilio (Leiden and Boston 2015), 573–630, Chapter 15, especially 585 and 610; H. Karge, 'Die Grabkult der Heiligen und apostolische Konkurenz. Pilgerkirchen im aquitanischen Kulturraum als Modelle für Santiago di Compostela', in *Santiago de Compostela: Pilgerarchitectur und bildliche Repräsentation in neuer Perspektive*, eds. B. Nicolai and K. Rheidt (Bern 2015), 345–61, especially 345–58.

[12] C. Andrault-Schmitt, 'Saint Martial of Limoges and the Making of a Saint', in *Romanesque Saints, Shrines and Pilgrimage*, eds. J. McNeill and R. Plant (Milton Park–New York 2020), 109–25, at 117.

[13] Kubach, *Romanik*, 1974 (as n. 1), 207; Kubach, *Romanesque*, 1988 (as n. 1), 118.

[14] Kubach, *Romanik*, 1974 (as n. 1), 9; Kubach, *Romanesque*, 1988 (as n. 1), 7.

[15] Andreas Hartmann-Virnich has, like Kubach, stressed the importance of examining the distribution of building types, parts and elements, but he presents such examining as a means of assessing and, where necessary, correcting the boundaries suggested by secular and ecclesiastical organisations, along with pilgrimages (*Was ist Romanik? Geschichte, Formen und Technik des romanischen Kirchenbaus* (Darmstadt 2004), 8, 60, and 262).

The Regional and Transregional in Romanesque Europe (2021), 19–33

DID *ZODIAQUE*'S REGIONAL PORTRAYAL CREATE A FALSE IMPRESSION AS TO THE NATURE OF ROMANESQUE?

Philip Bovey

The Zodiaque *collection of books, journals, and other material is, by any measure, the largest body of published images of Romanesque architecture and sculpture ever produced. The main series is organised on a regional basis. The quality of the photographs and their presentation is recognized but can be seen as creating a false impression of transregional unity. Given the power of images to exert a (largely subconscious) influence on our perception, we need to understand what inspired the vision and how it is conveyed. It had its genesis at a very particular moment in the political and religious history of France and reflected the ideas of the Benedictine monk who was the driving force behind the collection and of the main photographer, Dom Angelico Surchamp.*

The *Zodiaque* project is a collective term for the different publications which emerged from the Benedictine Abbey of La Pierre-qui-Vire in Burgundy between 1951 and 1998,[1] largely concerned with Romanesque, and, in particular, the unrivalled body of photographs which is its distinguishing feature. The *Directeur-Gérant* was Dom Angelico Surchamp (1924–2018) (Figure 3.1 and Colour Plate II (top)). Although arranged by region, the body of photographs has an unmistakable unity and can be seen as giving a false impression as to the existence of a transregional artistic style and approach in Romanesque. What I hope to show is that the unity of the portrayal is not concerned with regionalism or transregionalism in terms of architectural history but expresses a distinctive vision which, whether or not we share it, we need to understand.

ROMANESQUE AND 'FORM'

What appears to be the first published article on a Romanesque subject by Dom Angelico is dated October 1947.[2] It includes a comparative analysis (Figure 3.2) of the Christ in Glory in the porch at Saint-Savin-sur-Gartempe (Vienne) and a 'tableau' by the Cubist painter and theoretician Albert Gleizes, who was associated with La Pierre-qui-Vire and became Dom Angelico's teacher and a major influence on him. The title is *De la réalité des sens à la réalité de l'esprit*. Moving from the reality of the senses to the reality of the spirit is central to Dom Angelico's vision.

While 'Romanesque' had long been recognised as distinct from Gothic, around 1930 in France there developed a new emphasis on it as something important to study in its own right, rather than just a barbarous predecessor or a debased survival from the Antique. Mérimée had, of course, identified the significance of the Saint-Savin paintings as early as 1845, but the revival of interest seems to have come from a relatively small group, all of whom had a major influence on Dom Angelico.[3] What links them together is the concept of 'form'.

What is meant by 'form', is, of course, not a simple question. It is distinct from 'style', iconography, subject matter, or even signification (other than of itself). It can be 'Essence' or 'Reality', or simply 'Beauty'. There are many different ideas. These ideas are frequently associated with what are put forward as different ways of seeing (ways that in many cases interact directly with photography) and therefore of what we can know and understand. The best known considerations of this question are those of Henri Focillon, starting with his *Les Pierres de France* in 1919.[4] The turning point is probably his *L'Art des sculpteurs romans*, subtitled *Recherches sur l'histoire des formes*, in 1931,[5] followed in 1934 by *La vie des formes*.[6] In parallel, however, in 1923 Gleizes published *La Peinture et ses Lois* and then in 1931–32 delivered three lectures.[7] The first lecture, *Art et Religion*,[8] is in effect a summary of his major work *La forme et l'histoire*, although to his frustration that was not published until 1932.[9] It was Gleizes and also Jurgis Baltrušaitis (Focillon's son-in-law) rather

  DOI: 10.4324/9781003162827-3

FIGURE 3.1

Dom Angelico Surchamp OSB, at a reception given on 2 April 2012 to mark his appointment as Chevalier de la Légion d'honneur (Philip Bovey)

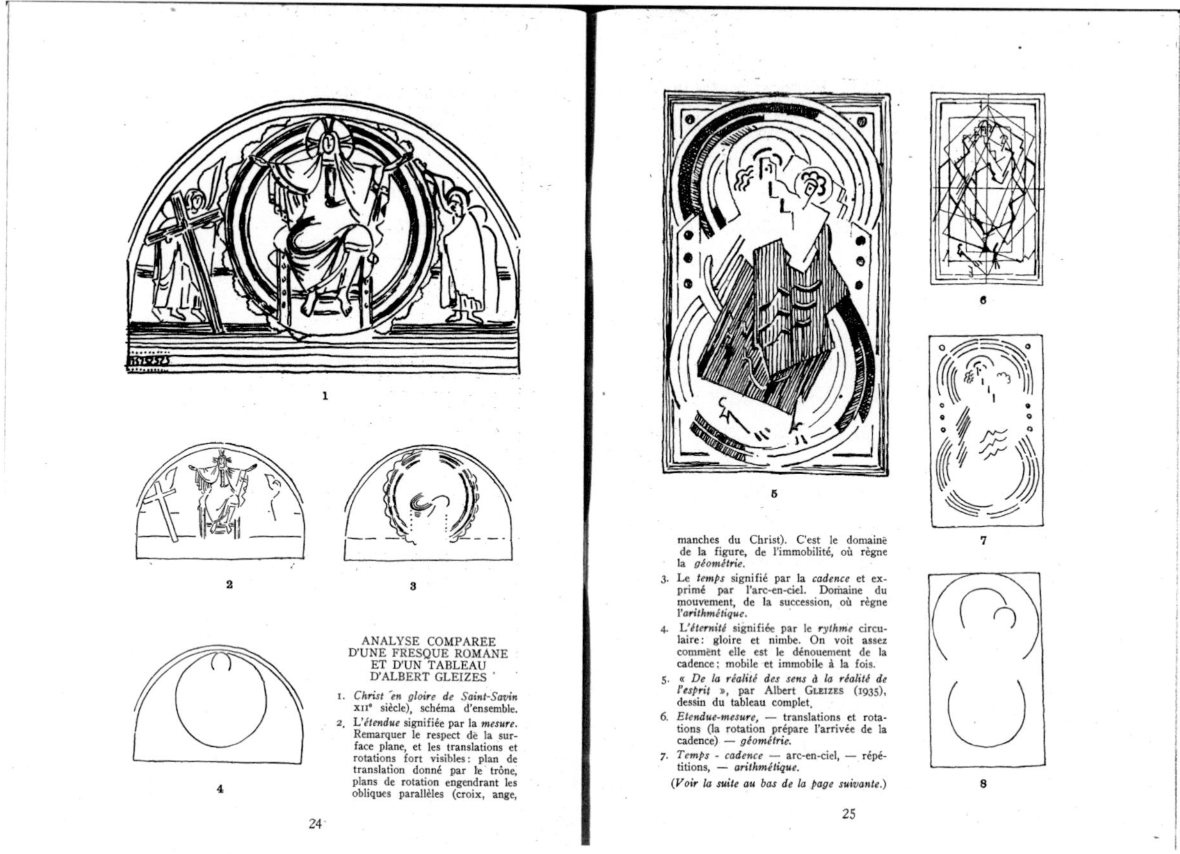

1

2

3

4

ANALYSE COMPAREE
D'UNE FRESQUE ROMANE
ET D'UN TABLEAU
D'ALBERT GLEIZES

1. *Christ en gloire de Saint-Savin* XIIe siècle), schéma d'ensemble.
2. L'*étendue* signifiée par la *mesure*. Remarquer le respect de la surface plane, et les translations et rotations fort visibles: plan de translation donné par le trône, plans de rotation engendrant les obliques parallèles (croix, ange,

24

5

6

7

8

manches du Christ). C'est le domaine de la figure, de l'immobilité, où règne la *géométrie*.

3. Le *temps* signifié par la *cadence* et exprimé par l'arc-en-ciel. Domaine du mouvement, de la succession, où règne l'*arithmétique*.
4. L'*éternité* signifiée par le *rythme* circulaire: gloire et nimbe. On voit assez comment elle est le dénouement de la cadence; mobile et immobile à la fois.
5. « *De la réalité des sens à la réalité de l'esprit* », par Albert GLEIZES (1935), dessin du tableau complet.
6. *Etendue-mesure,* — translations et rotations (la rotation prépare l'arrivée de la cadence) — *géométrie*.
7. *Temps - cadence* — arc-en-ciel, — répétitions, — *arithmétique*.

(*Voir la suite au bas de la page suivante.*)

25

FIGURE 3.2

Analyse comparée d'une fresque romane et d'un tableau d'Albert Gleizes from (A. Surchamp, 'L'Enseignement d'Albert Gleizes')

than Focillon who were the direct influence (at least initially) on Dom Angelico.[10]

As will be described, the project was not conventional 'architectural history'. The background is a theological debate as to the best way to respond to the perceived crisis of unbelief, and its express purpose was to contribute to that response by bringing people to an understanding of modern art and in particular Cubism. What Cubism is about is 'form', the replacement of illusionist art and Impressionism's recording of optical impressions with a study of the structure of objects by defining their form.[11] The logic may seem obscure. The steps are that conventional religious art was seen as a major part of the problem but that modern art provoked a hostile reaction from the public. On the other hand, the public did like Romanesque. Modern art had rehabilitated primitive art and notably Romanesque. The answer was therefore to bring the public to modern art through a greater understanding of Romanesque. As Dom Angelico said 'Romanesque art intervened'.[12]

The theological debate is often characterised as an argument between conservatives and progressives, with the conservatives in control of the Church hierarchy, prepared to use every possible disciplinary means to maintain their position until they comprehensively lost the battle in the opening stages of Vatican II.[13] That characterisation is not wholly untrue, but many on the other side were uncomfortable with what happened following Vatican II, and they appear to have included Dom Angelico. Either way, arguing for the removal of later 'excresences', whether theological or artistic (Figure 3.3), was a challenge to the establishment.[14]

How then is this objective reflected in the portrayal? I would suggest that the proper starting point is the physical form and presentation of the books. There are more than 200 books in the various series (including different editions). The main series is *La nuit des temps* ('From the Depths of Time' – the title is significant), arranged regionally, beginning in 1954 with *Bourgogne romane*[15] and concluding in 1999 with *Westphalie romane* (Figure 3.4).[16] Their distinctive 'architecture' was deliberate. Physically and in design they were the work of the monks themselves. As a consequence, while the project was very much subject to financial constraints, it was not subject to editorial or other external ones.

As Focillon said:

> What would the world be, other than brute reality, devoid of cathedrals and books? Books do not owe everything to the sublimity of the spirit that conceived them. I am not afraid to say that they are matter, and noble matter, matter worked by learned and diligent hands, matter that is ordered, fashioned, endowed with life at last by a technique that is an art. Travellers who describe famous cities talk about their inhabitants, and also about the houses where these inhabitants live. The houses where we house the thoughts of the masters, and secondly the thoughts of everyone, are what books are. [. . .] No art is closer to architecture than typography. Like architecture, it has as its first rule the right discernment and the right adaptation of materials; like architecture, it is based on a system of definite relationships, its economy is stable, it is repugnant to sinuous whims. Just as the architect of a palace distributes light and shade on the façades with a wise measure and, in the interior layout, balances light with shade for the needs of life, so likewise the creator of a book, in disposing of two contrary forces: the white of the paper and the black of the ink, assigns a role to each and harmony in combining them. There are, in architecture, large flat areas which are like the margins.
>
> There are, in a book, symmetries and alternations which are those of a builder. And so, is it not true that these two great works of man: a book and a house, must strive for the same essential virtue, the style, I want to say the order, gravity without sadness, majesty without emphasis, combined with an accent of nature and noble charm that fully satisfies the spirit?[17]

The size, binding, typography, printing process, and (with some exceptions) layout and format remained largely the same.[18] *La nuit des temps* is the least 'arty' of the different series. Some of the others are in a larger format with bigger type and more white space, and more obvious book design. Arguably, it is the apparent artlessness in the main series that contributed to its success. The result was something sufficiently special to be capable of being given as a Christmas or First Communion present and yet sufficiently everyday to be used as a guide by those visiting an area. In consequence, the books sold in huge numbers.

The presentation seems to be designed to take the reader on a visual journey. Each group of photographs is an invitation to contemplate without reference to the text. In many cases, where there are several photographs of the same church, it starts with a distant view, then the outside, then perhaps views in different directions internally and particular features. It is a rhythmical progression as if one were walking through, picking out bits and looking at them more intently.

This arrangement, both of the individual volumes and the series as a whole, raised issues for the academics: as, for example, in the following excerpted reviews in the *Bulletin Monumental*: 'the presentation of the text and images is a bit disconcerting, and of an astonishing fantasy, both by the variety of characteristics used and the justification only by exaggerated width or by deletion of the margins, especially for images, which are often remarkable' (Aubert); 'complicated layout that makes it difficult to identify images and use notes' (Salet); 'primitive formula' (Grodecki); 'seriousness and scientific quality [] sorely lacking in its early days. [. . .] "Romanesque myth" [. . .] had grown disproportionately large to the detriment of Gothic art. [. . .] The technical quality of the photographic reproductions must obviously be recognized, although it is regrettable that this quality too often prevails over their archaeological interest' (Erlande-Brandenburg); 'could not totally escape its original flaws' (Bousquet).[19]

Just as text depends on the distribution of black and white, the same is true of photographs, above all gravure plates, as used (in the form of rotogravure) throughout the collection. Gravure is an 'intaglio' process: the deeper the etched indentation the more ink and the blacker the result. Gravure plates are not made from finished photographs but from a positive with tones not intended to be final but to produce the desired tonality in the etching process. The process tends to increase the contrast significantly, so that darker areas get blacker, lighter areas get lighter, and intermediate tones are compressed. The negative from which the positive is made is likely to have been considerably worked on (normally in a different colour to make it easier for the retoucher) to remove (in the case of *Zodiaque*) wiring, 'excresences', and other fittings which could not physically be taken out. When it works (and the process is highly skilled), the result is an image with a liveliness, sparkle, and tactile feel that no other process

FIGURE 3.3

Saulieu; Saint-Andoche view of nave showing how lamps obscure the Romanesque capitals (Philip Bovey)

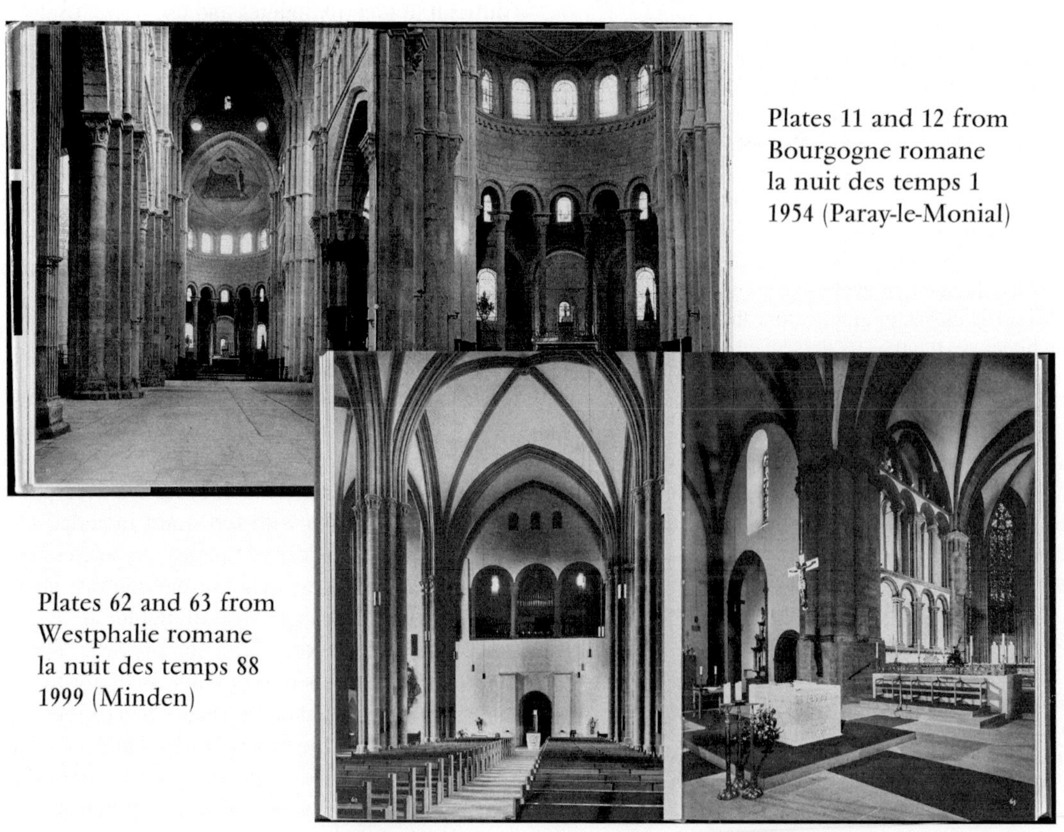

FIGURE 3.4

Comparison between the first and last volumes of La nuit des temps *(arranged by Philip Bovey)*

can produce. The gravure plates are thus not *reproductions* of photographs. They are the final photograph in multiple form.

With gravure, it does not matter if the highlights burn out. We accept the glow of sunlight through a window or round a door which looks awful in colour. Indeed, it is arguably closer to how we see it in real life. The result is to give the photographer and printer much greater freedom in how the tones are distributed in the final image. In particular, there is greater scope for the use of natural light to bring out the form as conceived by the artist.[20]

The plates were printed full page, without borders, and a general view was often followed by one or more details. For example, there are sixteen plates of details following the overall view of the tympanum at Moissac, several of them the same thing from different angles (see the discussion later of the exhibition *Art Roman du Soleil*, which featured these images).[21] Comparing the full-page treatment to an image with a margin and a caption, Dom Angelico said that the full page gives 'all the force, all the interiority of the figure. [. . .] [T]his consecration of the entire page to its sole presence, gives it a unique, incomparable power of radiation. There is no escape from it. It is necessary to face this look, this form that time has brought closer to us than far away, so much does it speak to our mentality of modern man'.[22] Similar considerations apply to moving from the general to a detail.

All of this undoubtedly contributes to the impression of uniformity in the subject matter. It is hardly surprising that everything can seem the same, particularly with groups of images that follow on without an obvious break. This impression may or may not have been intended to reinforce what Erlande-Brandenburg, in the passage previously quoted, calls the 'Romanesque myth', but either way the point is that it is the 'form' of the presentation that has the effect.

THE BEGINNING OF THE PROJECT

The project began not in 1954 with the books but in 1951 with a journal, *Zodiaque*, which continued in parallel. The most likely explanation as to why the new journal was launched when the Abbey already had a journal, *Témoignages*, to which Dom Angelico regularly contributed, seems to be that it was aimed at a different audience. Although there are lighter pieces, *Témoignages* is largely devoted to philosophy and theology for a specialist readership. The two journals were complementary, both directed to promoting the Christian faith in a modern unbelieving world but in different ways.

The new journal followed the vision of the Abbey's founder (le Père Jean-Baptiste Muard), which was distinct from mainstream Benedictinism. As described in an interview by Dom Angelico's brother monk and slightly younger contemporary, Dom Ghislain Lafont, the 'community, following the intuitions of its founder, had, from the beginning in 1850, a missionary aspect, kept an eye on the Church, on the world, and sought out how to bear witness to the faith'.[23] 'This orientation has continued throughout our history at La Pierre-qui-Vire, and many of the enterprises were marked by an evangelical concern for mission'.[24] Dom Angelico describes it as follows: 'Jean Baptiste Muard had an intellectual "vision": a house where there would be found three categories of religious, some devoted to prayer, others to preaching, and the third who worked in the community'.[25] The journal was not in any way intended as a commercial venture, although in the event the project was to prove extremely profitable for the Abbey.

The journal was launched at a time of controversy over the Dominicans' use of modern artists who were non-believers to produce sacred art for their new churches, the *Querelle de l'art sacré*, and the controversy is certainly relevant as part of the background but does not seem to have been the key factor.[26]

At a personal level, there was ill feeling between the Dominican co-editor of *L'Art Sacré*, Raymond Régamey, and Dom Angelico's teacher and mentor, Albert Gleizes, leading to a major row over Gleizes' comparative analysis of the St-Savin wall-painting (Figure 3.2). Régamey called it 'dessicated academicism'.[27] More important, although what the Dominicans and Dom Angelico were opposed to was the same thing, the *Saint-Sulpicien* religious art of the 19th century, what they were in favour of was different. Underlying that difference, there seems to be a difference of view as to the nature of 'form' and how we see. The Dominicans, and in particular Régamey's co-editor Couturier, were looking for 'Purity', the beauty of forms as forms without the slightest concession to moral, social, or pastoral intentions external to the work. They gave as examples the 'honeycombed curve of a[n unidentified] dam and the fresh, pure curve of a Sénanque capital'.[28] In contrast, although Plate 33 of *Zodiaque*'s *L'art Cistercien* could be the same capital, it is preceded by plates showing the approach to the abbey and the exterior.[29] There is no context, no materiality, in *L'Art Sacré*, what the *Zodiaque* volume calls the "simple beauty" which seizes the visitor. Couturier was dubious about a return to the past: 'The idealised collective world of the Middle Ages no longer existed, if it ever had'.[30] While, therefore, there is some connection it does not appear to be the whole story. As Cédric Lesec said, referring to the statement of intent in the first issue of the journal: 'The message of *Zodiaque* is more coded [i.e. than that of the Dominicans]. The choice of such a title is symptomatic in this respect'.[31]

That statement of intent combines a number of elements. Beginning with a quotation from Ramuz (Stravinsky's sometime librettist) – 'For one must be both savage and civilized; one shouldn't only be a primitive, but one must also be a primitive' – it refers to going back to the old in order to find the new.[32] 'This text could serve as a motto for our journal; it indicates well the meaning of our effort. By calling our journal *Zodiaque*, we intend several things. The first is the desire to return to a new conception of life, time, work and things, a new conception? Old more exactly, and – let's admit it – "primitive"'.[33]

This 'conception' is clearly derived from Gleizes's ideas discussed here. What it seems equally to be about is the thinking (the two are not unconnected) of the loose grouping of mainly Dominican and Jesuit French theologians known by their enemies in the Vatican as *Nouvelle Théologie* and by others as *Ressourcement* – 'going back to the sources' in order to make sense of the present.[34]

The concept of *Ressourcement* is said to have come from Charles Péguy: 'A revolution is a call to a more perfect tradition from a less perfect tradition, a call to a deeper tradition from a shallower tradition.[35] It means surpassing tradition in depth by going back, a search for deeper sources; in the literal sense of the word, a "resource". [. . .] [A] revolution [. . .] cannot succeed unless [. . .] it causes a deeper humanity than the humanity of the tradition which it opposes to arise and spring forth'.[36]

Described by his biographer Alexander Dru as 'the only poet of consequence during the last fifty years in France whose work has failed to arouse the smallest critical interest in this country' [i.e. Britain],[37] Péguy was a Dreyfusard socialist who became a Catholic and denounced both his former socialist friends (by then in Government) and the Catholic priesthood. Both, he said, turned *mystique* into *politique*. They failed to recognise the mystery at the heart of belief and tried to systematize it and apply rationalism to what cannot be rationalised.

Most of the Catholic establishment at the time had been strongly anti-Dreyfusard, with a few notable exceptions such as Étienne Gilson.[38] But as the opening words of the journal of Péguy studies launched in 1947 state, by then 'Péguy est à la mode', at least outside the conservative establishment. Dom Angelico refers to him frequently.[39] In particular, although his influence on Dom Angelico goes much wider, Péguy ran a subscriber-financed 'Cahiers', where he was constantly having to appeal for funds to maintain the high production and typographical standards, with which Dom Angelico clearly identified.[40]

French Catholic ordination training was generally deeply conservative.[41] 'The monastery, like all the Benedictine houses [. . .] was "ultramontane". One of the elements of this mentality [. . .] was the adoption, in obedience to Pope Leo XIII, of Thomism [i.e. the teaching of St Thomas Aquinas] as a major doctrinal orientation [. . .] the monks knew little or nothing about their own tradition'.[42]

Outside the monastery, Thomism was taught almost entirely from manuals, which digested and summarised it in ways that derived from post-Reformation Catholic theology, i.e. neo-Thomism (also called neo-Scholasticism). But that was not how the young monks in La Pierre-qui-Vire were taught. They:

> had no theology textbook and were constantly being sent back to the actual text of the works of Saint Thomas, the *Summa Theologica*, the *Quaestiones disputatae de veritate*, etc., [of] which the reading and study (in Latin!) took up a lot of [their] time[. . .] . [T]he mentality in which [they] approached Saint Thomas was directly inspired by two contemporary authors: Father [Marie-Dominique] Chenu and Étienne Gilson[. . .] . The first one happily situated Saint Thomas in the world of his time, in what he called the Mediæval Renaissance, with his evangelism, his interest in Scripture, his openness to the prevailing culture, its social developments. The second proposed for the idea of "being", unquestionably at the base of the Thomist construction, a convincing "existentialist" interpretation. Since Gilson was a neighbour, because he had a country house in the surrounding area, [the monks] sometimes benefited from his visit and his comments.

Chenu was a central figure in *Ressourcement* and a specialist on the 12th century.[43] Gilson was not a member of the *Ressourcement* group but was close to those who were. I will suggest here that Gilson's 'existentialism' is the key to the 'realism' which is central to Dom Angelico's *Zodiaque* vision. The same interview refers also to a great debt to the Jesuit, de Lubac, another of the leading *Ressourcemen*t theologians, and to an (unnamed) 'great, passionate and exciting brother' in the Abbey who taught the history of philosophy. There were also connections with the *Ressourcemen*t theologians through Gleizes.[44]

What is described are the seeds of the revolution that, with the ideas of Newman, became Vatican II, being taught to young men in the depths of a Burgundian forest at a time when, for the most part, Catholic France was unchanged.

Dom Angelico had originally intended to become a Dominican and would presumably have trained for the priesthood at Le Saulchoir. The then Regent of Studies was Marie-Dominique Chenu, who disagreed with the way Thomism was taught. He thought the way of understanding Aquinas was by reconstituting his work in its original setting. The Roman approach, he said, was polluted by 'centuries of baroque excrescences' and the overreaction to earlier attempts to reconcile faith and history. 'It is good Thomism', Chenu concluded, 'to do the history of Thomas's thought – to see its soul united to its body'.[45] In his position as Regent of Studies, Chenu's approach was a fundamental challenge to the authority of Rome. On 6 February 1942, he was removed from his post, and his book was placed on the Index. Dom Angelico went to La Pierre-qui-Vire seven months later. As he subsequently said, he later understood better how much he would have been tested if he had opted for the order of St Dominic![46]

Then, as Henri de Lubac described it, 'lightning struck' the Jesuits as well. In June 1950, de Lubac and four other professors at Lyon were removed from their posts and required to leave the Province. In August, the Pope published a thundering encyclical *Humani Generis*. It did not condemn the *Ressourcement* theologians (Jesuit or Dominican) by name, but there was no mistaking its target. It was a comprehensive denunciation of everything they stood for. It was not unprovoked! For example, the Dominican theologian Congar's *Vraie et Fausse Réforme dans L'Église* included an Appendix (omitted in later versions) on the 'mentality of the "right" and integrism in France' which nobody in authority could have tolerated.[47]

From the 'lightning strike' until Vatican II, *Ressourcement* effectively went underground.

Had *Zodiaque* openly allied itself with this movement, it might never have survived. Its intention was, as Lesec said, 'more coded'. However, the Abbey of La Pierre-qui-Vire had made its position clear in a note in *Témoignages* in 1947, in an issue devoted to existentialism. Commenting on a skirmish between the Jesuits and the hierarchy in the run-up to the 'lightning strike', received after the rest of the issue had been prepared, the note says that they do not agree with everything in the Jesuit response but strongly support its publication. They cite Newman's meditations on the church militant and the need for 'shock troops' to 'penetrate the modern thinking that must be conquered in Christ'. The story is set out in J. Mettepenningen, *Truth, Orthodoxy, and the Nouvelle Théologie: Truth as Issue in a "Second Modernist Crisis" (1946–1950)*.[48]

The Benedictines were less threatening to the hierarchy because they were not, as the Dominicans and Jesuits were supposed to be, shock troops. 'Primitivism' was seen as part of the original Benedictine character. Thus in the compendium volume *L'Europe des Monastères*,[49] Dom Angelico used as the introductory essay passages from Newman's *The Mission of the Benedictine Order*:

> To St. Benedict [. . .] let me assign the element of Poetry; to St. Dominic, the Scientific element; and to St. Ignatius [i.e. the Jesuits], the Practical. [. . .] Poetry delights in the indefinite and various as contrasted with unity. [. . .] [The Benedictine] spirit indeed is ever one, but not its outward circumstances. It is not an Order proceeding from one mind at a particular date, and appearing all at once in its full perfection, and in its extreme development, and in form one and the same everywhere and from first to last, as is the case with other great religious institutions; but it is an organization, diverse, complex, and irregular, and variously ramified, rich rather than symmetrical, with many origins and centres and new beginnings and the action of local influences, like some great natural growth; with tokens, on the face of it, of its being a divine work, not the mere creation of human genius. Instead of progressing on plan and system and from the will of a superior, it has shot forth and run out as if spontaneously, and has shaped itself according to events, from an irrepressible fulness of life within, and from the energetic self-action of its parts, like those symbolical creatures in the prophet's vision, which went every one of them straight forward, whither the impulse of the spirit was to go. [. . .]
>
> And when he [i.e. the Benedictine monk] began to build, his architecture was suggested by the scene – not the scientific and masterly conception of a great whole with many parts, as the Gothic style in a later age, but plain and inartificial, the adaptation of received fashions to his own purpose, and an addition of chapel to chapel and a wayward growth of cloister, according to the occasion, with half-concealed shrines and unexpected recesses, with paintings on the wall as by a second thought, with an absence of display and a wild, irregular beauty, like that of the woods by which he was at first surrounded.[50]

Here we have clearly a concept of diversity in unity from a time before scientific rationalism, one which underlies Dom Angelico's vision of Romanesque. That vision was firmly based on the thinking just described. Forty years later, in terms he would not have used at the time, he said:

> No doubt about it. I remain profoundly Thomist; not linked to neo-scholasticism, but to the actual Thomism, that is, to St. Thomas himself. For the simple reason that I am an unconditional defender of 'realism' in art. It is for me a true realism, no more and no less than that, of matter. Realism in painting, isn't it pictorial matter? For the art I practice, I therefore claim realism and to be 'realistic'. Without trying to copy nature, I try to use matter, with its quality of material, colour as colour, grain as grain, canvas as canvas. That is realism. I intend to work with reality itself, the real reality. But isn't that profoundly Thomist? When I discovered this Thomist realism, I understood with force that, alone, experience justifies thinking.[51]

In other words, he rejected the position of the hierarchy, neo-Thomism, and embraced that of (most of) the *Ressourcement* theologians, an approach to Thomas Aquinas in a historical context. More particularly, he derives this position from a concept of "realism" in art. Aquinas had nothing to say about art, and this can only have come from Gilson. Almost every word is an echo of Gilson's existentialist interpretation of Thomism.[52] Starting with his Gifford lectures in 1931–32, Gilson developed his analysis in *Methodical Realism* and *Thomist Realism*.[53] The fifth edition of his major work *Le Thomisme* then began with a new chapter on 'existence and reality'.[54] Finally *L'être et l'essence* brought it together.[55] These were all coming out as Dom Angelico was studying.

Gilson, whose aesthetic sensibility was modernist, then applied these ideas to art in *Painting and Reality* which he described as 'a pictorial approach to philosophy' (while refusing to call it 'Thomistic' because Aquinas had said nothing on the subject).[56] This he followed with *The Arts of the Beautiful*, dedicated to the memory of Focillon 'who knew the art of translating into the language of knowledge the forward thrusts of creation'.[57] Finally he published *Forms and Substances in the Arts*.[58] In 1951, Dom Angelico could not have known this second sequence of books, but the later preceding quotation seems to be a clear reference to them. It is possible that he heard Gilson on the subject when Gilson visited the Abbey. Certainly by 1952 he was expressly linking art with the philosophy of Realism and Being, referring to the physicality of Romanesque sculpture, its integration with the architecture, the loss of this vision in Gothic and later art, and the rediscovery of the vision in modern art.[59]

Very broadly Gilson's interpretation of Aquinas is that 'matter', created by God *ex nihilo*, exists and that we grasp its reality before we think about it (in Dom Angelico's words 'experience before thinking'). Descartes was wrong, and the neo-Thomists were wrong to follow him, in putting thought first. Matter cannot exist without 'form', and, more controversially, form (even the soul, which is the form of Man) cannot exist without matter (i.e. in the case of Man the body).[60] Artists give form to the material they are working with and thus create something capable of its own act of existence, through which we can grasp God. (Nature is not an artist; no organism emerges from her whose function is simply to give aesthetic delight. It follows that the idea that the artist's purpose is to imitate nature is also wrong.) The implications for how we should look at Romanesque are profound. The starting point is not the viewer's perspective (or indeed perspective at all). It is the artist's vision, directed to God and first grasped by the senses rather than the intellect, that matters. As in the title of Gleizes's Saint-Savin tableau (Figure 3.2), we move from the reality of the senses to the reality of the spirit. Seeking complete objectivity, it is the very opposite of modern art theory (much of which derives from France at the same period).

The second element in the statement of intent in the first issue of *Zodiaque* (see previous discussion) is the explanation for going back to the 'primitivism' of Romanesque, namely to reach out to a public starved of spiritual nourishment. Commenting later:

> [P]erformance [as a commercial publishing venture] was never our primary concern. There are two reasons for this which remain fundamental: the opening, through Romanesque art, to modern art – and, linked to this, a deliberately apostolic aim [. . .] to reach a public waiting for spirituality, a public which the Church can reach only through culture. In a world like ours, spiritual need is alive and well, but, more and more in my opinion, we will reach our contemporaries only through their leisure time, according to their interests. While some people have a negative view of tourists dragging their feet in the churches, I for one see this as an opportunity that should be taken advantage of.[61]

Given this objective, it is in no way surprising that the books were initially dismissed as popular tourist guides by architectural historians.

The third element is the explanation for the name *Zodiaque*:

> In advocating the zodiac, we are calling for a return to a true notion of time based on the laws of nature: to a normal life, inscribed in the God-given unfolding of the world of things. Art would be the first to benefit from this return, because, by rediscovering the natural conditions of time, we would be led to rethink the value and natural legitimacy of art, which would greatly enlighten the research and efforts of contemporary art.

It was equally important that it was a secular symbol which the Church had made her own: '*Zodiaque* wants to grasp in the art of our time all that may seem to it to be convertible into legitimate Christian art, even if it means rethinking in a new way the elements which it will seek to take advantage of in this way, and to indicate frankly the aspects which it will judge to be Christianly inadmissible or harmful'.

Recognising that those being addressed would need to be weaned off conventional religious art, on the back cover there was a quotation from St John Chrysostom (*c.* 380) about the primacy of the artistic vision and the fickleness of the ignorant crowd. The public needed to be led.[62]

The first Romanesque publication, *L'Étrange Aventure de la Cathedrale d'Autun* came in July 1951.[63] It told the story of how the 'beauté pauvre et vraie' of the cathedral had been spoiled by excrescences and how the sculpture had been covered over, not by the Revolution or by the State but by the Church itself, and then recovered.

There seems a clear analogy with the *Ressourcement* recovery of Thomism, one which did not need to be spelled out.

CUBISM AND FORM

As previously described, the concept of 'form' in the sense used in this piece is usually associated with Focillon, but it is equally at the centre of Cubist theory. Gleizes's summary of his *La Forme et L'Histoire* in *Spiritualité, Rhythme, Forme* was what inspired Dom Angelico.[64]

The concepts of Focillon and Gleizes are similar but subtly different. What is common is movement over time. This is not the same idea as the study of links and provenance. For Focillon, form expresses itself in the work of the individual craftsman (often unnamed), working with his hands at a particular time and place to create a physical object which embodies the living form and is not a mere copy or reproduction. It is not evolutionary or determinist or dictated by social forces.[65] It has a life of its own. It is significant that the only book in which Dom Angelico allowed a significant number of his images to be used outside *Zodiaque* was the reissue of Focillon's *L'art des sculpteurs romans*.[66]

Gleizes adds a spiritual and historical element. Again, the artist who expresses the form is an artisan working in a living tradition, but it is specifically Romanesque. Perhaps because his first encounter had been with neo-Thomism, Gleizes blamed Thomism for the replacement of the Romanesque vision of rhythm and movement in time by a static concept of space. However, the philosophical approach outlined above nonetheless accords closely with his teaching. It is from the physical reality of the stone and the paint to which the skill of the artisan has been applied that one can attain spiritual reality. Our task is to grasp the real living essence of what the artist created. It is not a nostalgic going back. It is a return to the originals from which, if we follow his precepts, we can create new and specifically Cubist art. Thomist realism is similarly about time in this sense. "Being" is the act of existence. While, being finite, artwork can of course be lost or destroyed, so long as it subsists it continues to 'be'.

The illustrations for Figures 3.5 and 3.6 are from *La Forme et L'Histoire*. Dom Angelico remained fascinated by the carvings at Gavr'inis and especially their physicality (Figures 3.7 and 3.8 show the originals).[67] André Breton compared Picasso's *Les Demoiselles d'Avignon*

FIGURE 3.5

Tumulus de Gavr'inis *(Gleizes,* La Forme et L'Histoire, *1932)*

FIGURE 3.6

'Cimabue: Musée du Louvre (Gleizes, La Forme et L'Histoire, *1932)*

FIGURE 3.7

Gavr'inis (C.-T. Le Roux)

FIGURE 3.8

Cimabue: Virgin and Child *(Paris, Musée du Louvre – wikimedia commons)*

FIGURE 3.9

Pablo Picasso: Les Demoiselles d'Avignon *(New York, MoMA – wikimedia commons)*

(Figure 3.9) to the Cimabue,[68] and Dom Angelico included it.[69]

Gleizes called his analysis *Translation and Rotation* (Figures 3.10–3.13).[70] 'To paint is to give life to a flat surface; to give life to flat surface is to endow its space with rhythm'.[71] He later refined 'rotation' as described here. His final book-length essay was written in 1948 (although not published until 1998).[72] But Dom Angelico could well have seen it in draft, or at the very least it would have been the basis for Gleizes's teaching when he studied with Gleizes in 1946 and 1947. It expands on how our eyes see and is directed at young artists at a more practical level than the earlier works.

Very briefly, 'translation' is the arrangement of overlapping geometrical planes to create a finite structured 'space'. 'Rotation' is then the movement of the eye within that space to coordinate the resulting forms in 'time' and so create 'rhythm'. It is a single operation which he separates for the purpose of clarity. The one produces the other, and both are necessary. Without rhythm, the space is dead. Without a structured space, the rhythm cannot give life. The verbal descriptions which accompanied the operations in Figures 3.10 to 3.13 are transcribed in the endnotes which are cited with each figure.

This combination of high philosophy, abstruse art theory, and popular evangelism is, I would argue, the basis of Dom Angelico's vision and explains why the project as a whole stands apart from conventional architectural history. But none of it is of the slightest relevance unless it is reflected in the photography, and it is to that, finally, that we must turn.

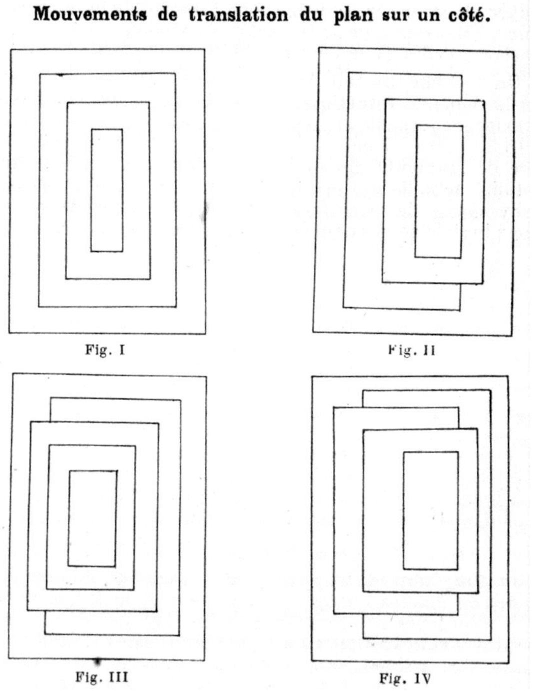

Mouvements de translation du plan sur un côté.
Fig. I
Fig. II
Fig. III
Fig. IV

FIGURE 3.10

Movements of translation of the plane to one side (Gleizes, La peinture et ses lois: ce qui devait sortir du Cubisme*, 1923)*[73]

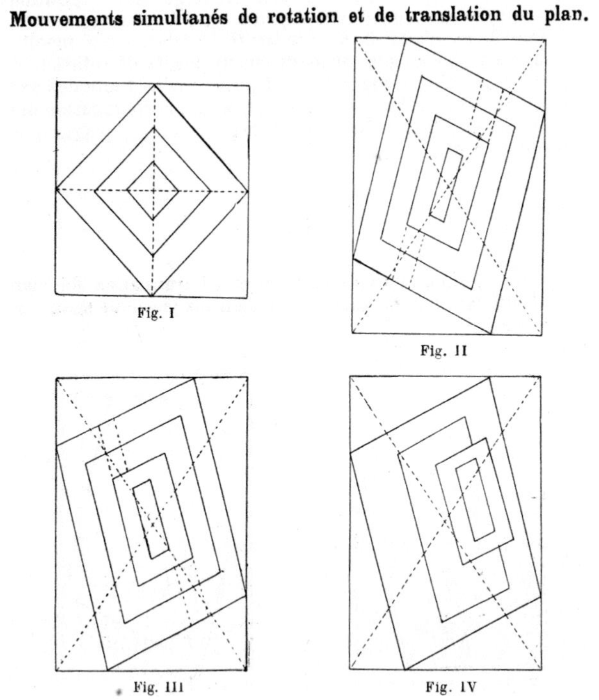

Mouvements simultanés de rotation et de translation du plan.
Fig. I
Fig. II
Fig. III
Fig. IV

FIGURE 3.11

Simultaneous movements of translation and rotation of the plane (Gleizes, La peinture et ses lois: ce qui devait sortir du Cubisme*, 1923)*[74]

Mouvements simultanés de rotation et de translation du plan aboutissant à la création d'un organisme plastique spatial et rythmique.
Fig. I
Fig. II
Fig. III
Fig. IV

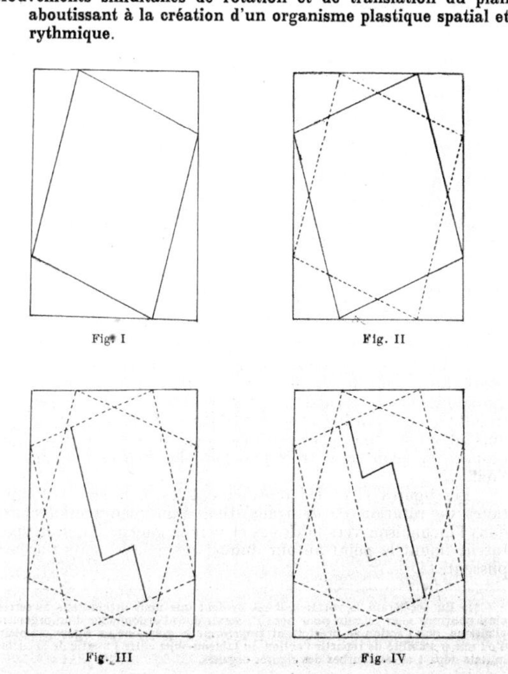

FIGURE 3.12

Simultaneous movements of rotation and of translation of the plane, resulting in the creation of a plastic spatial and rhythmic organisation (Gleizes, La peinture et ses lois: ce qui devait sortir du Cubisme*, 1923)*[75]

— 47 —
Fig. V
Fig. VI
Fig. VII
Fig. VIII

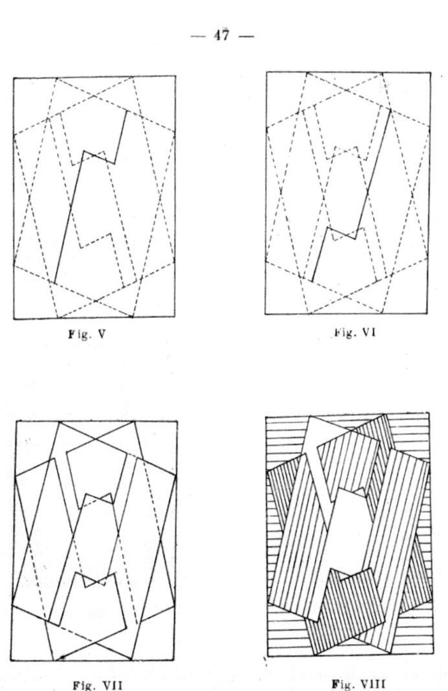

FIGURE 3.13

Simultaneous movements of rotation and of translation of the plane, resulting in the creation of a plastic spatial and rhythmic organisation (Gleizes, La peinture et ses lois: ce qui devait sortir du Cubisme*, 1923)*

Système plastique spatial et rythmique obtenu par la conjugaison des mouvements simultanés de rotation et de translation du plan et des mouvements de translation du plan sur un côté.

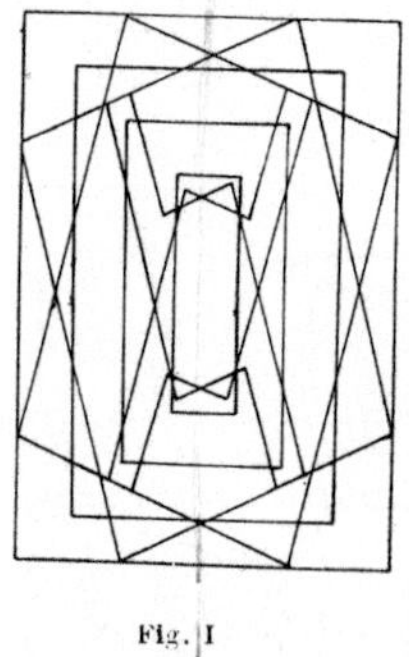

Fig. I

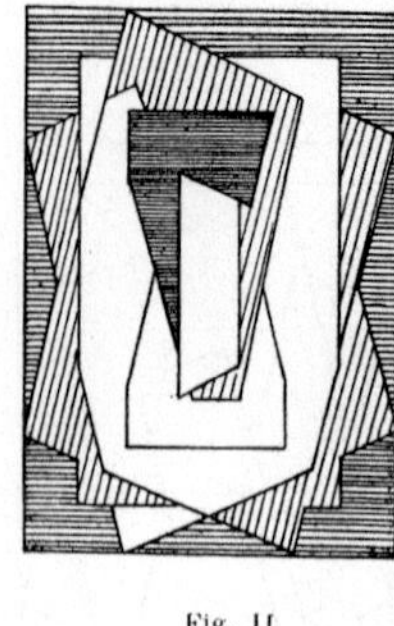

Fig. II

FIGURE 3.14

Spatial and rhythmic plastic system obtained by the combination of simultaneous movements of the rotation and translation of the plane from side to side (Gleizes, La peinture et ses lois: ce qui devait sortir du Cubisme*, 1923)*[76]

'THE EYE IS NOT A CAMERA'

The principles of translation and rotation can be applied to photography as a means of composing an image from what we see. This might be done by one who, as with Dom Angelico, had learned and practised the techniques as a painter. If we look without moving our eyes, we see an ellipse with indistinct edges. Our angle of vision is conventionally 53°, the same as a 'normal' lens on a camera. Outside the ellipse, we can see an area of about 120°, just bigger than the widest non-fisheye camera lens. Within this area we look around, particularly in a large interior such as a church, and assemble a picture as a whole in our brains. It is not a two-dimensional image on a plane surface like a painting or a photograph. Even with one eye, what we see is three-dimensional. We focus in on particular things which our brains then bring to the assembled image. They alter colours, tones, and even shapes (so that, for example, we do not see columns at the side as being wider than those in the centre) and eliminate distractions. The result is a selective composite view rather than a purely optical one. In effect, what we are seeing is the same thing simultaneously from different angles. In seeking to represent what we see, the task, whether of the painter or the photographer, is to render it in two-dimensional form.

Renaissance perspective operates (in the sense that it corresponds closely to what we see) in the central ellipse. It also works outside that area in the sense that it is *optically* what a camera with a fixed body sees. But it is not how we actually see. In our composite view, verticals do not converge, columns at the side are the same size as those in the centre, and the geometry of shapes is not distorted. In comparison, as David Hockney said, the [normal] camera is a 'paralysed cyclops'.[77] But it does not have to be so.

Using a 'normal' lens only gives us a small part of what we see in our heads. With a wide-angle lens, important central elements are small and far away. The answer (even now) is to use a specialist architectural camera with movements. It may be cyclopean, but it is not paralysed. The front and back can move in relation to each other so as to alter the way the planes overlap in the subject and their angles, i.e. 'translation'.

Obviously in photographing we cannot *create* in the way that a painter can, but we can *find* viewpoints, angles of view and framing which produce a distinctive image. Gleizes's refinement, which he arrived at in 1934, was to 'unleash rotation' by adding curved arabesques which 'summed up in a line the intentions that were contained in the different directed currents of the canvas', simplifying and unifying the composition and enabling the eye to penetrate, thus creating rhythm, form, and light.[78] Photographically we can do the same (easier with Romanesque than Gothic because it is more enclosed and the curves are there). In other words, we can arrange the elements so as to follow the way our eyes move. If it works, it creates a structure or scaffolding in our minds, establishing a space within which we can focus on individual features.

Long lenses are impracticable on an architectural camera (at least inside a building) and not easy to use generally. They also foreshorten, which may not be desirable. To capture details, we may therefore need another approach. After the Second World War (slightly earlier in Germany which was technically more advanced) with newer lenses and materials, different types of cameras, and a different approach to publishing, it became possible to do more than before.

There are three elements to this. The first is sequencing. In 1948 Dom Angelico wrote about what he called 'film fixe'(a continuous slide show).[79] He refers particularly to photographs of Mont Saint-Michel in what seems to have been both a book and a 'film fixe'.[80] In both there were a large number of photographs of the same place, and in the case of the book full page and beautifully printed. He went on to say that while the book and the film are complementary, the book relates to the solitary reader, the film to a collective audience and is therefore more suited to 'contemporary artistic education', in order to 'renew appreciation of the great laws of human aesthetic perception'.

It seems clear that these photographs were part of the stimulus for what became the *Zodiaque* project and likely that they were behind the decision to use photographs together in a sequence, even though they showed the same thing, rather than to produce a corpus of surviving monuments, as some architectural historians would have preferred.

The second element is showing the same thing from different angles and at different distances, using a combination of an architectural camera and a small hand camera. In other words, there are both internal camera movements and movement by the photographer.

The third element is to use the natural light by which the original artist would have seen his creation. Dom Angelico's running commentary over the years is full of disparaging references to photographing casts, as for example Deschamps had done, beautifully produced though it is.[81] What he wanted were the tactile qualities, the texture of the stone, the way the light moulded the shapes, and the inky voids, all of which the camera is uniquely capable of depicting from the original.

Being Dom Angelico, he went for the best in finding photographers, with whom he collaborated closely. What they were doing was not producing 'Cubist' photography, which would have added another layer, but applying the insights just described. His intention was to lead his viewers 'from the reality of the senses to the reality of the spirit'. He was not producing guidebooks or architectural history.

The photography moved up a level when in 1956 he engaged Jean Dieuzaide, also known as 'Yan'.[82] So far as I can discover, Dieuzaide is the only photographer ever to cite Thomist realism as a source for his inspiration![83] The collaboration only lasted six years, but during that time they produced *Quercy roman*, *Rouergue roman*, *Roussillon roman*, and *Catalogne romane* (two volumes), for which they won the Prix Nadar in 1961 for the best photographic book. When, because the Abbey either could not or would not pay enough, Dieuzaide decided not to continue, he agreed to teach Dom Angelico photography. As Dom Angelico later said, he 'owed him all he knew about photography'.[84]

The five volumes were the basis for a successful exhibition, Art Roman du Soleil, which brought together 180 photos, some of them in large format (up to 6 m^2) (Figure 3.14).[85] The exhibition followed the principles just outlined: for example, it began with sixteen photographs of Moissac, mostly different views of the south portal rather than the cloister, and continued with twenty-seven of Conques. In other words, it was not a survey of Romanesque in the region concerned but, like the books themselves, something designed to immerse the viewer. For example, it included Christ's head at Conques in profile, a view normally invisible. Dieuzaide is photographed, with Dom Angelico, standing on the second level of the tympanum to take it![86]

Installation de l'exposition « Art Roman du Soleil » à Vich en Catalogne juillet 1961

FIGURE 3.15

*Dieuzaide installing his photograph of the head of Christ from Moissac, probably 2 July 1961 (*Zodiaque*)*

The exhibition was critically acclaimed, and its intentions clearly understood. Thus:

> throughout the [. . .] exhibition, the gaze discovered a strangely new world, strangely present, rubbing against the grain of the stones, rushing under ignored vaults, flowing between pillars, bumping into walls, resting on landscapes vibrating with silence, only to return to get lost in the living labyrinth of sculpted figures and monsters. Before the photos of *l'art roman du soleil*, had we seen Romanesque art?[87]

To conclude, Dom Angelico was well aware that there is no single Romanesque style, which is why it is so difficult to define. As he said, it is varied and diverse across the countries, single and multiple, a spirit rather than a rigid pattern,[88] 'proteiform',[89] that is possessed of the same (real) 'essence' in different (material) guises. The project reflects a specific philosophical and artistic vision which can stand alongside conventional architectural history and, as such, may enable us to see Romanesque in a different and rewarding way.

NOTES

1 For a description of the original Abbey, see *Notre-Dame de la Pierre-qui-vire* (Paris 1923).

2 A. Surchamp, 'L'Enseignement d'Albert Gleizes', in *50 ans de Peinture – Le Cubisme et son Dénouement dans la Tradition*, ed. A. Gleizes (Lyon 1947), 17–30.

3 P. Mérimée, *Notice Sur Les Peintures De L'Église De Saint-Savin* (Paris 1845).

4 H. Focillon, *Les Pierres de France* (Paris 1919), especially 37–58.

5 H. Focillon, *L'Art des sculpteurs romans* (Paris 1931).

6 H. Focillon, *La vie des formes* (Paris 1934) translated as *The Life of Forms in Art* by C. B. Hogan and G. Kubler (originally published 1948, reprinted Princeton 1989).

7 A. Gleizes, 'La peinture et ses lois: ce qui devait sortir du Cubisme', *La Vie des Lettres et des Arts* (March 1923), 41. Later published separately (Paris 1924).

8 A. Gleizes, *Art and Religion, Art and Science, Art and Production.* Translated by Peter Brooke with an introduction and notes (London 1999).

9 A. Gleizes, *La forme et l'histoire* (Paris 1932).

10 J. Baltrušaitis, *La Stylistique Ornementale dans la Sculpture Romane* (Paris 1931).

11 D. H. Kahnweiler *The Sculptures of Picasso* (London 1949), second unnumbered page of text.

12 *Dom Angelico Surchamp – moine et artiste,* Beaux-Arts, hors-série (Paris 2012), 26.

13 A good general guide to the Second Vatican Council of the Roman Catholic Church is R. R. Gaillardetz, ed., *The Cambridge Companion to Vatican II* (Cambridge 2020).

14 Dom Angelico refers to the lamps installed in front of the capitals in Saint-Andoche de Saulieu as an example of current hostility to Romanesque. Dom A. Surchamp, 'En prodel arte Románico y su mensaje tan actual', *Románico: Revista de arte de amigos del románico*, 7 (2008), 48–60 at 50 (in response to X. Barral i Altet).

[15] R. Oursel, *Bourgogne Romane* (Saint-Léger-Vauban 1954). The series title is 'La nuit des temps', 1. This first volume is described by Dom Angelico as the bringing together, at the suggestion of the Tournus bookseller Léon Fernez, of different numbers which had appeared earlier. 'L'aventure de Zodiaque', *Revue Zodiaque*, 150 (1986), 10–11.

[16] U. Lobbedy, *Westphalie Romane* (Saint-Léger-Vauban 1999). The series title is 'La nuit des temps', 88.

[17] Henri Focillon's preface to M. Audin, *Le Livre – Son Architecture, Sa Technique* (Paris 1924), vii.

[18] The fonts used were specially acquired, and each had a distinct purpose in the presentation.

[19] See P. Plaignieux, 'Le double discours de l'image', in *Zodiaque – Le Monument Livre,* ed. C. Lesec (Paris 2012), 23–59. All references are to the *Bulletin Monumental*: 115 (1957), 303–04; 117 (1959), 85; 121 (1963), 210–12; 123 (1965), 172–75; 124 (1966), 228–30; 125 (1967), 443–46; 127 (1969), 345–46; 131 (1973), 66–68; 137 (1979), 74–75; 140 (1982), 57–59; 140 (1982), 256–58; 142 (1984), 464–65; 151 (1993), 528–30. The translations into English are mine.

[20] See Plates 8 and 9 and Dom Angelico's comments in 'Pour les Cinq Ans de Zodiaque', *Revue Zodiaque,* 29 (1956), 48. 'One could almost say that it [i.e. the one with artificial light] is not the same work'.

[21] M. Vidal, *Quercy Roman* (Saint-Léger-Vauban 1959) Plates 5–21. The series number is La nuit des temps, 10.

[22] See Dom A. Surchamp, 'Les points cardinaux', *Revue Zodiaque*, 64 (April 1965), 12. In contrast, he suggests, the image with a margin and a caption lost force in expression and in suggestion. A mixture of the image with other text in a third example took away its essence so that it became no more than an accompaniment to the text, with no more value than the words.

[23] G. Lafont, 'Tirer de son trésor de l'ancien et du neuf', *Lumière & Vie*, 300 (October–December 2013), 7–21.

[24] Anon, *The Life of Jean-Baptiste Muard* (London 1886), 392.

[25] Dom A. Surchamp, *L'art roman, Rencontre entre Dieu et les hommes, Entretiens avec Gwendoline Jarczyk* (Paris 1993), 183.

[26] Aidan Nichols, 'The Dominicans and the Journal "L'Art sacré"', *New Blackfriars*, 88/1013 (January 2007), 25–45.

[27] P. Brooke, *Albert Gleizes – For and Against the Twentieth Century* (New Haven 2001), 247–52.

[28] Marcel Billot in M. A. Couturier *Sacred Art* texts selected by D. de Menil and P. Duployé (University of Texas Press 1989), 11, referring to two articles from 1950 which follow: 'For the Eyes' and 'Purity'.

[29] Père A. Dimier '*L'Art Cistercien*' (Saint-Léger-Vauban 1962).

[30] Online description of the Couturier Collection at Yale University, https://web.library.yale.edu [accessed 31 October 2020].

[31] C. Lesec, 'Esthétique et Apostolat. Les Éditions Zodiaque', in *Le Livre et l'architecte*, eds. J.-P. Garric and E. Thibault (Mardaga 2011), 120.

[32] D. H. Pickering, 'Recollections of Stravinsky: Prose by C. F. Ramuz', www.musicandliterature.org/features/2018/10/30/stravinsky [accessed 1 November 2020].

[33] *Revue Zodiaque*, 1 (1953), 25–8. I am extremely grateful to the monks at La Pierre-qui-Vire for scanning the relevant pages for me, which were omitted when it was republished. They appear to be otherwise unobtainable. The translations are mine.

[34] The best general treatment in English is G. Flynn and P. D. Murray, *Ressourcement – A Movement for Renewal in Twentieth-Century Catholic Theology* (Oxford 2011).

[35] J. Wood, 'Ressourcement', in *The T&T Clark Companion to Henri de Lubac*, ed. J. Hilbert (Edinburgh 2016), 112.

[36] 'Avertissement', *Cahiers de la quinzaine*, ser. 5, 11 (1 March 1904), xxxvii.

[37] C. Péguy, *The Holy Innocents and Other Poems*, trans. Pansy Pakenham (London 1956) Introduction, 7.

[38] F. A. Murphy, *Art and Intellect in the Philosophy of Étienne Gilson* (Columbia 2004), 2.

[39] See, for example, *Cahiers de l'amitié Charles Péguy,* 1 (1947).

[40] 'Les dix ans de "la nuit des temps"', *Revue Zodiaque*, 63 (January 1965), 2, 8–10 and at the back. See also the quote on the back of *Revue Zodiaque*, 64 (1965).

[41] Lafont, 'Tirer de son trésor' (as n. 23), 7–21 at p. 9 (my translations).

[42] *Aeterni Patris*, 4 August 1879.

[43] See, for example, M.-D. Chenu, *Nature, Man, and Society in the 12th Century: Essays on New Theological Perspectives in the Latin West* (Chicago 1968).

[44] Brooke, *Albert Gleizes* (as n. 27), 275.

[45] This is a reference to one of the key elements in Thomist realism. The book itself is M.-D. Chenu, *'Le Saulchoir: une école de théologie'* (Le Saulchoir 1937) but is extremely rare, and I have not been able to access a copy. The quotations are from secondary sources.

[46] Surchamp, *L'art roman* (as n. 25), 178. Dom Angelico was comparing the difficulties faced by the Dominicans with their *l'Art Sacré* and his experience at La Pierre-qui-Vire with *Zodiaque*, but the one flows from the other.

[47] Y. Congar, *Vraie et Fausse Réforme dans L'Église* (Paris 1950), 43 n. 35. It seems to have been here that the link between *Ressourcement* and the passage in Péguy previously cited was drawn.

[48] Issue XIII '*Existentialisme*' mai 1947, 210–11 commenting on 'Réponse des *Recherches de Sciences Religieuses* aux "Études critiques" de la '*Revue thomiste*' mai–août 1946, sur la *Théologie et ses sources'*. There are three distinct elements here, first the *Témoignages* reference, followed by what the note was referring to exactly. However, stated and actual publishing dates were still disrupted after the war, and tracing the references was difficult. Mettepenningen sets out the sequence. Third, he sets the matter in context. This particular skirmish was a relatively small part of the much larger battle between the Ressourcement theologians and the Establishment. See J. Mettepenningen; 'Truth, Orthodoxy, and the Nouvelle Théologie: Truth as Issue in a "Second Modernist Crisis" (1946–1950)', in *Orthodoxy, Liberalism, and Adaptation: Essays on Ways of Worldmaking in Times of Change from Biblical, Historical and Systematic Perspectives*, ed. B. Becking (Leiden–Boston 2011), 149–82.

[49] J. Newman, *L'Europe des Monastères* (Saint-Léger-Vauban 1985). The title appears in the collection 'Les formes de la nuit'. Newman's name comes first on the title page, so that it appears as his work in library catalogues!

[50] J. Newman, 'The Mission of the Benedictine Order', in *The Atlantis – A Register of Literature and Science*, vol. I (London 1858), 1, no. I.

[51] Surchamp, *L'art roman* (as n. 25), 82.

[52] E. Gilson, *The Spirit of Medieval Philosophy*, trans. A. H. C. Downes (New York 1936).

[53] E. Gilson, *Methodical Realism – A Handbook for Beginning Realists* (1936 in French), translated by P. Trower (San Francisco 1990); E. Gilson, *Thomist Realism and the Critique of Knowledge* (1939 in French), translated by M. A. Wauk (San Francisco 1986).

[54] E. Gilson, *Le Thomisme* (1942–44 in French), translated as *The Christian Philosophy of St. Thomas Aquinas* by L. K. Shook (London 1961).

[55] E. Gilson, *L'être et l'essence* (Paris 1948), condensed version in English published as *Being and Some Philosophers* (Toronto 1952).

[56] E. Gilson, *Painting and Reality* (New York 1957).

[57] E. Gilson, *The Arts of the Beautiful* (New York 1965).

[58] E. Gilson, *Forms and Substances in the Arts* (first published in 1966), translated by S. Attanasio (Chicago 2001).

[59] E. Gilson, 'Destinée de l'art moderne', *Psyché*, 73 (November1952), 730–42.

[60] Compare with Chenu's conclusion previously quoted: 'It is good Thomism to do the history of Thomas's thought – to see its soul united to its body'.

[61] Surchamp, *L'art roman* (as n. 25), 90.

[62] F. W. Hohler, trans., *The Six Books on the Priesthood of St. John Chrysostom* (Cambridge 1837), Book V, 121–22.

[63] D. Grivot, *L'Étrange Aventure de la Cathedrale d'Autun* (Saint-Léger-Vauban 1951). Issued before they began to use gravure. The illustrations do not do justice to the photographs. A similar publication, with much better illustrations, was issued as the first in a new series in 1953: D. Grivot, *Autun* (Saint-Léger-Vauban 1953). The series title here was Travaux des Mois no. 1.

[64] A. Gleizes, *La Forme et L'Histoire* (Paris 1932), especially Plates 4 and 5; A. Gleizes, 'Spiritualité, Rythme, Forme', in *Confluences: Les Problèmes de la Peinture*, ed. G. Diehl (Lyon 1945)

section 6; J. L. Peudon, *Dom Angelico Surchamp Artiste, inventeur de Zodiaque* (Troyes 2014), 18 and from other sources.

[65] Focillon, *Vie des formes* (as n. 6).

[66] Focillon. *Sculpteurs romans* (as n. 5).

[67] The stone in questions is Jambstone R9, at Gavrinis (Morbihan). C.-T. Le Roux, 'The Art of Gavrinis Presented in Its Armorican Context and in Comparison with Ireland', *The Journal of the Royal Society of Antiquaries of Ireland*, 122 (1992), 79–108 at 100.

[68] See the letter of 12 December 1924 urging the collector Doucet to buy the painting. É.-A. Hubert, *Lettres à Jacques Doucet (1920–1926)* (Gallimard 2016).

[69] Dom A. Surchamp, 'En prodel arte Románico' (as n. 14), 49.

[70] The figures are taken from the 1924 version.

[71] A. Gleizes, 'La peinture et ses lois' (as n. 7), 41. For the translation, see P. Brooke, trans., *Gino Severini – From Cubism to Classicism; Albert Gleizes – Painting and Its Laws* (London 2001), 185. See also his website, which includes a translation of 'Spiritualité, Rythme, Forme': www.peterbrooke.org/form-and-history/texts/spirituality-rhythm-form [accessed October 2020], along with a great deal of other important material.

[72] A. Gleizes, *L'homme devenu peintre* (Paris 1998); translation by P. Brooke: *Painting and Man Become Painter*, www.peterbrooke.org/form-and-history/texts.

[73] The explanatory text which accompanies Gleizes's illustration is as translated below. The translations which follow are from Peter Brooke, *Painting and its Laws* (as n. 71), 188-92. We are very grateful to Peter Brooke for allowing us to use his translations.

'Movements of translation of the plane to one side: Since space and rhythm are perceptible to us through extension and movement, the first decisive action of the plastic order will be to put the brute matter that we have at our disposal – the flat surface - into movement. Simple and elementary movements to begin with, which we call *movements of translation of the plane* to one side, forwards and backwards (I); to the right (II); to the left (Fig III). These movements have changed the position and importance of the first plane as it moves away from the eye, thus creating a series of new planes which have emerged from the total plane, separated by an interval which can be understood physiologically by the organ that records the phenomenon, namely, the eye. This interval between the different planes that have been recorded reveals the space. It becomes equally possible to combine the three movements (IV) and thus to realise a space between the extensions in which there are movements going in contradictory directions.'

[74] Simultaneous movements of translation and rotation of the plane: 'Another movement is added to the first movement of translation – that of *rotation of the plane*. Thus, if we speed up the rotation, we will of course arrive at the circle; so we can remember, to be able to make use of it in the ordering of a plastic organism, that as the action goes faster it transforms the polygon into a circular figure. This gives us the possibility of sharing the action of the painting-object between the inertia of the initial surface from which we start and the curves of the figures or organs. Fig. I shows the outline of the plastic formation that derives from simultaneous movements of rotation and translation of the initial plane turned upon its own axis (the plane in this case being a perfect square). We have chosen in the space given by the whole plane three positions for the figures which are retained by the eye.

Figs II and III represent the simultaneous movements of rotation and translation of a rectangular plane, turning to the right and to the left – the spectator's eye determining the point round which these movements take place. Fig. IV represents the simultaneous movements of rotation and translation of a rectangular plane, in which the position of the spectator's eye is shifted to the left of the axis of the plane. [Translator's note reads: As in original. It seems to me that the terms 'left' and 'right' should be reversed.] We have not given a diagram to show the formal modifications necessary to the form of the plane in movements of rotation and translation in which the spectator's eye is shifted to the right [see translator's note above] of the axis of the plane. They can easily be imagined, as can the combination of the three movements as it was discussed in the previous section.'

[75] Simultaneous movements of rotation and of translation of the plane, resulting in the creation of a plastic spatial and rhythmic organism: 'In this third paragraph we have tried to show, in the simplest possible conditions, simultaneous movements of rotation and translation of the plane which result, with almost no effort on the part of whoever is directing the operation, in the creation of a spatial and rhythmic plastic organism. All we have done in Fig. VII is to specify, by removing some superfluous lines, what could already be guessed by the senses in the preceding Fig. VI; and in Fig. VIII, we have just filled in the planes or parts of the initial surface with different types of shading, following their direction. It seems clear that when the movement of the inert plane is followed by the eye of the spectator, it leaves in his mind a visible trace of its successive aspects whose different states of succession have been co-ordinated by the initial rhythmic cadence. As we remarked above, it is the states of succession that permit the perception of the space. The initial plane thus becomes a spatial and rhythmic organism.'

[76] Spatial and rhythmic plastic system obtained by the combination of simultaneous movements of the rotation and translation of the plane and of movements of translation of the plane from side to side: 'In the same spirit of simplification, we have tried here to realise mechanically, with hardly any personal initiative, a spatial and rhythmic plastic system through the combination of simultaneous movements of rotation and of translation, with movements of translation of the plane from side to side. All we have done is to bring together on one single plane all the movements which were described in the other paragraphs, and to separate out in the second figure the order of the elements which have thus been interwoven. The result is an organism which is a little more *complex* than the preceding, but which equally realises a spatial and rhythmic plastic system.'

[77] 'All you can do with most ordinary photographs is stare at them – they stare back, blankly – and presently your concentration begins to fade. They stare you down. I mean, photography is all right if you don't mind looking at the world from the point of view of a paralysed cyclops – *for a split second*' as told to Lawrence Weschler, Cameraworks (1984).

[78] P. Brooke, *Albert Gleizes – For and Against the Twentieth Century* (New Haven 2001), 175–80.

[79] 'Le rôle du film fixe dans l'enseignement artistique', *Témoignages XVIII – Tradition et Histoire* (July 1948), 443–51.

[80] *Le Mont Saint-Michel* (Paris 1947). This was published under the collection Charme de la France, Challamel, with a preface from É. Mâle.

[81] P. Deschamps, *French Sculpture of the Romanesque Period Eleventh and Twelfth Centuries* (New York 1930).

[82] J.-M. Le Scouarnec, *Jean Dieuzaide – La photographie d'abord* (Paris 2012), Chapter 11.

[83] *Revue Zodiaque,* 121 (July 1979), 11.

[84] Ibid., 1.

[85] There is a similar photograph to Figure 3.15, which is dated, showing Dom Angelico standing next to the Head, presumably on the same occasion. Figure 3.15 may therefore have been taken by Dom Angelico. See *Dom Angelico Surchamp – moine et artiste* (as n. 12), 21.

[86] J. M. Marquardt: *Zodiaque – Making Medieval Modern 1951–2001* (Pennsylvania University Press 2015), Plates 30 and 31.

[87] Review by Michel Roquebert, published November 1963, www.espritsnomades.net/arts-plastiques/jean-dieuzaide-yan-art-roman-du-soleil/ [accessed 1 November 2020].

[88] *Dom Angelico Surchamp – moine et artiste* (as n. 12), 24.

[89] Surchamp, 'En prodel arte Románico' (as n. 14), 57.

The Regional and Transregional in Romanesque Europe (2021), 35–45

ROMANESQUE SCULPTURE IN AQUITAINE

A HISTORY OF THE MARGINALISATION OF A WIDELY IMITATED REGIONAL SCULPTURAL STYLE

Marcello Angheben

The historiography of Romanesque sculpture in France holds that the most important creative centres are Burgundy and Languedoc. It has represented work in the former duchy of Aquitaine – namely Poitou, Saintonge, and Angoumois – as late, regional, largely ornamental, and unsympathetic to the paradigm for Romanesque portals, which should be provided with a tympanum. In order to restore this sculpture to a recognition of the importance it once commanded, the following paper will deal successively with the historiography, the chronology of Romanesque sculpture in Aquitaine and south-western France, and the question of portals without tympana, along with their iconography and artistic quality. One of the most important points is that what is found elsewhere on tympana was largely located at the top of the façades – namely theophanies. Furthermore, the west portal at Aulnay was the most influential in all Romanesque France, inspiring a total of nineteen portals which survive between Bordeaux and Tournai.

INTRODUCTION

The duchy of Aquitaine is unquestionably one of the richest centres of Romanesque art in Europe and is justifiably renowned for its monumental sculpture. The core of this production is situated in the Poitou, Saintonge, and Angoumois. On the exteriors of churches, this sculpture is concentrated on portals without tympana and across screen façades – façade-frontispieces in French. These are façades on which sculpture ascends as far as the summit and which are generally dominated by a theophany. In the historiography, this sculpture has tended to be either neglected or deprecated. If the reasons behind this intellectual positioning were not always explicit, they were articulated in unfavourable comparisons with the portals of Languedoc, particularly those of Toulouse and Moissac, which were considered to be the earliest in the south-west quarter of France and which were regarded as paradigms of what a Romanesque portal should be. By contrast, the portals of Aquitaine were thought to be later, more decorative, and less representational as the result of the lack of a tympanum. Their iconography was unsophisticated, and their artistic quality was low. Languedoc was thus considered to be a centre, and Aquitaine formed a periphery.

This appreciation rests largely on a misunderstanding of sculpture in Aquitaine and on a historiographical bias. In an attempt to redress the balance and argue for an appreciation of the legitimate place occupied by the sculpture of Aquitaine in the 12th century, it is necessary to very briefly address this historiography before turning successively to the chronology, the lack of tympana, the iconographic programs, and the aesthetic qualities of architectural sculpture here.

THE HISTORIOGRAPHY

In the historiography, various positions were enunciated regarding Romanesque sculpture in Aquitaine. In 1831, Arcisse de Caumont seemed to put portals and screen façades on an equal footing in terms of their significance in Romanesque.[1] Yet, in 1982, Marcel Durliat does not have a single word to say for Aquitaine in the chapter devoted to sculpture in his general survey of Romanesque, while in his 2010 book on Romanesque sculpture, Jean-René Gaborit gave little space to the region.[2] Meanwhile, in 1922, Émile Mâle considered the Elders of the Apocalypse at Saintes to have been inspired by those of Moissac but that they had 'lost any meaning and any dignity: they are no more than an infinitely repeated embroidery motif'.[3] In 1938, Henri Focillon gave a lot of attention to Aquitaine, but he pointed out, as a defect, that the sculptors of the Poitou did not create vast tympana which 'summarised Romanesque thought by amplifying it'.[4] To compensate for the lack of tympana, the artists fell back on the beauty of the treatment.[5] He thus implies a causal relationship between the lack of tympana and decorative richness.

By contrast, Arthur Kingsley Porter was enthusiastic and displayed an extensive knowledge and great respect

  DOI: 10.4324/9781003162827-4

for the sculpture of Aquitaine.[6] He included the majority of surviving examples in his great study of the sculpture of the pilgrimage roads and placed them in an international context. Curiously, Porter's intellectual curiosity is scarcely reflected in later publications, as in the works previously mentioned. Only those scholars directly involved in the study of this sculpture noted its significance. Mention in this respect must be made of the works of Marie-Thérèse Camus and Anat Tcherikover, the latter being the only scholar to propose a global chronology.[7] Among general surveys, only that by Éliane Vergnolle offers much in the way of praise for the originality of Aquitainian sculpture, even if the problem of chronology is largely avoided given the numerous uncertainties surrounding this issue.

THE CHRONOLOGY

The issue of chronology is very important because it enables us to determine the extent to which the sculpture of Aquitaine is genuinely inventive. From an epistemological point of view, the search for the oldest work is not without risk, as it can lead us to value early works above later ones and to consider the latter as falling within a peripheral or regional artistic category. Significantly, this trend affects Spain less than France, as the *tardoromanico* is widely valued there.

The chronology of sculpture in Languedoc and Aquitaine remains uncertain, despite the earlier dating models that have emerged in the last thirty years. The favoured date for the Porte Miègeville at Saint-Sernin in Toulouse, has moved from around 1115 to around 1100, underlining its status as the oldest historiated portal in south-western France.[8] For Moissac, the beginning of Abbot Roger's period of office in 1115 has been proposed for the south portal sculpture, though some still place this around 1130, just before Roger's death.[9] For Conques, the chronology has been pushed back from 1140–50 to 1110 or even before 1105.[10]

For Aquitaine, the first portal has been situated in Saint-Hilaire at Melle, by 1100.[11] The south and west portals at Aulnay were once dated very late, around 1175–95, in other words long after the earliest Gothic portals.[12] More recently, however, they have been dated to between 1120 and 1135, mainly because of documents that mention the building around 1120.[13] From my point of view, the one useful point of reference comes from the lateral portals of Tournai Cathedral, which were probably inspired by the portals of Aulnay as we shall see.[14] Basing his hypothesis on a dendrochronological analysis of the roof of the transept, Laurent Deléhouzée showed that this part of the

FIGURE 4.1

Saint-Jouin-de-Marnes: west front (Marcello Angheben)

building was finished in 1130, which means that the nave portals were realized around 1125 or even earlier.[15] If we admit this hypothesis and the influence of the portals of Aulnay, we must infer from it that the latter was completed around 1120. This dating remains hypothetical and demands a more thorough analysis, but it constitutes in my opinion a chronological landmark.

As regards screen façades, Saint-Jouin-de-Marnes is probably the first in Aquitaine (Figure 4.1 and Colour Plate II (bottom)). Several features suggest a chronology around 1100–10, as was first suggested by Anat Tcherikover: the relatively thin wall, the use of decorative masonry patterns on the gable, the absence of an arcade framing the figures in high relief, and the lack of any analogy with Aulnay.[16] This last question is fundamental because around 1100, St-Jouin would be contemporary with the earliest sculpted Romanesque portals. Finally, the façade of the cathedral of Angoulême can be dated between the beginning of the episcopacy of Girard in 1102 and the consecration of 1128.[17] As for the Saint-Jouin west front, we could date the earliest sculpture to the first decade of the 12th century or around 1120, in other words after the presumed completion of the great portals of Languedoc.

Although it seems likely that the portals of Languedoc precede the façades of Aquitaine, excepting perhaps that at Saint-Jouin, the relative chronology of the works cannot be established precisely. The most important point, however, is that the chronological gap is no more than a few years. It cannot imply that the sculptors of Languedoc were the great creators and that those of Aquitaine mere regional followers. We shall see, moreover, that from a stylistic point of view, the sculpture evolves gradually from one work to another. It therefore seems to me that it is better to conceive the link between both sets of monuments in terms of continuity rather than by seeing it as a centre precipitating a delayed regional or peripheral reaction.

THE QUESTION OF TYMPANA

On the epistemological side, one of the main problems has arisen from the idea that a Romanesque portal should contain a sculpted tympanum. In the 19th century, this idea was already deeply entrenched, so much so that restorers sometimes added tympana to Aquitainian portals, as at Pont-l'Abbé-d'Arnoult and Civray. This attitude arose from an essentially teleological model: portals with tympana became almost definitive after 1140 – after they were employed at Saint-Denis – and this in turn became a paradigm and model to be followed. As we cannot assess a work of the 1130s by the standards of the 1150s, the criticism was obviously misplaced. Meanwhile, Henri Focillon took a different aim. It wasn't that western French portals were deficient because they were retardataire. They were iconographically deficient. The superiority of the portal with a tympanum derives from its capacity to express apocalyptic visions, as at Moissac.

This line of argument fails to acknowledge the visual power of a screen façade. It extends the representational field to the major part of the surface of the façade rather than concentrating it around the door, and it places the divine vision as close as possible to the sky. This expressive strength is particularly significant when the uppermost theophany is a depiction of the Ascension as at Angoulême (Figure 4.2). By looking towards the summit of the façade, the spectator adopts the same point of view as the apostles who lean their head backwards to see Christ disappearing into the clouds.

With respect to portals strictly defined and comprising a tympanum, portals without a tympanum are obviously visually less powerful. On the interior south portal of Saint-Hilaire at Melle, Christ is hardly visible in the middle of a crowd of characters who are mostly anonymous and interchangeable. And on the south portal of Aulnay, no theophany appears in the middle of the thirty-one Elders of the Apocalypse (Figure 4.3). This work is moreover one of those that illustrates most clearly the taste for decorative effects which appeared in Saint-Eutrope at Saintes.[18] It seems, however, that the sculptors were conscious of the lack of visibility of these figures, given that on the western portal, another workshop deployed the characters in the curvature of the arch, so that they are less numerous and of significantly larger size (Figure 4.4). They thus tried to optimize the potential offered by the medium without modifying its structure. And if they didn't feel the need to add a tympanum, it may be because they wanted to evoke Roman triumphal arches, as was argued by Linda Seidel.[19]

The designer of Aulnay's west front knew in any case that there was an opportunity to carve larger figures on the side tympana and in the upper registers of the façade. If the façade of Aulnay has lost the sculptures of both upper levels, we know that it was enhanced with an equestrian rider as at Châteauneuf-sur-Charente and probably with a theophany as at Saint-Jouin-de-Marnes, Angoulême, Ruffec, or Notre-Dame-la-Grande in Poitiers. Among façades inspired by that of Aulnay, we can quote Fenioux where Christ is depicted above the portal, surrounded with the four beasts of the Apocalypse and flanked by a series of sainted figures, as we shall see on Spanish façades.

Whatever the qualities and the defects of the structure of this portal, the most important point is that, before the building of the façade of Saint-Denis, Aulnay's is the portal design which experienced the widest dissemination in France: nineteen portals in this manner survive, among which sixteen are in Poitou, Saintonge, and Angoumois.[20] On the other hand, the portal of Moissac directly inspired just five portals: Beaulieu, Souillac, Cahors, Lagraulière, and Ydes. The most remarkable aspect of this is that the portal of Aulnay was influential far beyond its immediate region. Southwards, we can quote the portals of Bordeaux and Blasimon (Gironde). And northwards, we can note a remarkable echo in Angers (refectory portal at Saint-Aubin) and, more surprisingly, in Tournai which was situated on the northern border of the kingdom of France.

FIGURE 4.2
Angoulême Cathedral: west front (Amelot/CESCM)

FIGURE 4.3
Aulnay: south portal (Marcello Angheben)

FIGURE 4.4
Aulnay: west portal (Marcello Angheben)

FIGURE 4.5

Tournai Cathedral: Porte Mantile (© Bureau de dessin Tilmant)

Both portals of the cathedral of Tournai were raised at the east end of a very long nave that was probably completed around 1120 (Figure 4.5).[21] The structure and motifs displayed on the Porte Mantille indicate that the sculptors knew Moissac, given that they adapted the theme of the Miser sitting on the shoulders of the devil which appears on the left jamb. But they also knew Aulnay, from which they reproduced several patterns. Among these is the bird standing on a lion – from the south portal – and the struggle of Virtues against Vices which they adopted from the west portal and applied to the second arch and to the jambs. As the sculptors of Tournai had no experience in creating historiated portals, we can imagine the following scenario: the canons sent one or more sculptors to France to look at certain recent works about which they had heard. The alternative, that they hired sculptors from south-west France, seems less likely.

The relevant point here is that the Tournai sculptors knew both types of portal. They could therefore have chosen a portal like Moissac, but they clearly preferred that of Aulnay: the portal lacks a tympanum, the sculpture is arranged longitudinally to follow the arches, and the portal was dominated by a central figure, perhaps the Virgin, in a configuration similar to that of the south nave entrance of Saint-Pierre at Melle. If my hypothesis is correct, the portals at Tournai would offer the best example of a patron external to Languedoc and Aquitaine opting, with full knowledge, for the Aulnay formula.

FIGURE 4.6

Carrión de los Condes: Santiago, west façade (Marcello Angheben)

To complete this overview, it is necessary to venture into Spain, while prefacing this by saying that the works that will be cited adopt the approach of the façades of Aquitaine but not the style or the iconography of Aulnay, so that the ties are weaker. In Jaca, Compostela, and León, historiated tympana were produced as early as 1100–10. By the second quarter of the century, a series of portals were conceived that dispensed with the tympanum. This is the case with the nave portal of Santa Maria at Uncastillo, whose arches host one of the most beautiful displays of non-biblical figures which, for convenience, I will here describe as marginal. The portal is, however, dominated by a Christ in majesty flanked by a saint.[22] The city of Carrión de los Condes has two portals which also adopt structural features that can be related to Aquitaine (Figure 4.6).[23] It is in the church of Santiago that they were applied the most faithfully, with a portal without tympanum and an arch hosting marginal figures. As for the theophany, it occupies the width of the upper register, with a Christ in glory flanked by beasts of the Apocalypse and twelve apostles. Faced with such a vision, it would be absurd to blame the designer of this façade for the lack of tympanum.

In Santa Maria at Carrión de los Condes, we find a similar structure, to which is added another theme peculiar to the sculpture of Aquitaine, as was noted by René Crozet: an equestrian rider to the right and Samson slaying the lion to the left.[24] It is important to note that in the centre of the upper frieze, the figure is not the Christ but Herod welcoming the Magi. The designer clearly preferred a continuous narrative sequence that leads the eye towards the Virgin and Child represented on the left side wall of the porch. He did, however, respect the principle according to which a hieratic figure should appear in the centre of the composition. Both façades of Carrión inspired others, such as the portal at Peranzacas de Ojeda, which only reproduces the arch decorated with marginal figures, and the façade of Moarves which replicates the frieze of Santiago but not the historiated arch.

By 1160, the portal at Sangüesa was one of very first in Spain to respond to the early Gothic portals, with column-statues and a historiated tympanum.[25] Without this tympanum, it would have been difficult to depict the theme of the Last Judgment. This formula cannot have been considered completely satisfactory because at a later stage another group of sculptors, related to the workshop of San Juan de la Peña, were hired to carve a second theophany, comparable to that of Santiago of Carrión and containing a *Maiestas Domini* and the apostles. In spite of the influence of early French Gothic, the designer remained attached to the concept of the screen façade and an upper theophany, demonstrating that the patrons must have considered this scheme as worthy as that of portals with tympana.

The expansion of Romanesque Aquitanian sculpture even reached England, as at Shobdon and Malmesbury's outer portal.[26] The decorative aspect of the latter, along with the absence of a tympanum, evokes Aquitainian compositions, even if the detailing is quite different. For the west doorway of Rochester, a designer eventually opted for a tympanum like that of Cluny, but he made a point of combining it with sculpted voussoirs as in Aquitaine and jamb statues like those of the first gothic portals.[27] Aquitanian sculpture has therefore been the subject of the widest expansion ever known in Romanesque art.

THE ICONOGRAPHY

The fourth aspect of Romanesque sculpture in Aquitaine I wish to mention concerns iconography. Henri Focillon's view is that the tympanum constitutes the most adaptable medium for the deployment of theophanies. The historiography, which neglected the façades of Aquitaine in favour of sculpture in Languedoc and Burgundy, implies the same, suggesting that the mediocrity of certain artists in Aquitaine, the inadequacy of the medium, and the taste for decorative profusion militated against sophisticated and complex programmes. This is how the façade of the Abbaye-aux-Dames in Saintes could be read, where figures are rough, small-scale, and embedded in invasive vegetation (Figure 4.7). When we compare this programme to that of Moissac, we nevertheless notice that it is at least as rich and that it conveys, in my opinion, comparable Eucharistic content (Figure 4.8).[28] Both programmes are focused on a vision of the Apocalypse. The visions centre on Christ – in glory at Moissac and under the guise of the Lamb at Saintes – surrounded by the Living Creatures and the Elders celebrating the celestial liturgy.

John's Apocalypse tells that the Living Creatures celebrate night and day the glory of God by singing a hymn stemming from the song of the seraphs (Isaiah 6:3): 'Holy, Holy, Holy, Lord God, Ruler of all, who was and is and is to come" (Revelation 4:8). In his commentaries on the Mass, Amalarius of Metz equates that hymn and the song of the seraphs to the liturgical Sanctus, even if the words are not exactly the same, and he adds that the Elders also take part to that praise.[29] The depiction of these apocalyptic characters can therefore be interpreted liturgically. The hypothesis is reinforced when seraphs and/or cherubs accompany the Elders as at Moissac and, above all, when the Elders hold a chalice as in both façades. At Saintes, it is confirmed by a motif widespread in Romanesque sculpture but almost never associated with a theophany: two birds drinking from a chalice. The theme of the Eucharist is thus explicitly expressed by the chalices held by the Elders and in which the birds are quenching their thirst.

Around the theophanies of Saintes and Moissac are narrative scenes. At Moissac, the walls of the porch host five scenes. At Saintes, the program includes the Massacre of the Innocents on the central portal and the Last Supper on the left arch, where an Apostle exposes a host, thereby re-emphasising the Eucharistic concerns of the

FIGURE 4.7

Saintes, Abbaye-aux-Dames: west portal (Marcello Angheben)

programme. The capitals depict the Fall, Samson wrestling with the lion, and other scenes of combat. Above the lateral arches, relief figures, of which only haloes remain, may have taken part in biblical scenes, as at Notre-Dame-la-Grande in Poitiers. Finally, the upper levels probably hosted an equestrian rider and a theophany. The programme at Saintes was therefore at least as complex as that of Moissac and is in no way intellectually inferior to the program to the south.

ARTISTIC QUALITY

The last issue I would like to touch on concerns artistic quality. If we compare the details of the carvings on the lateral arches at Angoulême, which are among the earliest from the façade, to those of Moissac, we notice that they reproduce certain popular conventions, like the double fold line incised on the legs or folds in the form of a dovetail (Figures 4.8 and 4.9). The sculpture at Angoulême is, however, more three-dimensional, the dovetails are softer, less angular, and above all, the pattern of the folds is less geometrical, more random and thus more naturalistic. The evolution is substantial, in the light of the relative chronology of these works. If we consider that they are a few years apart, we would adduce that the development is rapid and that the sculptors of Angoulême are immensely creative. If we suppose, on the contrary, a fifteen-year gap, we would reduce the extent of the creativity. In either case, it must be recognized that the sculptors of Angoulême are among the most talented of their generation and that they are concerned for greater realism. If we supposed that they worked at the same time as their colleagues at Moissac or just a little later, it would infer that they represent a remarkable acceleration towards naturalism, such that we should accord them recognition as leading artists.

My contention that there is continuity between Languedoc and Aquitaine is confirmed by a comparison of the Christ of the Ascension at Angoulême, also among the early works of the Angoulême sculptors, with that of Cahors (Figures 4.10 and 4.11). Both adopt the same pattern: the same narrow mandorla with a decorated edge, the section of mantle crossed on the breast, and plate-fold on either side of the legs. The Christ of Cahors is, however, more highly developed: the body and the head are less cylindrical, and the clothes are softer and more voluminous, in particular at the level of the right sleeve. If we consider that the portal of Cahors is older, we must deduce that the sculpture of Angoulême is a poor imitation. If not, the sculptors from Aquitaine should take their place within a progressive evolution that should not be solely considered the preserve of Languedocian art.[30]

FIGURE 4.8
Moissac: south portal tympanum (Amelot/CESCM)

FIGURE 4.9
Angoulême Cathedral: lateral tympanum (CESCM)

One last example will demonstrate the point. When we compare the Annunciation of Moissac to that of Notre-Dame-la-Grande, we immediately notice that the latter is more three-dimensional; the figures are more dynamic, and their movement is accompanied by softer folds. Historiographically, the relative importance of these works has depended on their chronology, and as this remains vague, the chronology is simply adapted to suit the point of view of the scholar for whom it is a concern. It is thus an extremely subjective matter.

In conclusion, I wish to underline three essential points. Firstly, the appetite for ornament and the evident mediocrity of certain sculptors in Aquitaine, as at the Abbaye-aux-Dames in Saintes, did not hinder the development of complex iconographical programmes. Secondly, we can establish that certain sculptors are among the more talented in early 12th-century France, even if their relative position depends on how we interpret the chronology. Most importantly, and for reasons which largely escape us, the west portal of Aulnay was the most influential of all French Romanesque portal compositions, both in terms of quantity and of transregional impact, since it was imitated from Tournai to Bordeaux. We should consequently give more weight to the views of 12th-century patrons, who massively favoured this formula, than to received historiographical opinion.

FIGURE 4.10

Angoulême Cathedral: west front, Christ Ascending to Heaven (Archives of the author)

FIGURE 4.11

Cahors Cathedral: north portal tympanum, Christ Ascending to Heaven (Marcello Angheben)

NOTES

[1] A. de Caumont, *Cours d'antiquités monumentales, professé à Caen en 1830. Histoire de l'art dans l'ouest de la France depuis les temps les plus reculés jusqu'au XVIIe siècle. Quatrième partie, Moyen Âge, architecture religieuse* (Paris 1831).

[2] M. Durliat, *L'art roman* (Paris 1982); J.-R. Gaborit, *La sculpture romane* (Paris 2010).

[3] É. Mâle, *L'art religieux du XIIe siècle en France. Étude sur les origines de l'iconographie du Moyen Âge* (Paris 1922, reprinted 1992), 380.

[4] H. Focillon, *Art d'Occident* (Paris 1938), 284. Neither did this scholar pay any more attention to Aquitainian sculpture in H. Focillon, *L'art de sculpteurs romans. Recherches sur l'histoire des formes* (Paris 1995, 1st ed. 1931).

[5] Focillon, *Art d'Occident* (as n. 4), 238.

[6] A. K. Porter, *Romanesque Sculpture of the Pilgrimage Roads* (Boston 1923), I, 303–42.

[7] M.-T. Camus, *Sculpture romane du Poitou: les grands chantiers du XIe siècle* (Paris 1992); A. Tcherikover, *High Romanesque Sculpture in the Duchy of Aquitaine. c. 1090–1140* (Oxford 1997); M.-T.Camus, É. Carpentier and J.-F. Amelot, *Sculpture romane du Poitou. Le temps des chefs-d'œuvre* (Paris 2009). See also J. Lacoste, ed., *L'imaginaire et la foi. La sculpture romane en Saintonge* (Saint-Cyr-sur-Loire 1998); R.A. Maxwell, *The Art of Medieval Urbanism: Parthenay in Romanesque Aquitaine* (University Park 2007); H. R. Silvers, 'Repulsive Rhetoric: Profanity in the Visual Vernacular of Village Churches of Romanesque Saintonge' (unpublished PhD thesis, University of Indiana, 2010).

[8] H. Pradalier, 'Saint-Sernin de Toulouse au Moyen Âge', *Congrès archéologique de France: 154 Toulousain et Comminges* (Paris 2002), 256–301; D. Cazes and Q. Cazes, *Saint-Sernin de Toulouse. de Saturnin au chef-d'œuvre de l'art roman* (Graulhet 2008).

[9] J. Wirth, *La datation de la sculpture médiévale* (Genève 2004), 26–35; I. H. Forsyth, 'The Date of the Moissac Portal', in *Current Directions in Eleventh- and Twelfth-Century Sculpture Studies*, eds. R. A. Maxwell and K. Ambrose (Turnhout 2010), 77–99; C. E. Besancon, 'The French Romanesque Portals of Moissac, Souillac and Beaulieu: A Response to the Papal Reform Movement and Popular Heresy' (unpublished PhD thesis, University of Southern California, 2013), 53–65.

[10] M. Angheben, *D'un jugement à l'autre. La représentation du jugement immédiat dans les Jugements derniers français: 1100–1250* (Turnhout 2013), 187–88; M. Castiñeiras, '*Didacus Gelmirius*, Mécène des Arts. Le long chemin de Compostelle: de périphérie à centre du roman', in *Compostelle et l'Europe: l'histoire de Diego Gelmírez*, ed. M. Castiñeiras (Milan 2010), 32–97. On p. 79, the author suggested that the portal had been carved before 1105.

[11] F. Werner, *Aulnay de Saintonge und die romanische Skulptur im Westfrankreich* (Worms 1979), 82–83; Tcherikover, *High Romanesque Sculpture* (as. n. 7), 24–25; Camus, Carpentier, and Amelot, *Sculpture romane* (as. n. 7), 433–34. See also Wirth, *La datation* (as. n. 9), 35–38, who criticised Tcherikover's chronology and the general trend in making monuments earlier.

[12] J. Chagnolleau, *L'église d'Aulnay de Saintonge* (Grenoble 1938).

[13] Werner, *Aulnay de Saintonge* (as. n. 11), 89–90; Tcherikover, *High Romanesque Sculpture* (as. n. 7), 53–61; Lacoste, *L'imaginaire et la foi* (as. n. 7), 73–85; Camus, Carpentier, and Amelot, *Sculpture romane* (as. n. 7), 414.

[14] M. Angheben, 'Des portails du groupe d'Aulnay aux portails latéraux de la cathédrale de Tournai', in *Les portails romans de la cathédrale de Tournai: contextualisation et restauration*, eds. F. Duperroy and Y. Desmet (Namur 2015), 71–85.

[15] L. Deléhouzée, 'La place des portails dans la chronologie du chantier roman de la cathédrale de Tournai', in *Les portails romans* (as. n. 14), 17–29.

[16] A. Tcherikover, *High Romanesque Sculpture* (as n. 7), 31 and 37. See also M.-T. Camus, 'Saint-Jouin-de-Marnes. Réflexion sur les chantiers romans de l'abbatiale', in *Congrès Archéologique de France: 159 Deux-Sèvres* (Paris 2004), 247–61.

[17] P. Dubourg-Noves, 'La cathédrale d'Angoulême', in *Congrès archéologique de France: 153, Charente* (Paris 1999), 37–68; Tcherikover, *High Romanesque Sculpture* (as n. 7), 62–67. G. Milanesi, *"Bonifica" delle immagini e "Propaganda" in Aquitania durante lo scisma del 1130–1138* (Verona 2013) argued that the sculpture is later.

[18] Lacoste, *L'imaginaire et la foi* (as. n. 7), 50–57.

[19] L. Seidel, *Songs of Glory. The Romanesque Façades of Aquitaine* (Chicago–London 1981).

[20] Argenton-les-Vallées (St-Gilles, Argenton-Château), Castelvieil, Chadenac, Civray, Corme-Royal, Échillais, Fenioux, Fontaine-d'Ozillac, Le Douhet, Melle (Saint-Hilaire), Parthenay (Notre-Dame-de-la-Couldre), Pont-l'Abbé-d'Arnoult, Saint-Pompain, Saint-Symphorien, Talmont, and Varaize.

[21] M. Angheben, 'Des portails du groupe d'Aulnay' (as n. 14).

[22] J. Lacoste, *Les maîtres de la sculpture romane dans l'Espagne du pèlerinage à Compostelle* (Bordeaux 2006), 69–75. See also the paper by Julia Perratore in this volume.

[23] Lacoste, *Les maîtres de la sculpture romane* (as. n. 22), 189–90; D. Rico Camps, 'Los maestros de Carrión de los Condes y San Vicente de Avila. Reflexiones sobre la decantación hispana de la escultura borgoñona', in *Maestros del románico en el Camino de Santiago*, ed. P. L. Huerta (Aguilar de Campoo 2010), 117–49.

[24] R. Crozet, 'Nouvelles remarques sur les cavaliers sculptés ou peints dans les églises romanes', *Cahiers de civilisation médiévale*, 1 (1958), 27–36; R. Crozet, 'Le thème du cavalier victorieux dans l'art roman de France et d'Espagne', *Principe de Viana*, 32 (1971), 125–43.

[25] R. Crozet, 'Remarques sur les relations artistiques entre la France du Sud-Ouest et le Nord de l'Espagne à l'époque romane', in *Actes du XIXe Congrès international d'histoire de l'art* (Paris 1958), 62–71; B. Müller, 'Santa María la Real, Sangüesa (Navarra). Die Bauplastik Santa Marías und die Skulptur Navarras und Aragóns im 12. Jahrhundert. Rezeptor, Katalysator, Innovator?' (unpublished PhD thesis, Humboldt-Universität, Berlin, 1997); A. Ancho Villanueva and C. Fernández-Ladreda Aguadé, *Portada de Santa María de Sangüesa. Imaginario románico en piedra* (Pampelune 2010).

[26] J. McNeill, 'Romanesque Sculpture in England and Aquitaine', in *Regards croisés sur le monument médiéval. Mélanges offerts à Claude Andrault-Schmitt*, ed. M. Angheben (Turnhout 2018), 357–68.

[27] It seems likely that the earliest iteration of the Rochester west portal had no tympanum, and that the tympanum one now sees there, along with the jamb figures, were part of an uprating of the portal in the later 1150s or 1160s. R. Baxter, 'The Construction of the West Doorway of Rochester Cathedral', in *Medieval Art, Architecture and Archaeology at Rochester*, eds. T. Ayers and T. Tatton-Brown (Leeds 2006), 85–96.

[28] M. Angheben, 'La théophanie du portail de Moissac: une vision de l'Église céleste célébrant la liturgie eucharistique', *Les cahiers de Saint-Michel de Cuxa*, 45 (2014), 61–82. See also M. Angheben, 'Romanesque Sculpture and Liturgy', in *Medieval Art*, ed. P. Piva (Milan 2010), 131–79.

[29] Amalarius of Metz, *Canonis missae interpretatio*, 40, and *Expositio missae 'Dominus vobiscum'*, 20, ed. J.-M. Hanssens, *Amalarii episcopi opera liturgica omnia* (Vatican City 1948–1950), I, 307 and 302.

[30] E. Bratke, *Das Nordportal der Kathedrale Saint-Étienne in Cahors* (Berlin 1977), 158–60, reached the same conclusions. And these have been accepted in particular by M. Durliat, 'La cathédrale Saint-Étienne de Cahors: architecture et sculpture', *Bulletin monumental*, 137 (1979), 285–340; M. Bénéjeam-Lère, 'La cathédrale Saint-Etienne de Cahors', *Congrès archéologique de France. 1989: Quercy* (Paris 1993), 9–69. However, it should be noted, as the above scholars also did, that the sculptors of Cahors have also been inspired by the porch of Moissac.

The Regional and Transregional in Romanesque Europe (2021), 47–67

THE *BALDACHIN-CIBORIUM*

THE SHIFTING MEANINGS OF A RESTRICTED LITURGICAL FURNISHING IN ROMANESQUE ART

Manuel Castiñeiras

To Romanesque viewers, a baldachin-ciborium *over the high altar was a rare and distinguished element in the liturgical furnishing of a church. Beginning in Rome, where ciboria had been established since the 4th century, the ciborium featured as a prominent sign in basilicas ad corpus or in sanctuaries above reliquary crypts (Old St Peter's, Sta Maria in Cosmedin, Lateran Basilica, Sta Maria Maggiore). Its use was restricted even in Romanesque Italy. Examples from the 11th and 12th centuries – such as those of Montecassino, San Nicola in Bari, or in the Abruzzi – should been seen as echoing Papal Roman settings. Outside Italy,* baldachin-ciboria *over high altars are exceptional and seem to be restricted to places and institutions especially concerned to advertise their adherence to papal authority as a guarantor of their rights. Thus the* baldachin *at Old St Peters is the symbolic and ideological model for those at Cluny, Ripoll, Cuixà, and Santiago de Compostela.*

Notwithstanding all this, as with other forms of 'prototype' and 'copy' the evocation of a prestigious model does not imply a facsimile, and in some cases the choice of materials and figurative ornamentation enhanced old meanings and added new content. Thus, in 11th-century Catalonia ciboria were described as the 'sancta sanctorum' of the Temple of Jerusalem, and their pictorial programmes introduced themes that were subsequently incorporated into Romanesque mural and panel painting. In certain later examples, as represented by the mid-12th-century replacement for the canopy at Ripoll or the twin ciboria at San Juan del Duero in Soria (Castile), the significance of the baldachin-ciborium *was updated either to reflect Eucharistic themes or to evoke the Holy Land and Christ's tomb in Jerusalem.*

At first glance, it might seem odd to focus on the *baldachin-ciborium* in a volume devoted to the regional and transregional in Romanesque art.[1] The subject neither belongs to a regional school, nor is it concerned with itinerant workshops or the export of artworks. The justification is that study of the distribution and typology of *baldachin-ciboria* in Romanesque Europe before 1200 enables one to address the issue of a type of liturgical furnishing that existed independent of geography and to investigate their relationship with the Rome of Constantine as markers of martyrs' graves or relics. Notwithstanding their roots in early Christian Rome, however, a singular approach diminishes the ontological status of the *ciborium*, which is characterized from the beginning by its polysemy. So the subject will be approached from more than one direction.

PRESTIGIOUS MODELS, DISTINCTIVE FEATURES AND POLYSEMY

In terms of its prestige, the most famous *ciborium* formed a part of the 4th-century theatrical scenery that attended the high altar at St Peter's in Rome, whose appearance can be reconstructed thanks to its depiction on the Pola Casket (5th century). The *ciborium* consisted of a trabeated superstructure supported on twisted columns. Two columns can be seen in the foreground and four in the background, linked by an architrave. The central area framed the tomb of Peter and was crowned by two intersecting arches from which a lamp is hung to indicate the burial place.[2]

The early Christian aedicule of Christ in the Church of the Holy Sepulchre in Jerusalem of *c.* 325–35 also belonged to this category. The Jerusalem example had a polygonal canopy crowned by an octagonal pyramidal roof supported on seven columns with spiral fluting. Each side was enclosed by railings, and the structure had a small porch (Figure 5.1). The appearance of the monument, which mostly survived until its destruction by the Fatimid Caliph Al-Hakim in 1009, is well documented thanks to its depiction on 6th-century pilgrims' ampullae found in Monza and Bobbio and is represented by the 5th-century stone model now in the Museum of Narbonne.[3]

The most distinctive features of the early aedicule of the Holy Sepulchre were the spiral-fluted columns and

  DOI: 10.4324/9781003162827-5

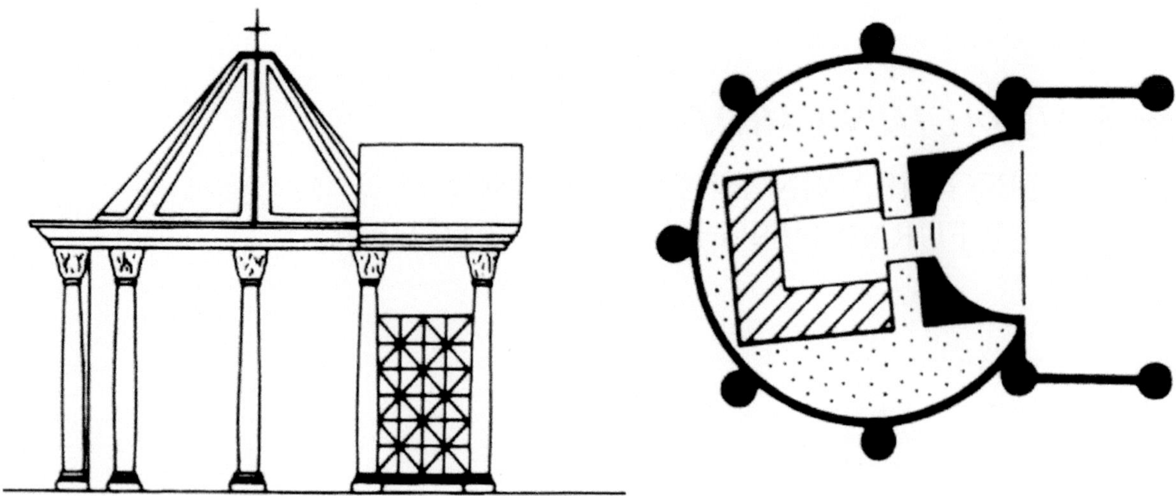

FIGURE 5.1
Jerusalem: Church of the Holy Sepulchre, the early Christian aedicule of Christ, c. *325–35 (Martin Biddle)*

the conical or pyramidal shape of its roof.[4] Both elements were imitated in the most prestigious *Christian ciboria* of the 6th century. Thus, according to the description of Paul the Silentiary (563), the Justinianic silver canopy in the Hagia Sophia in Constantinople was supported by four arches on silver columns which were spirally fluted and crowned by a pyramidal roof (*πύργος*) formed by eight triangular silver plates (Figure 5.2).[5] In the case of St Peter's in Rome, the high altar was rearranged by Pope Gregory the Great (580–604): a new *ciborium* in silver, with the distinctive pyramidal roof, was erected, while the six twisted columns from the earlier structure were repositioned to form a chancel screen (Figure 5.3).[6] The St Peter's *ciborium* was then remade several times during the Middle Ages; in the 9th century, it was substituted by one also in silver, which in turn was renewed in the 12th century and later replaced with a new *ciborium* between 1216 and 1227.[7]

These elements – the pyramid and twisted columns – and the material – silver – were symbolic bearers of meaning. The pyramidal summit had burial connotations, while the twisted columns and the use of precious metals were an allusion to the Temple of Solomon and the Ark of Covenant. However, the semantics of each part should be understood in the context of the whole, since the underlying significance of the *ciborium* derives from its privileged position by the high altar. It is a mark of holiness and acts as a persuasive metaphor for the bond between the Old and New Testament. Thus Basil the Great (329–79), in his *Historia Mystagogica*, explains the term *Κιβώριον* not only as a reference to the place where Christ was crucified, buried, and raised but as an evocation of the metallic and mystic Ark of Covenant. The author expands on the idea of *Κιβώριον* as the Holy of Holies on the basis of the etymology of the term. Thus, ***Κιβ*** *ἐστὶ κιβωτός* (*κιβ* is the ark) and ***οὖριν***, *φῶς κυρίον* (light of the Lord).[8] Similarly, Germanos I, Patriarch of Constantinople, in his *Mystagogia* of *c*. 730, insists on these two significations by saying that the *ciborium* is the shrine of the divine tomb, in which the canopy above is formed by the outstretched wings of the cherubim covering the Ark (Ezekiel 25[10–22]).[9]

Beyond this, the *ciborium* can be seen in micro-architectural terms as a reflection of the symbolism of the vaulted church within a neo-Platonic tradition. Thus, the Byzantine bishop Theodore of Andina comments in his *Protheoria* – an 11th-century treatise on the divine liturgy – that the *ciborium*, with its four columns and its domed canopy over the *mensa altaris*, marks the place between heaven and earth where salvation occurred. This sacred spot in the middle of the earth was the city of Jerusalem. However, as Theodore reminds us, not all churches have *ciboria*, but their function and meaning as a metaphor for the celestial dome over the altar can be represented by the vaulted semicircular apse above the *bema*.[10]

Fortunately, both in the Latin West and in Byzantium, the particular symbolism of these liturgical furnishings was solemnly celebrated and enriched through the genre of *ekphrasis*. Ekphrastic passages usually formed a part of homilies which were recited during the ceremony of consecration (*ἐγκαίνια*) – as in Paul the Silentiary's description of Hagia Sophia – or in annual commemorations of the event. These commemorations often provided an accurate description of an artwork, as in the 12th-century homily of Michael of Thessaloniki on Hagia Sophia.[11] At other times, as was the case with the famous sermon of the monk Garsies for Sant Miquel de Cuixà (*c*. 1043–46),[12] the text applies metaphorical and biblical meanings to the *ciborium* which help us understand its significance for the consecration of the new altar of the abbatial church in 1040.

Thus the polysemic potential of the *ciborium* is especially rich. This liturgical furnishing not only embodies concepts but is able to evoke both imaginary and real models. On the one hand, it was the place of Christ's sacrifice and resurrection, the city of Jerusalem, the Holy of Holies, and a celestial dwelling. On the other hand,

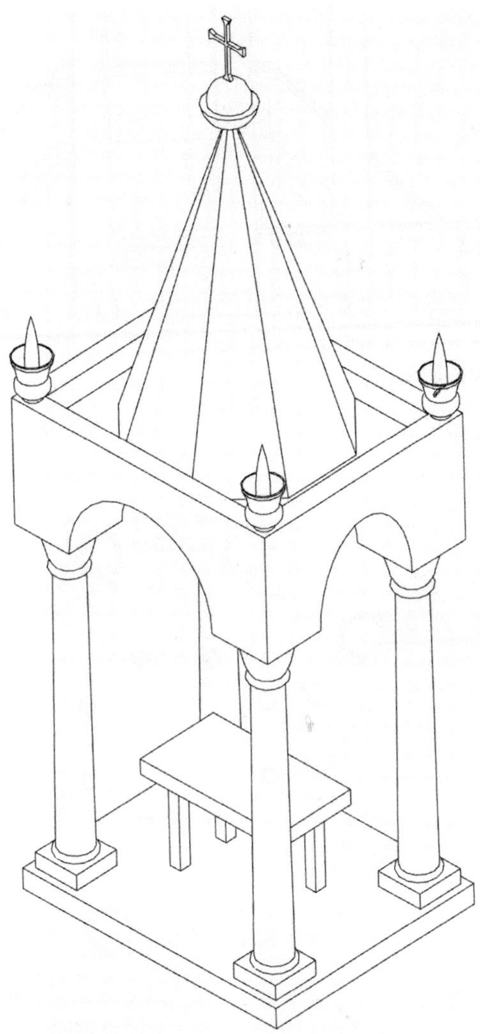

FIGURE 5.2

Constantinople, Hagia Sophia: reconstruction of the Justinianic furnishings, chancel, with the silver ciborium *(L. Fobelli,* Un tempio per Giustiniano*)*

certain *ciboria* were a citation of specific and prestigious artworks such as the aedicule of the Holy Sepulchre, the high altar of St Peter or the biblical Ark of the Covenant. None of these significations were exclusive, and, as we will see, they coexisted within the artwork as layers of meaning. Moreover, beyond its semantics, the *ciborium* functioned as a navigation mark within the topography of the church, highlighting the site of the high altar, marking the presence of a martyrial crypt or chamber of relics, or signifying a burial. A collection of short case studies should suffice to disclose the significance and function of the *ciborium* and the relevance of any one meaning over another.

THE GEOGRAPHY OF *CIBORIA* UP TO 1200

The prestigious precedents of the *ciboria* can be assessed through its dissemination across the Mediterranean.

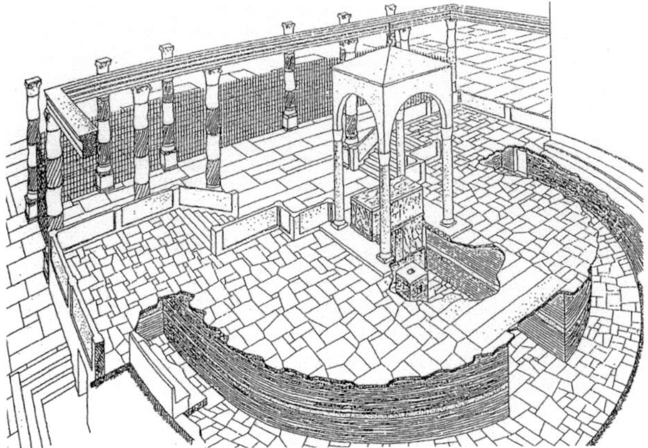

FIGURE 5.3

Rome, Old St Peter's: reconstruction of the high altar and the annular crypt during the papacy of Pope Gregory III (731-41) (Richard Krautheimer)

The canopy enjoyed a great success in Byzantium both as physical object and as a visual and literary topic.[13] In the orthodox tradition, the use of martyrial-shrines, the descriptions of the *ciborium* of Hagia Sophia, and its association with the liturgy encouraged the spread of canopies in the church and increased their liturgical uses.

In western Europe, at least before 1200, the *ciborium* is primarily an Italian phenomenon, with a particular concentration in central Italy (Lazio, Tuscany, Marche, Abruzzo, Molise) and across the Adriatic (from Puglia to Ravenna to Dalmatia). Although there are links here with Byzantium, especially along the Adriatic, this distribution must be largely related to the prestige of Roman altar-canopies as sacred markers both in basilicas *ad corpus* and in sanctuaries above reliquary crypts or chambers, as in the Lateran Basilica, Old St Peter's, San Crisogono, and others. Most of the Roman *ciboria* were renewed in the major basilicas during the Carolingian era – the Lateran Basilica in 809, Santa Maria Maggiore between 794 and 809, St Peter's in 809 – while the *Liber Pontificalis* to some extent chronicles the success of *ciboria* in Roman churches from this period onwards.

It seems to be during the Carolingian period that *ciboria* proliferated across the Italian Peninsula. Some examples – such as that at Santa Maria di Sovana (Tuscany), previously in the cathedral of St Peter at Sovana (Figure 5.4), and that of the basilica of Sant'Ippolito all'Isola Sacra, between Ostia and Porto – are interesting in that they show how ancient and prestigious types of outer coverings in silver were translated into stone. Both *ciboria* consist of four arches over four columns, with an octagonal roof crowned by a pinnacle.[14] The pyramid-shaped summit is reminiscent of that of the *ciborium* of the Hagia Sophia in Constantinople, which was probably known in Rome in the early Middle Ages.[15] As Anna Maria D'Achille has pointed out, the *ciborium* of Old St Peter's, with its simple quadrangular pyramidal crown, was the more usual model for churches within the *terra Petri* in Latium. This traditional shape even survived into the 11th and 12th centuries, as at Santa Pudenziana a

FIGURE 5.4
Sovana, Santa Maria: high altar, ciborium, *9th century (Manuel Castiñeiras)*

FIGURE 5.5

Tuscania, San Pietro: high altar, ciborium, *1093 (John McNeill)*

FIGURE 5.6

Milan, Sant'Ambrogio: high altar, ciborium *showing stucco relief of the Traditio Legis (10th century) (Manuel Castiñeiras)*

Visciano (Umbria), Santa Vittoria a Monteleone in Sabina, and, in partially reconstructed form, at San Pietro in Tuscania (Lazio) of 1093 (Figure 5.5).[16]

Outside of central Italy, Sant'Ambrogio in Milan provides a remarkable example of how this kind of furnishing could be used to draw attention to the church's status as a *basilica martyrium* (Figure 5.6). It is even possible at Milan to follow and single out the various alterations made to the monument during the early Middle Ages. First, a *ciborium* supported by four porphyry columns was raised around the year 500 over the burial area. Later, in the course of the work undertaken by Bishop Angilbertus II (825–50) in the apse area and contemporary with the installation of the luxurious golden altar of Vuolvinius, the *ciborium* was renewed with a domed canopy and four gabled *tympana*. Finally, in the second half of the 10th century, when a crypt was constructed beneath the high altar and the *ciborium* column bases were buried, the four *frontones* were lavishly decorated in polychromed stucco with scenes exalting the church of Milan and the saints buried in the immediate area, namely Gervase and Protase, and Ambrose.[17]

The emergence of narrative figuration on *ciboria* is a phenomenon that was picked up in the 11th and 12th centuries, with outstanding examples known from Sant Miquel de Cuixà (1040) and San Pietro al Monte in Civate (*c.* 1100). Civate (Lombardy) clearly reflects Sant'Ambrogio, with four gabled tympana lavishly decorated with stucco. However, its iconographical programme turns on the earlier concept of the *ciborium* as the place of the sacrifice and resurrection of Christ, arranging subjects such as the Crucifixion, the *Visitatio Sepulchri* (Figure 5.7) and the Ascension of Christ around the exterior faces. As a result, the earthly Jerusalem mingled with the Heavenly Jerusalem, which is evoked on the interior dome by the apocalyptical scene of the Triumph of the Lamb surrounded by saints. However, the most interesting aspect of the *ciborium* at Civate is that it is conceived as an element in an iconographic programme that embraces the entire church and reflects a liturgical itinerary that involves the nearby oratory of San Giovanni Battista (S. Benedetto), which belonged to the same monastic complex. Thus, in the same way that the painting in the *ciborium* dome is linked to other apocalyptical scenes in the church, such as Archangel Michael fighting the Dragon or the Heavenly Jerusalem, it has been argued by Paolo Piva that the stucco relief with the *Visitatio Sepulchri* is a direct citation of the Easter celebrations which probably took place in the oratory of San Giovanni.[18]

It is true that the geographical distribution of *ciboria* expanded in western Europe from the Carolingian period onwards. However, outside Italy, *ciboria* over high altars remained exceptional before 1200, with just a few examples north of the Alps known in the Carolingian and post-Carolingian periods (Centula, Auxerre, Le Mans, Heiligenstadt, Peterhausen, Sankt Gallen, Mainz) and a very restricted dissemination in French and Spanish Romanesque.[19]

FIGURE 5.7

Civate, San Pietro al Monte: ciborium *showing the relief of Visitatio Sepulchri and painted vault of* c. *1100 (Juan Antonio Olañeta)*

NEW READINGS OF SOME IBERIAN *CIBORIA*

Nevertheless, this paper is not intended to provide a comprehensive geography of the *ciborium* in Romanesque Europe. Rather it is intended to draw attention to its semantics. Scholars usually consider *ciboria* as exemplars of continuity from early Christian to Romanesque art and can understate other important aspects of these objects – shifts in meaning or variation in the handling of formal elements. As with other forms of 'prototype' and 'copy' in the Middle Ages, the evocation of a prestigious model did not imply a facsimile.[20] In most cases, the choice of materials, colour, and figurative ornamentation were intended to stress a particular interpretation of the symbolism of the canopy, sometimes deeply rooted in Early Christian traditions, at other times linked to new themes in 12th-century art.

In the case of the Iberian peninsula, the dissemination of *ciboria* during the 11th and 12th centuries is held to be concentrated in institutions which were especially concerned to display their adherence to papal authority as a guarantor of their rights – institutions such as the abbey of Santa Maria de Ripoll (Catalonia) or the cathedral of Santiago de Compostela (Glicia). Nevertheless, analysis of individual cases shows how these institutions were equally concerned to create a distinct sacred topography for their sanctuaries and did not hesitate to use a series of biblical metaphors that went beyond the Roman models. Moreover, the huge increase in the popularity of the pilgrimage to Jerusalem in the 12th century and the emerging doctrine of the 'Real Presence' of Christ in the Host promoted perceptions of *ciboria* as a commemorative complement to the sacrament of the Eucharist (Ripoll) or as an exotic evocation of the Holy Land and the Sepulchre of Christ (San Juan de Duero).

Olibas's *ciboria*: the *baldachin-ciborium* as a reminiscence of the Sancta Sanctorum of the Temple of Jerusalem and the performance of the divine liturgy

Unfortunately, almost nothing survives of the *ciboria* that were commissioned by Abbot Oliba for the Benedictine monastic churches of Santa Maria de Ripoll (1032) and Cuixà (1040). According to Imma Lorés, the only element that has come down to us from Oliba's *ciboria* is a pink base now kept in the cloister of Sant Miquel de Cuixà.[21] Its particular colour coincides with the description of the *ciborium* in Cuixà written by the monk Garsies around 1043–46: the structure was supported by four columns and bases whose reddish colour symbolized the blood of the martyrs and the brightness of Cherubims.[22]

A close reading of Garsies's text makes it clear that this peculiar furnishing was made of different materials – marble and wood with a silver and enamel covering – and conveyed a strong biblical symbolism (Figure 5.8). A few years earlier, the same Oliba had commissioned a *ciborium* for the high altar of the monastic church of Santa Maria at Ripoll (1032). This was made of wood and covered by silver plates, but in this case the liturgical 'set' included an altar frontal and lateral panels made of silver and decorated with precious stones and enamels:

> *In primis, in altare sancte Dei genitricis Marie tabulam coopertam auro cum lapidibus et esmaltis XVI; tabulas cooperta argento II, colunas ciborii coopertas argento, et desuper tabulam coopertam argento.*[23]

Although scholars have proposed a series of comparisons for these no longer extant liturgical furnishings, the lack of material evidence has hindered further research. It is likely, however, that with these imposing structures over the high altar, Oliba sought to dignify the status of the monastic church of Ripoll as a consequence of his two journeys to Rome – in 1011 and 1016–17 – to obtain Papal immunity for the abbey, as well as to seek confirmations of its possessions.[24] To this end, the silver altar frontal and canopy could have been seen as an evocation of the lavish furnishings of the great Roman basilicas, like St Peter's, the Lateran Basilica, or Santa Maria Maggiore. However, as is discussed in this chapter, Oliba seems to have been interested in enlarging their significance in order to create a particular *hierotopy* in his churches.

In this same period, the abbot of Cluny, Odilon (994–1049), offered a golden altar frontal (1016–24) and a *ciborium* (1035) to the high altar of the church of Cluny II, though the actual configuration of Odilon's high altar slightly differed to that of Oliba's sanctuary. It is worth noting that Cluny II is often invoked as the architectural model for the remodelling of the east end of the church of Cuixà.[25]

The remains of the high altar of Cluny II were found in excavations in 2006, allowing Christian Sapin to propose a reconstruction (Figure 5.9). The altar, which was located over a crypt, was constructed with a *fenestella confessionis* and was sheltered by a canopy supported by wooden columns covered in stucco.[26] Although Sapin invoked Carolingian models for the setting, the typology of the altar, its dedication to saints Peter and Paul, and the special status of Cluny as a monastery directly linked to Rome suggest an intentional reference to the canopy over the altar of St Peter in Rome or perhaps to Roman canopies in general, which were usually placed over an altar *ad corpus*.

Thus the absence of a crypt and *fenestella confessionis* at the main altars of Ripoll and Cuixà diminishes their capacity to evoke the impressive sanctuaries of Rome. In so saying, I do not intend to deny the Roman background of Oliba's enterprises but rather to suggest that the abbot altered the terms of reference of the model in order to attach a specific significance to his liturgical furnishing. It is no coincidence that in one of the bibles illustrated during Oliba's abbacy in the scriptorium at Ripoll, the *ciborium* acquired a special relevance.[27] This appears in a full-page miniature devoted to the consecration of the Temple of Jerusalem and is located at the end of the emotional Prayer of King Solomon (I Kings 8^{22-53}) (Paris, BN, Ms. Lat. 6, vol. II, f. 129v) (Figure 5.10). Once the Temple of Jerusalem had been completed, the king transferred the Ark of Covenant from Sion, placing it in the Holy of Holies (*Sancta Sanctorum)* (I Kings 8^{1-21}). At the consecration of the building, Solomon, raising his hands, sings a prayer to ask for the divine protection of his people (I Kings 8^{62-65}). The Tabernacle–Ark of Covenant was shaped like a flat-roofed *baldachin-ciborium* flanked by two monumental cherubs.

This is a direct reference to the three outstanding elements in Oliba's *hierotopy*. First, as the monk Garsies states of the *ciborium* at Cuixà, the canopy evokes the propitiatory of Moses (Ex. 25^{17}): '*construxit propitiatorium, ut Beatus Moysis, super altare artifici magisterio*' (he made a *propitiatorium* of masterful artistry above the altar, as did the blessed Moses).[28] Secondly, in the same text, the reddish columns are compared to the cherubs that, according to Exodus (25^{18-19}), cast their shadow over the Ark of Covenant: '*explicite in oraculo Cherubim gloriae obumbrantia sacrae venerationes figurans*' ('explicitly symbolizing the cherub casting its shadow of sacred veneration upon the oracle of his glory').[29] Finally, the top of the internal structure is described as a flat-wooden ceiling that is made of thirteen painted-timber boards: '*Interiori namque ambitu[. . .] preciosi ligni ordines XIII ad fixit, ut apostoli inter semitas iustorum abintus filium hominis in spiritu gloriae suae illustrarent*' ('As for the inner part [. . .], there are fixed thirteen precious wooden boards, so that the apostles pay tribute to the Son of Man in the spirit of his glory following from inside the path of the Righteous').[30]

This last distinction – a flat painted ceiling – led me some years ago to revisit one of the most extraordinary surviving examples of Catalan panel painting, the so-called 'Baldaquí de Ribes', now preserved in the Episcopal Museum of Vic (MEV 3884) (Figure 5.11). In my opinion, it is likely that this fragmentary piece, consisting of nine assembled boards, also originally formed the flat ceiling of a lost *baldachin-ciborium* supported by four columns, and not a cantilevered aerial *baldachin* as is usually believed. Having been produced in the abbey of Ripoll in the first third of the 12th century (1119–34), the Ribes panel probably echoed Oliba's now lost 11th-century *painted ciborium* ceiling.[31]

Anna Orriols recently proposed that features of the painted ceiling of Cuixà are evoked in a miniature from a manuscript of the Gospels produced at Cuixà *c.* 1120 (Perpignan, Médiathèque municipal, Ms. 1, fol.3).[32] The composition consists of a series of concentric circles within a quadrangular frame. At the centre is an *Agnus*

FIGURE 5.8

Saint-Michel de Cuixà: ciborium *of 1040, reconstruction drawing (Daniel Codina)*

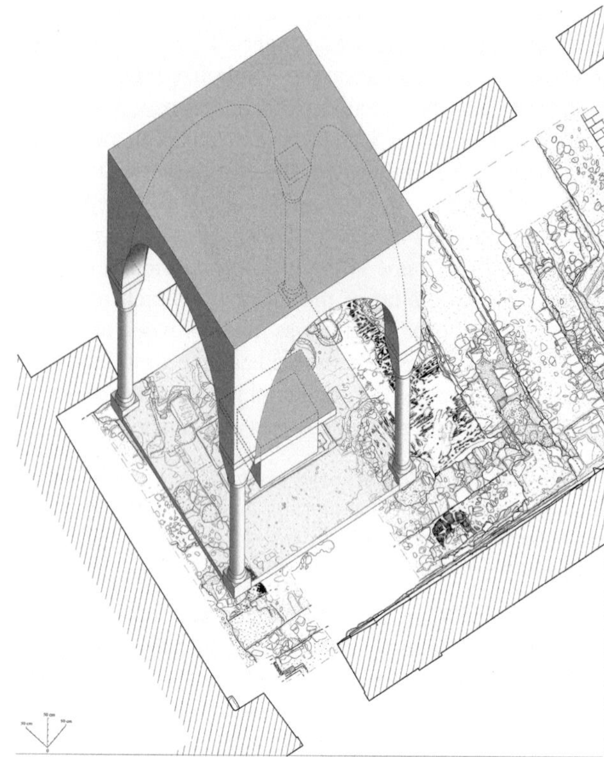

FIGURE 5.9

Cluny: reconstruction of the ciborium *of Cluny II (© CEM Christian Sapin)*

Dei surrounded by busts of sixteen haloed saints, which refer to the Apostles and the Righteous as mentioned by Garsies. Orriols argues that the drawing in the Cuixà Gospels recreates the painted ceiling of Oliba's *ciborium* by flattening what would appear to have been a domical structure (the circle) within a square (the quadrangular frame). In other words, the canopy would have been a little like the painted *ciborium* in San Pietro al Monte in Civate, in which is depicted a similar scene with the Adoration of the Lamb by martyrs.[33]

Nevertheless, it seems fundamentally unlikely that a wooden canopy made of painted boards, as described by Garsies and illustrated in the Bible of Rodes, would have been domical. The proliferation of flat wooden ceilings in 12th- and 13th-century Catalan panel painting hints at this and draws attention to the creativity of Catalan workshops. It was very probably around 1200 that the old Early Christian type of canopy altar was finally transformed in Catalonia into a peculiar hybrid known as the 'aerial *baldachin*' or '*baldachin*-plafond', as can be seen in the Baldaquí de Tost (*c.* 1220) (Barcelona, MNAC 3907 and Museu Episcopal de Vic 5166) (Figure 5.12). This unique structure literally hovers above the altar; its remarkable characteristic lies in being supported not by columns but by beams embedded into the apse wall. The result was a structural fusion between the common flat ceiling of ciboria as established in Catalonia from the early 11th century and a Byzantine *epistyle*. These peculiar hybrids, called *laquelaria* in texts, are probably the consequence of the translation into wood of textile canopies.[34]

Before moving on, one more aspect should be highlighted. The inner ceiling images of the Catalan canopies were not intended for public display, as were other monumental compositions in Romanesque art, but for restricted liturgical contemplation. These images were seen by the officiant during the Eucharistic liturgy, at the moment he raised his eyes and hands to recite the canon. In the case of abbeys such as Ripoll or Cuixà, where this kind of depiction was first invented, the images were also seen by the community of monks during the chant of the psalms since ciboria were included in the choir area. As Garsies stated, the illustrious bishop Oliba had created these images – '*non ad pompam et claritudine vulgi[. . .] sed in laudem duodecim apostolorum*' ('not to boast of magnificence before the common people but to praise the Apostles'.[35] As a result, the *ciborium* became a distinctive furnishing associated with monastic performance, and its more recondite depictions were thought to be seen with the eyes of the spirit.

This idea – that the viewing of the *ciborium* can be related to divine psalmody – is made clear in an illumination from the Bible of Rodes, namely that at the opening of the Psalms (Paris, BN, Ms. Lat. 6, vol. II, f. 130v) (Figure 5.13). The miniature shows a hooded figure sheltered by a *ciborium* reading a book on a lectern, while a woman approaches him in *proskynesis*. The scene has been interpreted as Jerome – author of the prologue to the Psalms – with Paula,[36] but it rather seems to me to be a depiction of King David in the dress of a Benedictine monk receiving tribute from the personification of Wisdom.[37] Thus David

FIGURE 5.10

Paris, Bibliothèque Nationale, Ms. Lat. 6, vol. II, f. 129v., Bible of Rodes, Sancta Sanctorum of the Temple of Solomon – propitiatorium, c. *1017–20 (© Bibliothèque Nationale, Paris)*

FIGURE 5.11

Vic, Museu Episcopal: 'Baldaquí de Ribes' (1119–34), ceiling of a ciborium*? (MEV 3884; ©Museu Episcopal de Vic)*

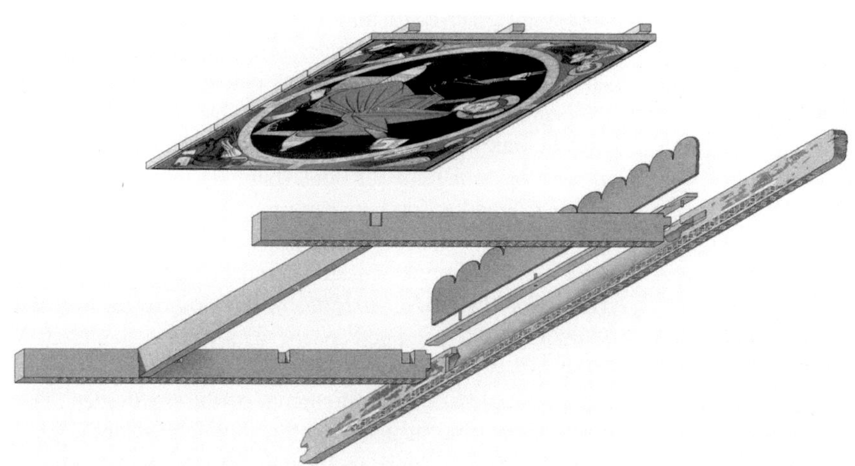

FIGURE 5.12

Sant Martí de Tost (c. *1220): reconstruction of the 'aerial* baldachin*' or '*baldachin-*plafond' (Jordi Ballonga)*

FIGURE 5.13

Paris, Bibliothèque Nationale, Ms. Lat. 6, vol. II, f. 130v, Bible de Rodes, King David with 'Wisdom' (?) (© Bibliothèque Nationale, Paris)

becomes the embodiment of the psalmody performed by the Benedictine community inspired by divine Wisdom.[38] The inclusion of the *ciborium* thereby acquires a special relevance by marking out the high altar of the monastic church around which the monks gather each day to chant Psalms to the Throne of Mercy represented by the *ciborium*.

It should also be remembered that the *ciborium* fulfilled an important function as an *attrezzo*, a tool or prop, in liturgy and paraliturgy, especially during the performance of liturgical dramas.[39] *Ciboria* were often equipped with complementary elements, such as hooks behind the arches from which curtains or lamps could be hung, as can be seen in the example at Isola Sacra.

Ultimately, the meanings attached to the altar canopies in Cuixà and Ripoll were multifaceted. Lying behind them was an understanding drawn from Early Christian and Byzantine art. The descriptions of the *ciborium* at St Peter's in Rome by Gregory of Tours and found in the *Liber Pontificalis*, as well as the descriptions of Hagia Sophia in Constantinople by Paul the Silentiary and the Patriarch Germanos, were full of the same biblical metaphors. The *ciborium* is Propitiatory, the Ark of Covenant, the Holy of Holies in the Temple of Solomon, the Throne of Mercy (Wisdom) and the Ark of the New Law. Building on this, it seems likely that the most specific message of this liturgical furnishing in Ripoll and Cuixà was its direct connection with the performance of the psalmody. The *ciborium* became, in a very exclusive and restricted monastic space, a true gate to Heaven.

Destroying and repairing the sacred: a new setting for the *ciborium* in Ripoll

Having established the important role developed by the *ciboria* in Ripoll and Cuixà within the daily prayer of their Benedictine communities, one can imagine how traumatic and painful the destruction of that of Ripoll could be for its community. This happened in 1141, when Ramon Berenguer IV, Count of Barcelona, had the silver *ciborium* melted down – 200 silver pounds in total – to produce metal to mint coinage. According to the records, the community of Ripoll was reluctant to go along with this and only finally agreed in exchange for a property in Molló. The monks subsequently saved the revenues raised by the Molló property in order to replace the *ciborium* as quickly as possible.[40]

This finally happened in 1151, when *Guillelmus*, the *prepositus* (prior) of the abbey, contracted a craftsman-silversmith, along with his assistants (*artifex cum sociis suis*), to restore the treasury and make a new *ciborium*.[41] The contract specifies the amount of silver to be used for the making of the new furnishing, which was to be distributed between the columns and the canopy: '*ego Guillelmus prepositus restauravi in ecclesia Sancte Marie [. . .] in columnis XII libras, et in cimborio septem libras et I solidum*'. Unfortunately, this second *ciborium* at Ripoll was disassembled between 1464 and 1465, when the monastery was plundered during the Catalan Civil War. Once again, the silver was melted down.[42]

The nature and composition of the second *ciborium* has generated controversy among scholars. In 1973, Xavier Barral i Altet, who was unaware of the 1151 document, identified a series of mid-12th-century limestone bases, along with some fragmentary sculpture preserved in the monastic lapidary collection, as belonging to an alleged *ciborium*.[43] The bases are richly carved with animal and human figures: a man between lions (base A) (Figure 5.14), four rampant lions (base B), four seated men (Base C), and a lion between men (base D).[44] Following on from this, in 2000, Jordi Camps attributed a small head of a lion kept in the Museu Nacional d'Art de Catalunya (Barcelona) (MNAC 202505) to this *baldachin*, hypothesizing that it belonged to one of the lions depicted in base A.[45] With respect to the upper part of the *ciborium*, Barral singled out six fragments of different sizes. The most interesting in understanding the iconographic programme of the *ciborium* are the carvings depicting two

FIGURE 5.14

Barcelona: MNAC, Base A of the ciborium *of Santa Maria de Ripoll,* c. *1151 (Museu Nacional d'Art de Catalunya deposit of the Bishopric of Vic. Jordi Camps)*

FIGURE 5.15

Ripoll, Museu de Ripoll: limestone relief belonging to the lost ciborium *of Santa Maria de Ripoll,* c. *1151 (Manuel Castiñeiras)*

angels. These probably belonged to the spandrels of an arch: one holds a Host decorated with a cross (fragment III) (Figure 5.15), whereas the other raises a censer (fragment IV).

There is no doubt that all these pieces were produced at Ripoll by the same workshops as were responsible for the renovation of the abbatial church and its dependencies in the middle of the 12th century. Thus the upper part of the *ciborium* has been attributed to the team responsible for the west portal (*c.* 1141–51), while the bases seem very close to the style of the capitals of the north gallery of the cloister (*c.* 1150–70).[46] Besides, both the subjects and motifs carved on these sculptured elements match the function and symbolism of a high altar *ciborium*. Thus the bases allude to the idea of salvation – Daniel in the lion's den (base A) – while the reliefs in the upper part exalt the Eucharist.[47] These reliefs feature angels wearing the Holy Host, while the censer might have been seen as a celestial echo of the terrestrial liturgy of the Canon of the Mass and the blessing of the altar. As Barral pointed out, the most convincing comparison for this imagery is the monumental *ciborium* commissioned by Abbot Eustazio for the church of San Nicola in Bari (1105–23), where angels bearing Hosts incised with crosses are positioned at the corners beneath the canopy (Figure 5.16).[48] Furthermore, as in Italian sanctuaries, on the occasion of the making of the *new ciborium* at Ripoll, the level of the sanctuary of the church was raised and paved with a magnificent mosaic in *opus sectile* that alluded to the creation of the world (Figure 5.17).[49]

Prior Guillelmus was in office during the abbacy of Pere Ramon (1134–53), and probably supervised work at the abbey over the 1140s. This included the magnificent stone portal, the vaulting of the nave, the elevation of the sanctuary, the choir mosaic, and the new *ciborium*. As such, it is highly likely that the fragments identified by Barral as belonging to the *ciborium* mentioned in 1151 were indeed from this *ciborium*. In my view, the monastic workshops assembled the new furnishing by combining elements in different materials. The sculptors carved the four bases and the upper reliefs in limestone, while the silversmiths were commissioned to make the columns and the ceiling of the canopy.[50] Joan Duran-Porta disagrees on this point and has proposed a *ciborium* made entirely in silver. In his opinion, a materially hybrid *ciborium* would not have been structurally stable, as the silver columns – especially if these were wooden columns coated in silver – would not have supported a partly stone upper superstructure. Moreover, Duran-Porta argues that the carved limestone fragments are more likely to have originally formed part of a sculptured portal.[51]

Nevertheless, both the bases – carved on all sides – and the reliefs, which appear to have been arch spandrels, are perfectly compatible with the structure and design of a *ciborium*. The original columns could also have been made from limestone, as with the rest of the fragments, but coated in silver to enrich their aspect. The sculptors at Ripoll were used to combining different techniques in their productions. Thus the west portal was polychromed in bright colours and the eyes of certain figures were filled with lead.[52] Both techniques are found in the bases. This suggests that the second Ripoll *ciborium* could have been a colourful furnishing, combining polychromed stone sculpture with a silver coating for the columns and ceiling.

Once in place, at the centre of the recently raised sanctuary, the new *ciborium* became a bearer of novel meanings. Standing over a floor that symbolized the earth and the sea, the altar canopy embodied the salvific mission of Christ through the Eucharistic. What we see here is no longer Oliba's canopy with its hints of the Temple of Solomon and the recitation of the divine Psalmody, but

FIGURE 5.16

Bari, San Nicola: ciborium, *capital with angels bearing host (1105–23) (Manuel Castiñeiras)*

FIGURE 5.17

19th-century drawing of the lost mosaic of Santa Maria de Ripoll by Josep Pellicer (From X. Barral I Altet, Els Mosaics medievals de Ripoll i de Cuixà*)*

a structure whose salvific programme probably responds better to the renewed function of the abbey as the pantheon of the counts of Barcelona, Ramon Berenguer III (d.1131) and Ramon Berenguer IV (d.1162) – a privileged place for the liturgical memory of the dead.[53]

Compostela: Gregorian reform and the heavenly Jerusalem

The Romanesque *ciborium* (1105–06) framing the high altar in the cathedral of Santiago de Compostela is known thanks to the 12th-century description included in the *Liber sancti Iacobi* (V, 9) and the *Historia Compostelana.*[54] It consisted of a magnificent two-storey canopy, supported on four columns, and was lavishly made in gold and silver and decorated with numerous depictions. Serafin Moralejo's seminal study of 1980 has become the platform from which an understanding of this monument is based, providing scholars with clues to its appearance via his reconstruction drawing (Figure 5.18).[55]

It was on this basis, when setting up the international exhibition, Compostela and Europe. The Story of Diego Gelmírez (2010), that a 3D-digital reconstruction of the high altar of the Romanesque cathedral in the time of Archbishop Diego Gelmírez (1100–40) was made. The *ciborium* was one of several artworks commissioned by Gelmírez to furnish the new sanctuary under construction at the beginning of the 12th century (Figure 5.19 and Colour Plate III (top)).[56] Gelmírez began with the building of a *confessio* (1105) at the east end and continued with the creation of a spectacular setting for the high altar of St James. The latter consisted of an altar frontal in silver and gold and a *ciborium* (1105–06), to which a pentagonal silver altarpiece (*tabula retro altaris*) was added, installed around 1137.[57] All this was positioned over the chamber containing the remains of St James and his disciples. The sanctuary in turn was enclosed by a monumental railing which served to highlight the holiness of the place.[58]

Moralejo associated the production of this furnishing in silver with the network of relations Gelmírez forged during his two journeys to Rome in 1100 and 1105.[59] As a result, Compostela became an international artistic centre, whereby craftsmen with different origins and expertise in different techniques were incorporated into the cathedral workshops.[60] Indeed, the complexity and variety of the iconographic programmes which embellished these objects are striking. The altar frontal depicted a Christ in Majesty, the twenty-four Elders of the Apocalypse, and the twelve Apostles. The *ciborium* included angels and personifications of Virtues surrounding the enthroned *Agnus Dei* on the interior and, on the exterior, depictions of four apocalyptic angels and prophets. On a second level there were Apostles and Evangelists, climaxing in an image of the Holy Trinity at the apex. Finally, the altarpiece encompassed representations of Christ displaying his wounds, St John, the Virgin, and the twelve Apostles.

The aim of this paper is not to dwell on the theological background to this astonishing iconographical display, however.[61] Rather, it is to review Gelmirez's *ciborium* in relation to *ciboria* more generally so as to pinpoint its distinctive emphases. In this respect, the description contained in the *Codex Calixtinus* is extensive and sufficiently rich in detail to make an excellent starting point.

> The ciborium which covers this worthy altar is wonderfully worked both inside and outside with paintings, and drawings and diverse kinds of things. For it is square, placed on four columns, and made with harmonious proportions in height and width. On the interior, in truth, in the first row are the particular virtues, represented as women, which Paul mentions – that is, eight. In each corner there are two. Above the head of each, angels stand erect, with raised hands, and hold the throne with is at the top of the ciborium. In the middle of the throne, the Lamb of God holds the cross with His foot. There are as many angels as virtues.

FIGURE 5.18

Santiago de Compostela: reconstruction drawing of the ciborium *of Gelmírez (Serafin Moralejo)*

FIGURE 5.19

Santiago de Compostela: digital reconstruction of the high altar of Diego Gelmírez for the exhibition, Compostela and Europe. The Story of Diego Gelmírez (2010) (Tomás Guerrero-Magneto Studio and Manuel Castiñeiras)

> In truth, on the exterior in the first row, there are four angels who proclaim the Resurrection of the Day of Judgement by sounding their trumpets. Two are on the front face and two are behind on the other face. On the very same row are four prophets, Moses and Abraham on the left face and Isaac and Jacob on the right, each holding in his hand scrolls with their own prophecies. In the upper row, the twelve apostles are seated in a circle. On the first face, on the front, the blessed James sits in the middle, holding a book with his left hand, and giving a blessing with his right. On this right is another apostle and on his left another in the same row. Similarly, on the right (face) of the ciborium there are three other apostles, an on the left (face) three, and at the back three in the same manner. On the roof, above, sit four angels as if guarding the altar. But in the four corners of this ciborium, where the roofing begins, are sculptured the Four Evangelists with their symbols.
>
> The interior is painted, and the exterior of the ciborium is sculptured as well as painted. At the apex of the exterior is erected a certain triple-arched finial in which the Holy Trinity is sculpted. In the first arch, which looks towards the west, is erected the person of the Father; in the second, which looks between the south and the east, is the person of the Son; and in the third arch, which looks towards the north, is the person of the Holy Trinity. Finally above this finial, is a shining orb in silver on which a precious cross is placed.
>
> (*Liber sancti Iacobi* V, 9)[62]

Serafin Moralejo argued that Gelmírez's primary intention in commissioning a monumental *ciborium* in gold and silver was the emulation of the high altar of St Peter's in Rome. The arrangement of the sanctuary – with a *confessio*, altar frontal, and *ciborium* of gold and silver – drew attention to the new basilica of St James at Compostela as an apostolic tomb. With this, Santiago evoked Roman basilicas *ad corpus*, in what amounts to an updated version of annular crypts, by concentrating the pilgrims' itinerary on an ambulatory around the sanctuary which gave onto a subterranean chapel devoted to Mary Magdalen behind the high altar. It was there that pilgrims could satisfy their wish to pray in a space beside the apostle's tomb, which itself remained inaccessible in a chamber beneath the high altar.[63]

The creation of this *hierotopy* in the basilica of St James fused concepts of itinerary and intertextuality, two features that helped to define the pilgrimage to Santiago in the years around 1100. Gelmírez laid out a sacred itinerary for pilgrims. They entered the basilica through the *Porta Francigena* (north portal) and, following the ambulatory, ended in the chapel of Mary Magdalen, wherein they prayed. Within this short circuit, pilgrims experienced the new basilica as an 'intertextual' phenomenon, with a double reference to St Peter's in Rome. First, outside the northern entrance, known as *Paradisus*, they beheld the marble twisted columns which decorated the façade of the *Porta Francigena* and constituted a direct citation of those of the double screen (or *pergola*) of the high altar of St Peter's. Second, once inside the cathedral, the experience of the *confessio* and the sight of the lavish altar frontal and *ciborium* reinforced the link between Compostela and Rome. Gelmirez himself visited the holy city on two occasions and enjoyed a privileged view of the high altar of St Peter's when he was consecrated a *subdiaconus* there in 1100.[64]

There is no doubt that the prestigious models invoked by Moralejo do help one better understand Gelmirez's intentions in the creation of this sacred topography. Moreover, analysis of certain details of the arrangements at Santiago demonstrates what Gelmirez saw and understood of the art of Rome around 1100. Both the twisted columns of the *Porta Francigena* and some of the ecclesiological motifs decorating their shafts (*barbarae ferae et vulpes hereticae*) owe more to contemporary compositions by Roman marble workers (*marmoristi*) – such as the spiral columns of Santa Trinità dei Monti and San Carlo in Cave *(c.* 1093) – than they do to the ancient columns of St Peter's.[65] Likewise, certain features of the *ciborium* differ from those of St Peter's and were inspired by coeval Roman art. Thus the depiction of prophets on the spandrels of the *ciborium* as custodians of the sanctuary is a common theme of 12th-century Roman triumphal arches, as with those of the upper church of San Clemente (*c.* 1118), Santa Maria in Trastevere (*c.* 1143) and Santa Maria Nova (1165–67).[66]

The description in the *Codex Calixtinus*, suggests that the upper part of the *ciborium* canopy in Santiago was a two-storey structure and not the pyramidal shape envisaged by Moralejo. The first level sheltered the twelve apostles with statues of the four evangelists at the corners, while the second consisted of three arches depicting the Trinity, in turn crowned by a cross over an orb. An octagonal shape for the first storey would fit well with the description and enable it to accommodate apostles and prophets.[67] Two-storey canopies with an octagonal shape were evidently a distinctive feature of 12th-century *ciboria* in Rome and southern Italy, as with those at San Nicola in Bari (1105–23) (Figure 5.20 and Colour Plate III (bottom)) and San Paolo fuori le Mura (1147).[68]

The process of transforming the pyramidal *ciborium* into a structural micro-architecture began in Rome and Latium at the beginning of the 12th century in the context of the Gregorian reform. Thus the *ciboria* at San Clemente in Rome and Sant'Anastasio a Castel Sant'Elia (Nepi) are polished structures in marble with an upper columnar storey crowned by a pediment as if to evoke the image of a church.[69] In the case of Bari, the upper part is more complicated, incorporating a double octagonal storey in an attempt to enrich its ecclesiological and eschatological meaning. The *ciborium* not only highlights the presence of the remains of Saint Nicholas below but acts as an evocation of the Heavenly Jerusalem which the chosen people of God address, as is recorded in the inscription at Bari: '*Arx hec par celis/Intra bone serve fideli/Ora devote Dominicum pro/ Pro te populoque*' ('This ark is akin to heaven/Come in good and faithful servant/ Pray devotedly to the Lord /for you and your people').[70]

At Santiago, the function of the *ciborium* as a landmark which highlighted the presence of a saint's burial is matched by Gelmirez's desire to turn Compostela into a metropolitan see with the support of papal Rome. The furnishing of the high altar was created in 1105–06 following his return from Rome, where he had been presented with a pallium.[71] Thus the *ciborium* exalted the role of St James among the apostles – James was depicted presiding over the apostolic college on the first row of the canopy – and claimed for Compostela the status of a metropolitan see, something that was finally granted by Pope Callixtus II in 1120. As at Bari, the structure might be also seen as a Heavenly Jerusalem. The depiction of the *Agnus Dei* above the altar, the angels blowing trumpets on the spandrels, and the twelve apostles on the upper part were all themes related to the book of Revelation, of which the Spanish church was accustomed through illustrations of Beatus's Commentary on the Apocalypse.[72] This Heavenly Jerusalem was crowned by a dogmatic image of the Trinity, ensuring the adherence of the Compostelan clergy to Rome and the ideals of the Gregorian reform, just as the nature of the Trinity had been recently discussed at the Council of Bari (1098) by Anselm of Canterbury.[73]

Ultimately, Gelmirez's *ciborium* was the creative outcome of combining both old and new traditions. The traditional apostolic canopy became a space to proclaim the adherence of Compostela to the church of the Gregorian Reform and embodied the Heavenly Jerusalem as a future reward to the faithful and to pilgrims visiting the sanctuary.

San Juan de Duero, the hospitallers, and the recollection of the Holy Land

The exotic character, orientalising features and placement of the two stone *ciboria* in the Hospitaller church of San Juan de Duero (Soria) have long exercised scholars, concerned as to their artistic provenance and symbolic function (Figures 5.21–5.23).[74] The *ciboria* are located to either side of the entrance to the apse above a stepped platform. Both are set against the east wall of the aisleless nave to shelter an altar and consist of a vault supported on four arches, in turn supported by four sets of clustered columns. Each support consists of four clustered columns, but while the north *ciborium* is crowned by a dome, the south *ciborium* carries a pyramidal roof.

From a purely practical point of view, the double *ciboria* of San Juan de Duero can be seen as examples of the functionality of canopies as a means of signifying side altars in aisleless churches, creating an equivalent to side apses. The same formula is found in the church of Sillenstede (Lower Saxony) in the middle of the 12th century and in the Galician Hospitaller church of San Xoán de Portomarín (1188–1220).[75] The side altars at San Juan de Duero were added around 1200 to an aisleless church of *c.* 1152, in which the nave was covered by a timber roof and only the principal apse was vaulted. Hence, the vaulted *ciboria* have been seen as echoing the vault over the high altar, in an attempt to provide secondary altars either for the use of the Hospitaller community – if indeed they were included in the chancel area – or for the faithful if they were placed to the west of the chancel screen, as has been suggested by Alexandra Sotirakis.[76]

Notwithstanding this, the question cannot be reduced to a discussion of functionality. The *ciboria* at San Juan de Duero possess features that far exceed their role as simple housings for side altars.[77] As Javier Martínez de Aguirre pointed out, this church is explicitly mentioned in a document of 1152 as belonging to the Order of St John of Jerusalem and as having been dedicated to the Holy Sepulchre.[78] At the end of the 12th century, the complex (*Domus Hospitalis*) was remodelled, an initiative which

FIGURE 5.20

Bari, San Nicola: ciborium *(1105–23) (John McNeill)*

FIGURE 5.21

Soria, San Juan de Duero: church interior with two ciboria, c. *1200 (Antonio García Omedes)*

FIGURE 5.22

Soria, San Juan de Duero: church interior, altar of John the Baptist (north ciborium*) (Antonio García Omedes)*

FIGURE 5.23

Soria, San Juan de Duero: church interior, altar of Our Lady (south ciborium*) (Antonio García Omedes)*

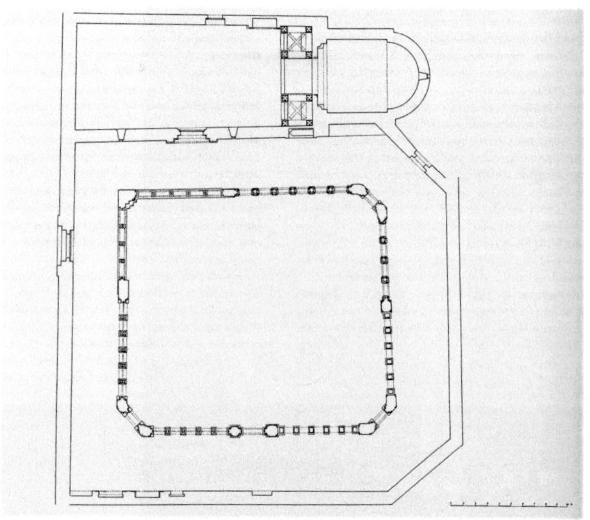

FIGURE 5.24

Soria, San Juan de Duero: ground plan (J. Nuño)

FIGURE 5.25

Soria, San Juan de Duero: capital with the Assumption of the Virgin from the southern ciborium *(*c. *1200) (Antonio García Omedes)*

FIGURE 5.26

Bethlehem, Church of the Nativity: mosaic on east wall of the south transept, detail of the Triumphal Entry into Jerusalem showing the Anastasis rotunda and Dome of the Rock, 1167–69 (Michele Bacci)

FIGURE 5.27

Jerusalem, Haram al-Sharif (Temple Mount), Qubbat al-Miraj: former baptistery of the Templum Domini (1143–53) (Manuel Castiñeiras)

included the building of the two *ciboria* and the construction of an ambitious cloister (Figure 5.24). In both cases, the workshop employed architectural models, iconographic types, and decorative elements which alluded to the church of the Holy Sepulchre in Jerusalem as it had been reconstructed by the Crusaders and, by extension, the transcultural art of the Latin Kingdom of Jerusalem. Thus the eccentric appearance of the *ciboria* in San Juan de Duero could have been derived from certain 12th-century structures in the Holy Sepulchre, such as the Chapel of the Franks or the apex of the aedicule over the tomb of Christ.[79] Moreover, the unusual plan and detailing of the cloister, whereby the angles of the galleries are chamfered as an octagon and pointed arches are used, suggest it tried to evoke the Crusader Holy Sepulchre, which is explicitly alluded to in the north gallery on a capital depicting the *Visitatio Sepuchri*.[80]

A longing for the Holy Land is common in buildings belonging to institutions of the Crusader Kingdom of Jerusalem throughout Europe during this period. The Iberian Peninsula is particularly rich in examples around 1200, as at Torres del Río (Navarra), the church of the Vera Cruz in Segovia (Order of the Holy Sepulchre), and the *Charola* of the convent of Christ in Tomar (Portugal) of the Knight Templars.[81] Most of the imitations and evocations of the architectural landscape of Crusader Jerusalem were based on established liturgical uses that allowed yearly re-enactments of the experience of the Holy Land.

In this respect, the dedications of the side -altars at San Juan de Duero should be considered. According to a visitation report of 1655, the south altar was dedicated to the Virgin, while the north was dedicated to St John the Baptist.[82] This is reflected in the narrative capitals of the *ciboria*. To the north is a capital showing Herod, Salome, and the beheading of John the Baptist, while to the south a series of capitals highlight the role of the Virgin in the history of Salvation with an Annunciation, Visitation, Nativity, Annunciation to the Shepherds, Epiphany, Massacre of the Innocents, Flight into Egypt, and Assumption of the Virgin (Figure 5.25).[83]

As a church belonging to the Order of St John of Jerusalem, the dedication of the side altars to St John and the Virgin Mary might have responded to the symbolic and liturgical uses of the Hospitallers. The three altars created a Deesis, with St John the Baptist on the left, Christ (Holy Sepulchre) at the centre, and Mary to the right. This is an uncommon configuration for an east end in Spanish Romanesque and should be seen as an evocation of the sacred topography of the Hospitallers in Jerusalem. Their hospital was in the Mouristan in Jerusalem – between the churches of St John and the Holy Sepulchre – and possessed two churches devoted to the Virgin. One was for male pilgrims (St Mary of the Latins) and the other for female pilgrims (St Mary Minor).[84] It is no coincidence that among this group of churches, the Deesis presided over the west portal of the church of St John the Baptist in the Mouristan, dated to the third quarter of the 12th century.[85] Moreover, the altar dedications were probably directly related to the liturgy of the Hospitallers, which, as is well-known, followed that of the Canons Regulars of the Holy Sepulchre. If the dedication of the high altar to the Holy Sepulchre ensured a perfect setting for the Easter rites, the side altars were appropriate for the commemoration of the liturgical year. Thus the capital with the Assumption in the south *ciborium* seems to evoke the antiphon ‘Asumpta est’, chanted at Prime and Nones in the *Officium quotidianum de Beata Maria Virgine*.[86] On a similar level, the dedication of an altar to John the Baptist corresponds to the importance given to his feast in the *proprium de sanctis*, in which the saint was commemorated on the eve (*vigilia*).[87]

Finally, turning to the question of the distinctive silhouettes of the two *ciboria*, this intentionally alluded to the Holy Land. The respectively domical and conical roofs echoed the skyline of Crusader Jerusalem, in which the rounded shape of the Dome of the Rock was often juxtaposed with the pyramidal upper part of the rotunda of the Holy Sepulchre (Figure 5.26).[88] Moreover, there were numerous free-standing domed structures in Jerusalem which could have served as inspirations for the Hospitallers to create evocative micro-architectures in the west. The Qubbat al-Silisah (Dome of the Chain) on the Haram al-Sharif (Temple Mount), for instance, was erected by the Umayyads and renovated by the Crusaders as the chapel of St James the Minor,[89] or the Qubbat al-Miraj, which was built between 1143 and 1152 as the baptistery of the *Templum Domini* (Figure 5.27).[90] This latter employs a whole repertoire of architectural forms – paired and clustered columns, pointed arches, domes, and intersecting arches – which seem to have been known by the masons at San Juan de Duero and were deployed in the *ciboria* and the cloister.[91]

In conclusion, the *ciborium* is a privileged bearer of meaning. Although Rome and Italy created the most prestigious models for the early and high Middle Ages and central Italy was the area in which the form was most widely embraced, *ciboria* were disseminated throughout western Europe, particularly from the Carolingian period onwards. It was most notably during the Romanesque period, however, that the early received meanings were enhanced, that new content was introduced, and that the *ciborium*'s liturgical functions were expanded. The transregional character of this furnishing allowed it to cross borders as a distinctive element within the layout of a church, emphasizing the importance of an altar, burial, or entire basilica, advertising adherence to papal Rome, or acting as an evocative appeal to far-distant lands.

NOTES

1 A *ciborium* is a quadrangular structure framing the altar. Ordinarily, it consists of four columns supporting a canopy. It is also sometimes referred to as a *baldachin*, though strictly speaking, this latter term – derived from the ancient Germanic name for the city of Baghdad (*Baldacco*) – should be limited to cloth canopies. See A. Hart, 'Ciboria and Tabernacles: A Short History', *Orthodox Arts Journal* (2018), https://www.orthodoxartsjournal.org [accessed 24 April 2021]; A. M. D'Achille, 'Baldacchino', in *Enciclopedia dell'Arte Medievale*, vol. III (Rome 1992), 29–36; A. M. D'Achille, 'Ciborio', *Enciclopedia dell'Arte Medievale*, vol. IV (Rome 1993), 718–35. All this notwithstanding, the terms 'ciborium', 'baldachin', and 'canopy' are frequently used by scholars as synonymous. In this article, I privilege the Latin term *ciborium*, commonly found in the medieval texts, over the term *baldachin*. See J. Bogdanovic, *The Framing of Sacred Space. The Canopy and the Byzantine Church* (Oxford 2017), 12–13. However, I used the term '*baldachin-ciborium*' in the title, the better to be understood by a general public.

2 J. B. Ward Perkins, 'The Shrine of St Peter and Its Twelve Spiral Columns', *Journal of Roman Studies*, XLII (1952), 21–33 at 22–3 and fig. 1; J. Toynbee and J. B. Ward Perkins, *The Shrine of St Peter and the Vatican Excavations* (London 1958), 202–07; M. Teasdale Smith, 'The Ciborium in Christian Architecture at Rome, 310–600 AD' (unpublished PhD thesis, New York University, 1968), 11; M. Teasdale Smith, 'The Development of the Altar Canopy in Rome', *Rivista di Archeologia Cristiana*, 50 (1974), 379–414 at 381–87; Bogdanovic, *The Framing of Sacred Space* (as n. 1), 184–85.

3 Hart, 'Ciboria and Tabernacles' (as n. 1); Teasdale Smith, 'The Development' (as n. 2), p. 389; M. Biddle, *The Tomb of Christ* (Stroud 1999), 1–73; Bogdanovic, *The Framing of Sacred Space* (as n. 1), 277–85. For the model of the *aedicule* of Christ in Narbonne, see P. de Palol Salellas, 'Una representación del Martyrium de Jesucristo en el Museo Lapidario de Narbona', *Archivo de Prehistoria Levantina*, V (1954), 1–7; A. Bonnery, 'L'edicule du Saint-Sepulcre de Narbonne. Recherche sur l'iconographie de l'Anastasis, *Cahiers de Saint-Michel de Cuxa*, 22 (1991), 7–42.

4 Bogdanovic, *The Framing of Sacred Space* (as n. 1), 272.

5 Paolo Silenziario, 'Descrizione della Santa Sofia', vv. 720–729 (Greek text with Italian translation), in *Un tempio per Giustiniano. Santa Sofia di Costantinopoli e la Descrizione di Paolo Silenziario*, ed. M. L. Fobelli (Rome 2005), 78–79, 157. See also Teasdale Smith, *The Ciborium* (as n. 2), 310; Bogdanovic, *The Framing of Sacred Space* (as n. 1), 113.

6 Later, Pope Gregory III (AD 731–741) added six more columns as an outer screen. Ward Perkins, 'The Shrine of St Peter and Its Twelve Spiral Columns' (as n. 2), 23–25, fig. 2. See also R. Krautheimer, *Roma. Profilo di una città* (Roma 1981), 111, fig. 70; S. De Blaauw, *Cultus et Decor. Liturgia e architettura nella Roma tardoantica e medievale: Basilica Salvatoris, Sanctae Mariae, Sancti Petri*, vol. II (Città del Vaticano 1994), 828; Bogdanovic, *The Framing of Sacred Space* (as n. 1), 113–14.

7 De Blauw, *Cultus et Décor* (as n. 6), vol. II, 482–83, 675.

8 Bogdanovic, *The Framing of Sacred Space* (as n. 1), 18. Likewise, St Jerome in his *Commentary of Ezekiel* (410 CE) presents the church as the Tabernacle and Temple of Jerusalem, in which the high altar is the new *propitiatorium* of the *sancta sanctorum*. Teasdale Smith, *The Ciborium* (as n. 2), 329.

9 Bogdanovic, *The Framing of Sacred Space* (as n. 1), 22–23. As for Hagia Sophia, the Justinianic church has long been seen as the new Temple of Solomon and the cathedral's collection of relics – the Rod of Moses, the ark of the covenant, the tablets of the Law – chime with this prototypical sacred space. R. Ousterhout, 'New Temples and New Solomons: The Rhetoric of Byzantine Architecture', in *The Old Testament in Byzantium*, eds. P. Magdalino and R. Nelson (Washington 2014), 223–55, 242–43.

10 Theodore of Andina, *Protheoria (De divinae liturgiae symbolis et mysteriis)* in *Patrologia Graeca*, 140, ed. J.-P. Migne (Paris 1887), cols. 441–44. See also Bogdanovic, *The Framing of Sacred Space* (as n. 1), 260.

11 C. Mango and J. Parker, 'A Twelfth-Century Description of St Sophia', *Dumbarton Oaks Papers*, 14 (1960), 233–45 at 239–40.

12 R. Ordeig i Mata, 'La documentació del monestir de Cuixà refernt a Oliba i als anys del seu abadiat', *Cahiers de Saint-Michel de Cuxa*, XL (2009), 39–51, 47.

13 Bogdanovic, *The Framing of Sacred Space* (as n. 1), 1–9, maps 1–5.

14 D'Achille, 'Ciborio'. Cf. L. Pani Ermini, 'Il ciborio della basilica di S. Ippolito all'Isola Sacra', in *Roma e l'età carolingia. Atti delle Giornate di studio, Roma 1976* (Roma 1976), 337–44.

15 This is a simple formal comparison. A polygonal roof also crowned the former aedicule of Christ in the church of the Holy Sepulchre in Jerusalem and was repeated in some of its copies in the early and high Middle Ages as with the 11th-century example at Aquileia. The *ciborium* at the Hagia Sophia was also seen in liturgical texts and descriptions as an evocation of the tomb of Christ.

16 D'Achille, 'Ciborio' (as n. 1), 718–35. See also E. Parlato and S. Romano, *Roma y el Lacio* (Madrid 1993), 212. The ciborium at San Pietro, Tuscania was partially reconstructed in the 19th century.

[17] C. Capponi, ed., *La basilica di Sant'Ambrogio a Milano. Guida storico-artistica* (Milan 2003), 35, 41, 45–47. See also, A. Sotirakis, 'Espaces voûtés du chevet dans l'architecture romane en Europe: formes et fonctions', vol. I (unpublished PhD thesis, Sorbonne Université-Università degli Studi di Firenze-Universität Bonn, 2020), 178.

[18] P. Piva, 'San Giovanni Battista del Sepolcro (A proposito di Civate e Monte Sant' Angelo)', *Arte Medievale*, series 3, V (2006), 55–56 and Figures. 13–14.

[19] When Justin Kroesen states that the *ciborium* is 'a European phenomenon', he assumes a chronology which extends into the 16th century and which therefore includes numerous Gothic examples scattered across Central and northern Europe, J. Kroesen, 'Ciborios y baldaquinos en iglesias medievales. Un panorama europeo', *Codex Aquilariensis*, 29 (2013), 189–222 at 190; J. E. Kroesen, *Staging the Liturgy. The Medieval Altarpiece in the Iberian Peninsula* (Leuven 2009); J. E. Kroesen and V. M. Schmidt, eds., *The Altar and Its Enviroment, 1150–1400* (Turnhout 2009). However, a census of *ciboria* in Romanesque Europe reveals a disproportionately large number of examples in Italy and a very restricted dissemination of the form in Spain, France, or Germany before 1200.

[20] R. Krautheimer, 'Introduction to an "Iconography of Medieval Architecture"', *Journal of the Warburg and Courtauld Institutes*, 5 (1942), 1–33.

[21] I. Lorés i Otzet, 'La sculpture de Saint-Michel de Cuxa à l'époque de l'abbé Oliba', *Les Cahiers de Saint-Michel de Cuxa*, XXXVIII (2007), 183–91, at 187 and 190.

[22] '*Bases, inquam, iuxta unius hominis incessum quatuor a calce procul altaris posuit, totidemque columnas e marmore rubicundi coloris e singularibus saxis in pedibus septem voluntaria fortitudine erexit,* ***explicite in oraculo Cherubin gloriae obumbrantia sacrae venerationis figurans****; et* ***in columnis martyrum gloriam praemonstrans, qui corporis passionis rubicundi****, spiritus puritate candidi, per undam baptismatis vel cruoris sui venerunt ad incrementa frugum iustitiae Dei*' (emphasis added), E. Junyent i Subirà, *Diplomatari i escrits literaris de l'abat i bise Oliba*, ed. Anscari Mundó (Barcelona 1996), 378 ('Cartasermó del monjo Garsies de Cuixà a l'abat Oliba', IV). For a translation of the text into French, see D. Codina, P. Bourgain, and M. Besseyre: '*Il en posa, dis-je, les quatre basses à une distance d'un pas depuis le bas de l'autel, et il éleva autant de colonnes de sept pieds de haut en marbre rouge et pierres spéciales, tout exprès pour symboliser les chérubins de gloire couvrant de leur ombre le lieu de la dévotion sacré: avec les colonnes, il proclame la gloire des martyrs qui, écarlates para la passion de leurs corps, blancs par la pureté de leur âme, en sont venus, baignés para l'eau du baptême ou de leur sang, à accroître les fruits de la justice divine*', D. Codina, P. Bourgain, and M. Besseyre, 'Lettre-sermon du moine Garsias de Cuxa à l'abbé Oliba', *Cahiers de Saint-Michel de Cuxa*, XL (2009), 65–76, 72. See also A. Orriols, 'The Artistic Patronage of Abbot Gregorius at Cuixà: Models and Tributes', in *Romanesque Patrons and Processes,* eds. J. Camps, M. Castiñeiras, J. McNeill, and R. Plant (Milton Park 2018), 159–74, at 168.

[23] Junyent i Subirà, *Diplomatari* (as n. 22), 396 ('Inventari del tresor de culte del monestir de Ripoll, després de la mort de l'abat bisbe Oliba', 1047). See also, M. Castiñeiras, 'El altar románico y su mobiliario litúrgico: frontales, vigas y baldaquinos', in *Mobiliario y ajuar litúrgico en las Iglesias románicas*, ed. P. L. Huerta (Aguilar de Campoo 2011), 11–75, 45.

[24] X. Barral i Altet, 'Culture visuelle et réflexion architecturale au debut du XIe siècle: les voyages de l'abbé-évêque et leurs conséquences', *Les Cahiers de Saint-Michel de Cuxa,* XLI (2010), 211–26.

[25] I. G. Torviso, 'La part oriental des temples del abat-bisbe Oliba', *Quaderns d'Estudis Medievals*, 23–4 (1988), 51–66.

[26] C. Sapin, 'L'abbaye Saint-Pierre-Saint-Paul de Cluny (Saône-et-Loire): sur les traces des premiers Cluny, découverte de l'autel de Cluny II', *BUCEMA*, 12 (2008), 1–2, https://doi.org/10.4000/cem.5772 [accessed 1 March 2021]; C. Sapin, 'L'autel de Cluny II. Sa decouverte (2006) et sa restitution', in *Kirche und Kloster, Architektur und Liturgie im Mittelalter: Festschrift für Clemens Kosch zum 65. Geburtstag*, eds. Klaus Gereon Beuckers and Elizabeth den Hartog (Regensburg 2012), 65–78, 69–71, 76–77.

[27] See the Bibles of Ripoll (Città del Vaticano, BAV, MS. lat 5729) and Sant Pere de Rodes (Paris, BNF, MS. lat. 6, I–IV). For a detailed description of these bibles, see A. Mundó, *Les Bíblies de Ripoll. Estudi dels mss. Vaticà, Lat. 5729 i París, BnF, Lat. 6* (Città del Vaticano 2002), Studi e Testi, 408. For an artistic analysis of the manuscripts, see P. Klein, 'Date et scriptorium de la Bible de Roda. État des recherches', *Les Cahiers de Saint-Michel de Cuxa*, 3 (1972), 91–102; R. Alcoy, 'Bíblia de Rodes', *Catalunya Romànica: X, El Ripollès* (Barcelona 1987), 292–315; M. Castiñeiras and I. Lorés i Otzet, 'Las Biblias de Rodes y Ripoll: una encrucijada del arte románico', in *Les fonts de la pintura romànica*, eds. M. Guardia and C. Mancho (Barcelona 2008), 219–60; M. Castiñeiras, 'Les Bibles de Ripoll et Rodes et les Ivoires de Salerne: la narration biblique sur des supports variés. Modèles, adaptations et discours', in *Les stratégies de la narration dans la peinture médiévale La représentation de l'Ancien Testament aux IVe-XIIe siècles,* ed. M. Angheben (Turnhout 2020), 67–100.

[28] Junyent i Subirà, *Diplomatari* (as n. 22), 378.

[29] Ibid.

[30] Ibid., 379.

[31] M. Castiñeiras, 'El Baldaquí de Ribes: un "incunable" pictòric del taller de Ripoll', in *Pintar fa mil anys. El colors i l'ofici del pintor romànic*, eds. M. Castiñeiras and Judit Verdaguer (Bellaterra 2014), 55–70, at 61 and fig. 8; M. Castiñeiras and J. Verdaguer, '*Le baldaquin de Ribes et la question des ateliers monastiques: un cas d'étude pour la connaissance de la technique de la peinture sur bois en Catalogne romane*', in *Arts picturaux en territoires catalans (XIIè–XIVè siècle). Approches matérielles, techniques et comparatives*, eds. Géraldine Mallet et Anne Leturque (Montpellier 2015), 199–235, at 209–10 and fig. 7.

[32] Orriols, 'Artistic patronage' (as n. 22), 167–68, fig. 13.14. For the description of Garsies see Junyent i Subirà, *Diplomatari* (as n. 22), 369–86.

[33] Orriols, 'Artistic patronage' (as n. 22), 168, Figures. 13.15–13.16.

[34] Castiñeiras, 'El altar románico' (as n. 23), 56–60; M. Castiñeiras, 'El baldaquí de Tost: una obra mestra de la pintura sobre taula', in *El cel pintat. El Baldaquí de Tost*, ed. M. Castiñeiras (Vic 2008), 33–54. See also: J. Gudiol i Cunill, *Els primitius. III. La Pintura sobre fusta* (Barcelona 1929), 352–53.

[35] Junyent i Subirà, *Diplomatari* (as n. 22), 378–79.

[36] Mundó, *Les Bíblies* (as n. 27), 282.

[37] In my view, this image of David and Wisdom should be reinterpreted in terms of monastic psalmody. The illustration follows formulas derived from early Byzantine portrayals of authors receiving divine inspiration such as that of the Evangelist Saint Mark in the Rossano Gospels (5th–6th centuries) or that of princess Anicia Juliana in the Vienna *Dioscorides*. M. Castiñeiras, '*Le Nouveau Testament de la Bible de Ripoll et les anciennes traditions de l'iconographie chrétienne: du scriptorium de l'abbé Oliba à la peinture romane sur bois*', *Les Cahiers de Saint-Michel de Cuxa,* XL (2009), 145–64, Figures. 11–13.

[38] M. J. Westerby, 'Religious Experience and Monastic Identity in Romanesque Sculpture at Santa Maria de Ripoll, 1030–1180' (unpublished PhD thesis, University of Wisconsin–Madison, 1994), 45–46.

[39] J. González Montañés, *Drama e iconografía en el arte medieval peninsular (siglos XI–XV)* (unpublished Ph.D. thesis, UNED, Madrid 2012), 110–11.

[40] '*[P]idio con instancia 200 libras de plata del tesoro de la Sacristia para el socorro de sus necesidades a cuya entrega se resitieron los monges, pero por fin condescendieron vencidos por sus instancias, y por temas de la escomunion fulminada por el obispo Oliba y otros obispos*', Barcelona, Biblioteca de Catalunya, ms. 430, f. 24v. Cf. X. Altés, 'La institució de la Festa de Santa Maria en dissabte i la renovació de l'altar major del monestir de Ripoll a mitjan segle XII', *Studia Monastica*, 44 (2002), 57–96, 64–65.

[41] '*Hoc est breve de Molione ad restaurandum thesaurum, quod ego Guillelmus prepositus restauravi in ecclesia Sancte Marie. Primum in cruce VI libras de argento et octo morabetinos maris, et in teste II^{as} libras, et in columpnis XII libras, et in cimborio septem libras et I solidum [. . .] Et artifex istius opere dispensavit cum sociis suis modiium tritici et XII solidos berguitanos, et cotidie inter argentum ab abluendum et sibi ad potandum II canadels*' (Paris, Bibliothèque Nationale, MS. lat. 5132, f. 104r). This text has drawn the attention of X. Altés (in 2002),

myself (in 2011 and 2013), and J. Duran-Porta (in 2015 and 2019) with regard to the making of a new *ciborium* at Ripoll, but our conclusions differ. See Altès, 'La institució' (as n. 40), 66, n. 44; Castiñeiras, 'El altar románico' (as n. 23), 48–49; M. Castiñeiras, 'The Portal at Ripoll Revisited: An Honorary Arch for the Ancestors', in *Romanesque and the Past*, eds. J. McNeill and R. Plant (Leeds 2013), 121–41, at 135; J. Duran-Porta, 'L'orfebreria romànica a Catalunya (950–1250)' (unpublished PhD thesis, Universitat Autònoma de Barcelona, 2015), 454–55; J. Duran-Porta, 'Deux baldaquins romans en argent à l'abbaye de Ripoll', *Revue de l'Art*, 204 (2019), 15–21.

[42] Altès, 'La institució' (as n. 40), 66, n. 44.

[43] X. Barral i Altet, 'La sculpture de Ripoll au XIIè siècle', *Bulletin Monumental,* 131 (1973), 311–59; X. Barral i Altet, 'El baldaquí del presbiteri', *Catalunya Romànica. X. El Ripollès* (Barcelona 1987), 256–57.

[44] Since 2011, these bases have been displayed in the Romanesque collection of the Museu Nacional d'Art de Catalunya (Barcelona), where they were deposited by the bishopric of Vic.

[45] J. Camps, 'Un fragment escultòric del Museu Nacional d'Art de Catalunya atribuible al baldaquí romànic de Ripoll', *Butlletín del MNAC*, 4 (2000), 113–17.

[46] Barral i Altet (as n. 43), 'La sculpture de Ripoll', 331. For the date of the cloister, see: J. Camps, 'La galeria nord-occidental i l'escultura romànica del claustre', in *Claustrum. Claustre medieval de Santa Maria de Ripoll* (Ripoll 2018), 187–211, at 206–09.

[47] B. Cayuela, 'Elementos del baldaquino de Santa Maria de Ripoll', in *El Románico y el Mediterráneo. Cataluña, Toulouse y Pisa (1120–1180),* eds. M. Castiñeiras, J. Camps, and I. Lorés (Barcelona 2008), 244–47.

[48] G. Cioffari, *Storia della basilica di S. Nicola di Bari. I. L'epoca normanno-sveva* (Bari 1984), 125, 137–38.

[49] X. Barral i Altet, *Els Mosaics medievals de Ripoll i de Cuixà* (Poblet 1971); X. Barral i Altet, 'El mosaic medieval de Santa Maria de Ripoll', in *II Colloqui d'història del monaquisme català. Sant Joan de les Abadesses 1970,* vol. II (Poblet 1974), 129–31; X. Barral i Altet, *Le décor du pavement au Moyen Âge. Les mosaïques de France et d'Italie* (Rome 2010), 266; M. Castiñeiras, *El Tapís de la Creació* (Girona 2011), 79–85.

[50] Castiñeiras, 'El altar románico' (as n. 23), 48–49; Castiñeiras, 'The Portal at Ripoll revisited' (as n. 41), 135–36.

[51] Duran-Porta, *L'orfebreria romànica* (as n. 41), 454–55; Duran-Porta, 'Deux baldaquins' (as n. 41), 15.

[52] Castiñeiras, 'The Portal at Ripoll revisited' (as n. 41), 137.

[53] For this renewed use of the abbey as a comital pantheon in the 12th century, see F. Español, 'Panthéons comtaux en Catalogne à l'époque romane. Les inhumations privilégiées du monastère de Ripoll', *Cahiers of Saint-Michel de Cuxa,* XLII (2011), 103–14.

[54] *Liber sanct Iacobi. Codex Calixtinus*, V, translation into Spanish by A. Moralejo, C. Torres, and J. Feo (Santiago de Compostela 1951), 567–68; *Historia Compostelana*, I, 18, ed. E. Falque Rey (Madrid 1994), 107.

[55] S. Moralejo, '*Ars Sacra* et sculpture romane monumentale: le trésor et le chantier de Compostelle', *Les Cahiers de Saint-Michel de Cuxa*, XI (1980), 189–238.

[56] The 3D-digital reconstruction was produced by Tomás Guerrero-Magneto Studio to be displayed in the exhibition, Compostela and Europe. The Story of Diego Gelmírez (Paris, Vatican City, Santiago de Compostela 2010). There was also a DVD edited by the Xunta de Galicia (2010) entitled, *Compostela y Europa. La historia de Diego Gelmírez*, which included a video with a digital reconstruction of the high altar of the cathedral of Santiago de Compostela. Research on the early iterations of the Romanesque high altar was published in a series of articles: M. Castiñeiras and V. Nodar, 'Para una reconstrucción del altar mayor de Gelmírez: cien años después de López Ferreiro', *Compostellanum. Estudios Jacobeos*, LV (2010), 575–640; Castiñeiras, 'El altar románico' (as n. 23), 16–44.

[57] The now lost furnishing was made of precious materials, sumptuously decorated by enamels and gems, and included an ambitious iconographic programme. Unfortunately, excepting the descriptions and two drawings, virtually no trace of the individual elements have survived. The *ciborium* was destroyed in the late Middle Ages (1462–76), while the altar frontal and altarpiece vanished in the second half of the 17th century. M. Taín Guzmán, 'Pervivencia y destrucción del Altar de Gelmírez en la época moderna', in *Compostela y Europa. La historia de Diego Gelmírez,* ed. M. Castiñeiras (Milan–Santiago de Compostela 2010), 166–81. For the silver altar frontal and the *ciborium*, there is an exhaustive account in the *Liber sancti Iacobi* (V, 9), while the appearance of the altarpiece, which is only mentioned in the *Historia Compostellana* (III, 44), is known thanks to two drawings made in 1656 by the well-known canon of the cathedral, José Vega y Verdugo. See *Historia Compostelana*, III, 44, ed. E. Falque Rey (as n. 54), 573–74; Taín Guzmán 'Pervivencia' (as n. 57); Castiñeiras, 'El altar románico'(as n. 23), 42, fig. 18.

[58] Castiñeiras and Nodar, 'Para una reconstrucción' (as n. 56), 593–99.

[59] Moralejo, '*Ars Sacra*' (as n. 55); S. Moralejo, 'El patronazgo artístico del arzobispo Diego Gelmírez (1110–40): su reflejo en la obra e imagen de Santiago', in *Pistoia e il Cammino di Santiago. Una dimensione europea della Toscana medievale*, ed. L. Gai (Pistoia 1987), 245–72.

[60] The second journey of Gelmirez to Rome in 1105 included a lengthy journey through France, with visits to several of the most important artistic centres of the period, such as Toulouse, Moissac, Conques (probably), Limoges, and Cluny. M. Castiñeiras, 'Jaca, Toulouse, Conques y Roma: las huellas de los viajes de Diego Gelmírez en el arte románico compostelano', in *O Século de Xelmírez, Actas del Congreso Internacional, Santiago*, eds. F. López Alsina, H. Monteagudo, R. Villares, and R. Yzquierdo Perrín (Santiago de Compostela 2013), 245–98; M. Castiñeiras, 'Diego Gelmírez, un committente viaggiatore: dalla Porta Francigena all'altare maggiore della Cattedrale di Santiago', in *Medievo: i committenti. XIII Convegno Internazionale di Studi, Parma,* ed. A. C. Quintavalle (Parma 2011), 268–80.

[61] Moralejo, '*Ars Sacra*' (as n. 55).

[62] A. Shaver-Crandell, Paula Gerson, and Alison Stones, *The Pilgrim's Guide to Santiago de Compostela: A Gazetteer* (London 1995), 93. The full text in Latin is: '*Cimborius vero qui hoc altare venerandum cooperit, mirabiliter picturis et debuxaturis speciebusque diversis deintus et deforis operatur. Est enim quadratus, super quattuor columpnas positus, altitudine et amplitudine congruenti factus. Deintus vero in primo ordine, quedam, spetiales virtutes in modum mulierum quas Paulus commemorat, octo scilicet, habentur; in uno qouque angulo, due sunt (1 Cor 13^{4-13} and Gal 5^{22}). Et super utrarumque capita angeli recti stantes habentur, qui manibus elevatis tronum qui est in summitate cimborii tenent. In medio vero troni, Agnus Dei, pede crucem tenens habetur; sed angeli tot sunt quot virtutes. Deforis vero in primo ordine, quattuor angeli habentur qui resurrectionem diei iudicii bucinantes bucinis pronuntiant. Duo sunt antea in facie et duo retro in alia facie. In eodem vero ordine quattuor prophete habentur, Moyses scilicet et Abraham in sinistrali facie et Ysaac et Iacob in dextrali, singuli singulos rotulos proprie prophetie manibus tenentes. In superiori vero ordine, XII apostoli sedent per circuitum. In prima facie in antea scilicet beatus Iacobus residet in medio, manu sinistra librum tenens et dextera benedictionem innuens. Ad cuius dexteram est alius apostolus et ad levan alter in ordine proprio. Similiter ad dexteram cimborii tres alii habentur apostoli et ad levam eius tres, et retro eodem modo tres. In coopertura vero desuper quattuor angeli sedent, quasi altare custodientes. Sed in quattuor cornibus eiusdem cimborii, incipiente coopertura, IVor evangeliste propriis similitudinibus sculpuntur. Deintus vero est depictus, deforis autem scultus et depictus cimborius. In cacumine vero eius deforis est quedam summitas erecta, tripliciter arcuata, in qua Trinitas deica est insculpta: in primo arcu qui respicit ad occidentem, persona Patris est erecta, et in secundo qui respicit inter meridiem et orientem est persona Filii, et in tercio arcu qui respicit ad septentrionem est persona Spiritus Sancti. Item vero super hanc summitatem est pomus argenteus lucifluus super quem crux ponitur preciosa*'. *Liber Sancti Jacobi. Codex Calixtinus*, eds. K. Herbers and M. Santos Noia (Santiago de Compostela 1998), 255–56.

[63] M. Castiñeiras, 'Topographie sacrée, liturgie pascale et reliques dans les grands centres de pèlerinage: Saint-Jacques de Compostetelle,

Saint Isidore de León et Saint Étienne de Ribas de Sil', *Cahiers de Saint-Michel de Cuxa,* XXXIV (2003), 13–36.

[64] S. Moralejo, 'La imagen arquitectónica de la Catedral de Santiago', in *Il Pellegrinaggio a Santiago de Compostela e la letteratura jacopea (Perugia 1983)*, ed. G. Scalia (Perugia 1985), 37–61; M. Castiñeiras, 'The Topography of Images in Santiago Cathedral. Monks, Pilgrims, Bishops and the Road to Paradise', in *Culture and Society in Medieval Galicia: A Cultural Crossroads at the Edge of Europe*, ed. J. D'Emilio (Leiden 2015), 631–94.

[65] M. Castiñeiras, '*Didacus Gelmirius*, patrono de las artes. El largo camino de Compostela: de periferia a centro del Románico', in *Compostela y Europa* (as n. 57), 30–31.

[66] Castiñeiras and Nodar, 'Para una reconstrucción' (as n. 56), 603. For Roman examples, see S. Romano, *La pittura medievale a Roma. Corpus. IV. Riforma e tradizione, 1050–1198* (Rome 2006), 209, 305, and 335.

[67] Castiñeiras and Nodar, 'Para una reconstrucción' (as n. 56), 603; Castiñeiras, 'El altar románico' (as n. 23), 29–31.

[68] G. Cioffari, *Storia della basilica di S. Nicola di Bari. I. L'epoca normanno-sveva* (Bari 1984), 125. The early 13th-century example at Santa Maria Assunta at Bominaco (Abruzzi) belongs to the same typology of two-storey columnar *ciboria*, with an octagonal summit, like that of Bari. For the example at San Paolo fuori le Mura, see C. Faldi Guglielmi, *Roma: basílica di S. Lorenzo al Verano* (Bologna 1966), 24.

[69] Parlato and Romano, *Roma* (as n. 16), 47, 285, Figures 7 and 89.

[70] For the inscription, see Cioffari, *Storia* (as n. 68), 125.

[71] The date of the furnishing of the high altar is provided by the inscription which was inscribed on the altar frontal: '*Hanc tabulam Didacus presul iacobita secundus/Tempore quinquenni fecit episcopii*' ('Diego the second who was prelate in Santiago, made this table when he turned five years in his bishopric'), *Liber Sancti Jacobi* (as n. 62), 255. In my opinion, the inscription refers to the anniversary of the official consecration of Gelmirez as bishop on 22 April 1101. Thus the altar frontal and *ciborium* could have been installed in April 1106, several months after the return of Gelmírez from his second trip to Rome in Autumn 1105, Castiñeiras and Nodar, 'Para una reconstrucción' (as n. 56), 585.

[72] For this tradition, see J. Williams, *The Illustrated Beatus. A Corpus of the Illustrations of the Commentary on the Apocalypses*, 5 vols. (London 1995–2003).

[73] Cioffari, *Storia* (as n. 67), 95–96.

[74] J. Martínez de Aguirre, 'San Juan de Duero y el *Sepulchrum Domini* de Jerusalén', in *Siete maravillas del románico español* (Aguilar de Campoo 2009), 111–48.

[75] J. Kroesen, *Seitenaltäre in Mittelalterlichen: Standort – Raum – Liturgie* (Regensburg 2010); Kroesen, 'Ciborios y baldaquinos' (as n. 19), 198.

[76] Sotirakis, *Espaces voûtés* (as n. 17), vol. I, 178–98, vol. II, 52–57.

[77] M. Castiñeiras, 'Iconografía e culto di San Nicola nella sponda occidentale del Mediterraneo (XI-XIII secolo)', in *I Santi venuti dal mare, Atti del V Convegno Internazionale di Studi*, ed. M. S. Calò Mariani (Bari 2009), 131–54, 141–46, Figures 15–19.

[78] '*Facio carta donationis et textum firmitatis Deo et Sancto Hospitali Iherusalem et ecclesie Sancti Sepulchri que in Sauria habet*', cited by Martínez de Aguirre, 'San Juan de Duero' (as n. 74), 148. This text is also mentioned and discussed by G. Boto Varela, 'San Juan de Duero', in *Claustros románicos hispanos*, eds. J. Yarza Luaces and G. Boto Varela (León 2003), 176–77. See also J. Nuño, Monasterio de San Juan de Duero, in *Enciclopedia del Románico en Castilla y León. Soria*, vol. III (Aguilar de Campoo 2002), 1036–58.

[79] Martínez de Aguirre, 'San Juan de Duero' (as n. 74), 123, n. 33.

[80] Ibid., 135–47, Figures 18–24.

[81] J. Martínez de Aguirre and L. Gil Cornet, *Torres del Río. Iglesia del Santo Sepulcro* (Pamplona 2004); J. Martínez de Aguirre, and L. Gil Cornet, 'Templars, Hospitallers, and Canons of the Holy Sepulchre on the Way to Saint James: Building at the Service of Lay Spirituality', in *Romanesque Saints, Shrines, and Pilgrimage*, eds. J. McNeill and R. Plant (Milton Park 2020), 291–301; E. Carrero Santamaría, 'Iglesias y capillas del Santo Sepulcro. Entre el lugar común historiográfico y la norma y práctica litúrgicas', in *Arte y patrimonio de las órdenes militares de Jerusalén en España: hacia un estado de la cuestión*, eds. A. López-Yarto and W. Rincón García (Madrid 2010), 321–34.

[82] O. Pérez Monzón, 'Presencia sanjuanista en la provincia de Soria', *Celtiberia,* XXXVIII (1988), 215–35 at 229.

[83] Martínez de Aguirre, 'San Juan de Duero' (as n. 74), 118–21.

[84] J. Murphy-O'Connor, *The Holy Land. An Oxford Archaeological Guide* (Oxford 2008), 63–65.

[85] A fragment of this group is kept in the Museum of the Greek Orthodox Patriarchate in Jerusalem: A. Heyman, 'Un reto para el "taller de Melisenda" la decoración de Santa María en el Valle de Josafat y el proyecto monumental de la Jerusalén cruzada', in *Entre la letra y el pincel: el artista medieval. Leyenda, identidad y estatus*, ed. M. Castiñeiras (Almería 2017), 272, fig. 16.

[86] C. Dondi, *The Liturgy of the Canons Regular of the Holy Sepulchre of Jerusalem: A Study and a Catalogue of the Manuscript Sources* (Turnhout 2004), 131–33.

[87] Rome, Biblioteca Apostolica Vaticana, MS. Barb. Lat. 659, 96v–97v, Dondi, *The Liturgy of the Canons* (as n. 86), 170.

[88] See, for example, the Triumphal Entry into Jerusalem in the mosaics of the church of the Nativity at Bethlehem (1167–69), M. Bacci, *The Mystic Cave. A History of the Nativity Church of Bethlehem* (Brno–Rome 2017), 188, fig. 55. Moreover, the silhouettes of the Temple of the Lord (i.e. the Dome of the Rock) and the Rotunda of the Holy Sepulchre were adopted by the Latin Kings of Jerusalem as the logo on their royal seals, D. M. Metcalf, 'Islamic, Byzantine, and Latin Influences in the Iconography of Crusader Coins and Seals', in *East and West in the Crusader States: Context, Contacts, Confrontations*, vol. II, eds. K. N. Ciggaar, A. Davids, and H. G. Teule (Leuven 1999), 163–75, 172–73, fig. 6.

[89] J. Folda, *The Art of the Crusaders in the Holy Land 1098–1187* (Cambridge 1995), 253–54, Plate 8.4.

[90] Ibid., 253–59, Plate 8A.5ab.

[91] Castiñeiras, 'Iconografía e culto di San Nicola' (as n. 77), 141–2, Figures 17–18. See also Martínez de Aguirre, 'San Juan de Duero' (as n. 74), 144.

The Regional and Transregional in Romanesque Europe (2021), 69–80

HILDESHEIM AS A NEXUS OF METALWORK PRODUCTION, *C.* 1130–1250

Gerhard Lutz

The North German episcopal city of Hildesheim, famed for Bishop Bernward's donations at the turn of the first millennium, experienced a flowering of luxury metalwork production between the second quarter of the 12th century and the middle of the 13th century, evidenced by the relic shrines of St Godehard and Epiphanius as well as other ambitious commissions.

Taking the bronze baptismal font of Hildesheim Cathedral of c. *1226 as a starting point, the following paper surveys Hildesheim's far-reaching and complex artistic contacts. The advantage in starting this way is that the font offers important insights into local production, Hildesheim's position in relation to other regional centres, and the city's access to well-connected European distribution markets.*

The second part of the article considers the early stages of this flowering. These are framed in relation to Helmarshausen, an influential Benedictine abbey in the upper Weser valley, well-known for its goldsmith Roger. Roger has been identified in the past with Theophilus, the supposed author of the famous treatise Schedula diversarum artium. More recent research, however, suggests that the Schedula was compiled by a monk of St Michael at Hildesheim. This brings Hildesheim as an intellectual milieu into focus, one which was characterized by far-reaching contacts that extended to Paris and the Mediterranean region. Thus, a multifaceted panorama of a 12th- and 13th-century cultural centre emerges. Building on this, the article advocates a stronger emphasis on the broader cultural and intellectual conditions at each site in order to better understand the artistic contexts themselves.

THE HILDESHEIM BAPTISMAL FONT

The main scene on the Hildesheim baptismal font shows the donor, Wilbrand of Oldenburg-Wildeshausen, in an episcopal robe kneeling before the Virgin Mary (Figures 6.1 and 6.2 and Colour Plate IV).[1] A charter, issued on 30 October 1226, sheds light on the background to its commissioning: Wilbrand, until recently Hildesheim's Cathedral Provost and from October 1225 bishop of Paderborn, donated the impressive quantity of 50 pounds of silver to the chapter of Hildesheim Cathedral.[2] With this Wilbrand apparently responded to the chapter's continuing complaints about his repeated absence during his time as provost, which had supposedly caused Hildesheim to suffer financial losses. The commissioning of the baptismal font is assumed to be directly related to this. As such, the work cannot have been created before 1225 when Wilbrand became bishop. The theologically complex pictorial program is unique and can most likely be attributed to the donor himself, who at the same time puts his knowledge in the centre.

Earlier research considered the stylistic classification of the font to be important, and the question was repeatedly discussed. Erwin Panofsky thought the corporeality of the figures suggested an indirect connection with French early Gothic sculpture, though one which had been arrived at through several intermediary nodes.[3] William Wixom followed this same model of the gradual spread of artistic forms, associating the baptismal font with the so-called Samson Master, the leading sculptor on the Middle Rhine in the second quarter of the 13th century (Figures 6.3 and 6.4).[4] He left open the question of whether the font was cast in a Lorraine workshop and then delivered to Hildesheim or was co-designed by a local artist who had intimate knowledge of work in Lorraine. Klaus Niehr, continuing this approach, also saw 'influences of French Gothic sculpture', but that 'on the way to Lower Saxony [. . .] a series of further transformations' took place.[5] Only recently has Michael Brandt been able to show that the connection was much more direct. The figures on the choir and transept of Reims Cathedral, begun around 1207, especially the famous atlases, must have been known to the maker of the Hildesheim font. (Figure 6.5).[6] This discovery stands in the context of a fundamental differentiation in our understanding of the

  DOI: 10.4324/9781003162827-6

FIGURE 6.1

Hildesheim Cathedral: baptismal font, dedication scene, c. *1226 (Dommuseum Hildesheim, M. Zimmermann)*

FIGURE 6.2

Hildesheim Cathedral: baptismal font, Wilbrand of Oldenburg in the dedication scene, c. *1226 (Dommuseum Hildesheim, M. Zimmermann)*

FIGURE 6.3

Hildesheim Cathedral: baptismal font, figure of Geon, c. *1226 (Dommuseum Hildesheim, M. Zimmermann)*

FIGURE 6.4

Maria Laach, Benedictine Abbey: Samson defeats the lion, Samson Master, c. *1220 (Rheinisches Bildarchiv/M. Menniken, E. Bauer)*

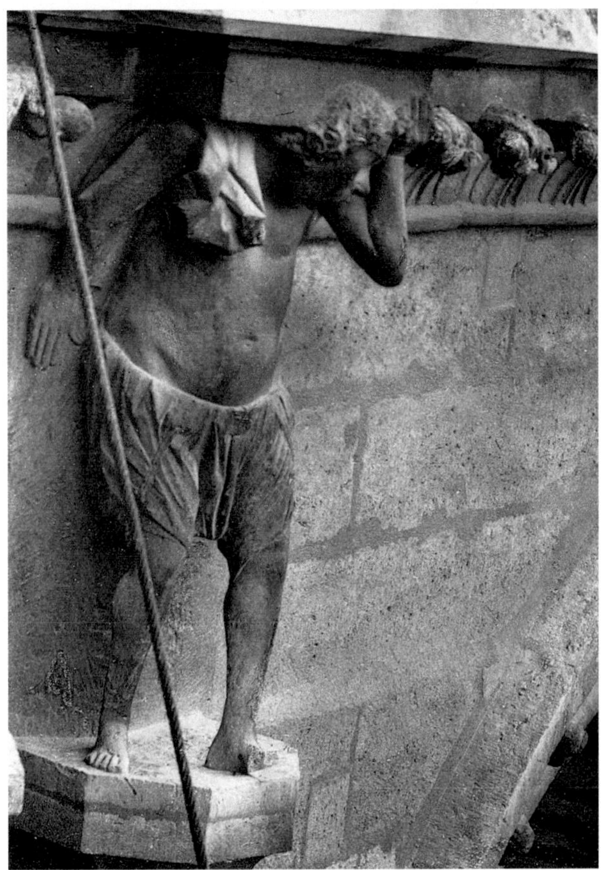

FIGURE 6.5

Reims Cathedral: Choir Atlante, c. *1225 (historical photo before 1914)*

dissemination of forms in the early 13th century from the Île-de-France through the Champagne to Lorraine and the Meuse region.

For the purposes of this paper, the question is how a transfer of artistic ideas from Reims to Hildesheim was effected. If we discount indirect mediation via sketches or models, we should consider, after Wixom, whether a stone sculptor who knew the Reims figures was directly involved in the creation of casting models. That this might be so is supported by the fact that very few years lie between the creation of the Reims sculptures and the Hildesheim cathedral font. At almost the same time, the appearance of sculptors closely familiar with the Reims sculptures can also be seen at Bamberg Cathedral.[7]

As one of the few datable large-format sculptural objects from the first half of the 13th century, the baptismal font lies at a point of intersection within Hildesheim's known artistic production.[8] The head of the lion of St Mark on the baptismal font, for example, shows similarities with the group of Hildesheim lion aquamanilia, thus supporting a close workshop link.[9] Furthermore, a monumental version of the head of the eagle of St John the Evangelist can be found on the eagle lectern from Hildesheim cathedral (Figures 6.6 and 6.7).[10]

Starting with the baptismal font, the following paper will present a number of perspectives and questions in a synthesis-like manner. What conclusions as to Hildesheim as an artistic centre does an elaborate work such as the font allow us to draw? What do we know about the production of metalwork in Hildesheim? How was Hildesheim connected, both in terms of trade routes and in terms of the exchange of knowledge and artistic contacts. In the second part of this paper, attention will be directed to the 12th century, the period in which the foundations for later development were laid.

HILDESHEIM AND THE HARZ REGION AS A EUROPEAN PRODUCTION CENTRE IN THE 12TH AND 13TH CENTURIES

A large part of the success of Hildesheim bronze work in the first decades of the 13th century is due to its capacity to produce technically and artistically high-quality vessels in large numbers. Their types had been established by the second half of the 12th century, and the earlier designs often remained models well into the 14th century, with no more than slight variations from object to object. A characteristic instance of this is the aquamanile in the form of a lion, an example of which was acquired by the Hildesheim Dommuseum in 2006 (Figure 6.8).[11] This belongs to the circle of the workshop of the baptismal font and is thus an important link to a large number of similar Hildesheim aquamanilia of this time.

At first glance, this looks like a clearly identifiable and traceable success story. The model for all these 'predators' was the bronze lion in the courtyard of the castle at Braunschweig (Brunswick), which the sources inform us was erected around 1166 (Figure 6.9).[12] This is generally accepted to have been made on site. The statue was commissioned by Duke Henry the Lion as a centrepiece of his residence. Did he engage artists and craftsmen from outside for this purpose, perhaps from Hildesheim? Or was there a more extensive tradition of bronze casting in Brunswick that Henry could draw on? And to what extent did this ambitious project create a local tradition? These are all questions which cannot be answered conclusively for now given the lack of clear evidence. Interestingly, the intensified reception of the lion form in Hildesheim seems not to have taken place until approximately sixty years later.[13] So why did the Brunswick castle lion not become the model for small-sized bronzes in Hildesheim before the 1220s? Perhaps our chronology is mistaken in this, and the dating of Hildesheim bronzes should be reexamined.[14]

Objects that can be precisely located and dated, such as the Brunswick castle lion or the Hildesheim baptismal font, are of particular importance in this. At the same time, they raise new questions. They are often of limited help in the precise differentiation of particular centres, especially since there are numerous other players to be considered in the region.

Besides Braunschweig, Magdeburg stands out as an important production centre.[15] In addition to the tomb slabs made for Archbishops Friedrich von Wettin

FIGURE 6.6

Hildesheim Cathedral: baptismal font, eagle head, symbol of St John the Evangelist, c. *1226 (Dommuseum Hildesheim, M. Zimmermann)*

(d. 1152) and Wichmann von Seeburg (d. 1192) in Magdeburg Cathedral,[16] the famous bronze doors in Novgorod, originally made for the cathedral of Ploçk (Poland) and presumably delivered in individual parts, were manufactured in Magdeberg.[17] The imperial city of Goslar, near the Harz mountains, had numerous churches and monasteries. The emperor's throne, dating back to the 11th century, the Krodo-Altar of around 1100, and, most especially, the market fountain and accompanying eagle should be cited as originating in Goslar.[18] And there are the other episcopal seats, such as Halberstadt in the east and Minden and Paderborn to the west. In all these places, an unknown number of workshops may have operated, although their production cannot be itemized due to the lack of clearly attributable work.[19]

The situation is further complicated by the fact that bronze vessels were often traded over long distances.[20] Only a few pieces have survived in the place where or for which they were made, such as the lion aquamanilia in the cathedral treasuries of Minden and Halberstadt.[21] However, for most objects, especially those in large museum collections, provenance is rarely traceable and usually goes no further than an art dealer or auction house.

A look at the distribution map of bronzes from Hildesheim and the Harz region shows that they were in great demand and enjoyed a wide circulation.[22] Connections with the Baltic Sea region and to Russia and Siberia have been repeatedly addressed in recent years.[23] There is less clarity regarding contacts to the west and south, however. Here the view is obscured by a persistent methodological bias, which we have already observed in the attribution of the Hildesheim baptismal font. Art in northern France and the Meuse region is said to have played the pioneering role, and the stylistic and formal innovations first encountered there, to the west, were emulated in areas east of the Rhine, sometimes with considerable delay. Also connected to this is the problematic historical picture of an eastward movement from the Holy Roman

FIGURE 6.7

Dommuseum Hildesheim: eagle lectern from Hildesheim Cathedral, Hildesheim, c. *1220/30, inv.-no. D 1984–2 (Museum, Florian Monheim)*

Empire in the course of the High and Late Middle Ages. It is difficult to fit centres like Hildesheim into this picture, when work originating here appears further west.[24]

All this can lead to questionable attributions, like the so-called head of Barbarossa in Cappenberg (Westphalia), in fact a reliquary of St John the Evangelist, which has been recently attributed to Hildesheim.[25] The head reliquary of St Vitalis in Gerresheim near Düsseldorf might be another such example, but its provenance is unclear.[26] These objects have to be reexamined in such a way that their technical and material aspects are studied.

Contacts can also be found south of the Alps, although these still raise many questions. The lion aquamanile from St Maria in Gradi in Viterbo, today in the Museo Civico, for instance, could be an export of the second half of the 12th century and could be from Magdeburg.[27] While the aquamanile in Viterbo may have been a merchant's item, brought down from the north and sold, the older segments of the bronze doors of San Zeno in Verona, probably dating from the 1130s, were possibly made by travelling artists from the Harz region, perhaps Hildesheim itself (Figure 6.10).[28] However, it is equally possible that the bronze reliefs were actually made in Hildesheim and subsequently sent over the Alps. That no more than a partial delivery arrived in Verona, while the remaining scenes were made by a workshop with a different background, may offer support to such a hypothesis.[29] And tucked away on one of the doors of San Marco in Venice is a lion's head of about 1230, which can also be attributed to a Hildesheim workshop (Figure 6.11).[30] The chandelier in Klosterneuburg Abbey was probably made by this same workshop.[31] Thus it becomes apparent that works from Hildesheim and the Harz region were either delivered

FIGURE 6.8

Hildesheim, Dommuseum: lion aquamanile, Hildesheim, c. *1220/30, inv.-no. 2006–01 (Museum, Florian Monheim)*

FIGURE 6.9

Braunschweig, Herzog Anton Ulrich Museum: castle lion monument, c. *1166 (Herzog Anton Ulrich Museum)*

FIGURE 6.10

Verona, S. Zeno: bronze doors, tree of virtues and tree of vices, c. *1130/40 (Gerhard Lutz)*

FIGURE 6.11

Venice, San Marco: Lion door drawer, Hildesheim workshop, c. *1230 (Joanna Olchawa)*

to many parts of Europe or that artists from these same regions travelled.

THE HILDESHEIM SENMURV

The second quarter of the 12th century offers several objects that might act as starting points for questions that shed light on our understanding of Hildesheim as an important art centre over the 12th and 13th centuries. Particularly significant is an aquamanile discovered a few years ago and acquired by the Hildesheim Dommuseum in 2015 (Figure 6.12 and Colour Plate V).[32] It is one of the early examples of the proliferation of bronze cast vessels from the first half of the 12th century.

The ornamentation of this aquamanile compares with Hildesheim bronzes, especially those from before 1150, such as the arm reliquary of St Gereon in the Dommuseum collection (Figure 6.13).[33] The form adopted for the vessel and the technique employed in making it also parallel the outstanding dragon now in the Kunsthistorisches Museum, Vienna, which in turn has been localised to Helmarshausen, a Benedictine monastery near the Upper Weser River, to which we will return.[34] In addition, there are remarkable parallels with the ornamentation of contemporary Islamic bronzes. Its unusual form also corresponds to this: the aquamanile has the shape of a hybrid creature of Persian origin – a Senmurv.[35] Thus, the question of the overarching contexts of this artistic flowering in Hildesheim, which began around 1130, is to be seen against a background of contacts with Islamic art.

The Senmurv seems to have been created at a time when the Hildesheim bronze workshops were experiencing an unprecedented boom. This expansion in production can be attributed to a number of factors.[36] First, Hildesheim is close to the Harz mountains, the major European mining site for copper in the 12th and 13th centuries. Copper mining provided Hildesheim with a major revenue stream, as Goslar, the major town closest to the Rammelsberg mining site, was in the diocese of Hildesheim. Institutions in Hildesheim became extremely wealthy as a result of this and had the money to be able to undertake outstanding commissions. In addition, with the canonization of Bishop Godehard in 1131, Hildesheim cathedral became a pilgrimage destination. Two major relic shrines were made for this purpose; one for Godehard, and the other for Epiphanius, patron of the diocese, both between *c.* 1130 and *c.* 1150. These economic and artistic factors were complemented by Hildesheim's prestigious cathedral school, a major educational centre with far-reaching contacts in France and elsewhere.[37] The high intellectual standards and geographical horizons of the Hildesheim clergy, particularly their close contacts in France, are documented by, among other things, Bruno, bishop from 1153 to 1161, who donated his library to the cathedral.[38]

Artistically, Hildesheim must have been in contact with the important art centres of the Meuse region, which had a leading position in the field of goldsmiths work and bronze casting, although little has survived within the area such as the famous baptismal font of Rainer of Huy, cast between 1107 and 1118 and now in the church of St Bartholomew at Liège. For the aquamanile in the form of a dove in the Museum Kolumba in Cologne, an origin in the Meuse region and a date in the first quarter of the 12th century has been convincingly suggested.[39] The shape of the dove and its two-dimensional engraved ornamentation connect the vessel on the one hand with Islamic objects and on the other hand with early Hildesheim bronzes. The diversity of contacts is

FIGURE 6.12

Hildesheim, Dommuseum: aquamanile in the form of a senmurv, Hildesheim, second quarter of 12th century, inv.-no. 2016–1 (Dommuseum, Florian Monheim)

FIGURE 6.13

Hildesheim, Dommuseum: arm reliquary of St Gereon, Hildesheim, c. *1130–40, inv.-no. L 1994–2 (Dommuseum, F. Monheim)*

evidenced by the fact that in 1196 Flemish settlers came to live at the Dammstraße in Hildesheim, west of the old town.[40] The settlement was apparently so successful that in 1232 more Flemish settlers arrived.[41] In this case, contemporary written sources explicitly mention cloth makers. However, it should be assumed that this is the tip of an iceberg and that it is not necessary to refer to Flanders cloth makers alone to explain artistic exchanges between the Meuse and Hildesheim.

HILDESHEIM AND HELMARSHAUSEN RECONSIDERED

At a date contemporary with the preceding one, the Benedictine Abbey of Helmarshausen on the upper Weser experienced its heyday.[42] The problems encountered in assessing the changing role of regional centres become readily apparent if one takes a comparative look at this monastery. In one sense, Helmarshausen is the antithesis of Hildesheim: here a flourishing episcopal city with far-reaching trade contacts, there a monastery located far from a city. In addition to important works of manuscript illumination, such as the famous Gospels of Henry the Lion, the Helmarshausen workshops are also credited with important goldsmith's work and objects in bronze.

The abbey has traditionally been viewed as a major artistic hub, important within the 12th-century resurgence in metalwork production east of the river Weser, wherein the central figure – the monk Rogerus – was identified with Theophilus, author of the famous treatise *Schedula diversarum artium*.[43] This is not the place to delve into the controversial questions around Theophilus and the *Schedula*, though one point in recent discussion is relevant to our context. It is now commonly understood that the text of the *Schedula* is not homogeneous. Rather, the technical parts have a composite character and were compiled from various older sources.[44] Citing a previously overlooked late 15th-century transcription in the Herzog August Bibliothek at Wolfenbüttel (Cod. Guelf. Helmst. 1127), Ilya Dines drew attention to a different version of the text which commences 'ego Northungus indignus', in addition to mentioning Theophilus.[45]

What do we know about Northungus? He was apparently a monk at Saint Michael in Hildesheim during the first quarter of the 12th century, and we know him from a manuscript with miscellaneous texts in the Staatsbibliothek Bamberg (med. 6). This miscellany must have been made after 1140 because of its references to bishop Bernhard, who was in office from 1130 to 1153, and abbot Dietrich of St Michael, who served from 1125 to 1140 and was already deceased – 'pie memorie' – when the miscellany was compiled.

Northungus seems to have been active as a teacher and physician, who collected texts for his student audience. His horizons were evidently broad, and he integrated contemporary works into his teaching, such as those by Stephen of Antioch, active in Antioch (modern Syria) and in southern Italy.[46] He also translated Arabic texts during the second quarter of the 12th century, at almost the same time as Northungus was active. This suggests the intellectual network around St Michael was capable of sharing in the rapid transfer of knowledge from the Mediterranean to Lower Saxony. Recent research on the *Schedula*, in which the author's education and horizon have increasingly come into the foreground, also points in this direction.[47]

Dines suggests that Northungus wrote the Prologues and the Third Book of the *Schedula* and then revised the rest of the material.[48] In the prologue to the first book, there is a passage where the special achievements of craftsmen of other countries and cultures are mentioned. The author particularly refers to the excellence of Islamic, or to be more precise of Arabic, metalwork: '*quicquid ductili vel fusili seu interrasili opere distinguit Arabia*' ('Arabia distinguishes itself by repoussé work, casting, or open work of diverse kinds').[49] In addition, the third book of the *Schedula* refers to the production of Spanish gold. This passage is possibly based on a text by the alchemist Abufalah, who lived in Sicily in the 11th century. Here, too, a translation from Arabic into Latin that is now lost may have been available to the author.[50] This harmonizes perfectly with what is known of the international outlook of Northungus and his interest in Latin translations of Arabic texts, as well as his contacts with intellectual circles in Italy and the eastern Mediterranean.[51] All this can be taken as indicative of a broader phenomenon common to cultural networks in the 12th century. It should be noted, however, that examples of this responsiveness to Arabic metalworking techniques as early as the second quarter of the 12th century are extremely rare.[52]

Arabic metalwork has been repeatedly cited in the context of contemporary work in bronze from Hildesheim. But the observation is isolated if one looks exclusively at the works themselves and possible contemporary trade contacts. It is only by including the broader intellectual-cultural background in and around Hildesheim that the phenomenon can be brought out of isolation. If this is done, we can observe a broader interest in texts ranging from medicine to technical treatises that were common in monasteries such as St Michael in Hildesheim.[53]

In addition to doubts over the localization of the *Schedula* to Helmarshausen, our understanding of the significance of the monastery for the goldsmith and for bronze art in the 12th century also requires renewed examination.[54] For the first half of the 12th century, thanks to the monk Roger and the supposed connection with Theophilus Presbyter, Helmarshausen has been afforded a pivotal role in the formation of what we understand as the art of Hildesheim over the ensuing decades.[55] Recent research has also posed some significant questions as regards the role of the monk Rogerus in this.

The central work in this is the portable altar in the cathedral treasury at Paderborn which mentions one Rogerus (Figure 6.14). In a forged charter made between 1215 and 1221, pretending to be of the year 1100, Rogerus the monk is mentioned as the artist of a scrinium – 'a brother of the same church [St Peter in Helmarshausen], Rogerus, had made in very fine work, to the honor of Saints Kilian and Liborius' – though Clemens Bayer has recently raised serious doubts whether the word 'scrinium' can refer to the surviving portable altar in Paderborn.[56]

What we know from different sources is that a Benedictine monk named Rogerus might have moved from Stavelot, to St Pantaleon in Cologne and finally to Helmarshausen.[57] Helmarshausen was flourishing during these decades and had far-reaching contacts, even among the monks themselves, with a congregation which included members from other countries, such as Sweden.[58] Thus Rogerus fits well with what is known of the cultural context of the monastery. But the only reference to mention a Rogerus as a goldsmith is the early 13th-century forgery. It is impossible to conclude from this alone that the aforementioned monk should be identified with a famous work of art, although the temptation is great, especially since the artworks associated with Rogerus show close links to the production of the Meuse region.

Other than the Paderborn portable altar, a core group of objects might be the product of the same workshop and directly related to the monastery via their provenance: the Modoaldus cross in the Museum Schnütgen in Cologne or the Gospel book from Helmarshausen, now in the Domschatz at Trier.[59] As regards the other works commonly cited in this context, Ursula Mende has conceded that the variety of forms found in them hints at a broader group of artists.[60]

Given this background, it seems possible that metalwork production at Helmarshausen issued from a temporary workshop on site that executed a limited number of projects.[61] It is equally possible that the objects were commissioned elsewhere. If we exclude the problematic Rogerus document, all that is left is a myth and an art-historical tradition based around it. Localization of this work to Minden, Paderborn, or Hildesheim, all episcopal sees with richer infrastructure and patronage, should not be ruled out. It should also be asked whether a thriving scriptorium, such as is known to have existed at Helmarshausen, necessarily extends to an equally flourishing workshop of goldsmiths and bronze casters? The latter encompass rather different technical and logistical conditions.

CONCLUSION

What does the example of Hildesheim tell us about metalworking centres in the 12th and 13th centuries? On the one hand, our impressions remain shaped in many details by an outdated view of the development of styles based on linear chronological and geographical sequences. On the other hand, we have a legacy of art-historical myths, against which the precise role of certain places should be re-examined.

Given the favourable documentary and epigraphic sources, Hildesheim can significantly enrich our picture of this epoch. Figures such as Northungus apparently had a European reach to their knowledge and were capable of assimilating contemporary texts from the Mediterranean. Knowledge of Arabian casting techniques could also have reached Central Europe via such axes of knowledge. However, the evidence suggests that not only writings but also objects must have reached Hildesheim. In essence, this paints a picture of an epoch that was more interconnected than traditional models have suggested. These contacts went beyond Europe, they included different cultures, and they enabled work from Hildesheim to be traded over long distances and for knowledge and exposure to artistic innovation to reach Hildesheim quickly.

The reassessment of medieval artistic production is by its nature an interdisciplinary endeavour in which a wide variety of methodological approaches are intertwined. As Hildesheim shows, current scholarly horizons are broadening, and the variety of factors to be taken into account is growing considerably. It is satisfying to conclude that this was no different for Northungus in the first half of the 12th century.

ACKNOWLEDGEMENTS

I am particularly grateful to Charles T. Little (New York), Joanna Olchawa (Frankfurt), and Nancy Wu (New York) for important comments.

FIGURE 6.14

Paderborn Diözesanmuseum: portable altar, Helmarshausen/Paderborn (?), c. *1120/30 (Paderborn Diözesanmuseum, A. Hoffmann)*

NOTES

[1] On the baptismal font, see J. Olchawa, *Aquamanilien: Genese, Verbreitung und Bedeutung in islamischen und christlichen Zeremonien* (Regensburg 2019), 119–23; Peter Barnet in P. Barnet, M. Brandt, and G. Lutz, eds., *Medieval Treasures from Hildesheim* (New Haven 2013), 104–07, no. 38; C. Höhl, *Das Taufbecken des Wilbernus* (Regensburg and Hildesheim 2009). On the technical details of the baptismal font, see especially P. Dandridge, 'The Hildesheim Baptismal Font: A Window into Medieval Workshop Practices', in *Cuivre, bronzes et laitons médiévaux: Histoire, archéologie et archéométrie des productions en laiton, bronze et autres alliages à base de cuivre dans l'Europe médiévale (12e-16e siècles) (Medieval Copper, Bronze and Brass: History, Archaeology and Archaeometry of the Production of Brass, Bronze and Other Copper Alloy Objects in Medieval Europe (12th–16th Centuries)*, eds. Nicolas Thomas and Pete Dandridge (Namur 2018), 205–17.

[2] H. Hoogeweg and K. Janicke, *Urkundenbuch des Hochstifts Hildesheim und seiner Bischöfe, Teil 2: 1221–1260* (Hannover and Leipzig 1901), 52, no. 115.

[3] E. Panofsky, *Die deutsche Plastik des 11. bis 13. Jahrhunderts*, 2 vols. (München 1924), vol. 1, 112.

[4] W. D. Wixom, D. F. Gibbons and K. C. Ruhl, 'A Lion Aquamanile', *The Bulletin of the Cleveland Museum of Art*, 61 (1974), 260–70; W. D. Wixom, 'A Lion Aquamanile in Cleveland', in *Intuition und Kunstwissenschaft. Festschrift für Hanns Swarzenski zum 70*, eds. P. Bloch and T. Buddensieg (Berlin 1973), 253–60.

[5] K. Niehr, *Die mitteldeutsche Skulptur der ersten Hälfte des 13. Jahrhunderts* (Weinheim 1992), 97; Martin Gosebruch followed a similar model for architecture: M. Gosebruch, *Vom oberrheinisch-sächsischen Weg der Kathedralgotik nach Deutschland* (Göttingen 1983).

[6] M. Brandt, 'Reims in Hildesheim: Die Bronzetaufe des Wilbernus', *Jahrbuch für Geschichte und Kunst im Bistum Hildesheim*, 74 (2006), 103–21. On the early building history of Reims cathedral see W. Tegel and O. Brun, 'Premiers résultats des analyses dendrochronologiques relatives aux boulins de construction', in *Nouveaux regards sur la cathédrale de Reims*, eds. Bruno DeCrock and Patrick Demouy (Langres 2008), 29–40; A. Prache, 'Le début de la construction de la cathédrale de Reims au XIIIe siècle', *Bulletin de la Société Nationale des Antiquaires de France* (2008), 334–46; A. Prache, 'Le début de la construction de la cathédrale de Reims au XIIIe siècle. L' apport de l'archéologie et de la dendrochronologie', in *Nouveaux regards sur la cathédrale de Reims*, eds. Bruno Decrock and Patrick Demouy (Langres 2008), 41–52, 205–06; A. Prache, 'New Dendrochronological and Archaeological Evidence for the Building Chronology of Reims Cathedral', in *Archaeology in Architecture: Studies in Honor of Cecil L. Striker*, eds. J. Emerick and D. Deliyannis (Mainz am Rhein 2005), 167–72. On the atlas figures, see most recently I. Kasarska, 'Les atlantes des arcs-boutants de la cathédrale de Reims', in *La cathédrale de Reims*, ed. Patrick Demouy (Paris 2017), 313–40; D. Schmengler, *Die Masken von Reims: Zur Genese negativer Ausdrucksformen zwischen Tradition und Innovation* (Berlin–München 2016). For another example of the Reims atlases serving as a model, see W. D. Wixom, 'A Thirteenth-Century Support Figure of a Seated Friar', *Wiener Jahrbuch für Kunstgeschichte,* XLVI/XLVII (1993/94), 797–802.

[7] More recently A. Hubel, 'Überlegungen zur "älteren" Bildhauerwerkstatt des Bamberger Doms und zum Stand der Forschung', in *Der Bamberger Dom im europäischen Kontext*, ed. Stefan Albrecht (Bamberg 2015), 7–41 at 36–38; P. Kurmann, 'Redemptor sive judex. Zu den Weltgerichtsportalen von Reims und Bamberg', *Bericht des Historischen Vereins Bamberg*, 143 (2007), 159–84; R. Suckale, 'Die

Bamberger Domskulpturen: Technik, Blockbehandlung, Ansichtigkeit und die Einbeziehung des Betrachters', *Münchner Jahrbuch der Bildenden Kunst*, N. F., 38 (1987), 27–82.

[8] Olchawa, *Aquamanilien: Genese, Verbreitung und Bedeutung in islamischen und christlichen Zeremonien*, 123–30.

[9] U. Mende, 'Aquamanilien im Umkreis des Hildesheimer Dom-Taufbeckens', in *Bild und Bestie: Hildesheimer Bronzen der Stauferzeit, Katalog der Ausstellung im Dom-Museum Hildesheim, 2008*, ed. Michael Brandt (Regensburg 2008), 195–208 (reprinted in *Ursula Mende: Gusswerke. Beiträge zur Bronzekunst des Mittelalters*, eds. M. Brandt, C. Höhl and L. Lambacher (Regensburg 2020), 397–411).

[10] Peter Barnet in Barnet, Brandt, and Lutz, *Medieval Treasures from Hildesheim*, 102–03, no. 37; Michael Brandt in M. Brandt, ed., *Bild und Bestie: Hildesheimer Bronzen der Stauferzeit* (Regensburg 2008), 384–87, no. 54.

[11] Barnet in *Medieval Treasures from Hildesheim* (as n. 10), 108–09, no. 39; Ursula Mende in Brandt, *Bild und Bestie: Hildesheimer Bronzen der Stauferzeit* (as n. 10), 374–77, no. 51.

[12] M. Brandt, 'Die Werkstatt des Burglöwen: Braunschweiger Bronzekunst oder Bronzekunst in Braunschweig?' In *850 Jahre Braunschweiger Burglöwe: Dokumentation der Tagung am 10. und 11. März 2017*, eds. B. Bei der Wieden, J. Luckhardt and H. Pöppelmann (Braunschweig 2019), 47–57; M. Gosebruch, *Der Braunschweiger Burglöwe: Bericht über ein wissenschaftliches Symposium in Braunschweig vom 12.10. bis 15.10.1983* (Göttingen 1985).

[13] Mende, 'Aquamanilien im Umkreis des Hildesheimer Dom-Taufbeckens' (as n. 9), 194–99.

[14] U. Mende, 'Zur Topographie sächsischer Bronzewerkstätten im welfischen Einflußbereich', in *Heinrich der Löwe und seine Zeit: Herrschaft und Repräsentation der Welfen 1125–1235. Katalog der Ausstellung Braunschweig 1995*, eds. J. Luckhardt and F. Niehoff (München 1995), 427–39 at 430 (reprinted in Ursula Mende, *Gusswerke* (as n 9), 82–95).

[15] On Magdeburg as a centre of bronze production see most recently Olchawa, *Aquamanilien: Genese, Verbreitung und Bedeutung* (as n. 1), 103–14. See also the essays by Ursula Mende in Brandt, Höhl, and Lambacher, eds., Ursula Mende *Gusswerke* (as n. 9), 199–263. For an overview of the centres, see U. Mende, 'Zur Topographie sächsischer Bronzewerkstätten im welfischen Einflussbereich', in *Heinrich der Löwe und seine Zeit. Herrschaft und Repräsentation der Welfen 1125–1235. Katalog der Ausstellung Braunschweig, 1995*, eds. J. Luckhardt and F. Niehoff (München 1995), 427–39 (reprinted in Ursula Mende, *Gusswerke* (as n. 9), pp. 82–95), 427–39.

[16] On early bronze tomb slabs see most recently J. Olchawa, ' "Cera" zu "era": Wolfhards Grabplatte und die Bronzegrabmäler vor 1302. Überlegungen zu Material und Technik', in *Die Bronze, der Tod und die Erinnerung*, eds. G. Lutz and R. Müller (Passau 2020), 179–98.

[17] Olchawa, *Aquamanilien: Genese, Verbreitung und Bedeutung* (as n. 1), 104–10; U. Mende, *Die Bronzetüren des Mittelalters: 800–1200*, 2nd ed. (München 1994), 74–83, 154–61.

[18] J. Olchawa, 'Der Greif in Goslar', in *Löwe, Wölfin, Greif: Monumentale Tierbronzen im Mittelalter*, ed. J. Olchawa (Berlin 2020), 181–200; U. Mende, 'Der Marktbrunnen in Goslar: Formanalyse und Entstehungsgeschichte. Mit einem Beitrag zum Bronze-Vogel vom Kaiserhaus', in *Goslar. Bergstadt – Kaiserstadt in Geschichte und Kunst. Bericht über ein wissenschaftliches Symposion in Goslar vom 5. bis 8. Oktober 1989*, ed. F. N. Steigerwald (Göttingen 1993), 195–250 (reprinted in Ursula Mende, *Gusswerke* (as n. 9), 464–507).

[19] Olchawa, *Aquamanilien: Genese, Verbreitung und Bedeutung* (as n. 1), 114–18, 40–41. On Minden see U. Mende, 'Minden oder Helmarshausen: Bronzeleuchter aus der Werkstatt Rogers von Helmarshausen', *Jahrbuch der Berliner Museen*, NF, 31 (1989), 61–85. On the basis of a detailed comparison, Mende concludes in this study that the works of inferior quality were created in Minden by followers of Roger von Helmarshausen.

[20] Mende, 'Zur Topographie sächsischer Bronzewerkstätten im welfischen Einflußbereich' (as n. 15), 430–31.

[21] Olchawa, *Aquamanilien: Genese, Verbreitung* (as n. 1), 379–80, no. 83 and 502–3, no. 140.

[22] Ibid., 138–40.

[23] C. Lübke, 'Von Mitteldeutschland bis in die Transkaspi-Region. Bronzeguss als Zeugnis der Beziehungen zwischen Mittel- und Osteuropa', in *Bild und Bestie: Hildesheimer Bronzekunst der Stauferzeit*, ed. Michael Brandt (Regensburg 2008), 131–42.

[24] See recently on this Olchawa, *Aquamanilien: Genese, Verbreitung* (as n. 1), 79–82.

[25] The reassessment of the head was discussed in detail at a conference in Cappenberg in 2019. On this so far there is only J. Lemmer, 'Tagungsbericht: Cappenberg: Der Kopf, das Kloster und seine Stifter, 27.09.2019–28.09.2019 Schloss Cappenberg', *H-Soz-Kult* (2020), www.hsozkult.de/conferencereport/id/tagungsberichte-8585. The publication of the conference papers is in preparation. The new interpretation can be found in M. Brandt, 'Das Cappenberger Kopfbild: Herrscher oder Heiliger?' In *Opus: Festschrift für Rainer Kahsnitz*, ed. W. Augustyn (Berlin 2019), 89–106.

[26] Brandt, 'Die Werkstatt des Burglöwen' (as n. 12), 52.

[27] Olchawa, *Aquamanilien: Genese, Verbreitung und Bedeutung* (as n. 1), 365–66, no. 74.

[28] Ibid., 95–99; Mende, *Die Bronzetüren des Mittelalters: 800–1200* (München 1994), 57–73 and 146–54.

[29] Olchawa, *Aquamanilien: Genese, Verbreitung und Bedeutung* (as n. 1), 99.

[30] U. Mende, *Die Türzieher des Mittelalters* (Berlin 1981), cat. no. 99, ill. 177.

[31] U. Mende, 'Romanische Bronzen: Hildesheim und sein Umkreis', in *Abglanz des Himmels: Romanik in Hildesheim: Katalog zur Ausstellung des Dom-Museums Hildesheim, Hildesheim 2001*, ed. Michael Brandt (Regensburg 2001) (reprinted in Ursula Mende, *Gusswerke* (as n. 9), 156–69 at 162).

[32] C. Höhl, G. Lutz, and J. Olchawa, eds., *Drachenlandung: Ein Hildesheimer Drachen-Aquamanile des 12. Jahrhunderts* (Regensburg–Hildesheim 2017).

[33] D. Kemper, 'Zu Reliquiartypen des 12. Jahrhunderts aus dem Hildesheimer Domschatz', in *Typen mittelalterlicher Reliquiare zwischen Innovation und Tradition*, eds. K. G. Beuckers and D. Kemper (Regensburg 2017), 81–99 at 92–95; B. Drake Boehm in *Medieval Treasures from Hildesheim* (as n. 11), 64–65, no. 20.

[34] Olchawa, *Aquamanilien: Genese, Verbreitung und Bedeutung* (as n. 1), 292–96; U. Mende, 'Das Wiener Greifen-Aquamanile: Eine Kleinbronze aus der Werkstatt Rogers von Helmarshausen', in *Helmarshausen und das Evangeliar Heinrichs des Löwen. Bericht über ein Symposion in Braunschweig und Helmarshausen vom 9. Oktober bis 11. Oktober 1985*, eds. M. Gosebruch and F. N. Steigerwald (Göttingen 1985), 109–32 (reprinted in Ursula Mende, *Gusswerke* (as n. 9), 17–33).

[35] S. Kuehn, 'On the Transcultural and Transreligious Dimension of the So-Called "Senmurw" ', in *Drachenlandung: Ein Hildesheimer Drachen-Aquamanile des 12. Jahrhunderts*, eds. C. Hoehl, G. Lutz, and J. Olchawa (Regensburg 2017), 103–26.

[36] For more details, see G. Lutz, 'The Canonisation of Bernward and Godehard: Hildesheim as a Cultural and Artistic Centre in the 12th and 13th Centuries', in *Romanesque Saints, Shrines and Pilgrimage*, eds. J. McNeill and R. Plant (Milton Park 2020), 41–52.

[37] For an overview see G. Lutz, 'The Cultural and Intellectual Context of the Benedictine Monastery of St. Michael's at Hildesheim in the Twelfth Century', in *The Stammheim Missal. Commentary to the Facsimile-Edition/Das Stammheimer Missale. Kommentar zur Faksimile-Edition*, ed. Kristen Collins (Luzern 2020), 297–303 with further bibliography.

[38] C. Heitzmann, 'Pro remedio animae meae: Mittelalterliche Bücherstiftungen am Beispiel Brunos von Hildesheim', in *Schätze im Himmel – Bücher auf Erden: Mittelalterliche Handschriften aus Hildesheim*, ed. M. E. Müller (Wolfenbüttel 2010), 155–60.

[39] Olchawa, *Aquamanilien: Genese, Verbreitung und Bedeutung* (as n. 1), 79–81, 268–69, no. 28.

[40] See O. Gerland, 'Die Dammstadt von Hildesheim', *Zeitschrift des Harz-Vereins für Geschichte und Altertumskunde*, 40 (1907), 372–92; T. Küntzel, 'Die Dammstadt von Hildesheim: Ideal und Realität einer hochmittelalterlichen Stadtgründung', *Concilium Medii Aevi*, 10 (2007), 1–32. On the history of Hildesheim in the 12th and 13 centuries: E. Bünz, 'Hildesheim um 1200 – Der Horizont einer Stadt', in *Bild*

und Bestie: Hildesheimer Bronzen der Stauferzeit, ed. Michael Brandt (Regensburg 2008), 115–30.

[41] R. Doebner, *Urkundenbuch der Stadt Hildesheim*, 8 vols. (Hildesheim 1881), vol. 1, no. 122; see also Küntzel, 'Die Dammstadt von Hildesheimn' (as n. 40).

[42] On the history of the abbey, see E. Freise, 'Adelsstiftung, Reichsabtei, Bischofskloster – Konvent der Kalligraphen, Künstler und Fälscher', in *Helmarshausen: Buchkultur und Goldschmiedekunst im Hochmittelalter*, ed. Ingrid Baumgärtner (Kassel 2005), 9–44.

[43] On Roger of Helmarshausen, see most recently H. C. Gearhart, *Theophilus and the Theory and Practice of Medieval Art* (University Park Pennsylvania 2017).

[44] M. Clarke, 'Reworking Theophilus: Adaptation and Use in Workshop Texts', in *Zwischen Kunsthandwerk und Kunst: Die Schedula diversarum artium*, ed. Andreas Speer (Berlin and Boston 2014), 72–89.

[45] I. Dines, 'The Theophilus Manuscript Tradition Reconsidered in the Light of New Manuscript Discoveries', in *Zwischen Kunsthandwerk und Kunst: Die 'Schedula diversarum artium'*, eds. A. Speer, M. Mauriège, and H. Westermann-Angerhausen (Berlin 2014), 3–10. The following passages summarize Dines's findings.

[46] C. V. Duzer, 'An Arabic Source for Theophilus's Recipe for Spanish Gold', in *Zwischen Kunsthandwerk und Kunst: Die Schedula diversarum artium*, eds. A. Speer, M. Mauriège, and H. Westermann-Angerhausen (Berlin–Boston 2014), 369–78 at 374.

[47] S. Kroustallis, 'Theophilus Matters: The Thorny Question of the "Schedula Diversarum Artium" Authorship', in *Zwischen Kunsthandwerk und Kunst* (as n. 45), 52–71.

[48] Dines, 'The Theophilus Manuscript Tradition Reconsidered' (as n. 45), 8.

[49] For a comparison of different editions, see http://schedula.uni-koeln.de/index.shtml [accessed 10 March 2021].

[50] Duzer, 'An Arabic Source for Theophilus's Recipe for Spanish Gold' (as n. 46), 371–72.

[51] Dines, 'The Theophilus Manusript Tradition Reconsidered' (as n. 45), 8.

[52] Duzer, 'An Arabic Source for Theophilus's Recipe for Spanish Gold' (as n. 46), 374.

[53] Lutz, 'The Cultural and Intellectual Context of St. Michael's at Hildesheim in the Twelfth Century' (as n. 37), 297–99.

[54] There is an extensive literature on Helmarshausen as an artistic centre. See more recently C. Stiegemann and H. Westermann-Angerhausen, eds., *Schatzkunst am Aufgang der Romanik: Der Paderborner Dom-Tragaltar und sein Umkreis* (München 2006); I. Baumgärtner, ed., *Helmarshausen: Buchkultur und Goldschmiedekunst im Hochmittelalter* (Kassel 2003); M. Gosebruch and F. N. Steigerwald, eds., *Helmarshausen und das Evangeliar Heinrichs des Löwen. Bericht über ein wissenschaftliches Symposion in Braunschweig und Helmarshausen vom 9. Oktober bis 11. Oktober 1985* (Göttingen 1992); Mende, 'Minden oder Helmarshausen: Bronzeleuchter aus der Werkstatt Rogers von Helmarshausen'; Mende, 'Das Wiener Greifen-Aquamanile: Eine Kleinbronze aus der Werkstatt Rogers von Helmarshausen'.

[55] M. Brandt, 'Made in Hildesheim? Überlegungen zur niedersächsischen Bronzekunst des Mittelalters', in *Drachenlandung: Ein Hildesheimer Drachen-Aquamanile des 12. Jahrhunderts*, eds. C. Höhl, G. Lutz, and J. Olchawa (Regensburg–Hildesheim 2017), 45–71.

[56] C. M. M. Bayer, 'Der Paderborner Dom-Tragaltar und die zu 1100 gefälschte Urkunde Bischof Heinrichs II. von Werl für die Abtei Helmarshausen', in *Schatzkunst am Aufgang der Romanik: Der Paderborner Dom-Tragaltar und sein Umkreis*, eds. C. Stiegemann and H. Westermann-Angerhausen (München 2006), 65–77. Reacting to this, see also M. Brandt, 'Roger von Helmarshausen – Zwischen Fakten und Fiktionen', in Ibid., 97–111.

[57] On the reconstruction of the *Vita* of the monk Rogerus, see E. Freise, 'Roger von Helmarshausen in seiner monastischen Umwelt', *Frühmittelalterliche Studien*, 15 (1981), 180–293; E. Freise, 'Adelsstiftung, Reichsabtei, Bischofskloster – Konvent der Kalligraphen, Künstler und Fälscher', in *Helmarshausen: Buchkultur und Goldschmiedekunst im Hochmittelalter*, ed. Ingrid Baumgärtner (Kassel 2005), 9–44 at 27–30.

[58] Freise, 'Adelsstiftung, Reichsabtei, Bischofskloster – Konvent der Kalligraphen, Künstler und Fälscher', 50.

[59] Still worth reading in the compilation and analysis of the objects is H. Fillitz, 'Rogerus von Helmarshausen', in *Helmarshausen und das Evangeliar Heinrichs des Löwen. Bericht über ein wissenschaftliches Symposion in Braunschweig und Helmarshausen vom 9. Oktober bis 11. Oktober 1985*, eds. M. Gosebruch and F. Neithart (Göttingen 1992), 43–62. More recently M. Peter, 'Neue Fragen und alte Probleme. Die beiden Paderborner Tragaltäre und der Beginn der Helmarshausener Goldschmiedekunst im 12. Jahrhundert', in *Schatzkunst am Aufgang der Romanik: Der Paderborner Dom-Tragaltar und sein Umkreis*, eds. C. Stiegemann and H. Westermann-Angerhausen (München 2006), 80–96.

[60] Mende, 'Minden oder Helmarshausen: Bronzeleuchter aus der Werkstatt Rogers von Helmarshausen' (no. 54), 83–5.

[61] On the question of the localization of workshops, see Mende, 'Zur Topographie sächsischer Bronzewerkstätten im welfischen Einflußbereich' (as n. 14), 431; Mende, 'Minden oder Helmarshausen: Bronzeleuchter aus der Werkstatt Rogers von Helmarshausen'.

The Regional and Transregional in Romanesque Europe (2021), 81–89

'MOSAN' METALWORK AND ITS DIFFUSION IN THE RHINELAND, FRANCE, AND ENGLAND

Aleuna Macarenko

The shrine of Saint Heribert, bishop of Cologne, the base of the cross of Saint-Omer, or the many enamelled plaques scattered today across American and European museums all bear testimony to the emergence of the champlevé technique in the valleys of the Meuse and Rhine in the first half of the 12th century.[1] *These objects, crafted in Mosan workshops or in ateliers of the Rhineland, in northern regions of present-day France or in England, exhibit a number of original and common traits.*[2] *To explain this phenomenon, early researchers – mostly Belgian specialists – invoked the extraordinary diffusion of so-called 'Mosan' art in the neighbouring regions, as well as in more distant territories, and its civilizing action within them.*[3] *Such an affirmation generated a heated debate, over time giving rise to reflections on more general questions such as the definition of style, the existence of regional and transregional schools of art, and the concepts of 'influence' and 'transfer'.*[4] *This paper aims to offer a historiographical survey of the abundant literature brought about by this discussion, until the most recent period.*[5]

BELGIUM AND MOSAN ART

'It is through Mosan art that begins the artistic history of our country', believed the Belgian historian F. Rousseaux.[6] Among the items gathered in 1881 for the *Exposition de l'Art ancien au Pays de Liège*, commemorating the fiftieth anniversary of Belgian independence, were featured numerous 12th-century goldsmith's works; indeed, the exhibition brought together, for the first time, a body of Mosan works, such as the shrines of saint Hadelin (Visé), Domitien and Mengold (Huy), and Remacle (Stavelot) (Figure 7.1 and Colour Plate VI).[7] The term 'Mosan' itself was coined by C. de Linas in his retrospective commentary on the event, published the next year under the title *Art et industrie de la région de la Meuse belge*. He used the term to name this art, which he described as being 'not of the Rhineland, nor Flemish nor French, despite being linked to all three by numerous affinities'.[8] Mosan production was presented again to the public for the seventy-fifth and then the hundredth anniversaries of Belgian independence, respectively, during the 1905 *Art ancien au Pays de Liège* exhibition and the 1930 *Art de l'ancien Pays de Liège et des anciens Arts Wallons* exhibition, thus becoming inextricably linked to the shaping of a national identity – Belgian, Walloon, and of Liège all at once.[9] The reasons given were powerful: is art not 'the manifestation of a nation's genius [. . .], its most delicate, most honest, most graceful expression?'[10] In this respect defining its special features, thus liberating it from the production of the neighbouring Rhineland, became, for the pro-Mosan Belgian researchers, a political challenge.

THE RHINELAND AND MOSAN ART

The diocese of Liège, the cradle of Mosan art, has always occupied an ambiguous place with respect to the Rhineland: Lower Lotharingia formed part of the German Empire, and the city and diocese of Liège in particular were placed under the authority of the archdiocese of Cologne. Indeed, Mosan art was originally perceived to be a mere expression of Rhenish art and not a specific production.[11] Surprisingly enough, it was two German authors, O. Von Falke and H. Frauberger, who were the first to try to define the specific traits of the figurative works that they perceived to be Mosan; these could be seen in the facial characteristics, in the flow of drapery and in the management of the characters' attitudes.[12] Simple recognition of the existence of a specific Mosan art was, however, not enough for Belgian authors; they wanted to proclaim the primacy and the superiority of what they considered to be the metalworking tradition 'of their region' over Rhenish production.[13] It is not surprising, then, to read authors such as M. Laurent state that:

> for two centuries, there was an art of which Mosan artists were known to be the masters. Some of them were unrivalled during their time, and one could point out long periods of time when the brightest centre of Germanic

  DOI: 10.4324/9781003162827-7

FIGURE 7.1

Stavelot altar, Bruxelles, Musées royaux d'Art et d'Histoire, inv. 1590: (© MRAH-KMKG, Brussels)

> art, as far as works in metal was concerned, was located not in the Rhineland but in the Meuse valley, and it was Walloon cities that showed the way to progress to the somewhat lazy Germanic workshops.[14]

No work of art illustrates this historiographical confrontation as well as the jewelled shrine holding the relics of Saint Heribert, bishop of Cologne (999–1024), kept in the church of Deutz abbey (Figure 7.2). As early as 1857, E. aus'm Weerth drew researchers' attention to this monument, which he considered to be a particularly striking testimony of Rhenish goldsmiths' work;[15] in 1902, the shrine was also attributed to 'German' art by the curators of the exhibition *Industrie- und Gewerbeausstellung Düsseldorf*, during which it was presented to the public.[16] O. Von Falke and H. Frauberger quickly opposed this attribution in their retrospective summary of the event, titled *Deutsche Schmelzarbeiten des Mittelalters*: according to them, the shrine obviously bore stylistic marks indicating its Mosan origin.[17] The conclusions of Von Falke and Frauberger immediately brought about excitement within the scholarly community, in particular among Belgian researchers, who were delighted by this unexpected alliance.[18] However, starting from the mid-1920s – perhaps as a consequence of the *Jahrtausendausstellungen* of Cologne and Aachen in 1925 which might have awoken nationalist feelings in many German authors[19] – opposing opinions emerged. For J. Braun and H. Beenken, the Saint Heribert shrine is undoubtedly a work of German art.[20] It was within this context of exacerbated historiographical confrontations and national sensibilities that H. Schnitzler proposed, in 1931, the *Zwei-Meister-Theorie*, which attributed the crafting of the Saint Heribert shrine to two goldsmiths, one from the Mosan region, another from the Rhineland, supported by arguments based on morphological, stylistic, and iconographic considerations.[21] This double origin, both German and Belgian

FIGURE 7.2
Saint Heribert shrine: Köln-Deutz, St Heribert. (© Katholische Kirchengemeinde St Heribert, Köln)

(truly 'Rhenish-Mosan'),[22] was also attributed to the shrine during its presentation to the public at the 1972 Rhein und Maas exhibition. After the event, however, the shrine of Saint Heribert would elicit only the occasional comment, as everything seemed to have been said and done about it. It was a study of the material state of the shrine – the first of its kind published on a medieval shrine[23] – that challenged and finally rejected Schnitzler's *Zwei-Meister-Theorie*. Performed during the restoration of the shrine during the 1980s and the 1990s, M. Seidler's research helped bring to light the numerous changes of plan which occurred during the creation of the object as well as the wide variety of techniques used to decorate it, showing that rather than 'two masters', the shrine had been worked on by a workshop, whose workers, armed with various skills, moved from project to project.[24] Seidler's conclusions fell in line with the observations previously made by D. Kötzsche about the shrine of Saint Servatius, produced in Maastricht, and the shrine of Charlemagne, which was produced by an Aachen-based workshop: by highlighting the use of the same punch to produce the decoration on the copper sheets that adorn both works, the German researcher managed to prove the presence of the same master goldsmith at both sites.[25] This opened the way for discussion about how mobile artisans and artists in the Rhenish-Mosan region during the 12th century really were, a question that is still being debated by researchers today.[26]

THE CHAMPAGNE REGION AND MOSAN ART

Pro-Mosan authors also turned their attention towards the lands surrounding the western borders of the diocese of Liège. 'The most beautiful works [of the 12th century]', wrote Count Borchgrave d'Alténa, 'are all ours, or very close to those that were found in our lands since the beginning'.[27] He added that a 'systematic exploration of the North of France would undoubtedly yield most interesting results'[28] for any researcher who would undertake the task of identifying all the works of Mosan metalwork, as he believed there to be many produced for regions such as Reims, the Pas-de-Calais, or Champagne and kept in France ever since the Middle Ages. This comment falls in line with a long historiographical tradition, the origin of which lies in the 19th-century reading of *Rebus in administratione sua gentis*, by Suger, abbot of

FIGURE 7.3

Saint-Bertin candlestick: Saint-Omer, Musée Sandelin, inv. 2800 bis (© MarcGIL-Projet e.thesaurus-Université de Lille/Université de Liège, Lille)

Saint-Denis (1122–51). In this, Suger describes a monumental base for a cross, which has since disappeared, decorated with enamelled typological figures, crafted by '*plures aurifabros Lotharingos*', sometimes five, sometimes seven, whom he had invited to his abbey.[29] The fact that 'Lotharingian' goldsmiths – quickly identified to be of 'Mosan' origin[30] – were summoned to work on this most prestigious project was seen as a sign of the appreciation enjoyed by the Mosan metal arts in neighbouring countries during the 12th century.[31] Soon the entirety of goldsmith's works and champlevé enamels in the north of France were attributed to Mosan workshops; we will simply mention here, as an example, the base of the cross of Saint-Omer (Figure 7.3) or some plaques kept today at the Louvre museum, which were recently reattributed to the artistic sphere widely described as 'northern'.[32]

The debate has focused, these past few years, on a group of nineteen enamelled plaques, kept at the Treasury of the cathedral of Troyes, adorned with typological scenes and portraits of evangelists[33] and today believed to be the *membra disjecta* of a processional cross (Figure 7.4 and Colour Plate VII (top)).[34] While they were undoubtedly crafted during the second half of the 12th century – there seems to be consensus today dating them 1160–80 – the production site of these plaques continues to be debated. A. Darcel (*Publications récentes sur l'émaillerie*, 1863) believed these objects to be 'of German origin';[35] J. Labarte (*Histoire des arts industriels au moyen âge et à l'époque de la Renaissance*, 1863–66) specified that they must be Rhenish;[36] soon after the publication of Ch. de Linas' *Art et industrie d'autrefois dans la région de la Meuse belge* (1882), they were to be seen as being 'Mosan'. It would not be until the 1950s that the existence of a 'peri-Mosan' production would be suggested – a subtle paradigm shift which gained a response in the literature dedicated to the enamels of the Treasury of Troyes. That these plaques were produced in Champagne, perhaps even in Troyes, was then no longer inconceivable

FIGURE 7.4

Saint Matthew: Troyes, Trésor de la Cathédrale, inv. 012 (© DRAC Grand-Est, Boulangé-Geffroy, Troyes Classified as Monument historique on the 1894/09/15)

for many authors, postulating the existence of 'migrating Mosan workshops'[37] or of local sites influenced by the art of the diocese of Liège.[38] That they could have been crafted by a non-Mosan enameller, however, was considered, by the very same researchers, a heresy, judging by the strong reaction[39] generated by M. Jottrand's proposal to recognize in these enamels the work of a local artist, 'with an original personality, distinct from that of Mosan enamellers'.[40] Yet nearly half a century later, it is this hypothesis that retains researchers' attention. In the exhibition catalogue for *Une Renaissance. L'art entre Flandre et Champagne, 1150–1250* (published in 2013 and now considered the main reference work for the study of the links between Mosan production and the art of the northern parts of France), S. Balace, C. Descatoire, and M. Gil reject the traditional historiography where 'the artistic relationships between the main production centres are analysed in terms of the influence of Mosan art on these regions'; they instead consider them being the result of 'parallel research studies, cross-influences, artistic kinships and workshop collaborations'.[41] For them, these exchanges generate close ties between the art of the Champagne and that of the Mosan region; ties that make it difficult to attribute works to one or the other of these styles, hence the authors' preference to call them 'northern'.[42] It remains to be seen what posterity awaits this term in future publications.

ENGLAND AND MOSAN ART

Just as in the Rhineland and in Champagne, valuable works of medieval metalwork and enamelling, exhibiting features similar to the 'Mosan' works, are also part of British collections; it is not surprising, then, that 'pro-Mosan' authors also attempted to attribute their conception, if not their crafting, to workshops of the Meuse valley. They did so, however, with a completely different mind-set from the one fuelling the debates regarding 'Rhenish-Mosan' or 'Franco-Mosan' art. Indeed, no confrontation is to be found in the abundant literature produced by Belgian and English scholars, but instead a discussion, enriched by mutual contributions from both parties.[43] This was perhaps due to the clear and undisputable geographical divide between the continental and the insular spheres, and perhaps also because the art of metalworking had been practiced on the British Isles since time immemorial.[44]

It is interesting to note within this context that the definition of a local champlevé production predated the questioning of possible links that could tie it to the Mosan area. The existence of a specifically English production of enamels during the 12th century – put forward as a hypothesis at the end of the 19th century by the French historian Marquet de Vasselot and by the British author S. Gardner[45] – was indeed recognized before the mid-20th century thanks to research conducted by H. P. Mitchell. In his *English Enamels of the Twelfth Century*, published in 1925, the author proposes a reading grid based on stylistic, iconographic, technical, and provenance criteria, carefully selected with the goal of distinguishing production in the British Isles from the contemporaneous continental production; many works previously believed to have been produced in the Rhineland or in the Meuse valley were thus attributed, mostly by the work of Mitchell's successors, to the Anglo-Norman domain.[46] The most famous example of this is, undoubtedly, the group of three closely related ciboria, today kept in London (The Balfour and Warwick ciboria, Victoria and Albert Museum) and New York (Malmesbury ciborium, Morgan Library & Museum) (Figure 7.5 and Colour Plate VII (bottom)).[47] In addition to their technical and stylistic features, and the use of a specifically English decorative vocabulary such as octopus flowers, the epigraphic inscriptions on the enamelled scenes of the ciboria, which closely resemble those painted in the 12th century on the vaults of the Worcester Cathedral Chapter-House, prove the English origin of these objects.[48]

Only from the second half of the 20th century onwards did researchers – spearheaded by K. E. Haney and N. Stratford – commit themselves to defining how the Mosan aesthetic could have spread within the Anglo-Norman world; in this respect, the question of the origin of the so-called Henry of Blois plaques, kept at the British Museum, has particularly preoccupied researchers (Figure 7.6).[49] These enamels, crafted for the bishop of Winchester, are undoubtedly executed in a Mosan style.[50] They were made by the same artist who executed a series of plaques of which twelve are known today, including the famous figure of Naaman dipping himself in the waters of the Jordan River, also kept today among the collections of the British Museum, as well as four plaques

FIGURE 7.5

Balfour ciborium: *London, Victoria and Albert Museum, inv. M.1:1, 2–1981 (© Victoria and Albert Museum, London)*

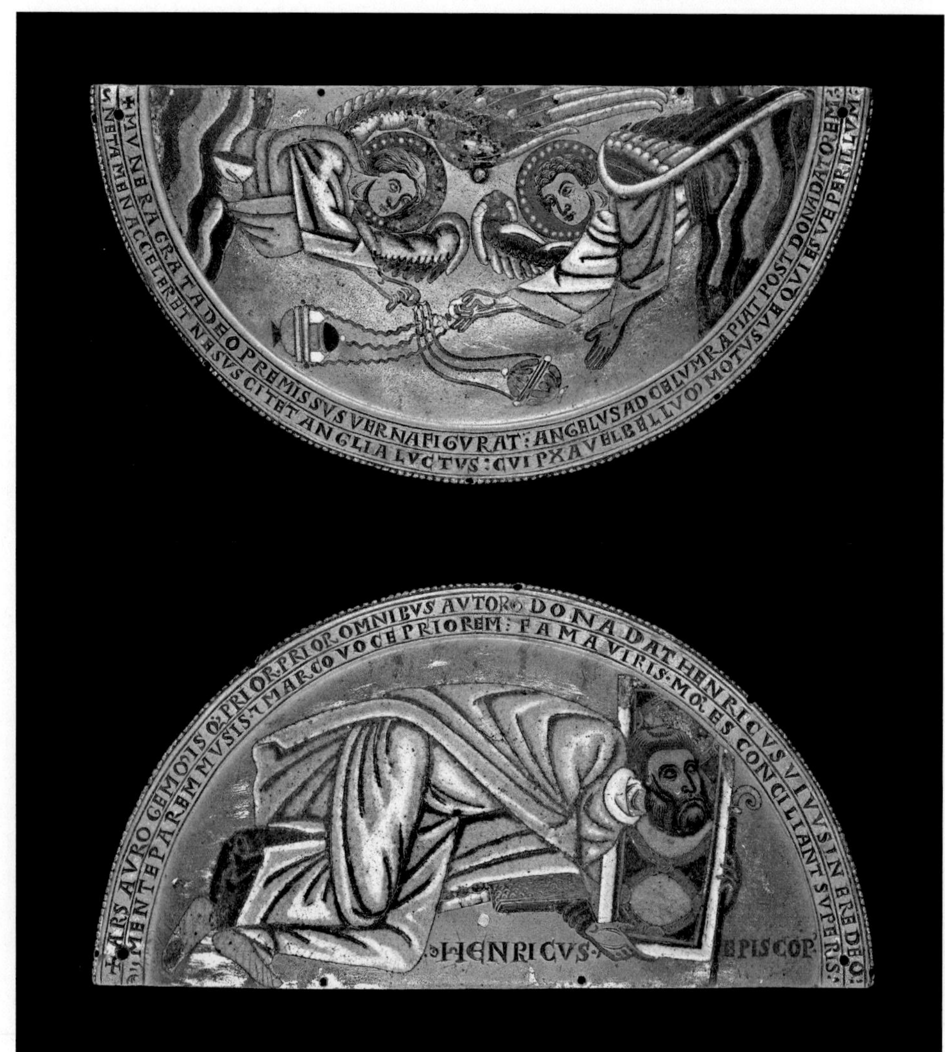

FIGURE 7.6

Henri of Blois plaques: British Museum, inv. M&LA 52,3–27, 1 (© The Trustees of the British Museum. All rights reserved)

in the Victoria and Albert Museum (known as the Rolls Plaques, depicting Samson and the Lion, Alexander's ascent to the Heavens, a man riding a camel, and Moses and the brazen serpent), four more in the Metropolitan Museum of Art in New York (bearing scenes of the life of Christ: the Baptism, the Crucifixion, the Holy Women at the Tomb, and the Pentecost), and three plaques in the Louvre Museum (depicting a centaur brandishing a hunting bow, a young man slaying a dragon, and the Saints Sebastian and Livinus).[51] Various hypotheses were put forward regarding the exact production site of those enamels. Were they fashioned in a continental workshop and imported to England?[52] Were they crafted by a Mosan artisan invited to work on English soil?[53] Were they made by an English artist trained in the art of enamelling in Lotharingia or who got acquainted with the Mosan aesthetic through models in circulation during the 12th century?[54] None of these theories can be affirmed today with any degree of certainty. Stratford considers that 'for the time being, as a working hypothesis it would seem that the Henry of Blois plaques were executed [. . .] by a Mosan goldsmith [. . .] perhaps in England'.[55] However, we lack compelling evidence which would allow us to confirm or definitively reject this hypothesis.

PHYSICOCHEMICAL ANALYSES COMING TO THE AID OF ART HISTORIANS

Despite the abundant literature generated by the question of exchanges between the Mosan region and its neighbouring territories – of which we have examined a small part in this paper – the debate has somewhat dried up during the recent years.[56] It seems that by using traditional art-historical approaches, such as studies of morphology, of style, or of iconography, researchers have reached the limits of these methods. A renewed methodology could, however, breathe new life into this research. Just as a material study of the shrines kept in Deutz, in Maastricht, and in Aachen allowed authors to provide answers to questions that were left unresolved by stylistic and iconographic observations alone, material analyses of the 'northern' enamels could undoubtedly aid researchers today in defining a specifically regional champlevé production. The application of laboratory analyses to the study of medieval enamels is nothing new: it was pioneered by P. England in 1986, during her study on the glasses and enamels of the Museum of Fine Arts in Boston, and by I. Freestone in 1993 with his compositional examination of medieval enamels kept at the British Museum.[57] Some twenty years later, I. Biron and her team launched, under the aegis of C2RMF, a colossal study project for 'southern' as well as 'northern' enamels, putting particular emphasis on the different practices within the latter group. The results of this study, published in 2015, are promising: while materials and techniques used by the northern enamellers are indeed homogeneous, slight variations do exist both in the glass composition and in the artist's touch, allowing researchers to distinguish works considered to be of Rhenish or Mosan origin from those that possibly originated in the northern regions of France or in England.[58] Future studies will undoubtedly bring additional responses to these questions.

Similar projects, dedicated to the study of goldsmith's work and aiming to break down methodological barriers, currently flourish across Europe. Indeed, the research group *Corpus scriniorum*, bringing together specialists from different fields, is calling for a material study of all the Romanesque shrines kept in Germany, Belgium, and the Netherlands, taking advantage of the restoration works planned or currently being performed on those shrines.[59] The secondary decoration – stamped, punched, or worked in *vernis brun* – is gaining more and more attention from researchers. The filigrees, common to the Rhenish, Mosan, and French jewelled works, have very recently been studied by H. Cambier, who demonstrated in her doctoral thesis that a combined analysis of their formal and material aspects allows for advancement of knowledge of the medieval shrines, on the one hand, and of the goldsmiths' practices, on the other.[60] An increase in multidisciplinary studies bears witness to the renewed vitality of research; in the coming years, they are sure to renew the debate around the art known as 'Mosan'.

NOTES

1 A. Lemeunier, 'L'orfèvrerie mosane', in *L'art mosan: Liège et son pays à l'époque romane du 11e au 13e siècle*, ed. B. Van den Bossche (Liège 2007), 107–35.

2 A. Lemeunier, 'De la Meuse à l'art mosan', in *L'art mosan* (as n. 1), 11–36.

3 'After causing all the centres in the Principality to blossom magnificently, [Mosan goldsmith's work] shone across borders, projecting far and wide the evidence of its vitality. In its wake came many foreign artists, initiated to our techniques and our forms of expression' (S. Collon-Gevaert, *L'orfèvrerie mosane au Moyen âge* (Bruxelles 1943), 6).

4 This reflection is expanded upon in S. Balace, 'Art mosan *versus* art de la France du nord. Essai historiographique', in *Une Renaissance. L'art entre Flandre et Champagne: 1150–1250* [exhib. cat.] (Paris 2013), 38–43.

5 For literature before 2009, S. Balace proposes in her doctoral thesis a more complete reading of the issue: S. Balace, 'Historiographie de l'art mosan' (unpublished PhD thesis, University of Liège, 2009, http://bictel.ulg.ac.be/ETD-db/collection/available/ULgetd-01112009-143217/, last consulted on 21 April 2020). A recent summary of some aspects of this thesis can be found in S. Balace, 'L'art mosan: regard historiographique', in *Art mosan (1000–1250). Un art entre Seine et Rhin? Réflexions, bilans, perspectives. Actes du colloque international* (Bruxelles–Liège–Namur 2015), 9–21.

6 F. Rousseau, *Introduction historique à l'art mosan* (Bruxelles 1942), 3.

7 The 'mosan' artefacts displayed in 1881 were primarily shrines, reliquaries, and various liturgical items (such as crosses, pyxides, and ciboria; see: *Exposition de l'art ancient au pays de Liège. Catalogue official* (Liège 1881)). Nowadays, one most readily thinks of enamelled objects as being 'mosan'; the most famous thereof are the portable altar of Stavelot (Brussels, Royal Museums of Art and History, inv. 20038605; see C. Dumortier and F. Van Noten, *La salle aux trésors. Chefs-d'oeuvre de l'art roman et mosan* (Turnhout 1999), 24–27) or the Stavelot Tryptich (New York, Morgan Library & Museum, inv. B3 002 C; see W. Voelkle, *The Stavelot Tryptich. Mosan Art and the Legend of the True Cross* (New York 1980).

[8] Ch. De Linas, *Art et industrie d'autrefois dans la région de la Meuse belge: souvenirs de la rétrospective de Liège en 1881* (Liège 1882), 12.

[9] J. Stiennon provides an interesting, although dated, summary of these exhibitions in J. Stiennon, 'L'art mosan, un âge d'or', in *La Wallonie, le pays et les hommes: lettres – arts – culture. Tome 1: des origines à la fin du 15e siècle*, eds. R. Lejeune and J. Stiennon (Bruxelles 1977), 230–303, esp. 236–40.

[10] J. Helbig, *L'art mosan. Tome 1: des origines jusqu'au 15e siècle* (Paris 1906), 5–6.

[11] On these questions, see A. Marchandisse and M. Suttor, 'L'histoire du pays mosan à l'époque romane (1000–1250)', in *L'art mosan* (as n. 1), 37–60; A. Lemeunier, 'De la Meuse à l'art mosan', Ibid., 11–36.

[12] O. Von Falke and H. Frauberger, *Deutsche Schmelzarbeiten des Mittelalters und andere Kunstwerke der Kunsthistorischen Ausstellung zu Düsseldorf 1902* (Frankfurt-am-Main 1904), esp. 61–88.

[13] The nationalist discourse using 'our goldsmiths/our region/our geniuses' abounds among the authors of that time; as an example: J. Borchgrave d'Alténa, 'À propos de l'art "mosan"', *Bulletin de la société royale d'archéologie de Bruxelles*, 24 (1951), 27–42; S. Collon-Gevaert, *L'orfèvrerie* (as n. 3), more specifically 24–26.

[14] M. Laurent, 'Note sur l'état de nos connaissances relativement aux arts plastiques dans la vallée de la Meuse, aux époques carolingienne, romane et gothique', *Annales du 21e Congrès de la Fédération Archéologique et Historique de Belgique* (Liège 1909), II, 67–79, esp. 68.

[15] E. aus'm Weerth, *Kunstdenkmäler des christlichen Mittelalters in den Rheinlanden* (Leipzig 1857), 8–13. His conclusions are echoed by F. Bock, *Das heilige Köln* (Leipzig 1858), 12. The shrine was previously described in *Organ der christlichen Kunst*, 5 (1855), 225–28, with no comment as to its origin.

[16] Among the abundant literature generated by the event, mentioning the shrine of Saint Heribert: S. Beissel, 'Die Kunstausstellung zu Düsseldorf', *Stimmen aus Maria Laach*, 67 (1902), 330–31; P. Clemen, *Die rheinische und die westfälische Kunst auf der kunsthistorischen Ausstellung zu Düsseldorf 1902* (Leipzig 1903), 26.

[17] Von Falke and Frauberger, *Deutsche Schmelzarbeiten* (as n. 12), 84–86.

[18] Helbig, *L'art mosan* (as n. 10), 63–64; M. Laurent, *Art rhénan, art mosan, art byzantin: la Bible de Stavelot*, Byzantion, 6/i (1931), 75–98; S. Collon-Gevaert, 'Les médaillons émaillés de la châsse de Saint-Héribert, à Deutz', *Annales de la Fédération archéologique et historique de Belgique*, 4 (1932), 145–48.

[19] This cause-result link was discussed by Laurent, *Art rhénan* (as n. 18), 75–98, esp. 80.

[20] H. Beenken, 'Schreine und Schranken', *Jahrbuch für Kunstwissenschaft*, 4 (1926), 65–107, esp. 69–86; J. Braun, *Meisterwerke der deutschen Goldschmiedekunst der vorgotischen Zeit* (München 1922), 12, was never convinced by Von Falke's and Frauberger's conclusions either.

[21] H. Schnitzler, *Die Goldschniedeplastik der Aachener Schreinswerkstadt chreinswe zur Entwicklung der Goldschniedekunst des Rhein-Maasgebiete in der romanischen Zeit* (Bonn 1931).

[22] Precisely this term had already been used to refer to the shrine of Saint Heribert by M. Creutz, 'Die Goldschniedekunst des Rhein-Maas-Gebietes', in *Belgische Kunstdenkmäller*, ed. P. Clemen (München 1923), 123–62.

[23] Although, in fact, the shrine of Charlemagne had already been subject to restoration between 1982 and 1986; however, the results of this study were not published until 1998 in F. Mütherich and D. Kötzsche, *Der Schrein Karls des Grossen: Bestand und Sicherung 1982–1988* (Aachen 1998).

[24] M. Seidler, *Studien zum Reliquienschrein des heiligen Heribert in Deutz (Stadt Köln): Rekonstruktion seiner Entstehung* (Bonn 1995). His conclusions were recalled in later publications, including in the most recent monograph: M. Seidler, *Der Schrein des Heiligen Heribert in Köln-Deutz* (Regensburg 2016).

[25] D. Kötzsche, 'Zum Stand der Forschung der Goldschmiedekunst des 12. Jahrhunderts im Rhein-Maas-Gebiet', in *Rhein und Maas – Kunst und Kultur – 800–1400* [exhib. cat.] (Köln 1973), II, 191–236, more specifically 198. See also R. Kroos, *Der Schrein des Heiligen Servatius in Maastricht und die vier zugehörigen Reliquiare in Brüssel* (München 1985), more particularly 104–24.

[26] See the activities of the group *Corpus Scriniorum* (L. Lambacher, 'Das Corpus Scriniorum – Stand und Perspektiven eines internationalen Forschungsprojektes', in *Corpus – Inventar – Katalog Beispiele für Forschung und Dokumentation zur materiellen Überlieferung der Künste*, ed. W. Augustyn (München 2015), 63–72).

[27] d'Alténa, 'À propos de l'art "mosan"' (as n. 13), 27–42, esp. 39.

[28] J. Borchgrave d'Alténa, 'À propos d'orfèvreries mosanes conservées en France', *Bulletin de la société royale d'archéologie de Bruxelles*, 58 (1947–1948), 47–63, esp. 53.

[29] J. Labarte, *Histoire des arts industriels au moyen âge et à l'époque de la Renaissance* (Paris 1864–66), III, 619–21. The text is most readily available in English in Erwin Panofsky, ed. and trans., *Abbot Suger on the Abbey Church of St.-Denis and Its Art Treasures*, 2nd ed. (Princeton 1979), 58–59.

[30] M. Laurent, 'Godefroid de Claire et la croix de Suger à l'abbaye de Saint-Denis', *Revue archéologique*, 19 (1924), 79–87.

[31] Before the concept of 'Mosan art' came to be: A. Pinchard, 'Histoire de la dinanterie et de la sculpture du métal en Belgique', *Bulletin des commissions royales d'art et d'archéologie*, 13 (1873), 308–65, esp. 332–38 (quoted in S. Balace, *Historiographie* (as n. 5), 440).

[32] See *Une Renaissance* (as n. 4), esp. 89, n. 25 (Paris, Musée du Louvre, dept. des Objets d'art, inv. OA 6275 and inv. 12007); 114–15, n. 47 (Saint-Omer, Musée de l'hôtel Sandelin, inv. 2800 bis). The use of the term 'northern' is discussed in n. 42.

[33] Troyes, Trésor de la Cathédrale, inv. 012, 013, 015-A and 015-B.

[34] C. Descatoire, 'Un ensemble d'émaux de la seconde moitié du 12e siècle: les plaques de la cathédrale de Troyes, influences et spécificités', in *L'œuvre de la Meuse*, ed. P. George (Liège 2015), 49–65.

[35] A. Darcel, 'Publications récentes sur les origines de l'émaillerie', *Gazette des Beaux-Arts*, 15 (1863), 295–96. The plaques were mentioned in earlier literature, but the authors never reflected upon their origin: E. Le Brun-Dalbanne, *Recherches sur l'histoire et le symbolisme de quelques émaux du trésor de la cathédrale de Troyes* (Troyes 1862), 264–72.

[36] Labarte, *Histoire des arts industriels* (as n. 29), 621–22.

[37] M.-M. Gauthier, 'Plaquettes semi-circulaires: scènes de typologie biblique', in *Art roman* [exhib. cat.] (Barcelona 1963), n. 429, 262–64; M.-M. Gauthier, *Émaux du Moyen Âge occidental* (Fribourg 1972), 177–78; 368, n. 120.

[38] H. Swarzenski, *Monuments of Romanesque Art: The Art of Church Treasures in North-Western Europe* (London 1954), 79; pl. 209, n. 486; F. Baron, 'Plaques semi-circulaires', in *L'art en Champagne au Moyen Âge* [exhib. cat.] (Paris 1959), 47–48, n. 93; N. Morgan, 'The Iconography of Twelfth-Century Mosan Enamels', in *Rhin-Meuse: Art et Civilisation, 800–1400* [exhib. cat.] (Köln–Brussels 1973), II, 263–78, esp. 271, note 5.

[39] F. Salet, 'Les émaux du trésor de la cathédrale de Troyes (compte-rendu)', *Bull. mon.*, 123/iii (1965), 250–51; L. Pressouyre, 'Réflexions sur la sculpture du 12e siècle en Champagne', *Gesta*, 9/ii (1970), 16–31; X. Dectot, 'Les tombeaux des comtes de Champagne (1151–1284). Un manifeste politique', *Bulletin Monumental*, 162/i (2004), 3–62, esp. 41, recently came back to this debate; the plaques are 'Mosan' according to the author.

[40] 1 M. Jottrand, 'Les émaux du Trésor de la cathédrale de Troyes décoraient-ils les tombeaux des comtes de Champagne?' *Gazette des Beaux-Arts*, 65 (1965), 257–64. Her thesis was echoed by E. C. Pastan, 'Fit for a Count: The Twelfth-Century Stained Glass Panels from Troyes', *Speculum*, 64/ii (1989), 338–72, esp. 352–53. This hypothesis was previously presented but not further developed by L. Grodecki in 'Les vitraux de Châlons-sur-Marne et l'art mosan', in *Relations artistiques entre la France et les autres pays depuis le haut Moyen Âge jusqu'à la fin du 19e siècle. Actes du 19e Congrès international d'histoire de l'art* (Paris 1959), 183–90, esp. 189.

[41] C. Descatoire and M. Gil, 'Un siècle de création. L'art des années 1150–1250 entre nord de la France, région mosane et Champagne', in *Une Renaissance* (as n. 4), 45–55.

[42] 'Septentrional', in French (Gil, 'Un siècle de création' (as n. 41), 44–55). In the context of the study of medieval enamels, N. Stratford (*Catalogue of Medieval Enamels in the British Museum II: Northern Romanesque enamel* (London 1993), 11), first used the term 'northern' in distinction to 'Limoges' work, sometimes referred to as 'corpus meridional' in French (see M.-M. Gauthier, *Émaux méridionaux. Catalogue international de l'Œuvre de Limoges* (Paris 1987)). As such, it should logically include other areas of northern Europe: not only the Mosan region and northern France but England and Germany as well. There is therefore a slight issue with the use of the term 'northern' in *Une Renaissance* (as n. 4), as the authors almost exclusively apply it to objects crafted either in the Mosan region or on French soil. Indeed, only one English object (and no German artefacts) is presented in the catalogue: a small chest, dated 1170–75, adorned with depictions of a *psychomachia*, now kept at the Treasury of the cathedral of Troyes (Troyes, Trésor de la Cathédrale, inv. 011; see: *Une Renaissance* (as n. 4), 107, n. 40).

[43] The sides are, incidentally, not clearly defined: many English authors make 'pro-Mosan' statements while some Belgian authors strive to demonstrate the existence of a specifically English champlevé production.

[44] H. P. Mitchell, 'English Enamels of the Twelfth Century (I)', *The Burlington Magazine for Connoisseurs*, 47 (1925), 163–70, esp. 164.

[45] J.-J. Marquet de Vasselot, 'L'orfèvrerie et l'émaillerie au 13e et au 14e siècles', in *Histoire de l'Art*, ed. A. Michel, II, 917–89, more specifically 972; S. J. Gardner, *Some Minor Arts as Practiced in England*, 1894; S. J. Gardner, *Burlington Fine Arts Club. Catalogue of a collection of European enamels from the earliest date to the end of the 17. century*, 1897 (cited in Mitchell, 'English Enamels' (as n. 44), 163–64).

[46] Some examples are provided in Gauthier, *Émaux du Moyen Âge* (as n. 37), 342, n. 80; 361 n. 113; Stratford, *Catalogue of Medieval Enamels* (as n. 42).

[47] London, Victoria and Albert, inv. M.1:1, 2–1981 and M.159–1919; New York, Morgan Library & Museum, inv. AZ047.

[48] Gauthier, *Émaux du Moyen Âge* (as n. 37), 158; 362–63; N. Stratford, 'Three English Romanesque Enamelled Ciboria', *Burlington Magazine*, 120 (April 1984), 204–19.

[49] London, British Museum, inv. M&LA 52,3–27, I.

[50] Von Falke and Frauberger, *Deutsche Schmelzarbeiten* (as n. 12), 72. The first authors to report the existence of the plaques considered them to be Limoges (G. Isaac, 'On an Enamelled Plate of the Twelfth Century, in the Possession of the Revd Henry Crowe', *JBAA*, 3 (1848), 102–05) or of Rhenish origin (A. W. Franks, 'On the Additions to the Collections of National Antiquities in the British Museum', *Journal of Archaeological*, 10 (1853), 9–11).

[51] The complete series of theses plaques – which depicted the life of Christ, accompanied by typological and symbolic scenes – must have decorated the same object: a cross, a retable, or an antependium. The plaques are, respectively: London, British Museum, inv. M&LA 84, 6–6,3 (see Stratford, *Catalogue of Medieval Enamels* (as n. 42), 53–58, esp. 57, 65); London, Victoria and Albert Museum, inv. M.53A-1988, M.53–1988, M.53B-1988 and M.59–1952 (see M. Campbell, 'The Rolls Plaques', *National-Art Collection Fund Review* (1989), 99–102); New York, Metropolitan Museum of Art, 17.190.430, 17.190.431, 17.190.419, and 65.105 (see Stratford, *Catalogue of Medieval Enamels* (as n. 42), 27, 28, 30, 57, 59–67); Paris, Musée du Louvre, OA 8097, OA 8098 and MRR253 (see Gauthier, *Émaux du Moyen Âge* (as n. 37), 132–33; 349).

[52] T. S. R. Boase, *The Oxford History of English Art III: English Art 1100–1216* (Oxford 1953), 170–71; *Ornamenta ecclesiae: Kunst und Künstler der Romanik I* [exhib. cat.] (Köln 1985), 130–32; 158–59, n. B 10.

[53] H. P. Mitchell, 'English Enamels' (as n. 44), 163–70, esp. 164; C. Oman, 'Influences mosanes dans les émaux d'origine anglaise', in *L'art Mosan*, ed. P. Francastel (Paris 1953), 155–60, esp. 155; H. Swarzenski, *Monuments* (as n. 38), pl. 195, fig. 446; H. Swarzenski, 'The Song of the Three Worthies', *Bulletin of the Museum of Fine Arts*, 56 (1958), 30–49; K. Haney, 'Some Mosan Sources for the Henry of Blois Enamels', *The Burlington Magazine*, 124 (1982), 220–30; N. Stratford, *Catalogue of Medieval Enamels* (as n. 42), 53–58, esp. 58. This idea was previously expressed by N. Stratford, 'The Henri of Blois Enamel Plaques', in *English Romanesque Art 1066–1200*, eds. G. Zarnecki, T. Holland and J. Holt (London 1984), 261–62, nos. 277 a and b.

[54] Gauthier, *Émaux du Moyen Âge* (as n. 37), 158; 360, n. 112; P. Lasko, *Ars sacra: 800 to 1200* (Harmondsworth 1972), 238.

[55] Stratford, *Catalogue of Medieval Enamels* (as n. 42), 53–58, esp. 58.

[56] With the exception, perhaps, of the discussions on the art of Champagne and the northern parts of France in *Une Renaissance* (as n. 4).

[57] P. England, 'A Technical Investigation of Medieval Enamels', in *Medieval Objects in the Museum of Fine Arts, Boston: Enamels and Glass*, eds. N. Netzer and H. Swarzenski (Boston 1986), XIX–XIV; I. C. Freestone, 'Appendix: Composition of Glasses', in *Catalogue of Medieval Enamels* (as n. 42), 37–45.

[58] I. Biron, *Émaux sur métal, de l'an mil au 19e siècle. Histoire, technique et matériaux* (Paris 2015).

[59] Lambacher, 'Das Corpus Scriniorum' (as n. 26), 63–72. The monumental study was published as part of the activities of the *corpus scriniorum*: D. Kemper, *Die Goldschmiedearbeiten am Dreikönigenschrein: Bestand und Geschichte seiner Restaurierungen im 19. und 20. Jahrhundert: mit Beiträgen zu Materialanalysen und Herstellungstechniken* (Köln 2014).

[60] H. Cambier, 'Les filigranes dans l'orfèvrerie de la région rhéno-mosane et du nord de la France (12e-13e siècles). Du geste de l'orfèvre à la signification du décor' (Doctoral thesis, University of Namur, 2020) [to be published].

The Regional and Transregional in Romanesque Europe (2021), 91–102

WINCHESTER'S HOLY SEPULCHRE CHAPEL AND BYZANTIUM

ICONOGRAPHIC TRANSREGIONALISM?

Cecily Hennessy

It is widely recognised that Byzantine iconography is present in the 12th-century paintings of the Holy Sepulchre Chapel at Winchester Cathedral. This paper argues that in the painting of the Entombment/Lamentation on the east wall, Christ is not being placed into the sarcophagus, which is some distance below but rests on a red stone while his body is anointed for burial. It is argued that features of this representation are dependent on events in Constantinople. The stone on which Christ's body was embalmed, known as the lithos, was brought from Ephesus to Constantinople by Emperor Manuel I (1143–80) in 1169–70. It was placed in the Chapel of our Lady of the Pharos and ten years later was moved to the Komnenian mausoleum at the Pantokrator monastery, and Manuel was buried next to it. After this time, the red stone itself is shown in Byzantine Lamentation scenes, with Christ laying on it. This paper proposes that this significant imperial and religious event, having influenced Byzantine iconography, was incorporated into the paintings in the chapel in Winchester. This leads to the question of who the patron may have been who is associated with this swift movement of iconographic influence. It is proposed that Henry the Lion (Duke of Saxony 1142–80, d. 1195), who visited Constantinople in 1172, is a likely contender.

The 12th-century paintings in a small chapel in Winchester Cathedral, known as the Holy Sepulchre Chapel, between the two northern piers of the crossing, are some of the most significant to survive in England.[1] The paintings on the east wall depict the Deposition, in the upper register, and the Entombment with references to the Lamentation of Christ in the lower register (Figures 8.1 and 8.2 and Colour Plate VIII (top)). These were formerly covered by later paintings said to be from the early 13th century, perhaps 1205–20, which show the same scenes and which are now placed on the west wall of the chapel, having been removed from the east wall in the 1960s.[2] While details of the 12th-century Entombment/Lamentation are disputed, this paper proposes that the scene portrays Christ laid out in death on the Stone of Unction, the *lithos*, a relic held in Constantinople in the late 12th century during the reign of Manuel I (1143–80) and shares some features with Byzantine iconography of the time. It goes further to suggest a western patron for the painting, one who had close connections with Manuel and the east, Henry the Lion (Duke of Saxony 1142–80).

In the upper scene of the Deposition, evidence of Byzantine iconography has been identified. For instance, it has been compared to that in a 10th-century Byzantine ivory diptych panel in Hanover showing the Crucifixion and Deposition (Figure 8.3).[3] The iconography is reversed but very similar.[4]

This discussion, however, focuses on the lower scene, the Entombment cum Lamentation which shows Christ laid out in death with a crowned Virgin Mary at his side kissing his hand. On the left and right, at his head and his feet, Joseph of Arimathea and another man grasp the corners of a cloth as they set down the body, with a further man to the right of the Virgin Mary, presumably Nicodemus, pouring oil from a jug and rubbing Christ's left leg. Between the Virgin and Nicodemus, an angel holds the chains of a censer.[5] Behind is a representation of Jerusalem in the distance.

In a scene to the far left are the Marys (two) coming to the tomb to find the Angel, who is apparently standing on the lid of a marble sarcophagus and pointing down to the sarcophagus with its 'dark empty interior', which appears to be below with the soldiers sleeping in front of it (Figure 8.4 and Colour Plate VIII (bottom)).[6] The sarcophagus extends to the right side, with the end of it shown in a perspectival angle revealing the space within it. The sarcophagus, therefore, appears to belong to the scene of the women at the empty tomb, itself a witness to the resurrection of Christ and not to the Entombment.

To the far right of the sarcophagus is a Harrowing of Hell scene (Figure 8.5). Christ appears dressed in white in three-quarters view, his right hand reaching down to raise the dead. Thus, there is a compression of three scenes in one register: an Entombment cum Lamentation, the Marys at the Tomb, and the Harrowing of Hell.

Comparative examples of the iconography of an angel seated at the empty tomb as the Marys approach can

DOI: 10.4324/9781003162827-8

FIGURE 8.1

Winchester Cathedral, Holy Sepulchre Chapel: Deposition and Lamentation/Entombment, east wall (© Cecily Hennessy)

be seen in two 12th-century English manuscripts, the *St Albans Psalter*, dated 1120–45, and the *Winchester Psalter* from the mid-12th century.[7] A further example is in the *Ingeborg Psalter*, whose origin is disputed, perhaps dated to *c.* 1195–1210, where the angel points to the tomb (Figure 8.6 and Colour Plate X).[8] In all these, there are three Marys, as in the western tradition, based on Mark 16[1]. In Byzantium, in this period, two Marys are normally shown, derived from Matthew 27[61]. Only two are apparent in the wall-painting, but it is impossible to determine if there were ever three. However, what is similar in these three manuscripts and the Winchester wall-paintings is the open and empty sarcophagus and, in the *Ingeborg Psalter*, the angel standing on the lid of the sarcophagus.

To focus on the Entombment cum Lamentation scene, its distinctiveness can be seen by looking at comparative examples from these same manuscripts. In Christ's Entombment in the *St Albans Psalter*, Christ's head is to the right, not the left, with Saint John at his feet (who is not present in this scene in the Winchester wall-painting), and his mother stands at his side embracing him; he is already shrouded and being lowered into the sarcophagus (Figure 8.7).[9] This is related to an earlier scene from Sant' Angelo in Formis, from the last quarter of the 11th century, where again Christ's head is to the right and the Virgin holds his head as he is lowered, fully shrouded; John also appears here, flanked by two older men, Nicodemus and Joseph of Arimathea.[10] In the *Winchester Psalter*, Christ's head is to the left, as in the Holy Sepulchre Chapel, and

FIGURE 8.2

Winchester Cathedral, Holy Sepulchre Chapel: Lamentation/Entombment, lower register east wall (© Cecily Hennessy)

FIGURE 8.3

Crucifixion and Deposition, Kestner-Museum, Hanover, inv. no. WM XXIa, 44b: (© State Capital of Hanover, Museum August Kestner, photographer: Chr. Tepper)

FIGURE 8.4

Winchester Cathedral, Holy Sepulchre Chapel: Marys at the Tomb, lower register east wall (© Cecily Hennessy)

the shrouding is nearly finished: his head and lower body are fully covered, and his feet are being tucked into the foot of the sarcophagus, while only his bare chest is still revealed (Figure 8.8).[11] Thus these three scenes show an Entombment, with Christ completely or nearly shrouded, being lowered into a sarcophagus.

In the *Ingeborg Psalter*, the comparable scene is not an Entombment but a Lamentation cum Anointing on the Stone of Unction (Figure 8.6 and Colour Plate X).[12] Christ's head is again to the left, and his body is partially draped, his torso showing but not his lower legs as in the Holy Sepulchre Painting. The cloth seems to be a burial shroud, not a loincloth, as in the wall-painting. In both, Christ's head is bare, not shrouded. In both, an angel swings a censer above the head of the figure in the centre, the Virgin Mary in the Winchester painting and one of the men in the *Ingeborg Psalter*. It has been suggested that in the original composition in Winchester a male figure, probably Nicodemus, was at Christ's side holding his hand. The Virgin was then substituted for Nicodemus, and the figure's position slightly moved so that her head was placed over the censer.[13] The restorers suggest that these changes appear to have occurred at the time of painting, as the scene is outlined in red and black on the lower plaster layer and the final plaster is applied in sections using fresco technique.[14] In the *Ingeborg Psalter* composition, there are a total of six figures in addition to Christ. The Virgin Mary stands on the far left, not in the forefront of

FIGURE 8.5

Winchester Cathedral, Holy Sepulchre Chapel: Harrowing of Hell, lower register east wall (© Cecily Hennessy)

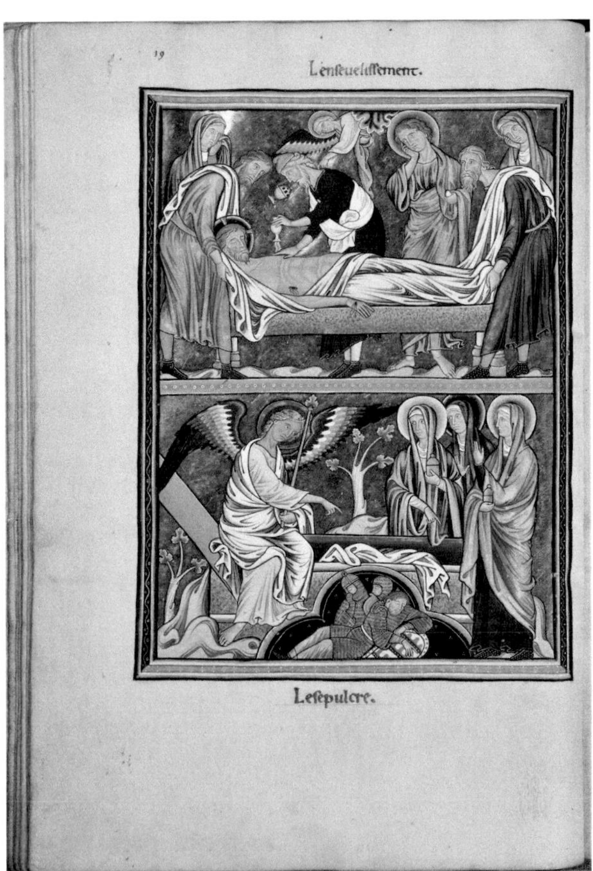

FIGURE 8.6

Lamentation and Anointing, Marys at the Tomb, Ingeborg Psalter, Chantilly, Musée Condé, MS 9, fol. 28v: Cliché CNRS – IRHT (© Bibliothèque du château de Chantilly (musée Condé))

the composition, and another woman, presumably Mary Magdalene, forms a pendant on the far right. John stands at Christ's side, with his hand to his face in a mourning gesture. Of the three older men, one is at Christ's side, anointing his torso, one at his head and one at his feet, holding the cloth and lowering the body. In comparison, in the Holy Sepulchre Chapel Paintings, the Virgin is in an intimate place, kissing Christ's hand. In both scenes, the event is prior to the burial – there is still much work to be done on the body, which is being anointed. In the *Ingeborg Psalter*, the shrouding is commencing with his feet, while in the Winchester wall-painting, the shrouding is yet to begin.

It has been recognised by David Park and by others that elements in the Winchester painting derive from Byzantine traditions, as was not uncommon in late 12th-century painting in parts of Europe, including England.[15] He notes that this scene is influenced not by the Byzantine representation of the Entombment, which does not feature a sarcophagus, but by the representation of the *Threnos* or Lamentation, which in the 11th and 12th centuries evolved from that of the Entombment.[16] This development was first outlined by Gabriel Millet and secondly by Kurt Weitzmann.[17]

Ninth-century Byzantine examples of the Entombment show Christ fully shrouded, being carried by two men into the cave-like tomb, as shown in a luxury 9th-century edition of the Homilies of Gregory of Nazianzus in Paris.[18] Similarly, in the marginal psalters, produced at various points from the ninth century, this same composition is used. Examples are found in both the 11th-century *Bristol Psalter* and *Theodore Psalter*, seemingly based on 9th-century models.[19] In Byzantium, the Entombment is rarely depicted with Christ being laid in a sarcophagus. When it is, the depiction may be making a reference to both the tomb and crib of Christ being an altar, a conceit devised by Germanus, the 8th-century patriarch of Jerusalem.[20] This composition is used in the 11th-century Crypt at Hosios Loukas and in an early 13th-century Gospel Book in Berlin.[21] In both examples, Christ is fully shrouded. Otherwise, the presence of a sarcophagus in the Entombment is a western concept. On occasions it is shown, as in the 11th-century Laurentian codex, one of the so-called *Frieze Gospels*, but in the Resurrection scene when Mary Magdalene discovers the empty tomb (John 20[1–9]) and not in the Entombment.[22]

In Byzantium, the Lamentation and the Entombment are never both shown in sequence, as the Lamentation took the place of the Entombment. As Weitzmann has discussed most clearly, there is a transition in the iconography from a scene where Christ is carried into the tomb, one with movement, to one where he is actually set down

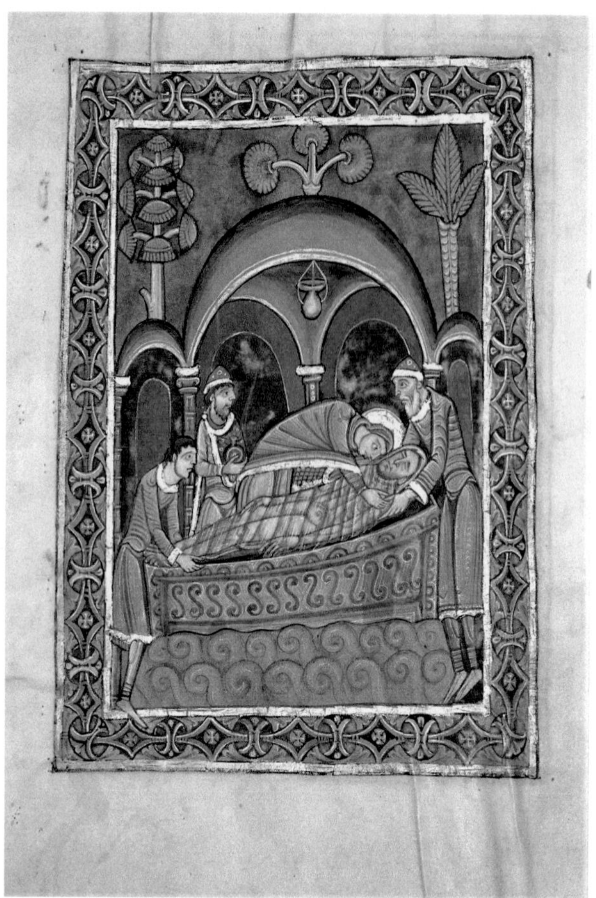

FIGURE 8.7

Entombment, St Albans Psalter, Dombibliothek Hildesheim, MS St Godehard 1, p. 48 (© Dombibliothek Hildesheim, HS St. God. 1 (Property of the Basilica of St Godehard, Hildesheim))

FIGURE 8.8

Entombment, Winchester Psalter, London, British Library, Cotton MS Nero C IV, fol. 23r (© British Library Board)

and lamented over. It is relevant to outline this progression as it highlights aspects of the Winchester wall-painting. Due to the influence of the apocryphal Gospel of Nicodemus, during the 10th and 11th centuries, the Virgin becomes included in the scene, lamenting.[23] Weitzmann therefore sees such works as an early 11th-century ivory panel, now in the Rosgartenmuseum, Konstanz, as an example of one of the first Lamentation scenes.[24] In this scene, Christ is carried towards the door of the tomb. The Virgin is at his head and her right leg looks as though she is both stepping forward and also preparing to kneel. The cloth on which Christ is laid and which is also being carried is raised from the ground. John, in the centre, kisses Christ's hand, and Joseph and Nicodemus carry his feet. Above, angels fly with covered hands. Christ is not shrouded but wears a loincloth. Similarities with the Holy Sepulchre Chapel painting are that Christ is in a loincloth and not shrouded, a figure kisses Christ's hand (here John, not the Virgin) and angels (here two, not one) appear above. This type of scene can also be seen in a late 12th- or early 13th-century manuscript in London (British Library, MS Harley 1810), which is based on earlier models.[25] Again, Christ is not shrouded, John kisses his hand, and the Virgin is present, cradling him in her arms, with the same action, both stepping forward and preparing to kneel. Similarly, a famous example is the Lamentation at Nerezi in the church of St Panteleimon, dated to 1164.[26] Christ's body is still raised from the ground as if being carried forward. The Virgin's leg is beneath Christ's, kneeling, as if perhaps cradling him in her lap while the men at his feet hold him up or perhaps lower him. The Lamentation comes to its full development in an example such as the 11th-century Gospel in the Vatican (MS gr. 1156) (Figure 8.9).[27] In the lower left image on the page, the Virgin kneels as she holds her Son and John kisses the hand of Christ. The body is no longer suspended in the air but rests on the ground.

To compare the Lamentation in this Vatican manuscript with the Holy Sepulchre Chapel wall-paintings, in the Byzantine Lamentation there is no embalming but rather simply a sorrowing over the death. In the Winchester wall-painting, Christ is being embalmed, as in the western tradition represented by the *St Albans Psalter* and the *Winchester Psalter*, though he is not shrouded but has fabric loosely wrapped around in the form of a loincloth, as in the Byzantine examples. However, in the Winchester painting, the Virgin has moved from embracing Christ's head to being at his side and has taken the

FIGURE 8.9

Scenes from Christ's Passion, lower left, Lamentation, Vatican, MS gr. 1156, fol. 194v (© Biblioteca Apostolica Vaticana)

place of John kissing his hand. She is crowned, which is not a feature of Byzantine iconography.

The closest comparison to the Winchester painting is perhaps the Lamentation in the *Ingeborg Psalter*.[28] In this scene, Christ's wound is visible as Joseph anoints his upper body. Christ is laid on a green stone, which is raised on feet at either end, and the legs of John and Joseph can be seen beneath it.[29] No sarcophagus is present. If in the Holy Sepulchre Chapel painting, the empty sarcophagus in the lower part of the composition is connected with the left scene, the Marys at the tomb, as has been suggested here, then it appears that Christ is also laying on a stone, the Stone of Unction, as in the *Ingeborg Psalter*, not being placed into a sarcophagus. The stone is visible as red and green, as though a layered stone. In the *Ingeborg Psalter*, it is just green. In the wall-painting, this stone is clearly not the lid of the sarcophagus, as this, on which the angel stands, lays over it at the far left (Figure 8.4).

The iconography of the Stone of Unction derives from Byzantine art and, as Spatharakis has argued, affected the portrayal of the Lamentation. The Stone of Unction, known as the *lithos*, was brought from Ephesus to Constantinople by Emperor Manuel I in 1169–70. Manuel purportedly carried it on his shoulders from the Boukoleon Harbour to the Chapel of our Lady of the Pharos, which housed the famous relics of the Passion. Some ten years later, it was placed in the Komnenian mausoleum at the Pantokrator monastery, and Manuel was buried next to it.[30] It was described by Niketas Choniates, a contemporary historian, to be red and as long as a human body and as being placed near Manuel's tomb on a pedestal.[31] John Kinnamos, Manuel's imperial secretary, described it as being the stone on which the Virgin had laid Christ and lamented over him.[32]

After this time, the stone is shown in Lamentation scenes, with Christ laying on it. The earliest example cited by Spatharakis is in the refectory of the Monastery of St John, Patmos.[33] This has been dated by some to about 1200 but by others to the second half of the 13th century.[34] The painting is not in good condition, but it is does appear that Christ is laying on a substantial stone. Significantly, instead of the inscription that accompanied the previous Entombment and Lamentation scenes, *'Ο 'Ενταφιασμός* the Burial, the scene is labelled *Ὁ Ἐπιτάφιος θρῆνος*, the Sepulchral Lamentation.[35] Later examples of the Lamentation include a throng of mourners, and often the scene is viewed from above, making the red stone very distinct. Examples are found in the Holy Mother of God Peribleptos church in Ohrid, dated to 1295, and in the exonarthex of the Katholikon at Vatopedi on Mount Athos, dated to

FIGURE 8.10

Oxford, Bodleian Libraries, MS Gr. th. f. 1, fol. 4r (© Bodleian Libraries, University of Oxford)

1312. A further scene from the 14th-century menologion manuscript at Oxford (Bodleian Library, MS Gr. th. f. 1), dated to 1322–40, shows it clearly (Figure 8.10 and Colour Plate IX).[36]

It is therefore apparent that the depiction of the Lamentation in the Holy Sepulchre Chapel shows the Stone of Unction, which became popularised in images at some point after 1169 when the stone arrived in Constantinople. The next question is how did this iconography arrive so quickly in Winchester? This issue may be associated with the artist or artists, with someone in charge of the commission or with the patron. It is perhaps logical to assume the iconography was developed in Constantinople, but indeed it may be the case that the artist or patron had seen or heard of the *lithos* and incorporated it as an innovation into the painting. We have no way of knowing with certitude. No research to date has been able to identify the artist or patron or any of their affiliations. Attempts to associate the artists of the Chapel with those of the *Winchester Bible* have not proved conclusive by any means.[37]

Regarding patronage of the paintings, there has been little discussion to date. One possibility has been tied to the assumption that Henry of Blois, bishop of Winchester, commissioned early stages of the *Winchester Bible* and so may have also have commissioned the wall-paintings.[38] However, Henry died in 1171, too early to be responsible for the Chapel paintings. The paintings have also been connected with the visit to England in 1185 of Heraclius, the Patriarch of Jerusalem, but the more secure evidence suggests that this meeting with Henry II took place in Reading, not Winchester, and that, as Park has argued, it is unlikely that the Chapel was made for this occasion.[39]

In terms of the function of the chapel, there was a growing tradition at this time for creating chapels representing the Holy Sepulchre in Jerusalem, in which the biblical events of Good Friday and Easter Sunday were enacted. As has also been pointed out by Park, there can be little doubt that the Winchester Chapel had this use.[40] We know that such enactments took place as early as 970 at Winchester due to a text recording the burying of the crucifix, the *depositio* used in the mass on Good Friday.[41] The *visitatio* performance of the Marys visiting the tomb took place on Easter Sunday.[42] Furthermore, the location of the chapel in the north aisle is the one used for Holy Sepulchre Chapels in other later medieval cases.[43] As again mentioned by Park, although a few are in France and Italy, most of the surviving examples of Holy Sepulchre Chapels are in Germany as, for instance, in St Cyriacus, Gernrode (Sachsen-Anhalt), dated 1100–30 and at the Externsteine (North Rhine-Westphalia), dated to perhaps 1130.[44] These were both formerly in the medieval Duchy of Saxony.

In terms of celebrated patrons of the arts of the 1180s who had roots in Saxony and extensive ties with England and particularly connections with Winchester, Henry the Lion stands out.[45] Furthermore he had experience of Constantinople and the East. He was Duke of Saxony (1142) and of Bavaria (1156) and married Matilda, the daughter of Henry II of England, in 1168 when she was twelve years old.[46] He twice visited Manuel I in Constantinople in 1172, while travelling to and from the Holy Land, where he spent June and July on a diplomatic pilgrimage. Matilda was then pregnant and remained in Braunschweig.[47] After a somewhat hazardous journey, he arrived outside Constantinople on Good Friday, 14 April 1172.[48] On Easter Sunday, Manuel welcomed him and his entourage, said to number 500 knights at the outset, in the hippodrome, in a reception normally used for kings. They then went from St Sophia along a purple-carpeted path with a brocaded canopy and gold lamps to a tent and then back to the church to hear mass while Henry sat on a throne below the emperor's.[49] Henry therefore celebrated Easter with Manuel, just two years after Manuel had secured the Stone of Unction.[50] At this time, as mentioned, the Stone was in the Chapel of the Pharos, with other relics of the Passion, and seeing these must have been especially potent at Easter.

Henry was given many gifts by Manuel and his wife Maria and left on a ship given by the emperor. On arriving in the Holy Land, he was feted by Amalric I, the Latin King of Jerusalem. Lavish gifts made by Henry include donating a large sum of money and three ever burning lamps to the Church of the Holy Sepulchre, paid for by the revenue from two houses.[51] He had the Holy Cross Chapel decorated with mosaics and its gates silver plated.[52] He also gave expensive presents to the Templars and Hospitallers, including 1000 silver coins to buy land to pay troops wages. He bought many valuable relics to take back with him.[53]

Visiting Manuel again on his return journey, he met him near Constantinople and spent several days together. He refused a gift of fourteen mules carrying treasures but accepted many holy relics along with precious stones.[54] It has been suggested by Regine Marth that Henry may have been the owner of the ivory diptych, now split between Dresden and Hanover (Figure 8.3), which has similar iconography to that in the Winchester paintings, and it could have been at this time that they came into his possession.[55]

Some ten years later, in 1182, Henry the Lion was exiled for three years by Frederick Barbarossa for failing to offer him support. Henry spent his time initially in Normandy with Henry II, went on a pilgrimage to Santiago in the autumn, celebrated Christmas at Caen in 1182 and stayed there in 1183.[56] In June 1184, Matilda went to England, and she gave birth to William, her youngest son, in Winchester in July or August.[57] William is known as William of Winchester and is the ancestor of all subsequent Welfs. Henry arrived in Winchester on 25 July. The exchequer records indicate that Henry II supported Henry the Lion during this period.[58] By October 1184, the emperor had pardoned Henry the Lion, but he stayed in England for the winter and only in the spring headed for Normandy and on to Braunschweig by Autumn.[59] William, still a baby, stayed in England, and his grandfather Henry II paid his expenses.[60] Matilda's daughter, likewise named Matilda, also stayed with her grandparents.

Henry again returned to England later, in 1189, the year following the fall of Jerusalem to Sultan Saladin. Frederick of Barbarossa, before joining the subsequent crusade, had received assurances from Henry that he would vacate his territories for three years. In early April 1189, at Easter, Henry left to join his sons Otto and William in England. Matilda stayed in Braunschweig and died that year on 24 June. When Henry arrived in England, he found Henry II was in Normandy, so he went there to meet him, and in July of that year Henry II died. Henry the Lion returned to England in August with the new king, Richard I, though he did not stay for long as he returned to Saxony to safeguard his rights.[61]

It is suggested, therefore, that Henry the Lion, in one of these two periods, either in 1184–85 (probably the more likely) or in 1189, was involved in the building and decorating of the Holy Sepulchre Chapel, perhaps to commemorate the birth of a son, or as a response to the loss of Jerusalem, or simply as a religious investment. Arguments for this are (1) that Henry was an ardent patron of the arts, (2) that there was a strong tradition of such chapels in northern Germany, (3) that Henry would have had a knowledge of the *lithos* and of Byzantine iconography acquired in Constantinople, and (4) the reference to the Stone of Unction can be accounted for in that Manuel I had so recently acquired it when Henry visited the Byzantine capital at Easter 1172.

A further argument to support this theory is Henry's use of Byzantine iconography in works he commissioned. Of these, a significant example is the luxury *Gospel Book of Henry the Lion*, which has been dated to the early 1170s, shortly after Henry's return from the east, but the date is more generally accepted as 1185–88.[62] For instance,

FIGURE 8.11

Wolfenbüttel, Herzog August Bibliothek, MS Guelf. 105 Noviss. 2°, fol. 171v (© Herzog August Bibliothek Wolfenbüttel: 171v)

in the dedication leaf showing the Virgin and Child in a mandorla, she is named in the upper border as 'theotocos', her Greek name meaning 'Mother of God'.[63] In the illumination in which Henry and Matilda are crowned by Christ, various features show adaption of Byzantine customs, such as the crowning itself and the holding of crosses (Figure 8.11).[64]

The relationship between the paintings of the Chapel and those in the *Winchester Bible* and at Sigena have often been discussed.[65] Whether or not one considers that the artists working on the *Bible* and the wall-paintings are the same artists, the stylistic overlaps suggest that the Chapel artist(s) were at least aware of the painting in the *Bible*. Christopher Norton's recent argument that the *Bible* left Winchester between 1184 and 1186 fits well with the dating of the Chapel paintings in the 1180s.[66] Similarly, Neil Stratford's position that the paintings at Sigena probably date to post-1188, would fit with this 1180s dating for the Chapel paintings.[67]

The political and religious magnificence of the Byzantine court was exemplified in the imagery that surrounded it. It is often said that Byzantine influence was filtered to England via the Norman kingdom of Sicily.[68] David Park, among others, has discussed this in relation to the Winchester wall-paintings, but the arguments presented here suggest that the influence comes more directly from Byzantium.[69] There are plenty of connections directly with the east if not specifically with artists, of whom there must have been some, but with patrons, who travelled widely, and with portable objects such as enamels, ivories, reliquaries, and manuscripts which were carried from court to court and from monastery to monastery. Henry the Lion is an excellent example of someone, who with ample finances to invest in buildings, in paintings, manuscripts, and *objets d'art*, assisted in the transmission of culturally specific iconography and style and may have been responsible for the use of cutting-edge iconography in the paintings in the Holy Sepulchre Chapel.

To conclude, this study suggests that the regional iconography and style of Byzantine art, already very present in the Romanesque west from the 11th century, had a very specific implementation in Winchester. If these arguments are correct, the lower register of the Holy Sepulchre Chapel paintings depict Christ laid out for embalming on the Stone of Unction, lately taken from Ephesus by Manuel I, housed in the imperial palace for ten years and then placed next to the emperor's own burial in the most prestigious of the Komnenian foundations in Constantinople. Either through knowledge of its depiction in scenes of the Lamentation or simply through sightings of it in Constantinople, it surfaces in representations of these paintings marking the events of Holy Week in Winchester. This, then, is an example of very swift transregional influence. It has been suggested that this knowledge of Byzantine relics and decorative programmes could have been carried to Winchester by Henry the Lion. Whether by him or by some other means, the choice of iconography reflects the great esteem held for the relics of Byzantium, especially those connected with the Passion, the significance of the emperor of the east, and the cultural initiatives associated with him.

ACKNOWLEDGEMENTS

I would like to thank in particular John McNeill and Richard Plant for inviting me to speak at the conference, Richard Plant for encouraging me to pursue this research and for bibliographic assistance, Sandy Heslop for conversations and suggestions for future developments, Andrew Budge for supplying articles, and Ivan Drpić for sending me his article prior to publication. I am also indebted to the late Ruth Macrides for alerting me to unpublished work and for her kindness.

NOTES

1 The paintings were restored in 1963 by E. Baker; see E. Baker, 'Wallpaintings in the Holy Sepulchre Chapel', *Winchester Cathedral Record*, 33 (1964), 10–12; E. Baker, 'The Holy Sepulchre Chapel, Winchester Cathedral', *Winchester Cathedral Record*, 34 (1965), 17–20; E. Baker, 'The Holy Sepulchre Chapel, Winchester Cathedral', *Winchester Cathedral Record*, 39 (1970), 29–31; E. Baker and R. Baker, 'Paintings in the Chapel of the Holy Sepulchre', *Winchester Cathedral Record*, 36 (1967), 21–5; see also W. Oakeshott, 'The Paintings of the Holy Sepulchre Chapel', *Winchester Cathedral Record*, 50 (1981), 10–14; the key published study is D. Park, 'The Wall Paintings of the Holy Sepulchre Chapel', in *Medieval Art and Architecture at Winchester Cathedral*, *BAA Trans*., 6, eds. T. A. Heslop and V. Sekules (Leeds 1983),

38–62, Figures III-XVI; significant works are M. Lee, 'Paintings in the Holy Sepulchre Chapel, Winchester' (unpublished MA thesis, University of London, 1975); K. Flynn, 'English Romanesque Wall Paintings' (unpublished MLitt thesis, University of Birmingham, 1980), esp. 139–206.

[2] See Park, 'Wall Paintings' (as n. 1), 38.

[3] Kestner-Museum, Hanover, Inv. No. WM XXIa, 44b; for recent discussion, see entry by R. Marth, *Heinrich Der Löwe und Seine Zeit: Herrschaft und Repräsentation Der Welfen 1125–1235: Katalog Der Ausstellung, Braunschweig 1995,* eds. J. Luckhardt and F. Niehoff (München 1995), D66, 254–56; A. Goldschmidt and K. Weitzmann, *Die Byzantinischen Elfenbeinskulpturen Des X. – Xiii. Jahrhunderts* (Berlin 1979), no. 40, 37, pl. 17; the pair to this panel is in Dresden and shows Christ appearing to the Marys and the Harrowing of Hell: Staatliche Kunstsammlungen, Grünes Gewölbe, Dresden; see Ibid., no. 41, 37, pl. 17.

[4] As pointed out by Lee, 'Paintings' (as n. 1), 10–11; and later by Park, 'Wall Paintings' (as n. 1), 44.

[5] Ibid.

[6] Quote in Oakeshott, 'Paintings' (as n. 1), 12; Flynn also suggested that the sarcophagus was empty, see Flynn, 'English Romanesque' (as n. 1), 188. Park did not agree; see Park, 'Wall Paintings' (as n. 1), 50–51, n. 110.

[7] For the *St Albans Psalter*, Hildesheim, Dombibliothek, MS St Godehard 1, p. 50, see O. Pächt, C. R. Dodwell and F. Wormald, *The St. Albans Psalter (Albani Psalter)* (London 1960), 93–94, pl. 31a; J. Geddes, *The St Albans Psalter: A Book for Christina of Markyate* (London 2005), fig. 41; for the *Winchester Psalter*, London, British Library, Cotton MS Nero C IV, fol. 23r, see F. Wormald, *The Winchester Psalter* (London 1973), 24–25, pl. 26. The manuscript has been digitized: www.abdn.ac.uk/stalbanspsalter/.

[8] For the *Ingeborg Psalter*, Chantilly, Musée Condé, MS 9, fol. 28v, see F. Deuchler, *Der Ingeborgpsalter* (Berlin 1967), 57–58, fig. 32; on the manuscript also see F. Deuchler, 'The Artists of the Ingeborg Psalter', *Gesta*, 9 (1970), 57–58; L. M. Ayres, 'The Work of the Morgan Master at Winchester and English Painting of the Early Gothic Period', *The Art Bulletin*, 56 (1974), 220, fn. 76, with references to reviews of Deuchler, *Der Ingeborgpsalter*, esp. M. Schapiro, *Cahiers de civilization médiévale*, 15 (1972), 153.

[9] For the *St Albans Psalter*, p. 48, see Pächt, Dodwell and Wormald, *St. Albans* (as n. 7), 62, 71–73, 93, pls 30a, 112b; Geddes, *St Albans Psalter* (as n. 7), fig. 39; also K. Collins and M. Fisher, eds., *St. Albans and the Markyate Psalter: Seeing and Reading in Twelfth-Century England. Studies in Iconography: Themes and Variations* (Kalamazoo 2017), fig. 7.

[10] O. Demus, *Romanesque Mural Painting*, trans. Mary Whitall (London 1970), 294–98, pl. 36.

[11] *Winchester Psalter*, BL, Cotton MS Nero C IV, fol. 23r; see Wormald, *Winchester* (as n. 7), 24, pl. 26.

[12] *Ingeborg Psalter*, Musée Condé, MS 9, fol. 28v; see Deuchler, *Ingeborgpsalter* (as n. 8), 55–57, fig. 32.

[13] Park, 'Wall Paintings' (as n. 1), 44.

[14] Baker and Baker, 'Paintings' (as n. 1), 25.

[15] Park, 'Wall Paintings' (as n. 1), 43.

[16] Ibid., 45.

[17] G. Millet, *Recherches sur L'iconographie de l'évangile* (Paris 1960), 489–516; K. Weitzmann, 'The Origin of the Threnos', in *De Artibus Opuscula XL: Essays in Honor of Erwin Panofsky*, ed. M. Meiss (New York 1961), 161–68; reprinted in K. Weitzmann, *Byzantine Book Illumination and Ivories* (London 1980), study no. IX.

[18] Paris, Bibliothèque nationale, MS gr. 510, fol. 30v; see L. Brubaker, *Vision and Meaning in Ninth-Century Byzantium: Image as Exegesis in the Homilies of Gregory of Nazianzus* (Cambridge 1999), 291–302, fig. 7.

[19] *Bristol Psalte*r, London, British Library, Add. MS. 40731, fol. 145r; S. Dufrenne, *L'illustration des psautiers grecs du moyen age, Pantokrator 61, Paris grec 20, British Museum 40731* (Paris 1966), 62–63, pl. 56; on the *Theodore Psalter*, London, British Library, Add. MS. 19352, fol. 116, S. der Nersessian, *L'illustration des psautiers grecs du moyen age, vol. 2. Londres, Add. 19.352* (Paris 1970), 45, pl. 70; Weitzmann, 'Threnos' (as n. 17), 481, fig. 6; Weitzmann argues that this is when first the Virgin's grief over the dead Christ is depicted.

[20] Germanus, *Patrologia Graecus*, 38, col. 253, in H. Maguire, 'The Depiction of Sorrow in Middle Byzantine Art', *Dumbarton Oaks Papers* 31 (1977), 123–74, at 139 and fn. 86: 'the altar is, and is called, the crib and tomb of the Lord'.

[21] For Hosios Loukas, see C. Connor, *Art and Miracles in* Medieval *Byzantium: The Crypt at Hosios Loukas and Its Frescoes* (Princeton 1991), 37–39, pl. 10; Berlin, Staatsbibliothek, MS gr. qu. 66, fol. 96r; also see B. Pitarakis, 'New Evidence on Lead Flasks and Devotional Patterns: From Crusader Jerusalem to Byzantium', in *Byzantine Religious Culture: Studies in Honor of Alice-Mary Talbot*, eds. E. Fisher, D Sullivan, and S. Papaioannou (Leiden 2012), 239–66, at 246.

[22] Florence, Laurenziana, Plut 6.23, fol. 209v; see T. Velmans, *Le Tétraévangile de la Laurentienne, Florence, Laur. VI. 23* (Paris 1971), 51, pl. 64 (John 20[1–9]).

[23] Her Lament occurs in the later recension, see B. C. Tischendorf, *Evangelia Apocrypha*, 2nd ed. (Leipzig 1876), 313; in Weitzmann, 'Threnos' (as n. 17), 486.

[24] Ibid., fig. 10; Goldschmidt and Weitzmann, *Byzantinischen* (as n. 3), no. 208, 75 pl. 68.

[25] London, British Library, MS Harley 1810, fol. 205v, based on a 10th-century model; Weitzmann, dates it to the 13th century, see Weitzmann, 'Threnos' (as n. 17), 484, fig. 11; on the manuscript, see *Byzantium: Treasures of Byzantine Art and Culture from British Collections*, ed. David Buckton (London: 1994), no. 194.

[26] I. Sinković, *The Church of St. Panteleimon at Nerezi: Architecture, Programme, Patronage* (Wiesbaden 2000), 1, 50–53, Figures X, XLVI, XLVIII, 47, 49.

[27] Vatican, MS gr. 1156, fol. 194v, dated to the third quarter of the 11th century; I. Spatharakis, 'The Influence of the Lithos in the Development of the Iconography of the Threnos', in *Byzantine East, Latin West: Art-Historical Studies in Honor of Kurt Weitzmann*, eds. D. Mouriki, C. F. Moss, and K. Kiefer (Princeton 1995), 435–41, Figures. 1–12, 436, fig. 4; also mentioned by Weitzmann, 'Threnos' (as n. 17), 486–87, fig. 16.

[28] Musée Condé, MS 9, fol. 28v, Deuchler, *Ingeborgpsalter* (as n. 8), 55–57, fig. 32.

[29] Deuchler associates this with the Stone of Unction in Constantinople, see ibid., 56, with references to related material.

[30] John Kinnamos, *Epitome rerum ab Ioanne et Alexio Comnenis gestarum*, ed. A. Meineke (Bonn 1836), 277.7–278.5; *Deeds of John and Manuel Comnenus by John Kinnamos*, trans., C. M. Brand (New York 1976), 207–08; Niketas Choniates, *Historia*, ed. J.-L. van Dieten (Berlin 1975), 222.76–86; *O City of Byzantium, annals of Niketas Choniates*, trans. H. J. Magoulias (Detroit 1984), 125; Spatharakis, 'Lithos' (as n. 27), 437–38; for recent work on the Stone of Unction, see I. Drpić, 'Manuel I Komnenos and the Stone of Unction', *Byzantine and Modern Greek Studies*, 43 (2019), 60–82; also M. A. Graeve, 'The Stone of Unction in Caravaggio's Painting for the Chiesa Nuova', *The Art Bulletin*, 40 (1958), 223–38, esp. 228.

[31] Choniates, *Historia*, 222 (as n. 30); *O City* (as n. 30), 125.

[32] Kinnamos, *Epitome rerum*, 277–78 (as n. 30); *Deeds* (as n. 30), 207.

[33] Spatharakis, 'Lithos' (as n. 27), fig. 6.

[34] A. K. Orlandos, Ἡ ἀρχιτεκτονικὴ καὶ αἱ βυζαντιναὶ τοιχουραφία τῆς Μονῆς τοῦ Θεολόγοι Πάτμου, Proceedings of the Academy of Athens 28 (Athens 1970), pl. 94; on the 13th-century date (trans. French), see 386–87; E. Kollias, 'Wall Paintings', in *Patmos, Treasures of the Monastery*, ed. A. D. Kominis, trans. D. A. Hardy (Athens 1988), 64, 65–66, fig. 37, who dates the layer to the last quarter of the 13th century.

[35] Spatharakis, 'Lithos' (as n. 27), 438.

[36] Oxford, Bodleian Library, MS Gr. th. f. 1, fol. 4r; see I. Hutter, *Corpus der byzantinischen Miniaturenhandschriften: Oxford Bodleian Library* (Stuttgart 1978), vol. 2, no. 1, 1–2, fig. 6.

[37] On this, see C. Norton, 'Henry of Blois, St Hugh and Henry II: The Winchester Bible Reconsidered', in *Romanesque Patrons and Processes: Design and Instrumentality in the Art and Architecture of Romanesque Europe*, eds. J. Camps, M. Castiñeiras, J. McNeill, and R. Plant (London 2018), 130; Oakeshott, 'Paintings' (as n. 1), 14; Oakeshott considered at this time that both the 12th and 13th century

paintings in the chapel were by the Morgan Master; Ayres 'Morgan Master' (as n. 8), 210, Figures 18–19, 212–13, 220.

[38] W. Oakeshott, *The Two Winchester Bibles* (Oxford 1981), 8 and n. 3; Norton, 'Henry' (as n. 37), 119, n. 7; on Henry of Blois as patron of the wall-paintings, see Baker, 'Holy Sepulchre' (1970) (as n. 1), 31.

[39] Ayres, 'Morgan Master' (as n. 8), 213; Ayres gives the dates 1180–86 for the Holy Sepulchre Chapel paintings, so fitting with this supposed visit; Park, 'Wall Paintings' (as n. 1), 51.

[40] Ibid., 50.

[41] The *Regularis Concordia*, drawn up at Winchester in 970, indicates that at that time the crucifix used in the Good Friday Mass was buried; see T. Symons, ed., *Regularis Concordia* (London 1953), 44; for references to such ceremonies at Winchester and elsewhere, see Park, 'Wall Paintings' (as n. 1), fn. 102; also T. A. Heslop, 'A Walrus Ivory Pyx and the Visitatio Sepulchri', *Journal of the Warburg and Courtauld Institutes*, 44 (1981), 157–60; J. E. A. Kroesen, trans. M. Kofod, *The Sepulchrum Domini Through The Ages: Its Form and Function* (Leuven 2000), 153–56.

[42] On liturgical drama, see S. Rickerby and D. Park, 'A Romanesque "Visitatio Sepulchri" at Kempley', *The Burlington Magazine*, 133 (1991), 27–31, at 28 and fns 6–8, with further references.

[43] See Park, 'Wall Paintings' (as n. 1), 50 and n. 106.

[44] On dating see ibid., 50; on Gernrode, see R. Budde, *Deutsche romanische Skulptur, 1050–1250* (München 1979), 36–38, pls 44–50; Kroesen, *sepulchrum domini* (as n. 41), 47–8, fig. 31; for the Externsteine, see Budde, *Deutsche*, 30–31, pl. 29; Kroesen, *sepulchrum domini*, 29, fig. 16.

[45] On Henry the Lion's patronage, see F. Niehoff, 'Heinrich der Löwe – Herrschaft und Repräsentation: vom individuellen Kunstkreis zum interdisziplinären Braunschweiger Hof der Welfen', in *Heinrich der Löwe* (as n. 3), vol. 2, 213–36.

[46] K. Jordan, *Henry the Lion: A Biography*, trans. P. A. Falla (Oxford 1986), 96; they were betrothed in 1165 when Matilda was aged eight or nine, see ibid., 144; also see C. Bowie, *The Daughters of Henry II and Eleanor of Aquitaine* (Turnhout 2014), 38–39, 69–70, with a date of 1167 for the marriage.

[47] Jordan, *Henry* (as n. 46), 150.

[48] Arnold of Lübeck, *Chronica Slavorum*, Monumenta Germaniae Historica, Scriptores rerum Germanicarum in usum scholarum, ed. M. Lappenberg (1868), bk. I, chap. 3, 18.

[49] On this, see E. Joranson, 'The Palestine Pilgrimage of Henry the Lion', in *Medieval and Historiographical Essays in Honor of James Westfall Thomson*, eds. J. L. Cate and E. N. Anderson (Chicago 1938), 146–225, at 183–85.

[50] Jordan, *Henry* (as n. 46), 152.

[51] For text, see Appendix, 'The Jerusalem Diploma of Henry the Lion', in Joranson, 'Palestine Pilgrimage' (as n. 49), 220–22.

[52] Ibid., 191; Arnold, *Chronica Slavorum* (as n. 48), bk. I, chap. 7, 21–22.

[53] Jordan, *Henry* (as n. 46), 151–53 with further references, 245; A. L. Poole, *Henry, the Lion: The Lothian Historical Essay for 1912* (London 1912), 56–57; for detailed analysis, see Joranson, 'Palestine Pilgrimage' (as n. 49).

[54] Jordan, *Henry* (as n. 46), 152–53; Joranson, 'Palestine Pilgrimage' (as n. 49), 203–05; also see H. A. Klein, 'Eastern Objects and Western Desires: Relics and Reliquaries Between Byzantium and the West', *Dumbarton Oaks Papers*, 58 (2004), 283–314, at 285.

[55] *Heinrich der Löwe* (as n. 3), vol. 1, 256.

[56] Jordan, *Henry* (as n. 46), 183; Poole (as n. 53), 89; Benedict of Peterborough, *Gesta Regis Henrici II*, ed. W. Stubbs (Rolls Series, XLIX, 1867), vol. 1, 288.

[57] Jordan, *Henry* (as n. 46), 184; Poole, *Henry* (as n. 53), 89.

[58] Ibid., 90; Jordan, *Henry* (as n. 46), 183; *The Great Roll of the Pipe for the Thirty-First Year of the Reign of King Henry II, A. D. 1184–1185* (London 1913), 206, 215, 218; R. W. Eyton, *Court, Household and Itinerary of Henry II* (London 1878), 256–57.

[59] Jordan, *Henry* (as n. 46), 185.

[60] For instance, *Pipe Roll 1184–1185* (as n. 58), 206, 218.

[61] Jordan, *Henry* (as n. 46), 188–89; Poole, *Henry* (as n. 53), 93–94; Arnold, *Chronica Slavorum* (as n. 48), bk. IV. chap. 7, 128.

[62] Wolfenbüttel, Herzog August Bibliothek, MS Guelf. 105 Noviss. 2°; *Heinrich der Löwe* (as n. 3), cat. No. D31, 206–10; for the later date, see R. Haussherr 'Zur Datierung des Helmarshausener Evangeliars Heinrichs des Löwen', *Zeitschrift des deutschen Vereins für Kunstwissenschaft*, 34 (1980), 3–15.

[63] Herzog Aug. Bib., MS Guelf. 105 Noviss. 2°, fol. 19r, *Heinrich der Löwe* (as n. 3), fig. 207; *The Gospels of Henry the Lion*, Sotheby's Catalogue (London 1983), 29.

[64] Herzog Aug. Bib., MS Guelf. 105 Noviss. 2°, fol. 171v; Sotheby's Catalogue (as n. 63), 68; discussed in O. B. Rader, 'Kreuze und Kronen: zum byzantinischen Einfluss im "Krönungsbild" des Evangeliars Heinrichs des Löwen', in *Heinrich der Löwe: Herrschaft und Repräsentation*, eds. J. Fried and O. G. Oexle (Stuttgart 2003), 199–238, on the crosses, 205–17, on the crowning, 217–33; J. Shepard, '"Constantinople Imaginaire" in Northern and Western Eyes: The Uses of Imperial Imagery to Twelfth-Century Outsiders', *Travaux et mémoires* (22) *Constantinople réelle et imaginaire autour de l'œuvre de Gilbert Dagron* 773–94, at 790–92.

[65] O. Demus first made parallels between the Morgan Master's work in the *Bible* and the wall-paintings, see O. Demus, *Romanesque Mural Painting*, 124–25, 509–11, colour pl. opp. 127; Ayres, 'Morgan Master' (as n. 8), 213; also see Oakeshott, 'Paintings' (as n. 1), with a theory that the Morgan Master as a young man painted the 12th-century paintings and later, after painting at Sigena, completed the 13th-century ones, 12–14; in the earlier W. Oakeshott, *Sigena: Romanesque Paintings in Spain & the Winchester Bible Artists* (London 1972), he states that, though similar, the wall-painting is not by any hand involved in the *Winchester Bible*, nor at Sigena, see 135.

[66] Norton, 'Henry' (as n. 37), 117–41, 123–25, 130, on the date of the wall-paintings, 130.

[67] N. Stratford, 'The Hospital, England and Sigena: A Footnote', in *Romanesque Patrons and Processes* (as n. 37), 109–16, at 114 and n. 13.

[68] As for instance, in O. Demus, *The Mosaics of Norman Sicily* (London 1949), 443–54, esp. 449–50; Park, 'Wall Paintings' (as n. 1), 43, 45; on the Morgan Master, see Ayres, 'Morgan Master' (as n. 8), 215, 220, on Sigena, see Oakeshott, *Sigena* (as n. 65), 82, 84, 107–13; O. Pächt, 'A Cycle of English Frescoes in Spain', *The Burlington Magazine*, 103 (1961), 162–75, esp. 172, 175.

[69] On this, see H. Klein, 'The so-called Byzantine Diptych in the Winchester Psalter, British Library, MS Cotton Nero C. IV', *Gesta*, 37 (1998), 26–43, at 35.

The Regional and Transregional in Romanesque Europe (2021), 103–118

TRANSREGIONAL DYNAMICS, MONASTIC NETWORKS

SANTA FEDE IN CAVAGNOLO, CONQUES, AND THE GEOGRAPHY OF ROMANESQUE ART

Michele Luigi Vescovi

The following article addresses the critical issues of the 'regional' and 'transregional' in Romanesque art and architecture in relation to monastic networks and does so through analysis of the church of Santa Fede in Cavagnolo (Piedmont) – a church likely to have been built in the first half of the 12th century as a priory of Sainte-Foy in Conques. By interrogating the institutional connection between the mother abbey (Conques) and its foundations across Europe, it explores the extent to which monastic networks, through the establishment of an institutional geography and the mobility of artefacts, masons, and models, provide an alternative paradigm to approach the question of transregional style in Romanesque art and architecture.

Geography has always played a critical role in the study of medieval, and in particular Romanesque art and architecture. Already in the first half of the 19th century, in an effort to classify Romanesque art according to the appearance and decoration of buildings, Arcisse de Caumont suggested the existence of '*régions monumentales*', based on the ancient provincial geography of France. He thus distinguished between different regional schools, the 'écoles' of Normandy, Brittany, Poitou, Burgundy, among others.[1] By the beginning of the 20th century, Arthur Kingsley Porter in *Romanesque Sculpture of the Pilgrimage Roads* suggested a new, revolutionary geographical model. As Porter explained, his work built on the theoretical framework provided by Joseph Bédier in relation to the formation of the *chansons de geste*: 'on the road to St James, M. Bédier has found the key which unlocks mediaeval literature'.[2] Rather than seeing Romanesque art as the product of different regions or nations, Porter explored the extent to which the pilgrimage roads to Santiago de Compostela provided a transregional platform for the creation and transmission of Romanesque sculpture.[3]

While some of these issues were subsequently redefined or abandoned, the current debate on Romanesque art constantly oscillates between different geographical models, ranging from the study of regional areas to the analysis of transregional, transnational or even global connections. Rather than falling to the wayside, consideration of the geography of art and of how geography might be understood in relation to the creation of art and architecture is still at the core of scholarly discussions. For example, in his provocative *Contre l'art roman?*, Xavier Barral i Altet argued against the idea of the circulation of artists, suggesting that 'Romanesque art appears to be an art closely related to the political system of the period, consisting essentially of territorial principalities, geographically limited and, politically, extremely divided'.[4] Romanesque art, he suggests, 'seems to correspond more to the local division [of political power] rather than to an art of distant exchange'. According to Barral i Altet, it is difficult to locate stylistic similarities beyond a local and regional level. Furthermore, he argues that the mobility of artists is an extremely restricted phenomenon and that the 'propagation of styles' is limited to defined geographical perimeters.[5]

From a different perspective, Eric Fernie also emphasises the importance of the geography of Romanesque architecture, suggesting that attention should be paid not only to political units, such as principalities and duchies, but also to 'the structures of government of the Church, in the form of its dioceses and especially archdioceses as well as its monastic orders'.[6] This statement calls attention to two intertwined issues. Fernie invites us to consider not only the political fragmentation of the period but also the administrative geography of the Church, one that was defined by dioceses and monastic orders. These two categories are distinct, as a diocese was as an essentially geographical entity with territorial boundaries, while a monastic 'order' offers a completely different type of geographical model, one potentially unconstrained by physical borders.

In the discussion of the geography of 'monastic orders' and its implications on the arts, the case of Cluny is extremely important. William III, duke of Aquitaine and count of Mâcon, founded an abbey at Cluny in 910, renouncing rights over the establishment, placing the

  DOI: 10.4324/9781003162827-9

abbey under papal protection and conceding to the monastic community the power to elect its abbot. In the following decades, Cluny was granted the privilege to take over and reform other monasteries at the request of their respective lay abbots (931). Subsequently, it was granted a privilege of exemption from ordinary diocesan jurisdiction by Pope Gregory V (998), a privilege which was later extended to all Cluniacs (1024).[7] Dominique Iogna-Prat emphasised that this privilege 'marked the real birth of the *Ecclesia Cluniacensis* [the Cluniac Church] as an ecclesiastical network of abbeys and priories', having at its centre the abbey of Cluny itself.[8]

In terms of geography, Cluny provides a model that goes beyond a binary definition of regional or transregional, even in relation to the structures of government of the Church discussed by Fernie. While a diocese can be defined geographically as confined to a particular locale, enclosed within borders (even though these might be flexible and mutable across time), Cluny offers a completely different structure, consisting of a network of abbeys and priories that transcends territorial entities. However, the Cluniac monastic network only rarely implied a clear artistic network. Although in 1938, Joan Evans suggested that the churches of the order shared 'certain ground plans' and that in these buildings we find 'a type of architecture commonly associated with Burgundy'.[9] More recently, Paolo Piva, in his exemplary analysis of Cluniac abbeys and priories in Lombardy, has argued that there were no precise Cluniac connotations imposed on the language of local workshops. Instead, Piva points out that the architectural solutions common in the majority of these buildings, such as a nave with three or four bays, crossing tower, and choir with communicating aisles, most likely relate to functional and structural concerns.[10]

This article addresses the critical issues of the 'regional' and 'transregional' in relation to 'monastic orders' or, rather, monastic networks. I would suggest adopting the term 'network' rather than 'order'. 'Order', according to the most recent debate on monasticism, refers to the legal-corporatist constitutional and organizational forms often adopted by new 'orders' (such as the Cistercians) or old congregations (such as Cluny, which only reshaped itself into an order in 1200).[11] The concept of 'network' instead takes into account the different range of potential connections between abbeys, their priories, and other churches associated with them.[12] I will focus my discussion of these issues by considering the church of Santa Fede in Cavagnolo (Piedmont) – likely built in the first half of the 12th century – which, I will argue, was a dependency of Sainte-Foy in Conques. By interrogating the institutional connection between the mother abbey (Conques) and its foundations across Europe, I explore the extent to which monastic networks, through the dynamics of foundations and the mobility of artefacts, masons and models, established what might be termed an institutional geography which provides an alternative model for how the question of transregional style in Romanesque art and architecture is approached.

SANTA FEDE, CAVAGNOLO

Santa Fede in Cavagnolo Po lies roughly 30 km northeast of Turin, in the modern region of Piedmont. The church, in the ancient diocese of Vercelli, provides a critical paradigm in relation to regional and transregional dynamics, as it has been alternatively read and understood either in its own local 'Lombard' context or in relation to Romanesque architecture in France. From the 19th century on, scholars such as Edoardo Arborio Mella, Fernand De Dartein, Adolfo Venturi, and Pietro Toesca have pointed to architectural elements in the church, such as the nave barrel vault, shaft rings, and billet mouldings over the arcades, that are alien to Lombard art and architecture.[13] More specifically, De Dartein posited that these features, '*caractères exotiques*' as he described them, were 'imported' from France.[14] In the following decades the presence of these 'exotic elements' was justified on the notion that Santa Fede in Cavagnolo was a priory of the abbey of Sainte-Foy in Conques. However, this connection was not developed any further.[15] Indeed, at the same time that some scholars were looking to France, others suggested that the church should be understood in its own 'local', Lombard context. Porter, for example, compared the portal of Santa Fede with the portal of San Pietro in Ciel d'Oro at Pavia and the style of the carvings with that of San Giorgio al Palazzo in Milan.[16] Along similar lines, many scholars were either unaware of or dismissed the reference to Cavagnolo's dependency of Conques, explaining the solutions adopted in Santa Fede as the result of 'regional' and local 'schools'.[17]

In the context of the present study, the relationship between Cavagnolo and Conques, often overlooked in discussions on the church, is extremely significant, as it inserts the site into larger debates on the regional and transregional, providing insight into the institutional nature of Santa Fede and the dynamics of monastic networks. Thus this connection should be carefully considered, starting with analysis of the dedication to Saint Faith, before addressing the complex constructional history of the building.

The dedication to St Faith (Santa Fede, Sainte Foy), the 4th-century martyr of Agen whose mortal remains were translated to Conques in the 9th century, was not common in the Italian peninsula during the Middle Ages.[18] Analysis of the *rationes decimarum*, the published volumes listing the tithes paid in Italian dioceses mainly in the 13th and the 14th centuries, reveals that, in addition to Cavagnolo, the dedication is otherwise restricted to Piacenza, Genoa, and Maddaloni (near Caserta).[19] It is worth noting that the tithe lists do not always offer the opportunity to develop a complete and satisfactory analysis of dedications. Foundations might have disappeared by the time these *rationes* were compiled. Furthermore, churches are occasionally identified by their toponyms alone rather than by their dedications. Nevertheless, the *rationes decimarum* offer a glimpse (albeit partial) at the rarity of the dedication to St Faith in the Italian peninsula. Surprisingly, however, the dedication was not uncommon in the ancient diocese of Vercelli. The feast day of St Faith is commemorated in the *Necrologio Eusebiano*, the medieval register of deaths belonging to the Cathedral of Vercelli. Moreover, in addition to Cavagnolo, two churches were dedicated to 'Santa Fede' in the 12th century: one in the suburbs of Vercelli and one at *Selvamora* (Greggio, 15 km north of Vercelli). The former was subject to the abbey of Fruttuaria, the latter to the abbey of Sannazaro Sesia.[20] Of all the sites dedicated to St Faith (if not related to her cult), the church of Cavagnolo alone survives in something like its medieval form.

Cavagnolo, however, not only carries the dedication to St Faith, it was also institutionally linked with Conques. At the end of the 19th century, Gustave Desjardins published the *cartulaire* of Sainte-Foy in Conques, including a 16th-century *pancarte* that listed all the abbey's dependencies, among which appears 'the priory of Santa Fede of Visterno, that is, Cavancholio'.[21] It should be noted that Cavagnolo is one of only two priories of Conques in the Italian peninsula listed on the *pancarte*; the second, dedicated to St Victor or St Simeon *de Currelis* or *Turretis* (probably in the diocese of Forlí, Emilia-Romagna), has not been identified.[22] The institutional relationship linking Conques and Cavagnolo is confirmed in an earlier document produced not in the mother abbey but in Piedmont. Santa Fede appears in the last will of John II, Marquis of Montferrat (r. 1338–72), where it is listed as 'the priory of Santa Fede, subject to the abbey of Conques in the diocese of Rodez; the priory is usually managed by one prior with two monks' ('*in villa Cavagnolii diocesis Vercell. Prioratus Sanctae Fidis, subjectus Abbatiae Monasterii Conchu. Bathen [sic! Ruthen]. Diocesis Ordinis S. Benedicti, qui prioratus est solitus gubernari per unum priorem cum duobus Monacis*').[23] This document is transcribed in the *Historia Montis-Ferrati* by Benvenuto da Sangiorgio (1450–1527). While the original document has not been located, its content, at least in relation to Cavagnolo, can be hardly contested. It is likely that the author had access to the original will, as is demonstrated by the transcription of the mistaken first letters of 'Ruthen'.

Thus, two distinct and independent sources record Santa Fede as a dependency, a priory, of the abbey of Conques. Unfortunately, however, the documentary evidence directly related to the priory is thin. Only two further documents, both dating from the end of the 13th century, can be related to it with confidence.[24] These were written on a single parchment, later reused for a protocol (or preamble) by the notaries of Monferrato, and subsequently housed in the Archivio di Stato in Alessandria, where it was rediscovered in the mid-20th century. The documents, one of which is dated 1281, relate to the permanent concession of land in 'Val Cavagnolo' (likely not far from the church) by the monastery of Cavagnolo to Giordano de Placio. This was signed in the presence of the prior of the monastery, Hugo Denavis, a single monk (*dominus* Archenbaldus) and two lay brothers.[25] The document explicitly asserts that Santa Fede is a monastery (a priory), but it is not possible to determine whether the four people listed comprised the entire resident monastic community. The acts of the pastoral visits of the bishops of Casale Monferrato suggest that the church had been abandoned by the monks by the 16th century, and it is probably in this period that its medieval documents were lost.[26]

AN ARCHITECTURAL PALIMPSEST

The surviving documentary sources, while significant in evidencing the institutional relationship between Conques and Cavagnolo, do not provide any further information as to the circumstances of the priory's foundation or chronology. Close analysis of the material structure of the church itself, however, sheds some light on these issues, as well as offers new insight into the institutional connection with Conques and the extent to which this impacted artistic production at the site.

The façade, the first element of the building encountered by a visitor, presents two types of masonry (Figure 9.1.) The lowest portion is built from large blocks of ashlar, finely squared and carefully jointed, while the upper part is constructed in brick. Two half-columns frame the central portal, dividing the façade into three parts. Between the left (north) half-column and the portal (partly covered by another semi-column), an inscription commemorates the death of the Presbiter Rolandus, on the eleventh day before the *Kalendae* of November (22 October): '*XI K(a)l(endae) Nove(m)bris ob[. . .] Rolandus P(res) b(iter)*' (Figure 9.2).[27] Unfortunately, *Rolandus* cannot be identified with anyone of this name who appears in the surviving ecclesiastical documents from nearby centres such as Vercelli, Casale Monferrato, or Asti, and the year of his death is not mentioned in the inscription.[28] *Rolandus*, however, appears in a second, later, inscription on the façade which probably refers to his role in the construction of the church ('*Dominus Rolandus [. . .] hic meritis ven[. . .] templi*'). The second inscription was carved *après la pose*, as it runs across different blocks of ashlar, and its *ductus* is not deep. The first inscription, by contrast, seems to have been carved *avant la pose*, in the lower portion of an ashlar, suggesting that these two epigraphic documents relate to different moments during the construction of the church.[29]

The portal (Figure 9.3 and Colour Plate XI) is framed by two half-columns, surmounted by carvings which depict an ox and a lion, to the left and right, respectively. The juxtaposition of these two animals on either side of a portal can be found at other sites both near and far, as, for example, at the Cluniac priory of Santa Maria in Calvenzano, near Lodi, or San Siro of Cemmo, in Valcamonica (Lombardy).[30] The destroyed abbey church of Notre-Dame des Moreaux near Poitiers boasted reliefs of two bishops of Poitiers (now in the Allen Memorial Art Museum, Oberlin, Ohio) flanking the portal on its west façade, identified by accompanying inscriptions as Adelelme (d. 1140) and Grimoard (d. 1142), standing respectively on a lion and an ox.[31] A further inscription

Figure 9.1

Cavagnolo, Santa Fede: façade (Michele Luigi Vescovi)

Figure 9.2

Cavagnolo, Santa Fede: facade inscription (Michele Luigi Vescovi)

Figure 9.3

Cavagnolo, Santa Fede: portal (Michele Luigi Vescovi)

FIGURE 9.4
Toulouse, Musée Saint-Raymond: 'chasse de Méléagre' (Ra 505a, Raphael Isla, CC BY-SA 4.0)

on the portal archivolt of Moreaux, now lost but recorded in the 19th century, linked the presence of these animals to the Temple of Solomon: 'As was the entrance to the Temple of Holy Solomon, so the entrance of this is placed between an ox and a lion'. According to the Book of Kings, the entrance to Solomon's temple was decorated with brass basins adorned with figures of oxen and lions (1 Kings 7[29]).[32] Thus, it is equally possible that the presence of carvings representing a lion and an ox at Cavagnolo might also reference the Temple of Solomon.

The tympanum is flanked by a pair of griffins facing inwards and two carvings representing a man and a woman. On the outer archivolt, an intricate braided and interlaced pattern forms twelve frames: at the top is a cross, towards which many of the animals and creatures inhabiting the surrounding space direct their attention. From left to right we can identify a rose, a pair of weasels, a hare, a camel, and a quadruped with prominent claws. On the right (south) of the cross are a griffin; Leviathan (?) eating two people; a basilisk (a cockerel with a snake's tail); a snake followed by a lamb; and an eagle. While it is clear that the cross forms the core of the representation (again, it is to this that the majority of the animals direct their attention), it is difficult to attribute a particular significance in the creatures chosen. However, if the carving that represents the legs of two naked figures emerging from the mouth of a monster is understood as Leviathan, that is the mouth of hell, this would offer an unusual frontal visualisation of this subject and a rare representation of it south of the Alps.[33] In the tympanum, two angels facing each other hold a mandorla/medallion containing the bust of Christ, shown beardless, with a cruciform nimbus and with his right hand raised in blessing. The lintel and the central archivolt are carved with vines carrying grapes. By highlighting the visual and substantial proximity between Christ and the grapes, the portal would seem to reference the Eucharist.[34]

Despite its apparent simplicity, the portal displays some noteworthy architectural features. It is framed by four independent columns, a layout extremely unusual south of the Alps, where engaged columns are usually employed. Furthermore, as noted by Emile Mâle, carved tympana (or, rather, carved lunettes) are extremely rare in the Italian peninsula.[35] Finally, in terms of style and iconography, the tympanum seems to allude to Roman and Late Antique sarcophagi, in particular those carved in Gaul. The graphic visualisation of the vine branches, for example, creating broad spirals with large leaves, recalls the same subject as represented on a sarcophagus redeployed in the cloister of Saint-Sernin in Toulouse or the so-called *chasse de Méléagre* in the same city (now Toulouse, Musée Saint-Raymond, Ra 505a). The cover of the latter presents a fascinating visual parallel with the tympanum at Cavagnolo, in the horizontal layout of the two angels holding, in this case, the *imago clipeata* of the Chi-Ro rather than the bust of Christ (Figure 9.4).[36] Furthermore, a similar range of visual elements (two angels holding the *imago clipeata* of the beardless Christ, and the overall horizontal layout) can be found on the high altar of Saint-Sernin at Toulouse, consecrated in 1096 and carved by *Bernardus Gelduinus* as the inscription carved around the *mensa* tells us.[37]

Santa Fede is very much an architectural palimpsest. The building consists of a five-bay nave and side aisles, with a non-projecting transept over the second bay from the east (Figure 9.5). The nave is covered by a barrel vault, while the aisles are groin vaulted. The piers consist of a rectangular core with an engaged half-column on each side. Similar to what has been noted for the façade, two types of masonry are employed consistently throughout

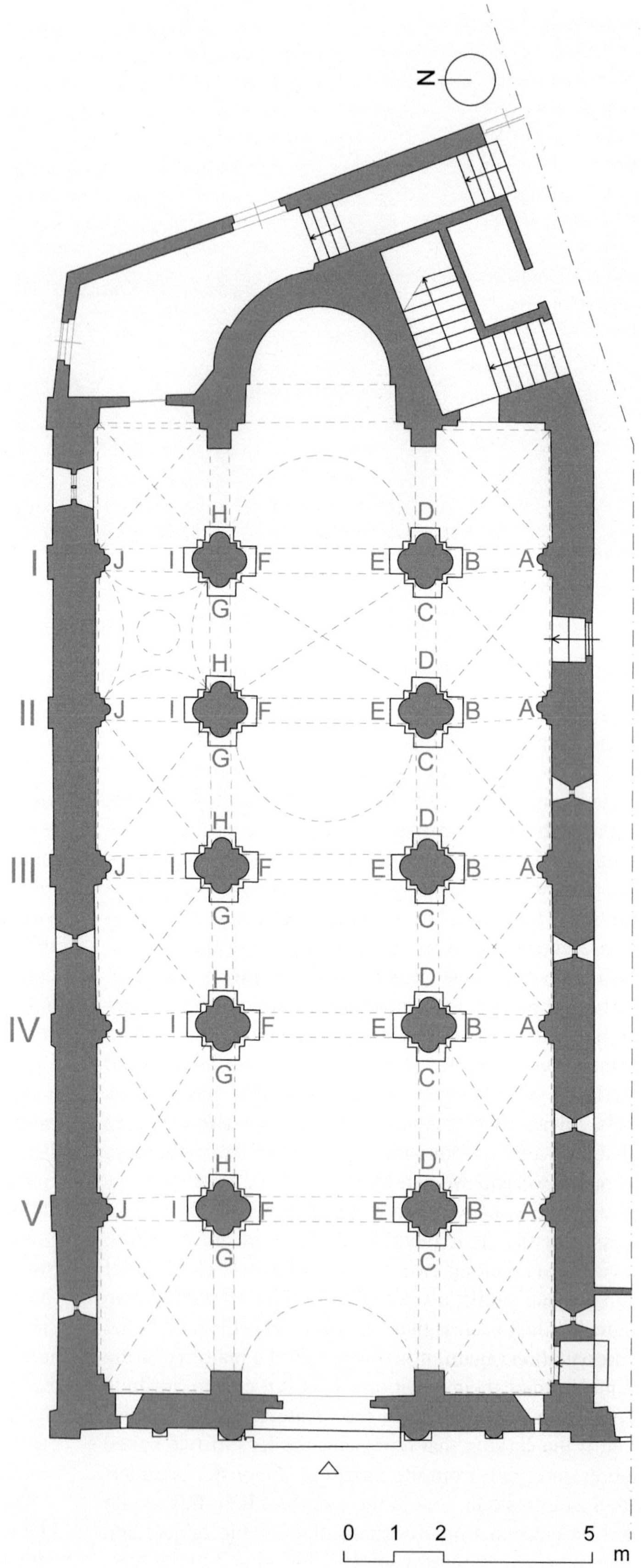

FIGURE 9.5

Cavagnolo, Santa Fede: plan (Drawing by Chiara Devoti, Monica Naretto). For reference, each capital at Santa Fede is identified by a Roman numeral followed by a letter. These relate to their positions within the building.

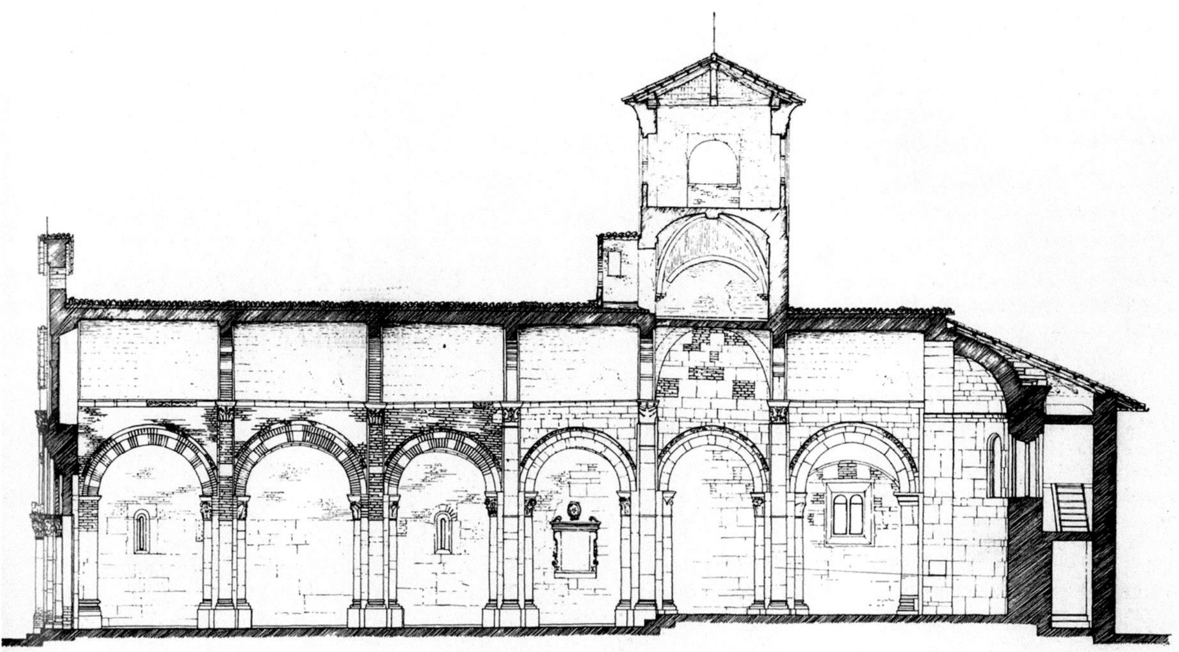

FIGURE 9.6

Cavagnolo, Santa Fede: sectional elevation (Drawing by Fernando Delmastro)

FIGURE 9.7

Cavagnolo, Santa Fede: north aisle to west (Michele Luigi Vescovi)

the building. The lowest portion of the west front and the north and south walls of the church are built using large blocks of ashlar, finely squared and carefully jointed; the upper parts of these areas are constructed with bricks. The apse and the eastern three bays of the clerestory use ashlar, while the three west bays of the clerestory employ bricks (Figure 9.6). Scholars have suggested that the use of two materials, ashlar and brick, denotes two different construction phases.[38]

This observation can be further substantiated by analysis of two additional factors, not fully addressed in earlier discussions of the site. The first relates to the piers, as those of the eastern part of the church (the easternmost three piers on the north and the easternmost two piers to the south) are peculiar (Figure 9.7). Here, the capitals supporting the transverse arches of the aisle vaults are set lower than those of the main arcade. In the piers in the western part of the church, by contrast, the three capitals are arranged at the same level. Furthermore, the capitals facing the aisles in the eastern bays are set at a lower level than the corresponding capitals of the outer aisle walls. The gap between the different levels of the sets of capitals has been filled by adding a masonry filler of around 0.4 m.

This unusual solution can only be explained by a change of plan in the course of construction. Such a change marks a precise stage in the building process: the intended project for the side aisles was modified when the three pairs of piers at the east end of the church had already been built and their capitals inserted into position, along with the lowest part of the outer north and south walls. Following the change, the transverse arches were then set at the same level of the main arcades; the level of the capitals of the piers still under construction (and those of the outer walls) was modified, even though this could not be done in the first three bays, where the capitals had been already installed. For this reason, sections of masonry had to be inserted in order to maintain a consistent springing level for the transverse arches.[39]

The two construction phases identified in the architecture can be further substantiated through consideration of the sculpture. The fifty carved capitals of the interior can be divided into two groups. One is characterised by the deep carving and soft treatment of the stone surface (Figures 9.8–9.10), creating a sharp contrast between light and shadow, particularly evident in the foliage or in the definition of the volume of the animals. The second group is distinguished by its harder treatment of surfaces and volumes and by a standardised decoration consisting of three flat vertical leaves (Figure 9.11). These two sets of capitals are located in different parts of the church. The first is found in the easternmost three bays and the portal, while capitals belonging to the second group are found in the western end of the church.[40]

The substantial formal differences between the two groups of capitals suggest that they have been carved by two distinct workshops. It is likely that these two workshops were not active at the same time but that one followed the other. The activity of the first workshop is confined to those parts of the church completed before the change just outlined, that is, the eastern part of the building and the lower part of the façade. Furthermore, this workshop left behind many unfinished capitals. For example, a foliate capital (Figure 9.12) was left as a work in progress, as the right leaf retains the holes left by the drill that were preparatory to carving a channel or fold within the leaf with a chisel. Another capital (Figure 9.13) was halted at an even earlier step of preparation, as here the volumes have been simply outlined, ready to receive the decorative elements.[41] Thus the change of plan could be linked to the departure of the first workshop from Cavagnolo. Moreover, this workshop moved to another site nearby, as its activity can be traced to the parish church of San Lorenzo in Montiglio, approximately 15 km south-east of Cavagnolo.[42]

But what are the origins of this first workshop? The capitals of Santa Fede are a reinterpretation of the Corinthian model, with two rows of superimposed flat leaves on the basket and volutes at the top. These do not find any similarities with 12th-century Corinthian capitals in Piedmont, such as those at Santa Trinitá da Lungi at Castellazzo Bormida, San Giacomo di Gavi, Santi Pietro e Giacomo at Castelnuovo Scrivia, Santa Maria Maggiore in Vercelli, or Sant'Evasio in Casale Monferrato.[43] The capitals of the first workshop of Santa Fede are indeed unique within the geographical context of northern Italy: the carving is deep and soft, and the design is completely different from contemporary artistic traditions in Milan, Como, or Pavia.

From this perspective, the institutional relationship between Cavagnolo and Conques might help in understanding and contextualising the sculptural anomalies of Santa Fede. In fact, the capitals at Conques and Cavagnolo share some similarities: for example, the proportions and the overall design of those exemplars with a basket decorated by two rows of superposed flat leaves and volutes (Figures 9.14 and 9.15). Furthermore, at both Cavagnolo and Conques, the volutes of many capitals are carved with an arboreal decoration (Figure 9.16, compare with Figure 9.12). The most interesting connection between the two sites, however, is suggested by a comparison between two capitals (Figures 9.17 and 9.18). Both of these are designed with two orders of flat leaves, and in each order a palmette alternates with a leaf, which carries a sphere at its apex. At Conques, the capital is located in the west aisle of the south transept, where the transept meets the nave of the church.[44] Furthermore, a very similar capital, which equally presents spheres at the apex of the leaves, appears in the portal of the south transept. Éliane Vergnolle has recently reconsidered the complex constructional history of the abbey church of Conques, suggesting that the transepts (in which these capitals are located) follows the model of Saint-Sernin in Toulouse, probably after 1060.[45] The Saint-Sernin model is not simply confined to the architecture of Sainte-Foy, as Vergnolle suggests that the capitals just discussed are also inspired by sculpture from Toulouse (Figure 9.19).[46]

The analysis of the material structures of Santa Fede reveals its complex constructional history. One workshop started building the church, adopting structural and decorative solutions which were uncommon in the local area, such as shaft rings and billet moulding over the arcade. In the course of construction, probably when the easternmost three pairs of piers had been raised and the lowest portions of the outer walls erected, this workshop left. While the reasons or events that could have led to their departure are unclear, mainly due to the lack of documentary sources for the priory, it is clear that many capitals have been left unfinished, with some at an early stage in their preparation and the organisation of the volumes. A second workshop then took over, introducing some modifications to the structure and creating a new decorative scheme for the capitals. Investigation of the first workshop reveals the intellectual complexity of the imagery deployed on the façade, which alludes to the Temple of Solomon and is inspired by Late Antique sculpture. Finally, analysis of the capitals shows that the first Cavagnolo workshop either followed models that had been employed already at Conques, or the masons themselves were connected to the mother abbey. The latter would allow us to make further conjectures related to the chronology of the foundation and construction of Santa Fede. The closest comparisons for Cavagnolo appear in the transept of Conques, built *c.* 1060–90 (Figure 9.18). While a date as early as this is unlikely for Santa Fede, its construction could follow, even loosely, this period. Thus the priory was likely to have been built in the opening decades of the 12th century.[47] However, the connection between Conques and Cavagnolo has deeper implications than a mere definition of the relative chronology of the

FIGURE 9.8

Cavagnolo, Santa Fede: capital I-c (Michele Luigi Vescovi)

FIGURE 9.9

Cavagnolo, Santa Fede: capital I-f (Michele Luigi Vescovi)

FIGURE 9.10

Cavagnolo, Santa Fede: capital II-d (Michele Luigi Vescovi)

FIGURE 9.11

Cavagnolo, Santa Fede: capital IV-e (Michele Luigi Vescovi)

building: it raises substantial issues related to geographical and institutional networks through the dynamics of foundation.

PRIORIES, DYNAMICS OF FOUNDATION, MONASTIC NETWORKS

Analysis of the documentary evidence proves that Cavagnolo was a dependency of Conques, at least by the time that Marquis John II (d. 1372) made his final will. Furthermore, the investigation of the material structures of the church – revealing the deployment of architectural and decorative solutions alien to the monumental landscape of Lombardy and the adoption of models for capitals employed at Conques – suggests that Santa Fede was a priory of Sainte-Foy from its foundation.[48]

Nothing is known about the foundation of Santa Fede. Unfortunately lost is the fragment of a Chronicle reporting 'the origin of the monastery of Santa Fede [. . .] composed by its monks', that Johannes Battista Moriondus, an 18th-century theologian and scholar, was able to read in Cavagnolo.[49] However, the *Cartulaire* of Conques and the collection of miracles of St Faith might offer comparative perspectives helpful to our understanding of the foundation of Santa Fede in Cavagnolo. The book of miracles offers many different reasons for the foundation of priories of Conques: a number of these miracles relates to the liberation of prisoners and, in at least two cases, the miracle was followed by the foundation of churches in honour of the saint. According to a miracle dating to the second half of the 11th century, a Saracen warrior living near Jerusalem was imprisoned in the area of Damascus. While in captivity, another prisoner from Aquitaine

FIGURE 9.12

Cavagnolo, Santa Fede: capital I-e (Michele Luigi Vescovi)

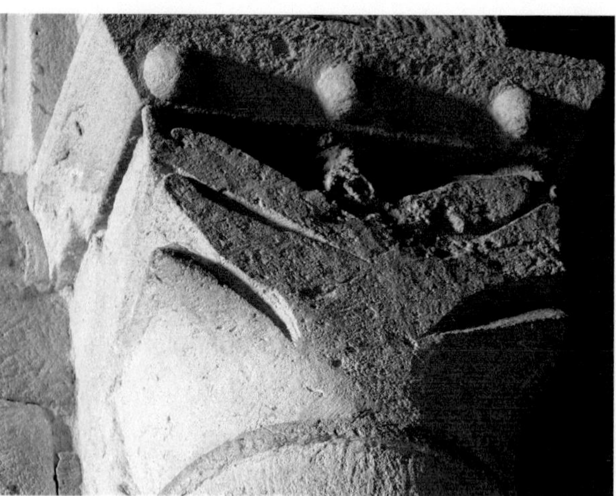

FIGURE 9.13

Cavagnolo, Santa Fede: capital II-f (Michele Luigi Vescovi)

FIGURE 9.14

Cavagnolo, Santa Fede: capital III-b (Michele Luigi Vescovi)

FIGURE 9.15

Conques, Sainte-Foy: north transept gallery, capital (Michele Luigi Vescovi)

explained 'that a virgin named St Faith was known to possess such great powers that she cured the blind, healed the sick, freed the enchained'.[50] The Saracen warrior invoked the saint, vowing to be baptised and to establish a church in her honour. After his liberation, he sent the fetters 'to a church that a brother named Robert had built in honour of St Faith on the bank of the Euphrates River', and he also travelled to Conques, where 'he hung in front of the martyr's tomb the hair shirt he had worn'.[51]

Another legend related to St Faith, probably recorded around 1107, narrates how Robert Fitzwalter and Sybil de Caneto were captured by bandits during a pilgrimage to southern France. After being miraculously liberated through the intercession of the saint, they went to visit her shrine in Conques. Once back in England, they established a church and priory in her honour, at Horsham St Faith.[52] Similarly, Jessica N. Richardson, in her analysis of San Leonardo at Siponto (Apulia), has argued that the church of San Leonardo itself, in its material structure, was a votive offering by Bohemond, Prince of Apulia and Antioch, himself imprisoned during a crusade in Turkey.[53] Furthermore, this and similar foundations are fundamental to our understanding of the geographical spread and increasing popularity of particular saints, such as Leonard of Noblat (Limousin), another patron of prisoners, whose cult of the Siponto foundation was growing at the time from a 'local' to a 'global' phenomenon.[54] In bringing together hagiographical narrations, the performance of miracles, and acts of foundation, Richardson suggests that the establishment of a church and its dedication to a particular saint could be read as a material *ex-voto*.

Yet the establishment of priories related to Sainte Foy might not only be linked to the miraculous liberations of prisoners performed on the saint's behalf. Their foundation can follow a visit or a pilgrimage to the mother abbey

FIGURE 9.16

Conques, Sainte-Foy: north transept gallery, capital (Michele Luigi Vescovi)

FIGURE 9.17

Cavagnolo, Santa Fede: capital, I-b (Michele Luigi Vescovi)

FIGURE 9.18

Conques, Sainte-Foy: south transept gallery, west aisle, capital (Michele Luigi Vescovi)

FIGURE 9.19

Toulouse, Saint-Sernin: capital #86 (Alain Escourbiac)

at Conques itself. According to the manuscript of the *liber miraculorum* at Sélestat (Bibliothèque Humaniste, 22), one of the best-preserved collections of the miracles of St Faith, Frederic, duke of Germany, with his two brothers, Count Conrad and Otto, bishop of Strasbourg, visited the abbey of Conques during a pilgrimage in southern France (1087–94). They were attracted there by 'the splendour of the miracles and the glory of St Faith'.[55] Once back in Alsace, according to the foundation document and their confirmations (1094–95), the brothers, together with their mother Hildegard, founded a church in Sélestat dedicated to the Holy Sepulchre, which they subsequently offered to the abbey of Conques together with lands, goods, and rights.[56] The connection between this priory and the mother abbey is also proven by the *liber miraculorum* itself, a copy of the original collection of miracles from Conques likely composed in Sélestat at the end of the 11th century.[57] Furthermore, according to this manuscript, Begon III, abbot of Conques, decided to send the monk Bertram to administer the new foundation in Alsace.[58]

All of these narrations offer fresh insights in the foundation of Conques's priories. The miracles often emphasise that liberated captives established priories and dependencies, such as those promoted by the Saracen warrior, by Robert Fitzwalter and Sybil de Caneto, or by Bohemond, prince of Antioch, on the banks of the Euphrates River, in England, and in Apulia, respectively. While the latter foundation relates to St Leonard rather than to St Faith, the dynamics highlighted are similar if not identical.

Considering the rarity of the dedication to St Faith south of the Alps and Conques's lack of dependencies in the Italian peninsula, it is tempting to suggest that Cavagnolo could also have been established as an *ex-voto* by a liberated prisoner. Unfortunately, however, the lack of written documentation on Cavagnolo from the early 12th century means this can be no more than a working hypothesis.

Nevertheless, in all these cases (including those related to liberated prisoners), the establishment of a priory follows direct contact with Conques (or, in the case of Bohemond, the abbey of Saint-Léonard-de-Noblat). The liberated prisoners and donors visit the mother-house and shrine of the saint, depositing objects related to their captivity; the hair shirt worn by the Saracen warrior; 'reade the life of Saint Faith and the miracles that God shewed for her there daily and hourely' (Robert Fitzwalter and Sybil de Caneto); or, like the sons of Hildegard, they are admitted to the monastic congregation by the abbot, participating in the spiritual goods of the abbey and of its dependencies.[59] Following this first contact, the abbot of Conques establishes local monastic communities by sending out monks from the mother abbey to the new priories, as with Bertram to Sélestat, or Barnard and Girard to Horsham-Saint-Faith.

The close connection with Conques, evidenced in direct contact between donors, patrons, and the mother abbey, relates also to the physical construction of a priory. In some cases, as mentioned in the discussion of Sélestat, the church was built by the donors and was consecrated prior to its donation to Conques, even though this structure was then replaced towards the end of the 12th century.[60] As in this example, monks from Conques occasionally took over pre-existing churches. But the combined analysis of documentary evidence and the narration of miracles show that this was not the only option.

Falco de Barta, in donating a *mansus* located in Vinairols (near the river Dordogne) to Conques (1076), mentions that in the same area at the time of his predecessors, there was a church dedicated to St Faith, subsequently abandoned, which was attracting a number of pilgrims. Thus Falco and his wife Florencia gave to Conques the *mansus*, a port on the river Dordogne, and part of the revenues from ships transporting salt, with the agreement that the monks should build a church there in honour of St Faith.[61] In another case, at the end of the 11th century, Oddo, Bernardus, Willelmus, and Poncius, sons of Raimondus Oddo and Lucia, donated a site ('Monte Sancto Johanni', identified as Saint-Jean de l'Union, Haute-Garonne) to Conques, where a church was once built, in order that it could be reconstructed directly by the monks themselves.[62] And in yet another instance, in the third quarter of the 11th century, Dodo de Samathan increased the donation his father had made to Conques in Perairols (likely identifiable in the commune of Saint-Martin-de-Villereglan, Aude), where a church and a *villa* had been built thanks to the virtues of St Faith and 'with great labour of the monks'.[63] Finally, in the miracle of the Saracen warrior previously discussed, it is explicitly mentioned that 'a brother named Robert had built a church in honour of St Faith on the bank of the Euphrates river'.[64]

All this evidence suggests that the construction of a priory was not the responsibility of the lay donors but instead of the monks of Conques. Other sources point towards an even more radical understanding of these dynamics: Amancuus donated, together with other goods, two *mansi* in Esclottes (diocese of Bazas, Gironde) on the precise understanding that 'the monk Deusdet or Petrus or Odolricus build here a church in honour of St Faith'.[65] According to a miracle in the fourth book of the collection of St Faith (probably dating to the mid-11th century), a monk named Deusdet 'constructed a church out of wood, and with humble equipment covered it with wooden beams' in a place called Sardan in the Bazadais.[66] It is not clear whether this monk is to be identified with the same '*Deusdet monachus*' requested by Amancuus to build a church in Esclottes.[67] Nevertheless, all these sources suggest not only that monks were sent from Conques but that these monks played an active role, at the very least, in the promotion of the construction of churches, if not in their material design and the building process itself. A potential visual counterpart to these ideas is offered by a capital in the cloister of Conques (Figure 9.20). It shows eight men, some of them with tools in their hands, emerging from an ashlar wall: Marcel Durliat has argued that this scene represents the construction of the cloister itself, and the tonsured heads might identify some of these figures as monks.[68]

MONASTIC NETWORKS AND ARTISTIC GEOGRAPHIES

Even though the documentary evidence for the foundation of Cavagnolo is lost, the surviving church, its capitals, and the artistic models they drew on point to the exceptionality of Santa Fede within its own 'region'. Yet this can be explained in the light of the dynamics of foundation. The examples just discussed suggest that, while donors might have different motivations for establishing a priory in any given area, there was often direct contact between the patrons themselves and Conques. Furthermore, the mother abbey sent out monks to these priories, and these monks were often responsible for promoting the construction of churches.

It is within this framework, as a part of the monastic network of Conques, that Santa Fede in Cavagnolo might be better understood. Unfortunately, unlike Cluny, Conques's monastic network has not been the subject of extensive scholarly investigation. The 16th-century *pancarte*, summarised by Desjardins in his 1879 publication, lists seventy-two priories in Europe, but it is necessary to add to this calculation all the churches subject to the abbey (or annexed to the different priories), recorded in the same document, which would bring the total to more than 150 sites. The *pancarte* is the only document listing all the dependencies of Conques, but even so it offers only a partial (and probably skewed) picture of this monastic

FIGURE 9.20

Conques, Sainte-Foy: cloister capital (Michele Luigi Vescovi)

network in the high Middle Ages, as by the time this document has been redacted, the mother abbey had probably already lost a considerable number of dependencies. For example, in the 12th century, in the ancient diocese of Toulouse alone, Conques possessed thirty churches.[69]

These numbers give an idea of the magnitude, geographical reach, and ramifications of the monastic network of Conques. Unfortunately, however, of the sites listed on the *pancarte*, only around twenty churches still retain any of their medieval fabric. Significantly, Cavagnolo is one of the best-preserved buildings within this group.[70] Due to the limited *corpus* of sites related to Conques's monastic network, it is not possible to prove beyond reasonable doubt whether the carvings at Cavagnolo directly issued from the mother abbey or if they were mediated through another priory. Neither it is possible to demonstrate whether the sculpture at Cavagnolo was carved by artists from Conques or one of its dependencies, or if it was simply the models, the design, which travelled across the Alps. Contrary to the example of Cluny, Cavagnolo shows that a monastic network could imply an artistic network. The layout of the portal with two independent columns on each side is alien to the Lombard tradition of the early 12th century, while it is well attested in Conques (Figure 9.21), in the surrounding region, and amongst its churches, such as Cristo de Catalàin (Figure 9.22).[71] The complexity of the tympanum suggests a dialogue with Late Antiquity, of a sort associated with Early Christian sarcophagi from or in Gallia. Finally, the capitals of the church have suggestive, if not convincing similarities with the decorative sculpture of Conques.

Artistic exchanges across the Alps were common during the Middle Ages. The mountains did not constitute borders or boundaries between different artistic traditions, as Enrico Castelnuovo has pointed out. The 12th-century cloister of Sant' Orso in Aosta, for instance, was carved by the same workshop (probably Lombard) responsible for work in the abbey church of Saint Martin d'Ainay (now in the suburbs of Lyon), while the altar of San Giusto at Susa, was made, according to the inscription on its front, by Peter from Lyon ('*Petrus Lugdunensis me fecit*').[72] Santa Fede can be understood from a similar perspective, exemplifying a transregional dynamic which was in part due to its geographical proximity with France. However, Santa Fede cannot be fully explained in terms of the 'regional' or 'transregional'. While these two categories might prove useful in classifying the different elements of the church, they fail to capture the significance, in terms of artistic geography, of the monastic network to which Santa Fede belonged.

In the analysis of the relationship between Cavagnolo and Conques, 'regional' and 'transregional' take on a new meaning. Here, the institution itself, through its network of priories, topographically diffuse but institutionally linked, constructs its own geography. The monastic network of Conques provides a distinct geographical model which transcends the borders of 'regions' as well as physical, political, or administrative boundaries. As such, it also provides a model for the geography of art which differs from the complex, if not problematic, framework of 'centre' and 'periphery', as outlined in 1979 by Enrico Castelnuovo and Carlo Ginzburg.[73] Castelnuovo and Ginzburg questioned the long-established model of the binary relationship between art and territory, exploring instead the interconnections between centre and periphery. The former could be seen as the place for artistic creation and the latter as receptive of delayed artistic inventions, if only superficially. Instead, such relations call attention to more nuanced factors, such as symbolic domination, the dynamics of works of art, artists, and patrons – connections that are much more fluid and whose changes of identity could be also connected to social and political modifications.[74] Yet in applying this model to the study of monastic networks, it is only on a superficial level that the mother abbey was the 'centre' and all the priories the 'periphery'. Rather, the network is liquid, providing for a more capillary flow and lateral contacts.

In a bull issued in 1100, Paschal II confirmed the abbey of Souvigny under his pontifical protection 'like a limb of the monastery of Cluny' ('*tamquam Cluniacensis coenobii membrum*').[75] This metaphor appears in pontifical documents addressed to other Cluniac houses, such as Binson, Beaulieu, and Saint-Martin-des-Champs; the same Paschal II in his privilege for Cluny of 1109 described the dependencies as 'adhering (to Cluny) like a limb to the head' ('*tanquam membra capiti adhaerentia*').[76] The analogy with limbs and head, employed also in the documentation related to Conques, finds a precise point of reference in the writings of St Paul.[77] In the First Letter to the Corinthians, the Apostle declares: 'For as the body is one, and hath many members; and all the members of the body, whereas they are many, yet are one body, so also is Christ' ('*Sicut enim corpus unum est, et membra habet multa, omnia autem membra corporis cum sint multa, unum tamen corpus sunt: ita et Christus*',

FIGURE 9.21

Conques, Sainte-Foy: south transept, portal (Michele Luigi Vescovi)

FIGURE 9.22

Garinoáin (Navarre), Cristo de Cataláin: façade (Antonio García Omedes)

I Corinthians 12[12]). In this passage, Paul compares the Christian community to the human body, in which all the members have a mutual relation and each has its proper place and function, emphasising the interdependence of parts and the whole. The metaphor of the body, evoked in the pontifical bulls and inspired by the writing of Paul, defines what I have here discussed as the monastic network of Conques. Like a body, a monastic network constitutes an individual organism: the different priories and dependencies, geographically spread, are like limbs of a body stretched over different locales, all belonging to the same organic unity.

ACKNOWLEDGEMENTS

The research for this article has been facilitated by the diocese of Casale Monferrato and the religious communities that, over many years, have cared for Santa Fede; the Marist Fathers and Brothers, followed by the Fraternitá Missionaria Siloe. I thank Monica Naretto, Chiara Devoti, Fernando Delmastro, Alain Escourbiac, and Antonio García Omedes for kindly providing drawings, plans, and photographs; the editors of this volume for their work on my text; and Laura Fernandez-Gonzalez for fruitful discussions about the geographies of art. Last but not least, my deepest gratitude goes to Jessica N. Richardson for providing a new theoretical framework for an understanding of church foundations as material *ex-voto* and for constantly pushing the boundaries of my intellectual curiosity. It is to her, my companion in travel, work, and life, that this article is gratefully dedicated.

NOTES

1 A. de Caumont, *Essai sur l'architecture religieuse du Moyen Âge, particulièrement en Normandie* (Caen 1825); A. de Caumont, *Histoire de l'architecture religieuse au Moyen Âge* (Paris 1841). The approach taken by de Caumont and its historiographical implications are further discussed by X. Barral i Altet, *Contre l'art roman? Essai sur un passé réinventé* (Paris 2006), 22–31. See also Claude Andrault-Schmitt, 'The Epistemological, Political and Practical Issues Affecting Regional Categories in French Romanesque Architecture', in this volume.

2 A. Kingsley Porter, *Romanesque Sculpture of the Pilgrimage Roads* (Boston 1923), I, 171.

3 J. Bédier, *Les légendes épiques: recherches sur la formation des chansons de geste* (Paris 1908–13). For the historiographical implications of *Romanesque Sculpture of the Pilgrimage Roads*, see J. Mann, 'Romantic Identity, Nationalism, and the Understanding of the Advent of Romanesque Art in Christian Spain', *Gesta,* 36 (1997), 156–64. For the debate on artistic geography at the beginning of the 21st century, see T. DaCosta Kaufmann, *Toward a Geography of Art* (Chicago 2004), 43–67.

4 Barral i Altet, *Contre l'art roman?* (as n. 1), 261: '*L'art roman apparaît plutôt comme un art très lié au système politique alors en place, essentiellement constitué de principautés territoriales, limitées géographiquement et très divisées politiquement*'.

5 Ibid., 261–65: '*L'art roman semble donc davantage correspondre à ce morcellement local qu'à un art d'échanges lointains*'.

6 E. Fernie, *Romanesque Architecture: The First Style of the European Age* (New Haven and London 2014), 27.

[7] D. Iogna-Prat, *Order and Exclusion: Cluny and Christendom Face Heresy, Judaism and Islam, 1100–1150* (Ithaca 2002), 26–27.

[8] Ibid.

[9] J. Evans, *The Romanesque Architecture of the Order of Cluny* (Cambridge 1938), 9.

[10] P. Piva, *Le chiese cluniacensi. Architettura monastica nell'Italia del Nord* (Milano 1998). For a recent reassessment of artistic production at Cluny and in Cluniac abbeys and priories more generally, see N. Stratford, ed., *Cluny 910–2010: onze siècles de rayonnement* (Paris 2010).

[11] G. Melville, *The World of Medieval Monasticism. Its History and Forms of Life* (Collegeville 2016), 158–79; G. M. Cantarella, 'È esistito un "modello cluniacense"?' In *Dinamiche istituzionali delle reti monastiche e canonicali nell'Italia dei secoli X–XII*, ed. N. D'Acunto (San Pietro in Cariano 2007), 61–85: 78–82.

[12] For example, Dominique Iogna-Prat has emphasised the difference between the *Cluniacensis Ecclesia* and what he termed the 'Cluniac nebula', distinguishing between the legal status of monastic houses institutionally dependent on Cluny from other generic connections with the Burgundian abbey (such as the adoption of the Cluniac customs). Iogna-Prat, *Order and Exclusion* (as n. 7), 54–75.

[13] E. Arborio Mella, 'Della badia e Chiesa di Santa Fede presso Cavagnolo Po', *L'Arte in Italia,* 2 (1870), 37–39; E. Arborio Mella, 'Cenno storico artistico sull'abbazia e Chiesa di Santa Fede presso Cavagnolo', *Il Politecnico,* 18 (1870), 684–88; F. De Dartein, *Etude sur l'architecture lombarde et sur les origines de l'architecture romano-byzantine* (Paris 1865–82), 448; A. Venturi, *L'arte romanica*, Storia dell'arte italiana, 3 (Milano 1904), 93; P. Toesca, *Il Medioevo*, Storia dell'arte italiana, 1 (Torino 1927), 532. For a more detailed discussion of the historiographical debate on Santa Fede, see: M. L. Vescovi, *'Monferrato' medievale. Crocevia di culture e sperimentazioni*, Ricerche di S/Confine, 4 (Verona 2012), 7–24 (in relation to the 'School of Monferrato'); C. Devoti, M. Naretto, *L'abbaziale di Santa Fede a Cavagnolo Po, Architettura dei monasteri in Piemonte*, vol. 4 (Savigliano 2015), 27–31, 49–60.

[14] De Dartein, *Etude sur l'architecture lombarde* (as n. 13), 448.

[15] A. Michel, *Histoire de l'Art depuis les premiers temps chrétiens jusqu'à nos jours*, I.2 (Paris 1905), 550–51.

[16] A. Kingsley Porter, *Lombard Architecture* (New Haven–London 1915–17), II, 276–78.

[17] A. Fissore Solaro, 'Romanico nel Monferrato e i suoi rapporti con la Saintonge', in *Archivi e Cultura ad Asti* (Asti 1971), 129–52; C. Tosco, 'Il Monferrato come scuola architettonica: interpretazioni critiche di un tema storiografico', *Monferrato Arte e Storia,* 9 (1997), 45–77. The connection with Conques is mentioned by S. Casartelli, 'Quattro chiese benedettine del XII secolo in Monferrato', *Atti del X Congresso di Storia dell'Architettura* (Roma 1959), 235–65.

[18] P. Sheingorn, ed., *The Book of Sainte Foy* (Philadelphia 1995), 1–32.

[19] For Cavagnolo, see M. Rosada, ed., *Lombardia et Pedemontium, Rationes Decimarum Italiae. Studi e Testi*, vol. 324 (Città del Vaticano 1990), 292; for Piacenza, see A. Mercati, E. Nasalli-Rocca, and P. Sella, eds., *Aemilia. Le decime dei secoli XIII–XIV, Rationes Decimarum Italiae. Studi e Testi*, vol. 60 (Città del Vaticano 1933), 409; for Maddaloni, see M. Inguanez, L. Mattei-Cerasoli, and P. Sella, eds., *Campania, Rationes Decimarum Italiae. Studi e Testi*, vol. 97 (Città del Vaticano 1942), 221; M. Rosada, ed., *Liguria Maritima, Rationes Decimarum Italiae. Studi e Testi*, vol. 425 (Città del Vaticano 2005), 48, 168, 214.

[20] The commemoration of the saint appears in G. Colombo and R. Pastè, eds., 'I necrologi eusebiani', *Bollettino storico-bibliografico subalpino*, 7 (1902), 366–74 at 367. For Santa Fede in Vercelli: Vescovi, *'Monferrato' medievale* (as n. 13), 87–88; G. Ferraris, *Le chiese stazionali delle rogazioni minori a Vercelli dal sec. X al sec. XIV*, ed. G. Tibaldeschi (Vercelli 1995), 114–15, n. 24, 181, n. 224. The location of this church is mentioned in a letter by Edoardo Mella to Carlo Promis, published in Devoti-Naretto, *L'abbaziale* (as n. 13), 51. For Santa Fede in *Selvamora*: A. Aina, *L'abbazia dei SS. Nazario e Celso* (Vercelli 1973), 37, 53; G. Ferraris, *La pieve di S. Maria di Biandrate* (Vercelli 1984), 614.

[21] R. Desjardins, *Cartulaire de l'abbaye de Conques en Rouergue* (Paris 1879), cxix: 'Prioratus Sanctae Fidis de Visterno seu Cavancholio (Cavanholio)'.

[22] Ibid., cxix.

[23] Benvenuto de Sancto Georgio, *Historia Montis-Ferrati ab origine marchionum illius tractus usque ad annum MCCCCXC, Rerum Italicarum Scriptores, 23*, ed. L. A. Muratori (Mediolani 1733), col. 570.

[24] Other documents, often related to this church by some scholars, probably refer to the church of Santa Fede in the suburbs of Vercelli: Vescovi, *'Monferrato' medievale* (as n. 13), 87–8, 126–7, n. 13.

[25] G. Pistarino, 'Documenti di storia monastica: Santa Fede di Cavagnolo', *Rivista di storia arte archeologia per le provincie di Alessandria e Asti*, 59 (1950), 144–52.

[26] Even though the site was abandoned by monks, the church did not seem to suffer in its material structures, as there are no major reconstructions or restorations recorded until the 19th century: Vescovi, *'Monferrato' medievale* (as n. 13), 89–92, 97–98; Devoti-Naretto, *L'abbaziale* (as n. 13), 41–48, 63–83.

[27] G. Romano, 'Asti e la "scuola del Monferrato"', in *Piemonte Romanico*, ed. G. Romano (Torino 1994), 199–214, 215 n. 124.

[28] Vescovi, *'Monferrato' medievale* (as n. 13), 104. Even if it cannot be proven, it is tempting to identify this *presbiter* with the *Rollandus*, probably a monk of Conques, who subscribed to a confirmation of rights to the abbey in *Palatio*, in the presence of Begon (the future abbot of Conques), in 1078: Desjardins, *Cartulaire* (as n. 21), 25–27.

[29] The first inscription could have been carved in the first half of the 12th century; the second finds comparison in the *tabula* of the Crucifix of Casale Monferrato, suggesting it dates to the second half of the 12th century: Vescovi, *'Monferrato' medievale* (as n. 13), 104, 133, n. 91.

[30] P. Piva, 'Santa Maria di Calvenzano (Vizzolo Predabissi)', in *Lombardia Romanica, 2, Paesaggi monumentali*, eds. R. Cassanelli, P. Piva and C. Maggioni (Milano 2011), 49–50; P. Piva, 'San Siro di Cemmo a Capodiponte', Ibid., 233–6.

[31] K. Horste, 'Romanesque Sculpture in American Collections. XX. Ohio and Michigan', *Gesta,* 21 (1982), 107–34 at 122–5.

[32] '*Ut fuit introitus templi sancti Salomonis, Sic est istius in medio bovis atque leonis*'. C. B. Kendall, *The Allegory of the Church: Romanesque Portals and Their Verse Inscriptions* (Toronto 1998), 99–100.

[33] For an analysis of this iconographic type, with a primary focus on Britain, see G. D. Schmidt, *The Iconography of the Mouth of Hell: Eight-Century Britain to the Fifteenth Century* (Selinsgrove–London 1995).

[34] For the relationship between façade sculpture and eucharistic themes, see M. Angheben, 'Scultura romanica e liturgia', in *Arte medievale. Le vie dello spazio liturgico*, ed. P. Piva (Milano 2012), 147–90 at 163–70.

[35] E. Mâle, *L'art religieux du XII*ᵉ *siècle en France* (Paris 1922), 274–76.

[36] For these sarcophagi, see, most recently, Q. Cazes and D. Cazes, *Saint-Sernin de Toulouse: de Saturnin au chef-d'œuvre de l'art roman* (Graulhet 2008), 28–36.

[37] Ibid., 195–206.

[38] Arborio Mella, 'Cenno storico-artistico' (as n. 13); F. Delmastro, 'Osservazioni sulla Chiesa di Santa Fede a Cavagnolo Po: per una ipotesi di lettura delle vicende costruttive dedotta dall'analisi delle murature', in *Le chiese romaniche delle campagne astigiane: un repertorio per la loro conoscenza, conservazione, tutela*, ed. L. Pittarello (Torino 1984), 301–13.

[39] For a more detailed investigation of the construction phases, see Vescovi, *'Monferrato' medievale* (as n. 13), 92–107.

[40] The differences between the two groups of capitals are further discussed in M. L. Vescovi, 'Officine transalpine: scultura a Santa Fede di Cavagnolo', in *L'abbaziale* (as n. 13), 32–40.

[41] The different stages in the production of Romanesque capitals are discussed by D. Valin Johnson, 'The Analysis of Romanesque Architectural Sculpture: Verifying the Steps of a Methodology', *Gesta*, 28 (1989), 11–20.

[42] Vescovi, *'Monferrato' medievale* (as n. 13), 109–23: the similarities between the two churches are strong, in particular in the carvings. However, the pier with a square core at Cavagnolo became a compound pier in Montiglio, and the decoration of the capitals is more profuse.

[43] Casale Monferrato (and Vercelli): ibid., 68; Castellazzo Bormida: G. Ieni, *SS. Trinità da Lungi di Castellazzo Bormida: una Fondazione*

mortariense in terra di Gamondio (Alessandria 1985); Gavi and Castelnuovo Scrivia: C. Franzoni and E. Pagella, *Arte in Piemonte. Antichità e medioevo* (Torino 2002), 174.

[44] C. Bernoulli, *Die Skulpturen der Abtei Conques-en-Rouergue* (Basel 1956), Plate 31; M. Durliat, *La sculpture romane de la route de Saint-Jacques* (Mont-de-Marsan 1990), 67; É. Vergnolle, H. Pradalier, and N. Pousthomis-Dalle, 'Conques, Sainte-Foy. L'abbatiale romane', *Congrès Archéologique de France. Monuments de l'Aveyron* (Paris 2011), 71–160: 102. In the numbering system of Christoph Bernoulli, this is capital #12. It is #109 in that established by Marcel Durliat and subsequently used by Éliane Vergnolle.

[45] Ibid., 117–18.

[46] Ibid., 107. For a discussion of the capitals of Saint-Sernin, see Cazes and Cazes, *Saint-Sernin de Toulouse* (as n. 36), 105–11.

[47] The sculpture of the first workshop at Cavagnolo is also in dialogue with other capitals at Conques, whose chronology relates to a slightly later constructional phase, probably towards the end of the 11th century (Figures 9.14 and 9.15).

[48] It has been suggested that Santa Fede is mentioned in a document of 743: B. Bardessono, *Santa Fede di Cavagnolo (Torino)* (Cavagnolo 1995), 20–21. However, the early date is the result of a transcription error, as the document dates from 1234: Vescovi, *'Monferrato' medievale* (as n. 13), 127 n. 13.

[49] J. B. Moriondus, *Monumenta Aquensia* (Torino 1790), II, 25: '*Inter Monferratensia Chronica recenseri possunt duo, quae ad Monasteria in ea ditione posita pertinebant. Primi fragmentum mihi fuit olim a quodam Cavagnolii Communitatis Consiliario ostensum, in quo agebatur de origine Monasterii S. Fidei in eo territorio extantis, quod nunc Mensae Episcopali Aquensi probante Rege nostro in perpetuo fuit a S. Pontifice unitum, ex quo concludi posset ab illius Monachis fuisse conscriptum; ubi autem integrum extet posteritas forte deteget aliquando*'.

[50] Sheingorn, ed., *The Book of Sainte Foy* (as n. 18), 235.

[51] Ibid., 236.

[52] K. M. Ashley, 'The Mural Paintings of Horsham Saint Faith, Norfolk: Secular Patronage and Monastic Memory', in *Out of the Stream: Studies in Medieval and Renaissance Mural Painting*, eds. L. Urbano Alfonso and V. Serrão (Newcastle 2007), 318–34.

[53] J. N. Richardson, 'Between the Limousin and the Holy Land: Prisoners, Performance, and the Portal of San Leonardo at Siponto', *Gesta*, 54 (2015), 165–94.

[54] Ibid., 168–69.

[55] J.-Y. Mariotte, 'La Comtesse Hildegarde, fondatrice de Sainte-Foy', *Annuaire. Les amis de la Bibliothèque Humaniste de Sélestat*, 44 (1994), 7–16.

[56] Ibid., 13–15. According to the first document (1094), the foundation was promoted by Hildegard with her sons, and at that stage the church dedicated to the Holy Sepulchre had already been consecrated by Otto, bishop of Strasbourg (and one of the donors). One year later (23 July 1095), the same Otto with his brother took over what had been started by his mother ('*quod mater nostra ad honorem Dominici Sepulcri in Schelestat et sanctae Fidei benigne incepit*'). Desjardins, *Cartulaire* (as n. 21), 405–06.

[57] L. Robertini, 'Le *Liber miraculorum sance Fidis* dans la tradition manuscrite entre Conques et Sélestat', *Annuaire. Les amis de la Bibliothèque Humaniste de Sélestat*, 44 (1994), 67–72.

[58] 'Livre des miracles de Sainte Foy. 1094–1994. Traduction des textes', *Annuaire. Les amis de la Bibliothèque Humaniste de Sélestat*, 44 (1994), 23. Also the abbey of Sainte-Foy in Conches-en-Ouche (Normandy) was founded by Roger de Tosny following a visit to Conques: A. Bouillet, *L'église Sainte-Foy de Conches (Eure) et ses vitraux: étude historique et archéologique* (Caen 1889), 2. I thank John McNeill for calling my attention to this example.

[59] Horsham, 'Houses of Benedictine Monks: The Priory of Binham', in *A History of the County of Norfolk: Volume 2*, ed. William Page (London 1906), 343–46; Sélestat, 'Livre des miracles de Sainte Foy' (as n. 57), 23.

[60] C. Vienney, 'Sélestat, église Sainte-Foy', in *Congrès Archéologique de France* (Paris 2006), 133–48.

[61] Desjardins, *Cartulaire* (as n. 21), 53–54: '*in tali convenientia ut monachi sanctae Fidis faciant ibi ecclesiam*'.

[62] Ibid., 336–37: '*aecclesiam nostram quae olim constructa fuit in alodio nostro de Monte Sancto Johanni que modo reedificatur a monachis Conchacensibus in honore sancti Johannis et sanctae Fidis virginis martyris*'.

[63] Ibid., 64–65: '*quia jam virtutibus sanctae Fidis et magno labore monachorum constructa est ibi ecclesia et villa admodum hedificata*'.

[64] Sheingorn, ed., *The Book of Sainte Foy* (as n. 18), 236; *Liber miraculorum Sancte Fidis*, ed. A. Bouillet (Paris 1897), 241: '*in ecclesiam quondam, quem in honorem sancta Fidis quidam frater, nomine Rodbertus, super ripam Euphratis fluvii construxerat*'.

[65] Desjardins, *Cartulaire* (as n. 21), 51: '*per talem convenientiam ut Deusdet monacus aut Petrus aut Odolricus faciant unam aecclesiam ibi in honore sanctae Fidis*'.

[66] *Liber miraculorum Sancte Fidis* (as n. 64), 212: '*Sancte Fidis in honore monachus nomine Deusdet ecclesiam que Sardanum dicitur, ligneo edificio in pago Basatensi prius construxit, et in humili machina tabulatis intexuit*'. Sheingorn, ed., *The Book of Sainte Foy* (as n. 18), 212. Deusdet is named as prior of Persa in 1060: Desjardins, *Cartulaire* (as n. 21), 401–02.

[67] For a different identification of this monk, see F. C. Taylor, 'Miracula, Saints' Cults and Socio-Political Landscapes: Bobbio, Conques and Post-Carolingian Society' (unpublished PhD thesis, University of Nottingham, 2012), 133–34.

[68] Durliat, *La sculpture romane* (as n. 44), 428–30.

[69] Desjardins, *Cartulaire* (as n. 21), xlvi–cxx (complete list of priories); civ–cv (priories in the diocese of Toulouse).

[70] Analysis of the list of priories and dependencies as summarised by Desjardins (Ibid., passim) has revealed that the following sites, once associated with Conques, still contain medieval remains. Saint-Hilarian-Sainte-Foy at Perse, Espalion; Saint-Martin, Flagnac; Saint-Védard, Coubisou; Sainte-Foi de Trébosc, Montrozier; La Roque Valzergues, Saint-Saturnin-de-Lenne; Saint-Martin, Brommes (all Aveyron); Sainte-Foy, Molompize (Cantal); Saint-Gal, Roffiac (Cantal); Saint-Blaise, Esclottes (Lot-et-Garonne); Saint-Pierre, Carsac (Dordogne); Sainte-Foy, Bains (Haute-Loire); Saint-Maurice, Saint-Maurice-d'Ibie (Ardèche); Notre-Dame-des-Planques, Tanus (Tarn); Sainte-Foy-du-Châtelet, Chambles (Loire); Saint-Victor-sur-Loire (Loire); Sainte-Foy, Sélestat (Bas-Rhin); Cristo de Cataláin, Garinoáin (Navarre); Santa Fe, Barbastro (Huesca); Horsham St Faith (Norfolk); Santa Fede, Cavagnolo (Piedmont).

[71] Conques, transept portal: Durliat, *La sculpture romane* (as n. 44), 68–70; Cristo de Cataláin: M. Castiñeiras, '*Didacus Gelmirius*, patrono delle arti. Il lungo cammino di Compostela: dalla periferia al centro del Romanico', in *Compostela e l'Europa. La storia di Diego Gelmirez*, ed. M. Castiñeiras (Milano 2010), 32–97 at 48.

[72] E. Castelnuovo, 'Scultori romanici sulle vie delle Alpi', in *Dal Piemonte all'Europa: esperienze monastiche nella società medievale* (Turin 1988), 21–42. F. Cervini, 'Cattedrali all'antica: l'autunno del romanico sulle Alpi occidentali', in *Medioevo: l'Europa delle Cattedrali*, ed. A. C. Quintavalle (Milano 2007), 586–97. On the cloister of Sant'Orso in Aosta see, most recently, W. Keil, 'Schrift und Bild zur Bildung? Die Kapitelle im Kreuzgang von SS. Pietro ed Orso in Aosta', in *Sacred Scripture/Sacred Space – The Interlacing of Real Places and Conceptual Spaces in Medieval Art and Architecture*, eds. T. Frese, W. Keil, and K. Krüger (Berlin–Boston 2019), 187–215.

[73] For this fundamental article, see the English version edited by Dario Gamboni: E. Castelnuovo and C. Ginzburg, 'Symbolic Domination and Artistic Geography in Italian Art History' (trans. M. Curie), *Art in Translation*, 1 (2009), 5–48. In relation to the subject of this article, the authors specify that 'the notions of "centre" and "periphery" would not have had for European monasticism the meaning that can be attributed to these terms after the year 1000' (p. 9).

[74] The model has been called into question, with Thomas DaCosta Kaufmann suggesting that it represents the 'colonizer's model of the world': DaCosta Kaufmann, *Toward a Geography of Art* (as n. 3), 163.

[75] G. Constable, *The Abbey of Cluny: A Collection of Essays to Mark the Eleven-Hundredth Anniversary of Its Foundation* (Münster 2010), 226.

[76] Ibid., 225, note 62, 228.

[77] Desjardins, *Cartulaire* (as n. 21), 54: '*ut sicut praecepta regalia monstrabant, perpetuo abbati Conchensi esset subditum et serviret sicut membra capiti*'.

The Regional and Transregional in Romanesque Europe (2021), 119–146

TIRON ON THE EDGE

CULTURAL GEOGRAPHY, REGIONALISM AND LIMINALITY

Sheila Bonde and Clark Maines with John Sheffer

The abbey of Tiron was established in the early 12th century on a liminal, forested site. In this paper, we adopt the strategies of cultural geography, regionalism, and liminality to situate the monastery within its marginal geographic location. The results of our archaeological excavations on the site, together with analysis of standing remains, and study of visual and documentary evidence, enable us to reconstruct the plan and elevation of the 12th-century church. We examine the contributions of local and extraregional supporters in shaping the church and its community. We also analyse the cultural geography of church construction at Tiron, investigating its local and transregional sources, building materials, modes of design and construction, as well as the varied sources for – and frames through which – its size, plan, and elevation may have been viewed and interpreted by its 12th-century community and sponsors.

INTRODUCTION

Tiron was founded by Bernard of Abbeville/Tiron in 1109 in a liminal zone at the intersection of three dioceses (Chartres, Le Mans, and Sées) and the major regions of Normandy, the Île-de-France and the Maine (Figure 10.1).[1] It lies within relatively underpopulated territory characterised by dense forests and was largely beyond the control of ecclesiastical and secular powers. The closest important town and diocesan seat was Chartres, 50 km to the east. The closest comital castle was Nogent-le-Rotrou, 15 km to the west.[2] The new abbey brought together a group of former itinerant hermits to create a new and stable community. This community quickly became an international order that included more than 150 dependent abbeys, priories, and parishes, as well as farms, mills, and other landed possessions (Figure 10.2). The mother-house of La Sainte-Trinité still stands, largely intact, a major monument of the medieval monastic reform (Figure 10.3).

Despite its importance, however, Tiron – both the order and the church – is notably absent from virtually all publications on Romanesque architecture. Three *Zodiaque* volumes – *Touraine romane*, *Val-de-Loire romane*, and *Île-de-France romane* – might have included the great abbey church of Tiron, but none does. On the maps that appear in the front of each volume, only the *Île-de-France romane* includes portions of its region, but Tiron itself does not appear.

How do we confront architecture that is 'not on the map'? We will argue that the perspectives of cultural geography, regionalism, and the anthropological notion of liminality can all contribute to an understanding of Tiron's marginal position in both the medieval and contemporary scholarly landscapes. Indeed, as we will show, Tiron's liminality was a key to its success in the Middle Ages as well as an important reason for its marginality in modern scholarship.

CULTURAL GEOGRAPHY

A regional approach typically assumes that surrounding geological and topographic conditions, as well as local traditions of construction, constrain or determine local styles. Art historians, especially those looking at medieval France, have tended to view Romanesque style through the lens of geographic regions. These regions (Burgundy, Provence, or the Île-de-France, for example) are presumed to provide the determining frame for stylistic development. Cultural geography, by contrast, rejects the notion of determinism. Rather, it places its focus upon the relationships among human agents acting within (or against) the natural environment to produce a 'cultural landscape'.[3] Power relations are seen as fundamental to spatial processes and the development of a sense of place and local identity.

In this paper, we will use the example of the mother church of the Tironensian congregation and view it as the monumental centre of a monastic cultural landscape created from the interactions between its natural environment and the actions of the community and its supporters – or,

  DOI: 10.4324/9781003162827-10

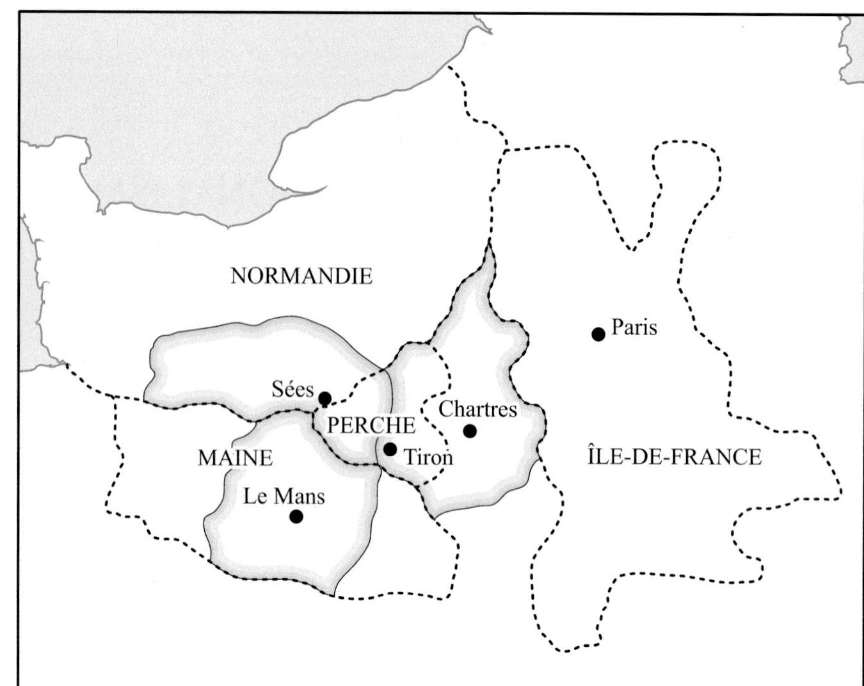

FIGURE 10.1

Map of dioceses and regional polities (Bonde and Maines – redrawn by Chris Kennish)

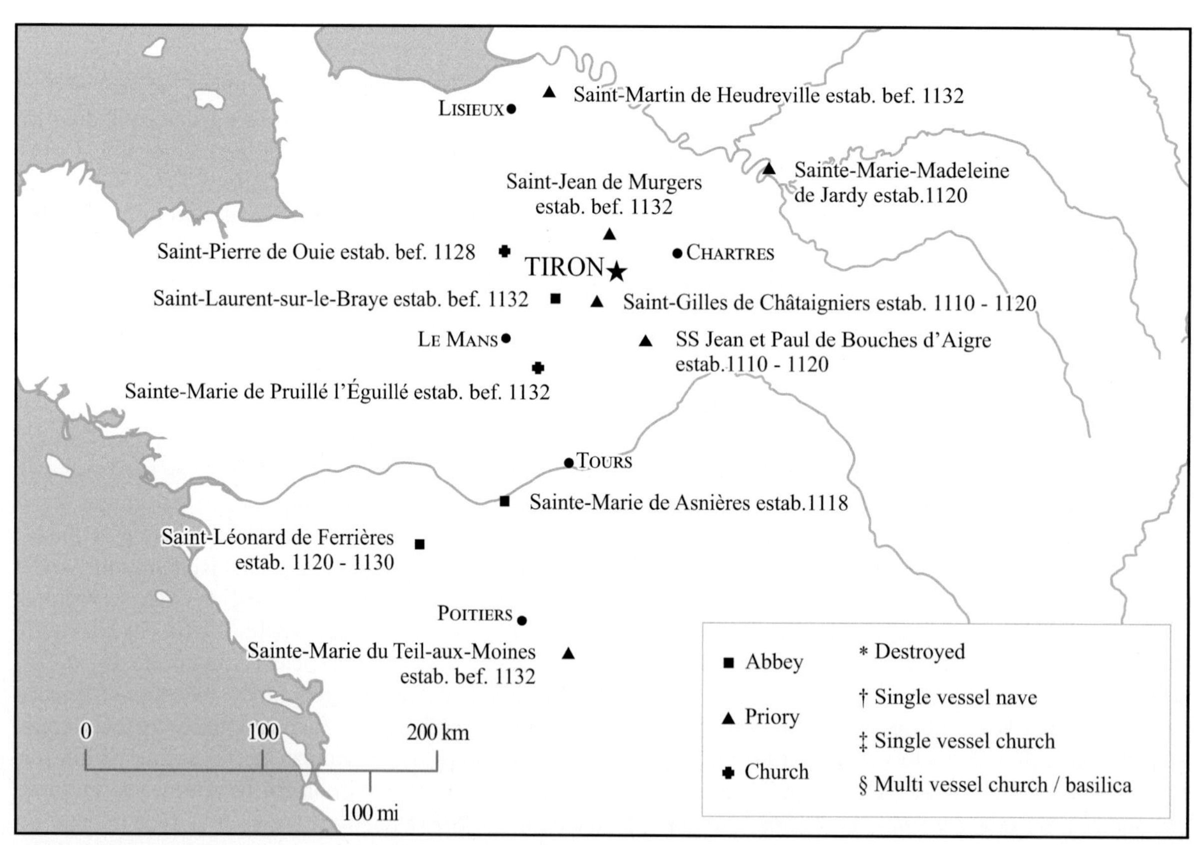

FIGURE 10.2

Tiron's church possessions in 1132 (Bonde and Maines – redrawn by Chris Kennish)

FIGURE 10.3
Aerial view of Thiron-Gardais (© Google Earth)

in the terms of cultural geography, a network of agents. As we will see, many members of the early community had regional and transregional experiences, and a number of its supporters were themselves situated extraregionally, factors that complicate any notion of Tiron's 'regionality'. The strategies of cultural geography will allow us to foreground the agency of extraregional individuals, as well as to suggest that both regional and transregional architectural traditions were important.

REGIONALISM AND 'CRITICAL REGIONALISM'

The concepts of regionalism and critical regionalism provide a complementary lens through which to view Tiron's place within the medieval landscape. Peter Lasko has offered a review of regionalism in French Romanesque, tracing its 19th-century roots in the thinking of Arcisse de Caumont and Viollet-le-Duc and seeing its continuation in much of subsequent scholarship.[4] Lasko pointed out both the reluctance and the inability of scholarship to define regions precisely. He proposed that we unplug the notion of regions as the determinants for architectural style, suggesting instead that architecture, shaped by the intersection of tradition and patronage, was the primary instrument in the definition of a region.[5] Working in the Gothic period rather than the Romanesque, Dany Sandron has offered a different approach to defining a geographic region and the study of its architecture. He suggested that the diocese constitutes the geographic region within which church architecture should be studied and that the key monument to understanding diocesan architecture should be the cathedral.[6] While Sandron's model usefully places the emphasis on ecclesiastical organization of the landscape, his view of the cathedral as the formal source for architectural development cannot be imposed in all cases. At Tiron, in particular, the peripheral location of the house, together with the power of other regional and extraregional forces, as we will see, changed the dynamic in important ways. Moreover, in formal terms, Tiron bears little resemblance to the Romanesque cathedral of Chartres.

One of the most influential sources to reinforce the notion of regions in French Romanesque has been the sixty-volume series, *La nuit des temps*, published by the monks of the abbey of Sainte-Marie de la Pierre-qui-Vire (Yonne).[7] The series materializes regions by mapping and dividing Romanesque architecture into separate regional volumes. As we have already noted, however, the *Zodiaque* series entirely overlooks Tiron which is located on the edges of several of its maps.

Contemporary architectural theory proposes what is often called 'critical regionalism' as a way of drawing attention to the globalizing and homogenizing weight of international modernism and to advocate for a renewed engagement with local styles and materials.[8] In the wake of the Postmodernist debate, critical regionalism has championed *place* as an essential force in shaping modern architecture and reconnecting it with cultural and local forces. In the words of Kenneth Frampton, one of its main proponents: 'The fundamental strategy of Critical Regionalism is to mediate the impact of universal civilization with elements derived [. . .] from the peculiarities of a particular place'.[9] Scholarship has tended to view 11th- and 12th-century Romanesque in France in much the same universalizing and monolithic fashion as globalizing international modernism. The Romanesque is often presented as a singular style, only gently mediated by regional materials and designs.

As we will see, however, Tiron uses resolutely local materials in combination with decidedly transregional forms. The individual 'agents' at Tiron (early abbots, members of the community, and patrons) were aware, through their travels and the exchange of knowledge, of architecture and ideas from other extraregional places. They actively chose regional and transregional styles, materials and technologies, or rejected them, providing medieval analogues to contemporary critical regionalist solutions. The cultural landscape and the great church of La Sainte-Trinité at Tiron results from decisions to blend transregional experiences with local tradition. We need to recognize the presence of these active choices rather than seeing only a passive determinism exerted by local styles.

LIMINALITY

Liminality is an anthropological concept, especially explored by van Gennep and Turner, denoting a transitional state in a ritual, in which the participant is neither the same as s/he was at its beginning nor as s/he will be at its end.[10] The spatial dimension of the concept includes borders, frontiers, no-man's-lands, disputed territories and crossroads, all places which people pass through but in which they do not live. The founders of the abbey of Tiron chose one such frontier territory but ironically embraced its liminality for a permanent establishment.

The monastery of Tiron was (and still is) liminal, set along the frontiers dividing Normandy to the west, the Île-de-France to the east and the Maine to the south (Figure 10.1). Today it is known as the *petit pays*, or micro-region, of the Perche-Thironnais.[11] Still sparsely populated today, during the 11th and 12th centuries the area was densely forested.

Tiron is also located liminally at the intersection of three diocesan boundaries. Distances from diocesan and regional centres are revealing. With an average day's travel at 40–50 km a day on horseback, Tiron was remote from almost all population centres. As we have already noted, Tiron was located 50 km to the west of its diocesan centre at Chartres and was even more remote from other cathedral towns: 90 km from Le Mans and 80 km from Sées. Few other monastic churches were in the vicinity, making the scale and presence of Tiron all the more surprising.[12] In addition, almost all of the 12th-century parish churches of the region were modest, unvaulted, and typically built of local materials. The nearby comital castle of Nogent-le-Rotrou was relatively close at 15 km, but the region held few other such fortified seats, with La Ferté-Bernard the next closest at 36 km away.

The liminality of Tiron on the edges of these religious and secular regions – and the relative emptiness of the territory – was palpable in the medieval as well as the contemporary experience. Medieval narratives, such as the 'Life of the Blessed Bernard of Tiron' consistently describe the region as one that is extensively forested. The following passage provides one example;[13] 'Bernard, man of God, secluded in the most solitary wildernesses of the forests of the Perche'.[14]

While descriptions of Bernard as a hermit, living and preaching in the forest, may have been a literary *topos* based on biblical precedents like John the Baptist and Old Testament prophets such as Jeremiah and Ezekiel, the early 12th-century reality of the Perche would have resonated equally with any contemporary familiar with it. Six of the first ten charters in the abbey's cartulary mention gifts of forest or use forests as boundary markers, confirming the wooded nature of the region.[15] Furthermore, the Cassini map, created in the 18th century, shows the region as having preserved much of its medieval forest cover (Figure 10.4).[16]

For a community of former hermits, liminality may have been a salient reason why Bernard and his followers saw advantages in the site of Tiron in the first place. The liminal setting of the abbey of Tiron makes it an interesting case study for investigating the relationship between the architecture of the church and its regional and transregional contexts. While its existence 'on the edge' has ensured its absence from most regional maps of Romanesque France, we wish to reposition its liminality as an active, 'critical regionalist' choice, which resonated with the hermits who selected it. This decision should help us recover ways to recognize Tiron as a major monument of the monastic reform movement during the Romanesque period.

THE ROMANESQUE CHURCH OF TIRON

The abbey of La Sainte-Trinité at Tiron was placed within this thickly forested, liminal micro-region. The Romanesque church was a simple but monumental structure more than 85 m long (Figure 10.5 and Colour Plate XII (top)). Its massive size contrasted strongly with the few parish churches and monasteries in the region. In plan, Tiron was an aisleless cruciform building with strongly projecting transepts, terminating in a comparatively short, flat east end that was flanked by two monumental towers 'shouldered' into and built integrally with the angles between the transept arms and the sanctuary. The nave and transept were tall, narrow, and wooden roofed. That the surviving crossing bay is not vaulted and shows no details in pier design to suggest that it ever was allows us to infer that the transept arms were unvaulted. As we have reconstructed the 12th-century plan (Figure 10.6), it is possible that the Romanesque sanctuary, partially supported on both sides by towers, may have been

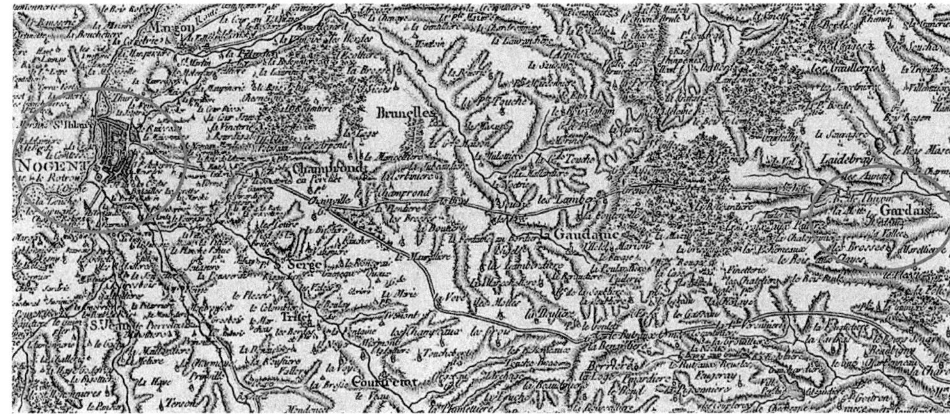

FIGURE 10.4

Detail of the Cassini map of the Perche showing Nogent-le-Rotrou, Tiron, and forest cover c. *1750*

FIGURE 10.5

Tiron: Romanesque church, view from the north (Bonde and Maines)

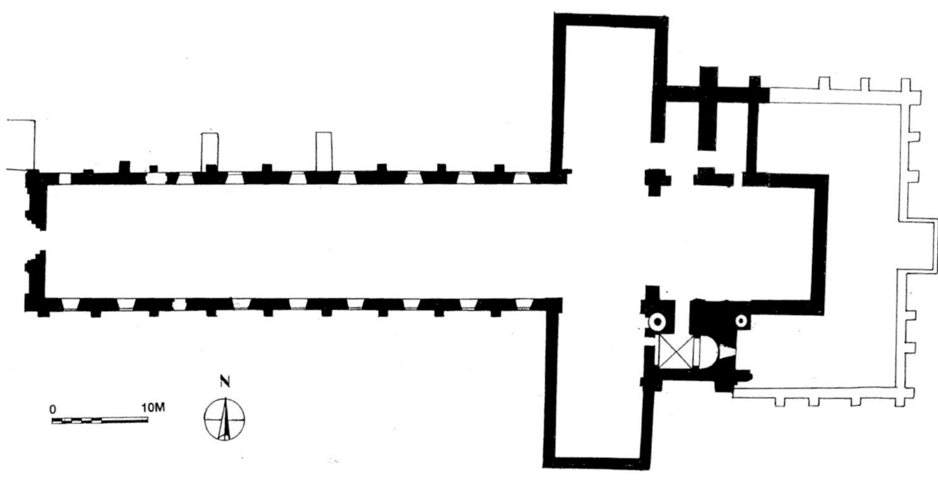

FIGURE 10.6

Tiron: reconstructed plan of the Romanesque church (Bonde and Maines

vaulted, even if the nave, crossing, and transept arms were not.[17] Our research and measurement of the south tower revealed that part of the curving wall of an internal apse on the ground floor had been cut away during the 15th-century construction of a Gothic chevet.[18] Decoration of the interior was minimal, and carving seems to have been limited to foliate and abstract capitals located in the choir and crossing arches.[19] As we will see, only the somewhat later west façade bears figural decoration in the form of relief sculpture, console heads, and historiated capitals.

SOURCES FOR THE STUDY OF THE 12TH-CENTURY CHURCH

Since the church survives today only in a fragmented state, we must draw on various sources in order to recover its original appearance. The most important source is, of course, what remains of the great 12th-century structure itself. The façade, nave, and crossing bay remain in elevation, as does the south tower. Vestiges of the north shouldered tower and parts of the north and south choir walls also survive.[20] The north tower only partly survives in elevation and may not have been as high as the tower on the south, but the arched opening giving onto the north transept arm does survive to its full height and is essentially identical to the opening of the tower in the opposite arm (Figure 10.7).[21] Excavations carried out by our research group in 2018 brought to light the foundations of the eastern closure wall of the 12th-century chevet (Figure 10.8).[22] Our research during that season now provides information on the phasing of the church and its surviving tower (see Figure 10.6). Our excavations also revealed that the foundations

FIGURE 10.7

Tiron: north transept arm east wall, showing the opening (now blocked) into the north shouldered tower and the small round-arched window above (Bonde and Maines)

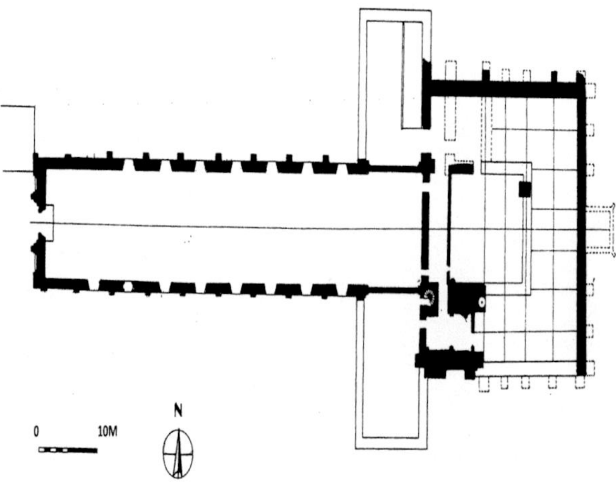

FIGURE 10.8

Tiron: plan of the church showing extant walls, including part of the foundation raft for the Romanesque chevet (Bonde and Maines)

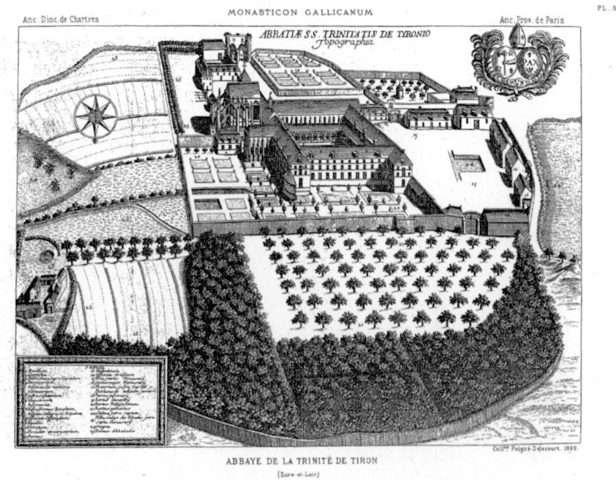

FIGURE 10.9

Tiron: Bird's-eye view of abbey (Monasticon Gallicanum, 1882 edition)

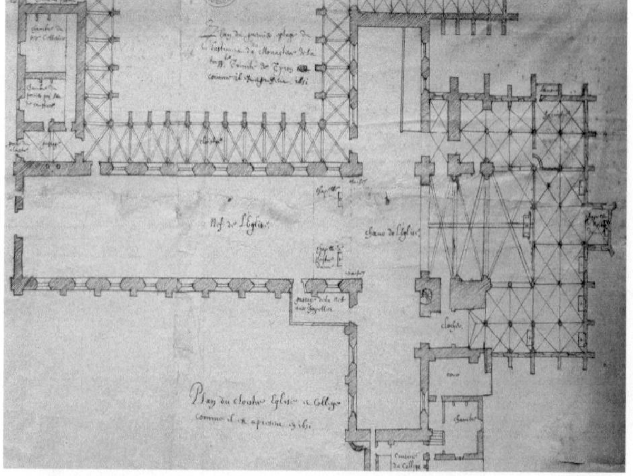

FIGURE 10.10

Plan of the church at Tiron (Dom Hilaire Pinet, 1651) (Archives nationales III. Eure-et-Loir, 4.2; photo by Arthur Panier)

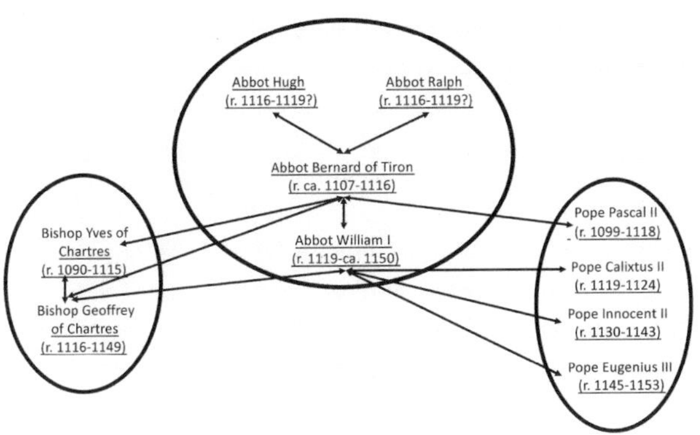

FIGURE 10.11a

Ecclesiastical support network for Tiron

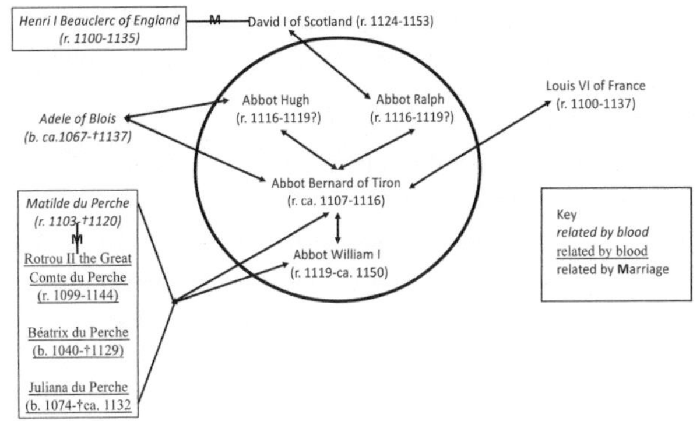

FIGURE 10.11b

Secular support network for Tiron

beneath the north wall of the Romanesque choir were as deep as those on the south side where the tower still survives. This discovery further supports the notion of twin shouldered towers.

A bird's-eye view of the abbey shown from the north is included in the *Monasticon Gallicanum* (Figure 10.9).[23] The Gothic choir, for which the engraving is most useful, collapsed in 1817.[24] It is not (yet) known when the transept arms were dismantled, though perhaps at the same time. Important pictorial information also exists in a set of eleven plans and one elevation drawn in 1651 by the Maurist monk, Hilaire Pinet, in preparation for an extensive series of alterations to the monastery.[25] These are now in the Archives nationales in Paris and include a reasonably accurate plan of the entire abbey site, a detailed plan of the church and cloister, and a series of plans of the cloister and claustral ranges that represent 'before' (the actual state) and 'after' (proposed Maurist alterations) states of the site.

Pinet's plan of the church and cloister is especially important for our analysis.[26] It represents the church as it was in Pinet's time – i.e. a 12th-century cruciform structure with a Gothic double-aisled, flat east end that includes a projecting axial chapel. In addition to providing a surprisingly accurate overall plan with vault lines and wall thicknesses indicated, the plan includes such details as the position of the night stairs, the location of altars, and a later alteration to the Gothic choir that incorporates a (presumably displaced) sacristy as well as the closure of the liturgical choir (Figure 10.10).

Beyond the material and visual sources, the abbey of Tiron is rich in surviving written records. Foremost among these documents is a mainly 12th-century cartulary with later additions and a number of separate medieval charters.[27] To these must be added the lives of the founder, Saint Bernard of Abbeville/Tiron.[28] Further information can be gleaned from contemporary texts such as the chronicle of the abbey of Saint-Maixent and the *Historia Ecclesiastica* of Orderic Vitalis.[29] These recount with varying degrees of chronological precision the foundation and growth of the abbey of Tiron.

THE 'AGENTS'

The sources just described allow us to perceive the roles played by members of the Tironensian community and by its regional and extraregional supporters in shaping the plan and elevation of the new church. Following the first of our theoretical frames, cultural geography, we will focus upon the relationships among the human 'agents' acting within (or against) the natural environment to produce Tiron's 'cultural landscape'. Our second theoretical frame, 'critical regionalism', will encourage us to view the choices made by Tiron's 'agents' as an active embrace – or rejection – of local factors in order to forge a new identity for the place.

As we will see, the 'agents' formed a network of people who knew one another either through personal contact, through family connections of blood or marriage, or by correspondence. Ecclesiastical and secular networks of the abbey of Tiron (Figures 10.11a and 10.11b) provided early support in the form of land and material resources, funds, privileges, and prestige.[30]

Agent I: Bernard of Tiron

Bernard of Tiron was probably born around 1050 in Abbeville or Ponthieu.[31] Little is known of his childhood though he was apparently a secular student before entering monastic life. While the *Vita* places him at Saint-Savin-sur-Gartempe, Orderic Vitalis claims he was in the monastery Saint-Benoît de Quinçay near Poitiers before becoming abbot of Saint-Cyprien in Poitiers, a monastery over which the abbey of Cluny had claims.[32] It is certain that Bernard became abbot of Saint-Cyprien in 1100, as three charters reveal his abbatial work there.[33] His appointment and consecration by Bishop Pierre II of Poitiers provoked a reaction from Cluny and led to him being deposed, despite a trip to Rome where he appealed his case before Pope Pascal II.[34] Details of Bernard's activity between 1102/04 and 1107 are lacking, but according to an entry of 1110 in the cartulary of Saint-Cyprien, he withdrew from that abbey to the 'wilderness', although the location of that particular 'desert' is unknown.[35]

Bernard of Tiron thus seems to have been a well-educated man, a member of a much larger religious reform movement and possessed of a charismatic personality. He was a man who moved around, not simply as a wandering hermit but also as a travelling ecclesiastic moving between monasteries in central and western France and reaching Rome at least once. His cultural and visual experience would have been comparatively broad and certainly transregional.

Agents II: Bernard's disciples

The *Vita Bernardi* makes clear that Bernard travelled with a group of followers.[36] He also seems to have attracted additional disciples during his travels in 'the wilderness', and we can assume that both men and women were among them. Some of these disciples may have left Saint-Cyprien with him. Foulon's research into eremitism in the Loire valley suggests that Bernard's travels took him northward through the forests of the Sarthe where he would have encountered other eremitic groups.[37] The cultural experiences of these men and women would, at a minimum, have extended across the west of France.

Individually, we know little of the early monks of Tiron, though they seem to have been numerous. Bernard's new order was notable in that it welcomed members of the artisanal classes, as Orderic Vitalis makes clear:

> A multitude of the faithful of both orders flocked to him there, and Father Bernard received in charity all who were eager for conversion to monastic life, instructing individuals to practice in the monastery the various crafts in which they were skilled. So, among the men who hastened to share his life were joiners and blacksmiths, sculptors and goldsmiths, painters and masons, vine-dressers and husbandmen and skilled artificers of many kinds.[38]

These artisans would have brought their own set of local traditions to bear upon the construction process of the new monastery.

Agents III: Bernard's successors

Bernard of Tiron died in April 1116, barely two years after Bishop Yves of Chartres and the cathedral chapter formally granted a carrucate of land at Tiron to the new community.[39] Little is known about Bernard's immediate successors, Ralph and Hugues. *Gallia christiana* provides a list of the abbots of Tiron, although the dates of accession and death are not given for all of them.[40] According to the authors of *Gallia christiana*, Hugues was chosen as abbot from among Bernard's close followers.[41] Abbot Hugues appears in only one charter, dated by Merlet to 1117–19.[42] Kathleen Thompson, however, uses Scottish documents to identify Abbot Ralph as the immediate successor to Bernard, a tradition confirmed by the 1123 mortuary roll of Vitalis of Savigny 'in which the monks of Tiron ask for prayers for their abbots Bernard and Ralph'.[43]

However the immediate succession to Abbot Bernard is resolved, by late 1119 the abbacy had passed to William I, who is addressed as abbot by Pope Calixtus II in a pancarte confirming Tiron in its possessions in November of that year.[44] William had probably been one of Bernard's followers in the wilderness. He became the great organizer-administrator of the Tironensian congregation and presided over the mother-house for at least thirty years.[45] Three papal confirmations of Tiron's holdings (Calixtus II in 1119, Innocent II in 1132, and Eugenius III in 1147) occurred during his abbacy, a time when the number of dependent churches (abbeys, priories and parishes) increased to more than eighty. By the end of Abbot William's long and impressive reign, the abbey of Tiron was the head of a rapidly expanding and still-growing congregation of reformed Benedictine monks.[46]

Agents IV: ecclesiastical patrons

One of the keys to the success of Bernard's Tironensian project resides in the early patronage the abbey received, which was notably ecclesiastical as well as secular. Ecclesiastical support flowed from the cathedral of Chartres, the centre of Tiron's diocese. In February of 1114, Bishop Yves and the cathedral chapter of Chartres gave:

> In the name of the holy and indivisible Trinity, I, Ivo, humble minister of the Church of Chartres, and Arnauldus, deacon, as well as the [whole] chapter of the Blessed Mary, wish it to be known to all, both now and in the future, what lord Bernard, the venerable abbot, with the congregation entrusted to his care, entreating us to grant them, we concede to them a carrucate [about 30 acres or about 12 hectares] of land of the lands of the Blessed Mary which is above the little river called Thironne in the parish of Gardais, for building a monastery and cloister et cetera necessary for the use of the brothers.[47]

Sometime before December 1115, at the request of Rotrou the Great, Count of the Perche, Bishop Yves consecrated a cemetery for the monks of Tiron:

> [W]e consecrated a certain communal cemetery that is sited above the river that is called Thironne for the use of certain religious monks who in the said place chose to lead a hermit's life and who had constructed a monastery there by the advantage of the place and of time.[48]

Bernard of Tiron died in April of 1116, two years after the gift of the cathedral chapter's land at Tiron. Of Bernard's death, the cathedral obituary states:

> Died Bernard, abbot of Tiron who, in that place built a church from its foundations and ordained there many monks in holy and religious ways.[49]

Whether this notice refers to a presumed initial wooden church or to the great 12th-century church is not known, although it is worth observing that the phrase '*de fundamentis*' is not typically used to refer to wooden buildings.

Thus Bishop Yves and his cathedral chapter were essential partners in the foundation of the new monastery at Tiron. Yves was an energetic reformer, one who was present at the Council of Poitiers in 1100, where he was likely to have first encountered Bernard.[50] Yves was in contact with other reformers through an active career as a letter writer and as a frequent traveller for his church.

Perhaps even more important to Tiron than Bishop Yves was his successor, Geoffrey of Lèves (1115–49).[51] Scholars are agreed that the Geoffrey who became bishop of Chartres was the same person as '*Gaufridus prepositus*' who signed Bishop Yves's foundation charter for Tiron.[52] This early relationship took on increased meaning when Geoffrey's election was contested by Count Thibaud of Blois-Chartres. The dispute was mediated in Geoffrey's favour by Abbot Bernard of Tiron and Robert of Arbrissel.[53] Geoffrey appeared in twenty-two Tironensian charters during his episcopacy (1115–49), which paralleled William I's abbacy (1119–*c*. 1150) almost exactly.[54] Geoffrey gave two parishes to Tiron, apparently directly, and gave three others that he first received from secular lords who held them unjustly. Ten gifts were recorded in his presence, or were confirmed by him, or were made 'by his hand'. Geoffrey also facilitated accords between Tiron and other houses or secular lords five times and gave land to the abbey himself once. Moreover, Geoffrey's support is spread over the fullness of his reign, extending from *c*. 1117 for the earliest charter to 1146 for the latest.

Yves, Geoffrey, and the chapter were not only implicated and strongly supportive of the new abbey, they brought their own reforming connections to bear upon it.

Agents V: secular patrons

Tiron's secular patronage was family connected as well as royal.[55] It focused upon the family of Rotrou II the Great (r. 1100–44), count of the Perche, an important border territory between Normandy and the Île-de-France, as we have noted.[56] Rotrou was married to Mathilda *fitz* Roy, an illegitimate but acknowledged daughter of King Henry I of England, making the count the king's son-in-law as well as his military ally.[57] Rotrou's mother was the former Béatrix de Roucy, a descendant of Carolingian nobility through her family.[58] His sister, Juliana, was the widow of Gilbert l'Aigle, who died in the sinking of the White Ship.[59]

In a charter dated 1116–19, recorded in the cathedral chapter in the presence of Bishop Geoffrey of Chartres, Rotrou made a variety of donations including a tithe of all his grain, use of his woodlands for firewood and for the monks' pigs, his holding at Arcisses with its mill and pond, the Luxvillat valley that is on the near side of the water, and the chapel with its garden, as well as 'timber in all his forests to build the monks' house'.[60] *Domus* may refer to the monks' church, or equally to any, or to all of the monastic buildings needed by the monks that may have originally been wooden structures. Given the need for scaffolding for large-scale construction and the fact that the church was an unvaulted, wooden-roofed structure, this passage suggests that construction on any or all parts of the monastery may have been under way by 1116–19.

Secular women were also important patrons. As KathleenThompson has pointed out, we know little about Rotrou's wife, the Countess Mathilda of the Perche.[61] She appears in charters with her husband in support of Tiron, but she was known to have also supported the Cluniac house of Saint-Denis in Nogent, presumably taking over that role from Béatrix who transferred her allegiance to Tiron. Countess Matilda may have been influential, along with her husband, in persuading Henry I Beauclerc to make generous gifts to the abbey and to confirm the gifts of others.[62]

Rotrou's mother, Béatrix of the Perche, was also an important supporter of the new abbey. She was born in Roucy in 1051, married Count Geoffrey II of the Perche in 1072, and died in 1129.[63] Béatrix's involvement with Tiron began long before she died. She was an active noblewoman involved with her county, with religious houses and with the new abbey. Geoffrey Grossus' *Life* tells us that the Dowager Countess Béatrix left the family castle in Nogent and moved to Tiron, where she lived in a house, perhaps located in the area west of the monastery proper, where a number of older structures still stand today:

> The above-mentioned Béatrix, who recognized Bernard's holiness, ceased to reside in her castle, once houses were built at Tiron. She lived at Tiron for the rest of her life and built the large basilica [sic] church with many cash outlays.[64]

Orderic Vitalis confirms Béatrix's role as an important patron of the new abbey.[65] Her patronage, however, cannot simply be tied to the decade of the 1120s, as might be assumed from Geoffrey's *Vita*. She witnessed charters on behalf of Tiron from at least 1114.[66] We do not know when Béatrix began supporting new construction financially, nor when she moved to Tiron to live out her life. While we can be reasonably certain that her support for the new house at Tiron extended from 1114 at the latest until her death in 1129, it may have begun several years earlier and could have continued after her death in the terms of her testament.

As Rotrou the Great's father-in-law, King Henry I Beauclerc of England also supported Bernard's new abbey, which lay near to his dukedom of Normandy. Probably before 1116, Henry gave 'the monks of Tiron a general exemption from tolls and customs throughout his lands'.[67] Further, the king regularly confirmed gifts made to Tiron by lords within his entourage in both Normandy and England: lands at Barton and Kington in England,[68] Grémonville in Normandy in 1115,[69] and Saint-Dogmaels in Wales.[70] Finally, in an undated charter, Henry gave 15 marks of silver annually at Winchester.[71]

King Henry's sister, the Countess Adela of Blois-Chartres, also contributed support to the new abbey. According to Geoffrey Grossus, the countess offered Bernard broader and better expanses of land on which to build his new monastery, although Bernard declined the offer.[72] Adela may have been acting for her son Thibaud when she twice made gifts of land to Tiron, once for land on which the priory of Saint-André d'Écoman was established and once for land for the priory of Saint-Eutrope de Montrion.[73] After Adela left the world for the convent of Marcigny in 1122, support for Tiron by the comital house of Blois-Chartres was continued by her son Thibaud.

Tiron's liminal geographic position between Normandy and the Île-de-France, and Henry Beauclerc's early support for the abbey, may have stimulated the patronage of Louis VI of France. Henry I and Louis VI were in conflict over border issues throughout the second decade of the 12th century. Louis's interest in supporting Tiron may thus have been intended to assert his influence in the region. Patronage of the French king began in 1115 when Louis gave Tiron four carrucates of land at Saintry (Essonne) and the wood of Melleray (Sarthe).[74] According to the *Vita Bernardi*, Louis VI also arranged for his two sons, Philip and the future Louis VII, to be baptised at Tiron.[75] The chapter of Geoffrey's *Life* in which this information appears and the chapters which precede and follow it effectively constitute a summary of the early elite patronage of Tiron.[76]

David I, Earl of Huntingdon and future King of Scotland (r. 1124–53), was the brother-in-law and courtier of King Henry I Beauclerc, who had married David's sister Mathilda. Given these family connections, it is not surprising that David also became interested in Tiron. According to Geoffrey Grossus, David came to Tiron not long after Abbot Bernard's death.[77] He left with twelve Tironensian monks to insert them into the community he had already founded at Selkirk, thereby making it a Tironensian house.[78]

The new and liminally situated foundation at Tiron thus attracted the highest and often competing levels of secular patronage from men and women of noble rank. No fewer than two monarchs and a future king could be counted among its patrons during the early days of the community. These secular patrons brought not only their own transregional connections, but they involved Tiron in an extraordinary network of cultural associations (see Figure 10.11).

THE CULTURAL GEOGRAPHY OF CHURCH CONSTRUCTION AT TIRON

The travels and the actions of the 'agents' – Bernard, his immediate successors and monks, as well as lords ecclesiastical and lords and ladies secular – combine to form the cultural context that helped to shape the great church at Tiron. These men and women also provided enough early support in both material and funding to suppose that permanent construction could have been under way by the middle of the second decade of the 12th century at the latest, in the year or two before the death of the founder, Bernard of Abbeville. The new church was forged from local materials and forms combined with transregional sources, modes of design, and construction styles.

The dating of construction

Uncertainty about precisely when Abbot Bernard and his followers arrived at the site of Thiron-Gardais – perhaps as early as 1107/09 and no later than 1113/14 – combined with date ranges provided by compositional and formal analysis of surviving parts of the church, make precise dating of the beginning of construction on La Sainte-Trinité difficult to achieve.[79]

By 1107, Bernard and his followers were in the diocese of Chartres, as was the former Cluniac monk, Pope Pascal II, whom Bernard had already met in Rome.[80] The chronicle of Saint-Maixent places Bernard's earliest settlement at Tiron in this year, and Reginald Perceae's gift to Bernard of land in the Loir valley was apparently made in the pope's presence.[81] It seems likely, as Thompson suggests, that Bernard was near the end of a process of negotiations with Count Rotrou the Great of Nogent-le-Rotrou, his wife Mathilde and mother Béatrix, as well as Yves, bishop of Chartres (r. 1090–1115), to establish a new monastic community in the Perche between the years 1107 and 1109.[82] Both Thompson and Cline argue that Bernard and his community were probably on the site where the monastery is today by 1109.[83]

Formal analysis makes it clear that the eastern parts of the church – choir and transepts – are older than the western parts. Written around the time of the formal act of foundation, Yves of Chartres's letter 283 announces the foundation to his diocese and also offers protection to the site and 'all its dependencies' and threatens a 'terrible condemnation' to 'all usurpers and abductors of its holdings'.[84] This language suggests a foundation process that was already under way before the date of the formal act of foundation.

Construction materials and building practice

Two types of stone were used in the construction of La Sainte-Trinité de Tiron. Our recent XRF (X-ray fluorescence; see the Appendix) analysis confirms that both stone types were quarried locally.[85] First, the walls of the nave are built largely of *moellons* of *grès fereugineux* (also known as *grès roussard*), a distinctive and very dense, iron-laden sedimentary rock characterized by its deep reddish-brown colour (Figure 10.12). The walls are reinforced by shallow buttresses composed largely of *moyen appareil* of the same stone set in much thinner beds of mortar than the walls. The *grès roussard* used at the site was imported from the quarry which we have identified as Blainville, only 3.6 km from Tiron (Figure 10.13). The type of construction used at Tiron, like the stone itself, is typical of the region. Rubble walls (*moellons* set in thick mortar beds and arranged in relatively regular courses)

FIGURE 10.12

Tiron: south nave wall showing grès roussard *in* moellons *and blocks of* moyen appareil, *interspersed with limestone blocks also of* moyen appareil *(Bonde and Maines)*

FIGURE 10.13

Postcard view of the grès roussard *quarry at Blainville (19th century)*

FIGURE 10.14

View of the limestone quarry of the Maquis de Plainville

are typical of churches and appear, for example, in the late 11th-century walls of the nave of Le Mans Cathedral as well as in the vestiges of the abbey of Étival, founded in 1109.[86]

Interspersed within the walls, buttresses, and window headers are dressed blocks of grey/cream limestone (see Figure 10.12). This stone is also used in neat *moyen appareil* courses in the piers of the crossing and the diaphragm arches of the transept arms. Our XRF analysis confirms that this stone, too, was quarried locally at the site known as the Maquis de Plainville, only 8 km distant from Tiron (Figure 10.14 and see Appendix).

FIGURE 10.15

Tiron: foundations of the north wall of the Romanesque choir during excavation in 2018 (Bonde and Maines)

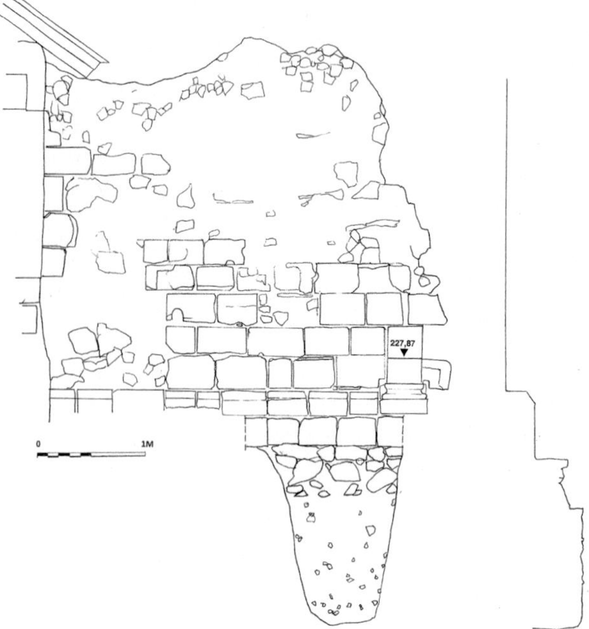

FIGURE 10.16

Tiron: stone-by-stone recording of north wall of choir (Bonde and Maines)

The walls and blind arcading of the Romanesque choir are also built with a mix of *grès fereugineux* and grey/cream limestone cut in blocks of *moyen appareil*. Bases and piers of the blind arcading are *grès*, but the capitals, which required more delicate carving, are limestone.[87] A similar mix of *grès* and limestone occurs in the crossing piers giving onto the transept arms, where the bases and nearly all courses of the shafts are *grès fereugineux*, but the capitals were limestone.[88] As on the south side, the mouldings and the diaphragm arch are carved from limestone.

The surviving three-story tower, on the south side of the church, is constructed entirely of greyish limestone in regular courses of *moyen appareil*. The tower is unquestionably integral with the rest of the church, since it shares walls with the choir and transept.

The foundations of the Romanesque church also reveal local knowledge of soil types. Our recent excavations at the bases of the walls of the Romanesque choir brought to light foundations of the *bloc volume* type, descending straight down or curving inward slightly to depths of 1.30–1.60 m below presumed interior circulation levels (Figures 10.15 and 10.16).[89] The foundations were roughly coursed masses of mostly *grès fereugineux*, faced with a sandy mortar. The foundations were deeply cut into and were bedded upon a very dense, naturally compacted clay that contained large quantities of silex. Such clays can sustain pressures of up to 40 metric tons/m^2, but even so, the foundations of the choir and its adjacent shouldered towers were surprisingly shallow.[90]

Recent excavations along the north side of the nave by Sophie Liégard revealed that these foundations descended only about 0.85 m below interior circulation layers.[91] Understanding the soils and the depth of the foundations of the church – choir and nave – at Tiron provides insights into the practical knowledge of the builders. While they would have had no scientific knowledge of soil capacities, they clearly and correctly thought that compacted clays could support not just the walls of the unvaulted nave but also the vaulted towers and choir. Knowledge of the foundations also provides an insight into the speed of construction since shallow foundations required less stone, less time to dig, and fewer personnel. Use of local stone, primarily *grès fereugineux*, for the nave and transept walls and locally available limestone for the heavy, vaulted towers also speaks to the immediate regional knowledge of the builders and implies that some of the masons in Bernard's early community came from the Perche itself.[92]

The aisleless cruciform plan

Given the plan and the massing of La Sainte-Trinité as we have reconstructed them, there are five essential characteristics of the church. First and foremost, the aisleless, cruciform plan; second, the unvaulted nave and transept; third, the shouldered towers and the absence of chapels visible on the exterior; fourth, the

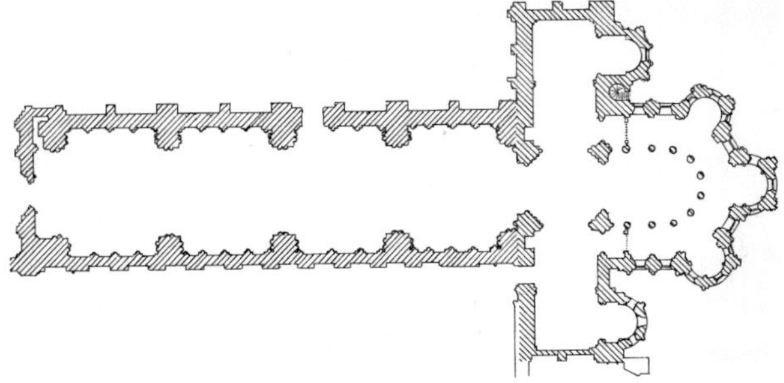

FIGURE 10.17

Fontevraud: plan of abbey church (after Jacques Mallet)

scale of the building whose length exceeds 85 m; and fifth, the combination of painted and carved decoration of the west portal.

We would argue that these characteristics have an intentional *iconography*. The aisleless cruciform plan is, of course, common across regions in western France and appears in cathedral churches like Angers and in monastic ones like Fontevraud or Cistercian Le Louroux and Chaloché (although these have more complicated chevets).[93] In that sense, the plan of Tiron is traditional in a transregional sense.[94] Single-vessel churches (nave and choir) are also typical of western France but particularly among *parish* churches. In this context, the choice of an aisleless mother church may reflect Abbot Bernard's ideas about the intentional simplicity and humility of his new order.

Second, single-vessel churches, some with transepts and some without, are remarkably common among churches which have an eremitic origin like Tiron. The obvious regional parallel is again the great abbey of Fontevraud founded by Bernard's friend and fellow preacher Robert of Arbrissel in 1101 (Figure 10.17).[95]

Further, there is another equally meaningful but transregional comparison that could have been influential in shaping Tiron. Saint Ambrose's so-called *Basilica Apostolorum* in Milan was an Early Christian building associated by relics and dedication with the *vita apostolica* so important to reformers of the late 11th and 12th centuries.[96] Indeed, the *Basilica Apostolorum* was the logical place in Milan when Saint Ambrose chose it for the burial of Saint Nazarius, a first-century Milanese martyr. Nazarius spent his life spreading Christianity throughout the western Empire and was thus himself an 'apostle'.[97] It was an aisleless cruciform church and was originally wooden roofed (Figure 10.18). Jill Franklin has linked the Ambrosian church to reform communities in early 12th-century England, as with the single-vessel, cruciform cathedral in York.[98] We would go further and link the plan to monastic churches with eremitic origins in western France, particularly Fontevraud, Notre-Dame d'Étival, Saint-Sulpice-le-Forêt, and Tiron whose founders had contact with popes and other Italian churchmen.

We know that Bernard went to Rome at least once before he came to settle at Tiron.[99] As an active reformer with an eremitic phase himself, it seems to us at least

FIGURE 10.18

Milan: plan of Basilica Apostolorum *(After Richard Krautheimer)*

plausible to suppose that Bernard of Tiron knew of the *Basilica Apostolorum*. Ambrose's church stood near the *Porta Romanorum* in Milan along the road that led to Rome, and Bernard may well have seen it on his journey. If this is the case, then the enormous, aisleless cruciform building of La Sainte-Trinité at Tiron would have embodied ideas of *vita apostolica* as Bernard and his followers might have understood it architecturally. It also testifies to the broad, transregional range of thinking and experience that came together to create La Sainte-Trinité de Tiron.

'Shouldered' towers

Features beyond the aisleless cruciform plan may also have been read by contemporaries as part of the iconography of Tiron's church. As described earlier, the three-story tower 'shouldered' into the angle between the choir and the southern transept arm still stands (Figures 10.19, 10.20a, and 10.20b). Not recognized from earlier plans, however, vestiges of a missing tower on the north side also survive. They include the part of its west wall that opened into the north transept arm which retains a small 'tunnel window' typical of tower construction (see Figure 10.7).[100] Part of another wall of the tower survives, less well preserved on the north side of the choir where a base and part of a shaft rising from it echo the Romanesque arcades of the 12th-century choir adhering to the inner wall of the opposite shouldered tower (see Figures 10.15 and 10.16). As previously discussed, the foundations of this wall are as deep as those on the south side where the tower still stands. Finally, Pinet's plan shows differently configured, massive walls where the north tower once was (see Figure 10.10). We see Pinet's plan as a confirmation of our interpretation of the standing remains and of the foundations belonging to a northern shouldered tower.

FIGURE 10.19

Tiron: south tower from the west (Bonde and Maines)

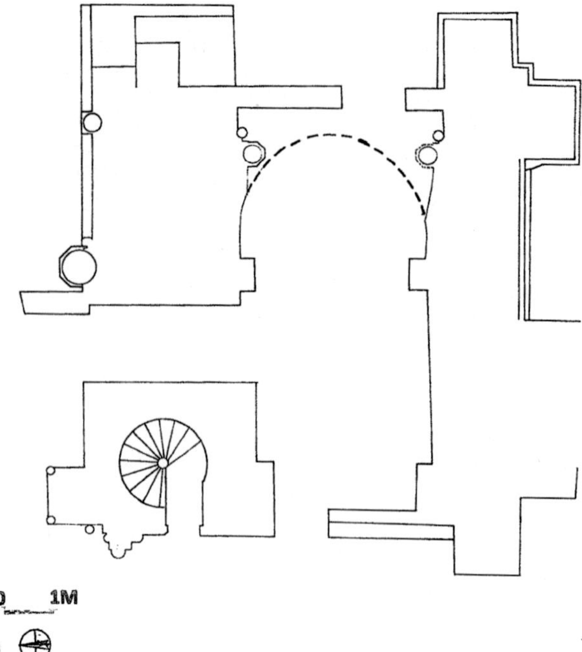

FIGURE 10.20a

Tiron: measured plan of the ground floor of the south tower (Bonde and Maines)

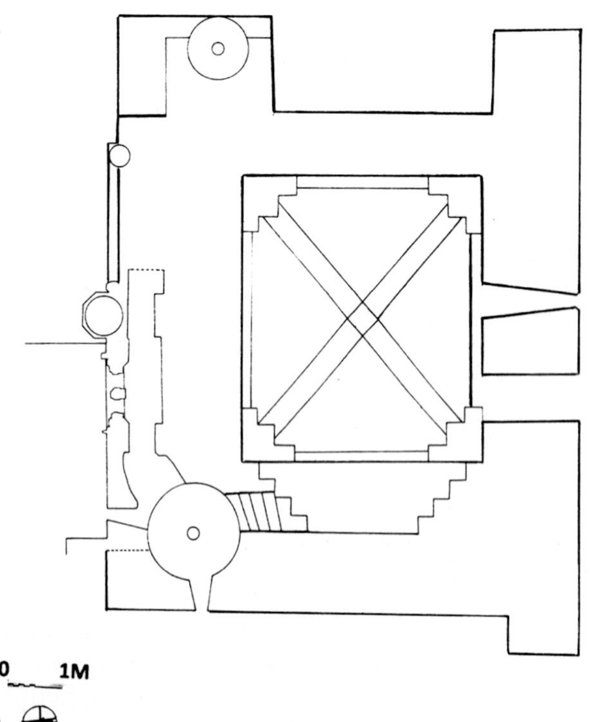

FIGURE 10.20b

Tiron: measured plan of the first floor of the south tower (Bonde and Maines)

While shouldered towers (or *tours jumelées*) are known throughout Europe, they are not a feature of Romanesque architecture in the west of France or in Normandy. They are, however, an important component of the elevations of 11th- and early 12th-century churches in the royal heartland of the Île-de-France, where they were built at a number of churches in royal lands including the Benedictine abbeys of Saint-Germain-des-Près and Morienval, as well as the collegiate church of Notre-Dame de Melun.[101] French royal patronage, beginning under King Louis VI in 1115, may help account for this feature and reflect another transregional dimension of the church in Tiron.[102]

FIGURE 10.21a

Tiron: capital à godrons *on north face of north-west crossing pier (Bonde and Maines)*

FIGURE 10.21b

Tiron: capital on the central column of the blind arcade on the south side of the Romanesque choir (Bonde and Maines)

Capitals and bases

The simplicity of the church's aisleless plan and the ruinous state of its east end ensure that there are fewer capitals and bases at Tiron than at many other sites. Nevertheless, three capitals and four bases survive in the 12th-century choir and transepts to provide limited material evidence for dating. The best-preserved capital in the eastern part of the church is found on the transept side of the north-west crossing pier (Figure 10.21a). It is a capital with *godrons* (known in Anglo-Norman England as a scallop capital – an ornamental form consisting of tapered tubular shapes).[103] This type of capital is widespread across Normandy in buildings such as Notre-Dame de Guibray and Lessay, both dated to the last quarter of the 11th century, and in buildings such as Saint-Georges de Boscherville and Saint-Martin in Ryes-en-Bessin, dated to the first quarter of the twelfth. The type also occurs in the Île-de-France, at for example Saint-Martin-des-Champs and Acy-le-Multien, but it is far less common in this region than it is in Normandy.[104]

The two other capitals are much less well-preserved and survive as part of the blind arcade on the south side of the 12th-century choir, one in the centre and the other at the west end (Figure 10.21b).[105] Sufficient remains of leaves survive to be able to assert that both were foliate capitals with the palmettes projecting in low relief.[106] The western capital had a vine or band motif near its base like several of the capitals in the abbey of Bernay or capitals from the chevet of Saint-Hilaire-le-Grand in Poitiers. Two foliate capitals from the mid-11th-century nave at Saint-Germain-des-Près in Paris, now authenticated by Plaigneux, can be used to suggest the original appearance of the Tiron capitals.[107]

The surviving imposts and bases confirm the connections with Normandy. Portions of the large impost blocks exist above both capitals, with the better preserved one at the west. The impost of the western capital, though damaged, reveals a profile consisting of a simple roll moulding incised below a broad filet and above a simple slightly curved chamfer. Analogous impost profiles are widespread in Normandy and elsewhere. While all four of the surviving bases are similar, the base that survives in the blind arcade on the north side of the choir allows us to see the full profile (see Figure 10.15). The four bases conform in a general way to the classical composition, but they have been greatly simplified. Bases of this simple type can be seen in the nave of the mid-11th-century church of Bernay and elsewhere in Normandy.

The testimony of written sources, combined with the limited material evidence of Tiron's capitals, imposts, and bases, encourages us to suggest that the choir and transepts were built between the years 1107/09 and 1125–30, and demonstrate the clear influence of both the nearby region of Normandy, as well as the kingdom of France, upon construction, design, and carving at Tiron. The style of the few sculptural survivals at Tiron can best be characterized as ranging from the contemporary (capital with *godrons*) to archaizing (bases and foliate capitals), a not surprising situation given a monastic reform context and little evidence of a local sculptural tradition in the Perche Tironnais.

FIGURE 10.22

Tiron: façade seen from the south west (Bonde and Maines)

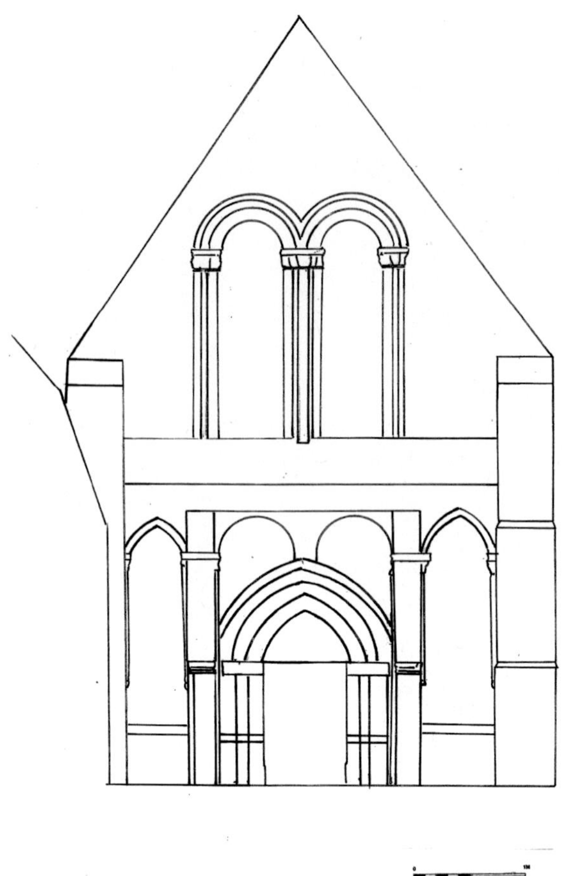

FIGURE 10.23a

Tiron: measured elevation drawing of the west façade of La Trinité (Bonde and Maines)

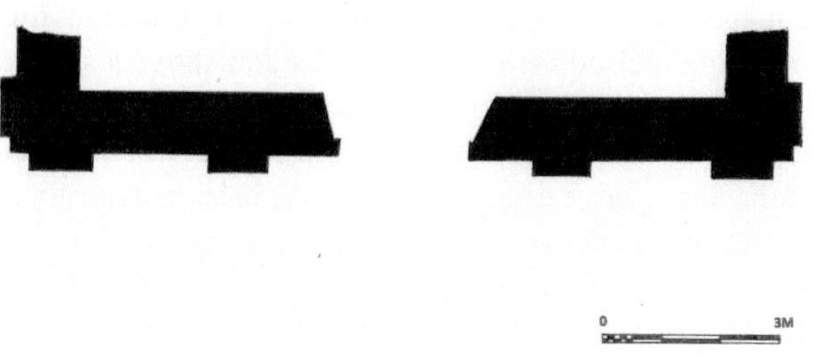

FIGURE 10.23b

Plan of phase I of the west façade (Bonde and Maines)

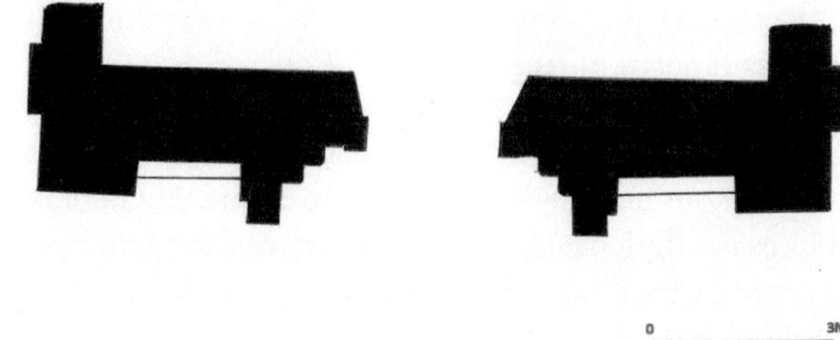

FIGURE 10.23c

Plan of phase 2 of the west façade (Bonde and Maines)

THE WEST FAÇADE OF LA SAINTE-TRINITÉ DE TIRON

The west façade of Tiron, as we see it today (Figure 10.22), is markedly later than the rest of the church. Chronologically, the façade can be seen to have been constructed in three phases. Initially the façade consisted of a simple, relatively thin wall, comparable in thickness to the lateral walls of the nave (Figure 10.23b). Its portal was likely a simple round-arched entry with or without a tympanum, perhaps with articulated jambs. Such doorways are found, for example, at the Tironensian priories of La Madeleine at Saint-Vincent de Réno (Orne) and Notre-Dame d'Yron (Eure-et-Loir) where the embrasures step back once to receive single columns that support a moulded archivolt.

The second phase thickened the façade wall by replacing the first portal with that we see today (Figures 10.23a and 10.23c). Blind arcades flank the portal in the lower zone, and additions were made to the four buttresses, allowing them to project further from the original façade wall. In the upper story, the second phase included the two lancet windows and their historiated capitals (Figures 10.22 and 10.23a). The two

FIGURE 10.24

Tiron: west portal (Bonde and Maines)

round-arched lancets, now blocked, once lighted the western end of the nave.

The final phase was a restoration, probably executed in the 19th century, when uncarved stones were inserted into the portal embrasures and voussoirs, and bricks were used in places in the buttresses (see Figure 10.22).

All of the portal, both the sculptural parts and the architectural frame, is built of a soft limestone, some blocks of which are greyish in colour and some are yellowish beige, but all came from the quarry at Plainville (see Appendix). Some of the latter blocks are likely to be restorations. The rest of the façade is built of *grès fereugineux*, save for the blind arcades and the lancet windows of the upper zone which are limestone.

The west façade is more richly decorated than the rest of the rather sober church. It also reflects a redirection of transregional influence, turning toward the east, toward Chartres and the Île-de-France (Figure 10.24). The embrasures of the portal step back to receive now lost column figures positioned on consoles borne on short, richly carved colonettes. The projecting angles of the embrasures are richly decorated, carved in continuous foliate and geometric patterns. The door jambs may also have borne figures in relief, as do the jambs of the lateral portal of Le Mans Cathedral.[108] Today, the only figural sculptures in the portal appear on the jamb blocks that correspond to the short colonettes of the embrasures. While badly eroded, each block bears an image of a seated author figure, perhaps representing either evangelists or Saint Benedict and Saint Gregory. These column and jamb figures originally supported three possibly figured or painted archivolts that framed the now missing tympanum. During the 19th century, one could apparently still see a painted figure of the Virgin surrounded by angels.[109] Some of the original upper jamb blocks, the entire capital course on each side of the portal, and some perhaps all the voussoirs have been replaced.[110]

Framing the portal on the inside of the buttresses are two thin colonettes that rise above the apex of the portal to terminate in abraded foliate capitals. Above each capital are curved courses that correspond to a pair, now missing, of blind arches that must once have joined to rest on a central console above the apex of the portal (see Figure 10.23a).[111] Two blind arcades borne on consoles composed of crowned heads articulate the wall between each pair of buttresses on either side of the portal. An analogous, if not precise, comparison to the composition of the lower zone façade design can be seen on the west façade of the cathedral of Le Mans.

Despite these losses, alterations, and repairs, Tiron's 'second' west portal compares favourably with Early Gothic portals at Chartres (1145–55) and Le Mans (*c.* 1140–50).[112] These features include short, highly decorated columns beneath statue-columns and highly decorated colonettes or arises between the statue columns. The sculpture is characterized by precise carving and deep drill work.

Four crowned console heads support the blind arcades that flank the central portal. They represent three kings and one queen (Figure 10.25). While they may relate to Old Testament monarchs, they may very likely (also) have been viewed by contemporaries as relating to the royal nature of Tiron's early patronage. The heads might thus represent King Henry I of England (r. 1100–35), King Louis VI of France (r. 1108–37), and King David I of Scotland (r. 1124–53). The lone female head is harder to identify (see Figure 10.25a). She could be read as Henry's wife, Queen Matilda (r. 1100–18) or his sister, Countess Adèle of Blois and Chartres (r. *c.* 1082–1137).[113] There is also the possibility that the female head represents Rotrou's wife (and Henry I's illegitimate but recognized daughter), also named Matilda (1102–67). It is unlikely that we will be able to confirm the identity of any of the heads, but for now we suggest that they were as likely to have been read as contemporary royal persons as Old Testament figures.

Despite the loss of detail due to erosion of the soft limestone, striking comparisons can still be made between these Tiron heads and those from the column-statues of the abbey of Saint-Denis, a comparison that reinforces the Île-de-France connection of the shouldered towers (Figure s 10.26a and 10.26b).[114] This second phase of the west façade consisted of the new portal, the arcading borne on consoles as well as the double lancets, suggesting a date later in the reign of Abbot William I, probably *c.* 1135–50.

The capitals of the clearstory lancets combine to form a frieze (Figure 10.27). All are inhabited; the groups in the centre and on the south (right) have sirens (bird

FIGURE 10.25

Tiron: four crowned console heads from the blind arcades flanking the west portal (a–d), arranged from north to south (Bonde and Maines)

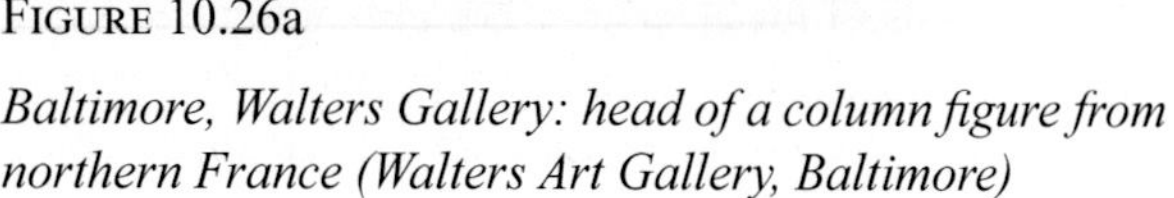

FIGURE 10.26a

Baltimore, Walters Gallery: head of a column figure from northern France (Walters Art Gallery, Baltimore)

FIGURE 10.26b

Tiron: crowned console head from the north blind arcade flaking the west portal (Bonde and Maines)

FIGURE 10.27

Tiron: Annunciation from clerestory capital frieze (Bonde and Maines)

FIGURE 10.28

Tiron: moralizing subjects from west front clerestory capital frieze (Bonde and Maines)

bodies with human heads). The remaining capital group, on the north (left) carries a conflated narrative consisting of three figures – one on each capital – that together affirm the Christian notion of the unity of the Old and New Testaments (Figure 10.28). Gabriel, the angel of the Annunciation with his right arm raised in a gesture of address, leans diagonally across the left capital to address the Virgin Mary seated on the central one. The figure of Mary holds a book in her right hand and raises her left hand in response to the angel but turns her gaze to the right to look at a second angel, probably another figure of Gabriel, who holds a short, flowering staff, a motif widely understood by art historians to represent the Rod of Jesse prophesied in the Book of Isaiah.[115] In the Gospel of Luke, Mary does not, at first, understand the significance of the words Gabriel has spoken to her.[116] Accordingly, the angel explains them at greater length. By directing her gaze at the second angel, Mary recognizes the fulfilment of Isaiah's prophecy in her, which she acknowledges to Gabriel in verse 38 of Luke's Annunciation narrative.

We do not know the medieval topography in front of the façade of La Sainte-Trinité. Today one approaches the façade from the south, descending a flight of stairs. If one also approached the façade in a similar way during the Middle Ages, it would explain the eccentric placement of this theologically central capital group. Set in the north embrasure (left) of the north lancet window, the image 'opens' toward the viewer approaching the church from the south or south-west.

This small, sculpted scene together with the image of the Virgin flanked by angels purportedly painted on the tympanum testify to Abbot Bernard's devotion to Mary described in literary sources. Capitals with stylistically similar sculptures appear in the western portal of Saint-Loup-de-Naud and on the interior capitals of Saint-Germain-des-Près. Capital friezes as a compositional device are well-known and occur around the middle decades of the 12th century at nearby Chartres, Notre-Dame-du-Fort in Étampes, Notre-Dame de Corbeil, and Saint-Pierre-au-Parvis in Soissons.

The second phase of the west façade at Tiron with its richly carved central portal and its clerestory capitals points to a shift in transregional influence toward the east. While the earlier capitals and bases of the nave and transepts looked primarily to Normandy, the west front follows Chartres and the Île-de-France, with the possibility that Le Mans may also have played a role. The death of Henry I in 1135 and the resultant civil war in England may have encouraged this eastward turn as Abbot William and his community continued their search for patrons during the expansion of the Tironensian order.

CONCLUSION

We have used the three lenses of cultural geography, regionalism, and liminality to reveal aspects of the early 12th-century church at Tiron and the later transformation of its west façade. Cultural geography helped us to see the ways in which Tiron's cultural landscape was shaped by conscious choices made by local/regional and extraregional 'agents' among the abbey's early community and supporters. The strategies of regionalism and critical regionalism have pushed us to identify networks of religious and secular influences. It has underscored the fact that the architecture of Tiron and, by implication, Romanesque architecture elsewhere were not a monolithic style determined by geography but rather one inflected by regional and extraregional forces. The notion of liminality leads us to see that the marginal location of the abbey of Tiron, namely its situation on the edges of three major regions and at the intersections of three diocesan boundaries, helped to shape its architectural form (see Figure 10.1). Its deserted landscape attracted a community of former hermits drawn to its secluded position, and invited patronage from competing secular rulers (Henry I Beauclerc and Louis VI) who intervened in this buffer zone for political expansion and influence.

The large scale of the new church at Tiron is especially notable in the underpopulated liminal zone of the Perche. Our analysis of regional building materials and construction techniques reflect local and immediately regional practice. The aisleless plan of La Sainte-Trinité as well as aspects of its elevation, like the shouldered towers, reflect the broader and more complicated transregional experiences of its founder and early patrons. The church is marked by the adoption of an aisleless cruciform plan which we have argued was read by contemporaries as having a multivalent iconography relating it to simple parish architecture, to western French traditions, to eremitic churches, and to the architecture of reform monasticism through contemporary ideas of the *Vita Apostolica*. The prominent shouldered towers link Tiron to the Île-de-France and its monuments. While its modest sanctuary capitals point to formal links predominantly with Normandy, its later west façade design and sculpture point again to the Île-de-France. La Sainte-Trinité should thus be seen as a major monument, participating in the architectural ideas of monastic reform in the eremitic tradition while reflecting high-level patronage.

In these ways, Tiron's position in the history of Romanesque architecture was determined by both regional and transregional factors over time. These were guided by the various agents involved in the establishment and development of the new monastery – Abbot Bernard of Tiron himself, his successor abbots, and his followers, who included at least some of the artisans responsible for building the church, Bishops Yves and Geoffrey of Chartres, Count Rotrou II the Great and his family, as well as the kings and queens of England, France, and Scotland. Despite its liminal position at the edges of Normandy, the Maine, and the Île-de-France and close to the boundaries of three dioceses, or perhaps because of it, Tiron's cultural landscape, and the critical regional choices made by its abbots and patrons mark it as a place of importance in the formation of ecclesiastical reform and Romanesque architecture.

In another sense, Tiron's geographic liminality was diminished by its success, as its spiritual standing became more 'central' over the course of the 12th century, and its geographic position relative to the struggle between Henry I and Louis VI made it a locus for royal patronage. Across the 13th century and beyond, as France took control of Normandy under King Philip Augustus and new forms of religious life, like the preaching orders, were established and flourished, Tiron's recent 'centrality' diminished, and the abbey retreated toward its original liminality, where we find it again today.

ACKNOWLEDGEMENTS

It is our pleasure to acknowledge the support of the mayor, Victor Provot, and the personnel of the Mairie of Thiron-Gardais. Brown and Wesleyan Universities helped to finance our excavation season in 2018. Our excavations were also aided by our team of students and volunteers: Katherine Concannon, Charlotte Rich, Charles Steinman, Daniel Villefailleau, Sam Wertheimer, and our field supervisor, John Sheffer, who contributed the stone analysis found in the Appendix to this study. Finally, we are pleased to acknowledge the organisational and editorial assistance of John McNeill and Richard Plant.

APPENDIX

XRF IDENTIFICATION OF THE QUARRIES USED TO PROVIDE STONE FOR TIRON

John Sheffer

METHODOLOGY

X-ray fluorescence (XRF) is a scientific method that uses X-rays to determine the chemical composition of a material and has been used for many years by geologists. Archaeologists and art historians have also used XRF to answer questions about composition and provenance. In this study, we used a wavelength XRF (WXRF) machine in the Wesleyan University Earth and Environmental Sciences Department. The purpose was to determine the elemental compositions of limestone and *grès roussard* samples from Tiron Abbey and two nearby quarries that were believed to be the source for the construction stone for Tiron.

During July 2018, the excavation team collected samples from different construction phases of the church at Tiron and collected samples from two nearby quarries: the limestone quarry at the Maquis de Plainville and the *grès roussard* quarry near Blainville. These samples weighed 5–35 g each. Multiple samples from the church had weathering varnish and plant growth that had to be removed. The samples were then brought back to Wesleyan University for processing and analysis.

After deposition at Wesleyan University, the samples were cleaned and examined for distinguishing characteristics. After cleaning, the samples were run through two pulverizing machines until each had produced about 8 g of sample that was an extremely fine powder. Next, 7 or 8 g of the powder were measured using an electronic scale with 0.001-g precision. Once a mass is properly measured in whole grams, the powder is transferred to a mortar with a number of wax pellets equivalent to the mass in grams. Using the mortar and pestle, the mixture is homogenized into a fine powder. This powder is transferred to a small aluminum dish and pressed by a 15-ton hydraulic press into a compact briquette. The purpose of this process is to create a homogenized sample that the X-rays can easily penetrate and from which they can also reflect.

Finally, the briquettes were placed in the XRF machine and irradiated. This determines the elemental abundance by using the secondary X-rays that the elements fluoresce when irradiated. Each element has a unique fluorescence energy that can be mapped as a wavelength, where the amplitude of the wave is proportional to the element's concentration in the sample (Shackley, 2017). The Bruker WXRF software at Wesleyan University automatically measures the wavelengths and amplitudes and outputs a data table eliminating the error involved in human readings of the reflectance wavelengths.

In order to make the data more easily comparable, elements whose values were equivalent to zero in a majority of samples were omitted from the final data table. Additionally, the oxide values that were presented in percentage form were changed into elemental parts per million (ppm) through a simple calculation that converted the percentage into ppm before cancelling the oxygen concentration.

RESULTS AND DISCUSSION

The results of this study can be seen in Tables A.1 and A.2. In order to fit the full chemical results onto one page, they had to be broken into two tables. This break is arbitrary and is made simply for formatting purposes. Because the WXRF measures principally trace elements, there is a great number of trace elements to be seen in the tables.

Looking at any single elemental composition would give an inaccurate understanding of the whole data set; therefore, in order to better understand the data as a whole, Graph A.1 has been included. This graph plots the elemental abundances of the limestone quarry sample against the elemental abundances of the five samples from the church at Tiron. Included in this graph is the line of best fit for each data set as well as the R^2 value for the line, which shows the degree of correlation for the data sets. As seen in Table A.3, the R^2 values for each of the included lines of best fit is within 0.004 of a perfect one-to-one ratio, which indicates that the quarry samples and the building samples have a strong correlation. A one-to-one correlation would mean that elemental compositions are identical. Since the data is trace element compositions of stone samples, a strong correlation of this data indicates nearly identical compositions. These correlations support the hypothesis that the monks of Tiron utilized the quarry at the Maquis du Plainville, during all construction phases, to build the church at Tiron.

In addition to determining the provenance of the limestone used in the church, we thought it prudent to determine the *grès roussard* provenance as well. Due to a lack of sample space in the WXRF, only two *grès roussard* samples could be run; one from the quarry in Blainville and one from the *grès roussard* foundations of the south tower at Tiron. Since these samples also yielded a multitude of elemental compositions, they were compiled into two tables (Table A.4 and Table A.5) for simplified viewing. Once again, the data was plotted on a scatter plot with a trend line, which can be seen in Graph A.3, whose R^2 value was used to determine the strength of the data's correlation. When plotted, the trend line has a value for $R^2 = 0.99972$, indicative of a very strong correlation.

CONCLUSIONS

After developing compositional fingerprints for samples of the limestone and *grès roussard* used to build the church at Tiron, as well as samples of limestone from the quarry at Maquis de Plainville, and of *grès roussard* from Blainville, it is clear that these building materials are very closely related if not the same.

As research on Tiron continues, the next step will be to collect and analyse more samples from the two quarries as well as from the church and claustral buildings, should the latter become available through excavation. The samples that have been collected are useful and allow for basic study, and the results of these tests support a local source hypothesis and will be used in a future architectural energetics study. The main purpose of further analysis would be to provide more support for the local stone source hypothesis and provide a more accurate location of the medieval phases of the local quarries.

More sample analysis of the church and monastic buildings (if evidence becomes available) could also add data and strengthen the correlation coefficient between all of the monastic building phases and the quarries. Finally, sampling the architectural fragments taken from the monastery site could provide insight into differences in the building practices of the Tironensian monks and their later Maurist reformers.

TABLE A.1

Limestone elemental compositions (Ti-As) [PPM]

Sample	*Ti*	*V*	*Mn*	*Fe*	*Co*	*Ni*	*Cu*	*Zn*	*Ga*	*As*
JTS15 TI2018	286.96	14.86	83.01	4363.63	8.00	6.57	9.69	23.38	2.17	2.70
JTS16 TI2018	527.20	18.07	66.41	5482.32	0.00	8.76	4.31	19.30	2.17	3.73
JTS18 TI2018	226.90	9.54	107.91	3156.04	5.72	3.28	1.08	16.24	2.17	–0.41
JTS20 TI2018	186.86	8.47	74.71	3259.76	3.43	6.57	3.23	22.36	1.09	–0.41
JTS21 TI2018	293.63	14.86	83.01	4311.77	1.14	6.57	10.77	17.26	2.17	2.70
JTS22 TI2018	493.84	17.00	83.01	5074.85	3.43	6.57	1.08	18.28	2.17	3.73
JTS23 TI2018	313.65	15.93	41.50	3126.41	3.43	5.47	9.69	20.32	2.17	4.77

TABLE A.2

Limestone elemental compositions (Rb-U) [PPM]

Sample	*Rb*	*Sr*	*Y*	*Zr*	*Nb*	*Mo*	*Cs*	*Ce*	*Pb*	*U*
JTS15 TI2018	17.09	309.69	5.11	18.79	1.65	0.78	0.07	59.21	4.67	0.93
JTS16 TI2018	18.10	294.99	5.11	44.50	2.64	0.78	1.41	47.03	2.34	0.93
JTS18 TI2018	12.06	313.89	4.09	15.82	2.64	1.56	3.41	61.10	8.15	2.78
JTS20 TI2018	11.06	255.10	4.09	13.84	2.64	1.56	0.63	58.27	6.99	0.93
JTS21 TI2018	13.07	349.58	4.09	16.81	1.65	0.78	0.63	67.74	6.99	0.93
JTS22 TI2018	18.10	248.80	6.13	47.46	3.64	0.78	0.44	55.44	2.34	1.85
JTS23 TI2018	11.06	191.06	4.09	17.80	1.65	1.56	0.44	38.70	16.23	0.93

TABLE A.3

R-squared values of the lines of best fit taken from Graphs A.1 and Graph A.2

Church sample number	*Maquis sample 1*	*Maquis sample 2*
JTS 15	0.99838	0.9986
JTS 18	0.99631	0.99667
JTS 20	0.99726	0.99752
JTS 21	0.99794	0.99825
JTS 23	0.99979	0.9999

Table A.4

Grès Roussard elemental composition (Sc-Ga) [PPM]

Sample	*Sc*	*Ti*	*V*	*Cr*	*Mn*	*Fe*	*Co*	*Ni*	*Cu*	*Zn*	*Ga*
JTS14 TI2018	15.99	473.82	126.72	38.31	0.00	100111.70	72.04	7.66	19.39	332.29	5.43
JTS9 TI2018	0.44	146.82	76.99	80.75	614.26	38487.40	73.18	6.57	3.23	19.30	2.17

Table A.5

Grès Roussard elemental composition (Sc-Ga) [PPM]

Sample	*As*	*Rb*	*Sr*	*Y*	*Zr*	*Nb*	*Mo*	*Ba*	*La*	*Ce*	*U*
JTS14 TI2018	301.90	70.04	21.00	70.15	41.53	20.64	10.56	52.28	36.50	26.80	30.70
JTS9 TI2018	163.17	10.01	80.40	70.15	31.64	10.65	00.78	182.22	10.43	11.50	10.85

Graph A.1

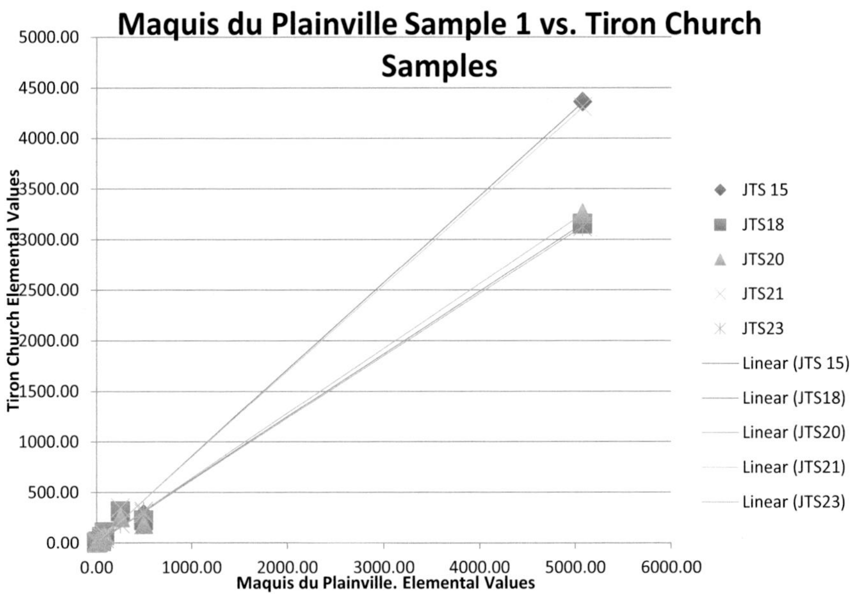

Graph A.2

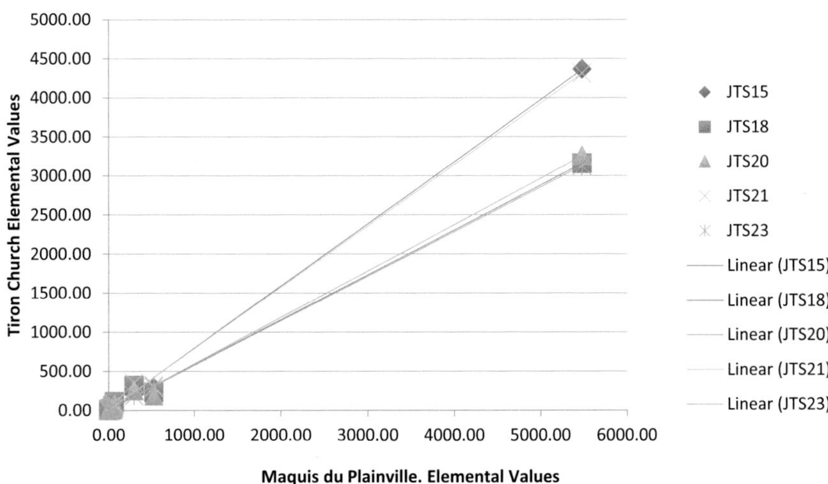

Graph A.3

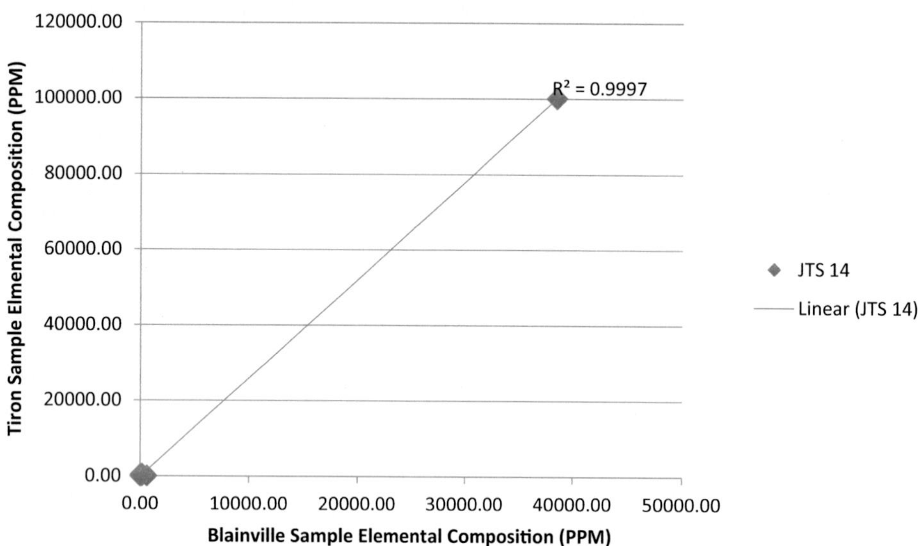

Graph A.4

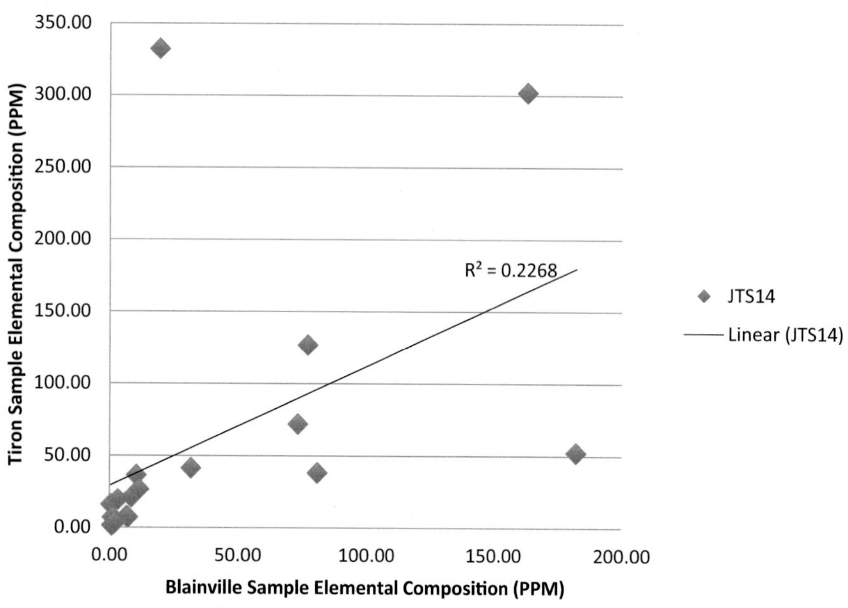

NOTES

1 The recovery of medieval diocesan and comital borders is quite complex. It is useful to note that the predominant counties in the early 12th century were Alençon, Chartres, Dunois, Évreux, and Maine.

2 While Chartres is well-known, Nogent-le-Rotrou has received relatively little scholarly attention. Research has largely focused on the Perche and the family of its counts. See K. Thompson, *Power and Border Lordship in Medieval France, the County of the Perche 1000–1226* (London 2002); S. Montagne-Chambolle and P. Siguret, eds., *Le pouvoir dans le Perche au temps des Rotrou* (Rémalard 2010), wherein discussion of the town appears in relation to the castle and its lords.

3 On cultural geography, see esp. Y.-F. Tuan, *Space and Place: The Perspective of Experience* (Minneapolis 1977); J. Wylie, 'Timely Geographies: "New Directions in Cultural Geography" Revisited', *Area*, 48 (2016), 374–77.

4 P. Lasko, 'The Concept of Regionalism in French Romanesque', in *Akten des XXV Internationalen Kongresses für Kunstgeschichte, III Probleme und Methoden des Klassifizierung*', ed. J. White (Vienna 1983), 17–25, reprinted in P. Lasko, *Studies on Metalwork, Ivory and Stone* (London 1994), 139–47. See also T. O'Keefe, *Archaeology and the Pan-European Romanesque* (London 2015), and the article by Claude Andrault-Schmitt elsewhere in this volume. Historians have also engaged with the concept of regions. See R. F. Berkhofer, 'Regions of Medieval France', in *Oxford Bilbiographies-Medieval Studies* (Oxford–New York 2010). For a critique, see B. Bedos-Rezak, 'French Medieval Regions: A Concept in History', *Historical Reflexions/Réflections historiques*, 19/2 (1993), 151–66.

[5] Lasko, 'Regionalism' (as n. 4), 147.

[6] D. Sandron, 'La cathédrale de Laon, un monument à l'échelle du diocèse', *La Sauvegarde de l'Art français*, 13 (2002), 22–39.

[7] J. T. Marquardt, *Zodiaque: Making Medieval Modern, 1951–2001* (University Park 2015). Prior to the Second World War, Marcel Aubert and Jean Verrier had a similar but even broader idea than the *Zodiaque* series. Their project, called *Les églises de France* was organised by *départements* and encompassed a longer time frame than simply the Romanesque. However, the series was never fully realized. Only six volumes were published before the war and one after. A decade after the *Zodiaque* series began, the multi-authored *L'art roman en France* (Paris 1961) followed essentially the same regional organization. On the *Zodiaque* series, see also Philip Bovey's article in this volume.

[8] See K. Frampton, 'Towards a Critical Regionalism: Six Points for an Architecture of Resistance', in *The Anti-Aesthetic. Essays on Post-modern Culture*, ed. H. Foster (Seattle 1983), 16–30.

[9] Ibid., 21.

[10] A. van Gennep, *The Rites of Passage* (Chicago 1960); V. Turner, 'Betwixt and Between: The Liminal Period in Rites of Passage', in *The Forest of Symbols: Aspects of Ndembu Ritual*, ed. A. van Gennep (Ithaca 1967).

[11] See F. Braudel, *The Identity of France, I: History and Environment*, trans. S. Reynolds (New York 1989), 37–57. For Braudel, a *pays* is 'an area [of the landscape] with its own identity, [. . .] visible not only in the particular features displayed in the landscape and in the many imprints man has left upon it, but also in a lived culture, "a way of life and a way of death"', 37.

[12] The abbey, subsequently Cluniac priory, of Saint-Denis at Nogent-le-Rotrou might appear to be an exception to the absence of important monastic houses in the immediate region of Tiron, but it is not. Founded *c.* 1030 by Count Geoffrey I, and given to Cluny by Count Rotrou II in 1080, the monks were supported by the family of the Rotrou. Saint-Denis was, however, quite quickly superseded by Tiron where Rotrou III acted as a co-founder and his mother and sister became major patrons. See K. Thompson, 'Sept textes pour une fondation, les premiers temps de Saint-Denis de Nogent-le-Rotrou', *Bibliothèque de l'École des chartes*, 160 (2002), 641–66 on the history of the priory.

[13] The life written by Gaufridus Grossus was first published by J.-B. Souchet, *Beati Bernardi Fundatori et I abbatis SS Trinitats de Tironoio ordinis sancti Benedictii, Vita auctore coaetano Gaufrido Grosso* (Paris 1649). The most accessible Latin edition (and facing French translation) is B. Beck, *Saint Bernard de Tiron, l'ermite, le moine, et le monde* (Cormelles-le-Royal 1998), 312–461; Beck, *Saint-Bernard*, 462–93, provides Latin editions and French translations of all other medieval narrative sources for Tiron. The *Vita* has been rendered into English: *Geoffrey Grossus, 'The Life of Blessed Bernard of Tiron'*, trans. with introduction and notes by R. H. Cline (Washington 2010). See also J. Delarun, 'La Vie abrégée de Bernard de Tiron', in *Entre texte et histoire. Études d'histoire médiévale offertes au professeur Shoichi Sato*, eds. O. Kano, J.-L. Lemaître, T. Adachi, Y. Nishimura, and M. Sot (Paris 2015).

[14] Cline, ed., *Life of Blessed Bernard* (as n. 13), para. 70, 77–78. Beck, *Saint Bernard* (as n. 13), 388: "*viro Dei Bernardo, in abditissimus Pertici silvarum solitudinibus latitanti*" and 389 for the French. On the forest in the Middle Ages generally, see R. Bechman, *Trees and Man, the Forest in the Middle Ages*, trans. K. Dunham (New York 1990).

[15] Tiron's cartulary is Chartres, Archives départementale d'Eure et Loir (ADEL), H 1374. An edition was published by L. Merlet, *Cartulaire de l'abbaye de la Sainte-Trinité de Tiron*, 2 vols. (Chartres 1883), which must now be read in conjunction with K. Thompson, 'The Cartulary of the Monastery of Tiron/Le cartulaire du monastère de Tiron', *Tabularia: Les cartulaires normands: bilan et perspectives de recherche*, 13 (2013), 65–123. The first ten charters include the foundation charter and the consecration of the abbey cemetery, as well as the gift of a parish church in a town. Six of the other seven mention forest or woods; all of them date to the period of Bernard's abbacy: Merlet, *Cartulaire* I, 14–15, charter 3, *de Foresta*; 16, charter 5, *omnia nemora mea*; 18, charter 7, *Preterea silvam de Meleriaco*; 19, charter 8, *cum iiii campis qui sunt citra aquam et nemus*; 20, charter 9, *sue proprie juxta Cohardum et boscum*; 22, charter 10, *Preterea sepefatus Odo totum nemus*. See C. Higounet, *Défrichements et villeneuves du bassin parisien (xie-xive siècles)* (Paris 1990), 312, 318, 327 and 329, on the forestation of the Perche.

[16] After 1350, records of deforestation (*défrichement* or land clearance) become relatively rare, presumably as a combined result of the beginning of the Hundred Years War, the recurrence of the plague, and a shift toward a cooler climatic period. See Higounet, *Défrichements* (as n. 15), for land clearance during the High Middle Ages in the greater Paris region. On map making in the early modern period, see J. Konvitz, *Cartography in France, 1600–1848, Science, Engineering and Statecraft* (Chicago 1987).

[17] No trace of vaulting exists on the outside of the crossing arches where they open onto the transept arms. O. Labat, in collaboration with P. Perrichon and A. Louis, revealed a small portion of the western wall of the south transept arm. O. Labat et al., 'Vestiges de l'abbaye de Tiron et du Collège militaire royal', Rapport de Diagnostic archéologique – Thiron-Gardais, 10–12 rue de l'abbaye, Chartres (unpublished report, 2015), 32 and 69–74. A parallel would be Notre-Dame-sur-l'Eau in Domfront (Orne), where the nave, crossing, and transept arms were not vaulted but the single bay choir and apse were.

[18] Reconstruction of the radius proves that the exterior wall was thick (as befits the first floor of a tower) but that the apse did not project beyond the plane of the exterior of the east tower wall. The presence of the apse makes it likely that the ground floor of this tower, which was open to the south transept arm, was a chapel.

[19] The nave walls, which are today plastered over, provide ample surfaces for painting. Future study may tell us whether the walls were originally painted as they are in the Tironensian priory of Notre-Dame d'Yron at Cloyes-sur-le-Loir (Eure-et-Loir).

[20] On shouldered towers, see P. Héliot, 'Sur les tours jumelées au chevet des églises du Moyen Age', in *Arte in Europe, Scritti di Storia dell'arte in onore Edoardo Arslan* (Milan 1967), 249–70.

[21] Both openings are today blocked, presumably to help stabilize the structure. The date of the infill is unknown but is likely to be 19th century.

[22] S. Bonde and C. Maines with the collaboration of A. Saintenoy and J. Sheffer, 'L'église-mère de la Congrégation bénédictine réformée de Tiron, Sondages archéologiques dans le chœur détruit de l'abbatiale, Prospections des zones des bâtiments claustraux' (unpublished field report, 2018, available at the Mairie de Tiron, the SRA du Centre-Val de Loire in Orléans and Brown and Wesleyan Universities), 29–79.

[23] See Dom M. Germain, *Monasticon Gallicanum*, ed. A. Peigné-Delacourt (Paris 1870), pl. 58.

[24] Oddly, the 'Table' of the *Monasticon* (as n. 23), 9 states, 'Église abbatiale détruite in 1793'. This was not the case in 1870 when the *Monasticon* was published, nor is it the case today.

[25] Paris, Archives nationales, NIII Eure-et-Loir 4–1–11. On Dom H. Pinet, see M. Bugner, *Cadre architectural et vie monastique des bénédictins de la congrégation de Saint-Maur* (Nogent-le-Roi 1984), 39, 40, 113, n. 151 and 114, n. 20. According to Bugner, Pinet made his profession in 1630 at La Trinité de Vendôme and died forty-five years later at Nogent-sous-Coucy. He was one of several *moine-architectes* who worked widely among Maurist houses in a variety of regions, including the Loire valley, Burgundy, the Beauce, Champagne, and the Beauvaisis. Pinet is thought to have drawn plans for Saint-Germer-de-Fly in addition to those of Tiron. On Pinet, see also C. Rich, 'Abbey Restorations Under the Maurist Reform: The Incorporation of Tridentine Canon Within Benedictine Monasticism', *Historical Narratives* (forthcoming). Another, more schematic, plan of Tiron dated 1780 and drawn by Dom G.-A. Huet also survives but is not sufficiently precise to help understand the church. Huet's plan is reproduced in Merlet, *Cartulaire* (as n. 15), I: xc, and by D. Guillemin, *Thiron, abbaye médiévale* (Montrouge 1999), 53.

[26] Paris AN NIII Eure-et-Loir (as n. 25), 4–2.

[27] For the cartulary, see, n. 15. A 17th-century copy (ADEL, H 1375) also exists. ADEL, H 1378 contains the confirmations of Popes Innocent II and Eugenius III.

[28] See n. 13.

[29] P. Marchegay and É. Mabille, *Chroniques des églises d'Anjou* (Paris 1869), 351–433; M. Chibnall, ed. and trans., *The Ecclesiastical History of Orderic Vitalis*, 5 vols. (Oxford 1969–80), IV, Books vii and viii, esp. viii: 330–31 et passim.

[30] On network theory, see J. Law and J. Hassard, eds., *Actor Network Theory and After* (Oxford and Keele 1999); B. Latour, *Reassembling the Social: An Introduction to Actor-Network-Theory* (Oxford 2005).

[31] For discussion of Bernard's early career, see K. Thompson, *The Monks of Tiron: A Monastic Community and Religious Reform in the Twelfth Century* (Cambridge 2014), 97–103; Beck, *Saint Bernard de Tiron* (as n. 13), 21–32; Cline, ed., *Life of Blessed Bernard* (as n. 13) xi–xvi, who use a range of written sources. See also the remarks in K. Thompson, 'The Other Saint Bernard: 'The Troubled and Varied Career' of Bernard of Abbeville, Abbot of Tiron', *Journal of Ecclesiastical History*, 60 (2009), 1–16.

[32] Another possibility favoured by both Cline and Thompson is that Bernard may have made his monastic profession at La Chaise Dieu and followed its abbot, Reginald, from there to Saint-Cyprien. See Cline, ed., *Life of Blessed Bernard* (as n. 13), xv; Thompson, *Monks of Tiron* (as n. 31), 98–99.

[33] L.-F. Rédet, *Cartulaire de l'abbaye de Saint-Cyprien de Poitiers, Société historique de Poitiers* (Poitiers 1874), 89 n°123, 182 n°285, 219–20 n°355.

[34] Thompson, *Monks of Tiron* (as n. 31), 102; Beck, *Saint Bernard de Tiron* (as n. 13), 28. See also Rédet, *Cartulaire Saint-Cyprien* (as n. 33), 43–47; Orderic Vitalis, *Ecclesiastical History* (as n. 29), IV, book viii, 329.

[35] According to his *Vita*, Bernard had two eremitic phases of which only the second concerns us here. See Beck, *Saint Bernard de Tiron* (as n. 13), §61–§62, 378–81; Cline, ed., *Life of the Blessed Bernard* (as n. 13), 67–69, and our article, S. Bonde and C. Maines, 'Hermits in the Forest: Western France and the Architecture of Monastic Reform', in *Other Monasticisms*, eds. S. Bonde and C. Maines (Turnhout forthcoming).

[36] Beck, *Saint-Bernard de Tiron* (as n. 13) §63–§66, 382–37; Cline, ed., *Life of the Blessed Bernard* (as n. 13), 70–73, on the followers and the forest.

[37] J.-H. Foulon, 'Les ermites dans l'ouest de la France: les sources, bilan et perspectives', in *Ermites de France et d'Italie, XIe–XVe siècle*, ed. A. Vauchez (Rome 2003), 81–113, esp. 85–94 and 99–113 on Bernard of Tiron. See also Bonde and Maines, 'Hermits in the Forest', (as n. 35).

[38] Orderic Vitalis, *Ecclesiastical History* (as n. 29), IV, book viii, 330–31: *'Illuc multitudo fidelium utriusque ordinis abunde confluxit, et predictus pater omnes ad conuersionem properantes caritatiuo amplexu suscepit, et singulis artes quas nouerant legitimas in monasterio exercere precepit. Vnde liberter conuenerunt ad eum fabri tam lignarii quam ferrarii, sculptores et aurifabri, pictores et cementarii, uinitores et agricolae, multorumque officiorum artifices peritissimi*'.

[39] *Gallia christiana in provincias ecclesiasticas. . .* (Paris 1744), VIII: 1263, on Bernard's death which repeats the notice in the obituary of Chartres Cathedral. The authors of *Gallia christiana* assert that the same passage appeared in the obituary of the abbey of Saint-Père de Chartres.

[40] *Gallia christiana* (as n. 39), VIII: 1262–68. Guillaumin, *Thiron* (as n. 25), 72, also provides a list of abbots that seems to be based on the list in *Gallia christiana* but that fills in the gaps in that earlier series.

[41] *Gallia christiana* (as n. 39), VIII: 1263, 'Hugo Bernardi disciplinis excultus'.

[42] Merlet, *Cartulaire* (as n. 13), I: 28–29, 'ego Adela, Blesensis comitissa, ea que dedi Hugoni, domno abbati Tyronensi'.

[43] Thompson, *Monks of Tiron* (as n. 31), 131–32. Beck, *Saint Bernard de Tiron* (as n. 13), 486: '*Anima domni Vitalis bonae memoriae viri et animae omnium fidelium defunctorum requiescant in pace. Amen. Orate pro abbatis nostris, Bernardo scilicet et Radulfo, et pro fratribus nostris omnibus*'.

[44] Merlet, *Cartulaire* I (as n. 15): 36, '*Calixtus episcopus, servus servorum Dei, dilectissimo filio Guillelmo, abbati monasterii Sancti-Salvatoris de Tyronio*'.

[45] Steven Vanderputten, *Monastic Reform as Process, Realities and Representations in Medieval Flanders, 900–1100* (Ithaca–London 2013), 97–101, on the roles of great reformers and their successors.

[46] Merlet, *Cartulaire* (as n. 15), I: xxi, 37–38 for the charter of 1119. William's last dated appearance occurs in both versions of the papal confirmation of Eugenius III, dated May 1147. Merlet, *Cartulaire* (as n. 15), II: ccxci, 60–63 and ccxcii, 63–67). Merlet suggests a date *c.* 1150 for an undated charter (*Cartulaire*, II: ccxcix, 72–74). William's apparent successor, Abbot Stephen first appears *c.* 1160 (*Cartulaire,* II: cccxiv, 87) See also Thompson, 'The Cartulary' (as n. 15), 119, n°324. On the two short abbatial reigns between Bernard and William, see Thompson, *Monks of Tiron* (as n. 31), 131–32; Cline, ed., *Life of the Blessed Bernard* (as n. 13), xxiii.

[47] Merlet, *Cartulaire* (as n. 15), I: 1–2. '*In nomine sancte et individue Trinitatis, ego Ivo Carnotensis ecclesie humilis minister, et Arnaudus decanus, necnon commune capitulum Beate Marie, notum volumus fieri omnibus tam futuris quam presentibus quod domnus Bernardus, venerabilis abbas, com grege sibi commisso parvitatem nostram humiliter adierunt, petentes ut eis concederemus carrucatam unam terre de terra Beate Marie, que est super rivulum qui dicitur Tiro, infra Gardiensem parrochiam, ad edificandum monasterium et claustrum et cetera usui fratrum neccesaria*'. This charter also appears, verbatim (apart from one or two variations in spelling), in E. de Lépinois and L. Merlet, *Cartulaire de Notre-Dame de Chartres, Société Archéologique d'Eure-et-Loir*, 3 vols. (Chartres 1862–1865), I: 117–18. What remains impressive is the list of witnesses. In addition to Bishop Yves and Deacon Arnaud, there follow the names of the cathedral cantor, its subdeacon and subcantor, six archdeacons, four provosts, the sacristan, the chamberlain, the abbot of Saint-Jean-en-Vallé, and six priests as well as Hugh of Saint-André.

[48] Merlet, *Cartulaire* (as n. 15), I: 13–14. '*consecraremus cujusdam cenobii cimiterium quod situm super rivum qui Tyron vocatur, ad usum quorumdam religiosorum monachorum, qui in eodem loco heremiticam vitam ducere elegerant*'.

[49] Lépinois and Merlet, *Cartulaire de Notre-Dame de Chartres* (as n. 47), III: 98. '*Necrologium B. M. Carnutensis – VII Kalendas Maii (25 avril), [Obiit] Et Bernardus, abbas de Tyro, qui ejusdem loci ecclesiam a fundamento construxit, et multos ibidem monachos sub sanctitatis et religionis norma congregavit*'.

[50] On Yves of Chartres, see C. Rolker, *Canon Law and the Letters of Ivo of Chartres* (Cambridge 2010). See also Beck, *Saint Bernard de Tiron* (as n. 13), 483–4 on Yves' letter 283 on the consecration of the monastic cemetery at Tiron.

[51] On Geoffrey, see L. Grant, 'Geoffrey of Lèves, Bishop of Chartres, Famous Wheeler Dealer in Secular Business', in *Suger en Question: Regards croisés sur Saint-Denis*, ed. R. Grosse (Paris 2004), 46–56.

[52] Merlet, *Cartulaire* (as n. 15), I: 2, n. 2; Cline, *Life of Blessed Bernard* (as n. 13), 83; Grant, 'Geoffrey of Lèves' (as n. 51), 47. For Geoffrey Grossus' assertion of the same, see Beck, *Saint Bernard de Tiron* (as n. 13), 396, para. 77.

[53] Grant, 'Geoffrey of Lèves' (as n. 51), 47–48.

[54] Merlet, *Cartulaire* (as n. 15), I: xiv, xviii, xxi, xxii, xxxviii, l, lxi, lxviii, lxxxi, cviii, cxxx, cxxxvi, clxiii, clxxxi, clxxxvi, cxcvi, ccxxii, ccxxvi, and *Cartulaire,* II: ccxxxiv, cclxix, ccxc.

[55] For a brief discussion of royal patronage as found in the abbey cartulary, see Thompson, 'The Cartulary' (as n. 15), 70; Thompson, *Monks of Tiron* (as n. 31), 114–15 and 120– 21 on Anglo-Norman and French royal patronage, respectively.

[56] For a genealogical chart of the Rotrou family, see Thompson, *Power and Border Lordship* (as n. 2), 6–7.

[57] Henry I married Matilda of Scotland in 1100. Among his many illegitimate children were two daughters, both of whom were named Matilda. On Rotrou's wife, Countess Matilda, see Thompson, *Power and Border Lordship* (as n. 2), 71–72.

[58] On Béatrix, see Thompson, *Power and Border Lordship* (as n. 2), 48.

[59] On Juliana, see Thompson, *Power and Border Lordship* (as n. 2), 74.

[60] Merlet, *Cartulaire* (as n. 15), I: 39. '*quod ego Rotrocus, comes Perticensium, dono Deo et monachis Tyronis, pro anima mea et animabus parentum meorum, unam magnam somam salis apud Mauritaniam, in unaquaque ebodmada perpetuo habendam, et deciman annone omnium horreorum meorum. Dono etiam monachis supradictus omnia nemora mea ad domos suas facienda et ad suum ardere, et cursum porcorum suorum, et pasturam peccorum suorum, et mediteriam de Arsiz [Arcisse], cum stagno et molendino, et vallem que est justa Luxvillat citra aquam, et capellam cum viridario*'.

[61] Thompson, *Power and Border Lordship* (as n. 2), 71–72; eadem, *Monks of Tiron* (as n. 31), 114.

[62] On Henry I's support for Tiron, see 127–28 below.

[63] www.myheritage.com/names/beatrice_roucy [accessed 16 November 2018]. We know of no document giving Béatrix's place of burial, though it seems reasonable to assume that it was at Tiron.

[64] Cline, ed., *Life of Blessed Bernard* (as n. 13), §81, 87 for the English translation used here. Beck, *Saint Bernard de Tiron* (as n. 13), 398, quotes the Latin: '*Supradicta vero Beatrix, ejus cognita sanctitate, castrorum suorum habitationem deserens, Tironii aedificatis aedibus quoad vixit deinceps habitavit; ibique ingentem Basilicam, multis expensis pecuniis, fabricant*'. Geoffrey Grossus goes on to say that Juliana, Béatrix's daughter and Rotrou's sister, continued her mother's patronage after the latter's death, contributing substantially to construction of the abbey's workshops (*officinarum nostrarum*). Cline, ed., *Life of Blessed Bernard* (as n. 13), 87, n. 15 thinks that Juliana also lived at Tiron with her mother. While the Life attributes additional patronage to Juliana, the text is not clear that Juliana lived at Tiron. As Thompson, *Power and Border Lordship* (as n. 2), 74, has reconstructed Juliana's career after the death of her husband, her residence in Tiron seems unlikely.

[65] Orderic Vitalis, *Ecclesiastical History* (as n. 29), IV, Book viii, 27, 330–31.

[66] Thompson, *Power and Border Lordship* (as n. 2), 47–48, 63.

[67] Thompson, *Monks of Tiron* (as n. 31), 115; Merlet, *Cartulaire* (as n. 15), I: 75, n° liv, which Merlet dates to *c.* 1122; but see Thompson, 'Cartulary' (as n. 15), 99, who says that the charter is 'undated but probably before 1116'.

[68] Merlet, *Cartulaire* (as n. 15), I: 29, 25, 41, n° xv and Thompson, 'Cartulary' (as n. 15), 99.

[69] Merlet, *Cartulaire* (as n. 15), I: 27–8, n° xiii and Thompson, 'Cartulary' (as n. 15), 99. See also Thompson, *Monks of Tiron* (as n. 31), 115.

[70] Merlet, *Cartulaire* (as n. 15), I: 43, n° xxv; Thompson, 'Cartulary' (as n. 15), 99.

[71] Merlet, *Cartulaire* (as n. 15), I: 41–2, n° xxvii; Thompson, 'Cartulary' (as n. 15), 101.

[72] Cline, ed., *Life of the Blessed Bernard* (as n. 13), 83–84, for the English, and Beck, *Saint Bernard de Tiron* (as n. 13), 396, §78. Geoffrey's assertion here is mentioned nowhere else.

[73] Merlet, *Cartulaire* (as n. 15), I: 28–29, number xiv, and 40–41, number xxiv, dated by the author to *c.* 1117–19 and *c.* 1119.

[74] Merlet, *Cartulaire* (as n. 15), I: 18, n° vii and Thompson, 'Cartulary' (as n. 15), 105.

[75] Beck, *Saint Bernard de Tiron* (as n. 13), §97, 416; Cline, ed., *Life of Blessed Bernard* (as n. 13), 103. '*Successoribus etiam suis post ejus obitum maximam reverentiam exhibuit ita ut ab eis liberos suos, Philippum videlicet, ac Ludovicum, postea Reges, sacro de fonte suscipi vellet*'. See also Thompson, *Monks of Tiron* (as n. 31), 121 and n. 112. Baptism of the king's sons at Tiron is known only from the *Life* and, if it occurred at all, must have happened after 1120 when the future Louis VII was born.

[76] Beck, *Saint Bernard de Tiron* (as n. 13), §96–§98, 416–18 and 421; Cline, ed., *Life of Blessed Bernard* (as n. 13), 102–06.

[77] See Beck, *Saint Bernard de Tiron* (as n. 13), §99, 418 and 423 for the Latin and French, respectively; Cline, ed., *Life of Blessed Bernard* (as n. 13), 106–07 and 106, n. 28 on David himself. No mention of Selkirk or David's visit to Tiron occurs in the cartulary, though David's place in Henry I Beauclerc's court and that king's presence in Normandy strengthens the possibility of a visit by the earl.

[78] When David became king, he created a second house, known today as Kelso, with monks from his first foundation. Kelso and its dependencies came, ultimately, to be independent of Tiron itself and seems to have led to the notion that the original foundation at Selkirk was abandoned. To us, this notion seems curious. It seems more likely that Kelso was founded from Selkirk and that Selkirk remained in existence, providing two communities to pray for King David's soul. In this regard, it is interesting to note that the 1516 *Livre blanc* lists both the abbeys of Rochaburgo (Kelso) and Selecherche (Selkirk). See Merlet, *Cartulaire* (as n. 15), II: 234–37. See also Thompson, *Monks of Tiron* (as n. 31), 88–89, on relations between Tiron and the Scottish houses.

[79] In this regard, it is useful to remember that the establishment of a monastery is not a simple formal event but rather a process. See S. Bonde and C. Maines, *Saint-Jean-des-Vignes: Approaches to Its Architecture, Archaeology and History* (Turnhout 2003), 55–83 and Vanderputten, *Monastic Reform* (as n. 45), 8–13.

[80] Thompson, *Monks of Tiron* (as n. 31), 106–07.

[81] Ibid., 107 and n. 61.

[82] Scholars have been concerned with uncertainties about the location of earlier sites in the area (Arcisse and Tiron-Brunelles, although these two may be the same) and about when Bernard and his followers arrived at any of them. It seems unlikely that either issue can be definitely resolved. From our perspective, the views expressed in Thompson, *Power and Border Lordship* (as n. 2), 56–58; eadem, *Monks of Tiron* (as n. 31), 103–22, seem the most convincing and rely on the widest number of sources. Cline, *Life of Blessed Bernard* (as n. 13), xviii–xxii makes a similar argument.

[83] See Thompson, *Power and Border Lordship* (as n. 2), 56–58 for an extended discussion of the date at which Bernard and his followers came to Thiron-Gardais. See also Thompson, *Monks of Tiron* (as n. 31), 109 and n. 67 and 111; Cline, ed., *Life of Blessed Bernard* (as n. 13) xviii–xxii; Beck, *Saint Bernard de Tiron* (as n. 13), 262–66, working primarily from the literary sources, argues for a date of 1114 for the beginning of occupation at Thiron-Gardais, where the abbey is today. See also G. Bonnebas, 'La fondation de l'abbaye de Tiron: sa place dans l'histoire des communautés régulières du diocèse de Chartres, des origines à 1180', *Cahiers Percherons*, 199 (2014), 35.

[84] Beck, *Saint Bernard de Tiron* (as n. 13), 483. '*Nos igitur ad conservandam tranquillitatem servorum Dei, praedictum locum cum appendicitis ejus ad petitionem praedicti comitis in tuitionem sanctae Carnotensis Ecclesiae et nostrum paterne suscipimus, et pervasores eorum atque distractores ante tribunal aeterni Judicis terribiliter condemnendos esse denunciamus, et in hac temporali Ecclesia, sine cujus communione ad illam aeternam perveniri non potest, eos a corpore et sanguine Christi patrimonium reformare humili satisfactione studuerint*'.

[85] Samples of *grès roussard* and limestone were taken at Blainville and Plainville quarries respectively during the summer of 2018, and were tested in May 2019 at Wesleyan University, using XRF technology. See Appendix.

[86] On Le Mans, see N. Gautier, ed., *La cathédrale du Mans, du visible à l'invisible* (Le Mans 2015), 78–89. There is very little scholarship on Étival. The church site is now private property and a working farm. Only the north transept arm with its one apse remain in elevation. On Étival, see Bonde and Maines, 'La Sainte-Trinité' (as n. 35).

[87] On the southern side remains of a Gothic capital and rib springer have been inserted into the shaft of a blind arcade column, presumably following the collapse of the choir in 1819.

[88] Both the north and south arches of the crossing bay were walled up when the transept arms were dismantled. Capitals of the four crossing piers have all been destroyed or removed, except for the transept side of the north-west pier. It is possible that capitals survive within the thickness of the walls now blocking the north and south arches.

[89] Bonde and Maines, 'L'Église-mère' (as n. 22), 64–79.

[90] Bearing capacity taken from the New York State building codes. See S. Bonde, C. Maines with R. Richards, 'Soils and Foundations', in *Architectural Technology Up to the Scientific Revolution: The Art and Structure of Large-Scale Buildings*, ed. R. Mark, gen. ed. (Cambridge 1993), 16–50, esp.18.

[91] S. Liégard, personal communication. See also S. Liégard, 'Thiron-Gardais – Cloître de l'abbaye, Intervention archéologique préalable à la reconstruction du cloître d'août à novembre 2016', *Le Collector, Ordre de Tiron*, 6 (2018), 5–6.

[92] Orderic Vitalis, *Ecclesiastical History* (as n. 29), IV, Book vii, 330–31, See above, p. 126 and n. 38.

[93] J. Mallet, 'La nef unique dans l'art religieux angevin', in *Anjou, Medieval Art, Architecture and Archaeology*, eds. J. McNeill and D. Prigent (Leeds 2003), 52–65.

[94] This may have been a specific instance of importance for Bernard. Very little seems to be known about the medieval church at Saint-Cyprien in Poitiers where Bernard was abbot. The few graphic images

and the Maurist drawing of the church that replaced it (Paris, Archives nationales N III Vienne, plan de Saint-Cyprien de 1691) hint at the form of the medieval church, which appears to have been an aisleless cruciform building. Saint-Cyprien is discussed further in Bonde and Maines, 'Hermits in the Forest' (as n. 35).

[95] For an overview see J. Mallet, 'La nef unique' (as n. 93), 52–65. On Fontevraud, see J.-M. Bienvenu and D. Prigent, 'Installation de la Communauté fontevriste', *Fontevraud Histoire-Archéologie*, I (1992), 15–22. See also Bonde and Maines, 'Hermits in the Forest' (as n 35).

[96] On the *Vita Apostolica*, Carolyn Walker Bynum, *Jesus as Mother, Studies in the Spirituality of the High Middle Ages* (Berkeley 1982), 102–04 et passim. See also the overview, E. F. McDonnell, 'The Vita Apostolica: Diversity or Dissent', *Church History*, 24/1 (1955), 15–31.

[97] On the saint, see Jacobus de Voragine, *The Golden Legend, Readings on the Saints*, trans. W. G. Ryan, 2 vols. (Princeton 1993), II: 18–21.

[98] See J. Franklin, 'Iconic Architecture and the Medieval Reformation: Ambrose of Milan, Peter Damian, Stephen Harding and the Aisleless Cruciform Church', in *Romanesque and the Past*, eds. J. McNeill and R. Plant (Leeds 2013), 77–94. See also J. Franklin, 'Augustinian and Other Canons' Churches in Romanesque Europe: The Significance of the Aisleless Cruciform Plan', in *Architecture and Interpretation: Essays for Eric Fernie*, eds. J. Franklin, T. A. Heslop, and C. Stevenson (Woodbridge 2012), 78–98. On the relationship between architecture and the Gregorian Reform, see, most recently, X. Barral i Altet, 'Art monumental roman et réforme grégorienne: plaidoyer contre une fiction historiographique très enracinée', in *Art et réfome grégorienne en France et dans la péninsule Ibérique*, ed. B. Franzé (Paris 2015), 41–56. Barral i Altet argues against the generalization of the idea of the impact of reform on art and in favour of studies that are locally focused, as we argue here.

[99] Orderic Vitalis, *Ecclesiastical History* (as n. 29), IV, Book vii, 328–29 'He fought an action in the Roman synod before Pope Pascal for the liberty of his church'. *In Romano sinodo contra Paschalem papam pro libertate aecclesiae litigavit*. Geoffrey Grossus would have Bernard going twice to Rome which is not supported elsewhere. See Cline, ed., *Life of Blessed Bernard* (as n. 13), 61–67, chaps. 55–60 for the English and Beck, *Saint Bernard de Tiron* (as n. 13), §55–61, 372–78 for the Latin.

[100] It is not simply that there is a small tower window in the transept wall; it is also that there is no trace of a longer 'transept window' which would otherwise have been present.

[101] Héliot, 'Sur les tours jumelées' (as n. 20), 249–70.

[102] Saint-Martin-des-Champs in Paris may also have had shouldered towers. A truncated tower survives on the north side of the church. On the south side, a tower seems to have been suppressed by the addition of an early modern structure.

[103] See M. Baylé, 'La sculpture romane dans la Normandie ducale', in *Les siècles romans en Basse-Normandie, Catalogue d'exposition* (Caen 1985), 55–63, esp. 61–62 on 'Le développement du géométrisme et l'apparition du chapiteau à godrons', of which the earliest for Baylé is found in the chapel of the Tower of London about 1080. Since Baylé was writing, a building break has been identified in St John's Chapel, making it far more likely that the double-cushion (or proto-scallop) capitals date from *c.* 1090 at the earliest. See J. Crook, 'St John's Chapel', in *The White Tower*, ed. E. Impey (New Haven–London 2008), 118–23.

[104] Artistic relations between Normandy and the Île-de-France have long been discussed. See M. Baylé, 'La place des sculptures de Saint-Germain-des-Prés (Paris) dans le cheminement des formes au xie siècle', in *De la création à la restauration. Mélanges en l'honneur de Marcel Durliat* (Toulouse 1992), 205–14; A. Prache, 'Les relations architecturales entre la Normandie, la Champagne septentrionale et le Soissonnais à l'époque romane' [Recueil d'études en hommage à Lucien Musset], *Cahier des Annales de Normandie*, 23 (1990), 337–50, containing a bibliography on related studies.

[105] The damage to these capitals is partly due to the relative softness of the limestone from which they are carved and partly, we assume, to the collapse of the Gothic choir in 1819.

[106] See M. Baylé, 'Les chapiteaux dérivés du corinthien dans la France du Nord', in *L'acanthe dans la sculpture monumentale de l'antiqué à la renaissance*, ed. L. Pressouyre (Paris 1993), 269–80.

[107] P. Plagnieux, 'L'abbatiale du XIe siècle de Saint-Germain-des-Prés: nouvelles perspectives de recherche', in *Saint-Germain-des-Prės, mille ans d'une abbaye à Paris*, eds. R. Recht and M. Zink (Paris 2015), 1–16 and esp. 12–16.

[108] On the portal at Le Mans, see M. Angheben, 'Le portail royal du Mans et l'évolution de la première gothique, entre les façades de Dijon et Chartres', *Cahiers de civilisation médiévale*, 60 (2017), 27–58.

[109] Merlet, *Cartulaire* (as n. 15), I: ciii. Merlet's information came evidently from the resident guardian, a man named Arsène Vincent. According to Merlet, *Cartulaire* (as n. 15) I: ciii, the original stone lintel was damaged (and is now replaced by the current wooden one).

[110] For example, the jamb courses above the console platform mask the rich carving of the arris of the embrasure step in a way that could never have been originally intended. The blocks of the capital courses and the archivolts are the same colour and texture as the replacement blocks in the jamb and are thus also likely to be replacement blocks.

[111] This console may, like the others, have ended in a sculpted head.

[112] On the *portail royal* at Chartres, see J. van der Meulen and J. Hohmeyer, *Chartres, Biographie der Kathedrale* (Cologne 1984), 228–43; M. E. Fassler, *The Virgin of Chartres* (New Haven 2010). On Le Mans, see Angheben, 'Portail royal du Mans' (as n. 108), who dates the portal between Saint-Bénigne and Chartres West.

[113] We are grateful to Kathleen Thompson for suggesting that the female head may represent Adela of Blois and Chartres.

[114] See W. W. Clark and T. G. Waldman, 'Money, Stone, Liturgy and Planning at the Royal Abbey of Saint-Denis', in *New Approaches to Medieval Architecture*, eds. R. Bork, W. W. Clark, and Abby McGehee [Avista Studies in the History of Medieval Technology, Science and Art, 8] (Farnham 2011), 63–75, which provides convincing evidence that the column-statues of Saint-Denis were likely to have been finished closer to 1130 than 1140.

[115] Isaiah 11^{1,10}.

[116] Luke I$^{26–38}$.

The Regional and Transregional in Romanesque Europe (2021), 147–156

FOUR ROMANESQUE CISTERCIAN ABBEYS IN LESSER POLAND

THE CONTEXT OF THEIR FOUNDATION

Tomasz Węcławowicz

This paper considers the four easternmost Cistercian Abbeys in Poland, at Jędrzejów, Koprzywnica, Wąchock, and Sulejów, all of them built relatively quickly and at a broadly similar date. The monastic churches at each site share the same groundplan, a well-established transregional plan type traditionally associated with Citeaux II.

Regional specificity depends on ideological context – in which respect the patron saints of these churches are important. These were chosen because they helped support the political aims of Krakow's duke or Krakow's bishop, or both. The patrons thus honoured were St Adalbert – the first patron saint of the Polish kingdom, St Florian, whose relics were brought from Italy to Krakow during the relevant period, and St Thomas Becket, whose cult was strongly promoted in the diocese of Krakow thanks to close contact between the local bishop and the English clergy. Moreover, in western Europe Cistercian monasteries were usually built in remote and inhospitable regions, so that the monks would not come into contact with laymen and could follow a life of strict religious discipline. In both Poland and Lesser Poland, Cistercian monasteries were always located by the seats of local rulers and were initially given an older church or a chapel.

Thanks to the initiatives of local bishops and lay founders, even such pan-European architectural forms and ideas as those promoted by the Cistercians thus acquired certain local and regional characteristics.

By the end of the 12th century, after the Cistercian order had spread throughout France and central and eastern Europe, the first monks were invited to Poland by Bishop Mathias of Krakow, following his correspondence with St Bernard of Clairvaux in *c.* 1146. As a result of the Bishop's request, four direct daughter-houses of Morimond were established in Lesser Poland. These were: Jędrzejów, Sulejów, Wąchock, and Koprzywnica, all in the uplands, north and north-east of Krakow and founded in a relatively short period of time, between 1150 and 1183. All these monasteries have survived, and despite frequent rebuilding, fires, and some Baroque transformations, they retain their medieval forms. Owing to the stylistic purity and the quality of their stone masonry, they exemplify a new and intriguing facet to the general picture of Romanesque art in Central Europe – a picture to which Alexandra Gajewski has drawn attention.[1] It is important to follow and develop some of her suggestions and to try to analyse some architectural features understood as transregional Cistercian forms taking into account the local background of these foundations.

Due to the stylistic purity of their architecture and the quality of their stone masonry these Cistercian Abbeys add a new and intriguing facet to the general picture of Romanesque art in Poland. In addition, they form a distinct group being connected by their 'Bernardine plan' (also known as the 'Citeaux II plan') with a straight east end and transepts opening onto rectangular chapels on each side of the choir. Typically their naves are basilical with the French *travée* system and two-storey interior elevations sometimes called Burgundian. (Figures 11.1 a–d and 11.2.).

The monastic buildings have survived only partially. The most recent archaeological investigations have shed new light on the original disposition of the cloisters and the function of the various rooms. It transpired that parts of the east range, including the Chapter-House, survive at Sulejów, Wąchock, and Koprzywnica (Figures 11.3 and 11.4 and Colour Plate XII (bottom)). In fact, it is now clear that the east range of all four cloisters was configured in a similar way. The narrow bay adjacent to the church was obviously used as the sacristy; next to that was the Chapter-House and a staircase leading to the dormitory. A room located underneath the staircase might have been used as a lockup or more likely a treasury. The narrow vaulted corridor next to the staircase served as a passage to a garden. Finally, the last room within the east range was probably used as the so-called *fraternia*, i.e. lay brothers' day room. (Figure 11.5) At all four abbeys, evidence has been found confirming the existence of dormitories extending across the upper parts of the eastern ranges. The previous layout of the other ranges are not

  DOI: 10.4324/9781003162827-11

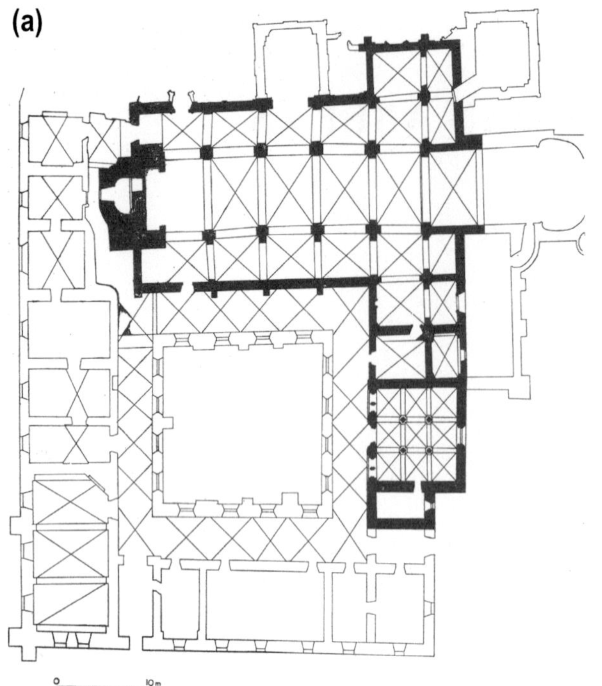

FIGURE 11.1a

Jędrzejów, Cistercian Abbey: ground plan (Chapter-House reconstructed). (Courtesy of the archives of the Department of Architecture History at the Warsaw University of Technology)

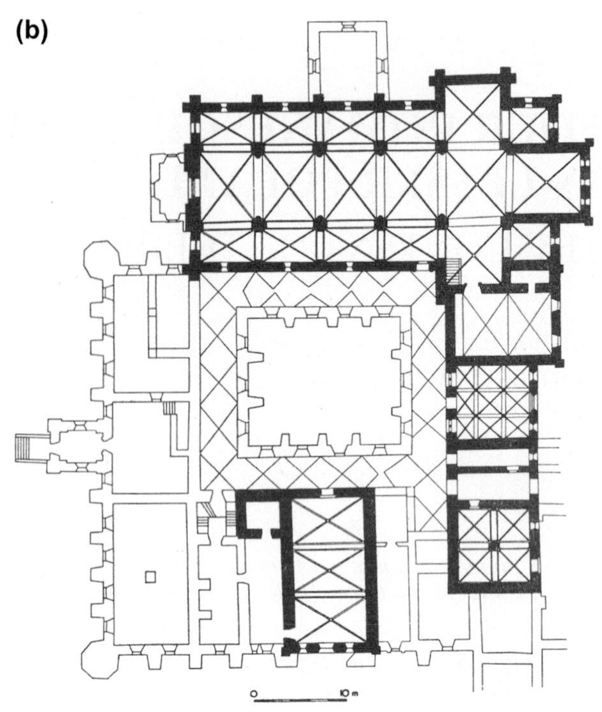

FIGURE 11.1b

Wąchock, Cistercian Abbey: ground plan (Courtesy of the archives of the Department of Architecture History at the Warsaw University of Technology)

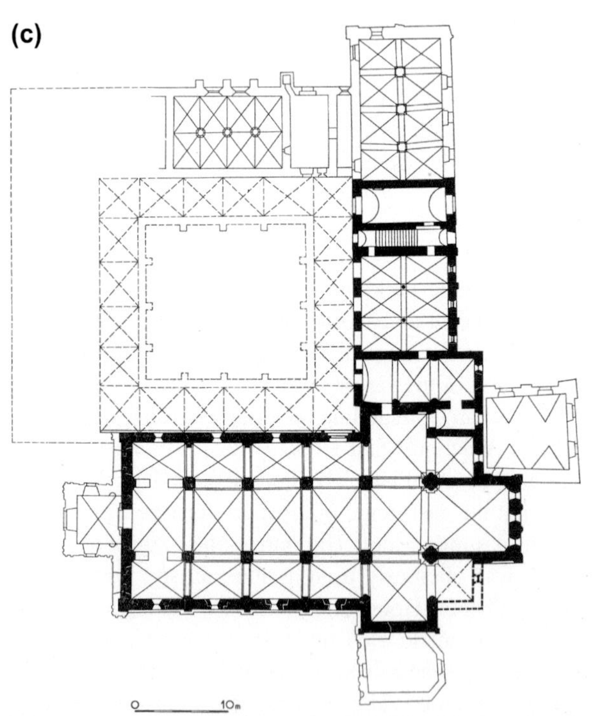

FIGURE 11.1c

Koprzywnica, Cistercian Abbey: ground plan (Courtesy of the archives of the Department of Architecture History at the Warsaw University of Technology)

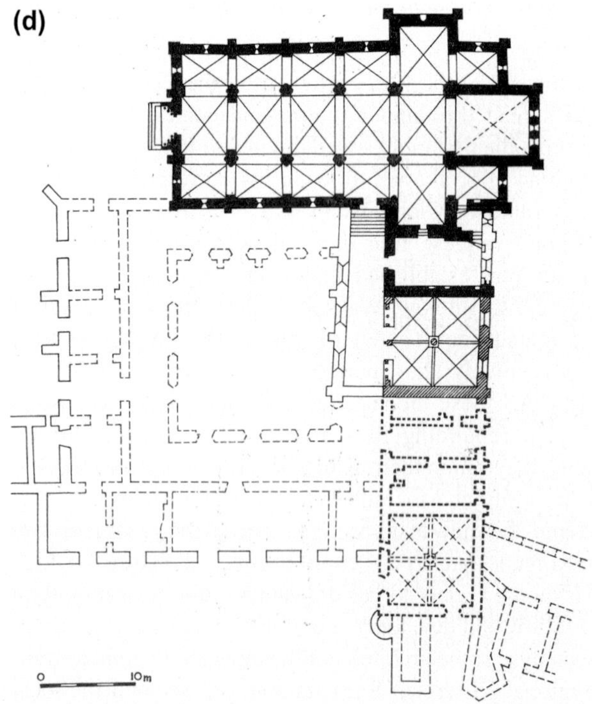

FIGURE 11.1d

Sulejów, Cistercian Abbey: ground plan (Courtesy of the archives of the Department of Architecture History at the Warsaw University of Technology)

FIGURE 11.2
Wąchock, Cistercian Church: the nave looking east (Photo: J. Kopka)

FIGURE 11.3
Wąchock, Cistercian Abbey: chapter-house (Photo: J. Kopka)

FIGURE 11.4

Koprzywnica, Cistercian Abbey: chapter-house (Photo: J. Kopka)

always clear because they were later remodelled or partly destroyed, but there are some fresh insights. The recent archaeological excavations at Jędrzejów and Koprzywnica have uncovered remains of previous refectories, situated at a right angle to the cloisters, in the same position as the surviving refectory at Wąchock.[2]

Traditionally it has been argued that the church at Wąchock has Italian provenance. Some late medieval sources described the mode of construction of the church walls – faced with dark pink and light-grey sandstone, arranged in horizontal rows – as '*modus italicus*'[3] (Figure 11.6). However, the links to Italy were probably indirect. The Hungarian monastery church in Bélapátfalva seems to be one of the important points in the network of influences at play here.[4]

Looking further at the churches in question, it is worth noting a couple of details. Their main portals are Romanesque (Figures 11.7 and 11.8); in Sulejów, it follows the Lombard type, with an oculus above (Figure 11.8).

The east ends of the presbyteries follow the common Cistercian scheme of three narrow windows with an oculus above (Figures 11.9 and 11.10). The interior elevations are of two stories with arcades of square or cruciform piers supporting round or slightly pointed arches and a low clerestory above a string-course (Figure 11.2).

One of the most fascinating aspects of these churches is the huge variety of corbel types and capitals of vaulting shafts. The differences between them provide another argument against the traditional hypothesis that a single workshop was responsible for the construction and decoration of all the four churches. There are various forms of capitals for the vaulting shafts, or rather the attached columns. They follow simplified, unusually reductive, and one may even say barbarized antique motifs, mostly of Corinthian and Byzantine derivation. These examples are unusual because of their extremely archaic appearance. Their origin is still subject to debate.

The Wąchock Chapter-House is probably the most beautiful and most richly decorated late Romanesque interior in Poland and showcases the style and skills of the unknown, possibly Italian (or Hungarian) stonemasons. Its square plan is divided into nine bays. Four columns stand on Attic bases. Their plinths are decorated with animal heads (or masks) and foliage. The capitals retain a Corinthian feel, having basket-shaped corner volutes terminating with rolled leaves. The mastery in the execution of their detail is astonishing. They are also surprisingly rich in calligraphic ornamentation (Figure 11.3). The corbels on the side walls have similar decoration. The vault construction is also unique. The vault webs are made from narrow stones the length of which is equivalent to the distance between the ribs. Presumably the architect was not yet familiar with Gothic construction methods and simply improvised a solution to the forms of a rib vault (Figures 11.3 and 11.5).

In contrast, the Chapter-House in Sulejów has fully developed Gothic rib vaults supported by short Romanesque column. It has Romanesque proportions, but its

FIGURE 11.5
Wąchock, Cistercian Abbey: lay brothers' day room (Photo: J. Kopka)

capital follows an Early Gothic form and floral ornamentation (Figure 11.11). Other unusual details include the arcade tracery between the cloisters and the Chapter-House at Wąchock. These resemble the simple late Romanesque forms which Lottlisa Behling described as *die Vorformen* and appeared here and there as early as by the middle of the 12th century. However, in Wąchock these details were executed later, possibly at the very end of this century (Figure 11.12).[5]

Since the end of the 19th century, Polish scholars have engaged in heated debate on the architectural models for Cistercian churches in Lesser Poland, which were associated with either Burgundy or Italy.[6] It has frequently been put forward that in many Cistercian abbeys the mother-house was the first and primary model for the monastic church of the daughter-house abbey. For instance, it is clear that some of the column capitals in Wąchock and Jędrzejów display similarities to those in the church of their mother-house at Morimond, whose details have survived in ruinous state. However, in my view this is purely coincidental and due to the use of a popular, commonly used form. Koprzywnica and Wąchock were linked to a hypothetical Italian workshop because the name of Simon, found carved respectively on a vault keystone and a wall, was associated with a Master Simon known to be active in Lazio.[7]

In a response to this Burgundian–Italian discussion, it should be pointed out that these churches are simply examples of fully developed Cistercian style. Their austere spirituality and restricted aesthetics, as well as the necessity to maintain formal uniformity, are usually defined as '*forma ordinis*'.[8] Cistercian architecture did not promote separation between territories such as Italy and Burgundy but rather exchange, interaction, and commonality. This can be regarded as transregional if we understand this as an exchange between regional arts and cultures. Some modern philosophers and sociologists have named such phenomena 'multiple attachments and identities' or 'cross-cutting identities'.[9] This is also reflected by the fact that although the Morimond mother house was in Burgundy, medieval written sources identify the majority of Cistercian monks at the Wąchock monastery as Italians.[10] The linking of some transcultural components is obvious here, and as a result it creates an architecture originating in differing workshops. Thomas Coomans, then, was perhaps correct when he suggested that this is not 'Cistercian architecture' but 'architecture of the Cistercians'.[11]

To better explain this problem, it may be helpful to follow some of Alexandra Gajewski's thoughts and to resort to the methodology of rhetoric and the so-called metalanguage of forms. Analogies between architecture

FIGURE 11.6

Wąchock, Cistercian Church: western façade (Photo: J. Kopka)

FIGURE 11.7

Koprzywnica, Cistercian Abbey: entrance to the church from the cloister (Photo: J. Kopka)

FIGURE 11.8

Sulejów, Cistercian Church: western façade (Photo: J. Kopka)

FIGURE 11.9

Sulejów, Cistercian Church: general view from north-east (Photo: J. Kopka)

FIGURE 11.11

Sulejów, Cistercian Abbey: Chapter-House, capital (Photo: J. Kopka)

FIGURE 11.10

Koprzywnica, Cistercian Church: eastern end (Photo: J. Kopka)

and language have been discussed especially in Central Europe by the followers of the so-called Viennese school of the history of art. Architectural elements can be understood as the text of culture in the way that words in sentences are. So a space, limited by walls, possibly can be analysed like rhetorical matter – as an art of expression, of fair and proper persuasion. Architectural patterns – such as those found in a Cistercian abbey church – can be compared with such rhetorical devices. Cistercian architecture is definitely textual, composed of constant, recurrent, and predictable spatial elements.[12] Therefore, we can say that the space of these churches was in some way 'expressed' by a *regula ordinis* before it was 'physically constructed'. The whole monastic space can also be seen as a rhetorical *dictum* or *proclamatio*.[13] There are sequences of rooms used in the rhythm of monastic life, determined by the rhythm of canonical prayers. It is a kind of *chronotopos*, which should be understood as the interplay of time and space, meaning the monasteries were created for Cistercians by Cistercians themselves using a universal spatial model based on their liturgy and a strict monastic rule.[14] It can be simply understood. Such a speculation relates to Coomans' general suggestion, already mentioned, that this is an architecture of the Cistercians, not a Cistercian architecture.

This is not to say that the abbeys of Lesser Poland lack any regional characteristics. Some scholars have emphasised that by the time the Cistercians came to Lesser Poland in the second half of the 12th century, the popularity of the order had waned. And yet the Cistercian churches in Lesser Poland, which were built relatively late, used traditional Romanesque forms. These are reflected by some architectural aspects of the buildings and in the history of their foundation. Firstly, all the churches follow a basilical system simplified in a Cistercian manner which pioneered the so-called pier-buttress system. In addition, the buttresses which support the clerestory wall are attached to the pillars. This Cistercian invention was spread in the 14th century as a regional feature in northern Bohemia, in Hungary, and in the monumental basilical churches of Krakow. The Wąchock church is evidently one of the early examples of this experimental technique.[15]

Second, Cistercian monasteries were usually built in remote and inhospitable regions, so that the monks would not come into contact with laymen and could more easily pursue a strict religious discipline. In Lesser Poland, indeed in Poland generally, Cistercian monasteries were located near the seat of a local ruler and initially given an

FIGURE 11.12

Wąchock: arcade tracery between cloister and Chapter-House (Photo: J. Kopka)

old church or a chapel.[16] This is why the western end in Jędrzejów church is "enclosed" by the early Romanesque apse of a previous church (Figure 11.13). The buildings and grange of Sulejów monastery are surrounded by the circular earthworks of the pre-existing stronghold of some local ruler. Under the pavement of the Chapter-House in Wąchock pre-Romanesque walls of a possible palace chapel were found.[17]

However, the most important aspect not yet raised by scholars is the ideological context of the abbeys' foundations and the role that the patron saints of these churches played in the process. The selection of each particular saint needs to be seen in the context of the political aims of either the ruler of Krakow, or its bishop, or both. The patrons thus honoured were: in Jędrzejów, St Adalbert, the first patron saint of the Polish kingdom; in Wąchock and Koprzywnica, St Florian; St Thomas Becket was chosen as the patron of Sulejów. All three patrons were martyrs. Adalbert was killed by Baltic pagans in north-eastern Poland, Thomas was killed in a dispute with King Henry II, and Florian was a Roman soldier tortured for his Christian faith. The relics of the latter were brought from Italy to Krakow in the 1180s to boost the significance and influence of the Krakow bishopric as well as the authority of Krakow's duke, Kasimir the Just (1138–94) among other Polish princes. According to the *legenda translationis*, St Florian wanted to defend Krakow against the Baltic pagans, despite the fact that Krakow is several hundred kilometres away from the pagan tribes' territories. St Florian's *patrocinium*, however, was repeated twice – in Wąchock and Koprzywnica. Thus the foundations and consecrations of both these monasteries can be seen in the context of the politics of that time.

The choice of Saint Thomas Becket as a patron in Sulejów also had a specific, local reason. His cult was avidly promoted by Bishop Vincent of Krakow (1150–1228). Bishop Vincent had been educated in France and studied for twelve years in Bologna after Thomas Becket left these places to become archbishop of Canterbury. After Thomas was assassinated and canonised (1173), he became one of the most popular martyrs of those times. George Zarnecki highlighted some close contacts which existed between Bishop Vincent and the English episcopate. In 1215 during the 4th Lateran Council, the Archbishop of York, Walter de Grey, presented the Krakow bishop with a spectacular gift in the form of decorative bronze doorknockers for the Cathedral Church.[18] One of these is still in Krakow Cathedral Museum. It is probable that Bishop Vincent was given not only doorknockers but also a Becket relic particle. Due to Vincent's initiative and his English connections, a new chapel in Krakow cathedral church dedicated to St Thomas Becket was founded,

FIGURE 11.13
Jędrzejów, Cistercian Church: remains of previous church, the western apse (Photo: J. Kopka)

and Sulejów Church was consecrated in the name of this martyr.

Becket's tragedy reminded Polish clergy that a century before, in 1079, Bishop Stanislaw of Krakow was also killed by the king. Bishop Vincent composed the legend of Stanislaw's martyrdom according to the Becket one.[19] Thus it can be said that the English St Thomas became in a sense the Polish St Stanislaw, the main Patron Saint of the Kingdom.

CONCLUSION

Searching for any regional features of Romanesque architecture in Lesser Poland is troublesome. There are actually only a few surviving imposing monuments and some typological groups, such as those with two apses (eastern and western), which Eric Fernie recently has written about.[20] The architecture of the four Cistercian churches, as just described, may be called transregional as it reveals the influence of various artistic regions. These churches could have been built in many places in Europe. Moreover, the architectural forms were complemented by a specific *chronotopos*, i.e. the Cistercian ceremonial rhetoric, celebrated in the monastic space. Thus, the long-standing dispute, whether these churches are Italian or Burgundian, is irrelevant and even unnecessary. The four Cistercian churches form a separate group, which cannot be called regional but that their regional characteristic can be seen in an immaterial aspect. Local ambitions and the promotion of the patron saints – St Adalbert, St Florian, and St Thomas – played a decisive role in the foundations. Recalling holy martyrs must also be seen in the context of the location of these abbeys: the easternmost in Europe. Thanks to the initiatives of local bishops and lay founders, such pan-European ideas and pan-European architectural forms have acquired local characteristics and ideological context.

NOTES

1 A. Gajewski, '(Rezension aus) Ewa Luzyniecka, Zygmunt Swiechowski, Robert Kunkel, the Architecture of Cistercian Abbeys. Morimond Filiation in Lesser Poland, Wroclaw 2008', *Kunst Chronik. Monatsschrift für Kunstwissenshaft Museumwesen und Denkmalpflege*, 63/5 (2010), 212–17; eadem, 'Identity on the Edge: The Architecture of the Cistercian Abbeys in Lesser Poland', in *Medieval Art, Architecture and Archaeology in Cracow and Lesser Poland*, eds. A Roznowska-Sadrei and T. Węcławowicz, BAA Trans XXXVII (Leeds 2014), 143–64, a highly erudite contribution.

2 B. Kwiatkowska-Kopka, 'Archaelogical Excavation at the Cistercian Monasteries of Jędrzejów, Szczyrzyc and Koprzywnica', in *Medieval Art, Architecture and Archaeology* (as n. 1), 165–74.

3 However, it has been recently pointed out by R. Quirini-Poplawski, *Rzeźba przedromańska i romańska w Polsce wobec sztuki włoskiej [Pre-Romanesque and Romanesque Sculpture in Poland and Italian Art]* (Krakow 2006), 149–59, that such decoration has an antique or Byzantine genesis and was not common in Cistercian Abbeys in Italy but occurs, for example, on Verona Cathedral and many early medieval buildings in Tuscany.

[4] A. Gergelyffy, 'L'églisse Abbatiale de Bélapátfalva avec un extrait du memoir de Ernő Szakál sur les travaux de Bélapátfalva', *Acta Historiae Artium Academiae Scientiarum Hungaricae*, 6 (1959), 245–75; eadem, 'L'architecture Cistercienne en Hongrie', in *Actes du XXIIe Congrès international d'histoire de l'art Budapest 1969*, vol. I (Budapest 1972), 481–85.

[5] L. Behling, *Gestalt und Geschichte des Masswerks* (Halle 1944), 14; G. Binding, *Masswerk* (Darmstadt 1989), 31–41.

[6] From W. Łuszczkiewicz, 'Opactwo Sulejówskie [Sulejów Abbey]', *Sprawozdania Komisyi do Badania Historyi Sztuki w Polsce Akademii Umiejętności w Krakowie*, I (1877), 33–42; until E. Łużyniecka, R. Kunkel, and Z. Świechowski, *The Architecture of Cistercian Abbeys: Morimond Filiations in Lesser Poland* (Wrocław 2008).

[7] K. Białoskórska, 'L'abbaye cistercienne de Wąchock', *Cahiers de civilisation medieval,* 5 (1962), 335–50; eadem, 'Polish Cistercian Architecture and Its Contact with Italy', *Gesta*, 4 (1965), 14–22.

[8] The classic term after M. Untermann, *Forma ordinis. Die mittelalterliche Baukunst der Zisterzienser*, Kunstwissenschaftliche Studien, 89 (München and Berlin 2001).

[9] D. Bell, *The Winding Passage: Essays and Sociological Journeys 1960–1980* (Cambridge, MA 1980), 243. See also W. Welsch, 'Subjektsein heute. Zum Zusammenhang von Subjektivität, Pluralität und Transversalität', *Studia Philosophica* 51 (1992), 153–82.

[10] J. Dlugosz, the Krakow cathedral canon and chronicler noted *c.* 1470 information about Italian monks at Wąchock. See: *Ioannis Dlugosz senioris canonici cracoviensis Liber beneficiorum dioecesis cracoviensis*, ed. A Przezdziecki, vol. 3 (Kraków 1864), 400–02.

[11] T. Coomans, 'Cistercian architecture or architecture of the Cistercians?' in *The Cambridge Companion to the Cistercian Order*, ed. M. Birkedal Bruun (Cambridge 2013), 151–72.

[12] This interpretation runs parallel to the considerations of M. Cassidy-Welch, *Monastic Spaces and Their Meanings: Thirteenth-Century English Cistercian Monasteries* (Turnhout 2001).

[13] The problem was elucidated first by A. Gajewski, 'Le Releq, ancienne église abbatiale. Entre rhétorique cistercienne et tradition locale', *Congrès Archéologique de France. Finistère* 167 (2007), 177–84. See also the papers by P. Binski and P. Crossley in, *Rhetoric Beyond the Words. Delight and Persuasion in the Art of Middle Ages*, ed. M. Carruthers (Cambridge 2010); for monasteries of Lesser Poland, see T. Węcławowicz, 'Cistercian Architecture and Rhetoric. A Preliminary Study', *Cistercium Mater Nostra*, 5 (2011), 25–34.

[14] See: M. J. Czajkowski and T. Węcławowicz, *Chronotopos monasticus: The Medieval Clock and the Rhythm of Monastic Life at the Mogiła Abbey near Krakow* (Krakow 2016).

[15] A literature review and discussion on this topic, see T. Węcławowicz, 'Royal Cathedral Church on Wawel Hill', in *Krakow. Jubilee of the Consecration 1364–2014* (Krakow 2014), 175–78.

[16] This unique feature was pointed out by K. Białoskórska, '*Czy o wyborze miejsca na założenie opactwa cysterskiego decydowały wskazania reguły. Między teorią a rzeczywistoscią* [Whether the Choice of Place for Foundation a Cistercian Abbey Was Determined by the Rule. Between Theory and Reality]', in *Cystersi w kulturze średniowiecznej Europy [Cistercians in the culture of medieval Europe]*, ed. J. Strzelczyk (Poznan 1992), 149–78 and by Gajewski, *Identity on the Edge* (as n. 1), 160.

[17] For the first report, see K. Białoskórska, 'Wąchock, woj. kieleckie. Opactwo OO. Cystersów', *Informator Archeologiczny: badania,* 9 (1975), 226.

[18] See G. Zarnecki, 'A Group of English Medieval Doorknockers', in *Miscelanea Pro Arte, Festschrift für Hermann Schnitzler zur Vollendung seines 6o. Lebensjahre,* eds. P. Bloch and J. Hoster [Shriften Pro Arte Medii Aevi – Freunde des Museums Schnütgen, vol. 1] (Düsseldorf 1964), 111–18. Revised version in G. Zarnecki, *Studies in Romanesque Sculpture* (London 1979); G. Zarnecki, T. Holland, and J. Holt, eds., *English Romanesque Art 1066–1200* (London 1984), 255–56. See also U. Mende, *Die Türzieher des Mittelalters* (Denkmäler deutscher Kunst, Bronzegeräte des Mittelalters, Bd. 2) (Berlin 1981), ns. 154 and 156.

[19] See D. von Güttner-Sporzynski, *Writing History in Medieval Poland: Vincentius Bishop of Cracow and the 'Chronica Polonorum'* (Turnhout 2017), part II of the 'Chronicle', chapter 20.

[20] E. Fernie, 'The Church of St Andrew, Krakow', in *Medieval Art, Architecture and Archaeology* (as n. 1), 17–27; E. Fernie, *Romanesque Architecture: The First Style of the European Age* (New Haven and London 2014), 167.

The Regional and Transregional in Romanesque Europe (2021), 157–169

THE CATHEDRAL OF CATANIA AND THE CREATION OF THE NORMAN COUNTY OF SICILY

TRANSREGIONAL AND TRANSALPINE MODELS IN THE ARCHITECTURE OF THE LATE 11TH CENTURY

Tancredi Bella

The foundation of the dioceses of Troina, Agrigento, Mazara del Vallo, Siracusa, and Catania under the guidance of French monks from Calabria and the construction of their cathedrals were important steps in Count Roger's political and ecclesiastical strategy for Sicily. A few years earlier, Roger had founded two abbeys in Calabria – Santa Maria at Sant'Eufemia and the Santissima Trinità in Mileto – both now unfortunately destroyed. However, it is possible to hypothesize that their plans were based on the model of Cluny II. This architectural plan was transferred, along with other architectural practices, to southern Italy via Benedictine monastic communities and thence to Sicily where it was used in the first Norman cathedrals.

In the light of new archival and archaeological research, much of it unpublished, this paper reconsiders the construction of the surviving Norman parts of the cathedral of Catania. The apses and transept, together with adjacent structures, survived at least two earthquakes. The original aisles will also be discussed briefly. The Norman status of the monument is reconsidered in relation to other Siculo-Norman cathedrals and to different contexts beyond the Alps.

THE BACKGROUND: CALABRIAN FOUNDATIONS

Before the Norman conquest of Sicily was complete, Count Roger of Altavilla undertook a programme of building work in Calabria. He founded the abbeys of Santa Maria at Sant'Eufemia (1062–65) and the Santissima Trinità in Mileto (1062–80). These now only survive as architectural ruins, but it is possible to recover their plans. A well-established Italian historiographical tradition sees these plans as having been based on the model of the apse-echelon of Cluny II (consecrated in 981). The plan was widely adopted in Normandy and then, it is alleged, transferred to southern Italy by Norman-trained Benedictine monks, thanks to Robert de Grandmesnil, former abbot of Saint Evroult-en-Ouche (Orne, Normandy), who moved down to southern Italy in 1061.[1]

Not much is known about the abbey of Sant'Eufemia. The nave may have been subdivided into three aisles, but this is uncertain. A barrel vault probably covered the lateral aisles, while the transept was tall, and the church had a tri-apsidal east end (Figure 12.1). The façade was finished with two towers. At the Santissima Trinità in Mileto, the nave was subdivided into three aisles, but these are longer than was the case at Sant'Eufemia. The transept gave onto three apses which, by contrast, were not as deep as those of Sant'Eufemia. The walls of the presbytery were precisely aligned with those of the nave.

SICILIAN CATHEDRALS OF THE 11TH CENTURY

As regards Sicily, scholars have always privileged the 12th-century cathedrals of the Norman Kingdom – that is the cathedrals of Cefalù, Monreale, and Palermo – in part because the first two at least have largely survived in their original medieval form. UNESCO recently underlined their status by listing the Arabic-Norman architecture of the west of Sicily.

The following study, however, is focused on the architecture of the late-11th-century cathedrals of Sicily and seeks to review the extent to which these are simplified versions of French churches transmitted through Calabria; an architectural production which has been described as 'colonialist'.[2] This historiographical tradition has coloured the evaluation of the buildings, most of which are now in ruins or were extensively altered in the post-medieval period.[3] Perceptions only began to change a little over a decade ago. First, Francesco Gandolfo published a brilliant paper on the cathedrals of the County of Sicily in relation to the cathedrals of the later Norman Kingdom. Then Caroline Bruzelius published an article which was partly anticipated by a paper she contributed to the British Archaeological Association's *Romanesque and the Mediterranean* conference in Palermo in 2012.[4] I now find myself on the same journey in studying the constructive problems posed by Catania Cathedral, in

  DOI: 10.4324/9781003162827-12

FIGURE 12.1

Sant'Eufemia, church of Santa Maria: view into apses (Tancredi Bella)

relation to other buildings dating from the period of the County.[5] At this same time, Margherita Tabanelli is reconsidering numerous aspects and contexts of the ecclesiastical architecture of Sicily and Calabria between *c.* 1060 and 1130.[6]

In 1080, Roger founded the diocese of Troina on what was then, perhaps, the most secure place available to him – a site at 1121 m above sea level to the west of Mount Etna. The cathedral was the first bishopric reestablished in Sicily, in the context of the projected conquest of southern Italy. The first bishop was a Benedictine monk, Robert, nominated by Roger. A strengthened relationship with the papacy was subsequently realised in 1088 when Pope Urban II visited Troina, confirming the importance of this diocese in the creation of the County.[7]

Troina cathedral was the earliest Norman architectural experiment in Sicily and might be seen as the formal expression of a new historical epoch. Its plan became a model for other cathedrals of the County and was perhaps the inspiration for the later and more elaborate constructions of the Kingdom (1130–98). Collapses, earthquakes, and reconstructions have altered its original form. In the modern age, the tower and façade (both probably of the second half of the 15th century), the presbytery (16th–17th centuries) and nave (18th century) were rebuilt. The famous representation of Oscar Mothes of 1883 shows the building standing on top of a rock, with the chevet encased in overhanging quadrangular forms following its modern reconstruction (Figure 12.2).[8] By comparing what is known with new data collected through careful measurement, geophysical analysis, and archival research, Fabio Linguanti is attempting to establish a new history of building as it was in the late 11th century.[9] It seems probable that Troina was not fully aisled, as has always been assumed, but rather that it was built with a single, wide, aisleless nave (Figure 12.3). The roof was probably wooden, and the transept was not particularly long but was taller than the nave. Portions of its walls survive. The transept gave onto three apses arranged in echelon, with an elongated central apse. Below there was a crypt. This reflected Norman and Calabrian models and had repercussions for the later architecture of the Norman Kingdom. This is evident, for example, in a similar plan having been adopted for the mid-12th-century priory of Sant'Andrea of the Holy Sepulchre in Piazza Armerina, in the centre of Sicily. The city was the site of numerous daughter-houses of the orders of Jerusalem in the 12th century. The church of Sant'Andrea was presumably founded in 1148 (Figure 12.4).[10] Analogies with the cathedral of Troina are evident but with the difference that the three apses are enclosed. The patron was the aristocratic Simone Aleramico, belonging to a family from Piedmont, who had settled in central-eastern Sicily in the service of the Altavilla dynasty, and in agreement with the order of the Holy Sepulchre in Jerusalem.

We know that the abbey and cathedral of Lipari (1085–91) in the Aeolian islands, as entrusted to the regency of Abbot Ambrogio, was also built with an aisleless nave, transept, and three oriented apses, the central apse being deeper that the two lateral apses. A crypt was also perhaps

FIGURE 12.2

Troina: cathedral, apse, and south transept (Tancredi Bella)

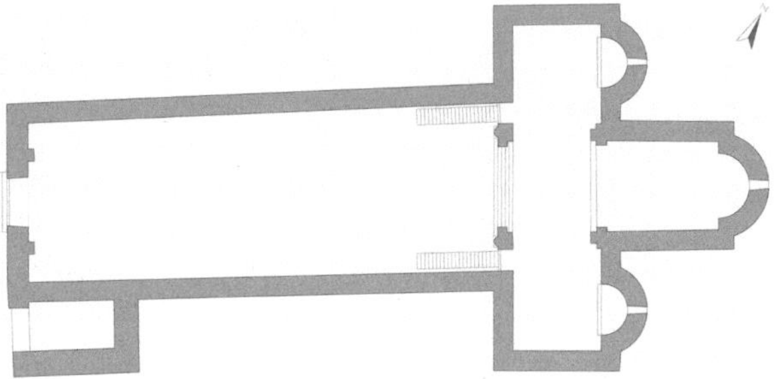

FIGURE 12.3

Troina: cathedral, plan (Fabio Linguanti, 2019)

FIGURE 12.4

Piazza Armerina, church of Sant'Andrea of the Holy Sepulchre: axonometric projection (Tancredi Bella)

FIGURE 12.5

Lipari: cathedral, south apse (Tancredi Bella)

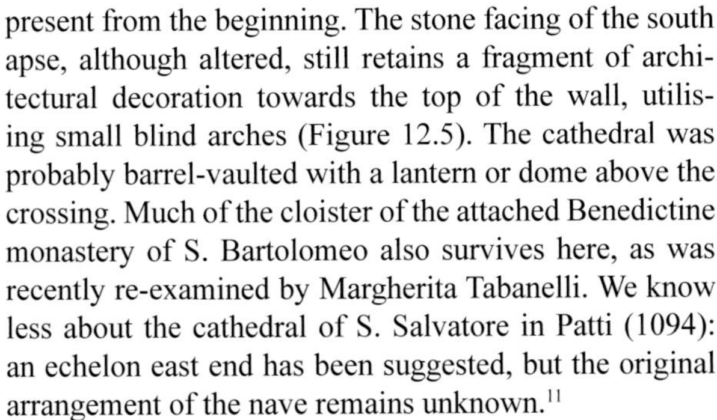

present from the beginning. The stone facing of the south apse, although altered, still retains a fragment of architectural decoration towards the top of the wall, utilising small blind arches (Figure 12.5). The cathedral was probably barrel-vaulted with a lantern or dome above the crossing. Much of the cloister of the attached Benedictine monastery of S. Bartolomeo also survives here, as was recently re-examined by Margherita Tabanelli. We know less about the cathedral of S. Salvatore in Patti (1094): an echelon east end has been suggested, but the original arrangement of the nave remains unknown.[11]

After Troina, Count Roger founded or refounded the dioceses of Agrigento, Mazara del Vallo, Siracusa, Catania, and Messina, often entrusting the staffing of their cathedral to French monks from Calabria.[12] The cathedral of Mazara (1086–93), whose diocese was assigned to Bishop Stephen of Rouen, a kinsman of Count Roger, was rebuilt after 1694. The building was begun in the late 11th century and was one of the most important created between the construction of the Santissima Trinità in Mileto and the foundation of the cathedral of Cefalù (1131), the first foundation of the Norman kingdom in Sicily. For a long time, it was thought that Mazara Cathedral had a columnar nave, aisles, a twin-towered façade, and three deep apses preceded by a square bay, demonstrating the adoption of the plan of Cluny II with a *chœur cloisonné*. However, recent and ongoing investigation has shown that this interpretation is partly wrong. The

FIGURE 12.6
Mazara: cathedral, north apse (Tancredi Bella)

nave was aisleless, and the north apse, detached from the main apse, was connected directly to the transept without an intermediate bay (Figure 12.6). The central apse, by contrast, is elongated to the east, and the solution adopted for the junction between the apse and the transept remains difficult to understand.[13]

The cathedral of Siracusa is less relevant to my immediate purpose, as in the Norman period it was largely left in its 7th-century Byzantine conformation, famously created through the transformation of the Greek Temple of Athena into a church. The first Norman bishop of Siracusa was called Roger. He originated from Provence and was previously the dean of Troina.[14]

As regards Agrigento (1087–94), Count Roger I commissioned Gerlando, called to Sicily from the Santissima Trinità at Mileto and originally from Burgundy, to found the cathedral in the highest part of the city, near the castle. However, it is again difficult to recover the late 11th-century plan. Only a few traces of the Norman fabric remain. Agrigento seems to have had a columnar aisled nave and transept, perhaps flanked by transept towers equipped with wall passages (of which portions have been lost in the south tower). There were three deep apses to the east of the transept.[15]

THE CATHEDRAL OF CATANIA

The Normans conquered Catania in 1071. However, it was not until 1091 that Count Roger ordered the construction of the new cathedral, entrusting the task to Ansger (Angerio), the former prior of Santa Maria in Sant'Eufemia in Calabria, the abbey that Roger had founded with Robert de Grandmesnil.[16] According to the chronicler Geoffrey Malaterra, himself a Benedictine monk from Saint-Evroult (Orne) writing while a member of the community at Catania, Ansger was from Brittany and had previously been a monk at the Benedictine abbey of Saint-Florent de Saumur (Maine-et-Loire).[17] On his return from a pilgrimage to Jerusalem, he entered the monastery of Sant'Eufemia in Calabria, where he assumed the post of prior. When he arrived in Catania, he was invited to found the new Benedictine monastery, built next to the new cathedral. Count Roger selected Ansger from the circle of his compatriots and appointed him abbot and bishop.[18] The diocese was then refounded by Urban II, on 9 March 1092.

The monastic cathedral was to be the religious and military centre of the new diocese. Its construction combined the interests of the Hauteville (Altavilla) family, the papacy in Rome and the Benedictine order. In Roger's political design, the building was an element in an essentially French domination of the local population (Greek and Muslim) in the south-eastern part of Sicily, an area that was particularly resistant to the new authority.[19]

Catania Cathedral was initially designed as an *ecclesia munita* – a fortified church – and was built with crenellated apses facing east (Figure 12.7 and Colour Plate XIII (top)). The location is significant: a building within the city walls but near the sea and the commercial port, between the Arab quarter and the parts of Catania occupied by the Jewish and Greek communities. It was thus at the heart of the *civitas* and formed the east side of the *platea magna* (the great square). The earthquake of 1169 caused significant damage, when the nave and transept roofs collapsed.[20] But it was the catastrophic earthquake of 1693 which resulted in the most far-reaching alterations to the medieval cathedral. This earthquake precipitated the collapse of the bell tower, built north-west of the church at the end of the 14th century, while the nave was almost entirely destroyed. Just the apses, transepts and parts of the façade survived.[21] Thus most of the eastern parts of the cathedral are Romanesque, although the apses carry later decoration on their interior faces. The reconstruction of the cathedral began in earnest in the 18th century.[22] The current appearance of the cathedral is due to a restoration, begun in the mid-20th century, taken up again in the 1980s and completed before 2000.[23] The documentation, not all of which has been published, is now preserved in state and private archives.

The Norman nave

It is not easy to distinguish the late 11th-century building from those parts rebuilt after the earthquake of 1169. In Troina, as mentioned above, recent investigation has confirmed that there was an aisleless nave. In Catania, the cathedral was certainly initially built to a Latin cross plan with an aisled nave and a monumental and strikingly tall transept. The east side of the transept was laid out with an echelon of three apses aligned with the nave aisles (Figure 12.8). However, the original nave arcade design remains uncertain and interpretation of the evidence is contested. When the floor was lifted during the restoration of 1955–59, deep excavations were undertaken to explore the subsoil. Two medieval pier bases were discovered with a rectangular core in the second and third intercolumniations of the nave north arcade (counting from the west), while another pier base was identified in the fourth intercolumniation but was not left exposed.

FIGURE 12.7

Catania Cathedral: aerial view from east (Tancredi Bella)

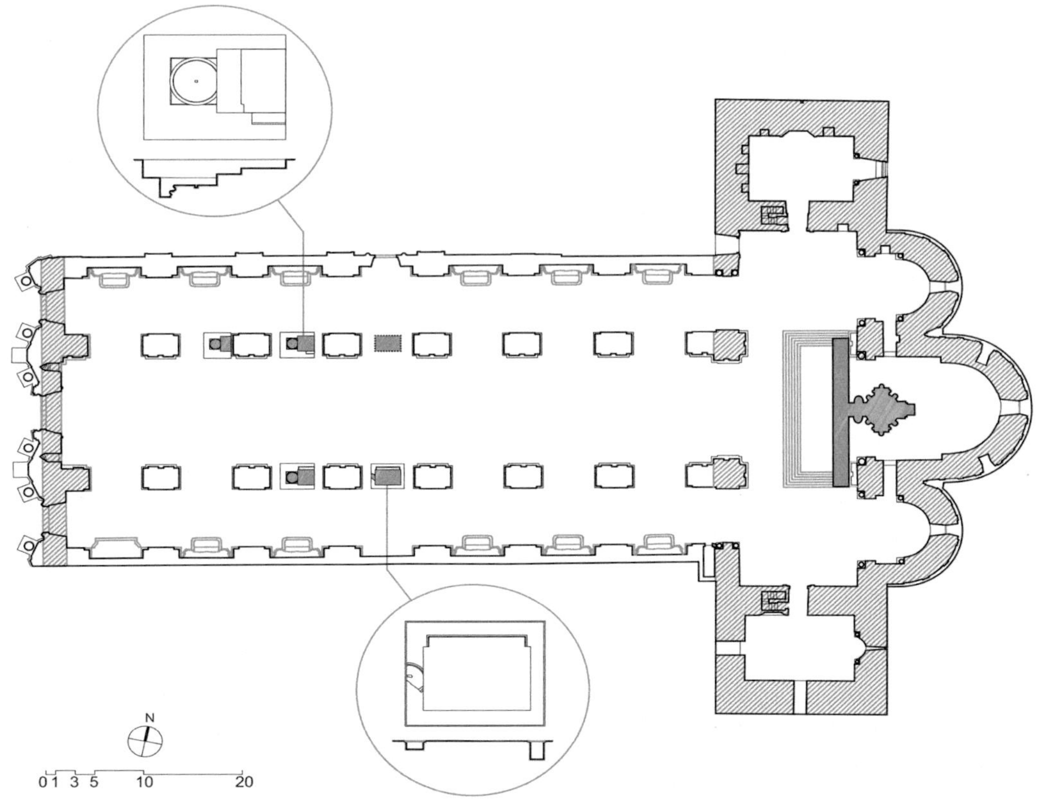

FIGURE 12.8

Catania Cathedral: plan showing the archaeological excavations and the crypt in projection (Tancredi Bella and Giovanni Giglia)

The third and fourth intercolumniations of the south arcade also yielded rectangular pier bases.[24] Full column bases located to the west of the rectangular piers were also found. Did columns also flank the rectangular piers to the east? It seems likely, though we don't yet have certain proof. The excavations determined the existence of at least three floor levels; the late 11th-century Norman level, more or less 1.25 m below the current pavement; a floor level around 0.5 m below the current pavement level which can be associated with changes made after the 1169 earthquake; and the 18th-century level – essentially the current level – which was established during the reconstruction that followed the earthquake of 1693.

Whether the original Norman arcade consisted of piers flanked by columns on both their west and east faces, or that the rectangular piers were inserted between pairs of closely spaced columns following the 1169 earthquake to reinforce the structure, has been a matter of dispute. Stefano Bottari thought the rectangular piers were insertions. But it was Francesco Gandolfo who first proposed that the piers might have been contemporary with the columns, a view subsequently developed by Caroline Bruzelius.[25] I agree with this recent reinterpretation, that the main arcade design utilised supports that arranged three elements on a longitudinal axis as column-pillar-column, and I am conducting further work in this regard. However, the reconstruction put forward by Gandolfo and Bruzelius has not met with universal agreement, and the argument that the design is a post-1169 rehash has been reiterated once more by Margherita Tabanelli.[26] Supports arranged as column-pier-column do not seem to have been used in Benedictine buildings in Calabria. Mileto employed spolia columns, while the arcade supports for Sant'Eufemia are unknown.[27] A similar solution to that proposed for the main elevation of Catania Cathedral is found at the junction between the outer walls of the aisles and the transept entry, where two spolia columns are set into the angle of the respond pier so as to create the same column-pier-column rhythm (Figure 12.9).[28] This same composition went on to be used in a similar position in Cefalù Cathedral as founded by King Roger II, and it seems possible that the original plan for Cefalù's nave was comparable to that of Catania. In the event, the construction of Cefalù's nave arcade was delayed, and the design was changed in the course of construction.

In support of the proposal for an initial nave arcade consisting of piers flanked by columns on their east and west faces, there is further, hitherto overlooked archaeological evidence. The base of the pier found during the 1957 excavation of the fourth intercolumniation in the south arcade appears in an unpublished drawing made during the excavation and now kept in the private archives of the architect Raffaele Leone, head of the Fabbriceria during the 1950s restoration work (Figure 12.10). This clearly shows that the shoulder of the pier has a small hollow on the east, indicating the presence of a column base, even though a whole column base was not found. Another unpublished drawing I only recently discovered shows an analogous detail for the comparable pier in the north arcade, confirming the likely presence of a column against the east face of the pier in addition to the known column bases to the west.[29] The recent georadar readings, carried out as part of the ground penetrating geophysical survey of the north side of the cathedral, have also attested that, in the fourth intercolumniation of the north arcade, there is material at −0.80 m and −1 m also east of the rectangular pier. These levels are similar to those visible for the western column bases from the excavations. Though one should obviously exercise caution in interpreting the survey, the report tends to support the

FIGURE 12.9

Catania Cathedral: north respond of the aisle entry to the north transept (Tancredi Bella)

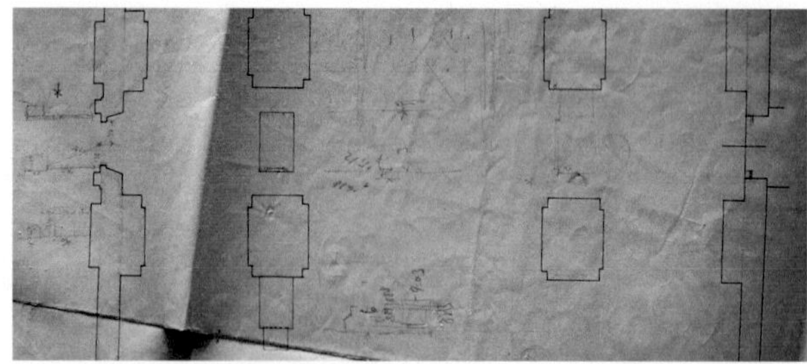

FIGURE 12.10

Catania Cathedral: Raffaele Leone's drawing of the archaeological excavations (Archivio Giacomo Leone)

hypothesis of a contemporary and initial support system organized as column-pier-column.[30]

If we accept that the piers had two columns set on their longitudinal faces in the first phase, a significant gap opens up between the design adopted for Catania Cathedral and that of SS Trinità in Mileto. Two contributors to the thinking behind the choice of this type of support might have been the abundance of antique columns among the ancient ruins of Catania and a desire for a strong support which did not renounce all classical refinement.[31] Bruzelius compared the resulting elevation with the mid-11th-century Benedictine church of Saint-Benoît-du-Sault (Indre), where columns flank rectangular piers.[32] This rather unusual solution is also present in other contexts. I have already drawn attention to a variant in the abbey church of Sant Pere de Rodes in Catalonia (first half of the 11th century). Here in the eastern bays, columns support arches to either side of the square core of the piers, set on bases taller than those of Catania (Figure 12.11).[33] Even in Normandy, one can find examples. At Notre-Dame de Bernay (about 1015–50), columns are used in conjunction with piers in the east elevation of the south transept.[34] The pier, or at least the respond, flanked by columns is present in 11th-century Romanesque architecture in Normandy, even if we find it used in different locations and combinations and almost always used for an aesthetic rather than a structural end.[35] We can therefore hypothesize that a transalpine model was chosen for Catania, but that it may not have been solely Norman. This model was then used in Sicily, without it first having been adopted in Calabria. The alternative is that the form may derive from the local architecture of Islamic Sicily, even more so if we consider that some construction workers may have been Arab and that Catania had certainly been a city with Islamic architecture, of which almost nothing is known. The comparison with the Aghlabid Great Mosque in Qairouan (late 11th century), in Ifriqiya (now Tunisia), is visually sustainable (Figure 12.12). Note in particular the door of Lalla Rayhana or the arcades of the narthex, placed before the mosque, with free-standing columns abutting the pier.[36]

The Apses

The cathedral's east end is compact. Crowned by an external walkway defended by a continuous battlement, restored over the centuries, it creates the impression of a fortified church. The imposing masonry is solid and, from a structural point of view, efficient. It is composed of large square or rectangular blocks of volcanic rock, reused like the columns, joined by thin layers of mortar in which one finds fragments of stone and brick.[37] The lateral apses are connected to the deeper central apse on the exterior through connecting niches which support the walkway. Sharply pointed blind arches frame the single-light windows, remodelled in the modern age with a rectangular profile, as can be seen in a splendidly informative drawing by the French architect Léon Dufourny, undated though no earlier than 1879 (Figure 12.13).[38] The windows were subsequently restored with pointed arches in 1955. The exterior east face rests on a slightly protruding tall base.

Inside, the apses are framed by pointed arches and are articulated by columns which are effectively cut into the in re-entrant angles of the apses. These were only rediscovered during the mid-20th-century restoration and are an early example of a composition which became immensely popular in the monumental architecture of Sicily, as at the Cappella Palatina in Palermo or the cathedrals of Cefalù and Monreale. At Troina, the central apse certainly extended considerably further east than the side apses, as is also the case at Cefalù. In Catania, on the other hand, there is much less distance between the central apse and the shorter side apses. The parallel with the plan of Cluny II is therefore less evident. In Catania, a short bay with a rising barrel vault precedes the apses, as in the Calabrian buildings. At the Santissima Trinità in Mileto, the bays separating the apses and the transept have a precise architectural identity, as they do in Norman examples of *chevet échelonné*.[39] Instead, at Catania, the bays that give onto the apses lack depth.

A further difference is that, unlike Mileto, the bays in front of the apses in Catania communicated with each other through tall and narrow passages (Figure 12.14 and Colour Plate XIII (bottom)). The southern passage was transformed into a chapel for the relics of Saint Agatha, the patron saint of Catania, at the end of the 15th century.[40] The northern passage is partially inaccessible, though it was originally possible to climb to the raised level of the central apse. This is a sophisticated system, known north of the Alps and widespread in Romanesque Normandy and the Loire Valley. In Catania, Gandolfo has argued it was adopted for liturgical reasons and to explicitly quote an architectural element from Cluny II and its derivatives.[41] However, this arrangement is not used at Mileto and was perhaps present only in Sant'Eufemia.[42] As much else at Catania can be seen to have come directly from Normandy, it is perhaps to Normandy that we should look for precedents. The problem is that 11th-century churches in Normandy with transepts do not spring apses directly from the east side of the transept. They conventionally have presbyteries with open arcades which, by definition, facilitate access between apses, as at Notre-Dame de Bernay or the parish church of Saint-Nicolas-de-Caen (11th–12th centuries).[43] Churches with apse-echelon east ends that lie directly east of the transept tend to be found further south, as at Chinon, the 11th-century abbey church of Baume-les-Messieurs (Jura), or the monastic church of St-Jouin-de-Marnes (Deux-Sevres) in its early-11th-century iteration.[44] It is possible to find Anglo-Norman churches with openings between otherwise solid bays immediately east of the crossing, as at La Trinité at Caen or the abbey of St Albans, so if the architect at Catania wished to refer to an Anglo-Norman precedent, it was possible to do so, but it had to be adapted to a T-transept type of plan. Catania was a pivotal city in the process of the re-Latinization of Sicily and of its reconnection with

FIGURE 12.11

Catalonia, Sant-Pere-de-Rodes: nave elevation (Tancredi Bella)

FIGURE 12.12

Qairouan (Tunisia), Great Mosque: door of Lalla Rayhana (Tancredi Bella)

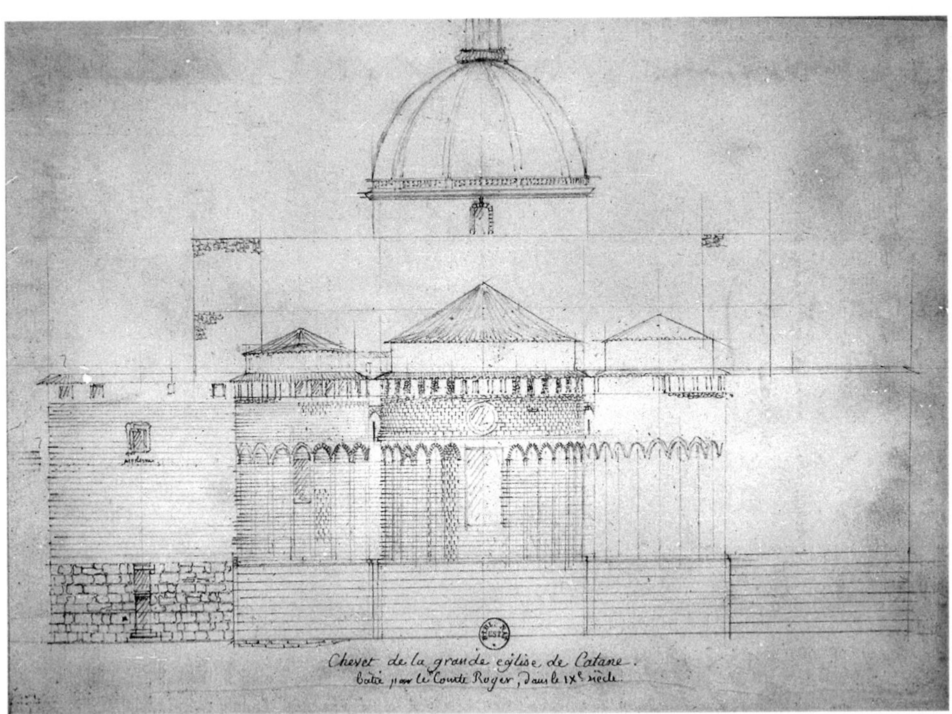

FIGURE 12.13

Catania Cathedral: Léon Dufourny's drawing of the exterior from the east (after 1879) (Partly redrawn by Giuseppe Pagnano, 2019)

FIGURE 12.14

Catania Cathedral: view of the apses from the mullioned window of the north transept (Tancredi Bella)

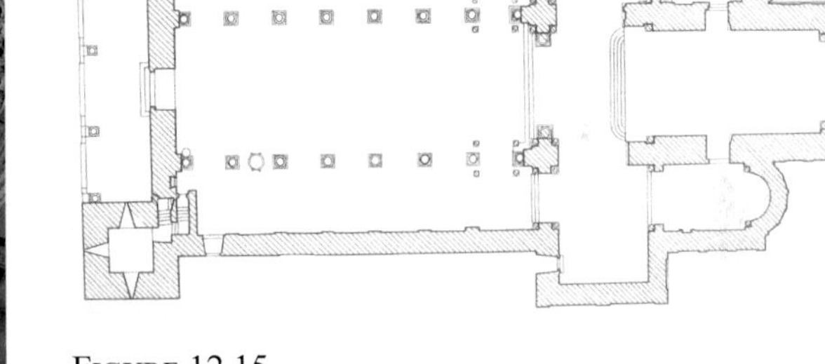

FIGURE 12.15

Cefalù Cathedral: plan (Tancredi Bella)

the authority of Rome. Ultimately, the model pioneered in Catania (absent in Troina) returned with the building of the cathedral at Cefalù (Figure 12.15).

The Crypt

Below the central apse are the remains of a crypt, discovered around twenty years ago but since then largely ignored by the scholarly community (Figure 12.8).[45] A narrow transverse corridor, built during the renovation of the presbytery at the end of the last century, gives access. The space is similar to a *tricora*, with a short, rectangular vestibule with convex terminations and a projecting apse. The plan is probably best described as a Greek cross inscribed within a circle. At the south end of the base, there is a niche which may have housed an altar, while the other walls are pierced with ten niches of varying sizes, all set at the same height, which were probably intended for the display of reliquaries of Saint Agatha. These probably date from the end of 14th century. The floor level is almost the same as that of the Norman nave: the faithful therefore had a direct, or at least a partial view of this space.

The nature of the crypt vault is uncertain, but the crypt must have been adapted from a small pre-existing

FIGURE 12.16

Catania Cathedral: upper room at first floor level in the north transept (Tancredi Bella)

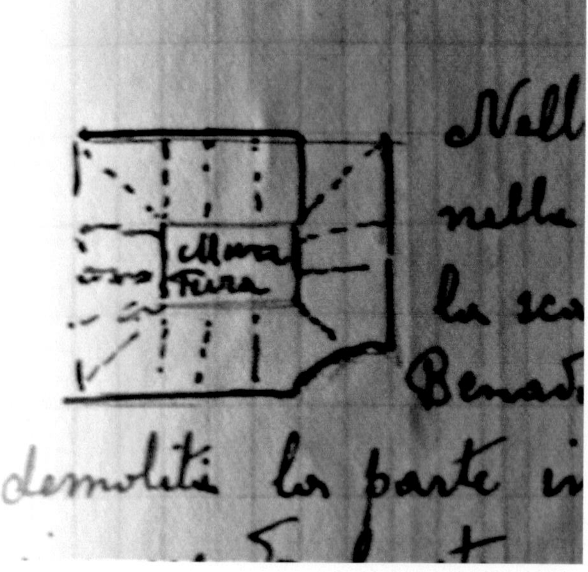

FIGURE 12.17

Catania Cathedral: Raffaele Leone's drawing of the south transept stair, before demolition in 1957–58 (Archivio Giacomo Leone)

FIGURE 12.18

Mazara Cathedral: west wall of the building attached to the transept seen from the south (Tancredi Bella)

building, perhaps part of a larger entity dating back to the Byzantine period. At a typological level, the plan resembles the cruciform *martyria* or mausolea of Late Antiquity, preceded by a narthex.[46] It is possible that its reuse was at the request the of Norman client.[47] The small structure, perhaps already linked to the Christian religion, perhaps even to the cult of Sant Agatha or the early martyrs of Catania, was then transformed into the crypt. This would then have housed the relics of Agatha after they were returned to Catania from Constantinople.[48] It was the sacred heart of the new cathedral, an essential element in a Norman strategy to reawaken devotion to Saint Agatha and foster a Catanian civic identity rooted in Roman Christianity.[49]

The transept and the two buildings to North and South

Two buildings, divided into two levels, flank the transept to the north and south (Figures 12.7 and 12.8).[50] They are lower than the transept but of the same depth and built to a rectangular plan. The walls are the same thickness as those of the transept and apses (about 3.30 m) and are demonstrably contemporary with the transept, at least in the basement portion.[51] The structures are linked to the apses through an upper walkway, which gives onto the roof terrace, while the homogeneity of the walls from north to south and, by extension, their contemporaneity have been demonstrated by analysis. The mechanical behaviour of the stonework of the buildings at the ends of the transepts is the same as that of the transepts.[52] On the ground floor of both the north and south buildings, there is a chapel, with single volume chambers at the first-floor level, though the latter do not connect with the transept.[53] The upper chamber to the south was restored in the last century, and that to the north is unexplored and has remained intact (Figure 12.16). At the top of each transept-facing wall there is a two-light window under three upper lancets.[54] Stairs, within the thickness of the wall, affords access to the first-floor chambers and then continue upwards. The upper southern stair was demolished in 1957–58, and there remains just a summary unpublished drawing of it (Figure 12.17). The north stair still exists in full. I think that, in the original late 11th-century plan, the architects intended a second floor, connected with the transept through mullioned windows, though either this was never built or it was subsequently demolished or collapsed. The received view is that these side buildings were intended as the bases for two towers, designed with a military purpose in mind.[55] I rather believe that they should be compared to the symmetrical towers placed above the transept ends of certain other Romanesque churches, as, for example, in Languedoc. There, the towers are closely connected to the roof, are equipped with slits, and have many internal levels, as at Sainte-Marie de Urgell and Saint-Pierre-et-Saint-Paul de Caunes.[56]

But in Catania, these side structures never exceeded the height of the transepts. Gandolfo recognised that the lateral transept chambers aren't congruent with the adoption of a fully French plan. They are instead specifically Sicilian. The idea was perhaps first used at Mazara cathedral where the terminal portions of the transept were configured as autonomous, lesser buildings, with functions and forms now unknown to us (Figure 12.18). The arrangement developed in Catania was then discarded in 12th-century Sicilian cathedrals. Walkways around the apses continued in use. However, this was a simpler system from that at Notre-Dame in Bernay, from Jumieges, or from that which took definitive form at St-Etienne at Caen, or, in a different tradition, from that assumed in the eastern walls of the transept of the abbey church of Saint-Bénigne de Dijon.[57] The two wall passages that run around the top of the transept of Cefalù Cathedral, considered unprecedented in Sicily, are – in my opinion – the development and improvement of a form first used in the 11th-century design of Catania.[58]

To conclude, I hope to have shown that there are differences between the plans and architectural solutions used in the cathedrals of the County in Sicily and those found in the most nearly contemporary churches of Norman Calabria. I also hope to have highlighted which references to transalpine and Norman models are sustainable and which are not. Above all, I hope to have shown how Catania Cathedral was undertaken at a critical moment. It was the monument in Sicily that directly drew on Norman tradition and that was prepared to experiment with new forms, not all of which were repeated and which transmitted much to the Cathedral of Cefalù, the first in the Kingdom, wherein reference to Normandy was now a second-generation legacy.

ACKNOWLEDGEMENTS

I should like to thank John McNeill, Claude Andrault-Schmit, Marcello Angheben, Claudia Guastella, and Edoardo Dotto; the architects Giovanni Giglia, Fabio Linguanti, and Antonio Zimbone; Monsignor Gaetano Zito (who sadly died in 2019 and who was previously director of the Archivo Storico Diocesano di Catania); Monsignor Barbaro Scionti (Cathedral of Catania); and the Archivio di Giacomo Leone.

NOTES

1 For Norman foundations in Calabria see C. Bozzoni, *Calabria normanna. Ricerche sull'architettura dei secoli undicesimo e dodicesimo* (Rome 1974), 21–30; G. Occhiato, *La SS. Trinità di Mileto e l'architettura normanna meridionale* (Catanzaro 1977); G. Occhiato, 'L'abbaziale normanna di Sant'Eufemia. Rapporti culturali e rispondenze architettoniche tra Calabria e Francia in età romanica', *Mélanges de l'École Française de Rome*, 93 (1981–82), 565–603; G. Di Gangi, 'Alcune note su un problema di architettura medievale: l'abbazia normanna di S. Eufemia – Scavo 1993', *Archeologia medievale*, 21 (1994), 343–51; G. Di Gangi, 'L'architettura religiosa di età normanna in Calabria', in *I Normanni* in finibus Calabriae, ed. F. A. Cuteri (Soveria Mannelli 2003), 65–74; G. Occhiato, 'Osservazioni in merito ad alcuni problemi interpretativi concernenti le scomparse abbaziali benedettine di Mileto e di Sant'Eufemia, in Calabria (XI sec.)', *Archivio storico per la Calabria e la Lucania*, 70 (2013), 27–48; M. J. Johnson, 'The Mausoleum of Bohemund in Canosa and the Architectural Setting of Ruler Tombs in Norman Italy', in *Romanesque and the Mediterranean*, eds. R. M. Bacile and J. McNeill (Leeds 2015), 151–66; M. Tabanelli, *Architettura sacra in Calabria e Sicilia nell'età della Contea normanna*, Esordi 1 (Rome 2019), 21–38. G. Loud, *The Latin Church in Norman Italy* (Cambridge 2007), especially 60–134.

2 On the architectural influence of Cluny II as conveyed from Normandy to Calabria and Sicily see A. Venditti, *Architettura bizantina nell'Italia meridionale. Campania-Calabria-Lucania* (Naples 1967), 892–955; G. Ciotta, *La cultura architettonica normanna in Sicilia* (Messina 1992), 87–133: M. D'Onofrio, 'Comparaisons entre quelques édifices de style normand de l'Italie méridionale et du Royaume de France aux XIe et XIIe siècles', in *Les Normands en Méditerranée dans le sillage de Tancrède*, eds. P. Bouet and F. Neveux (Caen 1994), 179–201.

3 T. Bella, 'La cathédrale normande de Catane (XIe siècle). Nouvelles données d'une recherche en cours', in *Regards croisés sur le monument médiéval. Mélanges offerts à Claude Andrault-Schmitt*, eds. M. Angheben, P. Martin, and É. Sparhubert (Turnhout 2018), 125–39, 487–88.

4 F. Gandolfo, 'Le cattedrali siciliane', in *Medioevo: l'Europa delle cattedrali*, ed. A. C. Quintavalle (Milan 2007), 191–207; C. Bruzelius, 'The Norman Cathedral of Sant'Agata in Catania', in *L'officina dello sguardo. Scritti in onore di Maria Andaloro*, eds. G. Bordi et al. (Rome 2014), 121–26.

5 T. Bella, 'Bâtir face à la mer. La cathédrale normande de Catane en Sicile. État de la question', *Les cahiers de Saint-Michel de Cuxa*, 48 (2017), 23–38; T. Bella, '*Ansgerius quod ego . . . Ecclesiae primus fundamina ieci.* La cattedrale normanna di Catania: materiali per un riesame', *Arte Cristiana*, 909 (2018), 404–21; T. Bella, 1091. Ecclesia munita intra moenia', in *Storia mondiale della Sicilia*, ed. G. Barone (Bari and Rome 2018), 123–27; T. Bella, *La cattedrale medievale di Catania. Un cantiere normanno nella contea di Sicilia* (Milan 2021).

6 Tabanelli, 'Architettura sacra' (as n. 1).

7 J. Becker, *Graf Roger I. von Sizilien. Wegbereiter des normannischen Königreichs* (Tübingen 2008), 172–76. On Troina see Gandolfo, 'Le cattedrali' (as n. 4), 191–94; L. Walker, 'Populating the Medieval Upland Landscape of Troina: a Review of Published Documentary Sources for the 9th–15th Centuries', in *Uplands of Ancient Sicily and Calabria. The archaeology of landscape revisited*, ed. M. Fitzjohn (London 2007), 115–42; M. Proietto and B. M. R. Spinella, 'Sulla politica ecclesiastica dei Normanni in Sicilia: il caso di Troina e Messina', in *Nelle terre dei Normanni. La Sicilia tra Ruggero I e Federico II*, eds. M. Congiu and S. Modeo (Caltanissetta and Rome 2015), 141–52.

8 O. Mothes, *Die Baukunst des Mittelalters in Italien von der ersten Entwicklung bis zu ihrer höchsten Blüthe. Mit 211 Holzschnitten u. 6 Farbendrucktaf* (Jena 1883), 525.

[9] F. Linguanti, 'La cattedrale di Troina tra 1643 e 1785. Nuove acquisizioni documentali', *Lexicon*, 25 (2017), 31–50; F. Linguanti. 'La cattedrale di Troina: prima sperimentazione architettonica normanna in Sicilia', *Hortus Artium Medievalium*, 25 (2019), 579–90.

[10] T. Bella, *S. Andrea a Piazza Armerina, priorato dell'Ordine del Santo Sepolcro. Vicende costruttive, cicli pittorici e spazio liturgico*, Ricerche, 6 (Caltanissetta 2012); Linguanti, 'La cattedrale di Troina: prime sperimentazioni' (as n. 9), 589–90.

[11] For Lipari see L. Bernabò Brea et al., 'Il monastero normanno di Lipari e il suo chiostro, Ricerche e scavi, 1954–1996', *Quaderni di archeologia dell'Università di Messina*, 2 (2001), 171–268; M. Cavalier, 'Il chiostro normanno di Lipari', in *Alle radici della cultura mediterranea ed europea. I normanni nello stretto e nelle Isole Eolie*, eds. G. M. Bacci and M. A. Mastelloni (Saponara Marittima 2002), 23–4; M. Tabanelli, 'Il chiostro di San Bartolomeo a Lipari: sperimentazioni progettuali e decorative nella prima comunità benedettina della Sicilia normanna', *Hortus Artium Medievalium*, 23/1 (2017), 318–28; Tabanelli, 'Architettura sacra' (as n. 1), 84–97. For Patti see R. Magistri and V. Porrazzo, *La cattedrale di Patti* (Messina 1990), 15–36; Tabanelli, 'Architettura sacra' (as n. 1), 97–8.

[12] On this critical subject, see H. Enzensberger, 'Fondazione o "rifondazione"? Alcune osservazioni sulla politica ecclesiastica del Conte Ruggero', in *Chiesa e società in Sicilia, l'età normanna*, ed. G. Zito (Turin 1995), 21–49; S. Fodale, 'Fondazione e rifondazioni episcopali da Ruggero I a Gugliemo II', in *Chiesa e società in Sicilia* (as n. 12), 51–61; N. Kamp, 'I vescovi siciliani nel periodo normanno: origine sociale e formazioni spirituali', in *Chiesa e società in Sicilia* (as n. 12), 63–89.

[13] Becker, 'Graf Roger I' (as n. 7), 187–88; C. Filangeri, 'La cattedrale del Santissimo Salvatore voluta a Mazara da Ruggero il Gran Conte, alla luce degli ultimi ritrovamenti', *Annali della Pontificia Insigne Accademia di Belle Arti e Lettere dei Virtuosi al Pantheon*, 2 (2001), 131–68; C. Filangeri, 'Annotazioni per la cattedrale di Mazara', *Annali della Pontificia Insigne Accademia di Belle Arti e Lettere dei Virtuosi al Pantheon*, 3 (2003), 129–44; C. Filangeri del Pino, 'Metamorfosi architettoniche', in *Trasfigurazione. La Basilica Cattedrale di Mazara del Vallo. Culto, Arte e Storia*, ed. L. Di Simone (Mazara del Vallo 2006), 164–89; Gandolfo, *Le cattedrali* (as n. 4), 195–200; Tabanelli, 'Architettura sacra' (as n. 1), 71–82.

[14] Becker, 'Graf Roger I' (as n. 7), 181–84.

[15] Ibid., 184–87; Gandolfo, 'Le cattedrali' (as n. 4), 194; C. Filangeri, 'La cattedrale di Agrigento fra le carte e le pietre dei suoi vescovi', in *La cattedrale di Agrigento tra storia, arte, architettura*, ed. G. Ingaglio (Palermo 2010), 55–62; A. M. Schmidt, 'Dalla cattedrale di Gerlando alla ecclesia munita', in *La cattedrale di Agrigento* (as n. 15), 63–71. Finally, see Tabaneli, 'Architettura sacra' (as n. 1), 82–84.

[16] G. Occhiato, 'Robert de Grandmesnil: un abate "architetto" operante in Calabria nell'XI secolo', in *Calabria bizantina. Testimonianze d'arte e strutture di territori* (Soveria Mannelli 1991), 129–207.

[17] Goffredo Malaterra, *De rebus gestis Rogerii Calabriae et Siciliae Comitis et Roberti Guiscardi Ducis fratris eius. . .*, ed. E. Pontieri (Bologna 1928); Becker, *Graf Roger I* (as n. 7), 176–81; J. Becker, *Documenti latini e greci del conte Ruggero I di Calabria e Sicilia* (Rome 2013), 92–96.

[18] On the life of Ansger, see G. T. Beech, 'The remarkable life of Ansger, a Breton monk and poet from the Loire Valley who became bishop of Catania in Sicily 1091–1124', *Viator*, 45 (2014), 149–75.

[19] B. Clausi and V. Milazzo, 'La città medievale: dai Bizantini agli Aragonesi', in *Catania. Storia Cultura Economia*, ed. F. Mazza (Soveria Mannelli 2008), 77–163; L. Arcifa, 'La città nel Medioevo: sviluppo urbano e dominio territoriale', in *Catania. L'identità urbana dall'antichità al Settecento*, ed. L. Scalisi (Catania 2009), 72–111.

[20] G. M. Agnello, 'Il terremoto del 1169 in Sicilia tra miti storiografici e cognizione storica', in *La Sicilia dei terremoti. Lunga durata e dinamiche sociali*, ed. G. Giarrizzo (Catania 1996), 101–27; L. Arcifa, 'La città medievale', in *Catania terremoti e lave dal mondo antico alla fine del Novecento*, eds. E. Boschi and E. Guidoboni (Bologna 2001), 36–64.

[21] E. Guidoboni, C. Ciuccarelli, and D. Mariotti, 'Catania alla fine del Seicento e i terremoti del gennaio 1693', in *Catania terremoti*, eds. E. Boschi and E. Guidoboni (as n. 20), 105–66.

[22] W. Krönig, *Il duomo di Monreale e l'architettura normanna in Sicilia* (Palermo 1965), 148–53; S. Calogero, 'La ricostruzione della Cattedrale di Catania dopo il terremoto del 1693', *Synaxis*, 12 (2004), 113–48; G. Pagnano, '*Melior de cinere surgo*: Catania 1693–1790', in *Catania. La grande Catania, la nobiltà virtuosa, la borghesia operosa*, ed. E. Iachello (Catania 2010), 70–87.

[23] G. Leone Uberti, 'I lavori di restauro del Duomo di Catania', *Rivista del Comune di Catania*, 4 (1957), 3–12; P. Lojacono, 'Il restauro del Duomo di Catania', *Tecnica e Ricostruzione*, XIV (1959), 249–57; R. Leone, *Notizie sul Duomo di Catania* (Catania 1962); D. Reale, *Gli ultimi scavi del Duomo di Catania* (Milan 1983).

[24] The explorations, begun in 1952, were made as the result of an agreement between the Soprintendenza, the Civil Engineers, and the Fabbriceria. The most substantial excavations were made in June 1957.

[25] Gandolfo, 'Le cattedrali' (as n. 4), 200–03. See the graphic reconstruction in Bruzelius, 'The Norman Cathedral' (as n. 4), 122. See also to C. Bruzelius and P. Vitolo, 'The Medieval Kingdom of Sicily Image Database', *Visual Resources. An International Journal on Images and Their Uses* (2002), 1–13.

[26] M. Tabanelli, '*Templum tota Sicilia maximum ab Angerio conditum*. La cattedrale di Catania tra XI e XII secolo', in *La lezione gentile. Scritti di storia dell'arte per Anna Maria Segagni Malacart*, eds. L. C. Schiavi, S. Caldano, and F. Gemelli (Milan 2017), 477–86; Tabanelli, 'Architettura sacra' (as n. 1), 59–71.

[27] S. Bottari, 'La Cattedrale di Catania', *Catania. Rivista del Comune*, 8 (1958), 53–59; Bruzelius, 'The Norman Cathedral' (as n. 4), 121–22; Occhiato, 'Robert de Grandmesnil' (as n. 16), 134–44 refers to French models in Calabrian architecture.

[28] Gandolfo, 'Le cattedrali' (as n. 4), 202–05. About the materials of the classical period, reused in the cathedral of Catania, see P. Pensabene, '*Il contributo degli elementi architettonici in marmo del Museo Civico di Castello Ursino alla storia dell'architettura romana di età imperiale a Catania*', in *Catania antica. Nuove prospettive di ricerca*, ed., F. Nicoletti (Palermo 2015), 471–506.

[29] See T. Bella, 'La Contea normanna e il mare. Il caso della cattedrale monastica di Catania: nuove precisazioni', in *Conoscere il mare per vivere il mare*, Atti del convegno di studio (Cagliari 2019), ed. R. Martorelli (Perugia 2019), forthcoming.

[30] The analyses using ground penetrating radar (GPR) were under my supervision and conducted by Bruno Billeci and Maria Dessì (Laboratory and Analysis of Cultural Heritage of the Department of Architecture, Design and Urban Planning of Alghero, University of Sassari) in May 2018, with the collaboration of Fabio Linguanti (Department of Architecture of the University of Palermo). See B. Billeci and M. Dessì, '*La diagnostica strumentale per la conservazione e la conoscenza. Un'applicazione al patrimonio medievale nel Mediterraneo*', in *Atti della Conferenza Nazionale sulle Prove non distruttive Monitoraggio Diagnostica* (Milan 2019), forthcoming. Previous surveys, particularly that conducted in 2003 by the University of Catania for other purposes, did not provide information on the Norman naves: S. Imposa and G. Mele, 'Ground Penetrating Radar Survey Inside the Cathedral of S. Agata in Catania (Eastern Sicily)', *International Journal of Architectural Heritage*, 5 (2011), 188–97.

[31] See A. M. Fallico, 'Capitelli antichi nella cattedrale di Catania', *Palladio*, 17/IV (1967), 171–82; Pensabene, '*Il contributo degli elementi architettonici in marmo del Museo Civico di Castello Ursino alla storia dell'architettura romana di età imperiale a Catania*' (as n. 28), 471–506.

[32] Bruzelius, 'The Norman Cathedral' (as n. 4), 123.

[33] Bella, 'Batir' (as n. 5), 26–27. On the building, see I. Lorés i Otzet, *El monastir de Saint Pere de Rodes* (Barcelona 2002), 11–36; J. McNeill, '*Veteres Statues emit Rome*: Romanesque Attitudes to the Past', in *Romanesque and the Past*, eds. J. McNeill and R. Plant (Leeds 2013), 5–8.

[34] V. Chaix, *Les églises romanes de Normandie. Formes et fonctions* (Paris 2011), 244–49.

[35] In this I am thinking of the upper part of the walls of Saint-Etienne at Caen or of the bell tower of the church of Secqueville-en-Bassin. See M. Baylé, 'Les monuments juifs de Rouen et l'architecture normande', in *Art et archéologie des Juifs en France médiévale*, ed. B. Blumenkranz (Paris 1980), 251–76.

[36] K. A. C. Creswell, *L'architettura islamica delle origini* (Milan 1958), 282–83; G. Michell, 'North Africa and Sicilia', in *Architecture of the Islamic World*, ed. G. Michell (London 1978), 215–22; F. Basile, *L'architettura della Sicilia normanna*, in *Storia della Sicilia*, vol. V, ed. R. Romeo (Naples 1981), 1–93 at 31–40; L. Hadda, *Nella Tunisia medievale. Architettura e decorazione islamica (IX-XVI secolo)* (Naples 2008), 5–21.

[37] G. Leone, *Il duomo di Catania. Un metodo di indagine per la determinazione delle caratteristiche meccaniche della muratura* (Catania 1995), 23; A. Salemi and G. Sanfilippo, '*Materiali e tecniche costruttive nella cattedrale: una storia narrata dalla materia*', in *Catania. Splendore del Barocco* (Catania 2004), 72–85.

[38] Paris: Bibliothèque National de France, P63050G. The drawing will be published in G. Pagnano, *Dufourny in Sicilia* (2019), forthcoming.

[39] In Normandy, it was usual to find two bays between the transept and the apses, as at Saint-Paul de Rouen, Cerisy-la-Forêt, and Saint-Étienne at Caen. See V. Chaix, 'Les chœurs cloisonnés du monde anglo-normand dans la seconde moitié du XIe siècle', in Ars auro gemmisque prior. *Mélanges en hommage à Jean-Pierre Caillet*, eds. C. Blondeau, B. Boissavit-Camus, et al. (Zagreb and Motovun 2013), 241–49.

[40] Agatha lived in the 3rd century and was martyred in Catania in 251, during the persecution of Decius, as was recounted in the later *Passio* (5th–6th centuries). Although local tradition identifies places within Catania with the life of Agata, there is no accurate information until after the Norman conquest, when the cult was reinvigorated as a tool of Christianization following Islamic domination: C. Crimi, 'Agata', in *Il grande libro dei Santi. Dizionario enciclopedico*, eds. E. Gueriero and D. Tuniz, 3 vols. (Milan 1998), 29–30; M. Stelladoro, *Agata. La martire dalla tradizione greca manoscritta* (Milan 2005); G. Zito, G. L. M. Millesoli, and G. G. Mellusi, *Una santa, una città: Agata e Catania in nuove fonti medievali* (Spoleto 2015).

[41] Gandolfo, 'Le cattedrali' (as n. 4), 201–02.

[42] Tabanelli, 'Architettura sacra' (as n. 1), 27–31.

[43] M. Lheure, *Le transept de la Rome antique à Vatican II. Architecture et liturgie* (Paris 2007), 90–91. Cefalù Cathedral is an example: Krönig, *Il duomo* (as n. 22), 188. A case outside Normandy is the church of Saint-Mexme de Chinon, where the apses were linked by passages. E. Lorans and X. Fehrnbach, eds., *La Collégiale Saint-Mexme de Chinon* (Chinon 1990), plan at 24. There are Carolingian precedents for cross-passages immediately east of the transept, as at St-Philibert-de-Grandlieu, and it may be these that lie behind the development of the scheme in the Loire Valley at the very beginning of the 11th century, as with Chinon or Saint-Jouin-de-Marnes. For a fuller discussion, see J. Mallet, *L'art roman de l'ancien Anjou* (Paris 1984), 282; A. Tcherikover, 'The Church of Saint-Jouin-de-Marnes in the Eleventh Century', *Journal of the British Archaeological Association,* 140 (1987), 15–16, plan at Figure 2. See also Chaix, 'Les chœurs' (as n. 39), 244–46.

[44] M.-L. Bassi, 'L'abbatiale romane de Baume-les-Messieurs (Jura). Premier résultats des recherches d'archéologie du bâti', in *Architettura dell'XI secolo nell'Italia del Nord. Storiografia e nuove ricerche*, Atti del convegno internazionale (Pavia 2010), eds., A. Segagni Malacart and L. C. Schiavi (Pisa 2013), 511–56. The cathedral of Mazara was also designed with an apse-echelon east end (with passages connecting the bays facing the apses), as was the Norman abbey of San Salvatore Telesino in Campania. This last foundation was linked to the abbey of Bec in Normandy through Abbot Jean, who came from there: F. Marazzi and A. James, 'Alle origini del monachesimo "normanno" in Italia meridionale. L'abbazia di San Salvatore Telesino (Benevento – Campania): ricognizione geofisica e analisi delle evidenze materiali', in *La mémoire des pierre. Mélanges d'archéologie, d'art et d'histoire en l'honneur de Christian Sapin*, eds. S. Balcon-Berry, B. Boissavit-Camus, and P. Chevalier (Turnhout 2016), 281–99.

[45] See Bella, 'Ansgerius quod ego' (as n. 5), 410–12; T. Bella, 'La Contea normanna' (as n. 29). The information given in Tabanelli, 'Architettura sacra' (as n. 1), 67–8 is incorrect.

[46] On early martyria, see A. Grabar, *Martyrium. Recherches sur le culte des reliques et l'art chrétien antique. Volume I. Architecture* (Paris 1946); R. Krautheimer, *Early Christian and Byzantine Architecture* (Middlesex 1975); R. Milburn, *Early Christian Art and Architecture* (Berkeley and Los Angeles 1988); M. J. Johnson, *The Roman Imperial Mausoleum in Late Antiquity* (New York 2009).

[47] For other Romanesque churches erected over pre-existing mausolea or oratories, see C. Sapin, *Les cryptes en France. Pour une approche archéologique, IVe-XIIe siècle* (Paris 2014), 34–36.

[48] C. Crimi, 'S. Agata a Bisanzio nel IX secolo. Rileggendo Metodio patriarca di Costantinopoli', in *Euplo e Lucia 304–2004*, eds. T. Sardella and G. Zito, Quaderni di Synaxis, 18 (Catania 2005), 143–64; C. Crimi, 'Sant'Agata a Bisanzio e oltre', in *Agata santa. Storia, arte, devozione* (Florence 2008), 247–50; C. Angelidi, 'Translationes Agathae. Note sur le culte d'une Sainte entre Byzance et la Sicile normande', *Néa Rhóme*, 9 (2012), 123–32; E. Bozoky, 'Translations de reliques prestigieuses d'Orient en Italie, fin du XIe -début du XIIIe siècle', *Cahiers d'études italiennes*, 25 (2017), http://journals.openedition.org/cei/3534.

[49] S. Tramontana, 'Sant'Agata e la religiosità della Catania normanna', in *Chiesa e società in Sicilia* (as n. 12), 189–202. On the medieval cult of Agatha, see P. Oldfield, 'The Medieval Cult of St. Agatha of Catania and the Consolidation of Christian Sicily', *Journal of Ecclesiastical History*, 62 (2011), 439–56; G. Zito, 'Su Sant'Agata nuovi documenti medievali a Catania: un lacerto di pergamena e un sigillo plumbeo', in *Una santa, una città* (as n. 40), 1–40.

[50] Gandolfo, 'Le cattedrali' (as n. 4), 200; Bella, 'Batir' (as n. 5), 29–32; Bella, 'Ansgerius quod ego' (as n. 5), 413–16.

[51] Krönig, *Il duomo* (as n. 22), 151.

[52] Lojacono, 'Il restauro' (as n. 23), 254; A. Salemi, 'Il corpus della Cattedrale: materiali e tecniche costruttive', in *La Cattedrale di Catania* (Catania 2009), 145–64.

[53] During the 1957–58 restoration the difference in height between the nave and transept was restored by means of three steps. The steps that predated the 1693 earthquake were found in the north aisle. Leone Uberti, 'I lavori' (as n. 23), 6.

[54] Krönig, *Il duomo* (as n. 22), 150–51; N. G. Leone, E. Mauro, C. Quartarone, and E. Sessa, 'Wahrzeichen des Feudalismus und Stupor mundi: Festungsbauten im Val Demone und Val di Noto. X.2. Catania', in *Arabisch-Normannische Kunst. Siziliens Kultur im Mittelalter*, eds. E. Schubert, S. Messina, and E. Mauro (Tübingen 2004), 296–301; Gandolfo, 'Le cattedrali' (as n. 4), 200–01. The upper windows were restored in the last century: Leone Uberti, 'I lavori' (as n. 23), 5.

[55] The towers in the thickness of the eastern walls of the Norman church of Santa Maria della Roccella in Calabria (late 11th century) have been compared to those of the Norman cathedrals of Mazara and Catania, extended to the full width of the transept ends. See K. Kappel, 'Architecture as a Visual Record? S. Maria della Roccella in Calabria', in *Romanesque and the Past,* eds. John McNeill and R. Plant (Leeds 2013), 67–76.

[56] For a similar conformation, see the 11th-century church of Sainte-Marie at Quarante (Hérault), where two symmetrical towers surmount the ends of the transept, but lower: A. Bonnery, 'Tours symétriques de chevet du Languedoc aux Pyrénées', *Les cahiers de Saint-Michel de Cuxa*, 27 (1996), 33–45; G. Boto and M. Sureda, 'Les cathédrales romanes catalanes. Programme, liturgie, architecture', *Les cahiers de Saint-Michel de Cuxa*, 44 (2013), 75–89; E. Fernie, 'Patronage, Romanesque architecture and the Languedoc', in *Romanesque Patrons and Processes*, eds. Jordi Camps, Manuel Castiñeiras, John McNeill, and Richard Plant (Milton Park 2018), 73–82.

[57] M. Baylé, 'L'architecture normande d'époque romane en France: sources et rayonnement', in *L'architecture normande en Europe. Identités et échanges su XIe siècle à nos jours* (Marseille 2002), 29–38; É. Vergnolle, 'Saint-Bénigne de Dijon. Cinquante ans de recherche sur l'abbatiale de l'an mil', *Bull. mon.*, 174 (2016), 131–64. On the wall passages at Boscherville see also T. Bella, 'La chiesa abbaziale di Saint-Georges de Boscherville in un carnet di Fernand de Dartein', *Ikhnos* (2019), 137–44.

[58] P. Héliot, 'La cathédrale de Cefalù, sa chronologie, sa filiation et les galeries murales dans les églises romanes du Midi', *Arte Lombarda*, 10 (1965), 19–39, and 11 (1966), 6–25; Gandolfo, 'Le cattedrali' (as n. 4), 204.

The Regional and Transregional in Romanesque Europe (2021), 171–187

'SCHOOL' OR 'MASONS' WORKSHOP'?

REFLECTIONS ON THE SO-CALLED *WORMSER BAUSCHULE* AND ON THE DEFINITION OF REGIONAL STYLE

Wilfried E. Keil

As is well-known, the definition of regional styles in Romanesque art and architecture has long been associated with the existence of 'schools'. The concept emerged in the 19th century, and this paper addresses the issues raised by the problematic category of 'schools' in relation to the so-called Wormser Bauschule *(Worms school of builders). The discussion will be focused on one particular decorative form invented in the workshop of Worms Cathedral at the beginning of the 12th century and then follows its deployment in other buildings in the city, in the region, and beyond – thus touching on issues related to transregional styles. This form, in German* Hornauslauf *(horn-stop), is a particular type of ending applied to the vertical profiles of pilasterstrips. Tracing the progressive use of the* Hornauslauf, *it will be asked how and by what means this form spread. Does this mark the activity of a 'school'? Or, rather, is 'school' the right concept by which to group and define different workshops active in the city of Worms, its region, and beyond? Should we talk about a 'school' or a specific workshop, or are some forms disseminated by single masons?*

THE ORIGIN OF THE TERM 'ROMANESQUE' AND THE DIVIDING OF REGIONS INTO 'SCHOOLS'

The definition of regional styles in Romanesque art and architecture has long been associated with the existence of 'schools'. This concept emerged in the 19th century and is closely linked to the spread of the term 'Romanesque'. Already in the late 18th century the English poet and scholar Thomas Gray (1716–71) pointed out that the architectural style before Gothic, named Norman or Saxon, was a degenerate style of Roman architecture.[1] William Gunn used the term 'Romanesque' for this architectural period in his book *An Inquiry into the Origin and Influence of Gothic Architecture*, which was written in 1813 and published six years later in 1819.[2] This, he explained, was using the English (and French) '*-esque*' of the Italian suffix '*-esco*' after the word 'Romano', the modern term used by citizens of Rome for those who were not native to the city.[3] Charles-Alexis de Hérissier Comte de Gerville (1769–1853) introduced the French term *roman* for this architecture in his notebook[4] and used it shortly afterwards in a letter of 18 December 1818 to Auguste Le Prévost (1787–1862).[5] The term found acceptance among other scholars and spread. In Germany, the term *romanisch* was used the first time by Sulpiz Boisserée in the year 1833.[6]

In 1824 Arcisse de Caumont (1801–73) used the term *roman* in his *Essai sur l'architecture religieuse au Moyen Age* and introduced it to a wider audience in France.[7] A few years later, in 1830, Arcisse de Caumont started his book series *Cours D'Antiquités Monumentales* with the subtitle *Histoire de l'art dans l'ouest de la France, depuis les temps les plus reculés jusqu'au XVIIe siècle*. The six text and six plate volumes were published between 1830 and 1841. In the fourth volume, *Moyen Age. Architecture religieuse*, which was published in 1831, he started to divide the geography of Romanesque architecture in France into schools.[8] In his publication *Abécédaire ou Rudiments d'archéologie* from 1850, he revised his classification and divided the geography of the Romanesque style in France into seven schools: Nord de la France (Champagne and Orléanais); Normandie and Bretagne; Poitou and Angoumois; Aquitaine; Auvergne; Bourgogne and Provence; provinces rhénanes.[9] Later classifications used that of Arcisse de Caumont as a basis and modified it.[10]

THE ORIGIN OF THE TERM *WORMSER BAUSCHULE*

This paper will address issues raised by the problematic category of 'schools' in relation to the definition of artistic regions, focusing on the so-called *Wormser Bauschule* (Worms school of builders), which derives from the Cathedral in Worms (Rheinland-Pfalz).

The origins of the term *Wormser Bauschule* cannot be defined precisely. However, in his 1887 inventory of

DOI: 10.4324/9781003162827-13

Worms and the surrounding area, Ernst Wörner wrote of Worms Cathedral and later churches which shared stylistic similarities, that they formed part of a *'Wormser Kunstrichtung*' (an 'art-movement of Worms') and that there was '*eine[r] in Worms blühende[n] Schule*' ('a flourishing school in Worms').[11] He added that there was an '*an dem Dombau mächtig gediehenen romanischen Bauschule*' (a vigorously thriving *Bauschule* at the cathedral building'), operating not only in the immediate area but also beyond.[12] Here he was clearly talking about a *Wormser Bauschule*, even if he did not use the exact term. Georg Dehio (1850–1932), one of the most famous German art historians and one of the inventors of modern cultural heritage preservation, mentioned for the first time a '*Wormser Schule*' (school of Worms) in his 1919 book *Geschichte der Deutschen Kunst.*[13] Shortly afterwards, in the year 1922, when Richard Hamann (1879–1961), the founder of Bildarchiv Foto Marburg, published his book on German and French art in the Middle Ages *Deutsche und französische Kunst im Mittelalter*, the term *Wormser Bauschule* was firmly established.[14] The term referred not only to the nave and the eastern parts of Worms Cathedral but also to other churches built within this tradition. Since then, the concept has never been properly contested, even though critical remarks have been made, and it reached its climax in the 1985 book *Wormser Bauschule 1000–1250* by Walter Hotz (1912–96).[15]

THE REGION, CHARACTERISTICS, AND FORMS OF THE *WORMSER BAUSCHULE*

The Oberrhein region (Upper Rhine Valley) is the area east and west of the Rhine between Basel (Basel-Stadt) and Bingen (Rheinland-Pfalz). The Worms area is understood in German scholarship to be a part of the *Kunstlandschaft*[16] of the Oberrhein,[17] more precisely the northern Franconian part,[18] which is also called Fränkischer Oberrhein.[19] If one had to define the area in which the *Wormser Bauschule* operated according to the buildings that Walter Hotz included in his book, this would cover the entire regions of Pfalz (Palatinate), Rheinhessen, North Baden, Alsace, and parts of the regions Schwaben (Swabia), Franken (Franconia), and Hessen (Hesse).[20] The concept of Romanesque 'schools', however, is French and is not commonly used in this sense in German architectural historical research.[21] Matthias Untermann has characterised the work of the so-called *Wormser Bauschule*. According to him, the school is to be understood as a training and recruitment context, which had a lasting effect in a region. Buildings which relate to the *Wormser Bauschule* either refer to the Cathedral or were built by craftsmen who were trained in Worms or who were influenced by Worms buildings.[22]

In this paper the problematic concept of *Wormser Bauschule* will be reassessed. To begin with, what is meant by the term *Wormser Bauschule*? Most of the standing parts of Worms Cathedral were built between 1106 and 1225, though there are still some parts of the former church, the Burcharddom, consecrated more than 1000 years ago in the year 1018, and some Gothic parts.[23] We might ask, however, which parts of the building are taken to be the product of the *Wormser Bauschule:* the nave and eastern parts, or should the western choir also be included?

Perhaps the easiest place to start is with the comparison used by Walter Hotz on a double-page spread in his book on the *Wormser Bauschule.*[24] There he compares the eastern façade of Worms cathedral with the eastern façade of the former monastery church St Laurentius in Seebach in Bad Dürkheim (Rheinland-Pfalz) (Figures 13.1 and 13.2 and Colour Plate XIV).[25] From the profiles of the jambs of the windows, pilaster strips, arched friezes, and the use of a band of sawtooth, it is obvious that most of the masons of Seebach belonged to the workshop of Worms Cathedral or at the least trained there. However, not only are the profiles of the jambs of each window on the eastern façade of the cathedral different from each other, but there was also a change in the building technique during the work.[26]

According to Walter Hotz, the peculiarity of a 'school' can be quantified by observing building processes (*Bauordnungen*) and proportional systems.[27] As characteristics of the so-called *Wormser Bauschule* Hotz mentions a wide variety of forms: ashlar masonry; the articulation of wall surfaces by cornices, arched friezes, often sawtooth bands, and vertical pilaster strips; the use of columned or stepped portals; the tendency to chamfer edges (except at the corners of buildings) or to profile them and use curved endings; the development of particular types of capital and ornament; and the use of imaginative figurative architectural sculpture.[28] He also includes more general forms: the structure of the walls of the towers and that they are often round, and the use of saddle roofs.[29] Hotz's listing is problematic because he also includes characteristics that were very widespread in the late Romanesque period, sometimes even beyond the borders of the Holy Roman Empire. A more precise and exclusive differentiation would have been more useful. Such a differentiation would have highlighted the problem of characterising the *Wormser Bauschule*. It is possible that Hotz was at least partially aware of this problem when he described the term *Wormser Bauschule* as a hypothesis. Two sentences later, however, he himself classifies it as useful and correct.[30] Matthias Untermann already emphasized that this attempt by Walter Hotz was never seriously discussed.[31] This may also be due to the fact that after the publication of Hotz's book the term '*Wormser Bauschule*' was considered problematic by some researchers and that therefore it was neither dealt with nor used.

Some of these forms were very widespread, among them monolithic columns, of which the still-existing ones in Worms include also the base and the capital. We know from written sources that Worms was famous for its columns and that they were exported to other regions. Columns were transported hundreds of kilometres to Sint-Truiden/Saint-Trond (Limbourg) in Belgium. Abbot Rudolf (1108–38) of Saint-Trond reported in *c.* 1110–20

FIGURE 13.1

Worms Cathedral: eastern façade (Wilfried E. Keil)

FIGURE 13.2

Seebach: eastern façade (Wilfried E. Keil)

that Abbot Adelard II (1055–82) ordered columns from Worms for the rebuilding of the church there, which were transported on the Rhine to Cologne and from there overland.[32] Inventive treatment of these monoliths can be seen in the gallery of the eastern façade of Worms Cathedral, on the well-known column of the architect with two animals.[33] These special monolithic columns make clear that there was a wide interest in the masonry of the workshop of Worms Cathedral.

THE INVENTION OF THE *HORNAUSLAUF* AT WORMS CATHEDRAL

This paper will focus in particular on one decorative form invented at Worms Cathedral at the beginning of the 12th century and then follow its deployment in other buildings of the city, in the region and beyond, thus touching on issues related to transregional styles. This form, for which the *Wormser Bauschule* is well-known, is called in German a *Hornauslauf* (which could be translated as 'horn-stop'). It is a particular type of ending applied to the vertical profiles of the pilaster strips and can be found on both the exterior and the interior of buildings. Usually the *Hornauslauf* is found at the bottom of the corner mouldings of a pilaster, forming a transition from the mouldings to the base. The angle of the pilaster is usually hollowed, flanked by rolls. The rolls curve in towards the corner at the bottom (Figure 13.9 provides a good example), ending in a point. The shape is like a horn, giving us the term *Hornauslauf*, combining the German words *Horn* (animal horn) and *Auslauf*, ending.[34] The *Hornauslauf* can end in different ways depending on the angle mouldings of the pilaster strip. Early uses of the form are found only at the end of pilaster strips, but it was later used on other elements, especially at the end of archivolts. The profile of a *Hornauslauf* itself cannot be reproduced simply by profile drawings. This would require a 3D model, and for comparisons, one would have to compare the 3D models of the individual *Hornausläufe*. Since the profiles are normally always a pointed continuation of the pilaster strip mouldings, the profiles of the pilaster strips are compared with each other (see e.g. Figure 13.3).

New dendrochronological investigations have shown that some of the eastern parts – the eastern façade and the towers – of Worms Cathedral were built in the 1130s in a single large construction campaign with most parts of the transept.[35] The dating of the transept to the 1130s has been known since dendrochronological analysis of the late 1970s and early 1980s as well as new dendrochronological investigations.[36] The upper parts and the gables of the north transept have been dated using wood from putlog holes from the exterior walls to between 1142 and 1145.[37]

There are also new dates for the inner eastern parts of the cathedral. These arc the result of palaeographic studies and documents, stylistic comparisons, and building archaeology (especially the connections of the towers to the sanctuary). This has allowed us to redefine the chronology of this part of the church, dating it to the beginning of the 12th century. It seems that the inner parts of the sanctuary were built between 1106 and 1110.[38] We have written sources of a consecration in 1110, which the emperor Henry V and many bishops attended, and the name of a patron, Adelbraht, a coiner, on the Juliana-relief.[39] We know this coiner from written sources, which belong to the first decade of the 12th century.[40] So first a sanctuary was built, and then about 20 years later, a new eastern façade with towers was added, so that the old sanctuary remained in large parts intact inside.

The pilaster strip with the Juliana-relief has the same angle-profile as those with a *Hornauslauf* in the eastern sanctuary, built at the same time (Figure 13.3, no. 1). On one of these, the bottom of the angles has a bearded man, which hides the moulding and especially its termination, though the beard partly follows the curves of the base (Figure 13.4). There are other human heads used as a transitional sculpture; on one the head, the neck and a part of the shoulder and the arms are visible (Figure 13.3, no. 2, and Figure 13.5). The arms are in the place where the 'horn' is on a *Hornauslauf*. On a further example, with the head of the ram, the *Hornauslauf* below the head is visible (Figure 13.6), and the similarity between the termination of the moulding and the horn of an animal is clear.

The eastern façade of Worms Cathedral has a different form of *Hornauslauf* to that inside the eastern sanctuary (Figures 13.3, n. 3, and Figure 13.7), apparently more developed. The profile is also different from that inside as can be seen by comparing numbers 1 and 2 with number 3 in figure 13.3. The roll-hollow-roll of the interior has been replaced by a cyma profile on the eastern façade, a new form in Worms, the origin of which is not yet known. The *Hornausläufe* on the east façade are also somewhat different. There is an original preserved (and a replaced one) with an additional scroll at the bottom of the *Hornauslauf* as decoration, which could be seen as reminiscent of a ram's horn. Perhaps a further elaboration was planned here or a reference to the *Hornauslauf* with the ram's head in the eastern sanctuary.

However, the implications of the new chronology of the eastern parts of the Cathedral still need to be investigated for the understanding of the so-called *Wormser Bauschule*: in particular, what the workshop of Worms did in the years between 1110 and *c.* 1130. Given the long break in construction of the eastern parts, the question arises whether Worms-trained masons and sculptors not only spread motifs such as the *Hornauslauf* but also developed them further at other buildings before returning to Worms and using them. It is also possible that an entirely new workshop was assembled around 1130 or one which mixed old and new masons. We are left with a number of possibilities: a new mason, who knows the cyma form elsewhere combined it with the *Hornauslauf*; a mason from Worms saw the cyma profile while

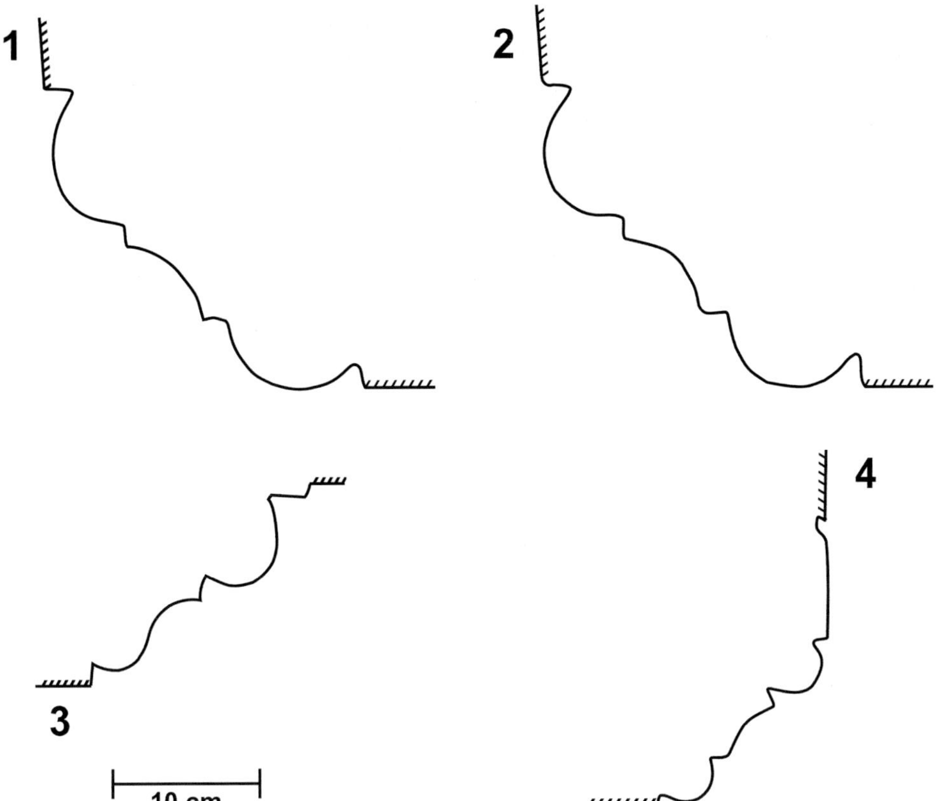

FIGURE 13.3

Worms Cathedral: drawings of profiles: (1) eastern sanctuary, pilaster strip, profile at the Juliana-relief; (2) eastern sanctuary, pilaster strip, profile with the Hornauslauf *with human head; (3) eastern façade, pilaster strip with* Hornauslauf*; (4) south aisle, former door to the Nicholas-chapel, south jamb (Wilfried E. Keil)*

working elsewhere; or perhaps the form was taken from a pattern book.

There are further developed examples at the Cathedral: at the bottom of the pilaster strips on the outer wall of the north aisle (dating to the 1160s[41]) are two different forms of the *Hornauslauf* side to side (Figure 13.8). The outer *Hornausläufe* (left in Figure 13.8) have a simpler design than the adjacent inner ones (right in Figure 13.8), where there is a fillet in the hollow. Inside the cathedral in the south aisle, one can find the *Hornauslauf* at the ending of the jambs of the former door to the chapel of St Nicholas, which is now blocked (Figure 13.3, no. 4, and Figure 13.9). The lunette above the door bears a relief of St Nicholas. This can be classified stylistically in the period of the former south portal, which dates from around 1160.[42]

From the new dating of the inner parts of the eastern parts of Worms Cathedral, it can be inferred that the *Hornauslauf* was invented at Worms Cathedral. While we as yet know nothing of the activity of the building works of Worms Cathedral between the construction of the inner and outer eastern parts, we might assume that the workshop of the Cathedral was working on other buildings in Worms during this time. Thus the further development of the *Hornauslauf* took place either at one of these projects or was continued with the construction of the eastern façade. This consisted in changes to the profile, which was no longer symmetrical, and the use of a cyma was introduced. Both variants, with and without a cyma, became common. Before this spread outside the workshop, the *Hornauslauf* cannot be taken for a characteristic of the *Wormser Bauschule*, as in these cases they are products of the workshop itself or works of masons trained in this workshop who worked locally.

THE DIFFUSION OF THE *HORNAUSLAUF*

In tracing the progressive deployment of the *Hornauslauf*, it will be questioned by what means the form spread: does this mark the activity of a 'school'? Or, rather, is 'school' the right concept to group and define the different workshops active in the city of Worms (Cathedral, St Andreas, St Paul, St Martin, Synagogue), in its region (for example Frankenthal, Seebach, Bechtheim (all Rheinland-Pfalz)) but also beyond the boundaries of the diocese of Worms? Does the term 'school' help, or does it tend to cause confusion because it suggests closer connections than were, in fact, present?

The *Hornauslauf* is found in the dioceses neighbouring Worms: Mainz (Rheinland-Pfalz), Metz (Moselle),

FIGURE 13.4

Worms Cathedral: eastern sanctuary, Hornauslauf *with human bearded men (Wilfried E. Keil)*

FIGURE 13.5

Worms Cathedral: eastern sanctuary, Hornauslauf *with human head (Wilfried E. Keil)*

FIGURE 13.6

Worms Cathedral: eastern sanctuary, Hornauslauf *with ram's head (Wilfried E. Keil)*

FIGURE 13.7

Worms Cathedral: eastern façade, Hornauslauf *(Wilfried E. Keil)*

FIGURE 13.8

Worms Cathedral: north aisle, exterior wall, pilaster strip, Hornausläufe *(Wilfried E. Keil)*

FIGURE 13.9

Worms Cathedral: south aisle, former door to the Nicholas chapel, east jamb, Hornauslauf *(Wilfried E. Keil)*

Speyer (Rheinland-Pfalz), Strasbourg (Bas-Rhin), and Würzburg (Bayern) but also in north Hesse, on the way toward Bamberg (Bayern) and at Bamberg Cathedral itself. A further distribution to the north and to the east seems probable but is not yet sufficiently investigated. By the later 12th and early 13th century, the *Hornauslauf* had become widespread. In 1963, Hans-Joachim Krause published a map to show its distribution (Figure 13.10).[43] At those places on the map marked with a cross, one can find a *Hornauslauf* with cyma, at places with a circle those without, and at places with a cross in a circle you can find both. The main region of the *Hornauslauf* is the Oberrhein area with Alsace and Pfalz (Palatine). There are some in Hessen (Hesse) and Mainfranken (Main-Franconia), in Sachsen (Saxony), Bayern (Bavaria), Austria, Bohemia, Hungary and Ukraine.

Rudolf Kautzsch thought that the origin of the *Hornauslauf* was in Alsace, but he used the now superseded dates for the Cathedral (from *c.* 1170 to *c.* 1215) and thought that most of the forms and architectural sculpture of Worms Cathedral had their origin in Alsace.[44] Hans-Joachim Krause had already refuted this assumption convincingly.[45] Following the old dating of the buildings, Krause wondered about the earlier occurrence of the *Hornauslauf* in Maulbronn (Baden-Württemberg), Bechtheim, and Münzenberg (Hessen), all of which relate to Worms Cathedral, and whether Worms could have been the starting point for the form.[46] He also examined the examples in the Saale-Mulde area, which are also earlier than those in Alsace, and concluded that the *Hornauslauf* must have originated in Worms or in the region of Worms and not in Alsace,[47] probably having its origin in the eastern sanctuary of Worms Cathedral.[48]

Because of the new chronology of the eastern parts of Worms Cathedral and new dating of the Romanesque parts of the cathedrals of Strasbourg and Bamberg, the whole structure of the dating of buildings in the upper Rhine valley is in need of revision.

The *Hornauslauf* at other churches in Worms

The workshop of Worms Cathedral was also active in the construction of other buildings in Worms and probably in some places nearby. It is only possible to present a few examples here. Inside the former collegiate church St Andreas in Worms, one can find the *Hornauslauf* in the sanctuary at the bottom of the outer jambs of the doors to the south and north tower. The profile consists of two

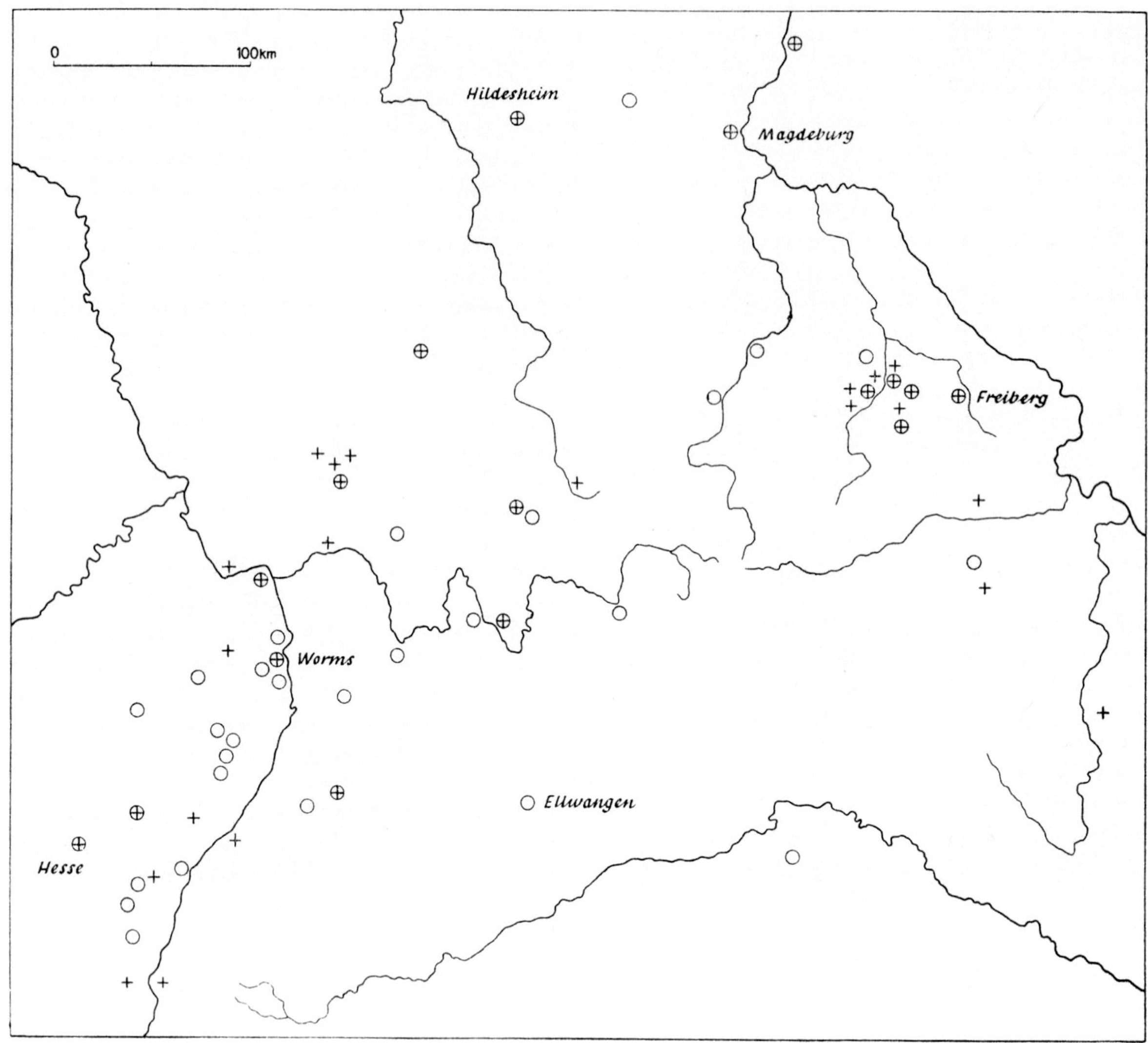

FIGURE 13.10

Occurrence of the Hornauslauf*: at the places with a cross, a* Hornauslauf *with cyma; at places with a circle, without cyma; at places with a cross in a circle, both (H.-J. Krause, 'Bemerkungen zum staufischen Neubau des Wormser Doms',* Wissenschaftliche Zeitschrift der Karl-Marx-Universität Leipzig*, 12 (1963), 445–62, at 454, Figure)*

rolls with a small-edged fillet between them. There is no cyma, and the design is most reminiscent of the profile inside the eastern sanctuary of the Cathedral, so it is possible that some parts of St Andreas were built before the eastern façade of Worms Cathedral and therefore before the 1130s. The *Hornausläufe* on the pilaster strips of the eastern façade of St Andreas are more similar to the ones at the eastern façade at the cathedral and can be dated in the 1130s or 1140s.[49] A similar date can be given to the *Hornausläufe* on the eastern façade of the former collegiate church of St Martin in Worms (Figures 13.11 and 13.12), which have very similar cyma forms to those on the eastern façade of the cathedral (Figures 13.3, no. 3, and Figure.13.7).[50] More *Hornausläufe* can be found inside the sanctuary of the collegiate church St Paul in Worms but with very flat endings, and the forms are imprecise in comparison to the ones at the Cathedral. Even though there is a cyma, it looks like a reduced version because of the ending. The sanctuary of St Paul can be dated *c.* 1200,[51] thus later than the consecration of the western choir of the cathedral in 1181.[52]

The *Hornauslauf* – regional and transregional

Of the wider distribution, regional and transregional, of the *Hornauslauf* only a few examples can be presented. Starting close to Worms, in Rheinland-Pfalz, on the east façade of the former nunnery St Laurentius in Seebach, the designs of the *Hornausläufe* are closely related to the east façade of Worms Cathedral, including scrolls at the base, as is the design of the whole façade (Figure.13.13). Although this additional decoration is different from the preserved *Hornauslauf* on the eastern façade of Worms Cathedral, it is probably derived from it (Figure.13.14). The cyma in Seebach is a little more developed than that at Worms (Figures 13.3, no. 3, and Figure.13.7) but still not as strong

FIGURE 13.11

Worms, St Martin: eastern façade, pilaster strip, Hornauslauf *(Wilfried E. Keil)*

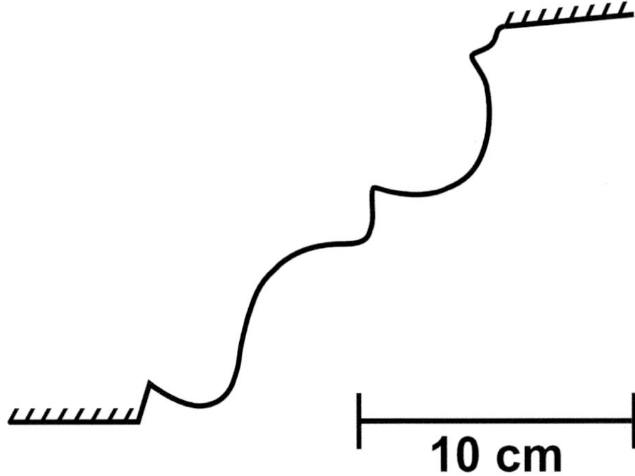

FIGURE 13.12

Worms, St Martin: eastern façade, pilaster strip, profile (Wilfried E. Keil)

as on the cathedral north aisle (Figure.13.8). In addition, the ending is less deeply cut and not as precise as on the east façade. According to the close similarity of the whole façade and similarities in the details, the sanctuary of Seebach dates shortly after the east façade of Worms Cathedral in the 1140s and was probably built by a workshop related to the Cathedral.[53] There are also *Hornausläufe* on the end of the jambs of the frame of the aumbry recess inside the sanctuary, which seem to date a little later.

The sanctuary of the parish church of St Lambert in Bechtheim was rebuilt between 1160 and 1170.[54] Here, the *Hornausläufe* at the bottom of the pilaster strips on the outer walls are imprecise, rather simplified versions, which do not look like a work of the workshop of Worms Cathedral but one influenced by it. Likewise on the portal of St Viktor in Guntersblum, built *c.* 1200,[55] there is a very simplified form of the *Hornauslauf* (Figure 13.15), though the shape is more precise than in Bechtheim, and the curved form is more like a horn, even if, because of restoration, this is not so obvious at first glance. It looks closest to the profile of the door to the Nicholas-chapel (*c.* 1160) in the south aisle of Worms Cathedral (Figures 3, no. 4, and 13.9).

Further from Worms but staying in the Upper Rhine Valley, the motif of the *Hornauslauf* is quite widely used at the Cistercian abbey of Maulbronn. It is found on the jambs of the west portal (see Figure 13.19), in the nave on the pilaster strips above the arcade piers, and on the gates of the rood-screen. We can, indeed, assume from the style and art of working that masons of Worms Cathedral worked in Maulbronn, which was built in large part from the mid-1160s to the beginning of the 1170s and was consecrated on May 14, 1178.[56]

Also in the Upper Rhine Valley, the *Hornauslauf* appears frequently in Alsace: for example at the former monastery of Saint-Pierre et Saint-Paul in Neuwiller-lès-Saverne (Bas-Rhin). At the ending of the jambs of the portal in the western wall of the south arm of the eastern transept, which dates *c.* 1180,[57] there are three different forms of the *Hornauslauf* (Figures 13.16 and 13.17). The one in the middle resembles examples in the eastern sanctuary of Worms Cathedral, and the outer is more like the form with a cyma on the eastern façade at Worms. The inner moulding is a new, reduced form, with a single quadrant roll though the base resembles the other two.

Further north from Worms, on the eastern exterior of St Mary, Gelnhausen (Hessen), the north and south portals and the pilaster strips of the towers have *Hornausläufe* (Figure 13.18). From dendrochronological investigations, we know that the roof of the western tower was built *c.* 1195 and that the roofs of the north arm of the transept and the sanctuary were built *c.* 1238/40.[58] The portal in the north aisle is dated *c.* 1225, and the north and south portals of the transept *c.* 1235.[59] Even though the church was built so late, the *Hornauslauf* is clearly derived from the cyma of Worms Cathedral (eastern façade and the inner ones outside the north aisle). Perhaps there were also *Hornausläufe* at the former church in Gelnhausen, assumed to be of the middle of the 12th century, and they were copied from them.[60]

Moving east from Worms, at castles such as Wildenburg in the Odenwald (Bayern), *Hornausläufe* were used on the jambs of the main portal (Figure 13.20), which is embedded in the gate tower and dates to between 1170 and 1180.[61] The form is also a very simplified one, which

FIGURE 13.13

Seebach: eastern façade, Hornauslauf *(Wilfried E. Keil)*

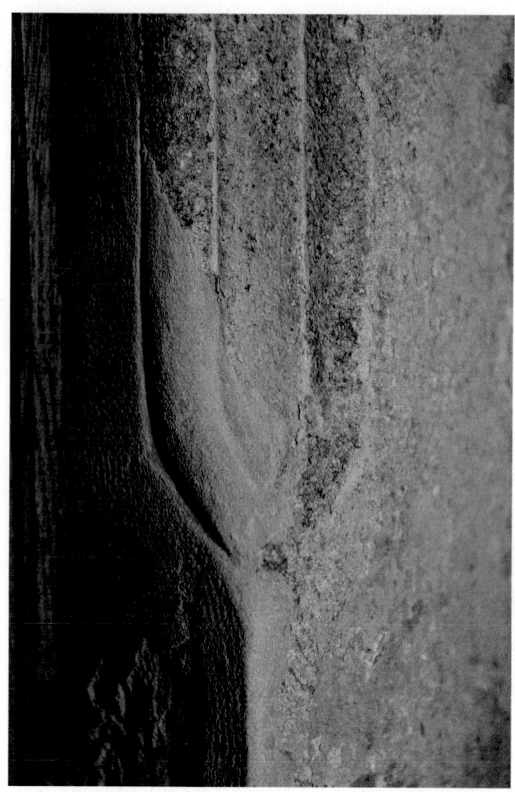

FIGURE 13.15

Guntersblum: west portal, right jamb, Hornauslauf *(Wilfried E. Keil)*

FIGURE 13.14

Worms Cathedral: eastern façade, Hornauslauf *with a scroll at the base (Wilfried E. Keil)*

looks most like Guntersblum (Figure 13.15) and the former door to the Nicholas-chapel (*c.* 1160) in the south aisle of Worms Cathedral (Figure 13.3, no. 4, and Figure 13.9). The shape, however, has almost no curvature like that of a horn and is more similar to a shape related to the *Hornauslauf*, which is the so-called *Schiffskehle* (ship's fillet).[62] But there are also 'classically' shaped *Hornausläufe* at Wildenberg castle. In the residential apartments to the left of the fireplace, there is a small niche whose profiles end at the sides at the bottom in *Hornausläufe* (Figure 13.21). This shows that there can be extremely different variants at one and the same building. Moving further east, and also later, *c.* 1190,[63] it occurs at Bamberg Cathedral (Bayern) on the Gnadenpforte, where it was used as an ending to the archivolts and also on the imposts of the small windows at the western apse (Figure 13.22).

To the north-east, at the former collegiate church of Wechselburg (Sachsen), there are *Hornausläufe* on the bottom of the pilaster strips on the western block, the aisles, the clerestory, and the jambs of the eastern and western open arches of the porch of the north aisle and inside the church at the bottom of the piers in the nave (Figure 13.23). The church dates in the third quarter of the 12th century.[64]

Still further from Worms at the baroque parish church of Szigetújfalu (Pest) in Hungary reused stones with *Hornauslauf* were found in 2010 from the abbey church at Ercsi built in the last third of the 12th century.[65] There are two stones with a precise shape of a *Hornauslauf* (Figure 13.24) like those from eastern façade of Worms

FIGURE 13.16

Neuwiller-lès-Saverne, Saint-Pierre et Saint-Paul: transept, south arm, western wall, portal, south jamb, Hornausläufe *(Wilfried E. Keil)*

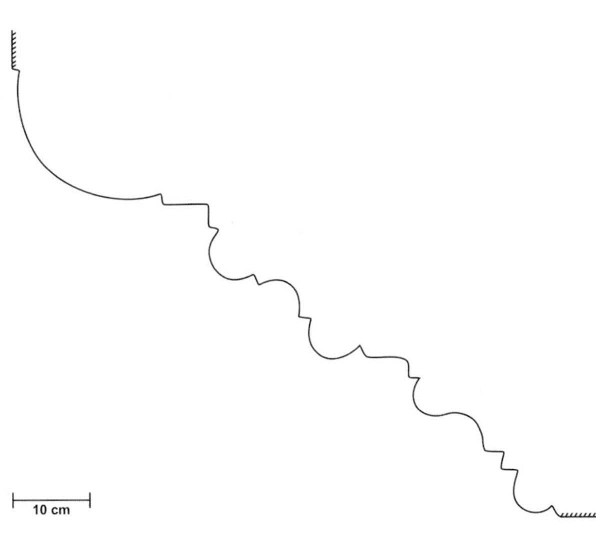

FIGURE 13.17

Neuwiller-lès-Saverne, Saint-Pierre et Saint-Paul: transept, south arm, western wall, portal, south jamb, Hornausläufe *(Wilfried E. Keil)*

FIGURE 13.18

Gelnhausen, St Mary Chapel: transept, south portal, eastern jamb, Hornauslauf *(Wilfried E. Keil)*

FIGURE 13.19

Maulbronn: west portal, south jamb, Hornauslauf *(Wilfried E. Keil)*

FIGURE 13.20

Wildenburg in the Odenwald: main portal at the castle, jamb, Hornauslauf *(Wilfried E. Keil)*

FIGURE 13.21

Wildenburg in the Odenwald: residental apartments, niche left of the fireplace, Hornauslauf *(Wilfried E. Keil)*

FIGURE 13.22

Bamberg Cathedral: western apse, window, jamb, Hornausläufe *(Wilfried E. Keil)*

FIGURE 13.23

Wechselburg, nave, pillar, Hornauslauf *(H.-J. Krause, 'Bemerkungen zum staufischen Neubau des Wormser Doms',* Wissenschaftliche Zeitschrift der Karl-Marx-Universität Leipzig, *12 (1963), 445–62, at 457, Figure.8)*

FIGURE 13.24

Székesfehérvár, Szent István Király Múzeum: former Ercsi Abbey, stone with Hornauslauf *(Béla Zsolt Szakács)*

FIGURE 13.25

Palágykomoróc/Palad'-Komarivtsi: south wall, portal, western jamb, Hornauslauf *(Béla Zsolt Szakács)*

Cathedral, which very probably originally belonged to a window and two others with a loosely cut form of a very simplified *Hornauslauf*,[66] which are more like the so-called *Schiffskehle* (ship's fillet). Ernő Marosi has already made the connection to Worms Cathedral for the two *Hornausläufe* with the precise profile.[67] At the parish church in Palágykomoróc/Palad'-Komarivtsi (Kárpátalja/Sakarpatska oblast) (Zakarpatska) in Ukraine near the borders with Slovakia and Hungary, heavily painted *Hornausläufen* have been discovered on a portal on the south side of the nave.[68] They appear at the bottom ends of the double-stepped archivolts and on the double-stepped jambs (Figure 13.25). The first documentary mentions of the church are from 1334 and 1335, but the building itself likely dates to *c.* 1280, when a noble family bought the land on which the church stands.[69] Even if these *Hornausläufe* are around 170 years later, they look as if the mason knew the ones on the eastern sanctuary of Worms Cathedral or ones whose design was very similar to those in Worms. It is possible, therefore, that the mason knew of the *Hornausläufe* of Szgetújfalu, which were less far away and oriented himself towards them.

WORMSER BAUSCHULE, WORKSHOP AND/OR SINGLE MASONS?

The design of the *Hornauslauf* seems to have originated in the inner parts of the sanctuary of Worms cathedral in the first decade of the 12th century. After that, the *Hornauslauf* first spread to the area near Worms and to the Upper Rhine Valley but also quite quickly to other nearby regions and to more distant places, eventually to more than 1000 km away in present-day Hungary and Ukraine. It is obvious that not all of these *Hornausläufe* were created by the workshop of Worms Cathedral itself. Because many buildings in the region around Worms had building elements that in their execution were reminiscent of those at the Cathedral and at other churches that were built in Worms at that time, the term *Wormser Bauschule* was introduced.

For Walter Hotz, the centre of the *Wormser Bauschule* was the mason´s workshop of Worms Cathedral. For him it was also a kind of school, in that the building trade was taught there and from there the craftsmen set out to work in other places. He used the term 'school' in the French tradition, set it up as a hypothesis for the period between

1000 and 1250, and emphasized that he considered this hypothesis to be useful and correct.[70]

In his book it becomes clear that Hotz wanted to create a category of the so-called *Wormser Bauschule*, which is larger than the mason´s workshop of Worms Cathedral. Even his characterisation of the elements that are typical of the so-called *Wormser Bauschule* is very problematic, as his list of features is long, and does not differentiate between what was common beyond Worms at the time and what was really typical of the mason´s workshop of Worms Cathedral. Through this analysis of a typical element of the so-called *Wormser Bauschule*, the *Hornauslauf*, it becomes clear that it spread far beyond the area that Hotz proposed for the *Wormser Bauschule*. This could possibly also be investigated for other elements.

The term *Wormser Bauschule* therefore does not seem to be appropriate for both regional and transregional use. The distant examples can no longer be explained by a 'school', but only by the transfer of forms between individual workshops or the traveling of individual masons. Matthias Untermann has already questioned whether it would not be better to speak of a *'Bauhütte'* (workshop) instead of a *'Bauschule'* (school of builders) for describing the regional and interregional dynamic of the transfer of forms. In using this term he considers both craftsmen and artists, as well as principals and patrons.[71] For Untermann the statement that the monastery at Maulbronn is at least in part a work of the *Wormser Bauschule* might be correct for the forms, but implies that there were stable networks connecting masons which did not exist between the 11th and 13th centuries.[72] He considers it would be better to think the craftsmen in Maulbronn had worked at Worms Cathedral or were trained there. In his opinion, the term *Wormser Bauschule* cannot be recommended.[73]

Whether a mason´s workshop like that of Worms Cathedral also worked outside Worms can only be clarified by detailed comparisons in the technique and style of individual forms, especially when the distance is more than 1000 km. Such transmissions can only be explained by a transfer of forms from one workshop to another or by the traveling of individual masons. It therefore seems to make more sense to examine these transfers and travels and to investigate more precise dependencies. In many of the buildings belonging to the so-called *Wormser Bauschule*, influences from other buildings or regions are also noticeable. In such cases, one cannot speak of buildings of the *Wormser Bauschule* because they show a combination of many influences. One finds in some – such as Bamberg Cathedral or Wechselburg – parts which are more and parts which are less closely related to Worms. While those elements not related to Worms might have been built by masons who were trained in another workshop, those parts using forms related to Worms might have been built by individual masons who were from the workshop of Worms cathedral itself, or by masons trained by someone who had been in the workshop, or by masons who had adopted Worms motifs simply from observation. There is also the possibility of transfer through pattern books which, however, have not been preserved from this time.

The concept of a 'school of builders' is a 19th-century invention that does not help in the study of regional and transregional styles, especially when the mixtures of different styles in a region are not taken into account. The question is whether one can even speak of a regional style if we do not know exactly what it is. One solution is to research the invention of a form in a certain region and its spread and to become aware that specific forms sometimes spread much further and faster than we think today. For this it is important that we pick out specific typical architectural elements and examine them as closely as possible. The long tried and tested method of profile comparison is particularly helpful here. With the help of technical aids such as a profile comb, profiles can be taken and reproduced very accurately. It is important that there is no distortion of the result by embellishing or copying the form as was partly the case in the past and is partly still the case today. For a direct comparison, even of complicated forms, photogrammetric 3D models can also be helpful. If these were made for a *Hornauslauf*, one could compare the *Hornauslaufe* directly and would not have to compare the mouldings above them.

The problem with using older research is that the drawings and plans are often not exact. Frequently measurements taken of one part were applied to the rest of the building without re-measurement, and even important churches such as Worms Cathedral and St Michael in Hildesheim do not have precisely measured plans.[74] For the investigation of the development of forms, we need exact drawings of profiles and also descriptions of the surface of the stones. By examining the traces of the working techniques of the masons, we will have a better chance to draw new conclusions, and in many cases it can be done without a scaffold.[75]

The investigation of single forms at different buildings is very important to get a better impression of the interchanges of workshops and the development of forms. As was shown in this paper for the research of one form, especially in the Romanesque period, we cannot think only of the regional; we need also to think of the transregional.

ACKNOWLEDGEMENTS

For discussions, I would like to thank Aquilante De Filippo, Michele Luigi Vescovi, and Richard Plant; for pictures and some literature on the eastern Europe examples, Béla Zsolt Szakács; and for corrections to my English, Richard Plant.

NOTES

1 T. Gray, 'Architectura Gothica', in *The Works of Thomas Gray*, 5 vols., ed. J. Mitford (London 1835–43), vol. V, 325–32.

2 W. Gunn, *An Inquiry into the Origin and Influence of Gothic Architecture* (London 1819), 6. For the difference in time between the writing and publishing, see page 1.

[3] Gunn, *An Inquiry into the Origin* (as n. 2), 6, 80.

[4] J. Nayrolles, *L'invention de l'art roman à l'époque moderne (XVIIIe–XIXe siècles)* (Rennes 2005, also PhD thesis, University of Toulouse 1994), 85.

[5] M. F. Gideon, 'L'invention de l'expression architecture romane par Gerville (1818) d'après quelques lettres de Gerville à Le Prévost', *Bulletin de la Société des Antiquaires de Normandie*, 42 (1934), 268–88, at 285–86; Nayrolles, *L'invention* (as n. 4), 86. For the whole process of the naming by Gerville, see Nayrolles, *L'invention* (as n. 4), 81–91.

[6] S. Boisserée, *Denkmale der Baukunst vom 7ten bis zum 13ten Jahrhundert am Nieder-Rhein* (München 1833), vii, 16, 24, 34.

[7] Arcisse de Caumont, 'Essai sur l'architecture religieuse au Moyen Âge, particulièrement en Normandie, communiqué à la Société d'Emulation de Caen, en décembre 1823, lu à la Société des Antiquaires de la Normandie, le 8 mai 1824', *Mémoires de la Société des Antiquaires de la Normandie*, 1 (1824), 535–677. For Arcisse de Caumont and his work, see V. Juhel, ed., *Arcisse de Caumont (1801–1873). Érudit normand et fondateur de l'archéologie français. Actes du colloque international organisé à Caen du 14 au 16 juin 2001 par la Société des Antiquaires de Normandie*, Mémoires de la Société des Antiquaires de Normandie, 40 (Caen 2004).

[8] A. de Caumont, *Cours d'Antiquités Monumentales professé à Caen. Histoire de l'art dans l'ouest de la France depuis les temps les plus reculés jusqu'au XVIIe siècle. 6 text volumes and 6 panel volumes* (Paris, Caen 1830–41), *IV: Moyen Age. Architecture religieuse* (Paris, Caen 1831), esp. 190–93. For the use of 'schools' in the analysis of French Romanesque see Andrault-Scmitt in this volume.

[9] A. de Caumont, *Abécédaire ou Rudiments d'archéologie* (Paris, Caen 1850), 138, 291–93.

[10] As an example, E.-E. Viollet-le-Duc used the classification of A. de Caumont and modified it in his *Dictionnaire*: E. E. Viollet-le-Duc, *Dictionnaire raisonné de l'architecture française du XIe au XVIe siècle. 10 volumes* (Paris 1854–68), vol. V (1861), 153–54 (école), 161–95 (église), at 163–68.

[11] E. Wörner, *Die Kunstdenkmäler im Grossherzogthum Hessen. Inventarisirung und beschreibende Darstellung der Werke der Architektur, Plastik, Malerei und des Kunstgewerbes bis zum Schluss des XVIII. Jahrhunderts. Provinz Rheinhessen. Kreis Worms* (Darmstadt 1887), 14, 26. H. Boos refers to E. Wörner in his use of the term: H. Boos, *Geschichte der rheinischen Städtekultur von ihren Anfängen bis zur Gegenwart mit besonderer Berücksichtigung der Stadt Worms*, 4 vols. (Berlin 1897–1901), vol. I, 278.

[12] Wörner, *Kunstdenkmäler* (as n. 11), 232.

[13] G. Dehio, *Geschichte der deutschen Kunst* (Berlin 1919), 243.

[14] R. Hamann, *Deutsche und französische Kunst im Mittelalter. Band 1: Südfranzösische Protorenaissance und ihre Ausbreitung in Deutschland auf dem Wege durch Italien und die Schweiz* (Marburg 1922), 95, 122. The term *Wormser Bauschule* was also used in the title of two unpublished PhD theses at the University of Marburg: E. Graf Solms-Laubach, 'Die Wormser Bauschule in Hessen und ihre Grundlagen in Deutschland und Oberitalien' (unpublished PhD thesis, University of Marburg, 1925); R. Hootz, 'Die ehemalige Klosterkirche Breitenau und ihre Beziehungen zur Hirsauer und Wormser Bauschule' (unpublished PhD thesis, University of Marburg, 1952). In his PhD thesis on St. Andreas in Worms, G. R. Kiewitt only occasionally uses the term *Wormser Bauschule*, see G. R. Kiewitt, 'St. Andreas und der Wormser Kreis. Baugeschichte des Andreasstifts und Auswirkung der Wormser Bautätigkeit um die Wende des 12. Jahrhunderts in der Pfalz und in Rheinhessen' (unpublished PhD thesis, Technische Hochschule Stuttgart, 1923). K. Nothnagel uses in contrast the term "*Wormser Schule*" in his PhD thesis from 1927. See Karl Nothnagel, *Staufische Architektur in Gelnhausen und Worms*, ed. F. Arens, Der Wormsgau, Beiheft 25 (Worms 1971; also: PhD thesis University of Frankfurt am Main 1927). For other monographs that deal with the *Wormser Bauschule*, see W. Hotz, *Die Wormser Bauschule 1000–1250: Werke – Nachbarn – Verwandte. Studien über landschaftsbezogene deutsche Baukunst* (Darmstadt 1985), 13–14.

[15] Hotz, *Bauschule* (as n. 14).

[16] For the use of the classification into *Kunstlandschaften* in the book *Architektur der Romanik* by H. E. Kubach, see 'Hans Kubach's Treatment of Regions in the Study of Romanesque Architecture' by Eric Fernie in this volume. Kubach did not use the term in this book; see H. E. Kubach, *Architektur der Romanik, Weltgeschichte der Architektur*, ed. P. L. Nervi (Stuttgart, Milano 1974). The translated Italian edition of the book was published earlier: H. E. Kubach, *Architettura romanica, Storia universale dell'architettura*, ed. P. L. Nervi (Milano 1972). For the English edition, see H. E. Kubach, *Romanesque Architecture, History of World Architecture*, ed. P. L. Nervi (New York 1975). The book was also published in French and Spanish. For Kubach's thoughts on the term *Kunstlandschaft*, see Chapter 6, 'Die Kunstlandschaft an Rhein und Maas', in *Romanische Kunst an Rhein und Maas, vol. 4: Architekturgeschichte und Kunstlandschaft*, eds. H. E. Kubach and A. Verbeek (Berlin 1989), 469–500.

[17] For the *Kunstlandschaft* Oberrhein (Upper Rhine Valley), see also Kubach, 'Die Kunstlandschaft' (as n. 16), 474–79.

[18] Hotz, *Bauschule* (as n. 14), 3.

[19] Ibid., 12.

[20] Ibid.

[21] In English research, the term 'school' is also rarely used for architecture and architectural sculpture. The best-known example is the Herefordshire School. See M. Thurlby, 'The Herefordshire School of Romanesque Sculpture (Almeley/Herefordshire 2013) and 'The Herefordshire School Revisited' by John McNeill in this volume. George Zarnecki developed the idea in his PhD thesis, 'Regional Schools of English Sculpture in the Twelfth Century' (unpublished PhD thesis, Courtauld Insitute of Art, University of London, 1950) and wrote later about a 'Yorkshire School'. See, for example, G. Zarnecki, 'A Romanesque Bronze Candlestick in Oslo and the Problem of the "Belts of Strength"', *Årbok. Kunstindustrimuseei i Oslo* (1963–1964), 45–66, at 52–54.

[22] M. Untermann, 'Kaiserdome oder Kunstlandschaft? Romanische Baukunst und regionale Identität', in *Kurpfalz und Rhein-Neckar. Kollektive Identitäten im Wandel*, eds. V. Gallé, J. Peltzer, B. Schneidmüller, and S. Weinfurter, Heidelberger Veröffentlichungen zur Landesgeschichte und Landeskunde, 13 (Heidelberg 2008), 51–62, at 58.

[23] W. Hotz, *Der Dom zu Worms* (Darmstadt 1981), 20; D. von Winterfeld, *Der Dom zu Worms*, rev. 3rd ed. (Königstein im Taunus 1994), 5; D. von Winterfeld, *Die Kaiserdome Speyer, Mainz, Worms und ihr romanisches Umfeld* (Würzburg 1993), 167. For the Ottonian Burcharddom, see M. Untermann, 'Der Burcharddom und die frühmittelalterliche Wormser Domkirche. Neue Beobachtungen und Überlegungen', *Der Wormsgau*, 34 (2018), 101–22.

[24] Hotz, *Bauschule* (as n. 14), Plates 22, 23.

[25] For Seebach, see note 53.

[26] For the first results of the investigations into the construction technique on the eastern façade of the cathedral in Worms, see W. Keil, 'Bemerkungen zur Bautechnik der Ostteile des Doms zu Worms', in *Der Dom zu Worms. Krone der Stadt. Festschrift zum 1000-jährigen Weihejubiläum des Doms*, eds. P. Kohlgraf, T. Schäfer, and F. Janson (Regensburg 2018), 75–80.

[27] Hotz, *Bauschule* (as n. 14), 15–18.

[28] Ibid., 18–19.

[29] Ibid., 19.

[30] Ibid.

[31] Untermann, 'Kaiserdome' (as n. 22), 58.

[32] V. Mortet, *Recueil de textes relatifs à l'histoire de l'architecture et à la condition des architectes en France, au Moyen Age. XIe–XIIe siècles* (Paris 1911), 157–58, no. XLVII, 1; O. Lehmann-Brockhaus, *Schriftquellen zur Kunstgeschichte des 11. und 12. Jahrhunderts in Deutschland, Lothringen und Italien* (Berlin 1938), 396, no. 1982. See also G. Binding, *Baubetrieb im Mittelalter* (Darmstadt 1993), 356; G. Binding and S. Linscheid-Burdich, *Planen und Bauen im frühen und hohen Mittelalter nach den Schriftquellen bis 1250* (Darmstadt 2002), 251–52, 357.

[33] W. E. Keil, 'Baumeistersäule', in *Die Staufer und Italien. Drei Innovationsregionen im mittelalterlichen Europa*, eds. A. Wieczorek, B. Schneidmüller, and S. Weinfurter, vol. II, Objekte (exhibition catalog) (Mannheim and Darmstadt 2010), 108–09; W. E. Keil, 'Die Baumeistersäule an der Ostfassade des Domes zu Worms', *Insitu. Zeitschrift für Architekturgeschichte*, 3 (2011), 5–18.

[34] For the longest reflection of the architectural motif *Hornauslauf* till now, see H.-J. Krause, 'Bemerkungen zum staufischen Neubau des Wormser Doms', *Wissenschaftliche Zeitschrift der Karl-Marx-Universität Leipzig*, 12 (1963), 445–62, at 455–60. R. Kautzsch named the motif *'schiffschnabelmäßige[s] Auslaufen'*. See: R. Kautzsch, 'Der Meister der Ostteile des Doms zu Worms', *Städel Jahrbuch*, 5 (1926), 99–114, at 105. O. Böcher describes it as 'schnabel- oder klauenförmiges Auslaufen eines gekehlten oder karniesförmigen Profils', see: O. Böcher, *Die Alte Synagoge zu Worms*, Der Wormsbau. Beiheft 18 (Worms 1960, also PhD thesis Mainz 1958), 56. I. Spille uses the term 'Wormser Kralle' ('Wormser claw'), which was created in a seminar by Fritz Arens. See I. Spille, 'Neuentdeckungen zur Datierung des Wormser Domes', *Der Wormsgau*, 13 (1979/81), 106–12, at 111 with n. 41. H.-J. Krause has pointed out that the *Hornauslauf* is not to be confused with the related but differently shaped '*Schiffskehle*' ('ship`s fillet'). See Krause, 'Bemerkungen' (as in this), 456.

[35] S. Bauer, 'Bauholzdaten und Gerüste des Mittelalters am Dom Sankt Peter zu Worms', *Der Wormsgau*, 34 (2018), 11–88, at 15–19, 59–63, 71 and plans 2–4 at 81–83. See also A. De Filippo, L. Schulten, and M. Untermann, 'Der Ostbau des Wormser Doms. Ergebnisse der bauhistorischen Untersuchungen 2007–2015', in *Der Dom zu Worms. Krone der Stadt. Festschrift zum 1000-jährigen Weihejubiläum des Doms*, eds. P. Kohlgraf, T. Schäfer, and F. Janson (Regensburg 2018), 27–42, at 31–32; L. Schulten and M. Untermann, 'Die Baugeschichte des Wormser Doms. Forschungsstand und neue Perspektiven', *Der Wormsgau*, 34 (2018), 89–99, at 98.

[36] In the upper parts of the transept they found some wood in the putlog holes which was dendrochronologically dated to the years from 1132 to 1137, see E. Hollstein, 'Dendrochronologische Datierung von Bauhölzern des Wormser Doms', *Neues Jahrbuch für das Bistum Mainz* (1979), 45–46; E. Hollstein, 'Neue Bauholzdaten des Wormser Doms', *Neues Jahrbuch für das Bistum Mainz* (1981), 125–34. S. Bauer examined the wood again and was able to partially confirm or slightly correct the data. Some wood could not be dated with complete certainty again. In general, there are no serious deviations that would affect a new dating. See Bauer, 'Bauholzdaten' (as n. 35), 19–22, 63–64, 71–72. S. Bauer was able to date newly removed wood from the putlog holes on the exterior of the transept from 1136 on. See Bauer, 'Bauholzdaten' (as n. 35), 22–26, 64–66, 72–73 and plans 5–6 at 84–85.

[37] Bauer, 'Bauholzdaten' (as n. 35), 22–26, 64–66, 72–73 and plans 5–6 at 84–85.

[38] M. Untermann, 'Der Ostbau des Wormser Doms. Neue Überlegungen und Befunde zu Bauabfolge und Datierung sowie zur Weihe von 1110', *Der Wormsgau*, 27 (2009), 189–203; M. Untermann and W. E. Keil, 'Der Ostbau des Wormser Doms. Neue Beobachtungen zu Bauabfolge, Bauentwurf und Datierung', *Insitu. Zeitschrift für Architekturgeschichte*, 2 (2010), 5–20. So far, this new classification has criticized only by Dethard Winterfeld in some parts. See D. von Winterfeld, 'Offene Fragen zur Baugeschichte des Wormser Doms', in *Der Dom zu Worms. Krone der Stadt. Festschrift zum 1000-jährigen Weihejubiläum des Doms*, eds. P. Kohlgraf, T. Schäfer, and F. Janson (Regensburg 2018), 43–45. Some of the criticisms can be answered in future publications without further research. The consecration of 1110 had already been cited in earlier research on the eastern parts, but for the entire eastern parts and with different arguments. For a historian's view, see F. M. Illert, 'Zur Geschichte des Domes (Regesten)', in *Der Dom zu Worms*, ed. R. Kautzsch (Berlin 1938), 9–49, at 25–26, 31–32; F. M. Illert, 'Zeitgeschichte und Dombau. Ein Beitrag zur Frage der Datierung des Wormser Dombaues', *Der Wormsgau*, 7 (1965/66), 9–36, at 23–24. From an art historian's view, announced with forthcoming arguments (which were never published), see R. Hootz, 'Zur Baugeschichte des Domes in Fritzlar', *Zeitschrift des Vereins für hessische Geschichte und Landeskunde*, 69 (1958), 66–86, at 85.

[39] For the relief with its inscriptions, see W. E. Keil, 'Remarks on Patron Inscriptions with Restricted Presence', in *Romanesque Patrons and Processes. Design and Instrumentality in the Art and Architecture of Romanesque Europe*, eds. J. Camps, M. Castiñeiras, J. McNeill, and R. Plant (London and New York 2018), 279–89, at 281–86.

[40] G. Bönnen, 'Dom und Stadt. Zu den Beziehungen zwischen der Stadtgemeinde und der Bischofskirche im mittelalterlichen Worms', *Der Wormsgau*, 17 (1998), 8–55, at 15 with n. 21.

[41] The dating comes from wood from the putlog holes of the interior north wall of the nave, which were dendrochronologically dated to the years 1162–63. See Hollstein, 'Dendrochronologische Datierung' (as n. 36), 45–46. S. Bauer was able to confirm the dates in her new dendrochronological analysis of the same wood. See Bauer, 'Bauholzdaten' (as n. 35), 21, 33, 63–64, 71–72. During the recent investigations, wood from putlog holes in the clerestory of the north side was analysed. In the first double bay from the east, the wood dates from the winter of 1141/42 and early summer 1145, and in the second double bay from winter 1163/64. See Bauer, 'Bauholzdaten' (as n. 35), 27–33, 66–68, 73–74, plan 7 at 85.

[42] The dating is given by the suggested construction progress and stylistic comparison with the north wall of the nave, where we have some wood from scaffold crossbars of the north wall of the nave. For the dendrochronological investigations, see note 41. W. Hotz dates the sculpture to around 1165, see W. Hotz, *Dom* (as n. 23), 75, footnote 123. D. v. Winterfeld dates the sculpture to perhaps before 1160, see v. Winterfeld, *Dom* (as n. 23), 16, 18; v. Winterfeld, *Kaiserdome* (as n. 23), 204.

[43] Krause, 'Bemerkungen' (as n. 34), 454, fig. 3.

[44] R. Kautzsch, *Romanische Kirchen im Elsaß. Ein Beitrag zur Geschichte der oberrheinischen Baukunst im 12. Jahrhundert* (Freiburg i. Br. 1927), 65. For this, see also R. Kautzsch, *Der Dom zu Worms* (Berlin 1938); R. Kautzsch, *Der romanische Kirchenbau im Elsass* (Freiburg i. Br. 1944).

[45] Krause, 'Bemerkungen' (as n. 34), 456.

[46] Ibid., 457.

[47] Ibid., 457–58. He used this argument to date Worms Cathedral earlier than some other researchers and dated the start of the construction works around 1140/50. This dating is obsolete since the dendrochronological investigations at the end of the 1970s.

[48] See also A. De Filippo, 'Die Bauskulptur des Mainzer und Wormser Domes und ihre Vorbilder in der Lombardei', in *Die Staufer und Italien. Drei Innovationsregionen im mittelalterlichen Europa*, eds. A. Wieczorek, B. Schneidmüller, and S. Weinfurter, vol. 1, Essays (exh. Cat.) (Mannheim and Darmstadt 2010), 150–60, at 154; A. De Filippo, 'Die romanische Bauskulptur des Wormser Doms', in *Der Dom zu Worms. Krone der Stadt. Festschrift zum 1000-jährigen Weihejubiläum des Doms*, eds. P. Kohlgraf, T. Schäfer, and F. Janson (Regensburg 2018), 47–59, at 48.

[49] D. von Winterfeld dates the rebuilding of the church between 1180 and 1200. See v. Winterfeld, *Kaiserdome* (as n. 23), 282. These dates do not work for the portals or the towers in the sanctuary or to the eastern façade. New results can be expected for St Andreas in Worms through Aquilante De Filippo's PhD thesis, which is currently in progress.

[50] The final consecration of the rebuilt church was in 1265. Von Winterfeld dates the new construction and conversion after 1200. See v. Winterfeld, *Kaiserdome* (as n. 23), 286. This is definitely too late. The east façade will have been started shortly after the beginning of the construction work on the aisles of the cathedral.

[51] D. von Winterfeld dates the rebuilding of the church to the beginning of the 13th century. See v. Winterfeld, *Kaiserdome* (as n. 23), 292. The dating here is also too late.

[52] W. Hotz, 'Die Wormser Domweihe von 1181. Zur Baugeschichte des staufischen Domes', *Neues Jahrbuch für das Bistum Mainz* (1981), 135–47. Previously, F. M. Illert had referred the consecration of 1181 to the western choir for archival reasons: Illert, 'Geschichte' (as. n. 38); F. M. Illert, 'Der Königschor des Wormser Domes. Versuch einer Deutung der Funktion des Westchores des Wormser Domes', *Der Wormsgau*, 2 (1934/42), 337–44, at 341; Illert, 'Zeitgeschichte' (as n. 38), 30, 32.

[53] D. von Winterfeld dates after 1160 and A. De Filippo dates *c.* 1160. See v. Winterfeld, *Kaiserdome* (as n. 23), 303; A. De Filippo, 'Seebach, ancienne église abbatiale Saint-Laurent', in *L'Alsace. Au coeur du Moyen Âge. De Strasbourg au Rhin supérieur XIe-XIIe siècles*, eds. M. Pottecher, J.-J. Schwien, J.-P. Meyer, and A. Freund-Lehmann (Lyon 2015), 140–41. Both datings are too late for the close similarities to the east façade of Worms Cathedral.

[54] Hotz, *Bauschule* (as n. 14), 103; v. Winterfeld, *Kaiserdome* (as n. 23), 304. The old datings of the sanctuary by H. Huth and J. Sommer to the first quarter of the 13th century are no longer acceptable because they are orientated by a very old dating of the west apse of Worms Cathedral. See H. Huth, 'Die romanische Basilika zu Bechtheim bei Worms', *Der Wormsgau*, 4 (1959/60, also PhD thesis, Heidelberg, 1956/57), 5–97, at 67–68, 75; J. Sommer, *Bechtheim, St. Lambertus* (Königstein im Taunus 1980), 24. The dating of Hotz may be a little too early.

[55] v. Winterfeld, *Kaiserdome* (as n. 23), 381. We have dates of 1201/02 from the dendrochronology of a wooden tension anchor in the north tower. See D. Krienke, *Kreis Mainz-Bingen. Verbandsgemeinden Bodenheim, Guntersblum und Nieder-Olm*, Denkmaltopographie Bundesrepublik Deutschland. Kulturdenkmäler in Rheinland-Pfalz, 18.2 (Worms 2011), 190.

[56] U. Knapp, *Das Kloster Maulbronn. Geschichte und Baugeschichte* (Stuttgart 1997), 52, 55, 59. The wood from the individual roof sections was felled between 1168 and 1172 according to dendrochronological investigations. See B. Lohrum, 'Die mittelalterlichen Dachwerke auf der Kirche und den Klausurbauten des Klosters Maulbronn', *Südwestdeutsche Beiträge zur historischen Bauforschung*, 2 (1994), 121–39, at 126–27.

[57] The church was reconstructed after destruction in 1177. See Hotz, *Bauschule* (as n. 14), 184; S. Braun, *Alsace romane* (Dijon 2010), 60; J.-Ph. Meyer, 'Neuwiller-lès-Saverne, église abbatiale Saint-Pierre-et-Saint-Paul', in *L'Alsace. Au coeur du Moyen Âge. De Strasbourg au Rhin supérieur XIe–XIIe siècles*, eds. M. Pottecher, J.-J. Schwien, J.-Ph. Meyer and A. Freund-Lehmann (Lyon 2015), 98. We have a document from 1192, which mentions construction works on the sanctuary. See Braun, *Alsace* (as in this note), 60; Meyer, 'Neuwiller-lès-Saverne' (as in this note), 98. J.-Ph. Meyer dates the transept, without giving reasons, to between 1205 and 1215 (perhaps because of the consecration of the main altar in 1251): Meyer, 'Neuwiller-lès-Saverne' (as in this note), 98.

[58] G. Wilbertz, *Die Marienkirche in Gelnhausen* (Königstein im Taunus 2000), 6.

[59] Wilbertz, *Marienkirche* (as n. 58), 12–13.

[60] For the dating of the former church of St Mary in Gelnhausen to the middle of the 12th century, see G. Wilbertz, *Die Marienkirche in Gelnhausen*, Veröffentlichung der Abteilung Architekturgeschichte des Kunsthistorischen Instituts der Universität zu Köln, 67. (Köln 1999, also PhD thesis, Köln), 40–41, 48.

[61] W. Hotz, *Burg Wildenberg im Odenwald. Ein Herrensitz der Hohenstauferzeit* (Amorbach 1963), 39; Hotz, *Bauschule* (as n. 14), 172.

[62] For Schiffskehle (ship's fillet), see also Krause, 'Bemerkungen' (as n. 34), 456.

[63] A. Hubel and M. Schuller, 'Überlegungen zur frühen Baugeschichte des Bamberger Doms', *Das Münster*, 56 (2003, Sonderheft Bamberger Dom), 310–25.

[64] Krause, 'Bemerkungen' (as n. 34), 457. There is a partial consecration recorded for the year 1168. H.-J. Krause, *Die Stiftskirche zu Wechselburg. 2. Teil Baugestalt und Baugeschichte, Corpus der romanischen Kunst im sächsisch-thüringischen Gebiet*, Series A, vol. II, 2 (Berlin 1972), 90–93. For the connection of the *Hornauslauf* in Wechselburg to Worms, see also Krause, *Wechselburg* (as in this note), 105–06. Near Wechselburg, the motif also occurs in the Romanesque Marktkirche of Chemnitz *c.* 1165/75. See Krause, 'Bemerkungen' (as n. 34), 457; Krause, *Wechselburg* (as in this note), 106. H.-J. Krause expresses the opinion that the form also exists in the Marienkirche in Freiberg, but it is different from the *Hornauslauf* and cannot count as one.

[65] B. Bodó and L. Farbakyné Deklava, 'Az Ersci Monostor Újabb Kőfaragványai', *Műemlékvédelem*, 55 (2011), 165–88 at 165, 169–70; E. Marosi, 'Az Ersci Monostor Kőfaragványaink Újabb Leletheihez', *Műemlékvédelem*, 55 (2011), 200–8 at 200, 206–7; B. Bodó and L. Farbaky-Deklava, 'Die neuestens freigelegten Steinskulpturen der Abtei Ercsi, Ungarn', *Acta Historiae Artium Academiae Scientiarum Hungaricae*, 52 (2011), 175–97, at 175, 181; E. Marosi, 'Bemerkungen zum neuen Fund von Steinskulpturen aus dem Kloster Ersci', *Acta Historiae Artium Academiae Scientiarum Hungaricae*, 52 (2011), 199–208. Today the stones are kept in the depot in Szent István Király Múzeum in Székesfehérvár. See: Bodó and Farbakyné Deklava, 'Ersci' (as in this n.), 167; Bodó and Farbaky-Deklava, 'Steinskulpturen' (as in this n.), 178.

[66] Bodó and Farbakyné Deklava, 'Ersci' (as n. 65), 179–80; Marosi, 'Leletheihez' (as n. 65), 196–97; Bodó and Farbaky-Deklava, 'Steinskulpturen' (as n. 65), 190.

[67] Marosi, 'Leletheihez' (as n. 65), 196–98.

[68] B. Z. Szakács, 'Palágykomoróc – Református templom', in. . . *ideje az építésnek. . .*, ed. T. Kollár (Budapest 2018), 175–85, at 181.

[69] B. Z. Szakács, 'Palágykomoróc, református templom', in *Középkori templomok a Tiszától a Kárpátokig*, ed. T. Kollár (Nyíregyháza 2013), 251–57, at 252, 257. Szakács, 'Palágykomoróc' (as n. 68), 175, 185.

[70] Hotz, *Bauschule* (as n. 14), 19.

[71] Untermann, 'Kaiserdome' (as n. 22), 58.

[72] Ibid., 58–59. The monastery at Maulbronn was several times mentioned as (partly) work of the *Wormser Bauschule*: P. F. Schmidt, *Maulbronn. Die baugeschichtliche Entwicklung des Klosters im 12. und 13. Jahrhundert und sein Einfluß auf die schwäbische und fränkische Architektur*, Studien zur deutschen Kunstgeschichte, 3 (Strassburg 1903); Hotz, *Bauschule* (as n. 14), 125–26, 129, 219; Ch. Kalko, 'Die Maulbronner Klosterkirche. Untersuchungen der Planwechsel unter Berücksichtigung des politischen und kulturellen Umfelds des Klosters', in *Maulbronn. Zur 850 jährigen Geschichte des Zisterzienserklosters*, Forschungen und Berichte der Bau- und Kunstdenkmalpflege in Baden-Württemberg, 7 (Stuttgart 1997), 117–61.

[73] Untermann, 'Kaiserdome' (as n. 22), 59.

[74] During the restoration and building archaeology, new measurements have been and are being taken, so that there will soon be a new, more detailed floor plan.

[75] For planning of the working process and stone surfaces in the Middle Ages, see particularly P. Völkle, *Werkplanung und Steinbearbeitung im Mittelalter. Grundlagen der handwerklichen Arbeitstechniken im mittleren Europa von 1000 bis 1500* (Ulm 2016).

The Regional and Transregional in Romanesque Europe (2021), 189–218

TOWARDS AN ANATOMY OF A REGIONAL WORKSHOP

THE HEREFORDSHIRE SCHOOL REVISITED

John McNeill

The following paper considers the composition and working methods of a sculptural atelier active in the southern Welsh Marches over the second quarter of the 12th century. Known as the 'Herefordshire School', the workshop specialised in small-scale commissions, producing portals, corbel tables, chancel arches, tympana, and fonts. Notwithstanding a general workshop tendency to favour repetition, the sculpture was inventive and open to external influence, a susceptibility which may be due to the way the workshop operated. It regularly collaborated with other masons, while its constituent workforce seems to have been flexible, expanding or contracting according to circumstance. It will be argued that the workshop's origins can be traced to Hereford Cathedral but that once formed all the churches for which the sculptors worked were either small or required relatively little carved stonework. In this it was essentially a child of the boom in masonry parish church construction. The type of sculptural workshop organization adopted by the 'Herefordshire School' was probably relatively common in early to mid-12th-century Europe.

The Herefordshire School is something of a *cause célèbre* in the tiny world of English Romanesque sculptural studies. It is well published; its rich and, for the most part, artfully deployed stock repertoire is easy to identify – and images of the churches of which the sculpture forms part are accessible online, thanks to the Corpus of Romanesque Sculpture in Britain and Ireland.[1]

There is general agreement that the 'Herefordshire School' is a specialist sculptural workshop. The term was first used in the 1930s, and, though initially it might have been intended to indicate a set of stylistic preferences shared across Herefordshire and neighbouring counties, it has come to be understood as referring to the output of a particular group of stone carvers and their immediate associates.[2] On this there is currently no dissent, and most recent discussion has concentrated on patronage, dating, and the order in which the buildings were constructed.[3] In particular, considerable effort has been lavished on attempts to determine formal sources for the sculpture and two related issues: identifying the lay patrons responsible for the churches for which the Herefordshire School provided sculpture, and accommodating the construction of those churches to outbreaks of violence during the reign of King Stephen (1135–54). Less interest has been shown in what the sculpture reveals as to workshop organization. What follows is an attempt to address that question and in so doing challenge a recent tendency to treat the workshop as a fixed and stable body.[4] That it was not seems clear. The workshop as a dynamic entity is a slightly different proposition for the Herefordshire School, however, offering a *modus operandi* at once flexible and suggestible and indicating a way in which novel sculptural ideas might be received and assimilated. It also has implications for the interaction of the workshop with patrons and for its resilience during periods of unrest. One aspect of this is the widely noted appearance of western French sculptural motifs and compositional methods in the work of the Herefordshire School. Despite the survival of sculpture attributable to the Herefordshire School at 20 sites, none are more than 70 km from Hereford. This combination of a regional base with an awareness of transregional sources makes the Herefordshire School a promising subject for an investigation of the potential for transmission and reception in a medium, architectural sculpture, in which the object itself is unlikely to circulate.

HISTORIOGRAPHY

Antiquarian interest in the sculpture can be traced back to the artist and ecclesiological polemicist, George Robert Lewis (1782–1871). In 1842, Lewis published *Illustrations of Kilpeck Church Herefordshire in a Series of Drawings Made on the Spot with an Essay on Ecclesiastical Design and a Descriptive Interpretation* and provided drawings of Kilpeck for a letter published in *Archaeologia* (Figure 14.1 and Colour Plate XV).[5] The letter was by

  DOI: 10.4324/9781003162827-14

FIGURE 14.1
Kilpeck, St Mary: south portal (John McNeill)

way of explanation for four plaster casts of figures from the chancel arch and south portal at Kilpeck exhibited at the Society of Antiquaries in London in April 1842, in which a comparison was made between the trousered 'welsh knights' at Kilpeck and similar figures at Shobdon and on the Eardisley font.

The exhibition at the Antiquaries was quickly followed up by Thomas Wright, who placed a short piece in the *Archaeological Journal*, alerting his audience to the 'still more remarkable' work at Shobdon, and offering a date of 'about 1135' for Kilpeck and 'about 1141' for Shobdon.[6] Wright also drew attention to a 'curious work in French' which the early 19th-century continuators of the *Monasticon Anglicanum* had spotted and published in 1830, the chronicle of Wigmore Abbey.[7] This described how Hugh I de Mortimer – the holder of extensive lands in the southern Welsh Marches – gave the *vill* of Shobdon to Oliver de Merlimond and that Oliver had a church built there which was consecrated by Robert de Bethune, bishop of Hereford (1131–48). Lewis again provided the illustrations for Wright's article, though it was not until 1852 that he finally raised sufficient funds from subscription to be able to publish what survived of the Romanesque church at Shobdon in full (see Figures 14.15–14.18).[8] Around this date, a set of plaster casts were also made of the reset sculpture from Shobdon, to be shown at the Crystal Palace following the Great Exhibition of 1851.[9] Meanwhile Wright, who had been investigating the history of the Herefordshire-Shropshire borderlands since the mid-1840s, published his history of Ludlow, in which he offered the first translation into English of the whole of the Wigmore Chronicle.[10]

So ended this opening flurry of interest in Herefordshire Romanesque sculpture. The scholarly world had been provided with a set of high-quality lithographs, two dates, a link to a third site (Eardisley), a London-based simulacrum of a crucial monument and an entrée into an unusually detailed narrative account of the foundation of a Victorine abbey at Shobdon.

The path from then to now was uneven. The British Archaeological Association based its 1870 annual congress in Hereford, inspiring Thomas Blashill to write a short article on Kilpeck and Rowlstone in which he surmised that since the Wigmore Chronicle states that Oliver de Merlimond undertook a pilgrimage to Santiago de Compostela while Shobdon was in building, his journey was probably relevant to the new style of the building.[11] Blashill also seems to have been the first to notice that the capitals of the west front of Leominster Priory and the font at Stottesdon, just over the border in Shropshire, belong in the stylistic orbit of Kilpeck, Rowlstone, and Shobdon.[12]

Virtually nothing more was then written on the subject until 1904, when Charles Keyser published his catalogue of English Romanesque tympana. Keyser grouped tympana and lintels by subject, and when it came to a discussion of images of Christ in Majesty, he put Shobdon alongside Rowlstone and the tympanum reset in a wall by the hospital of St Giles in Hereford, remarking 'they are almost certainly by the same guild of masons'.[13] He also repeated Wright's identification of Oliver de Merlimond as the patron of Shobdon and assigned all three tympana to the reign of King Stephen (1135–54).[14] Prior and Gardner added Castle Frome, averring that the Kilpeck south portal and the fonts at Eardisley and Castle Frome 'would seem to be from the same mason's hands', though they distanced these from the tympana at Rowlstone and Shobdon on the grounds that the latter were 'tentative'.[15]

It was left to Alfred Clapham to incorporate the tympana at Stretton Sugwas and Fownhope to work he identified as being by 'the curious Herefordshire school . . . one of the few cases in which a distinctive local style can be definitely recognised'.[16] In addition to expanding the corpus, this seems to be the first time the word 'school' was applied to the sculpture. Clapham no more defines what he means by 'school' than Keyser explains 'guild', so we are in the dark as to his intention, but his usage seems casual. He cannot have meant it in the way he wanted his readers to understand the term 'Norman school'.[17] That was a 'Romanesque school' as constructed and debated in 19th-century France. What was in, what was out, and whether it existed may have been points of contention, but French Romanesque schools endured for generations and were not confined to sculpture.[18] If anything, Clapham used 'school' to link a group of carved tympana in Herefordshire in much the same way the word was loosely used by 20th-century London art dealers to group unsigned works into stylistic circles. The term stuck, and the following year Arthur Gardner, in his commendably short and well-written 'handbook', took Kilpeck as 'the most conspicuous example of the school' and assembled a list of 'productions of this school' to put alongside it; namely the fonts at Eardisley, Chaddesley Corbett, and Castle Frome, and tympana at Rowlstone, Ruardean, Brinsop, Fownhope, and Shobdon, together with other sculpture at these same sites.[19]

This was how matters stood when George Zarnecki entered the discussion. Publication of the Herefordshire School over the second half of the 20th century was dominated by Zarnecki. The sculpture formed a substantial part of his doctoral thesis, and though Zarnecki never published his thesis, he synthesized and summarized much of it in two short books that came hard on its heels.[20] The Herefordshire School fell into the second of these books, where, with great clarity, Zarnecki laid out his thoughts in seven short pages.[21] He pointed to the relevance of architectural sculpture that had hitherto eluded mention at Aston (Herefordshire) and Rock (Worcestershire) and argued that three different sculptors could be detected at Shobdon and Kilpeck, one of whom he thought originated to the north and had first worked at Aston.[22] The workshop was a union of three sculptors, and they first came together at Shobdon. Work at Aston and Rock preceded this, and some work, the font at Stottesdon for example, may have been produced later and may have been by just the one sculptor.[23] Most importantly, he saw a direct relationship between the chancel entry at Kilpeck and the Puerta de las Platerias at Santiago

FIGURE 14.2

Kilpeck, St Mary: chancel entry, left jamb (John McNeill)

FIGURE 14.3

Santiago de Compostela, Cathedral: Puerta de las Platerias, left jamb of portal (Ramón Yzquierdo Peiró)

de Compostela (Figures 14.2 and 14.3) and between the tympana at Stretton Sugwas and Brinsop and the west front of Parthenay-le-Vieux (Deux-Sèvres).[24] Zarnecki decided this came about as the result of sketches made by a sculptor who travelled with Oliver de Merlimond to Santiago.[25] This sculptor he christened the 'Chief Master'. In Zarnecki's mind, the pilgrimage to Santiago was paramount and primary. Shobdon was the crucible of the Herefordshire School and Shobdon he thought 'most likely' to date between 1138 and 1143.[26]

There was an obvious chronological problem with this dating scheme, however. If Kilpeck was built around the time of its 1134 transfer to the Abbey of St Peter at Gloucester, 1138–43 was too late for Zarnecki's purposes. By the 1980s, Zarnecki's chronological model was starting to look strained anyway. He had already settled on earlier dates for several examples of English Romanesque sculpture at the Hayward Gallery's exhibition of English Romanesque Art, so the solution was to bring forward Shobdon as well, and in various articles he published in the 1990s, Zarnecki claimed that Oliver de Merlimond made his pilgrimage *c.* 1125 and that Shobdon had been consecrated in 1131 or 1132.[27] But this simply created another problem. Was it acceptable to admit the Wigmore Chronicle's account, highlighting Oliver de Merlimond's pilgrimage and the consecration of the church at Shobdon by Robert de Bethune, while dismissing the chronicle's claim that the events it recounts took place in the reign of King Stephen (1135–54)?[28] This was picked up by other scholars. First, Jim King argued that Kilpeck was earlier than Shobdon.[29] Then John Hunt questioned all moves towards an early dating for the Herefordshire School, and in a wide-ranging survey argued that the sculpture should be seen as developing over a period of roughly 30 years, between the mid-1130s and the 1160s, drawing attention to the relevance of martial and warlike imagery during the unsettled late 1130s and 1140s.[30] A new chapter was also opened with Malcolm Thurlby's publication of a book specifically devoted to the Herefordshire School.[31] Thurlby adopted an approach pioneered by Eileen Robertson Hamer – that the monuments wherein sculpture by the Herefordshire School are found should be grouped according to the holders of the land.[32] He was happy with Zarnecki's dating model, in the first edition of the book at least (reversing his views on which came first – Shobdon or Kilpeck – in the 2013 edition), and produced a remarkably accommodating account of the workshop's artistic background and influence that ran to 398 illustrations in the second edition.[33] Thurlby's inclusive method rarely accords importance to one parallel over another, but in the more recent study he does produce visual evidence to argue a case that he had earlier suggested: that work on the eastern bays of the nave of Hereford Cathedral was important in the formation of the Herefordshire School.[34]

DATING

The Herefordshire School

Few documentary dates are provided for churches associated with the Herefordshire School. The best-known is the earliest. According to the *Historia et Cartularium Monasterii Sancti Petri Gloucestriae*, Hugh, son of William FitzNorman, gave the church of St David at Kilpeck, together with the chapel of St Mary in the castle, to the abbey of St Peter at Gloucester in 1134, while Walter de Lacy was abbot (1130–39).[35] It is rare for charters recording the transfer of churches to monastic institutions to record whether the local church was recently built before it was conveyed or whether the monastic institution itself took responsibility for the physical construction or reconstruction, and the Gloucester chronicle says nothing about the physical condition of the church at Kilpeck.[36] However, it seems likely that it was complete by 1134 or at least that it was nearing completion by this date. The later confirmation charter shows that Hugh took a continuing and close interest in the church.[37]

In 1136, Miles of Gloucester granted land on the edge of Gloucester to a community of Augustinian canons from Llanthony, refugees from Welsh raids, where they founded a daughter-house known as Llanthony Secunda. Llanthony had been founded *c.* 1118, and encouragement either from Miles or from Robert de Bethune, who, before he was made bishop of Hereford, had been prior of Llanthony Prima (*c.* 1123–31), may have prompted Ralph de Baskerville, a recent recipient of Miles of Gloucester's largesse, to grant the churches of Eardisley and Stretton Sugwas to Llanthony Secunda.[38] The grant was confirmed by Pope Innocent II in April 1142.[39]

Hereford Cathedral was occupied by Geoffrey Talbot in 1140, in alliance with Miles of Gloucester, an operation which saw the cathedral used as an instrument of war.[40] The bishop, Robert de Bethune, remained loyal to King Stephen through 1140 and was forced out of Hereford, though during his exile he was able to arrange an exchange of land in Hereford and gave eight acres to Gilbert Foliot, Abbot of Gloucester, for the building of a new church of St Guthlac.[41] This was outside the city walls and some way to the north of the earlier site. At some point early in 1141, probably after King Stephen's defeat and imprisonment at the Battle of Lincoln on 2 February, Bishop Robert of Bethune went over to Matilda's side and was able to reclaim his cathedral. The church of St Guthlac was then amalgamated with St Peter at Hereford, forming a dependent priory of St Peter's at Gloucester, which was formally recognised in 1143.[42] In a charter dated to between 1148 and 1155, Roger, earl of Hereford, gave land previously forming part of the honour of Walter de Lacy outside St Owen's Gate in Hereford to St Guthlac's priory.[43] This is the land on which the hospital of St Giles stood.

Shobdon is the subject of a foundation story, carried in the Wigmore Chronicle, which limits the dates at which the church could have been built.[44] The prologue opens with a statement that what follows is an account of the foundation of Wigmore Abbey, whose origins are then traced to the church at Shobdon, while the account proper opens with the words, 'In the time of King Stephen'.[45] It could therefore be argued that since Victorine canons were introduced after the church was built, the restriction to Stephen's reign only applies to Shobdon's status as a monastery – i.e. the period after Victorine canons were sent from Paris. However, the implication of the account's opening words is that the events immediately described belong to the reign of Stephen and the account opens with the building of the church at Shobdon. This last is the interpretation followed here. Henry I died on 1 December 1135, and while Stephen came over to England quickly and was crowned on 22 December, a start on Shobdon before 1136 can be ruled out if one follows the line taken above. The *terminus ante quem* for the church's completion is provided by the death of Miles of Gloucester in 1143 in a hunting accident.[46] The Wigmore Chronicle is a rich source of information, and the main lines of its narrative repay rehearsal.

The Chronicle traces the origins of the Victorine abbey of Wigmore back to a church originally founded at Shobdon by Oliver de Merlimond, the steward and former tutor to Hugh de Mortimer, lord of Wigmore. It tells us that Oliver held land at Ledicote by right of birth and that Hugh had given him the neighbouring *vill* of Shobdon while also presenting Oliver's son, Odo, with the living of the church at Aymestry.[47] Since there was then no parish church at Shobdon, simply a wooden chapel subject to Aymestry, Oliver resolved that a new church should be built. Having arranged for Shobdon's independence on payment of an annual pension of two shillings, Oliver undertook the construction of the church, but as he wished to undertake a pilgrimage to Santiago ('*de prendre le vyage al seinct Jakes en pelrimage*'), he confided responsibility for the work at Shobdon, together with the necessary funds ('*tota la cure del overayne od espenses necessaires*') to a knight, Bernard.[48] Oliver reached Santiago, and on his return he lodged at the abbey of Saint-Victor in Paris before crossing back to England. Then, when the church at Shobdon was wholly complete ('*quant sa eglise fut tote parfete*'), he approached Robert of Bethune, bishop of Hereford (1131–48) and humbly asked that he consecrate it.[49] It was only after this had happened that Oliver began assembling an endowment with a view to introducing a small community of canons from Saint-Victor to the church. His first request was refused, but once he had secured the active support of Robert of Bethune, himself a former Augustinian abbot, Gilduin, Abbot of Saint-Victor, agreed to despatch two canons. Oliver then vested the canons with the promised endowment, and the canons were installed in a house adjacent to the church ('*un mesun assez honeste pres de l'eglise*').[50]

Things began to sour thereafter, and the rest of the chronicle is a depressing account of quarrels, broken promises, and exile. From our point of view, the most significant of these disputes are those that pitched the bishop, Robert de Bethune, against the earl of Hereford,

Miles of Gloucester, and the great and violent quarrel (*'un discord trop grant et hidous'*) that alienated Hugh de Mortimer I from Oliver de Merlimond.[51] Both these quarrels took place in 1143.

By early 1143, Miles was short of funds, and in order to continue supplying troops for Matilda's cause, he imposed a levy on the churches of Herefordshire.[52] Robert de Bethune objected, excommunicated Miles, and placed the city of Hereford under interdict. The Wigmore Chronicle tells us that, at Oliver de Merlimond's suggestion, the bishop then came to Shobdon and lived with the canons at his own expense until such time as he was reconciled with the earl and returned to the city. The cause of Oliver de Merlimond's estrangement from Hugh de Mortimer I is left unsaid. The chronicle says nothing about the issues at stake, merely noting that the dispute began shortly after the quarrel between Miles and Robert of Bethune (*'bien tost après'*) and that Oliver left Hugh and allied himself with Miles, who at that time was his friend (*'que esteit adunke son amy entire'*).[53] When Hugh realised this, he summoned Oliver and when Oliver failed to appear, fearing Hugh's malice and cruelty (*'la malice et la cruelté de son seigneur'*), Hugh seized his possessions, including those that had been made over to the canons.

It is not difficult to understand why Hugh de Mortimer moved against Oliver, however. When Robert de Bethune was driven out of the see of Hereford in 1140, he remained loyal to King Stephen. Early in 1141 he switched sides. If Oliver was able to shelter the bishop and broker a settlement with Miles, he must have switched sides as well.[54] Hugh, along with most of the barons in the far north of Herefordshire, remained loyal to the king. As Shobdon was in a territory largely loyal to Stephen, midway between the Lacy honour at Weobley and the Mortimer stronghold of Wigmore, its position was precarious. Matters came to a head with the death of Robert de Bethune in April 1148. Whatever hope the canons entertained that their lives would improve seem to have been diminished by this, prompting the English prior-elect, Robert, to reflect on his position. He was now permanently deprived of the bishop's counsel, Oliver de Merlimond was unable to support him, and he was maligned by Hugh de Mortimer I (*'ledengé et avily par sire Hugh de Mortemer'*). It was too much to bear, and at some time between April and July 1148 Robert returned to Paris.[55] Though there was an attempt to move to Aymestry, and a Victorine abbey did ultimately re-emerge at Wigmore, the summer of 1148 effectively marks the end of Shobdon as the viable seat of a Victorine community.

One other group of churches has a general bearing on the issue of date and indeed patronage for the Herefordshire School. A workshop known by analogy with the Herefordshire School as the 'Dymock School' was active at a broadly similar date, their output being concentrated along the borders of Gloucestershire and Herefordshire, to the south of Ledbury.[56] The sculpture associated with the Dymock School is simpler than that of the Herefordshire School and appreciably more repetitive. It favours two elements in particular; a volute capital with a stepped tongue descending along an angle, and a tympanum featuring a centralised and symmetrical tree (Figure 14.4).

FIGURE 14.4

Dymock, St Mary: south portal tympanum (John McNeill)

The most distinguished surviving church for which the workshop provided the sculpture, St Mary's, Kempley, was the subject of dendrochronological analysis in 1998. This initially yielded a felling date of between 1114 and 1144 for the west door and *c.* 1120–50 for the roof, though Dan Miles was subsequently able to narrow the date brackets for the construction of the roof to 1128–32.[57] As it happens, Kempley is the earliest timber roof still standing in England. An outlier among the Dymock School churches, the chapel of St James, Postlip (Gloucestershire) was founded *'tempore hostilitatis'* according to a charter confirming the grant of the chapel to Winchcombe Abbey.[58] Postlip is east of the river Severn and was unaffected by the Welsh Uprising of 1136, so the hostilities will have fallen between 1139 and 1148 and most likely between 1139 and 1144.[59]

The evidence suggests that the Dymock School was probably in existence before the Herefordshire School but that their work overlapped. The chronology and topography help explain how they occasionally share compositions – the tympanum over the south portal at Kilpeck is the outstanding example.

Thus the Herefordshire School evidently formed in a period of peace, sometime before 1134, and endured periods of violence and disruption; it was active at some point between 1136 and 1143 at Shobdon, *c.* 1142 at Eardisley and Stretton Sugwas, and after 1148 for the Hospital of St Giles.[60] Because war is seen as inimical to church building, there has been a tendency to discount dates between the Welsh uprising of 1136 and the early 1140s in relation to Herefordshire School work.[61] However, as William of Newburgh remarked, '[I]t is remarkable that a much greater number of monasteries, for both sexes, were founded in England, during the short time that Stephen reigned, or, more properly speaking, obtained the title of king, than had been for a century preceding'.[62] Jonathan Turnock has also drawn attention to the 'boom in building work and sculptural patronage during the 1140s' in neighbouring Gloucestershire.[63] Charter or chronicle evidence for Postlip, Upleadon, and Beckford make clear that the churches or chapels there were built as the result of hostilities. Turnock even argues that the

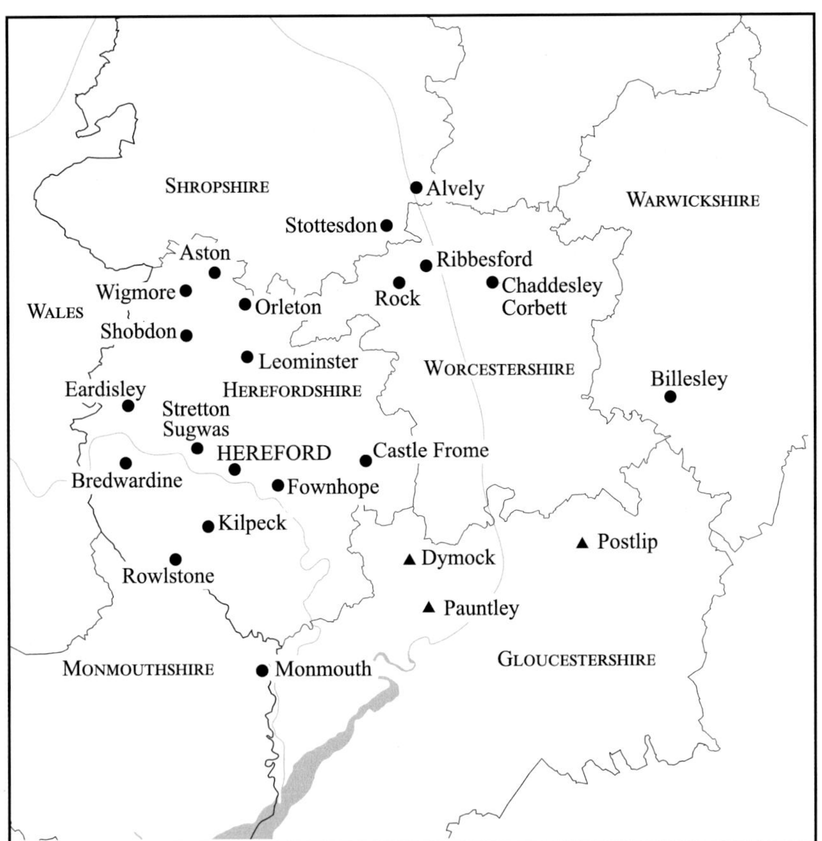

FIGURE 14.5

Map of sites mentioned in the text: Herefordshire School sites marked with dots; Dymock School sites marked with triangles (Chris Kennish)

nave of the church of St John the Baptist at Beckford (formerly Gloucestershire, now Worcestershire) is the oratory built by the canons of Ste-Barbe-en-Auge (Normandy) on their return following the hostile seizure of the manor of Beckford by William Beauchamp *c.* 1141.[64] The Ste-Barbe Chronicle maintains the canons deliberately positioned the oratory within the protective boundary of the priory, and as the priory was around 60 m north-east of the surviving parochial nave, it is entirely possible this was indeed the oratory built by the canons. If so, it draws attention to the likelihood that some of the structures built for the relief of parishioners either during or immediately after outbreaks of violence were substantial masonry chapels. Beckford was a two-cell design with an elaborate chancel arch and tympana over the north and south nave portals.[65] Bishops and monastic patrons regularly founded cemeteries of refuge with unlicensed chapels to offer sanctuary during the 1140s.[66] There was a well-documented group south of Leominster, for example, which became sufficiently established to warrant a letter from Pope Adrian IV (1154–58), writing on behalf of Reading Abbey, pointing out that chapels erected in time of war should not prejudice the rights of its parish churches.[67] The point is that what might have been regarded as temporary or emergency structures such as these were solid and durable. Parish church building was on an upswing during the first half of the 12th century anyway, and though it is likely that hostilities interrupted work at a local level, at least for the immediate duration of the violence, there is no evidence for a cessation of building between 1136 and the early 1150s. If anything, the circumstances of war favoured church building.[68]

PATRONAGE

The majority of churches with sculpture by the Herefordshire School are local churches (Figure 14.5). There is just one instance of work on a monastic church which may have been co-ordinated by outside parties – the Herefordshire School provided sculpture for the west front of the priory at Leominster which had been refounded by Henry I and given to Reading Abbey.[69] No other building campaigns seem to have been anything other than locally resourced, for although the tympanum reset in a wall by St Giles Hospital in Hereford was on land granted to St Guthlac's, Bishop Robert de Bethune was involved in arranging compensation for the destruction of the earlier site of St Guthlac. As Roger, earl of Hereford's, grant of the land on the which the hospital stood was awarded in the company of the next bishop of Hereford, Gilbert Foliot, it is likely the bishops of Hereford retained an interest. The jurisdiction and status of the hospital in the 12th century is unclear. John Leland described it as 'a Chapell of St Gyles, first founded for Lazers, now converted to the use of other poor folke. The Burgesses be Patrons of it'.[70] One should also perhaps attach a caveat to the sculpture at Billesley (Warwickshire), Alveley (Shropshire), and Monmouth. This is loose, or repositioned, and its initial setting is uncertain.[71] But at every other site where there is work that can be associated with the Herefordshire School, the sculpture is either *in situ* or its original disposition is obvious. In all these cases, the buildings in question are parish churches.[72]

As it is widely held that most rural 11th- and 12th-century parish churches were built at the behest of local lords, the hunt has been on to identify the patrons.[73] Eileen Robertson Hamer devoted a thesis to this question, and lay patronage of church building was taken up by Jonathan Turnock in a recent thesis on Gloucestershire over a similar period.[74] However, the patterns which emerge from the data are not especially clear. Recent studies have been too narrowly framed to answer whether and why patrons favour one sculptural workshop over another. They have either taken a particular style of sculpture as a starting point, without examining the existence and viability of alternative local styles and workshops, or they have examined the apparent preferences of the patrons within geographical boundaries that neither coincide with the land holdings of major tenants nor the working practices of sculptural workshops. This has been compounded by a tendency to err in two directions. On the one hand, as the identity of the holder of a manor at a given date is often uncertain, scholars are drawn to the names and not the lacunae.[75] On the other hand, the filter for many studies of 12th-century architectural sculpture is a particular sort of sculpture, so patrons who do not commission buildings that conform are excluded. Take, for instance, the three barons cited as attendant on Miles of Gloucester as earl of Hereford in Matilda's grant of the earldom: Robert de Chandos of Snodhill, Richard de Cormeilles of Tarrington, and Hugh of Kilpeck.[76] Hugh, we believe, was responsible for the church of Kilpeck, whose abundant sculpture is described below. Richard de Cormeilles was responsible for the church of Tarrington, generously equipped with two nave portals and a chancel arch but sparingly detailed, and Robert de Chandos was responsible for Peterchurch, a magnificently spacious four-cell church with virtually no sculpture to speak of.[77] These are very different parish churches built within a generation by three barons who knew one another and attended the earl of Hereford's court. They could constitute a study in contrasting outcomes. To be convincing, a survey aimed at weighing the limits to patronal influence should take account of every church on all the manors of more than one significant landholder.[78]

As the focus of this paper is workshop practice, however, it should be stressed that though the evidence for positive workshop preference is limited, it does exist. A striking example is the deployment of sculptors from the Dymock School to provide the sculpture for both St John at Pauntley and the chapel of St James at Postlip.[79] The buildings are 30 km apart, on opposite sides of the River Severn. But whereas Pauntley is close to several other churches with sculpture by the Dymock School, Postlip is not. What appears to link the two is that the respective manors were held by William de Solers at the likely date of construction.[80] It is much more difficult to see a preference for one group of sculptors over another if one moves up the patronal scale to the level of Miles of Gloucester and his son Roger.

In order to shed some light on this, we require a detour into the fickle patterns of manorial tenure in early 12th-century Herefordshire. Miles of Gloucester came from a family of royal administrators with land in Gloucestershire, Herefordshire, and Monmouthshire.[81] The principal offices they held were those of castellan of Gloucester and sheriff of Gloucestershire, but the family also developed responsibilities in south Wales. On his marriage to Sybil, daughter of Bernard de Neufmarché, in 1121, Miles became lord of Brecon.[82] He succeeded his father as sheriff of Gloucestershire *c.* 1126, and by 1130 had become sheriff of Staffordshire as well. Along with another royal servant, Pain *fitz* John, sheriff of Herefordshire and Shropshire, he dominated royal administration in the south-west midlands. The two are coupled in the *Gesta Stephani*, which accuses them of operating in a harsh and acquisitive manner.[83] They were also linked through the legacy of the Lacy family. In 1115 King Henry I approved the marriage of Pain *fitz* John to Sybil Talbot, niece and heiress to Hugh I de Lacy.[84] This brought over seventy manors scattered across Herefordshire and Shropshire under Pain's control, along with three significant castles at Ludlow, Weobley, and Ewyas Lacy. But as Pain was killed in a Welsh ambush in 1137, and King Stephen allowed Sybil Talbot to remarry, the old Lacy barony did not remain undivided. The northern manors around Ludlow were stripped out. Nevertheless, Stephen approved the marriage of Miles of Gloucester's son, Roger, to Cecily, the daughter of Pain and Sybil Talbot, meaning that many of the Herefordshire manors went to Roger.[85] A mere two years after his son's marriage, Miles of Gloucester deserted the king and switched his allegiance to Matilda, being rewarded with the title earl of Hereford in 1141. Two years after that, Miles was killed in a hunting accident, and his son, Roger, succeeded to his lands and the title, earl of Hereford.[86]

By 1143, the majority of landholders in Herefordshire were united in their support of Matilda, the exception being a handful in the north and west, of whom the most significant were Hugh de Mortimer at Wigmore and William de Braose at Radnor and Kington.[87] It does not follow that the tenants on the former Lacy estates were themselves united, however, or at one with Miles or Roger of Gloucester. A disinherited son, Gilbert de Lacy, along with his kinsman, Geoffrey Talbot, had managed to regain control of Weobley, and many of the former Lacy tenants supported Gilbert de Lacy's claim to the Lacy estates.[88] There were thus three rivals with designs on more of the Lacy barony than they were individually able to control. Joce de Dinan in Ludlow, Gilbert de Lacy in Weobley, and Roger in Hereford. The enmity that existed between them was entirely separate to whatever loyalty they felt to Matilda or Stephen.

This is the unstable world in which the Herefordshire School worked. It raises difficult questions as to how barons with substantial numbers of manors allotted resources among their manorial estates and how decisions on parish church building were taken. To return to Miles of Gloucester and his son Roger, all three churches in their manor of Great Barrington (Gloucestershire) – Great Barrington, Little Barrington, and Windrush – were rebuilt between *c.* 1135 and *c.* 1160.[89] Only the sculpture at Windrush survives, but it is carved from Taynton stone and relates to portal designs in Oxfordshire.[90] The church at Barnsley (Gloucestershire), built as a chapel of Bibury on a manor held by Miles and Roger, dates from before 1151 and employed two sculptural workshops. The internal sculpture is similar to the sculpture at the west end of the nave of St Peter's, Gloucester (now Gloucester Cathedral), while the corbel table is by a different workshop which seems to have been responsible for several churches in the Cotswolds.[91] Quenington (Gloucestershire), built on another manor held by right of marriage by Roger of Gloucester, is different again, with tympana over both the north and south nave portals carved by a workshop also responsible for South Cerney.[92] The churches that Miles or Roger had built on their Gloucestershire manors varied in the amounts of sculpture they demanded. Nor is there a clear consistency in its type or application.[93]

Of the manors in Herefordshire which may have passed into Roger's hands following his marriage to Cecily – and there is uncertainty about how many of these he controlled – two, Rowlstone and Castle Frome, contain sculpture by the Herefordshire School, while other manors which he is assumed to have inherited from his father, such as English Bicknor or Mansel Lacy, contain sculpture from the second quarter of the 12th century which has nothing to do with the Herefordshire School.[94] There is no evident concern to cultivate a particular workshop here on Miles's or Roger's parts. Among the major landholders, only the Mortimers stand out, where among surviving churches Aston, Orleton, Rock, and Ribbesford all contain Herefordshire School sculpture. Aston and Orleton are close to the Mortimer's principal residence at Wigmore, while Ribbesford and Rock were held from the Mortimers by Walter de Ribbesford.[95] Shobdon is considered below, but the manor had been granted to Oliver de Merlimond by Hugh de Mortimer in the first place.

In general, it seems to be at the level of the lesser tenant, among 'the knightly class', that one can detect workshop preference, though this may not be saying much more than that the key determinant was locality. The most striking candidate is Ralph de Baskerville. Like William de Solers at Postlip and Pauntley and Walter de Ribbesford at Ribbesford and Rock, Ralph de Baskerville held a handful of manors – five when he acceded to his father's estates: Eardisley, Stretton Sugwas, Brobury, Yazor, and Yarsop, to which he added Orcop, Treaddow, and Westfield (all Herefordshire). The latter were granted by Miles and Roger of Gloucester in or shortly after 1137.[96] He was also in possession of the manor of Bredwardine by the early 1140s. In a confirmation charter issued by Pope Innocent II on 30 April 1142, we learn that Ralph had given the churches or chapels of Eardisley, Yazor, Stretton Sugwas, Cusop, and Orcop, along with various specified tithes to the priory of Llanthony Secunda.[97] The church at Orcop is 13th century, and Yazor only survives in a late medieval (and ruinous) form. However, Eardisley and Stretton Sugwas retain significant work by the Herefordshire School, and although the only sculpture to survive at Cusop is a carved impost on one side of the chancel arch, the impost uses a Herefordshire School pattern.[98] Put another way, every one of the churches Ralph gave to Llanthony Secunda which retain 12th-century fabric contain sculpture by the Herefordshire School. Ralph de Baskerville's inherited honour was relatively compact. The patrimonial estates lay west of Hereford, and the acquisition of Bredwardine consolidated his hold on lands around Eardisley and Brobury. Cusop is a western outlier, right on the border with the lordship of Brecknock. The estates Ralph acquired at Orcop, Treaddow, and Westfield after 1137 are at a significant remove and are potentially relevant to the commissioning of new work. Not only did they bring new resources, they are in Archenfield, south of Hereford.[99] Orcop is within 8 km of Kilpeck.[100]

Patronage at a knightly level tends to be subregional, although, as with William de Solers or, following his advancement, Ralph de Baskerville, knights might find themselves with holdings that are 30 or 40 km apart. If one takes a bottom-up approach to the question of patronage and considers it in terms of workshop recruitment, the results point to different means and motives. For William de Solers, the Dymock School was simply the established local workshop. He liked it, and either he or whoever acted for him asked them to produce sculpture for a church at some remove from their base. The fact that the area around Postlip was the scene of recent and continuing violence may have been a contributory factor. For Ralph de Baskerville, it seems likely he became aware of the Herefordshire School after he acquired interests in Archenfield, and the decision to commission the workshop to produce sculpture for Eardisley and Stretton Sugwas was directly inspired by his sight of Kilpeck. For Walter de Ribbesford, the most probable link is that he was introduced to the Herefordshire School through the administrative offices of his tenant in chief, Hugh de Mortimer.[101]

Whether there are conclusions to be drawn from this is questionable. At best, the evidence is unequal. Far more can be said about the buildings than can be deduced as to the wishes of the patron. The evidence presented here suggests that at the level of the tenant in chief, the fact of parish church building was more important than the detail, whereas subtenants developed loyalties to specific regional or local workshops.[102]

FORMATION

Even taking into account the establishment of a priory at Kilpeck following the 1134 grant of the church to St Peter's at Gloucester, there is nothing in the local circumstances to account for the appearance of such extraordinary sculpture. Neither of the major set pieces, a chancel entry with carved saints on the jambs and a portal which juxtaposes two supports of a different section beneath a single capital, is known to have been repeated in Romanesque England (Figures 14.1, 14.2, 14.7–14.9 and Colour Plate XV).[103] However, both history and style suggest Kilpeck is the Herefordshire School's earliest surviving independent commission.

The church sits to the north-west of an open space otherwise bounded by an outer castle bailey and a post-medieval house known as Kilpeck Court. The castle and the village were planned together and are thought to have been first established between *c.* 1075 and *c.* 1100 under William *fitz* Norman.[104] As space was made for a church on the current site, the first building was presumably of timber, with the same true of the original tower and palisade on the castle motte.[105] This arrangement of castle, house, and church around an open public space is a striking piece of Anglo-Norman planning, and though ownership of the predecessor to Kilpeck Court is unknown, the holder of the manor is the obvious candidate as the proprietor of castle, church, *and* Kilpeck Court prior to 1134. Kilpeck Court certainly had nothing to do with the priory. That was built 350 m to the south-east of the church, beyond the village boundary.[106] The secondary positioning of the priory suggests that the initiative for the construction of a stone church came from the manorial lord and occupant of Kilpeck Court and was underway in advance of its transfer to Gloucester in 1134. By then, Kilpeck was held by Hugh, son of William *fitz* Norman (also known as Hugh of Kilpeck). He was one of three barons nominated to be attendant on the earl of Hereford in Matilda's grant of the earldom to Miles of Gloucester, though a relative measure of Hugh's resources is that his two fellow barons commanded knight service from nineteen and ten fees respectively. Hugh commanded service from one and a half.[107] As was said previously, the local circumstances were relatively modest.

Zarnecki thought he could detect 'at least three different hands at work' on the church.[108] One he called the 'Chief Master' and believed him responsible for the six figures on the jambs of the chancel arch, as well as a number of corbels, particularly of heads arranged along the west side of the church facing the castle. A second he called the 'Aston Master', as he thought he had earlier worked at Pipe Aston, well to the north near Wigmore. This sculptor was responsible for the four left-hand roundels of the outer order of the south portal and the magnificent serpents of the outer jambs (Figures 14.6 and 14.8–14.9). The inner order of the south portal, along with the rest of the outer order, was the work of a sculptor from Reading Abbey (Figure 14.6).[109] Zarnecki's division of the workshop into constituent hands, with principal sculptors taking on the most prominent sculpture, is not an approach many scholars would now pursue, in part because it is impossible to prove empirically, in part because the evidence suggests that specialist architectural sculptors worked in small teams and collaborated on particular capitals or jambs.[110] There are, however, discernible differences in handling in most substantial 12th-century sculptural *ateliers*, and if we are to investigate workshop organization, a discussion of the division of hands is a reasonable place to start.

While judgements will be inevitably subjective, the main disagreements I have with Zarnecki's attributions are over the assignment of parts and the background of the sculptors involved. The precisely outlined forms, drilled irises, and small-scale detailing of the motifs used on the voussoirs and most of the outer order, for example, seem to me more likely to be the work of a sculptor from Old Sarum than to have anything to do with Reading. I also do not share Zarnecki's ambivalence as to whether the half-columnar element of Kilpeck's jambs is by the same sculptor as the outer serpents. The south portal jambs are characterized by smooth, rounded forms of extraordinary plasticity. So powerfully sculptural are they that the underlying architectonic skeleton has been part dissolved. The liberties taken with the relief planes are too insistent to have been designed and worked on by more than one sculptor. Beyond this, there are overlaps within and between the finishing of many of the carved elements, and it is doubtful the individual sculptors strictly segregated their work. The capitals of the south portal have more in common with the voussoirs than the jambs, for instance, while, moving in the opposite direction, the motif between the ears of the outer order label-stops has less in common with the sculptor responsible for the rest of the voussoirs and more in common with the sculptor who carved the jambs. In addition, many of the corbels have been smoothed into shape but are sparingly detailed and have a soapy quality far removed from the south portal or chancel arch. These are not the work of the principal sculptors, and there must have been a pool of assistants or non-specialist mason carvers within the workshop at this stage, who took on some of the minor sculpture.

Given what survives of Anglo-Norman sculpture over the first third of the 12th century, three strands establish the sculptors' credentials. The most significant is Hereford Cathedral. The use of animal masks to join beaded roundels in the outer order of the south portal arch, the foliage design of the right half-column, and the interlace patterns used on the west window at Kilpeck relate directly to work at Hereford Cathedral, where these motifs appear in the crossing and eastern two bays of the nave (Figure 14.10).[111] This sculpture forms the immediate local background to Kilpeck's south portal, while the work of the Chief Master is essentially a development of the type of figurative work found in Hereford's central apse capitals.[112] Wreath-like circular foliate designs were used on the Hereford apse and make a return at certain Herefordshire School commissions, in addition to which there is some sculpture from the cathedral, most notably a damaged capital featuring two affronted birds from the north choir aisle (Figure 14.11) which broadly parallels the carved birds at Herefordshire School sites such as Rowlstone and Castle Frome.[113] Taken together, the evidence suggests that at least two of the sculptors at Kilpeck had previously worked at Hereford Cathedral. However, it is important to qualify this. Plenty of motifs

FIGURE 14.6
Kilpeck, St Mary: south portal tympanum (John McNeill)

FIGURE 14.7
Kilpeck, St Mary: chancel entry (John McNeill)

at Kilpeck cannot be found at Hereford, and the handling is very different. The sculpture is contained by the architecture at Hereford in a way that it is not at Kilpeck.

The second strand concerns Old Sarum (Figures 14.12–14.14). These parallels are well-known, but it is worth pointing out that they are highly selective. Most surviving carved stonework from Old Sarum is geometric and seems to have been of no interest to the Herefordshire School.[114] The similarities that exist, however, are arresting and are found in a handful of corbels excavated from Old Sarum Cathedral along with another composition by a Sarum team of sculptors – the north portal of All Saints, Lullington (Somerset).[115] Both sites throw up carvings that are close to particular corbels at Kilpeck, and the parallels extend to the voussoirs of the south portal. One aspect specifically links Old Sarum with Kilpeck; the multiplication of concentric or parallel contours around eyes, mouths, and across cheeks. These are treated in an identical way, in that the rounded contours above the eye are cut as flat receding planes, whereas the lines around the mouth consist of multiple narrow ridges. It is sufficiently close to suggest a working familiarity with architectural sculpture in or from Old Sarum on the part of the sculptor Zarnecki associated with Reading. There is something else at work in the Old Sarum style of sculpture as well, a compositional aspect that sits behind its surface finish. It is confined to the voussoirs and concerns the way in

FIGURE 14.8

Kilpeck, St Mary: south portal left jamb (John McNeill)

FIGURE 14.9

Kilpeck, St Mary: south portal right jamb (John McNeill)

several of the creatures are turned on themselves to form taut compositions akin to letters – S, O, D, and U shapes (Figure 14.6). As applied to arches, these forms are novel, and they first emerged in the Poitou and Saintonge during the 1120s.[116] The best parallels for Kilpeck are with the west front of Notre-Dame-la-Grande in Poitiers (see the third and fourth voussoirs to the right and the second from the left in Figure 14.6 and various voussoirs in the second and fourth orders of the central arch in Figure 14.22).[117] This raises a question to which – short of the discovery of new caches of Romanesque sculpture – there is no answer. Was a familiarity with Notre-Dame-la-Grande a feature of sculpture at Old Sarum? Or had a direct link opened between the Herefordshire School workshop and Poitiers by the early 1130s, before (as is argued here) renewed contact was made preparatory to Shobdon. The animated letter forms are distinctive, but they are also fairly simple.

The third strand is constructional and iconographic. Kilpeck's tympanum depicts the Tree of Life (Genesis 2^{8-9}; Revelation 2^{7}) and is cut from several stones, the lowest of which rests directly on the embrasures and is carved with a different pattern in the manner of a lintel. Both the construction and the imagery are features of the Dymock School.[118]

Kilpeck was granted to St Peter's, Gloucester in 1134, so if it was conveyed shortly after completion, a starting date between *c.* 1130 and *c.* 1132 is possible. As it is likely that two of the principal sculptors had worked at Hereford Cathedral, one possible scenario is that the Herefordshire School workshop formed as the result of a break in construction, though given the rather constrained and repetitive formats of the eastern nave capitals at Hereford and the facility with which forms overlap at Kilpeck, there is almost certainly a lost intermediary. This putative intermediary could have formed part of the cathedral; a south nave aisle portal, perhaps, or pulpitum screen, or it could have been elsewhere.[119] Hereford Cathedral was begun under Bishop Reynhelm (1107–15), while the tower which was occupied in 1140 as a platform from which to bombard the castle must have been the crossing tower.[120] Thus the eastern two bays of the nave, essential to buttress the crossing tower, were complete by 1140. At some date between the 1107–15 start and 1140, there was a break in building work. The archaeological evidence is now clearest in the third bay west of the crossing in the nave at arcade level.[121] The capitals of the nave bays west of this point are scallop capitals, whereas the capitals of the eastern two bays, along with the crossing, are varied. It is the originals of these capitals that were probably the work of at least one of the two sculptors responsible for Kilpeck's south portal. This shift in Hereford's sculptural vocabulary marks a pause in the building of the nave at a position which is not uncommon, as breaking the east-west sequence of building here allows for the construction of the lower stage of the crossing tower and roofing of the transepts.[122] Building work may not

FIGURE 14.10

Hereford Cathedral: detail of nave north arcade capital (John McNeill)

FIGURE 14.11

Hereford Cathedral: unlocalised respond capital (John McNeill)

FIGURE 14.12

Kilpeck, St Mary: apse corbel (John McNeill)

FIGURE 14.13

Old Sarum, Cathedral: excavated corbel (with kind permission of Salisbury Museum ©)

FIGURE 14.14

Lullington, All Saints: north portal voussoir (John McNeill)

FIGURE 14.15
Shobdon: chancel arch (G. R. Lewis)

have ceased altogether at Hereford but could have been switched to the lower stage of the crossing tower, though as the Romanesque crossing tower no longer survives, it is impossible now to determine the length, if any, of a pause in construction.

Notwithstanding those caveats, the see of Hereford Cathedral was vacant between 1127 and 1131, and that might have had an effect. By 1130, Pain *fitz* John and Miles of Gloucester were sufficiently concerned by the prolonged interregnum that they petitioned Henry I to appoint Robert de Bethune, then prior of Llanthony, to the see. Robert was initially unwilling, and only the intervention of Pope Innocent II persuaded Robert to accept. He was then consecrated bishop in June 1131.[123] Interregna are often disrupters of building work, and if this happened at Hereford, as comparable interregna closed down building campaigns elsewhere, it might have been the pretext that persuaded a small group of specialist architectural sculptors to branch out and take on work away from the cathedral.[124]

SHOBDON

All three of the principal sculptors who worked at Kilpeck also worked at Shobdon. The date at which they started was no earlier than 1136, while the church was complete by 1142 at the latest.[125] In terms of the demands made on the workshop, Shobdon was a step up from Kilpeck. The church called for two portals, each adorned with a monolithic figurative tympanum, and was designed with a chancel arch of striking breadth supported on six carved columns (Figure 14.15).[126] Assuming Shobdon was also built with a corbel table, the church will have deployed around twice the amount of architectural sculpture used at Kilpeck. The problem in assessing this is that Romanesque Shobdon was largely demolished in 1751–52, after which the chancel arch and two portals were re-erected to form a picturesque 'eye-catcher' around 400 m north of the original church.[127] These are now heavily eroded, and the sculptural detail is best seen in the drawings George Lewis published in 1852, though two points should be borne in mind when examining the carving in this way (Figure 14.16).[128] First, when it was recomposed in the 18th century, the arches of the two portals were separated from their tympana to form a five-part arrangement centred on the former chancel arch. Second, Lewis further isolated the arches in his drawings by representing them without their supporting columns and capitals. The Anglo-Norman compositional arrangement has thus been severely compromised. The removal and reconstruction of the carved set pieces from Romanesque Shobdon hinders any assessment of how well they were integrated into the building and makes it difficult to determine whether all the carved stonework – including the bread-and-butter Anglo-Norman geometric patterns used for the chancel arch – was provided by the Herefordshire School workshop. For that, one wants more of the incidental sculpture, particularly the window capitals. However, the nearly identical chancel arch at Rock (Worcestershire) does suggest that the Herefordshire School teamed up with a group of mason carvers at Shobdon, who dressed the ashlar and mass-produced the simpler geometric carving and mouldings (see Figure 14.28). Despite the losses, a lot of carving survives, and the approach evident at Kilpeck, whereby each of the principal sculptors takes responsibility for constituent parts while working across those same parts, is also evident at Shobdon. Thus Zarnecki's Chief Master sculptor carved both tympana, though the devil beneath the cross in the Harrowing of Hell tympanum could equally be the work of the sculptor responsible for the jambs at Kilpeck. The arches which formerly framed the tympana seem to have been primarily the work of the Chief and Aston Masters, with the more repetitive elements presumably portioned out to assistants. The columns supporting the chancel arch were shared between the principal sculptors, with obvious quotations from both the jambs and the outer order of voussoirs at Kilpeck on columns two and four (Figure 14.16a and b), namely the linked roundels and ribbed tunics, and what appears to be a merging of the styles of the two on column six (Figure 14.16c). The columns also see an increased role given to a foliage repertoire which had been in the background at Kilpeck, where it is confined to a few corbels and plaques, but which at Shobdon blossoms into the superbly controlled spirals of column one (Figure 14.16e). These are of a quality and discipline that would not be amiss in Rome, and they are joined in column three by an early example of the type of inhabited foliate column becoming popular in France and otherwise appearing in England at Wolvesey Palace and Lincoln Cathedral (Figure 14.16d).[129] All this suggests a renewal of models. Not only were figurative tympana

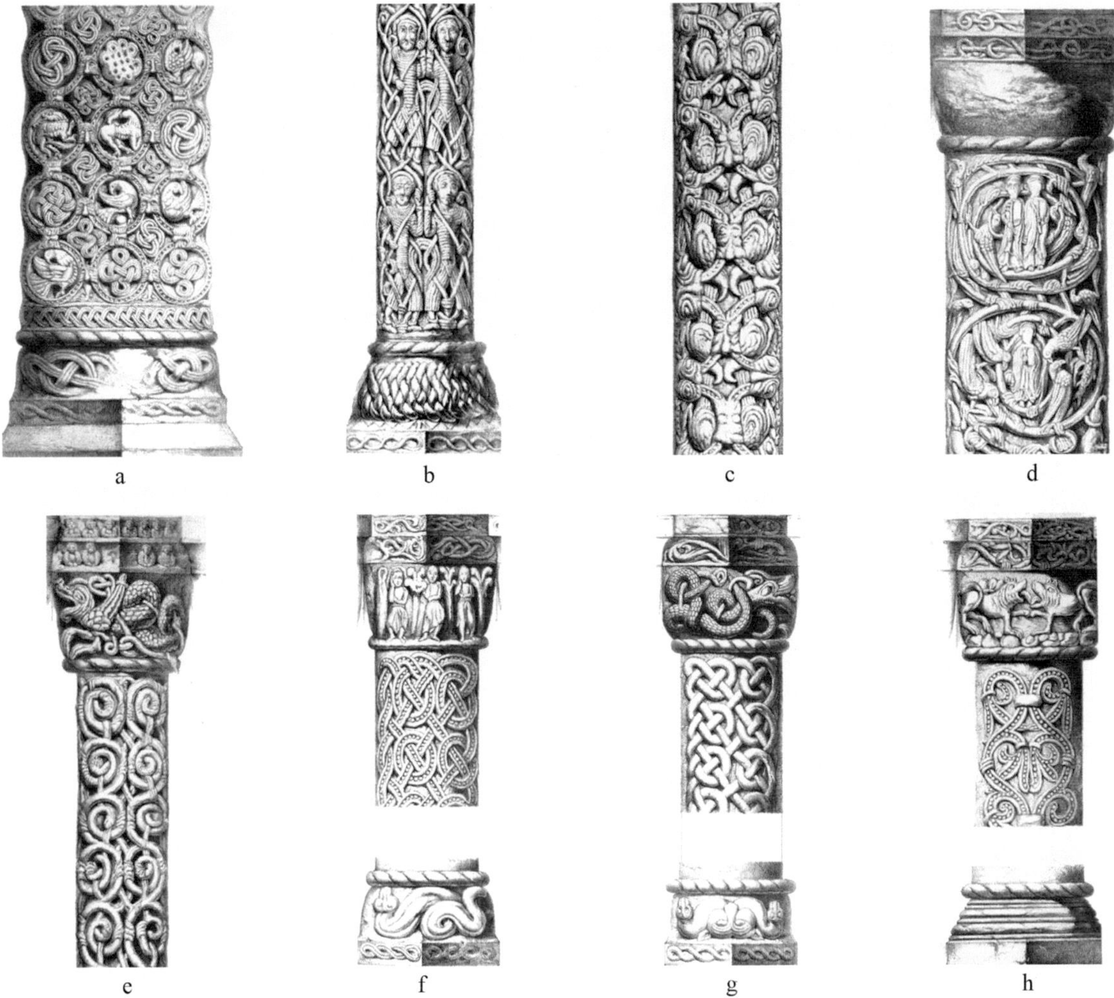

FIGURE 14.16

Shobdon: chancel arch columns (G. R. Lewis): (a) column 4; (b) column 2; (c) column 6; (d) column 3; (e) column 1; (f) left arch column 1; (g) left arch column 3; (h) right arch column 4.

absent from Kilpeck, the slender inhabited foliate column is a compositional type that is ultimately Antique and as a relatively newly revived architectural device it must have been encountered by the workshop before it was used at Shobdon. This is not intended to diminish the inventive capacity of the workshop or its preparedness to experiment. The adaptation of the Kilpeck repertoire to certain columns is both astonishing and unexpected, as is the extension of foliate and interlace designs to the bases. However, the workshop's virtuosic ability to transpose familiar motifs across forms is revealed precisely because of an increase in the formal range.

ENCOUNTERS WITH AQUITAINE

The *nec plus ultra* among Shobdon's new compositions is found on the portal arches (Figures 14.17 and 14.18). Radial voussoirs had been used at Kilpeck, but those at Shobdon are vastly more sophisticated and develop an aesthetic approach to arch composition that derives directly from western France. This aesthetic concerns the relationship between modularity, movement, and variety.[130] At Shobdon we are treated to four different approaches to the grouping of voussoirs around the two arches that originally contained the tympana. The inner order of the left arch is modular, repeating a single theme whereby each voussoir consists of a simple interlace pattern. The inner order of the right arch is a multi-motif arch. The middle order of the right arch is essentially a type of multi-motif arch with a notable tendency towards grouping individual voussoirs according to their subject (compare with Figure 14.19 and Colour Plate XVI (top)). Thus, the archivolt is divided into three parts by two pairs of embracing figures who are themselves reversed so that the outer figures advance inwards: splitting as 7 voussoirs (quadrupeds), 1 voussoir (embracers), 8 voussoirs (mostly figures), 1 voussoir (embracers), 7 voussoirs (fish and quadrupeds).[131] Finally, the middle order of the left arch takes a quadruped and pushes it through a variety of gymnastic poses, injecting a mesmerizing sense of movement into what is, essentially, a single subject. In the world of radial voussoir construction, that is a very adventurous thing to do.

FIGURE 14.17
Shobdon: right arch (G. R. Lewis)

FIGURE 14.18
Shobdon: left arch (G. R. Lewis)

Figure 14.19
Saint-Mandé-sur-Brédoire: south portal (Luke Purser)

Figure 14.20
Leyre, San Salvador: west portal archivolts (John McNeill)

The underlying approach to the arrangement of forms around an arch at Shobdon – the facility with which the shifting relationships among voussoirs, motifs, and orders are handled – is unparalleled in Anglo-Norman England. This is instructive, as there are instances elsewhere in Europe in which the compositional principle underlying the arrangement of voussoirs in an arch appears to be western French but where the carving can be shown to be by a local workshop. A case in point is the west portal at San Salvador de Leyre (Navarre) (Figure 14.20 and Colour Plate XVI (bottom)).[132] Though undated, this best fits the period around 1125. The arch at Leyre brings together a variety of different archivolt designs in an eye-catching demonstration of the potential of the radial voussoir. But the sculptors themselves are not western French. There is enough overlap between the motifs on the capitals and those of the voussoirs to show they are by a single workshop, while the capitals are closely related to a former portal from the Romanesque west front of Pamplona Cathedral whose sources in turn can be traced back to Toulouse and Santiago de Compostela.[133] Indeed, so close are the Leyre and Pamplona capitals that some of the same sculptors must have worked at both sites. This Leyre/Pamplona workshop could have originated anywhere along the '*camino*' between Toulouse and Santiago, but the likelihood is that they are local – and from Navarre.

The lesson of Leyre is that once the principles of varied radial voussoir construction had been understood, new variations might be initiated anywhere. Bridging the hollow, as happens in the inner order at Leyre, for instance, was not something that was done in Aquitaine, nor does one find creatures trapped behind rolls, as at Santa Maria de Uncastillo (Aragon) or a roll used as a bench, as at Morlaàs (Béarn).[134] Arches featuring elaborate and varied radial voussoirs initially came about through a process of combination anyway, the mixing of mouldings with geometric patterns, and were further developed in western France through the addition of foliate or animate motifs organized according to modular systems. Thus it is no surprise to find sculptural workshops beyond western France adapting the form by populating the arches with motifs they individually favoured. The process of adaptation was architectural as well as sculptural. The athletic quadrupeds of Shobdon's left arch are projected over a roll, whereas western French designers had long since abandoned rolls. Even so, from a compositional perspective, the Shobdon arches are more thoroughly western French than anything else to survive in England. Shobdon also relates to one composition in particular – the new west façade added to Notre-Dame-la-Grande at Poitiers *c.* 1130 (Figures 14.21–14.22).[135] One can find parallels throughout the west front – the athletic writhing quadrupeds of the upper window or within the arched corbels of the stringcourse above the figurative frieze (top of Figure 14.22) the straggly foliate plaques, the quotation of one of the most celebrated of Poitevin sculptural compositions – the embracers – the discipline with which variety is controlled around the different arch orders. Most telling are the superb dogs of the right-hand blind arch, which invest that arch with a tremendous sense of elasticity and movement and which seem likely to have been the jumping off point for the Shobdon sculptor's decision to take a single animal type – the quadruped – and enhance the sense of movement by treating it as a multi-motif arch.

Thus it seems likely that one (perhaps two) members of the Herefordshire School workshop had recently acquired first-hand experience of western French arch construction. What distinguishes Shobdon is that the archivolts do not simply imitate the surface effects of portals in Aquitaine. Shobdon's archivolts also conform to the principle that orders in an arch are contrasted and that cross-rhythms are contributed by the subtle use of repeats. As an example of the assimilation of a technical and aesthetic system, this goes far beyond the deployment of letter-like forms on a handful of voussoirs at Kilpeck. Indeed, in its underlying handling, Shobdon is more western French than Leyre. So thoroughgoing is it that until recently I thought one of the sculptors *was* western French, though I now think that unlikely.[136] How the transposition came about is arguable. For Zarnecki, it was the result of a sculptor in Oliver de Merlimond's retinue who made sketches of architectural sculpture as he travelled through Aquitaine *en route* to Compostela.[137] But for a sculptor familiar with the basics of radial voussoir composition, sketches would have been unnecessary. It was not the motif that was translated to Shobdon but the method. Take a single animal type and vary the pose. That is something an experienced sculptor would understand *in potentia* and carry back in the mind.[138]

This brings us back to George Zarnecki's contention that the Wigmore Chronicle provides the answer to how western French sculpture arrived in the Welsh Marches. Oliver de Merlimond's pilgrimage to Santiago certainly offers a possible context for an awareness of sculpture in Aquitaine and draws attention to an important force for cultural exchange in 12th-century Europe. However, Oliver's own pilgrimage was undertaken after the church at Shobdon had been begun.[139] Decisions as to the design of this church will have been taken at the outset, following which building work was supervised by Bernard the Knight. At a pinch, the infusion of new approaches to archivolt design could have arisen if a sculptor had accompanied Oliver as far as Aquitaine and then returned with fresh ideas for the portals, but as work was already underway this ought to have been reflected by an absent hand in Shobdon's chancel jambs – where there is none.[140] That particular conjecture seems highly improbable. It runs against the order of events the Chronicle is so careful to relate.

Related to this is a second contention. Zarnecki decided that the styles of the principal sculptors of the Herefordshire School were at their most marked at Shobdon, and this was a sign they were 'here assembled for the first time to work as a team'.[141] Zarnecki's model for the Herefordshire School was one in which the compositional and stylistic resources of the workshop were there at the beginning, at Shobdon, and that its subsequent trajectory

FIGURE 14.21

Poitiers, Notre-Dame-la-Grande: west front south arch (John McNeill)

FIGURE 14.22

Poitiers, Notre-Dame-la-Grande: west front west front, detail of stringcourse, left and central arches (John McNeill)

was marked by a working out of those resources. Everything that was European arrived as a result of Oliver's pilgrimage to Santiago, so if there was anything western French or Spanish at Kilpeck, this further confirmed that it postdated Shobdon. The real clincher was that the jambs of the chancel arch at Kilpeck were modelled on the marble columns of Puerta de las Platerías at Santiago (Figures 14.2 and 14.3).[142]

This is not only historically unlikely, however, it confuses matters. In the first instance, the relationship between Santiago and Kilpeck can be dismissed. There is no connection – at least not at a formal or stylistic level. The figures at Santiago stand beneath individual arcades and are arranged around a column. They are unrelated to Kilpeck. The second area of concern, Aquitaine, is an issue, and Zarnecki is right to point out there are links that tie Kilpeck to western France. It is evident in the use of radial voussoirs and of animals which bite their tails or are formed into letter shapes. But this was an avenue that was already open. The motifs in question are exclusive to the south portal arch, and their detailing, if not the specific compositions, corresponds to work at Old Sarum and Lullington. Unlike the arches at Shobdon, which in our current state of knowledge were without precedent in England, elements of the vocabulary visible in the Kilpeck portal had already taken root in Wiltshire and Somerset.[143] They may even have been fully developed there. The rather circumscribed and highly selective deployment of western French forms at Kilpeck is far more likely to have come about before Shobdon than after.

This difference in approach to arch composition at Kilpeck and Shobdon underpins any view one might take of the workshop dynamics. Zarnecki's vision was of a Herefordshire School that assembled with three principal sculptors and a large repertoire and that, following a dazzling debut at Shobdon, its output steadily homogenized. This is not how I see the Herefordshire School over the 1130s. Rather than narrowing, it strikes me that in its early commissions the Herefordshire School repertoire broadened. First, it broke away from its origins as part of the Hereford cathedral *chantier* to take on Kilpeck and then, following other work perhaps, it produced the carved stonework for Shobdon. First-hand exposure to contemporary western French sculpture between Kilpeck and Shobdon was a part of the broadening. This encounter was not the first to link the Herefordshire School with Aquitaine, but it was appreciably more profound, and it involved at least one sculptor whose earlier work at Kilpeck had shown no sign of familiarity with such exotic material.

MODUS OPERANDI

None of the other churches where the Herefordshire School worked individually conserve as much sculpture as Shobdon or Kilpeck. To judge by the loose voussoirs and relief plaques mounted in the north nave wall at Rock, there was a second Romanesque portal there, while fragmentary carved shafts at Eardisley and Orleton are also likely to be from now-vanished portals.[144] How much more has been lost it is difficult to say, but the overall level of survival is likely to be high. Far more Romanesque fabric survives as a proportion of that built in the West Midlands than in, say, East Anglia. There are up to twenty sites with evidence for Herefordshire School sculpture. In the absence of dates, the order of the work is unclear, but its quantity is impressive and cautions against compressing it into anything less than two decades. Some sites are closely related; Eardisley and Stretton Sugwas, for example, are churches donated to Llanthony Secunda before April 1142, where the respective font and tympanum were carved in a virtually identical manner.[145] The *Majestas* tympana at Shobdon, Rowlstone, and St Giles Hospital belong to a group which evidently runs through a decade or more, given a probable date of no earlier than

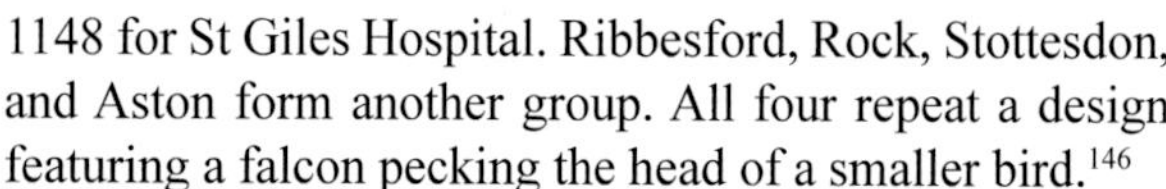

Figure 14.23

Eardisley, St Mary Magdalene: font (John McNeill)

Figure 14.24

Castle Frome, St Michael: font (John McNeill)

1148 for St Giles Hospital. Ribbesford, Rock, Stottesdon, and Aston form another group. All four repeat a design featuring a falcon pecking the head of a smaller bird.[146]

It is difficult to distinguish between individual hands in many of these commissions, and for most of the sites the idea of an individual hand is misleading, as the sculptors worked in pairs across compositions. At a simple level, a single sculptor might take on a carved section. The serpents on the Chaddesley Corbett font are clearly by whichever sculptor carved the jambs of Kilpeck's south portal. But for a more demanding composition, working methods could be tangled. The drapery style adopted for the figures on the Eardisley font, for instance, is comparable to that of the trousered warriors of the left portal jamb at Kilpeck, but the treatment of the heads is quite different (Figures 14.8 and 14.23). Instead, the Eardisley heads are a similar shape to those of the chancel entry figures at Kilpeck and also the egg-shaped heads of John the Baptist and Matthew on the Castle Frome font (Figures 14.2, 14.23, and 14.24), though their facial expression is different again, and the finish is appreciably more austere. Meanwhile, to extend the parallel to the Castle Frome font, the drapery of John the Baptist or the winged figure of Matthew at Castle Frome is not like Eardisley. The boxy pleats are instead like the chancel entry figures at Kilpeck, even if the drapery of the crouching atlas figures at Castle Frome is almost exactly like that of the figures on the Eardisley font. Moreover, the heads of all figures on the Castle Frome font are almost identical. This suggests that the Eardisley and Castle Frome fonts involved two of the same principal sculptors from Kilpeck – Zarnecki's Chief and Aston Masters, perhaps with an assistant – but that the way they divided up the work differed from font to font.

On the face of it, the Herefordshire School's working practices varied considerably. The larger commissions – Kilpeck, Shobdon, and Rock – called on significant resources. Other sites required no more than one principal sculptor. Several buildings – Leominster, Aston, and Rowlstone – show evidence of breakdown, with sculpture either left unfinished or clumsily reworked to fit, presumably after the sculptors had left. We may, of course, be missing a grand project from the late 1140s or early 1150s. One such could have been the chapel of the hospital of St Giles. This was centrally planned, like the castle chapel at Ludlow, and will have required a portal to frame the tympanum, window capitals, and a chancel arch.[147] A now heavily weathered Romanesque double capital depicting Christ the Good Shepherd has been reset close to the surviving Herefordshire School tympanum and presumably came from the hospital precinct. But St Giles is the only candidate that obviously presents itself. Otherwise, the Herefordshire School seemingly failed to find commissions in the 1140s that matched the ambition of those of the 1130s. To some extent, this perhaps reflects the difficulties of working during the 1140s, but it also highlights that at a parish church level, Kilpeck and Shobdon were exceptional in their demand for sculpture. There are differences in the handling of the sculpture between projects, and it is reasonable to conclude that flexibility was a necessary condition for workshop operation.

The poles in the Herefordshire School's operations are best illustrated in the contrast between Kilpeck and Aston. At Kilpeck the level of co-operation between the sculptors and the quarry supplying the stone, as well as between the sculptors and the masons building the church, was exceptional. The south portal jambs, for example, from a point just above the bases up to and including the capitals are monoliths (Figures 14.8 and 14.9).[148] These are blocks of stone of a size only otherwise associated with tomb slabs, cross-shafts, or liturgical furnishings in the first half of the 12th century. The carving is also uncommonly well fitted together, compared with the brutal chopping of the abaci on the inner side of the west portal at Leominster Priory or the incompetence of Rowlstone. So tightly coordinated is the masonry at Kilpeck – see the correlation of the left jamb capital of the south portal with the exterior wall plane for example – that the sculptors must have supervised the integration of the carved stonework when it was mortared into the building. Indeed, including the apse vault and the wall head (the corbel table supports a continuous carved architrave which the Herefordshire School almost certainly supplied), the sculpture informs the architecture to such an extent it is appreciably more likely that the head of the sculptural workshop took overall responsibility for the building rather than a mason or carpenter.[149] Kilpeck may be our earliest intimation of the Herefordshire School as a sculptural workshop, but its operating methods were clearly well worked out at this stage.

Aston sits at the opposite end of the scale. Zarnecki thought Aston predated Kilpeck and Shobdon because the relief of the tympanum is shallow. However, the relief is shallow because the tympanum is unfinished (Figure 14.25). The horizontal setting-out line marking the top of the chequerboard register is still visible beyond the limits of the chequerboard, and the modelling of the faces has barely been started. Indeed, the Aston north portal composition as a whole is unconvincing. The tympanum is not set well to the rear or behind the arch as would be conventional, there are no capitals, and the imposts are of a different stone, a friable greensand identical to similar imposts at Ribbesford, yet are still overlong. It is most unlikely the portal was designed to be as it is. It has the hallmarks of a hurried improvisation.[150]

The extremes occupied by Kilpeck and Aston point to different levels of organization in the building of parish churches. At the tightly organized end of the scale, a supervisor, or *procurator*, took charge. The Domesday entry for Fownhope, for instance, lists the church and follows this up with '*Ibi prepositus et faber et carpentarius*': an overseer, sculptor (?), and carpenter.[151] This suggests that a timber church was under construction at Fownhope in 1086 with the *prepositus* supervising work on behalf of the patron. Thanks to the Wigmore Chronicle, we know that Shobdon was supervised by Bernard the Knight who was given '*tota la cure del overayne od espenses necessaires*' – literally 'the curation of the operation and the necessary expenses' – by Oliver de Merlimond.[152] This is not unlike the administration of great church building, except that the tendency there was for a senior member of the religious community to take on the role rather than a lay overseer.[153]

If the great church model was followed at parish church level, there will have been a master of works. This was often the head of the masons, though it need not be. Most importantly, it is someone who knows the scale, detailing, and position of the fixed elements which make up the building, for which reason it is usually the architectural designer of the church. The number of artisans involved in building a parish church was far smaller than for a great church, and it may not have been necessary for a master craftsman to coordinate the masons, sculptors, and carpenters (along with tilers, plumbers, glaziers, and smiths where needed in the later stages of building). That could have been done by the overseer. But at a practical level, the craftsmen require measurements, and the components once made have to be set into position. High levels of coordination, as at Kilpeck, imply there was an effective master who supervised the critically important assembly whereby set-piece compositions, such as portals or roof trusses, were integrated. The sculpture at Kilpeck is so fundamental to defining openings, wall planes, and supporting the roof that it makes most sense for the *de facto* master of works to be the head of the sculptural workshop. In all probability, the Herefordshire School took primary responsibility for the building of the church. The same will have been true of Shobdon.

Where levels of coordination are low, it is fair to assume that the Herefordshire School was not exercising supervision. At Leominster, for example, the Herefordshire School provided the capitals for the exterior and interior faces of the west front, producing a selection of both old and new designs.[154] The overall plan did not call for a great deal of carved stonework. The exterior window and portal arches are mostly plain, and the portal jambs are uncarved half columns. One imagines the priority and iconographical focus was the glazing of the immense single west window. Most unusually, however, the interior face of the west portal also carried highly worked sculpture, with the Herefordshire School apparently collaborating with a group they had not worked with previously, who produced the geometric capitals. Unlike the exterior portal capitals, these interior capitals are not all the same size, and the measurements given to the Herefordshire School sculptors were evidently wrong (Figure 14.26). The result was that the capitals do not fit but were pressed into service regardless. The layers and setters simply spliced in additional stones and arbitrarily cut and rearranged the abaci. Rowlstone is not dissimilar.[155] The Herefordshire School provided a string-course which extended the line of the chancel arch abaci across the inner face of the chancel arch and east wall of the nave. It consisted of a simple arrangement of upright volutes and birds which, for some opaque reason, narrowly avoided settling to affronted pairs. Nor was the pattern coordinated with the length of wall available so that both ends of the frieze disappear, leaving fantails in their wake (Figure 14.27). The smaller projects, those where the Herefordshire School are providing less than half the quantity of sculpture found at Kilpeck, are most prone to these misjudgements.

On the whole, the evidence suggests that subsequent to Shobdon, the Herefordshire School workshop divided into subgroups. The Old Sarum connection largely fades away. These subgroups may have acted in concert

FIGURE 14.25

Aston, St Giles: south portal (John McNeill)

elsewhere, at St Giles Hospital, for example, but the workshop was mostly divided after *c.* 1140.[156] Ribbesford and Rock are the most revealing as to workshop organization during this phase in the life of the Herefordshire School. The churches are around 7 km apart and are likely to have been constructed at roughly the same date, either following on one from the other or contemporaneously.[157] Three sculptors were involved: the Shobdon foliage specialist who worked at Rock, the Aston Master who supervised the design of some of the chancel arch capitals at Rock and may have been responsible for the tympanum at Ribbesford, and a second foliage sculptor who worked at Ribbesford.[158] The foliage designs used on the capitals at Ribbesford derive from the spiral tendrils used in the main apse arch of Hereford Cathedral, designs which were already established within the Herefordshire School repertoire, but they are so crudely and repetitively detailed at Ribbesford that it is likely they were the work of a third sculptor. This implies the sculptors were working in pairs, with the Aston Master working alongside a different foliage specialist at each of the two churches.

Rock is the grander of the two. It is entirely built of ashlar, with shafted windows, a lavish north portal, and a majestic chancel arch with four archivolts whose sequence of geometric designs is identical to the chancel arch at Shobdon (Figures 14.15 and 14.28). As at Shobdon, the capitals and bases supporting the chancel arch were the work of specialist sculptors; indeed Rock is the only Herefordshire School church other than Shobdon to employ lavishly decorated bases. But unlike Shobdon, the Herefordshire School sculptors had little involvement with Rock's north portal (compare Figures 14.29 and 14.30).[159] The foliage specialist probably carved the imposts, but the capitals are routine scallop designs with two exceptions. The inner pair are column swallowers and of an unusual sort in which the upper lip breaks upwards beneath the nose – something which is paralleled to the east at Elkstone (Gloucestershire) and Monkton Farleigh (Wiltshire).

Several possible scenarios fit these circumstances. The one I propose is that Rock and Ribbesford followed on immediately from Shobdon and that the Aston Master and the main foliage specialist within the workshop were called to Rock by the mason carvers who produced Shobdon's chancel arch. The two workshops already had experience of collaboration, and the patron, Walter de Ribbesford, was almost certainly aware of the manner in which Shobdon had been built.[160] The Herefordshire School offshoot produced the elaborate sculpture for the chancel arch supports along with a font at Rock, while the mason carvers took overall responsibility for the church. They repeated their Shobdon chancel arch design, but in the later stages, despite receiving a Herefordshire School foliate impost for the north portal, the mason carvers felt short of a specialist and recruited a sculptor from east of the river Severn, who contributed the column-swallowers.

FIGURE 14.26

Leominster: priory, inner face of west portal (John McNeill)

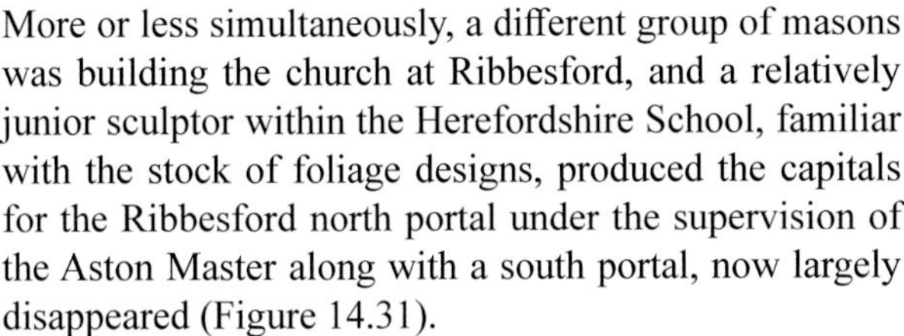

More or less simultaneously, a different group of masons was building the church at Ribbesford, and a relatively junior sculptor within the Herefordshire School, familiar with the stock of foliage designs, produced the capitals for the Ribbesford north portal under the supervision of the Aston Master along with a south portal, now largely disappeared (Figure 14.31).

Nor does the trail go cold at Ribbesford. Thanks to the fortuitous deployment of imposts carved from greensand at Aston, some 35 km to the west of Ribbesford, it seems likely that Aston was the next undertaking. These imposts are of an identical size and shape to two reset greensand imposts at Ribbesford – a stone type which the Herefordshire School otherwise eschewed. The Aston Master had already completed one free-standing piece of sculpture, now used as a font and redeployed inside the church, and was working on a tympanum when the project had to be radically simplified. The portal was redesigned to work without capitals, and the imposts were substituted. This particular sequence of work then comes to an end.

The above scenario is obviously highly speculative, and I simply put it forward for repudiation by others. We should sift through possible working models in instances where enough work survives if we are to make any progress in understanding how Romanesque sculptural workshops operated in the first half of the 12th century. Notwithstanding the caveats that attend when no more than fragments survive, as at Fownhope, Billesley, or Alveley, the later history of the Herefordshire School tends to be one in which sculptors worked in twos or threes on smaller-scale projects – as was obviously the case with the fonts. The Rock-Ribbesford-Aston sequence just outlined was untypical in the sense that there is a falling away in the quality and detailing of the sculpture which may have been due to the short-lived circumstances of war. It underlines, however, the way the workshop could operate with two principal sculptors – the Aston Master and the Shobdon foliage specialist – and then continue with just the single principal sculptor and an assistant. This sort of flexibility was probably crucial to its operation.

FIGURE 14.27

Rowlstone, St Peter: nave east wall to north (John McNeill)

CONCLUSION

As far as the evidence allows, the Herefordshire School seems to have emerged from a great church *atelier*. An origin in a large architectural workshop would account for its training, but thereafter, whether through choice or lack of alternative opportunity, it specialized in providing sculpture for parish churches. The workshop was capable of collaborating with masons to take on overall responsibility for the construction of small-scale buildings and reached a peak with four principal sculptors at Shobdon, perhaps between *c.* 1136 and *c.* 1139. Work was sporadically affected by the civil war of King Stephen's reign, principally in 1140–42, but the Herefordshire School continued to produce carved stonework through the 1140s. Most or probably all of the projects which involved the workshop after Shobdon demanded less carved stonework, and the workshop contracted, tending to deploy no more than two or, at most, three sculptors at a time. In practical terms, it may have split into offshoots – though perhaps retained a capacity to come back together if warranted by a sufficiently large commission, such as St Giles Hospital in Hereford. At least one of the later projects generally attributed to the Herefordshire School – Brinsop – is, in my opinion, problematic.[161] The level of finish and shaping of the stone is so poor as to call into question involvement on the part of the original core of principal sculptors.[162] This may represent an attempt to keep the workshop in operation under the direction of one of the assistants, but if so, it does not seem to have lasted for any length of time.[163] Thereafter, the short-lived proliferation of work that exaggerates familiar Herefordshire School motifs probably marks the demise of the workshop.[164]

Although their repertoire was more elaborate than other sculptural workshops operating outside great churches in Anglo-Norman England, and the Herefordshire School seems to have subcontracted the production of geometric sculpture, aspects of the workshop structure and *modus operandi* are mirrored elsewhere. Jill Franklin has drawn

FIGURE 14.28

Rock, St Peter: chancel arch (John McNeill)

FIGURE 14.30

Rock, St Peter: north portal (John McNeill)

FIGURE 14.29

Rock, St Peter: chancel entry south capitals (John McNeill)

FIGURE 14.31

Ribbesford, St Leonard (John McNeill)

attention to the existence of a workshop in Norfolk with a more restricted repertoire which eschewed figurative sculpture, and indeed tympana, but which worked for a variety of patrons across an area which stretched for over 80 km east to west.[165] Little research has been undertaken into workshop organization in the 11th or early 12th centuries, so it is difficult to form a view as to how typical the Herefordshire School might have been on a European stage, but small-scale specialist architectural sculpture workshops had certainly begun to form by the beginning of the 12th century in France. Neil Stratford tentatively suggested that in the case of local churches in southern Burgundy, the old mason carvers gave way to specialist architectural sculptors over the first quarter of the 12th century, though churches in which sculpture was an optional extra, provided by the more gifted masons as and when required, continued to be built into the middle of the 12th century and beyond.[166] The evidence is best for western France, where the demand for architectural sculpture expanded hugely over the first half of the 12th century and can be seen at a local church level from *c.* 1100.[167] The number of sculptural workshops active at any one time increased, and in addition to small teams of sculptors combining in order to fulfil a major commission, the more substantial workshops could create sufficient sculpture to equip a local church with a façade, window capitals, a corbel table, and elaborate apse and crossing capitals. A celebrated case is the First Aulnay workshop which, having completed the eastern parts of St-Pierre at Aulnay, can be followed producing sculpture in significant quantities for several local churches.[168] A successor workshop, the Third Aulnay workshop, worked across a much wider area and collaborated with other workshops over a period of roughly twenty years.[169]

The workshop responsible for the crossing of St-Eutrope at Saintes seems to have spawned an offshoot, which goes on to work at numerous parish churches in the southern Saintonge.[170] One could continue – the situation in Castile seems similar, if at a slightly later date – but hopefully the point is made.[171] Although local conditions will affect the precise ways in which teams of architectural sculptors could work, the essential *modus operandi* of the Herefordshire School was one that would have been familiar to architectural sculptors working in France and Spain. It is the best example of a regional workshop to have come down to us from Anglo-Norman England.

ACKNOWLEDGEMENTS

I particularly wish to thank Julian Luxford, Lloyd de Beer, and David Robinson for commenting on a draft of this paper; Richard Plant for his astute and constructive editing; and Manuel Castiñeiras for many stimulating discussions over the course of a three-day trip to Herefordshire. The paper is dedicated to John Osborn, generous sponsor of the BAA's Romanesque conference series and Herefordshire resident.

NOTES

1 The Corpus of Romanesque Sculpture in Britain and Ireland is an online record of Romanesque stone sculpture surviving in Britain and Ireland. It was established in 1988 and is organized on a site basis. The corpus now covers the overwhelming majority of sites associated with the Herefordshire School. See www.crsbi.ac.uk/about [accessed 18 November 2020].

2 As far as I am aware, the term 'Herefordshire School' was first used by Alfred Clapham. A. Clapham, *English Romanesque Architecture: II After the Conquest* (Oxford 1934), 142. See discussion below.

3 See, in particular, G. Zarnecki, 'The Future of the Shobdon Arches', *Journal of the British Archaeological Association*, 146 (1993), 87–92; G. Zarnecki, 'The Priory Church of Shobdon and Its Founder', in *Studies in Medieval Art and Architecture presented to Peter Lasko*, eds. D. Buckton and T. A. Heslop (Stroud 1994), 211–20; J. King, 'The Parish Church at Kilpeck Reassessed', in *Medieval Art, Architecture and Archaeology at Hereford, British Archaeological Association Transactions*, vol. XV, ed. D. Whitehead (Leeds 1995), 82–93; G. Zarnecki, 'La sculpture romane des "marches galloises"', in *L'architecture normande au Moyen Age*, ed. M. Baylé (Caen 1997), 91–109; G. Zarnecki, 'The Romanesque Sculpture of the Welsh Marches', in *Medieval Art: Recent Perspectives*, eds. G. Owen-Crocker and T. Graham (Manchester 1998), 61–88; M. Thurlby, *The Herefordshire School of Romanesque Sculpture*, 1st ed. (Little Logaston 1999); J. Hunt, 'Sculpture, Dates and Patrons: Dating the Herefordshire School of Sculpture', *Antiquaries Journal*, 84 (2004), 185–222; R. Wood, 'The Romanesque Tympanum at Fownhope, Herefordshire and the Functioning of the Herefordshire School of Romanesque Sculpture', *Transactions of the Woolhope Naturalists' Field Club*, 53 (2005), 51–76; J. C. Hillaby, *Leominster Priory: Priory and Borough c.660–1539* (Little Logaston 2006); M. Thurlby, 'Reflections on the Herefordshire School of Romanesque Sculpture', *Ecclesiology Today*, 40 (2008), 20–29; R. Baxter, 'Whose Heritage? The Problem of the Shobdon Arches', *Journal of the British Archaeological Association*, 163 (2010), 154–76; M. Thurlby and B. Coplestone-Crow, *The Herefordshire School of Romanesque Sculpture with a History of the Anarchy in Herefordshire*, 2nd ed. (Little Logaston 2013); J. Turnock, 'The Earls of Hereford and Their Retinue: A Network of Architectural and Sculptural Patronage in Twelfth-Century England, *c.* 1130–1155', *Gesta*, 59 (2020), 131–67.

4 To some extent, this is an illusion fostered by conferment of a name. Zarnecki certainly realized that as the workshop contracted, it operated less as a corporate body and more as two principal sculptors who were capable of working separately. G. Zarnecki, *Later English Romanesque Sculpture 1140–1210* (London 1953), 14–15.

5 G. R. Lewis, *Illustrations of Kilpeck Church Herefordshire in a Series of Drawings Made on the Spot with an Essay on Ecclesiastical Design and a Descriptive Interpretation* (London 1842); J. Gage Rokewode, 'A Letter from John Gage Rokewode, Esq., F.R.S., Director, to Sir Henry Ellis, K.H., F.R.S., Secretary, on the Sculptured Figures of Welsh Knights at Kilpeck Church in Herefordshire', *Archaeologia*, 30 (1842), 62–63. The drawings by G. R. Lewis are opposite page 62.

6 T. Wright, 'Remains of Shobdon Old Church, Herefordshire', *Archaeological Journal*, 1 (1845), 233–37. Wright's date of *c.* 1135 for Kilpeck was based on the record of the donation of the church to the abbey of St Peter at Gloucester in 1134 in the *Historia et Cartularium Monasterii Sancti Petri Gloucestriae*, quoted in Rokewode, 'A Letter' (as n. 5), 62.

7 W. Dugdale, *Monasticon Anglicanum*, eds. J. Caley, H. Ellis, and Rev. B. Bandinel, vol. VI (London 1830), 344–48. The Wigmore Chronicle survives in a single copy, and the manuscript which contains it is now in Chicago; University of Chicago Library, MS 224. This is written in a 14th-century hand and is a translation into French of an account originally written in Latin. Internal evidence suggests the main history of the foundation was compiled around 1185, to which a second section was added bringing the story up to *c.* 1250. A better critical edition to that in the *Monasticon Anglicanum*, together with a translation, can be found in J. C. Dickinson and P. Ricketts, eds. 'The Anglo-Norman Chronicle of Wigmore Abbey', *Transactions of the Woolhope Naturalists' Field Club*, 39 (1967–69), 413–45.

8 G. R. Lewis, *The Ancient Church of Shobdon Illustrated and Described* (London 1852).

9 The casts are thought to have been made in 1852–54, though all but the cast of the Christ in Majesty tympanum perished in the fire which destroyed the Crystal Palace in 1936. The trustees of the Crystal Palace donated the surviving tympanum to the Victoria and Albert Museum in 1938, where it is now exhibited in the Cast Court. See http://collections.vam.ac.uk/item/O40938/copy-of-a/ [accessed 2 May 2020].

10 T. Wright, *The History of Ludlow and Its Neighbourhood* (Ludlow 1852), 102–32.

11 T. Blashill, 'On the Churches of Kilpeck and Rowlstone', *Journal of the British Archaeological Association*, 27 (1871), 489–95. '[Shobdon] was built, in 1141, by Oliver de Merlemond, who while it was building made a pilgrimage to the famous shrine of St James at Compostella (Santiago) in Spain; and as his journey would also take him through all those districts of France in which ecclesiastical architecture was then most successfully practised, it may fairly be conjectured that his travels influenced the general style of his new building' (p. 489).

12 Ibid., 490, 495.

13 C. Keyser, *A List of Norman Tympana and Lintels* (London 1904), lxiii. The last-mentioned tympanum showing Christ in Majesty is now mounted in a wall that belongs to a terrace of 18th-century almshouses on St Owen's Street, Hereford – by the site of St Giles Hospital – and is assumed to have once adorned the portal of the hospital chapel. The chapel was excavated in 1927 and was found to have a circular nave. RCHME, *An Inventory of the Historical Monuments in Herefordshire, Volume 1, South West* (London 1931), 130–31.

14 Keyser, *List of Norman Tympana* (as n. 13), lxiv.

15 E. Prior and A. Gardner, *An Account of Medieval Figure-Sculpture in England* (Cambridge 1912), 167, 171. I am grateful to Julian Luxford for supplying me with these references when access to libraries was difficult.

16 Clapham, *English Romanesque Architecture* (as n. 2), vol. II, 142.

17 Ibid., 141 for example.

18 See Claude Andrault-Schmitt, 'The Epistemological, Political, and Practical Issues Affecting Regional Categories in French Romanesque Architecture' in this volume.

[19] A. Gardner, *A Handbook of English Medieval Sculpture* (Cambridge 1935), 58–60.

[20] G. Zarnecki, 'Regional Schools of English Sculpture in the Twelfth Century' (unpublished PhD thesis, University of London, 1951); G. Zarnecki, *English Romanesque Sculpture 1066–1140* (London 1951); G. Zarnecki, *Later English Romanesque Sculpture* (as n. 4).

[21] Zarnecki, *Later* (as n. 4), 9–15.

[22] Ibid., 14–15 and 10. In addition to Zarnecki's incorporation of Aston, Ribbesford, and Rock into the Herefordshire School corpus, a damaged tympanum and fragmentary relief from a Harrowing of Hell were discovered in 1980, reused in the 17th-century vestry of All Saints, Billesley (Warwickshire), and sculpture by the workshop was recognised at the former Bell Inn at Alveley (Shropshire). R. K. Morris, 'The Herefordshire School: Recent Discoveries', in *Studies in Medieval Sculpture*, ed. F. H. Thompson (London 1983), 198–201; J. Hunt and M. Stokes, 'Sculpture and Patronage in a Shropshire Manor: A Group of 12th-Century Sculptures from Alveley', *Journal of the British Archaeological Association,* 150 (1997), 27–47.

[23] Zarnecki, *Later* (as n. 4), 14.

[24] Ibid., 12–13.

[25] 'Thus, it becomes clear that the reference to the journey of Oliver de Merlimond to Compostela is of great significance and we must assume that one of the sculptors employed by him was included in his retinue. While on the journey he obviously made sketches of a number of decorative schemes in France and Spain, which he later used at Shobdon, Kilpeck and other places'. Ibid., 12.

[26] Ibid., 10.

[27] Compare, for example, the dates offered for stone sculpture by 'G.Z.' in G. Zarnecki, J. Holt, and T. Holland, eds., *English Romanesque Art 1066–1200* (London 1984) with the dates offered for the same works in Zarnecki, *Later* (as n. 4). For the early Shobdon dates, see Zarnecki, 'Shobdon and Its Founder' (as n. 3), 216; G. Zarnecki, 'Sculpture of the Welsh Marches' (as n. 3), 72; G. Zarnecki, 'Shobdon Arches, Shobdon', *Corpus of Romanesque Sculpture in Britain and Ireland,* www.crsbi.ac.uk/view-item?i=2436&WINID=1588524 [accessed 2 May 2020].

[28] Zarnecki didn't seem troubled by this. A clue as to why may be found in Paul Crossley's obituary of George Zarnecki; 'Peter Kidson recalls George declaring, perhaps mischievously, that if he had to choose between a date in a document and a date for what his eye for style told him, he would always trust his eye'. P. Crossley, 'George Zarnecki 1915–2008', *Biographical Memoirs of Fellows of the British Academy*, XII (2013), 441.

[29] King, 'Kilpeck Reassessed' (as n. 3), esp. 89–91.

[30] Hunt, 'Sculpture, Dates and Patrons' (as n. 3).

[31] Thurlby, *Herefordshire School* (as n. 3).

[32] E. R. Hamer, 'Patronage and Iconography in Romanesque England: The Herefordshire School in Context' (unpublished PhD thesis, University of Chicago, 1992). The criterion for inclusion in Thurlby's *Herefordshire School* is the sculpture, as the title suggests, and though patronage has been adopted as a means of organizing the material, it is not entirely clear why.

[33] Thurlby and Coplestone-Crow, *Herefordshire School* (as n. 3), see especially xvii and the chapters entitled 'Sources, Inspiration and Models' and 'Other Works'.

[34] Malcolm Thurlby first suggested this in 1984, though it is explored much more extensively in his 2013 publication. M. Thurlby, 'A Note on the Romanesque Sculpture at Hereford Cathedral and the Herefordshire School', *Burlington Magazine,* 126 (1984), 233–34; Thurlby and Coplestone-Crow, *Herefordshire School* (as n. 3), 62–67. Zarnecki noted the similarities but thought Shobdon preceded the east bays of Hereford Cathedral's nave. Zarnecki, 'Sculpture of the Welsh Marches' (as n. 3), 74. See also Hunt, 'Sculpture, Dates and Patrons' (as n. 3), 199–200.

[35] '*Eodem etiam anno [1134] Hugo, filius Willelmi, filii Normanni, dedit Deo et Sancti Petro, et monachis Gloucestriae, ecclesiam Sancti David in Kylpec, cum capella Sanctae Mariae de Castello, et omnes capellas et ecclesias suas et terras quae as eas pertinent ut in kalendario infra in K. littera patet*'. W. H. Hart, ed., *Historia et Cartularium Monasterii Sancti Petri Gloucestriae,* Rolls Series, XXXIII, vol. I (London 1863), 16.

[36] There are examples of both. At Long Sutton (Lincolnshire), rights to the church, together with a new site, were transferred to the Cluniac Priory of Castle Acre, who then built a masonry church at Long Sutton. D. Owen, *Church and Society in Medieval Lincolnshire* (Lincoln 1990), 5. By contrast, St Andrew, Weaverthorpe (Yorks, East Riding) was built by Herbert of Winchester, as recorded by inscription, and a short time later, *c.* 1121, Herbert's son, William, granted the church to Nostell Priory. C. Norton, *Saint William of York* (Woodbridge 2006), 43–45.

[37] In the company of Roger of Hereford, Hugh petitioned Bishop Gilbert Foliot for a charter confirming the endowments of Kilpeck Priory made by him in favour of the abbey of St Peter, Gloucester. J. Barrow, ed., *English Episcopal Acta VII: Hereford 1079–1234* (Oxford 1993), no. 73. The charter is dated to between 1148 and 1155. Hugh was probably concerned to seek confirmation from the bishop to bring his donation into line with the decree of the 1102 Council of Westminster that monks should not accept churches except from bishops. As Brian Kemp noted, by the middle of the century, 'if the donor did not do so it became customary for monasteries to seek diocesan confirmation of grants'. B. Kemp, 'Monastic Possession of Parish Churches in England in the Twelfth Century', *Journal of Ecclesiastical History,* 31 (1980), 137–39. It is notable that Hugh of Kilpeck took the lead.

[38] D. Williams, 'Llanthony Prima Priory', *The Monmouthshire Antiquary,* 25 (2009), 13–50.

[39] W. Holtzmann, *Papsturkunden in England,* vol. I (Berlin 1930), no. 26.

[40] Geoffrey Talbot drove the clergy out of the cathedral and used its tower to bombard the royalist garrison in Hereford Castle. 'At one time it was visible that catapults [*balistas*] were being put up on the tower from which they had heard the sweet and pacific admonition of the bells, at another that missiles were being shot from it to harm the king's garrison'. K. Potter and R. Davis, eds., *Gesta Stephani* (Oxford 1976), 108–11. Given its proximity to Wales, Herefordshire experienced instability early in the reign of King Stephen, and the Welsh uprising of 1136 was the prelude to many years of fighting along the Welsh borders. The area, along with Bristol and the Severn Valley, also became a power base for the Empress Matilda's supporters, after the daughter of Henry I landed in England in 1139 to prosecute her claim to the English throne. King Stephen had confided the county of Hereford in Robert de Beaumont, earl of Leicester, but there is little evidence he wielded much regional authority, and, following Miles of Gloucester's successful capture of Hereford Castle, Matilda installed Miles of Gloucester as earl of Hereford. The most disruptive period to affect Herefordshire was from 1138 to 1141. See H. Thomas, 'Violent Disorder in King Stephen's England: A Maximum Argument', in *King Stephen's Reign (1135–1154),* eds. P. Dalton and G. White (Woodbridge 2008), 139–70, esp. map 7 on 165; B. Coplestone-Crow, 'The Anarchy in Herefordshire', in Thurlby and Coplestone-Crow, *Herefordshire School* (as n. 3), 1–36, esp. 11–24; O. Creighton, D. Wright, M. Fradley, and S. Trick, 'Faith and Fortification: The Church', in *Anarchy: War and Status in Twelfth-Century Landscapes of Conflict*, eds. O. Creighton and D. Wright (Liverpool 2016), 185–218; C. Hopkinson, 'The Mortimers of Wigmore 1086–1214', *Transactions of the Woolhope Naturalists' Field Club,* 46 (1989), 183.

[41] The church of St Guthlac had been given to Gloucester by Hugh de Lacy before 1096 but was wrecked in 1140 in the attack on Hereford Castle, when its cemetery was also desecrated. B. Coplestone-Crow, 'The Anarchy in Herefordshire', in Thurlby and Coplestone-Crow, *Herefordshire School* (as n. 3), 14.

[42] J. Barrow, 'Clergy in the Diocese of Hereford in the Eleventh and Twelfth Centuries', *Anglo-Norman Studies,* 26 (2003), 47.

[43] D. Walker, *Charters of the Earldom of Hereford 1095–1201,* Camden Miscellany XXII 4th series, I (Cambridge 1969), charter 18. The date bracket is provided by the consecration of Gilbert Foliot as bishop of Hereford on 5 September 1148 and the death of Roger, earl of Hereford, in 1155.

[44] For a full critical edition and introduction, see Dickinson and Ricketts, 'Wigmore Chronicle' (as n. 7), 413–46.

[45] Ibid., 420.

[46] D. Walker, 'Miles of Gloucester, Earl of Hereford', *Oxford Dictionary of National Biography* (Oxford 2004), online edition (odnb/10820) [accessed 7 May 2020].

[47] Dickinson and Ricketts, 'Wigmore Chronicle' (as n. 7), 422. For an assessment of the value of the Wigmore Chronicle for Shobdon, see J. McNeill, 'Romanesque Sculpture in England and Aquitaine', in *Regards Croisés sur le monument medieval: Mélanges offerts á Claude Andrault-Schmitt*, ed. M. Angheben (Turnhout 2018), 356–59.

[48] Dickinson and Ricketts, 'Wigmore Chronicle' (as n. 7), 422.

[49] Ibid., 422.

[50] Ibid., 422–24.

[51] Ibid., 424.

[52] Walker, Miles of Gloucester (as n. 46).

[53] Dickinson and Ricketts, 'Wigmore Chronicle' (as n. 7), 424.

[54] Oliver remained in the Angevin camp and can be found as a witness to charters issued by Roger, successor to Miles as earl of Hereford. See Walker, *Charters of the Earldom of Hereford* (as n. 43), charters 68, 73.

[55] Dickinson and Ricketts, 'Wigmore Chronicle' (as n. 7), 426.

[56] Zarnecki knew this as the 'Bromyard Group', on the basis the workshop was responsible for the font at St Peter, Bromyard (Herefordshire), but it is now usually referred to as the 'Dymock School'. Dymock is within the area where most of the workshop's output is to be found and a former rector of St Mary, Dymock, Eric Gethyn-Jones, wrote a monograph on their work. E. Gethyn-Jones, *The Dymock School of Sculpture* (Chichester 1979).

[57] B. Morley and D. Miles, 'Nave Roof, Chest and Door of the Church of St. Mary, Kempley', *Antiquaries Journal,* 80 (2000), 294–96. For the 1128–32 date of the roof, see D. Miles, 'Tree-Ring Dates', *Vernacular Architecture,* 39 (2008), 135–46; R. Harris and D. Miles, 'Romanesque Westminster Hall and Its Roof', in *Westminster II: The Art, Architecture and Archaeology of the Royal Palace, British Archaeological Association Transactions,* eds. W. Rodwell and T. Tatton-Brown, vol. XXXIX (Leeds 2015), 47.

[58] J. Turnock, 'Reconsidering the Reign of King Stephen: A Contextual Study of Sculpture Created in Gloucestershire Between 1135 and 1154' (unpublished MA thesis, University of Durham, 2014), 114–18. The thesis is available online at http://etheses.dur.ac.uk/11024 [accessed 9 May 2020].

[59] Ibid., 163–64.

[60] See Thomas, 'Violent Disorder' (as n. 40), passim, though map 7 on 165 makes clear how the years around 1140–42 saw the greatest recorded number of acts of war to affect the southern Welsh Marches.

[61] See, for example, King, 'Kilpeck Reassessed' (as n. 3), 90–91.

[62] William of Newburgh, *Historia Rerum Anglicarum,* ed. H. Hamilton, Rolls Series, LXXXII/I (London 1856), Book I, Cap. XV, 45. For an assessment, see J. Burton, 'English Monasteries and the Continent in the reign of King Stephen', in *King Stephen's Reign (1135–1154),* eds. P. Dalton and G. White (Woodbridge 2008), 98–114.

[63] Turnock, 'Reconsidering the Reign of King Stephen' (as n. 58), 165–66.

[64] Ibid., 127–38.

[65] G. L. Pearson, 'St John the Baptist, Beckford', *Corpus of Romanesque Sculpture in Britain and Ireland,* www.crsbi.ac.uk/view-item?i=9041&WINID=1589721300374 [accessed 14 May 2020].

[66] B. Coplestone-Crow, 'The Anarchy in Herefordshire', in Thurlby and Coplestone-Crow, *Herefordshire School* (as n. 3), 30–31.

[67] B. Kemp, ed., *Reading Abbey Cartularies* (London 1986), I, 132, no. 147.

[68] See O. Creighton et al., 'Faith and Fortification' (as n. 40), though the chapter focuses on churches as fortifications and has disappointingly little to say about parish churches.

[69] Kemp, *Reading Abbey Cartularies* (as n. 67), I, 33–36, no. 1. The charter dates to 1125, and, though spurious in the form in which it was reproduced in the Reading cartulary, Brian Kemp argues it mostly reflects the 1125 original.

[70] John Chandler, ed., *John Leland's Itinerary: Travels in Tudor England* (Stroud 1993), 220. See also note 43 above.

[71] On Billesley, see Morris, 'The Herefordshire School: Recent Discoveries' (as n. 22), 198–201. On Alveley, see Hunt and Stokes, 'Sculpture and Patronage in a Shropshire Manor' (as n. 22), 27–47. There is sculpture which may also come from the same source as the Alveley sculpture at Lower Farm, Romsley, around a mile south. See Thurlby and Coplestone-Crow, *Herefordshire School* (as n. 3), 192–94. The tympana at Brinsop and Stretton Sugwas (both Herefordshire) are also *ex-situ*, but it is clear in both cases that they originally formed part of the churches where they are reset.

[72] They are Kilpeck, Shobdon, Rowlstone, Castle Frome, Eardisley, Fownhope, Stretton Sugwas, Cusop, Brinsop (?), Orleton, Aston (all Herefordshire), Rock, Ribbesford (Worcestershire), Chaddesley Corbett (Worcestershire), Ruardean (?) (Gloucestershire), Stottesdon (Shropshire), and Monmouth (Monmouthshire).

[73] On links between local lords and parish churches, see C. F. Davidson, 'Written in Stone: Architecture, Liturgy, and the Laity in English Parish Churches, *c.* 1125–*c.* 1250', vol. 1 (unpublished PhD thesis, University of London, 1998), 87–93; J. Blair, 'Introduction: From Minster to Parish Church', in *Minsters and Parish Churches: The Local Church in Transition 950–1200*, ed. J. Blair (Oxford 1988), 1–19; R. Gem, 'The English Parish Church in the Eleventh and Early Twelfth Centuries: A Great Rebuilding?' in *Minsters and Parish Churches* (as n. 73), 21–30.

[74] Hamer, 'The Herefordshire School in Context' (as n. 32); Turnock, 'Reconsidering the Reign of King Stephen' (as n. 58). Jonathan Turnock has also recently examined the ecclesiastical patronage of Miles of Gloucester and his son, Roger, across their various estates. Turnock, 'The Earls of Hereford and their Retinue' (as n. 3).

[75] Thus it is argued that the sculpture at Alveley was commissioned by Guy Lestrange between *c.* 1155 and *c.* 1160, for what appears no other reason than that the holder of the manor before 1155 is unknown. Hunt, 'Sculpture, Dates and Patrons' (as n. 3), 206–08. Or, for Brinsop, 'on the basis of documentary evidence alone, it is logical to conclude that Miles and Sybil were the patrons of the sculpture', by which assumption, the sculpture at Brinsop is dated to before 1144. As Miles's successor to the manor of Brinsop is uncertain, the alternative, that we do not know who commissioned the 12th-century church, is evidently unpalatable. Turnock, 'The Earls of Hereford and their Retinue' (as n. 3), 162–63.

[76] D. Walker, 'The "Honours" of the Earls of Hereford in the Twelfth Century', *Transactions of the Bristol and Gloucestershire Archaeological Society,* 79 (1960), 209–10 and *Red Book of the Exchequer*, vol. I, Rolls Series, IC, ed., H. Hall (London 1896), 283–84.

[77] For Tarrington, see R. Baxter, 'St Philip and St James, Tarrington', *Corpus of Romanesque Sculpture in Britain and Ireland,* www.crsbi.ac.uk/view-item?i=3450&WINID=1603723517550 [accessed 25 October 2020]. For Peterchurch, see R. Baxter, 'St Peter, Peterchurch', *Corpus of Romanesque Sculpture in Britain and Ireland,* www.crsbi.ac.uk/view-item?i=9934&WINID=1603723517550 [accessed 25 October 2020].

[78] Jeff West suggested a similar approach some time ago: that a keener sense of the interaction between 12th-century patrons and parish church builders would emerge if surveys encompassing many patrons with differing resources at their disposal were made and examined across a wide geographical area. See J. K. West, 'Architectural Sculpture in the Parish Churches of the 11th- and 12th-Century West Midlands: Some Problems in Assessing the Evidence', in *Minsters and Parish Churches* (as n. 73), 159–68. Though I disagree with his conclusions, Jonathan Turnock is to be congratulated for taking up this challenge in respect of the earls of Hereford, extending his examination of their architectural patronage in Gloucestershire to their patronage as a whole. Turnock, 'The Earls of Hereford and Their Retinue' (as n. 3).

[79] Turnock, 'Reconsidering the Reign of King Stephen' (as n. 58), 114–22.

[80] This is likely to be *c.* 1140–45. Postlip was built '*in tempore hostilitatis'* (see n. 58).

[81] Walker, 'Miles of Gloucester' (as n. 46).

[82] Coplestone-Crow, 'The Anarchy in Herefordshire' (as n. 3), 8. See also D. Walker, 'Miles of Gloucester, Earl of Hereford', *Transactions of the Bristol and Gloucestershire Archaeological Society,* 77 (1958), 66–84.

[83] Potter and Davis, *Gesta Stephani* (as n. 40), 148–49, 158–61.

[84] J. F. Mason, 'Pain *fitz* John', *Oxford Dictionary of National Biography* (Oxford 2004), online edition (odnb/9615) [accessed 12 May 2020].

[85] It seems that Roger only gained control of the marriage portion which Pain had allotted his daughter. This has been calculated to be no more than approximately 20% of the Lacy fief. Walker, 'The "Honours" of the Earls of Hereford' (as n. 76), 186–88.

[86] Potter and Davis, *Gesta Stephani* (as n. 40), 159–60.

[87] Coplestone-Crow, 'The Anarchy in Herefordshire' in Thurlby and Coplestone-Crow, *Herefordshire School* (as n. 3), 24–25.

[88] Gilbert de Lacy's father, Roger, had been banished for rebellion in 1096, and the Lacy barony passed to Gilbert's uncle, Hugh I de Lacy (died *c.* 1115). Gilbert's claims to the Lacy estates were subsequently passed over by Henry I, but within weeks of Stephen's accession, Gilbert came to England to press his claims. Stephen seems to have been no more welcoming than Henry I, however, so Gilbert allied himself with a cousin, Geoffrey Talbot, and went on the offensive, seizing Ludlow in 1138 while Geoffrey Talbot captured Weobley. Ludlow was quickly lost, but though Geoffrey Talbot died in 1140, Gilbert managed to retain Weobley.

[89] Turnock, 'Reconsidering the Reign of King Stephen' (as n. 58), 54–61, Turnock, 'The Earls of Hereford and their Retinue' (as n. 3), 134.

[90] J. Newsom, 'Beakhead Decoration on Romanesque Arches in the Upper Thames Valley', *Oxoniensia,* 78 (2013), 71–86.

[91] Turnock, 'Reconsidering the Reign of King Stephen' (as n. 58), 48–54; Turnock, 'The Earls of Hereford and their Retinue' (as n. 3), 134, 145.

[92] Turnock, 'Reconsidering the Reign of King Stephen' (as n. 58), 65–75 and 86–92; Turnock, 'The Earls of Hereford and their Retinue' (as n. 3), 133–34, 137–51. See also L. Abel Smith, *A Short Guide to St. Swithin's Church, Quenington* (Quenington 2010). The church on Roger's manor at Dymock employed the Dymock school, though it is likely this had been completed by 1137, the date at which Roger gained an interest in the manor.

[93] Jonathan Turnock has argued that there is consistency in the sculpture and that the recurrence of beakhead, flower-like motifs, frontal chevron, and geometrically enriched shafts constitutes a 'distinctive repertoire' and 'that the earls of Hereford arranged for the emergence of a certain repertoire of sculptural motifs at their churches'. Needless to say, I cannot agree, not least because none of the seventeen sites covered in the tables on pp. 166–67 combine all four of the elements he selects for emphasis in his conclusion. Turnock, 'The Earls of Hereford and their Retinue' (as n. 3), 164–67.

[94] For Rowlstone, see Thurlby and Coplestone-Crow, *The Herefordshire School* (as n. 3), 169–74. For Castle Frome, see H. W. Davis, C. Johnson and H. Cronne, eds., *Regesta Regum Anglo-Normanorum 1066–1154,* II (Oxford 1956), 308. The fabric of the church at Castle Frome could be earlier than the celebrated font, and as the church had been granted to the abbey of St Peter at Gloucester early in the 12th century, it may have been a representative of St Peter's at Gloucester who commissioned the font. For English Bicknor and Mansel Lacy, see Turnock, 'The Earls of Hereford and Their Retinue' (as n. 3), passim.

[95] W. Page, ed., *Victoria History of the County of Worcestershire, IV* (London 1924), 297–317 and 319–28.

[96] B. Coplestone-Crow, 'The Baskervilles of Herefordshire: 1086–1300', *Transactions of the Woolhope Naturalists Field Club*, 43 (1979), 18–39 at 21–22; B. Holden, *Lords of the Central Marches* (Oxford 2008), 93–95.

[97] W. Holtzmann, *Papsturkunden in England,* vol. I (Berlin 1930), no. 26.

[98] R. Baxter, 'St Mary, Cusop', *Corpus of Romanesque Sculpture in Britain and Ireland,* www.crsbi.ac.uk/view-item?i=7572&WINID=1589740552971 [accessed 27 May 2020]. The pattern used on the impost is the same as at Rowlstone and on a west portal abacus at Leominster Priory. Ralph de Baskerville's possession of Cusop seems to have been overlooked in the literature.

[99] Archenfield was a semi-autonomous Welsh district, or *commote*, which lay outside the English hundredal and shire system. Its customs were described in a separate section of the Domesday account for Herefordshire, and it was only absorbed into the diocese of Hereford at the end of the 11th century. Barrow, 'Clergy in the Diocese of Hereford' (as n. 41), 39. Even so, the bishops of Llandaff continued to claim jurisdiction over Archenfield during the episcopacy of Bishop Urban (1107–34), the first Norman appointee to the see. C. Brooke, 'The Archbishops of St David's, Llandaff and Caerleon-on-Usk', in *Studies in the Early British Church,* eds. N. Chadwick et al. (Cambridge 1958), 224–25.

[100] The whole of Archenfield had been granted to Roger of Gloucester on his marriage to Cecily, daughter of Sybil de Lacy and Pain *fitz* John, in 1137 – and Roger evidently granted out three Archenfield manors to Ralph de Baskerville. The Baskervilles were steadfast in the affinity of Miles and Roger of Gloucester throughout the 1140s.

[101] At the date that Rock and Ribbesford were likely to have been built, Oliver de Merlimond was probably still steward to Hugh de Mortimer I.

[102] Turnock takes the opposite view and sees great landholders as artistic torchbearers for 12th-century parish churches, particularly in the matter of the application of sculpture, and that where they led, their subtenants followed. His argument in relation to the earls of Hereford rests on the repeated use of specific non-figurative sculptural forms. This invests the forms in question with an associative value. Turnock, 'The Earls of Hereford and Their Retinue' (as n. 3), 164–65.

[103] Anglo-Norman chancel entries occasionally employ *en-delit* shafts with geometric decoration, or even polished marble shafts, but only Shobdon followed Kilpeck in finding a use for figured jambs and even here the figures are entangled warriors, not saints. Kilpeck's south portal jambs are difficult to characterise architectonically, so deep is the relief, but they seem to have been conceived as an outer pilaster against an inner half-column. If so, the form is associated with pre-Conquest churches, as at Stow (Lincolnshire) or St Bene't, Cambridge.

[104] The village is a planned Anglo-Norman settlement, retaining good evidence for its shape and layout as the castle and most of the village had been abandoned by the 16th century at the latest. Designed as an irregular T, the castle occupies the cross stroke with the rectangular village enclosure to the north-east and the church positioned between the castle and the enclosure. E. Impey, 'The Buildings on the Motte at Kilpeck Castle, Herefordshire', *Archaeologia Cambrensis,* 146 (1997), 101–08 and plan at 102. Not the least remarkable of the church's features is that its west front appears hostile to the castle. It has no portal, largely plain walls and three projecting dragon heads, their mouths dramatically open to reveal tongues about to uncoil, as if to 'protect' the church. The antithetical posturing is clearly intentional, though there is no reason to suspect it refers to contemporary enmity between the castellan and church. The 1134 grant makes clear that relations were cordial. Rather it should probably be understood as offering generic protection for the church against secular encroachment.

[105] Any buildings on the motte were replaced by a masonry shell keep in the last quarter of the 12th century. Impey, 'Kilpeck Castle' (as n. 103), 106.

[106] See note 35 and C. J. Robinson, *A History of the Mansions and Manors of Herefordshire* (London 1872), 157. The priory was dissolved in 1422. The successor to that priory, known as Priory Farmhouse, lies outside the village enclosure and is largely 17th century. No provision for a priory was made within the castle-church-village enclosure and it follows that the initiative came as part of the development of Kilpeck under Hugh rather than being a hangover from an earlier and unresolved scheme. That no adjustment was made to the enclosure to accommodate the priory suggests Hugh intended it to be kept at arm's length. Notwithstanding the existence of an unexcavated raised platform some 70 m south-west of Priory Farmhouse, often held to have been the site of the monastic buildings, it seems likely that the 'priory' was more akin to a monastic grange. RCHME, *An Inventory of the Historical Monuments in Herefordshire, Volume 1* (as n. 13), 159–60.

[107] Walker, 'The "Honours" of the Earls of Hereford' (as n. 76), 209–10 and *Red Book of the Exchequer* (as n. 76), vol. I, 283–84. Bruce Coplestone-Crow has now revised the figures for the knights' fees available to the three barons attendant on the earls, which he estimates at 16½ for Robert de Chandos, 11¼ for Richard de Cormeilles, and 4¼ for

Hugh of Kilpeck. Thurlby and Coplestone-Crow, *Herefordshire School* (as n. 3), 17–19. While the increase in Hugh's resources is considerable, the disparities remain large.

[108] Zarnecki, *Later* (as n. 4), 10. See also Ron Baxter's admirably judicious summary in the CRSBI entry; R. Baxter, 'St Mary, Kilpeck Herefordshire', *The Corpus of Romanesque Sculpture in Britain and Ireland*, www.crsbi.ac.uk/view-item?i=11497&WINID=1590843518064 [accessed 19 May 2020].

[109] From a purely formal perspective, Zarnecki was concerned to account for the appearance of beakhead at Kilpeck, and its attribution to a Reading sculptor must have been affected by familiarity gained during his organization of the 1948 excavation at Borough Marsh which resulted in the discovery of large numbers of beakhead voussoirs from the cloister at Reading. Kilpeck is the only Herefordshire School site where beakhead is found, and, given Zarnecki's belief that Shobdon came first, he needed an outside sculptor to account for beakhead. Reading fitted the bill, though there are few formal similarities between the beakheads at each site.

[110] The search for individual hands in Romanesque sculpture smacked of inappropriate connoisseurship to many scholars. See D. Glass, *The Sculpture of Reform in North Italy, ca 1095–1130* (Farnham 2010), 1–4. On one possible model for specialization and collaboration within mid-12th-century sculptural workshops, in this case in central and northern France, see R. Baxter, 'The West Portal of Angers Cathedral', in *Anjou: Medieval Art, Architecture and Archaeology, British Archaeological Association Transactions,* eds. J. McNeill and D. Prigent, vol. XXVI (Leeds 2003), 138–50.

[111] Hereford Cathedral was extensively restored between 1843 and 1847 under Lewis Cottingham, and most of its Romanesque sculpture was replaced. The replacement sculpture was closely modelled on the original work, however, and seems reliable. In a number of cases, it can be checked as some of the Romanesque work which was removed survives. D. Whitehead, 'The Mid-Nineteenth-Century Restoration of Hereford Cathedral by Lewis Knockalls Cottingham, 1842–1850', in *Medieval Art, Architecture and Archaeology at Hereford, British Archaeological Association Transactions*, vol. XV, ed. D. Whitehead (Leeds 1995), 176–86; Thurlby, 'A note' (as n. 34), 233–34.

[112] The original capitals from the apse entry arch are now mounted on brackets in the retrochoir. Given their position, they presumably date from early in the construction phases at Hereford Cathedral, say *c.* 1115. The relief is shallower than at Kilpeck, and the drapery is simply incised, but the facial types and certain poses are similar. The figures on the chancel entry at Kilpeck are essentially a forcefully three-dimensional development of this work.

[113] I am immensely grateful to Dr Richard Plant for pointing me to the probable original position of this capital and discussing its wider relevance.

[114] M. Thurlby, 'Sarum Cathedral as Rebuilt by Roger, Bishop of Salisbury, 1102–39: State of Research and Open Questions', *Wiltshire Archaeological and Natural History Magazine,* 101 (2008), 130–40; J. McNeill, 'William St John Hope and the Fate of the Romanesque Sculpture from Old Sarum', in *Balancing the Account: Prior and Gardner and the Study of English Medieval Sculpture*, ed. P. Lindley (forthcoming).

[115] King, 'Kilpeck Reassessed' (as n. 3), 86–87; Thurlby and Coplestone-Crow, *Herefordshire School* (as n. 3), 86–89. R. Stalley, 'A 12th-Century Patron of Architecture: A Study of the Buildings Erected by Roger, Bishop of Salisbury', *Journal of the British Archaeological Association,* 124 (1971), 75–77.

[116] See A. Tcherikover, *High Romanesque Sculpture in the Duchy of Aquitaine c. 1090–1140* (Oxford 1997), 115–17.

[117] M-T Camus and C. Andrault-Schmitt, eds., *Notre-Dame-la-Grande de Poitiers: l'œuvre romane* (Paris 2002), 249–334. For a good selection of details, see Figures 312–14 and 434–73.

[118] For the constructional arrangement, see Pauntley and Postlip (both Gloucestershire). For the Tree of Life tympana, see Dymock, Kempley, Rochford, Yatton. . . . Gethyn-Jones, *The Dymock School* (as n. 56), Plates 19–20. The capital on the south side of Kilpeck's chancel arch also features a low register of ornament just above the necking in the manner of Dymock School capitals.

[119] The obvious omission is figurative sculpture. This is relatively important in the work of the Herefordshire School but is largely absent from its apparent sources. Even at Hereford Cathedral, surviving Romanesque figurative sculpture is now confined to the apse capitals, which will date from early in the cathedral's construction, together with a handful of masks across the eastern arm and the animals set in roundels in the eastern bays of the nave.

[120] See n. 40 and R. Plant, 'The Cathedral Church of St Mary and St Ethelbert, Hereford: Aspects of Its Romanesque Fabric' (unpublished MA thesis, University of London, 1994). The tower housed bells, which makes it virtually certain the account, refer to the crossing tower and not the towers over the eastern presbytery aisle bays. The eastern two bays of the nave will predate the construction of the tower, while the style of the nave capitals to the west indicates there was a building break at this point.

[121] Richard Plant tells me there is clear evidence of a break between bays one and two at gallery level also. Personal communication.

[122] See, inter alia, Durham Cathedral.

[123] J. Barrow, 'Robert de Béthune', *Oxford Dictionary of National Biography* (Oxford 2004), online edition (odnb/23724) [accessed 21 May 2020].

[124] For a celebrated instance of the effect of a vacancy on a major building campaign, see E. Fernie, 'The Architecture and Sculpture of Ely Cathedral in the Norman Period', in *A History of Ely Cathedral*, eds. P. Meadows and N. Ramsay (Woodbridge 2003), 95–98.

[125] The completion of the church predated the arrival of Victorine canons, which can be no later than 1142 and was possibly significantly earlier.

[126] The Lewis engraving shows forty-two voussoirs for the inner order of the chancel arch at Shobdon as against twenty-two voussoirs for the inner order of the chancel arch at Kilpeck.

[127] A. Brooks and N. Pevsner, *Buildings of England, Herefordshire* (London and New Haven 2012), 596–98. Baxter, 'Whose Heritage?' (as n. 3), 161–76.

[128] Lewis, *The Ancient Church of Shobdon* (as n. 8).

[129] For Wolvesey see, Zarnecki, Holt, and Holland, *English Romanesque Art* (as n. 27), 183 (cat no 147). For Lincoln, see G. Zarnecki, *Romanesque Lincoln* (Lincoln 1988), 21–35.

[130] Much the best study of the types and organisation of radial voussoirs is A. Tcherikover, 'Romanesque Sculpted Archivolts in Western France: Forms and Techniques', *Arte Medievale,* 2nd series, 3 (1989), 49–75.

[131] A good example of this sort of thematic grouping of motifs is Saint-Mandé-sur-Brédoire (Charente-Maritime), near Aulnay.

[132] F. Quadrado Lorenzo, 'Tres esculturas de Leire y sus relaciones con temas ecsctológicos', *Príncipe de Viana,* 54 (1993), 229–45; C. Fernandez-Ladereda, ed., *El Arte Románico en Navarra* (Pamplona 2004), 95–102.

[133] The capitals are now in the Museo de Navarra in Pamplona. The best recent assessment is M. Etcheverry, 'Le portail occidental de la cathédrale de Pampelune et Maître Esteban: Relecture d'un mythe historiographique', *Cahiers de Saint-Michel de Cuxa,* XLV (2014), 83–92.

[134] See J. Perratore, 'Crossing the Pyrenees: Migration, Urbanisation, and Transregional Collaboration in Romanesque Aragón', in this volume.

[135] See M-T Camus and C. Andrault-Schmitt, eds., *Notre-Dame-la-Grande de Poitiers: l'œuvre romane* (Paris 2002), 249–334. For a good selection of details, see Figures 312–14 and 434–73.

[136] McNeill, 'Romanesque Sculpture in England and Aquitaine' (as n. 47), 363–64.

[137] Zarnecki, *Later* (as n. 4), 12–13.

[138] For a consideration of memory and the mnemotechnical method in relation to sculpture in the Auvergne, see T. le Deschault de Monredon, 'Formación, Viaje y Memoria Visual: Los Escultores de Auvernia y su Evolución Artística', in *Entre la Letra y el Pincel,* ed. M. Castiñeiras (Barcelona 2017), 121–34, esp. 130–34.

[139] Dickinson and Ricketts, 'Wigmore Chronicle' (as n. 7), 422.

[140] Sculpture will have been required early in the building process whichever order of construction was adopted for Shobdon. If the usual east-west sequence was followed, the chancel entry will have been

required within a matter of months of the start of work. If the church was built from west to east, the portals will have been required quickly.

[141] Zarnecki, *Later* (as n. 4), 10.

[142] Ibid., 12. For an account of the marble columns, their subject matter, and significance, see M. Castiñeiras, 'Un adro para un bispo: modelos e intencións na fachada de Praterías', *Semata,* 10 (1998), 231–64.

[143] Elaborate and varied arches constructed from radial voussoirs were also in use at Reading Abbey by the time Kilpeck had been started. R. Baxter, *The Royal Abbey of Reading* (Woodbridge 2016), 215–97.

[144] For Orleton, see R. Baxter, 'St George, Orleton', *Corpus of Romanesque Sculpture in Britain and Ireland,* www.crsbi.ac.uk/view-item?i=5146&WINID=1591797529319 [accessed 5 June 2020].

[145] The headstops that terminate the hood-mould at Stretton Sugwas were not carved by the sculptor(s) responsible for the tympanum, while the upper and lower interlace borders of the font at Eardisley are identical to those at Chaddesley Corbett (Worcestershire) and will have been provided by the same assistant sculptor.

[146] For convenient illustrations, see Thurlby and Coplestone-Crow, *Herefordshire School* (as n. 3), 49. The design was probably first used on column four of the chancel entry at Shobdon and was also repeated on the southern window capital of the west front at Leominster Priory.

[147] The foundations of the 12th-century chapel of St Giles were discovered during a road-widening scheme in 1927. See the plan published in RCHME, *Herefordshire, Volume 1* (as n. 13), 130–31.

[148] The east jamb is monolithic from the point it sits on the bases to the abacus. The west jamb monolith is slightly shorter, and the lowest 100 mm are not part of the main monolith.

[149] The only carved stonework I think the Herefordshire School sculptors may not have provided was that used for the chancel and apse arches. The geometric patterns used for the chancel arch seem fairly standard and were widely used in chancel arches across the southern Welsh Marches and Gloucestershire.

[150] Aston is a candidate for a building campaign which was part abandoned or scaled back as the result of war. The church stands on the road from Wigmore to Ludlow and may have become caught up in the serious disturbances of 1140–41. See P. McGurk, ed., *The Chronicle of John of Worcester, Volume III* (Oxford 1998), 276–77.

[151] *Domesday Book. 7, Herefordshire* (Chichester 1975), 29.2. *Faber,* literally 'maker', has been translated as 'smith' but could just as easily have been intended to mean sculptor; *faber* seems to be the trade term used for sculptors. As Dodwell pointed out, the term 'sculptor' was rarely used in the 11th or 12th centuries, unlike *pictor* or *caementarius*. See C. R. Dodwell, 'The Meaning of 'Sculptor' in the Romanesque Period', in *Romanesque and Gothic: Essays for George Zarnecki*, vol. I, ed. N. Stratford (Woodbridge 1987), 49–61.

[152] Dickinson and Ricketts, 'Wigmore Chronicle' (as n. 7), 422.

[153] See R. Gem, 'Function, Condition and Process in Eleventh-Century Anglo-Norman Architecture', in *Romanesque Patrons and Processes*, eds. J. Camps et al. (Milton Park 2018), 1–13; E. Fernie, *The Architecture of Norman England* (Oxford 2000), 283–84.

[154] Zarnecki, *Later* (as n. 4), 13–14; Thurlby and Coplestone-Crow, *Herefordshire School* (as n. 3), 215–24.

[155] G. Zarnecki and R. Baxter, 'St Peter, Rowlstone', *Corpus of Romanesque Sculpture in Britain and Ireland,* www.crsbi.ac.uk/view-item?i=8155&WINID=1591817291818 [accessed 6 June 2020].

[156] For St Giles, see above and n. 13.

[157] There is uncertainty over the identity of the manorial tenants at the likely date of their construction, though both were probably held by Walter de Ribbesford from Hugh de Mortimer, *Victoria History of the County of Worcestershire, IV* (as n. 95), 297–317 and 319–28.

[158] The tympanum is badly eroded, but even though the silhouette of the left-hand archer has much in common with work attributable to the Aston Master, the overall composition is uncharacteristically cumbersome.

[159] The two major sculptors – the Aston Master and the foliage specialist at Rock – possibly worked in partnership as a Herefordshire School splinter group in this area over several years, as the two were also jointly responsible for the font at Stottesdon, just over the border in Shropshire.

[160] Ribbesford and Rock were held from Hugh de Mortimer, in all likelihood by Walter de Ribbesford, *Victoria History of the County of Worcestershire, IV* (as n. 95), 297–317 and 319–28. It is thus likely that Walter knew Oliver de Merlimond. It is also likely that Ribbesford and Rock were begun before Oliver de Merlimond and Hugh de Mortimer fell into 'discord'.

[161] G. Zarnecki, 'St George, Brinsop', *Corpus of Romanesque Sculpture in Britain and Ireland,* www.crsbi.ac.uk/view-item?i=2736&WINID=1591817431954 [accessed 6 June 2020]; Thurlby and Coplestone-Crow, *Herefordshire School* (as n. 3), 203–08. Jonathan Turnock has recently pointed out that Brinsop was held by Miles of Gloucester through his marriage to Sybil de Neufmarché and has suggested that the sculpture was commissioned by Miles – thereby dating it to no later than 1143. Turnock, 'The Earls of Hereford and Their Retinue' (as n. 3), 162–63.

[162] Ruardean is another of these possible tail-end commissions, produced late in the life of the workshop in a style that follows the Stretton Sugwas tympanum but where no attempt was made to smooth the rear ground of the tympanum or even frame the composition.

[163] Throughout this paper, the term 'Herefordshire School' has been confined to the output of a specific workshop. This workshop did not obviously spawn imitators, so it is difficult to point to a 'school of the Herefordshire School'. Brinsop and Ruardean come closest to this, in my opinion, in that the sculpture which survives at both churches is closely based on the 'Herefordshire School workshop', but the technical handling of the stone is at some remove from the workshop sculpture. I am grateful to Richard Plant for pressing me on this point.

[164] The carvings in question exaggerate a few selected motifs and are not the work of the Herefordshire School. The tympana at Romsley and Pedmore (both Worcestershire), and fonts at Holt (Worcestershire) and Brecon Priory are good examples. For illustrations, see Thurlby and Coplestone-Crow, *Herefordshire School* (as n. 3), 231–34, 243 and 249.

[165] J. Franklin, 'The Romanesque Sculpture of Norwich and Norfolk: The City and Its Hinterland – Some Observations', in *Norwich: Medieval and Early Modern Art, Architecture and Archaeology, British Archaeological Association Transactions,* eds. T. A. Heslop and H. Lunnon, vol. XXXVIII (Leeds 2015), 135–61.

[166] N. Stratford, 'Romanesque Sculpture in Burgundy. Reflections on Its Geography, on Patronage, on the Status of Sculpture and on the Working Methods of Sculptors', in *Artistes, Artisans et Production Artistique au Moyen Age*, ed. X. Barral i Altet (Paris 1990), III, 235–63, esp., 242–45.

[167] The pioneering studies were those of René Crozet, much of the work being brought together in R. Crozet, *L'art Roman en Saintonge* (Paris 1971), 118–80. For the dating model as now more generally accepted, see Tcherikover, *High Romanesque Sculpture* (as n. 116), passim.

[168] The best example is Salles-lès-Aulnay, but there are others. M-T. Camus et al., *Sculpture romane du Poitou: Le temps des chefs-œuvres* (Paris 2009), 417–21; Crozet, *L'art Roman en Saintonge* (as n. 167), 175–76.

[169] Tcherikover, *High Romanesque Sculpture* (as n. 116), 139–40.

[170] See Arces-sur-Gironde, Beurlay, Conzac and Marignac J. Lacoste, eds., *L'imaginaire et la foi: la sculpture romane en Saintonge* (Saintes 1998), 65–68, 95–96, 149–52, 223–24.

[171] See, in particular, the proliferation of sculptural workshops around Segovia.

The Regional and Transregional in Romanesque Europe (2021), 219–233

CROSSING THE PYRENEES

MIGRATION, URBANIZATION, AND TRANSREGIONAL COLLABORATION IN ROMANESQUE ARAGON

Julia Perratore

Historians studying the transfer of artistic ideas across the Pyrenees during the 11th and 12th centuries habitually return to the same phenomena to describe how and why ideas travelled – most notably pilgrimage and monasticism. While it is undeniable that both played significant roles in facilitating the movement of artists, they were not the only forces that enabled creative connections. The late 11th and 12th centuries in Aragon, for example, saw the kingdom's transformation into a major participant in the Christian conquest of Iberia. The settlement and urbanization of the growing kingdom undertaken during this period demanded churchbuilding on a wide scale. In light of this, the linked phenomena of migration and urbanization also should be considered as major factors in the transfer of artistic ideas. In this paper, I present an instance of transregional cooperation at the worksite of Santa María de Uncastillo (Zaragoza), carried out by stone sculptors trained on either side of the Pyrenees, as the product of both urbanization and migration. On the one hand, the demands of urbanization brought about the project upon which the various sculptors collaborated. On the other, the sculptors themselves were migrants – and perhaps eventually settlers – whose collaboration enacted on a small scale the broader goals of urbanization throughout the kingdom.

During the second quarter of the 12th century, the sculptors decorating the church of Santa María de Uncastillo (Figure 15.1) in Aragon, Spain, experimented with architectural decorations new to the Iberian Peninsula. They bestowed the building with a riot of vivacious, not-strictly-sacred figures from the eaves of the apse to the capitals of the choir. On the south portal (Figure 15.2), they carved into tiered archivolts to maximize the number of such figures that they could display.

These features – one, a tendency toward profane subjects, and two, the use of the figured archivolt – are both typical of church decoration in western France. It has long been argued that sculptors trained in Aquitaine introduced these features to Uncastillo, where they worked on the church of Santa María alongside another group of sculptors trained in Aragon. More specifically, I see the *chantier* of Santa María de Uncastillo as the crucible for a highly successful collaboration between sculptors trained on either side of the Pyrenees. At Uncastillo, these sculptors accomplished an unusually seamless fusion of Aquitanian and Aragonese styles and iconographic repertoires, creating a new, transregional style. So successful was the cooperation among Santa María's artists that deciphering the organization of the worksite remains a particular challenge.

What prompted the trans-Pyrenean meeting of minds (and hands) in Uncastillo? The answer is not to be found among the phenomena that typically explain artistic transfer between France and Iberia during the Romanesque period – most notably, pilgrimage and monasticism. Uncastillo lies at a remove from both the Camino de Santiago and the paths of powerful monastic networks. Rather, the answer seems to be rooted in the social changes that shaped Uncastillo throughout the 11th and 12th centuries. During this period, Uncastillo grew from a frontier fortress-settlement into a leading town of the Aragonese hinterland, a process that took place in the wake of the Kingdom of Aragon's conquests of Muslim-ruled territory. I propose that the experiences of migration and community formation that fostered Aragon's post-conquest urban growth both inspired and supported the transregional artistic collaboration taking place in Uncastillo.

While pilgrimage and monastic networks were important motors of long-distance artistic transfer during the Romanesque period, we must acknowledge that ideas could travel with transplanted people as well as with pilgrims and monastic envoys. In seriously considering migration in Aragon as an additional conduit of artistic transfer, I take up a challenge posed by Frances Terpak. In a provocative study published in 1988, Terpak explored the possibility that, beyond pilgrimage, urban growth incentives offered in places such as Jaca, Aragon's royal capital, enticed artists to move there.[1] The evidence of Uncastillo may flesh out further the relationship between artistic transfer, migration, and urbanism. Of course, it is

  DOI: 10.4324/9781003162827-15

FIGURE 15.1

Santa María de Uncastillo: view from the south-east (Julia Perratore)

FIGURE 15.2

Santa María de Uncastillo: south portal (Julia Perratore)

almost impossible to uncover the individual motives of now-anonymous sculptors. Nonetheless, we can trace the movement of styles and hands and consider them in light of contemporary population changes.

THE URBANIZATION OF UNCASTILLO

The incredible carved imagery of Santa María de Uncastillo cannot be explained by a single, programmatic, concept, yet its many figures and vignettes surely held deep significance for its medieval viewers. On the sculpted south portal alone, musicians and acrobats perform, couples misbehave, shoemakers and tooth pullers ply their trades, and merchants sell their wares (Figure 15.3). Meanwhile, men tame monsters, otherworldly oddities lurk, and creatures familiar and invented contort and intertwine. Not to be outdone by the profane and fantastic forms around them, Jesus, Mary, and Joseph flee to Egypt, while Adam and Eve exit Eden at the point of

Figure 15.3

Santa María de Uncastillo: carved archivolts, south portal (Julia Perratore)

Figure 15.4

Santa María de Uncastillo: Expulsion from Paradise, capital, south portal (Julia Perratore)

a hostile angel's sword (Figure 15.4). This imagery was as concerned with daily life and its temptations as it was with catechism and lay spirituality, relying variously on the biblical, the popular, the mundane, and the fantastic to reach viewers.[2] Above all, it aimed to keep the faithful in the fold by addressing those aspects of existence that related to the dynamic and complex social life of Uncastillo. This was important because it was an urban, largely lay audience, supported by the secular clergy, which encountered these carvings every day.

Even if the term 'urban' tends to conjure in modern minds huge, bustling cities, teeming with people and crowded with buildings, the few hundred souls living in 12th-century Uncastillo surely felt themselves to be living somewhere big, populous, and important, with an increasingly complex built environment. The impetus for its growth, whatever its exact dimensions, came in large part from the dramatic political, economic, and social changes experienced in the Kingdom of Aragon at this time. By the beginning of Santa María de Uncastillo's construction in the 1130s, Aragon had just emerged from an intensive period of conquest, beginning with the capture of Huesca in 1096 and culminating in the fall of Zaragoza in 1118 and Tudela in 1119.[3] Given these broad territorial gains, achieved in a relatively short time frame, the kings of Aragon swiftly initiated the lengthy process of settling newly acquired land. As part of their strategy for securing the land and attracting new inhabitants, they founded new towns and added boroughs to existing towns. The kings offered law codes, privileges, and tax exemptions to incentivise settlement.[4] These initiatives stimulated widespread migration, with settlers coming from as far as the lands beyond the Pyrenees and, more frequently, from as near as the surrounding countryside to inhabit urban space.[5] The post-conquest period in Aragon thus saw unprecedented urbanization, in step, if at a slightly more urgent tempo, with the growth of towns across western Europe.

With Aragon's population in a state of flux, 'community' was both a fluid concept and a fragile reality that could be defined variously along municipal, neighbourhood, or confessional lines. For the Christian inhabitants of Aragon's growing towns, congregational worship in parochial churches and neighbourhood chapels reinforced a sense of community belonging. The multiplication of churches in Uncastillo – six survive from the 12th century – attests very clearly to the desire for close-knit neighbourhood communities.[6] Spirited church decorations, such as those found at Santa María, could accentuate a sense of belonging by offering commentary on townsfolk's experiences as a community. Viewers would have absorbed, if not an iconography of urbanism, per se, then a body of imagery heartily in support of urbanism and its attendant processes of community formation.

Uncastillo played a leading role in the urbanization of northern Aragon during the 11th and 12th centuries. Its eponymous castle had served as a Christian stronghold along the frontier with Muslim-ruled Al-Andalus from as early as the 10th century, making it strategically important to the conquest of the Ebro River Valley.[7] Well before the removal of the frontier, around the mid-11th century, a nascent but ambitious urban settlement had already begun to surround Uncastillo's fortress.[8] Precocious in comparison with other frontier settlements, Uncastillo's early urban growth enabled it to take on a leading role in the region. On the one hand, it modelled processes of urbanization for other towns. On the other, the group of sculptors at work on several of its six fine Romanesque churches, which punctuate its various intra- and extramural neighbourhoods, also decorated many other churches in the surrounding region, including both Aragon and Navarre. Uncastillo served as an artistic pivot point between Aragon and Navarre due to its location close to the border between these two territories, which until the death of King Alfonso I (1104–34) were ruled as one. Even after the split between the two lands, Uncastillo, firmly within the Kingdom of Aragon's territory, remained part of the diocese of the Navarrese city of Pamplona.[9] Its importance to both sides of the border throughout the Middle Ages seems to have contributed to Uncastillo's privileged status in the region, and its artists freely moved across political borders to work throughout the diocese.

A CRUCIBLE OF TRANSREGIONAL COLLABORATION

Santa María's sculpture can be dated firmly within the second quarter of the 12th century. A donation by King Ramiro II dated to 1135 indicates that Santa María's construction was already under way at this point.[10] The Bishop of Pamplona consecrated the church in 1155, a reasonable date for the project's completion, though not necessarily the definitive end of works.[11] The church underwent a series of renovations between the 16th and 18th centuries that have effaced the original western façade and caused the displacement of a number of sculptures, though the original sculpted ensemble of the apse, nave, and south flank exterior is still remarkably intact, revealing much about the progress of work. In the discussion that follows, I separate the extant sculpted ensemble into four zones: the apse exterior, including the corbel-table and window capitals; the apse interior, including the capitals of the choir and triumphal arch; the nave interior; and the south portal.

Scholars have long sought to separate Santa María's stylistic strands and characterize the nature and number of its sculptors' contributions. One thing many authors agree on is the consistency with which the sculptures were executed. Having observed a strong stylistic unity in Santa María's sculptures, some scholars have described them as the work of a single sculptor, the Uncastillo Master, or at least have viewed the Uncastillo Master as the head of a single workshop.[12] Other studies have argued for multiple masters and workshops successively contributing to the church.[13] As I will demonstrate, I believe that two sculpture workshops – one from Aquitaine and one from Aragon – came together at the Santa María worksite. These sculptors, the successors of those responsible for the famed trans-Pyrenean pilgrimage monuments of *c.* 1090–1110, may have been acquainted with each other already, given the spirit of cooperation in the work of their itinerant teachers. In Uncastillo, they joined forces to form their own, local, atelier.

The following discussion begins with the east end of the church, the likely starting point of construction, and concerns the first two zones of decoration completed: the apse interior and exterior. There, a distinct style characterizes the small window capitals found inside and outside the building, as well as the series of figural corbels under the eaves of the roof. The figure style of these sculptures is characterized by small, squat bodies supporting large heads with oval faces, strong jaws, chiselled cheekbones, prominent eyes, shallow foreheads, and jug-handle ears (Figure 15.5). Men's hair is generally short and wavy, while women's hair is straight and long. The male figures generally wear long, split robes. Sleeves are frequently adorned with decorative strips encircling the upper arms. Bands of two or three raised ribs consistently indicate drapery folds. These highly stylized folds stretch across the garments in parallel, horizontal rows, while the skirts of long tunics are vertically subdivided into panels by a single or double rib.[14] Expressive details of the faces are also notable: for example, on the corbel-table, the puckered lips of two kissing lovers or the open mouth of a singing fiddler (Figure 15.6).

It is difficult to say if the many foliate capitals on the apse exterior and interior are also part of the same style group, but a few details suggest that they are. For example, a capital in the apse interior depicting confronted lion fighters shares the same figure style with the exterior sculptures, and it compares favourably in turn with a small capital of confronted lions also inside the apse. On an interlace capital found in the apse interior, tiny masks in the upper corners are cruder versions of many of the faces of the corbel-table. These details, though limited, nonetheless support the possibility that the same sculptor or sculptors executed the non-figural window capitals inside and outside the building in addition to the corbel figures.

As Jacques Lacoste has persuasively argued, the apse carvings' style very closely corresponds to that of a cluster of monuments from Gascony, leading him to propose that a sculptor trained in the Béarn contributed substantially to Santa María. According to Lacoste, this artist was the Oloron Master, who was responsible for sculptures from the west portal of Sainte-Marie d'Oloron and the chevets of Lacommande (Béarn) and Sainte-Engrâce (Soule) – completed in that order during the 1130s.[15] Overall, the similarities among the figures on the Santa María apse and those of Lacommande (Figure 15.7), Oloron (and particularly the west portal's second archivolt, Figure 15.8), and Sainte-Engrâce are very compelling. Moreover, the Béarnais sites display an abundance of profane subjects rendered with a marked playfulness. For example, sirens in the chevet at Lacommande sing with lips wide (Figure 15.9), much like Uncastillo's singing fiddler (Figure 15.6). Though Lacoste dated these works to the 1130s, Peter Scott Brown has convincingly suggested placing Lacommande slightly earlier, in the 1120s, warranting a shift of Lacoste's chronology by a few years.[16] In light of this, I propose that a small Béarnais atelier (and not a single sculptor, as Lacoste suggested) arrived in Uncastillo sometime in the early to mid-1130s to begin work on the apse.

Inside the chevet of Santa María, we also find a group of four capitals that I will refer to as the triumphal arch capitals because they are located in the narrow bay separating apse from nave. The style of these capitals is very different from that of the Béarnais work in the apse. Two of the capitals unmistakably follow in subject and composition carvings from the porch and narthex of Saint-Pierre de Moissac.[17] Depending on the dating of this part of the Moissac church – in the 1130s, as many scholars suggest, or some years earlier, according to Ilene Forsyth – we may interpret the sculptures as either a brand-new sensation in the Romanesque world that other artists were keen to copy or as new classics with real staying power. Either way, the capitals are clearly indebted to Moissac's sculptures, though the iconography of the Death and Torment of the Miser (Figure 15.10), depicted in such detail on the abbey's porch, has been condensed and reconfigured to fit the format of a single capital. There is also on one of the capital's corners the added detail of a man carrying a fish – another subject imported from north of the Pyrenees. So striking is this capital's resemblance to the sculpture of Moissac and its environs that one of the first authors to write about it argued that a member of the Moissac atelier travelled to Uncastillo to execute the sculptures.[18] More convincing, however, is Laura Torralbo's suggestion, based on style, that the sculptors were trained in Aragon.[19] While these sculptors could have seen Moissac in person, a pattern book provided by the Gascon atelier – which had its own links to Moissac – could have formed the basis of the capitals' design just as effectively.[20]

Where the building's east end is concerned, both Lacoste and Torralbo's theories have merit. I believe the actual scenario likely results from their combination: sculptors trained on opposite sides of the Pyrenees came to Uncastillo in roughly the same period of time (early to mid-1130s) to contribute to the eastern end of the church, thus inaugurating the building's decorative work. Though each workshop brought its own style to the east end, perhaps we may observe in the selection of triumphal arch iconography a first manifestation of transregional, cooperative work at Santa María, in which Aragonese artists adapted models shared by their Gascon colleagues. Yet the Gascon workshop dominates the east end, suggesting that its master oversaw the entire decorative ensemble at least during the early stages of building – a view that I will complicate here.

Continuing into the nave, we see further evidence of a different atelier at work. There, the execution of the large foliate capitals is notably different. The vegetal and

FIGURE 15.5

Santa María de Uncastillo: corbel with a man and woman, apse exterior (Julia Perratore)

FIGURE 15.6

Santa María de Uncastillo: corbel with a singing fiddler, apse exterior (Julia Perratore)

interlace motifs in the apse are organically composed, soft, and only loosely symmetrical. In contrast, the foliate capitals of the nave are rigidly symmetrical and crisply carved. An additional feature of the nave capitals is the inclusion of a beaded pattern on stems and leaves. While the capitals of the apse windows seem to have been made by the same sculptors responsible for the apse exterior, the carvings of the nave interior compare more favourably with carvings in the triumphal arch and on the south portal. For example, the beaded patterning on some of the nave capitals is also found on the triumphal arch capital depicting a lion fighter and cavalier. To take another example, the treatment of the eagles on a nave capital can be compared with the carving of a harpy on the south portal's lower archivolt. Mouldings also support a comparison: the pattern on two impost block mouldings in the nave is identical to that of a moulding that separates the first and second archivolts of the south portal. Though few, these details suggest the nave and portal sculptors belonged to the same workshop.

Before commenting further on the shift of style, it is worth noting that on the exterior of the building, on the south flank, a faint but distinct break in the masonry is visible at precisely the juncture between apse and nave – just to the left of the westernmost buttress in the narrow forebay previously mentioned. At the very least, the break suggests a short-lived pause in construction. There is no obvious evidence of a break inside the building, though the unique appearance of a small number of mason's marks in the interior vault and exterior south wall of the first bay of the nave, corresponding to the resumption of work after the break, perhaps hints at some change in the building process. Whatever the reason for this break, it does seem to correspond to a reorganization in the execution of the building's sculptures, as the evidence of hands indicates. This evidence may be found among the nave sculptures, as already noted, but on the south portal the stylistic shift becomes even clearer. It is there that the first, tentative collaboration on the church interior – the sharing of a model for the triumphal arch capitals – seems to have led to artistic collaboration on a much larger scale.

In contrast to what the apse reveals, many aspects of the portal style relate closely to the work of sculptors

FIGURE 15.7

Lacommande: Adoration of the Magi, capital, apse interior (Julia Perratore)

FIGURE 15.8

Sainte-Marie d'Oloron: detail, second and third archivolts, west portal (Julia Perratore)

active in Aragon, specifically in Jaca and Huesca, during the 1110s and 1120s.[21] The considerable achievements of this workshop include the Jaca Cathedral cloister, Huesca's church of San Pedro el Viejo (Figure 15.11), and the sarcophagus associated with Doña Sancha, the royal abbess of Santa Cruz de la Serós (Figure 15.12).[22] The figure style is characterized by longer proportions, rubbery limbs, and round faces with large eyes and wide nostrils. Apart from the shared style, another clear link between Jaca and Uncastillo can be seen in the left-hand jamb capitals of the Santa María portal. Notably, these adapt iconography from the Doña Sancha sarcophagus. The left-hand capital's trio of clerics carrying out a funerary rite, paired with an image of a soul's ascension in the arms of angels, has strong links to representations of clergy and ascension on the front of the sarcophagus. Meanwhile, the pair of lion fighters and rider depicted on the jamb's centre and right-hand capitals, respectively,

FIGURE 15.9

Lacommande: singing sirens, detail of a capital, apse interior (Julia Perratore)

FIGURE 15.11

Huesca: angels displaying the chrismon, tympanum, north portal, San Pedro el Viejo (Julia Perratore)

FIGURE 15.10

Interior of Santa María de Uncastillo: torment of the miser, capital, triumphal arch (Julia Perratore)

recall the combat scene and single lion fighter on the other side of the sarcophagus.[23]

Even though Aragonese style and iconography take on a new dominance here, the south portal nonetheless should be seen as a merging of Aragonese and Aquitanian elements. Ingredients of the Aquitanian figure style are still visible on the portal, most notably in the drapery. In addition to the crescent-shaped ridges associated with Aragonese work, there is also liberal use of the rib-fold so typical of the Gascon sculptors' output (Figure 15.13). The types of garments worn by the figures on the apse corbels are also repeated on the portal. These consistencies have brought many scholars to see the south portal as an extension of the apse and have prompted some to see all of the sculpture as the work of a single, unified workshop. It truly seems that the portal carvers deliberately united the two zones of the church and, in so doing, fused two styles. Perhaps we even find Aquitanian and Aragonese sculptors sharing the work on single carvings.[24]

The evidence for a large-scale collaboration between two workshops trained on opposite sides of the Pyrenees is most evident, however, in the overall architectonic framework of the portal, specifically in the form of the carved archivolt. Here the typically Aquitanian archivolt decoration is used for the first time in Aragon. In Lacoste's view, the Oloron Master shared the idea with the Uncastillo Master (responsible for the portal) during his time at work on the apse.[25] Yet the south portal is a complex, elegant, and highly successful finished product. It does not register as the work of sculptors new to the form who followed either the verbal instructions of a transient sculptor or a few pages of a pattern book for guidance. Rather, it suggests that the portal framework was planned and orchestrated, if not solely executed, by masons and sculptors who already had experience working with figural archivolt carving. This is particularly evident in the middle archivolt (Figure 15.3), in which a series of carved figures seem to sit 'behind' a torus moulding. This clever detail is formally sophisticated, unlikely to have been devised by the newly initiated.

Moreover, in addition to drawing from the Jaca repertoire for subject matter, the portal sculptors also drew from Aquitanian reserves of profane imagery, already seen among Santa María's apse corbels. A number of the portal's archivolt figures emulate or respond to the corbels, even seeking to rival the apse sculptures in their depth of anecdotal detail. The many apse corbels depicting *jongleurie*, for example, are matched by a band of performers at the apex of the portal on the outer archivolt (Figure 15.3). A corbel showing a man indelicately reaching under the bodice of a woman's dress, turning her upside down in the process (Figure 15.5), seems to have an echo in the portal carving of a man touching the chest of a crouching woman (Figure 15.14). In this example, the voussoir not only mimics subject matter but also riffs on the corbel's topsy-turvy composition by grounding the woman and curving the man's body. One almost gets the sense of a competition enacted between the sculptors of

FIGURE 15.12

Jaca, Convento de las Benedictinas: sarcophagus associated with Doña Sancha (Julia Perratore)

FIGURE 15.13

Santa María de Uncastillo: two angels carry a soul to heaven, detail of a capital, south portal (Julia Perratore)

FIGURE 15.14

Santa María de Uncastillo: voussoir with a man and woman, outer archivolt, south portal (Julia Perratore)

the different zones of the church. Yet the portal carvers seem to have drawn from the apse corbels in more ways than one. On the outer archivolt (Figures 15.3 and 15.14), each voussoir is carved as if it were a corbel, following the corbel profile and filling the spaces with figures exactly in the manner of the corbels on the apse (Figures 15.5 and 15.6). This is an unusual approach to archivolt carving, allowing for a depth of relief that truly makes the portal come to life. Perhaps in this detail we see the portal sculptors adapting Béarnais corbel templates to the curve of the archivolt.

This evidence suggests the continued involvement of the Gascon master and his workshop, even if they do not seem to have played a primary role in the portal's carving. I think we see the Gascon Master taking on a different role instead, one pertaining more to the orchestration of the portal work than to its execution, a subject to which I will return. Whatever the specific relationship between the sculptors, the south portal constitutes a complex but harmonious synthesis of Aquitanian and Aragonese architectonic, stylistic, and iconographic contributions. The finesse with which the portal's designers seem to have selected and combined aspects of their repertoires certainly suggests a strong, trusting, and amicable working relationship among skilled workers of different backgrounds. Different hands may be visible on the portal, but they worked in concert. The closely knit working practices developed between the apse and nave of Santa María de Uncastillo resulted in the confection of a consistent, streamlined transregional style on the portal.

The overall coherence of the sculptural work at Santa María also suggests that collaboration was not the whim of sculptors who had just arrived on the scene. The easy blend of elements suggests a longer period of familiarity with Aquitanian work on the part of the Aragonese sculptors and vice versa. Perhaps this can be explained by prior contact between the Aragonese and Béarnais sculptors, as members of a professional network that had long been nurtured by the sculptors of monuments along the Camino de Santiago. As Brown has observed, the cathedrals of Jaca and Oloron are not without similarities.[26] In fact, Brown suggested that, taken together, their sculptures point to a long-term artistic relationship established well before the opening of the Uncastillo worksite. Thus, the Santa María collaboration may not have marked the first encounter between the Aragonese and Béarnais sculptors.

URBANIZATION, MIGRATION, AND THE ACTIVITY OF SCULPTORS

Whatever the degree of acquaintance between the Aquitanian and Aragonese sculptors prior to their arrival in Uncastillo, their convergence at Santa María likely was orchestrated by the project's patrons. Though the evidence is circumstantial, it seems the initial patrons of Santa María were the *tenentes*, or lords, of Uncastillo during the 1120s and 1130s: Gaston IV, Viscount of Béarn, and his wife, the Aragonese princess Doña Talesa. The coincidence of their taking up the *tenencia* of Uncastillo at around the time of Santa María's construction is significant.[27] Gaston IV was one of several Aquitanian nobles who had fought alongside Alfonso I, playing a key role in the conquest of the Ebro River Valley during the first quarter of the 12th century.[28] The reward for his service was the *tenencia* of a number of sites in Aragon. Gaston was *tenente* of Uncastillo until his death around 1130. His son Centulle succeeded him briefly, but Doña Talesa eventually took over the *tenencia* herself until 1136.[29]

Gaston and Talesa had been active patrons of the arts during their early life together in Béarn. Among other projects, they built a hospital at Lacommande, where Santa María's Gascon sculptors had worked prior to going to Uncastillo.[30] Moreover, Talesa had grown up in Jaca, which had been a major Romanesque construction site for much of her youth. She certainly would have been familiar with the Jaca sculptors' decoration of the new Cathedral and other churches in the town. In fact, I am inclined to think that it was Talesa who hired the sculptors for Santa María, given that her husband was perpetually off on campaign during the last years of his life. She may have sought to hire Béarnais sculptors with whom she had already worked in conjunction with members of the Jaca atelier whose work she knew so well.

The fact that the Uncastillo sculptors came from both husband's and wife's respective homelands may at first glance seem a bit too pat, but I view it as a bit of savvy diplomatic manoeuvring on the *tenentes*' part. Perhaps the combination was a careful choice, aiming to celebrate and perpetuate good relations between Aquitaine and Aragon under Alfonso I. Alfonso already valued his Gascon knights' support, but Gaston and Talesa had a powerful feudal role to promote, while Talesa had bonds of blood and marriage to honour. They both served to gain esteem in the eyes of the king by bringing prosperity and success to the town that they had been charged to nurture. On the one hand, the Gascon sculptors were a reminder of the Aquitanians' role in the post-conquest development of the kingdom. On the other, the Aragonese sculptors were associated with a number of royal projects. In this, Santa María echoes the visual choices of the earlier church of San Martín de Uncastillo, which emulates Jaca Cathedral directly through its distinctive south portal tympanum and other sculptures that follow the Jaca style.[31] In light of these observations, the combination of sculptors from north and south of the Pyrenees, brought together at the worksite, had the potential to communicate a message of political unity. However, this unity would seem to have dissolved by the later 1130s, when, after the deaths of both Gaston and his son, as well as that of Alfonso I, Talesa fell out of favour with the new king, her cousin Ramiro II.[32] It is unclear whether or not Talesa would have continued to serve as patron of Santa María, though it is tempting to view the masonry break between apse and nave as a result of her reversal of fortune. Beyond politics, if we imagine the lords of Uncastillo playing a principal role in the urbanization of the town – in attracting settlers and convincing them to stay – then the collaboration visible at Santa María actively celebrates migration, enacting in the stone of the principal parish church the benefits of social dynamism.

It is evident that a number of sculptors initially active at Santa María later went on to work at other churches in the area. To better assess their activity collectively, we can follow three sculptors working in similar style to other, nearby sites. First, we can pick up the trail of the master sculptor responsible for many, if not all of the sculptures from the apse of Santa María. This is the Gascon master who almost certainly started his career in Béarn. I propose that after working on the apse of Santa María, he went only as far as the northern end of town, where he contributed sculpture to the church of San Miguel de Uncastillo. San Miguel's south portal was removed in the early 20th century and is now in the collection of the Boston Museum of Fine Arts.[33] The portal's current location does tend to distance San Miguel from artistic discussions of Uncastillo and the surrounding region, but the stylistic links to Santa María's apse sculptures are striking. The Gascon sculptor's hand is especially evident in the carved figure of St Michael in the tympanum (Figure 15.15), who haggles with the devil over a soul. Michael's large

FIGURE 15.15

San Miguel de Uncastillo: St Michael and the devil vie for a soul, tympanum, south portal (Museum of Fine Arts, Boston. Museum purchase with funds from the Francis Bartlett Donation of 1912, 28.32. Photograph © 2021 Museum of Fine Arts, Boston)

head, strong jaw, thick, almost pursed lips, and shallow forehead make him resemble very closely the diminutive figures from the Santa María apse corbels. The Gascon's hand is not the only one evident at San Miguel, but this sculptor played a leading role in the portal's carving. Perhaps he moved on to this project after completing work on the Santa María apse.

Yet there is also the close formal relationship between the Santa María and San Miguel portals to consider. Even a brief glance at the San Miguel portal is enough to understand that it has a great overall affinity with that of Santa María, most especially through its tiers of figured archivolts (Figure 15.16 and Colour Plate XVII).[34] Though it is unfair to call it a copy, San Miguel does echo Santa María in many ways. This raises the possibility that the Gascon master was the *magister operarius* charged with overseeing work at Santa María and San Miguel concurrently, moving back and forth between projects as he walked the length of the town, sharing templates among worksites while contributing substantial carving to San Miguel. There is no clear explanation as to why this sculptor would have left off carving Santa María in order to move on to San Miguel, but it is nonetheless evident that he did. This is significant, however, because though San Miguel's sculpture is often seen as a later, derivative imitation of Santa María, the stylistic evidence rather suggests the San Miguel portal was carved sometime between the 1140s and 1150s, more or less concurrently with work on Santa María.

Next, we can trace a second sculptor's activity beyond Santa María. This sculptor was, in my view, a principal contributor to Santa María's portal, carving jamb capitals and voussoirs of the outer archivolt. This sculptor also decorated the west portal of San Martín de Unx, located just across the border in Navarre.[35] The figures on the Unx portal display his signature style, which includes delicate bodies with narrow shoulders and arms squeezed against their torsos, as well as large, flat heads with long, straight hair, and flattened drapery panels separated by vertical ribs.[36] This sculptor's work is also found at the extramural church of San Lorenzo de Uncastillo, now in ruins along the north road out of town.[37] San Lorenzo's south portal, though very badly eroded, nonetheless displays the hand of this sculptor on its tympanum, a depiction of the martyrdom of St Lawrence (Figure 15.17). This sculptor also seems to have worked on the different projects concurrently. Santa María was consecrated in 1155, and San Martín de Unx in 1156, suggesting that their portals were decorated more or less at the same time. The precise chronology is not essential to pin down, and since neither the Unx nor the San Lorenzo projects appear to have been very large jobs, they could reasonably have been accomplished within the same time frame. The journey from Uncastillo to Unx is also a relatively short one, allowing

FIGURE 15.16

San Miguel de Uncastillo: south portal (Museum of Fine Arts, Boston. Museum purchase with funds from the Francis Bartlett Donation of 1912, 28.32. Photograph © 2021 Museum of Fine Arts, Boston)

for the tackling of multiple projects at once. And though no documents provide parameters for the construction of San Lorenzo, the sculpture's style suggests its decoration should not be put very far into the 1160s.

A third sculptor working in the same style also seems to have roamed locally, producing capitals for several sites in the immediate area. His personal style, which included snub-nosed figures wearing garments with bunched rib folds, is close to that of the other sculptors. Like his colleagues, he also worked elsewhere in Uncastillo, contributing capitals to the decoration of San Martín's apse, which was eventually finished *c.* 1179.[38] Before working at San Martín, however, he went to Sangüesa, a few dozen kilometers to the north in Navarra.

FIGURE 15.17

San Lorenzo de Uncastillo: Martyrdom of St Lawrence, tympanum, south portal (Julia Perratore)

FIGURE 15.18

Santa María la Real de Sangüesa: Martyrdom of St John the Baptist, capital, apse interior (Julia Perratore)

The construction of Santa María de Sangüesa, at the heart of a busy pilgrimage town that also benefitted from royal patronage, was a major undertaking to which a number of sculpture workshops contributed. Our sculptor worked inside the church's east end, which Clara Fernández has dated between the 1130s and 1150s.[39] The figures of his capitals have curiously large, upturned noses and clown-like, downturned mouths, as seen, for example, in a capital representing the beheading of St John the Baptist (Figure 15.18).[40] Apart from facial features, the Sangüesa carvings recall the Santa María portal style in their sometimes awkward arrangements of figures, as well as their lively drapery effects. In addition, some of the vegetal capitals in the Sangüesa apse, with their sharp edges and strict symmetry, compare favourably to capitals from the Uncastillo nave. There is also a capital depicting the Flight into Egypt at Sangüesa that matches very closely the composition of the capital of the same subject at Santa María de Uncastillo. Finally, this artist also carved capitals for the apse of San Esteban in Sos, just north of Uncastillo, including a version of the Expulsion of Adam and Eve that closely follows the capital depicting this subject at Santa María de Uncastillo.[41]

I take the time to follow these three sculptors to emphasize that after they arrived in Uncastillo, they remained local. They settled in or around Uncastillo, and they made it their lives' work to decorate churches there, or no farther than a day or two's journey away from there. In this, the activity of the Uncastillo-based sculptors largely supports Beatrix Müller's assertion that the town was a small regional centre of sculpture production.[42] I agree, affirming that, upon converging at the worksite of Santa María, a newly united team of sculptors active within the surrounding region made Uncastillo their home base. The shared, transregional style developed at Santa María was not long-lived, perhaps surviving intact for a generation, but it was disseminated by a handful of sculptors who worked around the diocese of Pamplona.

While it may not seem to be a priority to identify hands when considering the broader social phenomena behind artistic creation, I describe the dissemination of the Uncastillo style in these terms precisely because I think it is crucial to remember that the Uncastillo sculptors were people with individual experiences, not mere conduits of style. They were people who, at this time and in this place, may have been presented with significant choices concerning their futures. Whatever the exact size of the workshop formed at Uncastillo and whatever the specific nature of its organization, its sculptors were transplants from Aquitaine and elsewhere in Aragon. Their remaining in or around the town echoed broader patterns of settlement in Uncastillo, particularly in comparison with other migrant tradespeople building lives in the growing urban centre. Perhaps they remained because they enjoyed the financial and social benefits that came of staying. While we cannot know for certain, it is nonetheless worth entertaining the possibility that Uncastillo's sculptors were themselves migrants who became settlers.

To what extent would sculptures created through transregional collaboration have been understood as such by contemporary viewers? While medieval townsfolk looking at Santa María may not have assessed the style as we do today, I think it possible that they could have registered the coherence of the sculpture insofar as they knew the background of the sculptors themselves. Townsfolk living during the mid-12th century saw the church under construction and watched its decorations take shape. Uncastillo was not so large that they would not have known who was working on the church and where they came from. It is possible that the sculptors' different origins were common knowledge even a few generations after the churches' completion, part of the building's oral history. In other words, though we do not know the sculptors' identities, they were not anonymous in the 12th century. They likely would have been well known to local people, especially as they seem to have remained local, working on the churches in town and nearby. Knowing that Uncastillo's churches were the products of sculptors of different origins and that the sculptors represented different regional cultures surely had a positive impact upon townsfolk.

The heyday of Uncastillo's transregional style may have been limited to the workshop's greatest period of activity in Aragon and Navarre around mid-century, but a next generation of sculptors from the workshop went on to work further afield. In his work on San Vicente in Ávila, Daniel Rico has explored the possibility that sculptors trained in Uncastillo contributed to this church, far away in Castile.[43] Closer to home, José Luís García Lloret has proposed that a sculptor from Uncastillo innovated the style associated with the so-called San Juan de la Peña Master. This style would come to decorate dozens of urban churches in Aragon during the second half of the 12th century, further disseminating a Romanesque art of urbanism across the kingdom.[44]

Even though Uncastillo's transregional style had a limited geographic scope, its sculptors significantly shaped the Romanesque in Aragon in other ways. For example, the hagiographic tympana at San Miguel, San Lorenzo, and later San Felices de Uncastillo would be emulated in at least two other nearby towns, Luna and Biota, suggesting the importance of patron saints in articulating community identity.[45] The enthusiastic incorporation of profane forms at Santa María and San Miguel de Uncastillo, particularly in representations of music, would become part of the repertoire of the San Juan de la Peña workshop, found in places like Ejea and Agüero. Finally, the figural carved archivolt would become a feature of parish churches not just in Aragon and Navarra but also across the Iberian Peninsula, especially in Palencia and Burgos. While it would be folly to trace the origin of all of these changes in the Iberian Romanesque to Uncastillo alone, it is nonetheless clear that the town's sculptors played a significant role in promoting its forms and subjects in their work.

Considering artistic transfer across regional boundaries through the lenses of urbanization and migration reminds us that artistic ideas travel from one place to another for many reasons and by many different means, some of which may concern an artist's personal destiny. It is not often that we remember to consider anonymous medieval artists as motivated individuals. Yet when people travel in search of a different or improved life, there lies great potential for ideas to converge and for artistic creation to spark. We may see evidence of this in Uncastillo, though admittedly there are several unknown factors, which are themselves significant obstacles to seeing the decoration of Santa María clearly. Nonetheless, thinking of the sculptors as drawn by the promise of migration might be useful insofar as sculptors can be thought of as generators and selectors of some of the imagery in the sculpted ensemble. It would be unwise to suggest the sculptors were Santa María's principal image coordinators, but to completely exclude sculptors from such decisions seems unnecessary. In the case of Uncastillo, artists' perspectives as new townsfolk may have infused their work with new insights.

ACKNOWLEDGEMENTS

For their feedback and encouragement in my own early work on the subject of artists and migration, I would like to thank Robert A. Maxwell, Therese Martin, and Amanda Dotseth. For their questions, comments, and further conversation on this and related topics during the conference in Poitiers, I particularly thank John McNeill, Sandy Heslop, Elizabeth Valdez del Álamo, Manuel Castiñeiras, Meg Bernstein, and Verónica Carla Abenza Soria.

NOTES

[1] F. Terpak, 'Pilgrimage or Migration? A Case Study of Artistic Movement in the Early Romanesque', *Zeitschrift für Kunstgeschichte*, 51 (1988), 414–27. For the urbanization of Jaca, see L. H. Nelson, 'The Foundation of Jaca (1076): Urban Growth in Early Aragon', *Speculum*, 53 (1978), 688–708.

[2] For an overview, see D. L. Simon, 'La escultura de San Miguel y Santa María de Uncastillo: Historietas de la vida cotidiana', in *La escultura románica: Encuentro transpirenaico sobre patrimonio histórico artístico* (Uncastillo 2007), 75–97.

[3] The classic account of the Aragonese conquest is A. Ubieto Arteta, *Historia de Aragón: La formación territorial* (Zaragoza 1981).

[4] C. Laliena Corbera, 'La articulación del espacio aragonés y el Camino de Santiago', in *El Camino de Santiago y la articulación del espacio hispánico*, ed. C. Laliena Corbera (Pamplona 1994), 85, 100–03. See also R. Betrán Abadía, *La forma de la ciudad: Las ciudades de*

Aragón en la Edad Media (Zaragoza 1992), 234; E. Piedrafita Pérez, *Las Cinco Villas en la Edad Media (siglos XI–XIII)* (Zaragoza 2005), 98–105. For broad discussions of territorial settlement and urbanism in post-conquest Aragon, see C. Stalls, *Possessing the Land: Aragon's Expansion into Islam's Ebro Frontier Under Alfonso the Battler 1104–1134* (Leiden 1995); P. Sénac, *La frontière et les hommes: Le peuplement musulman au nord de l'Ebre et les débuts de la reconquête aragonaise* (Paris 2000); C. Laliena Corbera, *Pedro I de Aragón y de Navarra* (Burgos 2001).

[5] For the importance of migration in Aragon, see L. H. Nelson, 'Internal Migration in Early Aragon: The Settlers from Ena and Baón', *Traditio*, 40 (1984), 131–48. For settlers from north of the Pyrenees, see C. Fernández-Ladreda Aguadé, 'El Camino de Santiago en Navarra: Pamplona, Sangüesa y Estella', in *Los Caminos de Santiago: Arte, Historia, Literatura*, ed. M. C. Lacarra Ducay (Zaragoza 2005), 30. For discussion of 12th-century demographics in Aragon, see A. Ubieto Arteta, 'Sobre demografía aragonesa del siglo XII', *Estudios de Edad Media de la Corona de Aragón*, 7 (1962), 578–98. As for Uncastillo, the majority of the names mentioned in the 12th-century Cartulary of Santa María are Aragonese in origin, suggesting most inhabitants came from the region, though it does also record a number of inhabitants with francophone names. For the onomastic evidence, see A. J. Martín Duque, 'El cartulario de Santa María de Uncastillo (siglo XII)', *Estudios de Edad Media en la Corona de Aragón*, 7 (1962), 647–740.

[6] J. Perratore, 'The Saint Above the Door: Hagiographic Sculpture in Twelfth-Century Uncastillo', *Journal of Medieval Iberian Studies*, 9 (2017), 72–98.

[7] Piedrafita, *Cinco Villas* (as n. 4), 36–38.

[8] Betrán, *Forma* (as n. 4), 154–58.

[9] J. Goñi Gaztambide, *Colección diplomática de la Catedral de Pamplona* (Pamplona 1997) doc. 203. This document of 1137 confirms the diocese of Pamplona's holdings. See also J. Goñi Gaztambide, *Historia de los Obispos de Pamplona I. Siglos IV–XIII* (Pamplona 1979), 385–89.

[10] Francisco Abbad Ríos, *Las iglesias románicas de Santa María y San Miguel de Uncastillo* (Zaragoza 1955), xiii.

[11] Martín, 'Cartulario' (as n. 5), 677–79.

[12] J. Gudiol Ricart and J. A. Gaya Nuño, *Ars hispaniae: Historia universal del arte hispánico. Arquitectura y escultura románicas,* 5 (Madrid 1948), 154; J. Lacoste, 'La decoration sculptée de l'église de Santa María de Uncastillo (Aragon)', *Annales du Midi*, 83 (1971), 155–56, 163–65, 168–72; B. Müller, 'La arquitectura plástica de Santa María la Real de Sangüesa (Navarra)', *Principe de Viana*, 57 (1996), 232, 247–82.

[13] For example, Abbad Ríos, *Las iglesias* (as n. 10), vi.

[14] P. S. Brown, 'Portal, Sculpture and Audience of the Romanesque Cathedral of Sainte-Marie d'Oloron' (unpublished PhD thesis, Yale University, 2004), 107–10.

[15] J. Lacoste, 'La sculpture romane n'avait pas de frontière: l'oeuvre d'un sculpteur béarnais en Aragon', *Revue de Pau et du Béarn*, 32 (2005), 81. For Lacoste's assessment of the Oloron Master's work at Sainte-Marie d'Oloron, see J. Lacoste, *Les grands oeuvres de la sculpture romane en Béarn* (Bordeaux 2007), 93–114; for Lacommande, ibid., 145–62; and for Sainte-Engrace, ibid., 163–81.

[16] Brown, 'Portal' (as n. 14), 140–59.

[17] I. H. Forsyth, 'Narrative at Moissac: Schapiro's Legacy', *Gesta*, 41 (2002), 71–93.

[18] A. Surchamp, 'Sur quatre chapiteaux de Santa Maria de Uncastillo', *Zodiaque*, 83 (1970–71), 2–14.

[19] L. Torralbo Salmón, *La escultura románica de Santa María de Uncastillo* (Uncastillo 2003), 27–36.

[20] Lacoste, *Grands oeuvres* (as n. 15), 136–40.

[21] D. L. Simon, 'Le sarcophage de Doña Sancha à Jaca', *Les Cahiers de Saint-Michel de Cuxa*, 10 (1979), 107–24.

[22] For discussion of the stylistic link to San Pedro el Viejo, see D. Ocón Alonso, 'Los maestros de San Pedro el Viejo de Huesca: un ensayo de aproximación a los procesos de creación artística en la escultura románica', *Actas III coloquio de arte aragonés* (1985), 90–91.

[23] D. Simon, 'L'art roman, source de l'art roman', *Les Cahiers de Saint-Michel de Cuxa*, 11 (1980), 253–54.

[24] Lacoste, 'Decoration sculptée' (as n. 11), 164. Lacoste suggested this during his initial assessment of the portal, which he saw as the product of a single workshop.

[25] Lacoste, 'Sculpture romane' (as n. 15), 89–90.

[26] Brown, 'Portal' (as n. 14), 141–49.

[27] Torralbo, *Escultura* (as n. 18), 14–15, 41–42.

[28] J. M. Lacarra, 'Gastón de Bearn y Zaragoza', *Pirineos: Revista del Instituto de Estudios Pirinaicos*, 7/xxiii (1952), 127–34.

[29] Ibid., 131.

[30] P. Tucoo-Chala, *Quand l'Islam était aux portes des Pyrénées: De Gaston IV le Croisé à la Croisade des Albigeois, XIe-XIIIe siècles* (Biarritz 1994), 87–88, 132, 214–17.

[31] D. L. Simon, 'Source' (as n. 23), 263–65; See also J. Mann, *Romanesque Architecture and its Sculptural Decoration in Christian Spain, 1000–1120: Exploring Frontiers and Confronting Identities* (Toronto 2009), 156–58.

[32] F. Balaguer, 'La vizcondesa del Bearn Doña Talesa y la rebelión contra Ramiro II en 1136', *Estudios de Edad Media de la Corona de Aragón*, 5 (1952), 100–02.

[33] For San Miguel, see W. Cahn, *Romanesque Sculpture in American Collections*, vol. I (New York 1979), 115–19; M. A. Zapater Baselga and A. Gil Orrios, 'La portada meridional de la iglesia de San Miguel de Uncastillo, actualmente en el Museo de Bellas Artes de Boston (Massachusetts USA.)', *Suessetania*, 15–16 (1996–97), 232–33.

[34] Lacoste, 'Decoration sculptée' (as n. 12), 166.

[35] Gudiol and Gaya, *Ars hispaniae* (as n. 12), 154; Abbad, *Las iglesias* (as n. 10), xii; Lacoste, 'Decoration sculptée' (as n. 12), 167; Müller, 'Santa María la Real' (as n. 12), 166–69; C. Fernández-Ladreda Aguadé, J. Martínez de Aguirre and C. Martínez Álava, *El arte románico en Navarra* (Pamplona 2002), 140–48.

[36] Lacoste, 'Decoration sculptée' (as n. 12), 167.

[37] For discussion of San Lorenzo, see M. A. Zapater Baselga et al., 'La iglesia románica de San Lorenzo de Uncastillo (Zaragoza)', *Suessetania*, 20 (2001), 94–100.

[38] A. De Egry, 'Esculturas románicas en San Martín de Uncastillo', *Archivo Español de Arte*, 36 (1963), 181–87; Müller, 'Santa María la Real' (as n. 12), 173–74.

[39] Fernández-Ladreda, Martínez de Aguirre and Martínez, *Navarra* (as n. 34), 134–39.

[40] Lacoste, 'Décoration sculptée' (as n. 12), 167.

[41] Müller, 'Santa María la Real' (as n. 12), 169–70; C. Martínez Álava, 'Iglesia de San Esteban', *Enciclopedia del románico de Zaragoza*, eds. J. Martínez de Aguirre, M. A. García Guinea, and J. M. Pérez González, vol. II (Aguilar de Campoo 2010), 609–11.

[42] Müller, 'La arquitectura plástica' (as n. 12), 232, 247–82; B. Müller, 'Santa María la Real, Sangüesa: Die Bauplastik Santa Marías und die Skulptur Navarras und Aragóns im 12. Jahrhundert' (unpublished PhD thesis, Humboldt-Universität zu Berlin, 1997), 159–81, 231–33.

[43] D. Rico Camps, *El románico de San Vicente de Ávila* (Madrid 2002), 105–06, 123.

[44] J. L. García Lloret, 'Las fuentes del arte románico del Maestro de San Juan de la Peña: La iglesia de San Felices de Uncastillo', *Suessetania*, 21 (2003), 83–96.

[45] Perratore, 'Saints' (as n. 6), 72–98.

The Regional and Transregional in Romanesque Europe (2021), 235–248

TRANSREGIONALISM AND PARTICULARITY IN ROMANESQUE WOODCARVING IN 12TH-CENTURY CATALONIA

Jordi Camps i Sòria

One of the cornerstones of the study of Romanesque art in Catalonia has been its connections with major artistic centres and with wider European styles. In the field of polychrome woodcarving, studies have been based on typological comparison: different groups of sculptures have been defined according to workshops, areas, and chronology. Although the different types produced correspond to those developed more widely in Europe, they present iconographical and stylistic variations that are clearly specific to Catalonia.

Majestats *form one of the most significant series in Catalonia, which raises the question of how far a prestigious image such as the* Volto Santo *in Lucca could have influenced them: worship of the* Passio Ymaginis Domini *is recorded in places such as Girona and Vic in the 10th and 11th centuries. A question arises: how was the production of three-dimensional images introduced to Catalonia in the 12th century? A striking case is that of the* Christ of Mijaran, *the only surviving element from a superb Descent from the Cross. Some details of the works in its series are similar to the paintings from Taüll. Diversity in carvings of the Virgin is also notable. A group from La Cerdanya indicates the existence of a specific model in a particular area. Its masterpiece is the* Virgin of Ger, *stylistically similar to the figure of an archangel in Cologne.*

INTRODUCTION

That the artistic production of the regions of Romanesque Europe evolved in somewhat uniform ways is an obvious assertion. Those works, or groups of works, which display marked characteristics, however, can be harder to assess. It is often difficult to determine which conceptual components generated them, what role was played by the specific (local, regional) historical context, or patron, source of inspiration, or artist. Moreover, in a single area, numerous variations appear over time, hard to contextualize and date, despite similar compositional and iconographical features. Differences can be apparent not only in technical and stylistic aspects but also in key elements of the iconography, the attributes, the dress and pose of the figures, and the distribution of colour.[1] The purpose of this study is to address these questions as they relate to the Romanesque wood carving of Catalonia, while bearing in mind aspects that are typical of the region or its specific territories.[2]

It is not always easy to determine the origins of types beyond the aspects that shaped overall trends in the Romanesque period. For individual works one might ask whether they were based on a prestigious model, perhaps now lost, or created by a highly influential artist or workshop. Taking a wider view, the influence of transregional currents or the mobility arising from pilgrimage and the worship of relics or diplomatic contacts might also have contributed, as, indeed, might Rome, with its papal or conciliar decisions.

It is, in fact, quite easy to detect a series of groups, related both by typology and style, in different areas of the Catalan bishoprics and counties, some circumscribed to delimited areas. This is the case with the carvings of the Virgin and Child, with clearly defined series such as those from the bishopric of Urgell (or from La Cerdanya),[3] those in the group of the Virgins of Montserrat and Barcelona Cathedral,[4] among many others. In another field it is interesting to gauge the importance of a type of triumphant crucifix, in Catalonia called *Majestats*, spread mainly over the north-eastern sector (including the area that since the 17th century has been part of France, Roussillon). On the other hand, in the westerly area the *Christus Patiens* was extensively adopted, which developed, with different variants, from at least the middle of the 12th century.[5] However, one must bear in mind that we have information about the date or patron for very few of these works, making it difficult to establish a relative chronology before the mid-13th century. Moreover, with respect to contacts with centres or workshops outside Catalonia, there are not enough points of reference to determine many certain cases. However, the series of Madonnas covered in tin is revealing: there are two or three in Catalonia (Thuir, Plandogau) and an important centre of production for these objects was the

  DOI: 10.4324/9781003162827-16

FIGURE 16.1

Plandogau: statue of the Virgin and Child (Barcelona, Museu Frederic Marès, MFM 656. Museu Frederic Marès. © Foto: Guillem F-H)

Auvergne region. (Figure 16.1) This enables us to speak of a relatively homogeneous production shared between different regions quite far from one another, despite the compositional and technical differences between the pieces. The hypothesis of importation, associated with the Marian pilgrimage routes, is acceptable. However, in this case we are referring to works dated to the beginning of the 13th century.[6]

THE UNCLEAR ORIGINS OF THREE-DIMENSIONAL IMAGES IN CATALONIA

As is well known, documentary and physical evidence has survived in Europe for the existence of three-dimensional images from the early Middle Ages. There is reference to an image from Clermont-Ferrand, made by the architect and goldsmith *Aleamus* or *Adelelmus*, for the Cathedral consecrated in 946 by Bishop Stephen II.[7] We should also bear in mind surviving works, among them the reliquary image of Sainte-Foy in Conques, with its long history and the numerous transformations that have enriched it,[8] and Ottonian examples that have been preserved, such as the Gero Crucifix or the Golden Madonna of Essen. From a slightly later period, there are statues like the Crucifix of Tongeren, dated to about 1100,[9] and controversial examples, such as Notre-Dame de Bon Espoir in Dijon,[10] or the Volto Santo di Sansepolcro.[11]

FIGURE 16.2

Sant Miquel de Cuixà: nativity crypt (Jordi Camps)

In Catalonia, it is difficult to demonstrate that any of the surviving examples belong to the 11th century, although it cannot be categorically denied that they might have existed and been replaced.[12] In fact, this absence of preserved or documented examples, with some dubious exceptions, should make us question the reasons for the late appearance of three-dimensional images, in relation to other areas of Europe.[13] I shall therefore work from the premise that the earliest free-standing woodcarvings in Catalonia are datable to the second quarter of the 12th century onwards.[14] However, sources relating to the cult of the Virgin Mary in Catalonia take us to an earlier period, that of Oliba (d. 1046), abbot of Ripoll, and Sant Miquel de Cuixà, and bishop of Vic. The architectural plan used for the construction of the west area in the enlargement of the abbey church of Sant Miquel de Cuixà is significant, with the design of the lower level based around the Nativity Crypt. (Figure 16.2) Moreover, the image of the *Maiestas Mariae* – the enthroned Virgin – in the Cuixà Gospels (*c.* 1100), could evoke a now-lost three-dimensional image of the Virgin and Child, an idea suggested by Mathias Delcor and developed by Anna Orriols.[15] Oliba and Cuixà lead us to Ripoll and to the possible link between the mid-11th-century illumination of the codex *De locis sanctis de Beda* (and other texts) and the lost sculpture of the monastery.[16] I shall deal in a later section with the aspects that have to do with this matter, though the information we have about altars dedicated to the Virgin Mary in Cuixà, Ripoll and Vic does not correspond to the examples of recorded and/or conserved Marian statues. The one in Cuixà is from the Gothic period, that from Ripoll is difficult to classify as it is lost, while the one of Santa Maria la Rodona in Vic is datable to about 1200 and was attached to an altar structure.[17]

The problem is with three-dimensional images, since the situation is different in the case of two-dimensional representations. For example, the 11th-century altar frontal in Girona Cathedral, promoted first by Countess Ermessenda and later by Guisla, had a central register occupied by a *Maiestas Mariae*.[18] The appearance of the *Maiestas Mariae*, often coordinated with an Epiphany, is

FIGURE 16.3

Sant Cristòfol de Beget Church: Majestat *of Beget (Jordi Camps)*

the focus of several Catalan pictorial ensembles dating to the first third of the 12th century.[19] Documents also suggest the existence of an image of a crucifix in Estamariu (a few kilometres from La Seu d'Urgell), in a church dedicated to the Holy Face (*ad ipso Vult de Estamariz*), in the last third of the 11th century.[20] The terminology may give rise to doubts but is suggestive of a carved image in the church at that date.

THE *MAJESTATS*: FROM THE *PASSIO YMAGINIS DOMINI* TO THE *VOLTO SANTO* IN LUCCA

One of the factors that distinguish Catalonia from other regions in the Romanesque period is the large number of surviving images of *Christus Triumphans*, known, in modern times at least, as *Majestats*.[21] It is a type related to the prestige of the *Volto Santo* in Lucca, although there are examples in other places in Italy and in Europe more widely. Among the outstanding examples is the *Majestat* of Beget, one of the few that is still an object of worship.[22] This presents the components that define the type: the *manicata* tunic, the arms outstretched horizontally, and the solemn facial expression, ignoring the pain of suffering (Figure.16.3). Belonging to the same group is the Batlló *Majestat*, of uncertain origin (Figure.16.4).[23] Most of the surviving *Majestats* come from north-eastern Catalonia, from Roussillon to the valleys of La Cerdanya and Andorra, and as far as El Vallès (near Barcelona), where we find such a singular work as the image in Caldes de Montbui.[24]

Above all, however, the theme was depicted in Sant Quirze de Pedret (near Berga, in the foothills of the Pyrenees) (Figure 16.5).[25] No trace of this painting now remains, but it is very significant that a Crucifix in Majesty should have been adopted as part of a highly ecclesiological cycle, associated with the Gregorian reform, shortly after 1110.[26] There is also the stuccoed Christ from Sant Joan de Caselles (Andorra), together with the painted figures of Longinus and Stephanon, which can be dated no later than 1150 (Figure 16.6 and Colour Plate XVIII).[27]

In looking for sources, it should be noted that some Limoges enamel plaques from the 13th century have a Catalan provenance, notably the one from Sant Joan de les Abadesses. Also perhaps relevant was a crucifix covered in silver in the chapel of Saint-Sauveur in Saint-Martial in Limoges for which a tunic was made, suggesting it was of the *Majestat* form.[28] While the references are from the early 13th century, it is interesting to bear this example in mind, seeing as contacts have been detected between Limoges and some Catalan works of art from approximately 1100 onwards. Finally, in this framework of contacts with the French Midi, and specifically with the Auvergne region, we must remember the reliquary Christ of Saint-Michel d'Aiguilhe (Haute-Loire), which has been typologically associated with the Catalan majesties.[29]

FIGURE 16.4

Majestat Batlló *(© Museu Nacional d'Art de Catalunya, Barcelona. Photographers: Calveras, Mèrida, Sagristà)*

FIGURE 16.5

*Sant Quirze de Pedret: remains of a painted crucifix (*Majestat *typology) (disappeared since 1937) (© Fundació Institut Amatller d'Art Hispànic. Arxiu Mas)*

The use of images like the *Volto Santo* in Lucca has been associated with the context of the Gregorian reform, as an image of the triumph of the Church.[30] Moreover, the association of the Lucca crucifix with its legendary origin, in the eastern Mediterranean, and sculptor, Nicodemus, could link in Catalonia with the cult of the *Passio Ymaginis Domini* recorded as early as the 10th and 11th centuries. This idea has been reinforced by Michele Bacci, who stressed the importance of the celebration of the dedication of the Lateran basilica in Rome to the Saviour.[31] These diverse arguments could explain the adoption of this type of Christ on the Cross over a large area in Catalonia.

The Catalan *Majestats* show other distinctive features: first, on the crosses themselves which have survived, there are eloquent images and inscriptions. A detailed article by Marcel Durliat also stressed the association with the Apocalypse through the golden belt,[32] something that can be interpreted in works as significant as the *Majestat Batlló*.[33] Some examples present the figures of Mary and Saint John the Evangelist at the ends of the front of the cross; on quite a few there is a tetramorph on the back and the Lamb of God in the centre, with inscriptions that insist on its Christological and sacrificial meaning. As Manuel Castiñeiras has recalled in a study of the cross from Bagergue (Aran), the inscriptions on the backs of the crosses of some of these images evoke their cult function during the celebration of Easter. The invocation of the Lamb of God in fact appears in codices such as the Sacramentaries of Vic and Ripoll, among others. The idea of triumph could moreover constitute an argument against the Cathar heresy.[34] However, we do not know what form the image of Christ would have taken on the cross of Bagergue, particularly when all the known crucifixes from Val d'Aran conform to the *Christus Patiens* type.

Other factors must also be considered when analysing the sources, the foreign models, and the significance of the Catalan *Majestats*. First is that images of the same type continued to be made after the 12th and 13th centuries, but the term *Majestat* applied to an image was not recorded until the 17th century.[35] Second is that the association with the dedications to the Saviour has also been detected in later versions of the *Christus Patiens*, also, according to legend, attributed to Nicodemus and of an eastern origin (*Sant Crist* of Balaguer, *Santíssim Crist del Salvador*, in València). At the same time, it is interesting to point out that on the Berardenga altar frontal (1215), now in Siena, the depiction of the Christ of Beirut does not wear the tunic of the Lucca crucifix or of the *Majestats* but is only dressed in a *perizonium*.[36]

FIGURE 16.6

*Sant Joan de Caselles (Andorra), Crucifixion: stucco relief (*Majestat *typology) (Jordi Camps)*

I am well aware that types and meanings do not always remain stable. It may be that the Catalan *Majestats* adopted a prestigious model, and, in keeping with a general context like works in Lucca and Rome, they were adapted to other functions depending on the specific determinants of each place.

THE PRODUCTION OF A WORKSHOP CLOSE TO THE VALLEYS OF ARAN, BOÍ, AND EL PALLARS

One of the best examples of the spread of iconographical models combined with a clear technical and stylistic uniformity is the group of carvings of crucifixes, of Descents from the Cross, and of other types of objects found in the valleys of Aran, Boí (Ribagorça) and in parts of the counties of Pallars. All the works have been grouped together around a 'workshop', noted for producing Descents from the Cross, located between the Aran and Boí valleys, in the Pyrenees.[37] The most complete group, after which the workshop has been named, is the one from Erill la Vall now in the MNAC in Barcelona and in the Museu Episcopal de Vic (Figure 16.7).[38] It is composed of seven figures, which sets these groups apart from those known from the rest of Europe in the Romanesque period.[39] The figures are marked by a powerful abstract simplification of the physical features, the gestures, and the clothes of the figures. The work that stands out is the spectacular Christ of Mijaran, an extraordinary torso that is the only vestige of an impressive group that comes from one of the most important churches in Aran (Figure 16.8 and Colour Plate XIX). We must, however, bear in mind that the historical context of the Aran valley is very different to that of the Boí valley. Geographically north-facing in the Middle Ages, it depended on the Occitan bishopric of Comminges (Haute-Garonne). It is feasible to think that in this region or further north in Languedoc, there might have been other groups, now lost, acting as models or points of reference.[40]

The images from the valleys of Aran and Boí show interesting correspondences with the mural painting in the area. Similarities have been noted between the veil (or *maphorion*) that covers the head of the Virgin Mary or of the Marys in the groups carved in the Boí valley (Erill la Vall, Durro, and Santa Maria in Taüll) and the image of Mary in the apse of Sant Climent in Taüll.[41] These similarities may be interpreted in two ways: either to justify a date for the carvings close to that of the paintings or to propose the maintenance of a tradition, or a nod back to the past, if we consider that the carvings are later than the paintings. The closeness between the works can also be seen in the rendering of the male torso, as it is treated in the carved images of Christ. In particular the remarkable schematic formulation of the thorax, and the detail of depicting the xiphoid process on the sternum, as traits characteristic of these figures (Figures 16.8 and 16.10), something we do not see in other almost-naked images of Christ in Catalonia. Again we may note parallels in wall-paintings, such as with the depiction of the chest of Lazarus in the apse of Sant Climent (Figure 16.9), or to some figures of the damned in the depiction of Hell in Santa Maria in Taüll.[42] Work is still being done to determine what the guidelines of the iconographical programme in these churches were and what rituals their creation eventually generated. There are signs that works made with different techniques and in different formats were part of a common coordinated programme, in which the architectural decoration, the murals, and the sculpted imagery would be associated. This, however, lies in the realm of hypothesis, and more research must be undertaken.

The group from Aran and Boí is also interesting because it spreads beyond the boundaries of a valley or a bishopric (being found in the dioceses of both Comminges and Urgell). At the same time, the fact that the most outstanding work is from a centre also associated with Languedoc poses the question of the models or of a prestigious point of reference, now lost.

The dating of these groups has revolved around different events, often detached from the phase of the mural paintings which were produced during the episcopacy of Bishop Ramon of Roda de Ribagorça, who consecrated the churches of Taüll in 1123. The promotion of those works is also associated with the Erill family, feudal lords

FIGURE 16.7

Erill la Vall (Vall de Boi): Descent from the Cross group (Museu Episcopal de Vic, MNAC. © Museu Nacional d'Art de Catalunya, Barcelona. Photographers: Calveras, Mèrida, Sagristà)

of much of the valley and its surrounding area. However, we have no further information to enable us to explain the appearance of the groups of carvings, beyond what has been mentioned in relation to liturgical drama or that the groups emerged in response to the Cathar heresy. Later, 13th-century examples provide some continuity and some development of the iconography and composition. These include the crucifixes in Perves and Manyanet, which emphasise Christ's suffering by accentuating the wound in Christ's side. Both Perves and Manyanet were domains of the barons of Erill, at least in the later Middle Ages, and these characteristic traits, seem to have formed part of the image projected by the lords of themselves.

We perhaps ought to be talking about something similar with the examples in El Pallars, because there were other types of images as well as the more theatrical examples of the Descent from the Cross. Many examples of the *Christus Patiens* kept the cross, like the one from Salardú (Val d'Aran) or the more monumental ones from Mur (Figure 16.10), Llimiana and Montmagastre, all three of which were lost during the Spanish Civil War.[43] Perhaps this has prevented them from enjoying the historiographical attention they deserve. Whatever the case, altar furniture and other kinds of objects were also produced in the area, such as the surprising Saint John the Evangelist, of unknown provenance, conserved in Vilafranca del Penedès.[44]

THE VIRGIN OF RIPOLL, NOW LOST, AS A MODEL?

The importance of Ripoll and the correspondences between the illustrated, painted, and carved works produced both in the centre itself and in places a great distance from the monastery have long been noted in the art-historical literature.[45] It is well known that some 11th century illustrations of the Bible were used as models for the reliefs on the façade, which has been interpreted in part as an evocation of a glorious past.[46] Moreover, that similar repertoires and stylistic solutions were used in stone sculpture, wood carvings, and panel painting, as part of a coordinated programme, above all in the second and third quarters of the 12th century, has also long been confirmed.

The image of the Virgin and Child from Ripoll which survived until the early modern period was analysed by Narcís Camós in the 17th century before being lost during the popular revolt of 1835. According to his description, also reflected in the composition on an

FIGURE 16.8

Sant Miqueu de Vielha (Val d'Aran): Christ from Mijaran (vestige of a Descent from the Cross)

FIGURE 16.9

Lazarus, Sant Climent de Taüll (MNAC) (© Museu Nacional d'Art de Catalunya, Barcelona. Photographers: Calveras, Mèrida, Sagristà)

early 13th century seal from the abbey, the Ripoll carving would have presented the figure of the Child facing and inclined towards Mary.[47] We might therefore doubt that the image described by Camós belonged to the Romanesque period. On the other hand, the Marian statues from centres associated with Ripoll or its surrounding area retain a rigid and frontal composition, quite monumental, conceived as *Sedes Sapientiae*. The most prestigious case is that of Montserrat, then a priory affiliated to Ripoll, to which we could add those from Matamala (Figure 16.11) and Llaés, among others.[48] The graphic documents of the famous Montserrat image conserved from the late Middle Ages clearly show a sculpture marked by the front-facing positions of both figures and by the importance of the throne. The carving itself was the object of devotion from the last third of the 12th century onwards, as a consequence of the miracles that were attributed to it; later, King James I granted indulgences to its pilgrims.[49] From the church of Matamala, which also depended on Ripoll (at least in the 10th and 11th centuries), comes an image that shows a composition similar to that of Montserrat, as does that

FIGURE 16.10

Santa Maria de Mur: crucifix (lost in 1936) (After Rafael Bastardes, Les talles romàniques, as n.5, 306)

from Llaés. The latter is geographically very close to Ripoll, although it depended on the monastery of Sant Joan de les Abadesses. It is significant that images from churches very close to Ripoll or from centres associated with the monastery were so similar to each other.

Studying works according to typological criteria does not always make it possible to draw firm conclusions, but coupling such analysis with consideration of other links, of their relationships of dependency, or of the role of their patrons may contribute to strengthening the signs of links between types and works from different centres. To this intriguing line about the original type of the Virgin of Ripoll and its role as a model, it is necessary to add that the plaster (or stucco) sculpture of the Virgin and Child from the cloister of Ripoll is a perfect example of the compositional type that I am talking about (Figure 16.12).[50] The relief, inscribed in a tympanum, was designed with a clear sense of monumentality, in which the size of the throne reinforces its symbolic nature. The dating of the tympanum is disputed, although it was probably made later than the examples previously mentioned, but it demonstrates the use of this compositional type at Ripoll. We are obviously in the realm of hypotheses, but we should also bear in mind the events that took place in Ripoll around the middle of the 12th century, among them the establishment of the Saturday Feast of the Virgin Mary, in 1157.[51]

FIGURE 16.11

Museu Episcopal de Vic: statue of the Virgin and Child from Matamala (© Museu Episcopal de Vic)

THE CHRIST FROM 1147: AN ISOLATED CASE?

In this to-ing and fro-ing of stylistic contacts and iconographical and typological options, one crucifix does not seem to be comparable with any other works (Figure.16.13 and Colour Plate XX). This is the Christ from 1147, a *Christus Patiens* which, having lost its polychromy, stands out for the very careful composition and treatment of the surfaces, especially the head and the facial features.[52] Restoration work in 1952 revealed a reliquary, where among the packets of relics, two fragments of parchment were found, one of which provided the date of the carving's consecration, 1147. It is initially surprising that, being a work associated with the bishopric of Urgell, it is apparently a *unicum*. We do not even know which building it was made for. It has been said that it could be from Andorra, but for the moment no documents have appeared to enable us to demonstrate this. The case

FIGURE 16.12

Ripoll: stucco relief of the Virgin and Child (Jordi Camps)

rests on the similarities in the modelling of the heads and the facial features with the Virgin of Santa Coloma in Andorra (Figure.16.14), perhaps the best-known work of sculpture of the highest quality from the valleys of Andorra in the 12th century. A detailed analysis of the treatment of the head, the eyes, and the hair also enables us to see traits in common with the stone sculpture in the cathedral, despite the fact that this, sculpted from granite, has a rough appearance. If we agree that the similarities are significant, once again as in Ripoll (or in the Boí valley), we can speak of general coordination at workshop level or at the level of the patrons of the cathedral or the bishopric. Finally, we should be wondering about the possibility of there once again being important models beyond the Pyrenees. In this respect, I shall venture to add that, due to its facial features, with the low forehead and the hair close to the clearly sunken eyes, we can see a certain similarity to sculpture from Toulouse from around 1100 and works which followed in the early decades of the 12th century.

A GROUP OF CARVINGS FROM LA CERDANYA IN THE LAST QUARTER OF THE 12TH CENTURY

The final group to be considered has been dated to the last quarter of the 12th century and seems to depend on the old boundaries of the bishopric of Urgell. It consists above all of a series of statues of the Virgin and Child. It is a clear example of the development of a type in a specific territorial area, marked at the same time by an undeniable stylistic homogeneity. The main examples come from La Cerdanya.[53] The figures are characterized by a frontal but not very rigid composition, with narrow shoulders and occasionally the head slightly inclined. The seat is a sort of bench, far from the more monumental thrones in other series. Mary is dressed in a garment that has been described as a chasuble, something that gives the groups a priestly meaning. This situates the figure as the image of the Church, as Tim Heilbronner has argued.[54] Among the most remarkable examples of this variant are the Virgins

FIGURE 16.13

Museu Nacional d'Art de Catalunya: crucifix from 1147, detail (Jordi Camps)

FIGURE.16.14

Santa Coloma d'Andorra (Andorra): Virgin of Santa Coloma d'Andorra (© Fons: Patrimoni Cultural d'Andorra. Photographer: Àlex Tena)

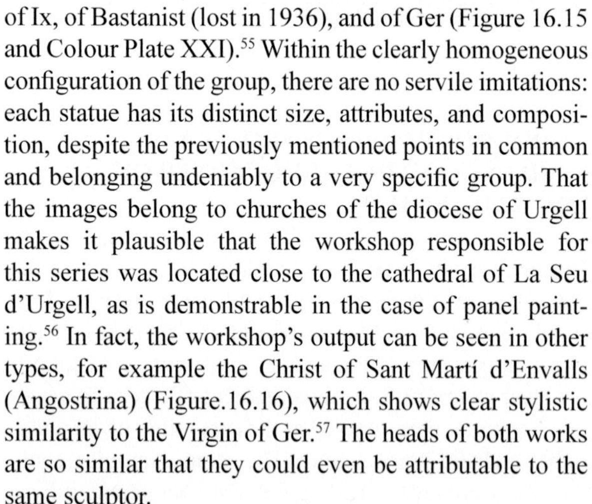

of Ix, of Bastanist (lost in 1936), and of Ger (Figure 16.15 and Colour Plate XXI).[55] Within the clearly homogeneous configuration of the group, there are no servile imitations: each statue has its distinct size, attributes, and composition, despite the previously mentioned points in common and belonging undeniably to a very specific group. That the images belong to churches of the diocese of Urgell makes it plausible that the workshop responsible for this series was located close to the cathedral of La Seu d'Urgell, as is demonstrable in the case of panel painting.[56] In fact, the workshop's output can be seen in other types, for example the Christ of Sant Martí d'Envalls (Angostrina) (Figure.16.16), which shows clear stylistic similarity to the Virgin of Ger.[57] The heads of both works are so similar that they could even be attributable to the same sculptor.

But we can go even further in the analysis of this group and the Urgell workshop. We might wonder about the circumstances in which works of such high quality could have been created in a Catalonia, apparently lacking a powerful tradition of sculptural imagery. In this respect, one must not forget that architectural sculpture in stone was being renewed thanks to the stimuli coming from the north side of the Pyrenees, from Languedoc and Provence especially. We should therefore consider the surprising similarities between the figure of an angel from Cologne, associated with a *Visitatio Sepulchri* group, and the Virgin of Ger, notably in the carefully carved facial features, even though they represent different characters.[58] The image from Cologne has been dated to about 1180, so if we accept this parallel with the group from La Cerdanya, we have an approximate chronological framework. The great quality of the Ger image poses the question of where its sculptor or the carving itself could have come from. A comparative study of the technique and the materials used in the works could help to give us some answers to these questions and to consider or reject hypotheses such as the importation of works or the arrival of a foreign sculptor or workshop. This in fact is the accepted thesis for the statues covered in tin from Thuir and Plandogau, closely related to images from the Auvergne, which might well be imported.

CONCLUSIONS

Elucidating the specific factors that, in a limited area like Catalonia, could have given rise to the creation of

Figure 16.15

Museu Nacional d'Art de Catalunya: Virgin from Ger (Cerdanya) (© Museu Nacional d'Art de Catalunya, Barcelona. Photographers: Calveras, Mèrida, Sagristà)

Figure 16.16

Barcelona, Sant Martí d'Envalls, Institut Amatller d'Art Hispànic: head from the crucifix (© Fundació Institut Amatller d'Art Hispànic. Arxiu Mas)

variants easy to associate with particular geographical and historical spaces is a complicated exercise. The compartmentalization of power in counties, viscounties, bishoprics, and so on may provide a first explanation. Motifs associated with the wishes of a patron or of an outstanding personality or intellectual could have determined the different iconographical and stylistic choices of themes as widespread as the Virgin and Child, the Crucifix, or the groups of the Descent from the Cross. Liturgy and the general affairs of the Church, such as responses to heretical movements, must have had an impact on the production of diverse types and on the way they developed throughout the 12th and 13th centuries. It is clear that artistic options over and above the territorial boundaries, often long-lasting, were also adopted. The most revealing case is that of the works grouped around the Christ of Mijaran that gave rise to different kinds of works from the Aran Valley to the south of El Pallars. Some works could be related to churches associated with the lords of Erill (and at different periods), but others belong to faraway territorial areas, though related through factors proper to the feudal world. The fact that a specific area could have employed a sculptural type for reasons of a family's image does not prevent us from seeing in those solutions a tendency broader in scope, even transregional, for which many points of reference and models have been lost. This, in fact, is what historians have observed in the case of mural painting or architectural sculpture.

There are sources for generically understanding the function of some images, beyond their presence in liturgical drama, their relationship with the altar, or their role with regard to relics or pilgrimage. The *Majestats* could have been associated with the *Passio Ymaginis Domini*, while their iconography seems to point to a specific meaning, different from the typological model of Lucca or others which might have served as a source. This does not rule out the possibility of a prestigious example being used as a model, reworked and adapted to a new context. The groups of the Descent from the Cross, with their unusual composition of seven figures, are also an example of the adoption of a type addressed to a specific function and symbolism without overlooking other more general content. In both cases, scholars have put forward hypotheses referring to a specific historical and ecclesiastical context. Nor should we forget the presence of images in processions and the value attached to a three-dimensional image in that context.

Much of the significance that is currently attached to some of the images of worship in Catalonia may be due more to their long history and to events taking place after the time when they were created rather than to the importance they enjoyed in the period when they were created. In very few cases has it been possible to detect the continuous prestige of a 12th century image after the time of its creation. There can be no doubt that the paradigmatic image is the Virgin of Montserrat. The carving, modified and restored on several occasions, could be from either the late 12th century or the first third of the 13th. It is still the centre of a sanctuary that attracts many Christian faithful (and tourists) and one of the country's religious symbols. It is realistic to think that the Ripoll model was important, given Montserrat's filiation to the great Pyrenean abbey. Over time, Montserrat itself became a prestigious reference, as is demonstrated by similar examples from the area near the monastery and from Barcelona. We ought to study to what extent these dynamics were due to more widespread phenomena, since there were centres of Marian worship as powerful as Le Puy, undoubtedly echoed in Catalonia or Chartres, elsewhere in Europe.

With respect to the roles of patrons and makers, there is little documentary evidence, from the 12th century associated with images.[59] What evidence we have comes from the 13th century: in 1218, Abbot Ramon de Banyeres ordered the Virgin of Sant Cugat del Vallès to be made, and he deposited relics in it ('*in capite huius ymaginis*').[60] In 1251, not far from Ripoll, a layman called Dolcet appears as a patron of the descent from the Cross of Sant Joan de les Abadesses, which he entrusted to the canon Ripoll Tarascó, even stating the material to be used, fir wood.[61]

Regarding the functioning of workshops, analysis of the works makes it possible to develop some hypotheses. The circle of Aran, Boí, and El Pallars provides clues to coordinated production or interaction between different media in one case at least, as has been proposed for groups of carvings from the Boí Valley and the mural paintings in Taüll. The production of a workshop, understood in a broad sense, could cover different types of objects and uses. In this case, Ripoll offers the most decisive examples, often analysed: from the production of the *scriptorium* to the liturgical furniture there are interactions, also reflected in the production of woodcarving. More work needs to be done on other centres, such as La Seu d'Urgell. Not far away, in Solsona the similarities between the stone Virgin of the Cloister and a wooden image of the Virgin and Child, almost certainly associated with an altar table, are telling. Beyond the continuous dynamics of the centres of production, there are also indications of works whose form is due to foreign artists or imports, a phenomenon widely accepted in other artistic fields.

There is still much work to do in this field. The technical study of the works, the review of documentation and the comparison with works from other artistic areas will provide new information to make it possible to classify works and to interpret variants and how they evolved. We must learn more in order to assess the role of centres beyond the Pyrenees in order to configure fully the broad panorama of the production of woodcarving in Catalonia.

ACKNOWLEDGEMENTS

This work derives from the research developed for the project "Movilidad y transferencia artística en el Mediterráneo Medieval (1187–1388). Artistas, objetos y modelos" – Magistri Mediterranei (HAR2015-63883-P).

NOTES

[1] The images have lost some of their supports or some key elements, such as the crosses in the case of numerous crucifixes or altar structures that were presided over by images of the Madonna (see, in this respect, F. Gutiérrez Baños, J. Kroesen, and E. Andersen, eds., *The Saint Enshrined. European Tabernacle-Altarpieces, c. 1150–1400* (Bellaterra 2020).

[2] Among the numerous general works dedicated to Romanesque wood carving in Catalonia see W. W. S. Cook and J. Gudiol Ricart, *Pintura e imaginería románicas* (Madrid 1950), 294–333 (2nd ed., 1980, 279–317); E. Junyent, 'La imatgeria', in *L'art català*, vol. I (Barcelona 1957), 191–204; C. Llarás, 'La talla', in *Catalunya Romànica*, vol. XVII (Barcelona 1998), 117–26J. Camps, 'Imágenes para la devoción. Crucifijos, descendimientos y vírgenes en la Cataluña romànica: tipologías y talleres', in *Mobiliario y ajuar litúrgico de las iglesias románicas*, coord. P. L. Huerta (Aguilar de Campoo 2011), 77–103.

[3] T. Heilbronner, 'The Wooden "Chasuble Madonnas" from Ger, Ix, Targasona, and Talló. About the Iconography of Catalan Madonna statues in the Romanesque period', *Locus Amoenus*, 9 (2007–2008), 31–50; by the same author, *Ikonographie und zeitgenössische Funktionhölzerner Sitz madonnen im romansichen Katalonien* (Hamburg 2013).

[4] J. de C. Laplana, 'La imatge de la Mare de Déu de Montserrat al llarg dels segles', in *Nigra Sum. Iconografia de Santa Maria de Montserrat* (Barcelona 1995), 15–39; F. X. Altés et al., *La imatge de la Mare de Déu de Montserrat* (Barcelona 2003).

[5] M. Trens, *Les majestats catalanes* (Barcelona 1966); R. Bastardes, *Les talles romàniques del Sant Crist a Catalunya* (Barcelona 1978); M. Durliat, 'La signification des Majestés catalanes', *Cahiers Archéologiques*, 37 (1989), 69–95; J. Camps, 'Romanesque *Majestats*: A Typology of Christus Triumphans in Catalonia', in *Envisioning Christ on the Cross. Ireland and the Early Medieval West*, eds. J. Mullins, J. Ní Ghrádaig, and R, Hawtree (Dublin 2013), 234–47.

[6] I. H. Forsyth, *The Throne of Wisdom. Wood sculptures of the Madonna in Romanesque France* (Princeton 1972), 179–80, fig. 124; P. Ponsich, 'La Vierge de Thuir et les relations artistiques entre la région auvergnate et les pays catalans à l'époque préromane et romane', *Les Cahiers de Saint-Michel de Cuxa*, 25 (1994), 51–71; J.-R. Gaborit, 'La Vierge de Thuir et ses 'soeurs': un cas de production sérielle à la fin de l'époque romane', in *Le plaisir de l'art du Moyen Âge. Commande, production et réception de l'oeuvre d'rt. Mélanges en hommage à Xavier Barral i Altet* (Paris 2012), 522–29.

[7] M. Goullet and D. Iogna-Prat, 'La Vierge en Majesté de Clermont-Ferrand', in *Marie. Le culte de la Vierge dans la Société Médiévale*, eds. D. Iogna-Prat, É. Palazzo, and D. Russo (Paris 1996), 383–405; J.-C. Schmitt, *Le Corps des images: essais sur la culture visuelle au Moyen Âge* (Paris 2002), 182–88, fig. 21.

[8] Danielle Gaborit-Chopin, É. Taburet-Delahaye, *Le Trésor de Conques* (Paris 2001).

[9] E. Mercier, 'New Research Findings on 11th–Early 13th-Century Polychrome Wood Sculpture at the Royal Institute for Cultural Heritage, Brussels', *Medievalista*, 26 (2019), http://www2.fcsh.unl.pt/iem/medievalista/MEDIEVALISTA26/mercier2606.html.

[10] N. Bertoni Cren, 'La sculpture sur bois polychrome des XIe et XIIe siècles en Bourgogne. Art and art history' (unpublished PhD thesis, Université de Bourgogne, 2013), NNT: 2013DIJOL030, particularly 44–59, 148–51.

[11] A. M. Maetzke, ed., *Il Volto Santo di Sansepolcro: un grande capolavoro medievale rivelato dal restauro* (s.l. 1994).

[12] For example the reliquary head of saint Eudald in Ripoll (for which an amount of gold had been destined), referred to in an inventory of the year 1008, though the work was probably not carried out (see J.-M. Sansterre and P. Henriet, 'De *l'inanimis imago* à l'*omagem mui bella*: méfiance à l'égard des images et essor de leur culte dans l'Espagne médiévale (VII–XIII siècle)', *Edad Media. Revista de historia*, 10 (2009), 37–92, particularly 50–53; and J. Duran-Porta, 'L'orfebreria romànica a Catalunya (950–1250). Volum I. Estudis' (unpublished PhD thesis, Universitat Autònoma de Barcelona, 2015), 364.

[13] For this question, see especially J.-M. Sansterre and P. Henriet, 'De *l'inanimis'* (as n. 12), particularly 44–45, 50–53, and 59.

[14] Currently there is no doubt that the Virgin of Bell-lloc (Cerdanya) is more than likely a late case of technically coarse workmanship rather than an early example. M. Delcor, *Les Vierges romanes de Cerdagne et Conflent dans l'Histoire et dans l'Art* (Barcelona 1970), 89–93; more recently, G. Dalmau and C. Roge-Bonneau, '045 Dorres. Vierge à l'Enfant, dite Vierge Noire, dite aussi Nostra Senyora de Belloch', in *Vierges à l'Enfant médiévales de Catalogne: mises en perspectives; suivi du Corpus des Vierges à l'Enfant (XIIe-XVe siècle) des Pyrénées-Orientales*, eds. M.-P. Subes and J.-B. Mathon (Perpignan 2013), 268–69.

[15] M. Delcor, *Les Vierges romanes* (as n. 14), 57–62; A. Orriols, 'De la icona al llibre. Algunes notes sobre imatges de la Verge transportades als manuscrits', *Lambard. Estudis d'art medieval*, XV (2003), 135–56; also G. Dalmau and C. Rogé-Bonneau, '042 Corneilla-de-Conflent. Notre-Dame de la Crêche dite aussi Nostra Senyora del Pessebre', in *Vierges à 'l'Enfant*, eds. M.-P. Subes and J.-B. Mathon (as n. 14), 262–63.

[16] Arxiu de la Corona d'Aragó, ms. Ripoll 151, f. 154. See A. Noguera, *Les marededéus romàniques de les terres gironines* (Barcelona 1977), 152–54; A. Orriols, 'De la icona' (as n. 15), 149–51.

[17] Museu Episcopal de Vic (MEV 17143). See M. dels S. Gros, *Museu Episcopal de Vic. Romànic* (Sabadell 1991), 88–89; M. Sureda, '15. St Mary "the Round"', in *North & South. Medieval Art from Norway and Catalonia 1100–1350*, eds. J. Kroesen, M. Leeflang, and M. Sureda (Zwolle 2019), 126–27.

[18] F. Español, 'El escenario litúrgico de la catedral de Girona (s. XI-XV)', *Hortius Artium Medievalium*, 11 (2005), 213–32, particularly 218–220.

[19] M. Angheben, 'La Vierge à l'Enfant comme imatge du prêtre officiant. Les exemples des peintures romanes des Pyrénées et de Maderuelo', *Codex Aquilarensis*, 28 (2012), 29–74.

[20] M. Trens, *Les majestats* (as. n. 5), 38; C. Baraut, 'Els documents dels anys 1051–1075 conservats a l'Arxiu Capitular de la Seu d'Urgell', *Urgellia*, VI, 1983 (1984), 7–243, particularly 115–17 and 127–29; C. Baraut, 'Els documents dels anys 1076–1092 conservats a l'Arxiu Capitular de la Seu d'Urgell', *Urgellia*, VII (1987), 7–218, particularly 213–14; C. Gascón Chopo, 'Estamariu als segles XI i XII: el desplegament del domini comtal', in S*ant Vicenç d'Estamariu. Tresor retrobat* (Lleida 2013), 19–23, particularly 19 and n. 7; M. Jorba, *Les majestats de la Cerdanya* (La Seu d'Urgell 2017).

[21] M. Trens, *Les majestats catalanes* (as n. 5); R. Bastardes, *Les talles romàniques* (as n. 5); M. Durliat, 'La signification' (as n. 5), 69–95.

[22] J. Camps, 'Majestat de Beget', in *Convidats d'honor. Exposició commemorativa del 75è aniversari del MNAC*, eds. C. Mendoza and M. T. Ocaña (Barcelona 2009), 96–101; I. Lorés et al., 'La sculpture romane catalane sur bois: étude et restauration du Christ de Casarilh et de la Majesté de Beget', *Les Cahiers de Saint-Michel de Cuxa*, 43 (2012), 101–11.

[23] Museu Nacional d'Art de Catalunya (MNAC 15937). J. Folch i Torres, 'Una "Majestat" romànica', *Gaseta de les Arts*, 1/4 (December 1928), 1–2; 'Majestad Batlló', in *El romànic i la Mediterrània. Catalunya, Toulouse i Pisa (1120–1180)*, eds. M. Castiñeiras and J. Camps (Barcelona 2008), 270–73.

[24] M. Trens, *Les majestats* (as n. 5), 115–20.

[25] Ibid., 135, pl. 31; see, also, M. Guardia and C. Mancho, 'Pedret, Boí, o dels orígens de la pintura mural romànica catalana', in *Les fonts de la pintura romànica*, eds. M. Guardia and C. Mancho (Barcelona 2008), 117–59, in particular 125–26, fig. 2.

[26] M. Castiñeiras, 'Il Maestro di Pedret e la pintura lombarda: mito o realtà', *Arte Lombarda*, 156 (2009), 48–66.

[27] M. Durliat, 'La signification des Majestés' (as n. 5), 84–86.

[28] É. Taburet-Delahaye, 'Christ d'applique', in *L'Oeuvre de Limoges. Émaux limousins du Moyen Âge* (Paris 1995), 184–85.

[29] F. Enaud, 'Découverte d'objets-reliquaires à Saint-Michel d'Aiguilhe (Haute-Loire)', *Bulletin monumental*, 122 (1964), 37–67; O. Poisson, 'Crist reliquiari de Saint-Michel d'Aiguilhe', in *El romànic*, eds. M. Castiñeiras and J. Camps (as n. 23), 416.

[30] M. Bacci, 'Nicodemo e il Volto Santo', in *Il Volto Santo in Europa. Culto e immagini del Crocifisso nel Medioevo. Atti del Convegno internazionale di Engelberg (13–16 settembre 2000)*, eds. M. C. Ferrari and A. Meyer (Lucca 2005), 15–40.

[31] M. Bacci, 'Le *Majestats*, il *Volto Santo* e il *Cristo di Beirut*. Nuove riflessioni', *Iconographica. Studies in the History of Images*, 13 (2014), 45–66.

[32] M. Durliat, 'La signification des Majestés' (as n. 5), 43.

[33] The analyses carried out on the belt of *Majestat Batlló* reveal the use of tin which, with the application of a varnish that would have given a golden appearance (M. Campuzano et al., 'Noves aportacions a l'estudi de la Majestat Batlló: identificació i caracterització de la policromia subjacent', in *Butlletí del Museu Nacional d'Art de Catalunya*, 11 (2011), 13–31, particularly 23, fig. 13).

[34] M. Castiñeiras, 'La cruz pintada de Bagergue: Cristo, serpiente, cordero y león', in *Progettare le arti. Studi in onore di Clara Baracchini*, eds. L. Carletti and C. Giometti (Pisa 2013), 21–30.

[35] It would be necessary to review the documentation of the whole of the Middle Ages in Catalonia to definitively confirm or refute this statement.

[36] M. Bacci, 'The Berardenga Antependium and the Passio Ymaginis Office', *Journal of the Warburg and Courtauld Institutes*, 61 (1998), 1–16, fig. 1.

[37] R. Bastardes, *La representació del Sant Crist al Taller d'Erill* (Barcelona 1977).

[38] J. Camps and J. M. Trullén, 'Descente de la Croix d'Erill la Vall', in *Catalogne romane. Sculptures du Val de Boí*, eds. J. Camps and X. Dectot (Paris–Barcelona 2004), 82–85.

[39] B. Schälicke, *Die Ikonographie der monumentalen Kreuzabnahmegruppen des Mittelalters in Spanien* (Berlin 1975); R. Bastardes, *Els davallaments romànics a Catalunya* (Barcelona 1980); in J. Camps and X. Dectot, *Catalogne romane* (as n. 38).

[40] J. Camps, 'Escultura d'epòca romanica ena Val d'Aran', in *Aran me fecit. Des Mèstres constructors ara recèrca deth patrimòni sacre*, ed. E. Ros (Vielha 2018), 25–28, in particular 27–28 (English translation: 325–28, specially 328).

[41] A. K. Porter, *Spanish Romanesque Sculpture*, vol. II (Barcelona 1928), 14.

[42] See illustration in www.museunacional.cat/en/colleccio/hell-santa-maria-de-taull/mestre-del-judici-final/015859-000.

[43] R. Bastardes, *Les talles* (as n. 5), 300–11.

[44] VINSEUM. Museu de les Cultures del Vi in Vilafranca del Penedès, inv. 3358. See J. Camps and A. Miguélez, 'Yo, Juan. La recuperación de una talla procedente del románico catalán', *Románico. Revista de Arte,* 21 (December 2015), 26–33.

[45] M. Castiñeiras and J. Camps, 'Figura pintada, imatge esculpida. Eclosió de la monumentalitat i diàleg entre les arts a Catalunya, 1120–1180', in *El romànic*, eds. M. Castiñeiras and J. Camps (as n. 23), 133–47.

[46] M. Castiñeiras, 'The Portal at Ripoll Revisited: An Honorary Arch for the Ancestors', in *Romanesque and the Past*, eds. J. McNeill and R. Plant (Leeds 2013), 121–41.

[47] N. Camós, *Jardín de María plantado en el Principado de Cataluña* (Barcelona 1949) (reprint of the work published in Barcelona in 1657 and reprinted in Girona in 1772), 368–72.

[48] Museu Episcopal de Vic (MEV 1404 and MEV 4914). See E. Bargalló, 'Santa Maria de Matamala', in *Catalunya Romànica*, vol. 10 (Barcelona 1987), 150–51; M. Gustà, 'Sant Bartomeu de Llaés', in ibid., 348–51.

[49] C. Sánchez, 'La peregrinación a Montserrat en los siglos XII y XIII: Génesis de una cultura devocional mariana', *Porticum. Revista d'Estudis Medievals*, 1 (2011), 28–43, in particular 40.

[50] M. Sureda, 'Les lieux de la Vierge. Notes de topo-liturgie mariale en Catalogne (XIe–XVe siècles)', in *Vierges à l'Enfant*, eds. M.-P. Subes and J.-B. Mathon (as n. 14), 39–69, particularly 61–62.

[51] F. X. Altés, 'La institució de la festa de Santa Maria en dissabte i la renovació de l'altar major del monestir de Ripoll a mitjan segle XII', *Studia Monastica*, 44, 1 (2002), 57–96.

[52] Museu Nacional d'Art de Catalunya (MNAC 15950). J. Ainaud, 'La consagració dels Crists en creu', *Liturgica*, 3 (1966), 11–20. See also J. Camps, 'Imágenes relicario de los siglos XII y XIII en Cataluña', in *Imagens e Liturgia na Idade Media*, coord. C. Varela (Lisboa 2016), 125–44, particularly 128–31.

[53] Cook, Gudiol, *Pintura e imaginería* (as n. 2, 1980), 290–95.

[54] T. Heilbronner, 'The Wooden Chasuble Madonnas' (as n. 3), 39–41.

[55] Museu Nacional d'Art de Catalunya (MNAC 65503). See J. Camps, 'Imatge de la Mare de Déu de Ger', *Prefiguració del Museu Nacional d'Art de Catalunya* (Barcelona 1992), 149–50.

[56] M. Castiñeiras, 'Entorn als orígens de la pintura romànica sobre taula a Catalunya: els frontals d'Urgell, Ix i Esquius', *Butlletí del Museu Nacional d'Art de Catalunya*, 9 (2008), 16–41.

[57] Institut Amatller d'Art Hispànic Collection, in Barcelona (see M. Durliat, *Christs romans du Roussillon et de Cerdagne* (Perpignan 1956), 43, fig. 17–18.

[58] Bode Museum (Berlin). Illustrated as Cat. 'J. 32 Un ange assis', in *Rhin-Meuse: art et civilisation 800–1400*, ed. A. von Euw (Bruxelles 1972), 301.

[59] In a general sense, see M. Castiñeiras, 'Patrons, Institutions and Públic in the Making of Catalan Romanesque Art During the Comital Period (1000–1137)', in *Romanesque Patrons and Processes. Design and Instrumentality in the Art and Architecture of Romanesque Europe*, eds. J. Camps, M. Castiñeiras, J. McNeill, and R. Plant (Oxford and New York 2018), 143–58.

[60] Museu de Terrassa, MdT 38. (See D. Ferran and A. Pladevall, 'Sant Cugat del Vallès', in *Catalunya Romànica*, vol. 18 (Barcelona 1991), 184–86).

[61] F. Español, 'Sant Joan de les Abadesses durant els segles del Romànic', in *El monestir de Sant Joan de les Abadesses*, eds. M. Crispí and M. Montraveta (Sant Joan de les Abadesses 2012), 47–82, particularly 75–81.

The Regional and Transregional in Romanesque Europe (2021), 249–259

ROMANESQUE WOODCARVERS AND PLASTERERS IN THE ABRUZZI

THE MEDITERRANEAN CONNECTION

Gaetano Curzi

In the 12th century, wooden doors, iconostasis screens, altars, thrones, and chests were carved and painted in Lazio, Campania, and the Abruzzi, following a tradition that had probably first developed in the previous century at Montecassino under Desiderius. Indeed, in his Chronicle, Leo Marsicano proudly describes the various different materials and techniques which Desiderius used and where, in addition to marble and precious metals, wood seems to have played an important role. The iconostasis, for example, consisted of a wooden beam that was splendidly carved and decorated with silver, gold, and purple but which did not survive the earthquake of 1349. A scaled-down version of this survives in the church of Santa Maria in Valle Porclaneta, which had belonged to Montecassino since 1064.

It is similarly of interest to note the wooden doors at the Greek abbey at Grottaferrata, at Santa Maria in Cellis and San Pietro in Albe, all of which show evidence of an awareness of Muslim forms and of work from the opposite side of the Adriatic Sea in the first half of the 12th century. Analysis of these works, especially in the light of recent discoveries, illuminates the close relationship that existed between the Abruzzi, Campania, and Apulia in this period.

In a similar vein, work that can be associated with the workshop of Ruggero, Roberto, and Nicodemo will be considered. This workshop was responsible for stucco ciboria and pulpits (at San Clemente al Vomano, Santa Maria in Valle Porcaneta, and Santa Maria del Lago a Moscufo) decorated with elaborate scrolls and imaginative ornamental motifs that reveal long-range influences.

The Abruzzi hinterland has preserved a rare group of wooden liturgical furnishings from the second quarter of the 12th century, originating from places only a few dozen kilometres apart and linked by the ancient Via Claudia-Valeria. Moreover, if we broaden the outlook to encompass a larger portion of the central Apennines, the number of artefacts preserved or recalled in sources increases still further.[1] This area was culturally dependent on Montecassino (Lazio), and almost all the buildings that will be mentioned were linked to the Benedictine world.[2]

The importance of wood in the reconstruction of the famous abbey promoted by Desiderius from 1066 onwards is therefore germane. According to the Chronicles of the monk Leo Marsicano, wood was not only used as a building material but, together with marble and precious metals, increased the magnificence of the church, which contained carved and painted choir stalls.[3] A reflection of these stalls has been seen by scholars in a panel (Figure 17.1) found in the early 20th century among the ruins of San Vincenzo al Volturno (Molise). However, the circumstances of this discovery, the excellent state of preservation and style of the relief, makes it unlikely that the rediscovered panel really is a fragment from a set of Romanesque choir stalls, and it therefore makes me doubt that it can be used to give an idea of what the Montecassino stalls looked like.[4]

In addition to the choir stalls, Montecassino was furnished with a fine wooden staircase which gave access to the ambo.[5] The pulpit was also entirely made of wood and was described as tall, majestic, and covered with purple and gold foils.[6] Wooden pulpits evidently continued to be made in later years, as can be seen from the four late 13th-century wooden columns now at the Victoria and Albert museum in London, which have probably come from Salerno (Campania).[7]

The iconostasis in Montecassino was made up of a beautifully carved wooden beam, this too decorated with gold and purple, supported by six columns covered with silver foil and adjoining a bronze beam:

> *Fecit itaque [. . .] trabem quoque nichilominus fusilem ex ere cum candelabris numero quinquaginta [. . .], ampadibus subter in ereis uncis ex eadem trabe triginta et sex dependentibus. Que videlicet erea trabes ereis eque brachiis ac manibus sustentata trabi lignee, quam pulcherrime sculpi et auro colorumque fucis interim fecerat*

DOI: 10.4324/9781003162827-17

FIGURE 17.1

Montecassino, library: wooden panel from San Vincenzo al Volturno (Gaetano Curzi)

FIGURE 17.2

Santa Maria in Valle Porclaneta: iconostasis and pulpit (Archivio DILASS)

FIGURE 17.3

Santa Maria in Valle Porclaneta: iconostasis, lintel (Archivio DILASS)

FIGURE 17.4
Santa Maria in Valle Porclaneta: iconostasis, detail of the lintel (Archivio DILASS)

FIGURE 17.5
Pofi, Sant'Antonino: detail of the lintel (Archivio DILASS)

> *Desiderius exornari, commissa est, et supra sex columnas argenteas quattuor et semis in altitudine cubitos habentes et octos libras per singulas in ipsa chori fronte constituit.*[8]

As such, the ensemble must have appeared like goldsmith's work, evoking the memory of the monumental *fastigium* donated by Constantine the Great to the Lateran Basilica in Roma, lost in 410 but celebrated in the *Liber pontificalis*.[9]

The life of the iconostasis of Montecassino was probably also cut short, either by looting on the part of Roger II and Frederick II or by the earthquake that destroyed the abbey in 1349.[10] Nonetheless, the literary description can be supplemented by works which took the Montecassino iconostasis as a model. Émile Bertaux had already recognized a small-scale replica of the work in the iconostasis which divides the interior of the church of Santa Maria in Valle Porclaneta (Abruzzo), a dependency of Montecassino since 1064 (Figures 17.2–17.4).[11]

This consists of two plutei made by 1150, the date which appears on the pulpit near to the one on the left (Figure 17.2). Above, there are four 13th-century columns, which replaced wooden columns probably damaged by an earthquake. At the top is an extraordinary lintel (Figure 17.3) datable to around the middle of the 12th century, formed by oak beams arranged horizontally

FIGURE 17.6

Celano, Museo d'Arte Sacra della Marsica: wooden doors from San Pietro at Alba Fucens (Archivio DILASS)

FIGURE 17.7

Celano, Museo d'Arte Sacra della Marsica: detail of the right valve from San Pietro at Alba Fucens (Archivio DILASS)

onto which a central panel is inserted.[12] The decoration of the lower strip is composed of an interweaving pattern which generates eleven major clipei alternating with twelve smaller rhomboids each with a flower at the centre. A scroll marks the passage to the upper register. This is divided into thirty arches completed by another volute with six figures holding books on the left and six *telamones* on the right. In the middle (Figure 17.4), the regular course is interrupted by three large arches crowned with cherubs.

We don't know what was depicted within the arcades, Hahnloser suggested that an iconographic programme centred on the *Deesis* was developed in the arches, flanked by saints and surmounted by angels and the *Etimasia*. The lower clipei meanwhile accommodated a feast cycle.[13] The iconographical reconstruction is based on the second version of the *pala d'oro* at Saint Mark's, Venice, which Hahnloser dates to the early 12th century and which in turn took the iconostasis of Montecassino as a model. Thus Santa Maria in Valle Porclaneta would have been closely modelled on Montecassino, and is, perhaps, not an isolated case in the region. The *Chronicon Casauriense* recalls that by 1093, a wooden door and a beam were installed in the choir of the abbey of San Clemente in Casauria (Abruzzo), with painted pictures of the Saviour, the apostles, the prophets, the Passion and Agnus Dei, indirectly confirming the reconstruction proposed by Hahnloser for Santa Maria in Valle Porclaneta.[14]

Despite the loss of the painted scenes, the iconostasis from Santa Maria in Valle Porclaneta offers considerable points of interest. Firstly, it has preserved microscopic traces of red, blue, ochre, and black colour, which point to it once having had a very bright appearance.[15] What is more, the decorative structure of the lower part can be found in a monumental oak lintel in Sant'Antonino a Pofi (Lazio). This too originally formed part of an iconostasis inspired by that of Montecassino (Figure 17.5).[16] Here, the clipei contain busts of saints, of which a few traces survive, while there are more substantial remains of painting among the plant motifs where we find intense reds and blues, a bright yellow close to gold, and fragments of a silver foil. The overall effect, as at Santa Maria in Valle Porclaneta, must have been extremely precious, recalling the bronze, silver, gold, and purple of the prototype at Montecassino.

The diffusion of this type of work across a much wider geographical area is suggested by a pair of wooden pillars, probably part of an iconostasis, in Sant'Adriano at San Demetrio Corone (Calabria),[17] where the *opus sectile* floor is very similar to that of Montecassino.[18]

In the following decades in central-southern Italy, in the wake of the construction project started by Desiderius, the use of carved wood for different types of liturgical furnishings became widespread. In Santa Maria in Vulturella, between Lazio and the Abruzzi, a panel in high relief represents the consecration of the sanctuary and the vision of St Eustace, the latter event having taken place in the surrounding woods. The lower part of the panel was divided into boxes by a grid of semi-precious stones, of which the imprint remains, transforming this work into a precious piece of furniture.[19] It probably dates to the beginning of the 13th century and originally, perhaps, formed the front of a *confession*. It recalls the pulpit and the iconostasis at Montecassino, where the side altars

FIGURE 17.8

Grottaferrata, Abbey of San Nilo: wooden doors (Gaetano Curzi)

FIGURE 17.9

Celano, Museo d'Arte Sacra della Marsica: wooden doors from Santa Maria in Cellis (Archivio DILASS)

were also covered with wooden panels, probably carved and painted to withstand comparison with the high altar and repoussé silver.[20] In Montecassino, as at the abbey of Farfa (Lazio), sources describe the presence of various relief icons, finished with painting and metal leaf.[21] We can obtain an idea of their appearance through the interesting figure of St Valerio now in the bishop's palace at Tivoli (Lazio), dated to *c.* 1138, or through the image of Christ the Saviour in the parish church of Castelchiodato (Lazio), which perhaps came from Farfa.[22] These are both reliquary images. The holes for the relics can still be seen, but in both cases questionable restoration has brought the wood back into view, eliminating modern repainting of poor quality but which gave the idea of the colourful vivacity of their original appearance.

The chronicle of the Benedictine monastery of Subiaco (Lazio) on the other hand testifies that in 1069 Abbot John gave the monastery a carved wooden arch of great beauty to contain books,[23] a piece of information that recalls the illustration of an *armarium* decorated in a famous codex of Rabanus Maurus made at Montecassino around 1030.[24] The only object of this sort to survive is an exotic cypress chest from Terracina, an important harbour close to Montecassino, though in this particular case, it is uncertain as to whether the chest was originally meant to contain books, documents, or relics.[25]

A similar interest in the representation of fights between men and fantastic animals, as is found on the chest, turns up on the surviving wooden doors (Figure 17.6 and Colour Plate XXII) from the church of San Pietro, on the hill overlooking the Roman city of Alba Fucens (Abruzzo), rebuilt by the mid-12th century in a style recalling once again Montecassino, on which depended the adjacent local monastery of Sant'Angelo.[26]

Severely damaged by the earthquake of 1915, the maple door is made up of two leafs, split into twenty-eight square compartments by moulded frames occupied by a variety of foliate motifs, from the rinceaux pattern which runs continuously along the entire outer edge, to the stylized leaves of the horizontal bands, up to the elegant wind-blown acanthus of the vertical axis. The square panels are organized in horizontal registers and are filled with figures in high relief, starting with the symbols of the Evangelists at the top, followed by David and Samson and a tribute to a holy bishop (Figure 17.7). In the third register, a pair of bulls precedes two knights. In the fourth re-register are a man armed with a club, a centaur, and two deer. The fifth register continues the representation of animals, probably inspired by oriental textiles, while the bestiary continues at the bottom of the door valves where early illustrations show a fantastical

FIGURE 17.10

Celano, Museo d'Arte Sacra della Marsica: detail of the wooden doors from Santa Maria in Cellis (Archivio DILASS)

animal facing frontally. A similar series can be found on the other side of the Adriatic on the doors of St Nicholas at Ohrid in North Macedonia (now in the National History Museum in Sofia).[27] These are difficult to date, as the doors seem to consist of pieces from different periods, though it is likely that for the most part they date back to the 12th century.

The affronted pairs of knights and animals in these works, glorifying hunting and spiritual combat, are to be interpreted as a metaphor for the struggle between good and evil and are well suited to a liminal position, separating the outside world from sacred space. This was also a theme developed in the bronze doors which spread through southern Italy in the Romanesque period. However, it is the formal geometric framework and setting of the bronze doors which seems to have been more influential and certainly seems to have inspired the wooden door of the Greek abbey of San Nilo in Grottaferrata (Lazio). This dates to the early 12th century and is still in its original context, consisting of a marble frame of classical inspiration, surmounted by a mosaic.[28] The door here is made up of two leaves decorated with foliate and geometric motifs which frame plain rectangular panels (Figure 17.8), recalling not only the doors of antiquity but those imported into southern Italy from Constantinople.[29] The latter lie behind the imprint of a cross, perhaps originally metal, and the numerous protuberances in the shape of studs arranged at short regular intervals, which at Grottaferrata obviously do not secure the metal plates but have a purely ornamental function.[30]

The great surprise at Grottaferrata, is the different width of the two leaves, particularly given the geometric regularity of the surface design. The left-hand door is clearly narrower. The consistency of the whole rules out the possibility of the two doors being of different origin. Moreover, a similar asymmetry can be found a few years later at Santa Maria in Cellis near Carsoli (Abruzzo), a monastery on the boundary between Lazio and the Abruzzi, donated to Montecassino in 1060.[31]

The doors from Santa Maria in Cellis are made of a light, resistant, and extremely compact wood, so much so that the carvings recall work in ivory (Figure 17.9). The surface, however, has been unfortunately corroded by exposure to the elements, particularly noticeable in the lower part, where there are signs of erosion caused by rainwater. Even so, traces of colour remained on the doors into the early 20th century.

The two leaves are framed by an elegant rinceaux pattern, which in turn contains a cycle of the childhood of Christ arranged from left to right and from top to bottom. A reversal of the narrative sequence characterizes the fourth register, where the Baptism precedes the Presentation at the Temple, while the fifth (and lowest) pair are almost illegible but appear to depict standing figures who seem in some cases to be wearing monastic dress.

All scenes are accompanied by explanatory inscriptions (Figure 17.10). On the left leaf, these are positioned in the decorative strip, while on the right leaf the identifying inscriptions are arranged within the narrative panels themselves, and the lettering between the panels consists of a long commemorative text. Only the first two lines of this are legible, containing the date of the door: '*Anno d(omi)ni millesimo centesimo tricesimo s(e)c(un)do, indic(tione) X [e]pac(ta) XII*'. What is striking here is that the year is accompanied not only by the indiction date but also by the much rarer calculation of the *epacta*, a figure related to the difference between the number of days in a given calendar year and those of the lunar year. This calculation is attested in the Abruzzi in a manuscript dating back to the early 9th century and in an epigraph dated 1151 that is discussed on the following page.[32] The text then continues for another four lines, where it was possible to read, between sequences of indecipherable letters, *beate Mariae, Iohannes*, and *Stefanus*, suggesting that it contained information on the dedication of the church, the names of the artist and the patron. The difference in width cannot be traced back to a different origin for the two leaves, which prompts us to look for alternative explanations, perhaps linked to the function of the portal itself. This can be used and seen differently, according to whether the doors are opened or closed. It is also possible that certain liturgical ceremonies required

FIGURE 17.11
San Clemente al Vomano: ciborium *(Archivio DILASS)*

FIGURE 17.12
San Clemente a Casauria: lapidarium, fragment from the lost ciborium *(Gaetano Curzi)*

the partial opening of the door, limited to a single leaf, which, however, had to be large enough to allow the passage of a procession, an image, or a statue. Different measurements characterise the leaves of the bronze door of Augsburg cathedral and, before their restoration in 1908, the wooden doors of the cathedral of Split, executed in 1214 by the painter Andrea Buvina.[33]

Recent studies have also demonstrated that wooden doors were not an economic substitute for those in bronze. Through polychromy, wooden doors could take on a similarly precious appearance.[34] It is for this reason that significant numbers of these artefacts were produced by different workshops in particular parts of Europe. This was the case in the Auvergne, for instance, or the Central Apennines, where all the works examined have common prototypes and draw on a common decorative repertoire but are never produced by the same workshop.[35] Even when it comes to the three masterpieces surviving in the Abruzzi, all made in the second quarter of the 12th century in a circumscribed area, the differences are more evident than the similarities. It is simply that the doors were made in a given artistic landscape, within which common elements can be found, even between works in different media and made using different techniques.

In this respect, we might turn to examine the work of a family of plasterers active in the Abruzzo during the 12th century in buildings linked to the Benedictine order.[36] Their first known work is the *ciborium* at San Clemente al Vomano (Figure 17.11), made between the fourth and fifth decades of the 12th century and signed by Robert and his father Roger.[37] The *ciborium* is a square structure resting on four columns linked by arches. In the upper part, there are two staggered octagons, the lower one lightened by rows of intersecting arches while the upper octagon is articulated by horseshoe arches. The upper octagon is, in turn, twisted through half a revolution, creating a sense of gyratory movement in a work which is entirely covered by refined stucco work consisting of foliage trails containing allegorical figures.

At the same period, the two artists were responsible for providing new liturgical furnishings at San Clemente a Casauria, where just a few fragments now survive (Figure 17.12).[38] In 1150, Robert, together with Nicodemus, perhaps his brother, appear as the creators of the pulpit of Santa Maria in Valle Porclaneta (Figure 17.2).[39] The ornamental repertoire is enriched here with liturgical themes and references to the Old Testament. In the same church, above the altar, is another *ciborium* which, in terms of its layout and decorative taste, is modelled on that of San Clemente al Vomano, an exception being made for the arcade, which has a trilobe profile similar to that of the Moscufo pulpit (Figure 17.13).[40] Although no inscription has survived at Santa Maria in Valle Porclaneta, it can therefore be associated with this pulpit and attributed to Robert and Nicodemus. In 1151, Nicodemus appeared alone in an inscription at San Martino sulla Marrucina in the inscription just mentioned in relation to the presence of the *epacta*. The inscription formed part of a lost *ciborium*:

> *Anni Domini millesi/mo centesimo L I indic/tione XIII epacta I m(en)s(e)/f(e)b(ruarii) inienii certus varii/Nicodemus magistrus/hoc levigarum Nicode/mus adq(ue) atque dolarum et fa/cies homnium volucrum/pecodu(m) que conectem inge/nio patrioq(ue) labore refle/ctet hoc Benedictus op[us] /dum fecit m(en)te fideli horat/ut a domino mereatur/premia cel.*[41].

The text defines Nicodemus as *magister* and attributes to him a knowledge of the profession due to the teachings of his father, who may have been Roger himself, suggesting

Figure 17.13
Moscufo, Santa Maria del Lago: pulpit, West side (Achivio DILASS)

FIGURE 17.14

Moscufo, Santa Maria del Lago: pulpit, South side (Achivio DILASS)

FIGURE 17.15

Canosa, Mausoleum of Bohemond: bronze doors (Gaetano Curzi)

the possibility of a family workshop of which he became the *leader*.

His signature is also to be found in 1159 on the pulpit of Santa Maria del Lago in Moscufo, a work which develops the solutions already developed in Santa Maria in Valle Porclaneta (Figures 17.13 and 17.14).[42] The significantly better state of preservation of the Santa Maria del Lago pulpit, which even retains elements of its original polychromy, enables us to appreciate its greater three-dimensionality. Its iconographic programme is also appreciably more elaborate than earlier compositions by the workshop, with quotes from classical sculpture, as with the thorn puller at the corner of the parapets. The last work to survive from this family workshop is the pulpit of Santo Stefano a Cugnoli, which is a replica of Moscufo made some seven years later in 1166.[43]

In short, this group of works was created over a period of roughly thirty years by three sculptors, employing a refined and eclectic language which has its roots in the figurative culture of Norman southern Italy, in particular Puglia and Campania, where the classical tradition was susceptible to Byzantine and Islamic influences.

The relatively eclectic sources of the *ciborium* of San Clemente al Vomano has induced some scholars to identify the Roger of the inscription as Roger of Melfi, the creator of the bronze doors of the mausoleum of Bohemond at Canosa (Puglia), predating 1122 and rich in Islamic quotations (Figure 17.15).[44] However, despite the dense web of references that can be grasped among these works, I do not believe that these two Rogers are one and the same person, Nor do I agree with the attribution to Roger, author of the *ciborium* of San Clemente al Vomano, of the wooden doors of Carsoli and San in Albe.[45] Although the latter share the rare use of the *epacta* and several decorative themes with the stucco works, they are not notably close, and any correspondences are attributable to their shared figurative horizon, along with the tendency of trade to favour technical practices which are in some steps similar. The more standardised decorative parts of the works of Roger, Robert, and Nicodemus, came about through the use of wooden moulds, for instance, a technique also to be found in stuccowork of the Norman period from Calabria and Sicily.[46]

A positive mould in carved wood, on which the clay could be modelled in negative, was also used in the complex operation of casting the bronze doors for the Mausoleum of Bohemond. The ornamental bands in 'chip carving' here were originally highlighted by red and black surface colouring, of which traces were discovered during the most recent restoration (Colour Plate XXIII).[47] It is striking that we find this type of two-dimensional relief in the wooden doors of Grottaferrata (Figure 17.8) and of San Pietro in Albe (Figures 17.6 and 17.7). Ultimately, it reflects a taste that some scholars consider to be of Andalusian origin, from where, after the 10th century, it spread to much of Europe.[48] One might think once again of the wooden doors of the Auvergne.

Given the versatility of carved wood, both as a production tool for bronze and stucco and as a vehicle for independent sculpture, it was capable of promoting exchanges of techniques and repertoires, preserving an eclectic character that could still to be found at the end of the 12th century. This is evident in the chair of Montevergine, an extraordinary work whose Islamic-style discs once again recall the doors to Bohemond's mausoleum.[49] That Montevergine was not alone at this date is also suggested by a panel now in the United States which was originally part of a throne or a chest, perhaps originating in southern Italy and decorated with animals inside *rotae* in the manner of oriental textiles.[50]

These reflections on eclecticism and technical skill take us back to where we started, that is to Montecassino as a centre of art and culture. According to Amatus of Montecassino, Desiderius enlisted workers from Byzantium and the Islamic world.[51] But he did not limit himself to using them to embellish the abbey. Leo Marsicanus assures us that he made sure that a large number of young people at the monastery were also educated in the arts, thus training masters who became skilled in working gold, silver, bronze, iron, glass, ivory, wood, stucco, and stone.[52]

NOTES

1 G. Curzi, *Arredi lignei medievali. L'Abruzzo e l'Italia centromeridionale. Secoli XII–XIII* (Cinisello Balsamo 2007).

2 G. Curzi, 'Ipotesi sull'origine cassinese di alcune botteghe romaniche di intagliatori del legno', in *Cantieri e maestranze nell'Italia medievale*, ed. M. C. Somma (Spoleto 2010), 157–86.

3 Leone Marsicano, *Cronaca di Montecassino,* eds. F. Aceto and V. Lucherini (Milan 2001), Book III, 26–33. For the reference to the choir stalls – '*Fecit et sedilia lignea in circuitu chori cum dossalibus eorum scalptura simul et pictura decora*': see *Chronica Monasterii Casinensis* (MGH, Scriptores, XXXIV, 1980), 384.

4 É. Bertaux, *L'art dans l'Italie méridionale* (Paris 1903), I, 212; P. Toesca, 'Reliquie d'arte della badia di S. Vincenzo al Volturno', *Bullettino dell'Istituto Storico Italiano*, 25 (1904), 1–84; A. Pantoni, *Le chiese e gli edifici del monastero di San Vincenzo al Volturno* (Montecassino 1980), 153; Curzi, 'Ipotesi sull'origine cassinese' (as n. 2), 176–78.

5 '*Sed et gradum nichilominus ligneum eiusdem operis extra chorum in ambonis modum satis pulchrum constituit*': *Chronica Monasterii* (as n. 3), 384.

6 '*Fecit quoque et pulpitum ligneum ad legendum sive cantandum longe priori prestantius et minentius, [. . .], idque diversis colorum fucis et auri petalis de pulchro pulcherrimum reddidit*': *Chronica Monasterii* (as n. 3), 403–04; *Cronaca di Montecassino* (as n. 3), 73.

7 J. Pope-Hennessy, *Catalogue of Italian Sculpture in the Victoria and Albert Museum* (London 1964), 7–9; P. Williamson, *Catalogue of Romanesque Sculpture. Victoria and Albert Museum* (London 1983), 68–77; F. Negri Arnoldi, 'Scultura italiana al Victoria and Albert Museum I', *Commentari*, 21 (1970), 17–26; A. Braca, 'Le colonne lignee del Victoria and Albert Museum di Londra', in *San Pietro a Corte. Recupero di una memoria nella città di Salerno* (Salerno 2000), 43–56; A. Braca, 'La scultura lignea medievale nel salernitano: presenze e problemi (secc. XII–XIII)', in *L'arte del legno in Italia. Esperienze e indagini a confronto*, ed. G. B. Fidanza (Perugia 2005), 201–16.

8 *Chronica Monasterii* (as n. 3), 403–04; *Cronaca di Montecassino* (as n. 3), 71.

9 *Le Liber pontificalis*, ed. L. Duchesne (Paris 1886), I, 172.

10 H. Bloch, *Monte Cassino in the Middle Ages* (Rome 1986), I, 70–71.

11 Bertaux, *L'art dans l'Italie méridionale* (as n. 4) II, 554–55; Curzi, *Arredi lignei* (as n. 1), 65–78; I. Trizio, *La chiesa di Santa Maria in Valle Porclaneta: la vicenda storico-costruttiva e l'uso di strumenti innovativi per la gestione della conoscenza* (Florence 2017).

12 Curzi, *Arredi lignei* (as n. 1), 65–70; for a different dating, see A. Trivellone, 'La decorazione scultorea medievale della chiesa abbaziale di S. Maria in Valle Porclaneta presso Rosciolo', in *La Terra dei Marsi. Cristianesimo, cultura, istituzioni*, ed. G. Luongo (Roma 2002), pp. 411–26.

13 H. R. Hahnloser, 'Le oreficerie della Pala d'oro, la nuova montatura di Bonesegna (1342) e del "Maestro Principale" (1343–1345)', in *Il tesoro di San Marco, I, La Pala d'oro*, ed. H. R. Hahnloser (Florence 1965), 81–114.

14 '*In cujus tempore magna Crux, que est in choro Ecclesie Sancti Clementis erecta, miro opere facta est atque depicta, que in magna veneratione tam a fratribus, quam a multis aliis habetur, eo quod ad honorem pretiosi ligni crucis Christi circa sibi devotos multum sit exaudibilis. Fecit etiam domnus Iohannes Abbas trabem, ubi Salvatoris yconas et ymagines prophetarum, et apostolorum, passionem quoque Domini, et Agnum Dei laudabili depincxit opere, ac in sublime levans super eiusdem chori ianuam ordinavit*': *Liber instrumentorum seu chronicorum monasterii Casauriensis seu Chronicon Casauriense*, eds. A. Pratesi and P. Cherubini (Rome 2017–18), I, 1099.

15 E. Sonnino, 'S. Maria in Valle Porclaneta. Note sulla storia conservativa e le caratteristiche tecnico-stilistiche di alcune opere attraverso in loro restauro', in *La Terra dei Marsi* (as n. 12), 427–36.

16 G. Curzi, 'Un frammento di iconostasi lignea-ai margini della Terra di san Benedetto. La trave intagliata della chiesa di Sant'Antonino a Pofi (Frosinone)', *Arte Medievale*, 3rd series, 6 (2007), 65–74.

17 Curzi, *Arredi lignei* (as n. 1), 84.

18 X. Barral i Altet, *Le décor du pavement au Moyen Âge: les mosaïques de France et d'Italie* (Rome 2010), 373.

19 Curzi, *Arredi lignei* (as n. 1), 95–102.

20 *Chronica Monasterii* (as n. 3), 403–04; *Cronaca di Montecassino* (as n. 3), 73.

21 Curzi, 'Ipotesi sull'origine cassinese' (as n. 2), 173–74.

22 G. Curzi, 'Secundum unguentum est devotionis. Il rilievo con il Salvatore e due donne a Castelchiodato', in *Immagine e ideologia, Studi in onore di Arturo Carlo Quintavalle* (Milan 2007), 184–90.

23 '*[Iohannes] fecit arcile ad recondendum libros sculptum mira pulchritudine [. . .]: Chronicon Sublacense*', in *Rerum Italicarum Scriptores*, ed. L. A. Muratori (Milan 1738), XXIV, 938.

24 Montecassino, Library, Casin, 132, 96.

25 G. Curzi, 'La cassa lignea di Terracina tra Riforma e crociata', in *Terracina nel medioevo*, eds. M. T. Gigliozzi and M. Nuzzo (Rome 2020), 105–12.

26 Curzi, *Arredi lignei* (as n. 1), 15–46.

27 I. Gergova and A. Paribeni, 'scheda n. 70', in *Tesori dell'arte cristiana in Bulgaria*, ed. V. Pace (Sofija 2000), 193–94.

28 M. Andaloro, 'Le porte lignee medievali in Abruzzo e nel Lazio', in *Le porte di bronzo dall'antichità al secolo XII*, ed. S. Salomi (Rome 1990), 325–40.

29 A. Iacobini, ed., *Le porte del Paradiso. Arte e tecnologia bizantina tra Italia e Mediterraneo* (Rome 2009).

30 This type of door can be found as late as the 14th century, an example being the unpublished wooden doors of San Francesco at Corvaro di Borgorose (Lazio), between Roma and L'Aquila, where the frames, plain panels, and fleurons reflect a desire to link up with the classical line of Abruzzi sculpture reaching back to the 12th and 13th centuries.

[31] Curzi, *Arredi lignei* (as n. 1), 47–64.

[32] Karlsruhe, Badische Landesbibliothek, Aug. perg. 229, *c.* 184r; C. Tedeschi, 'Un centro scrittorio nell'Abruzzo franco. Il ms. *Aug. perg.* 229 e il monastero di S. Stefano in Lucana', *Bullettino dell'Istituto Storico Italiano per il Medioevo*, 116 (2014), 1–23.

[33] For Augsburg, see U. Mende, *Die Bronzetüren des Mittelalters 800–1200* (München 1983), 34–40. For Split, see V. Gvozdanovich, 'Split Cathedral's Wooden Doors', *Commentari*, 29 (1978), 47–62.

[34] X. Barral i Altet, 'Riflessioni sull'elaborazione, la diffusione e le funzioni iconografiche delle porte lignee decorate negli edifici religiosi romanici', in *Abruzzo. Un laboratorio di ricerca per la scultura lignea, Studi Medievali e Moderni*, 15 (2011), 365–93.

[35] For the Auvergne, see W. Cahn, *The Romanesque Wooden Doors of Auvergne* (New York 1974).

[36] M. L. Fobelli, 'Ruggero, Roberto e Nicodemo', in *Enciclopedia dell'Arte medievale* (Rome 1999), X, 201–04; G. Ferrante, *La "firma" d'artista nel Medioevo: il caso di Ruggero, Roberto e Nicodemo* (Civitavecchia 2018). A. Ghisetti Giavarina and M. Maselli Campagna, *Le fondazioni benedettine in Abruzzo e Puglia* (Naples 2007).

[37] F. Bologna, 'San Clemente al Vomano. Il ciborio Ruggiero e Roberto', in *Documenti dell'Abruzzo Teramano, 2, La valle del medio e basso Vomano* (Roma 1986), I, 299–339; F. Coden, 'L'arredo liturgico di San Clemente al Vomano e la sua influenza in terra abruzzese', in *Un Medioevo in lungo e in largo: da Bisanzio all'Occidente (VI–XVI secolo). Studi per Valentino Pace*, eds. V. Camelliti and A. Trivellone (Pisa 2014), 127–37.

[38] I. C. Gavini, *Storia dell'architettura in Abruzzo* (Milan-Rome 1927–28), 196.

[39] F. Gandolfo, *Scultura medievale in Abruzzo. L'età normanno-sveva* (Pescara 2004), 69–75; S. Caranfa, 'Precisazioni intorno alla data di esecuzione dell'ambone di S. Maria in Valle Porclaneta', *Bullettino della Deputazione Abruzzese di Storia Patria*, 90 (2000), 125–33.

[40] Ibid., 69–75.

[41] Ibid., 69; Curzi, *Arredi lignei* (as n. 1), 55–56.

[42] F. Bologna, 'Ambone di Nicodemo, 1156. Santa Maria del Lago. Moscufo', in *Documenti dell'Abruzzo Teramano: 6, Dalla valle del Fino alla valle del medio e alto Pescara* (Teramo 2003), I, 335–40; Gandolfo, *Scultura medievale* (as n. 39), 76–83.

[43] F. Gandolfo, 'L'uso dei modelli in una bottega di stuccatori abruzzesi alla metà del XII secolo', in *Medioevo: i modelli*, ed. A. C. Quintavalle (Milan 2002), 319–29; L. Aventin, 'Des images au service de la parole. Le programme iconografique de Rosciolo, Moscufo et Cugnoli (Abruzzes, 1157–1166)', *Cahiers de civilisation médiévale*, 46 (2003), 301–26.

[44] Bologna, 'San Clemente al Vomano (as n. 37), 324–33; F. Aceto, 'Una fucina di cultura araba nel XII secolo: la bottega di Ruggiero da Melfi', *Rassegna del Centro di Cultura e Storia Amalfitana*, 17 (1999), 85–112.

[45] Bologna, 'San Clemente al Vomano' (as n. 37), 314–33; F. Aceto, 'L'Abruzzo e il Molise', in *La scultura d'età normanna tra Inghilterra e Terrasanta. Questioni storiografiche*, ed. M. D'Onofrio (Roma-Bari 2001), 49–70.

[46] C. Nenci, 'Gli stucchi italiani, nuove ricerche su alcune opere in stucco dell'Abruzzo', in *Stucs et décors de la fin de l'antiquité au Moyen âge (Ve–XIIe siècle)*, ed. C. Sapin (Turnhout 2009), 269–83. G. Di Cangi, C. M. Lebole Di Cangi, and C. Sabbione, 'Scavi medievali in Calabria: Gerace 1', *Archeologia medievale*, 18 (1991), 587–642.

[47] A. Cadei, 'La porta del mausoleo di Boemondo a Canosa tra Oriente e Occidente', in *Le porte del Paradiso* (as n. 29), 429–69.

[48] 1 K. Watson, 'The Kufic Inscription in the Romanesque Cloister of Moissac in Quercy: Links with Le Puy, Toledo and Catalan Woodworkers', *Arte medievale*, 3rd series, 1 (1995), 7–27; eadem, *French Romanesque and Islam, Andalusian Elements in French Architectural Decoration* (Oxford 1989).

[49] Curzi, *Arredi lignei* (as n. 1), 86–95; F. Gandolfo and G. Muollo, *Arte medievale in Irpinia* (Rome 2013), 103–11.

[50] The panel is now in the Fogg Art Museum in Cambridge (Massachusetts). See C Bornstein-Verzár, 'Catalogue Number 45', in *The Meeting of Two Worlds. The Crusades and the Mediterranean Context. Catalogue of the Exhibition* (Ann Arbor 1981), 72–73; *Le Crociate. L'Oriente e l'Occidente da Urbano II a San Luigi. 1096–1270*, ed. M. Rey-Delqué (Milan 1997), 296, 399.

[51] '*Et pour ce qu'il non trova in Ytalie homes de cert art, manda en Costentinnoble et en Alixandre pour homes grex et sarazins; pour aorner lo pavement de la eglize de marinoire entaillié et diverses paintures*': Amatus of Montecassino, *Storia de'Normanni* (Rome 1935), 375.

[52] '*Et quoniam artium istarum ingenium a quingentis et ultra iam annis magistra Latinitas intermiserat et studio huius inspirante et cooperante Deo nostro hoc tempore recuperare promeruit, ne sane id ultra Italie deperiret, studuit vir totius prudentie plerosque de monasterii pueris diligenter eisdem artibus erudiri. Non autem de his tantum, sed et de omnibus artificiis, quecumque ex auro vel argento, ere, ferro, vitro, ebore, ligno, gipso vel lapide patrari possunt, studiosissimos prorsus artifices de suis sibi paravit*': *Cronaca di Montecassino* (as n. 3), 57.

The Regional and Transregional in Romanesque Europe (2021), 261–272

A COUNTRY WITHOUT REGIONS?
THE CASE OF HUNGARY

Béla Zsolt Szakács

During the Middle Ages, the Kingdom of Hungary was among the larger countries of Latin Christianity. Subsequently, geographers divided the kingdom into regions (Transdanubia, Upper Hungary, Transylvania, and the Great Hungarian Plain). Although these divisions are geographically useful, the medieval monuments of the Kingdom of Hungary do not necessarily follow their logic. Among known Romanesque churches, certain features can be found throughout the country ('Lombard' ground plans, western towers, and six-lobed rotundas). While a special style developed in western Hungary, where buildings were enriched with stone carvings featuring acanthus and palmette motifs in the 11th century, this style became widespread by 1100. Micro-regions – the Saxon Lands in Transylvania, for example, or the region around Ják – can be detected though their local styles do not develop to form a larger regional dialect. Regions within Hungary did not function as autonomous units, nor was there a powerful local aristocracy. Administration was centralised, and the nobility, which had estates in different parts of the country, often moved between regions. This probably explains the strong interregional artistic connections within the country.

INTRODUCTION

> This province, called Pannonia since Antiquity, is surrounded by forests and mountains, with an extraordinarily huge plain inside, crossed by rivers of clear water. It is rich in woodland, full of wild animals, and the natural beauty of its territory is as pleasant as its fertile fields are abundant. Thus, it is as seemly as God's Paradise or the fair land of Egypt.[1]

These words were written by Bishop Otto of Freising in the middle of the 12th century. The 'province' he outlined broadly corresponds to the medieval Kingdom of Hungary, which, by the time Bishop Otto was writing, was one the largest countries in Europe.[2] Modern geographers describe the area as the Carpathian basin, a territory which in turn they divide into regions.[3] The land to the east of the Danube is hilly and comparable to its southern neighbour, Slavonia, between the rivers Sava and the Drava. The mountainous region in the north, which roughly corresponds to present-day Slovakia and the Transcarpathian part of Ukraine, was traditionally known as Upper Hungary. In the east, the smaller basin surrounded by mountains is Transylvania. While in the middle of the Carpathian Basin is a large plain, crossed by the rivers Danube and Tisa.

The first geographical description of the Hungarian Kingdom was written in 1536 by Nicolaus Olahus, a significant humanist and subsequently the archbishop of Esztergom (1553–68).[4] He also divided Hungary into four regions, starting with Transdanubia and Slavonia, continuing with Upper Hungary and the territory between the Danube and the Tisa and ending with Transylvania and the rest of the Great Plain. Although this differs slightly to the divisions adopted by later geographers, Olahus clearly acknowledges the existence of regions within the kingdom.

The larger European medieval polities, like France or the Holy Roman Empire, acknowledged what amount to regions in the Middle Ages (Saxony, Swabia, Normandy, Aquitaine, etc.), regions which, at least in the 19th century, worked as art-historical units, and even neighbouring Poland consisted of well-defined provinces, such as Lesser Poland, Silesia, Greater Poland or Mazovia. It therefore seems logical to suppose that the various regions of Hungary would also have given rise to discernible regional approaches to Romanesque during the 11th and 12th centuries.

Notwithstanding this, scholars who deal with medieval Hungarian art have been surprisingly reluctant to discuss the question of regional style. Early scholarship, up to the end of the 20th century, was concerned to deal with Hungarian Romanesque art on a national level.[5] The first groundbreaking attempt to offer an overview of the medieval artistic heritage of a Hungarian region was an exhibition dedicated to the art of Transdanubia, held in 1994–95.[6] This inspired another important venture,

  DOI: 10.4324/9781003162827-18

a volume of collected essays dedicated to the southern part of the Great Plain.[7] Local researchers have continued in smaller areas in eastern Hungary and Transylvania.[8] And, more recently, I have compiled a catalogue of 250 Romanesque churches in Transdanubia together with an introductory essay.[9] It was during this research that I found myself having to confront the problem of regionalism in Hungarian Romanesque.

ARCHITECTURAL ARRANGEMENTS

'Benedictine' ground plans, western towers, and centrally planned churches

From the very beginning, Hungarian scholars have tried to find national characteristics in the Romanesque architecture of the country. Arnold Ipolyi and Imre Henszlmann realized in the second half of the 19th century that many of the churches built in Hungary between the 11th and 13th centuries adopted a particular layout, which they referred to as the 'Benedictine ground plan'.[10] This type of architectural arrangement, also known as the 'Lombard ground plan' in earlier literature, consists of a three-aisled basilica without transepts, which terminates in three semicircular apses that spring in line with each other (Figure 18.1). The first dateable monument of this type was founded by King Géza I in 1075 at Garamszentbenedek (today Hronský Beňadik in Slovakia).[11] Géza I's younger brother, King Saint Ladislas I, founded a similar Benedictine Abbey at Somogyvár in 1091.[12] Others, such as Sárvármonostor, Ellésmonostor, or Dombó (today Rakovac, Serbia), cannot be dated precisely but fit well into the period around 1100.[13] These latter monasteries were founded by local aristocratic and ecclesiastical prelates.

The ground plan proved popular for a surprisingly long period. Monasteries of the late 12th and early 13th century frequently adopted this plan type.[14] However, the term 'Benedictine ground plan' is clearly misleading, since other monastic orders and institutions used the same architectural plan. It was especially popular among cathedrals, attested by those at Vác (*c.* 1070s), Pécs (1100 and after), Eger and Győr (both 1100 or after).[15] Looking at the map (Figure 18.2), it is evident that this type was in use throughout the country. Similarly, there are no regional tendencies implicit to the chronology or institutional type. The only exception is Transylvania, where no examples of this type of plan have yet been identified. On the other hand, the plan type was immensely popular in Italy, Dalmatia, most of the western Mediterranean, and southern Germany (where it is sometimes called the 'Bavarian church type'). In this respect, Hungary is part of a larger, southern European trend.[16]

However, these basilicas are often connected to a pair of towers at the west. The arrangement of these towers is often seen as peculiar to the Hungarian Kingdom.[17] The ground floors of the towers are usually open to the aisles as well as to the entrance hall. Thus much of the weight of the tower is held by a single compound pier. This open spatial arrangement is also usually repeated at first floor level, where the tower chambers are unified with the western gallery, and all three compartments look down onto the aisles.[18] The open ground-floor type is also subject to chronological change. The earliest examples can be dated to the middle of the 12th century, as at the cathedral of Esztergom and the Benedictine monastery of Nagykapornak.[19] Other monasteries, such as Ákos or Harina (Acâş and Herina in Romania) followed on in the years to either side of 1200 (Figures 18.3–18.5).[20] The golden age of this architectural arrangement is the early 13th century, when it is found in a number of Benedictine Abbeys. Some of the Premonstratensian houses also deployed the arrangement over the same period. Lesser monasteries of the Premonstratensians, such as in Bény (Bíňa, Slovakia) and Mórichida, reduced the aisles but kept the twin towers with an open ground floor. Parish churches also occasionally used this reduced version, as with Nyitrakoros (Krušovce, Slovakia) in the north[21] and Küküllővár (Cetatea de Baltă in Romania) in Transylvania, later drastically modified.[22] These buildings are again distributed all over the country, without any sign of regional preference (Figure 18.6). This particular combination, twin western towers opposite to a tri-apsidal east end, is unknown in the Mediterranean but was in use in southern Germany, the Czech Kingdom, and occasionally in Poland. Nevertheless, it is unquestionably in Hungary that the type was most popular during the High and Late Romanesque periods.

There is another variation when it comes to adapting twin towers to aisleless naves. In certain cases, the nave was flanked by a pair of towers to its north and south. This seems to have been especially popular with Benedictine Abbeys in the late 12th and early 13th centuries (Kána, Tereske, Bozók (Bzovík, Slovakia), and Jánosi (Rimavské Janovce, Slovakia). Interestingly, all four examples are in central Hungary, around and to the north of present-day Budapest (Figures 18.6 and 18.7). This seems to be a regional phenomenon, though distributed across a very limited area and over a short period.[23]

In addition to longitudinal architectural arrangements, there is a very particular centralised church type that is peculiar to Hungary. These rotundas, perfectly circular from the exterior but six-lobed from the interior, can be dated to between the middle of the 12th century and the end of the 13th century.[24] Until recently, just four were known, all situated in the eastern half of the kingdom: three buildings near the river Tisza and a fourth in Transylvania (Figure 18.8). Thus for a long time they were thought to be characteristic of eastern Hungary. However, a fifth rotunda was recently excavated in western Hungary, at the ruins of the Benedictine monastery of Almád.[25] As such, the six-lobed rotunda seems to have been another speciality of Hungarian Romanesque architecture distributed across the country (Figure 18.9).

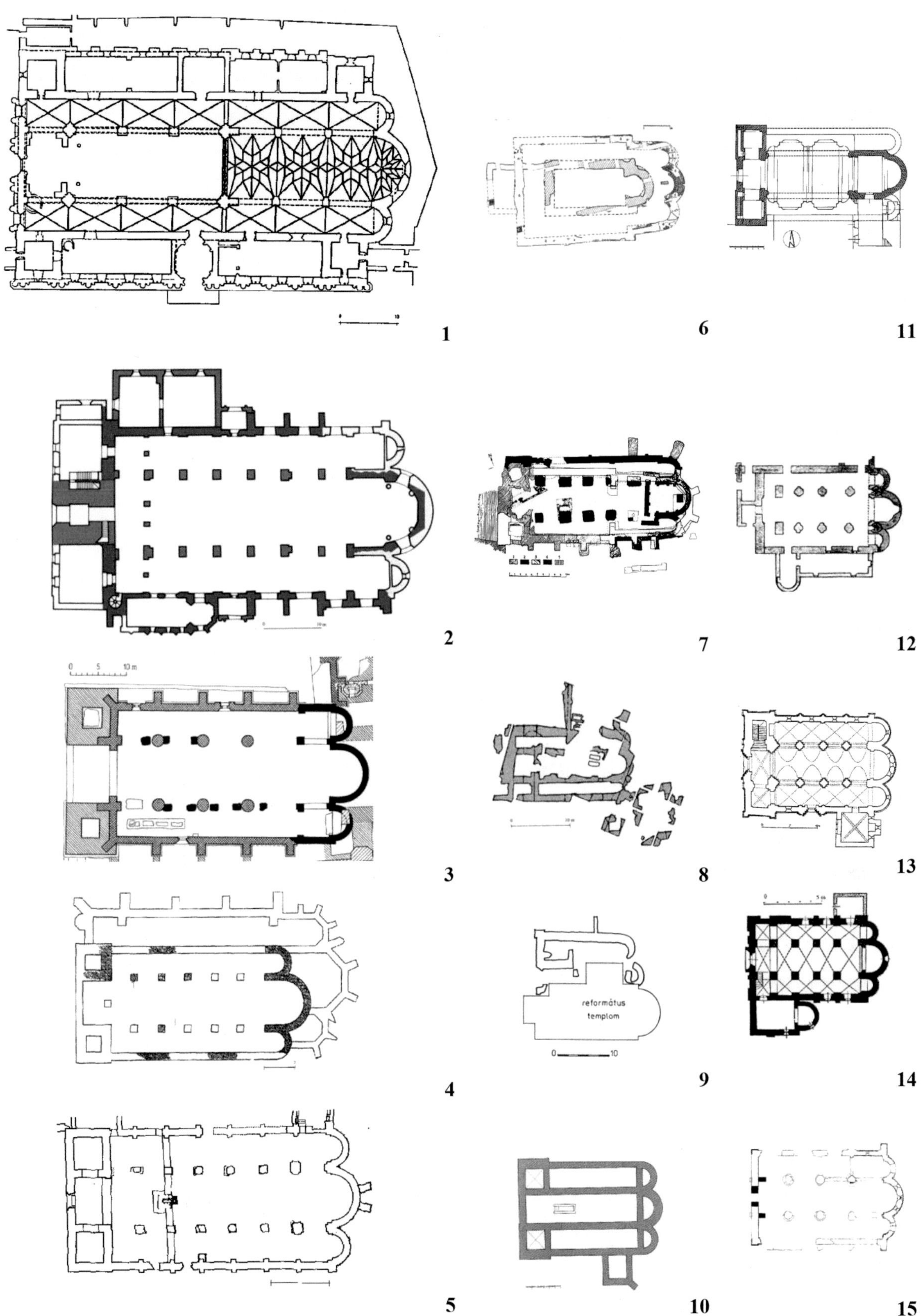

FIGURE 18.1

Examples of the Benedictine ground plan ((1) Pécs, (2) Győr, (3) Eger, (4) Garamszentbenedek, (5) Somogyvár, (6) Sárvármonostor, (7) Dombó, (8) Ellésmonostor, (9) Monostorpályi, (10) Vasvár, (11) Nagykapornak, (12) Kaplony, (13) Lébény, (14) Deáki, (15) Aracs) (After Béla Zsolt Szakács 2004)

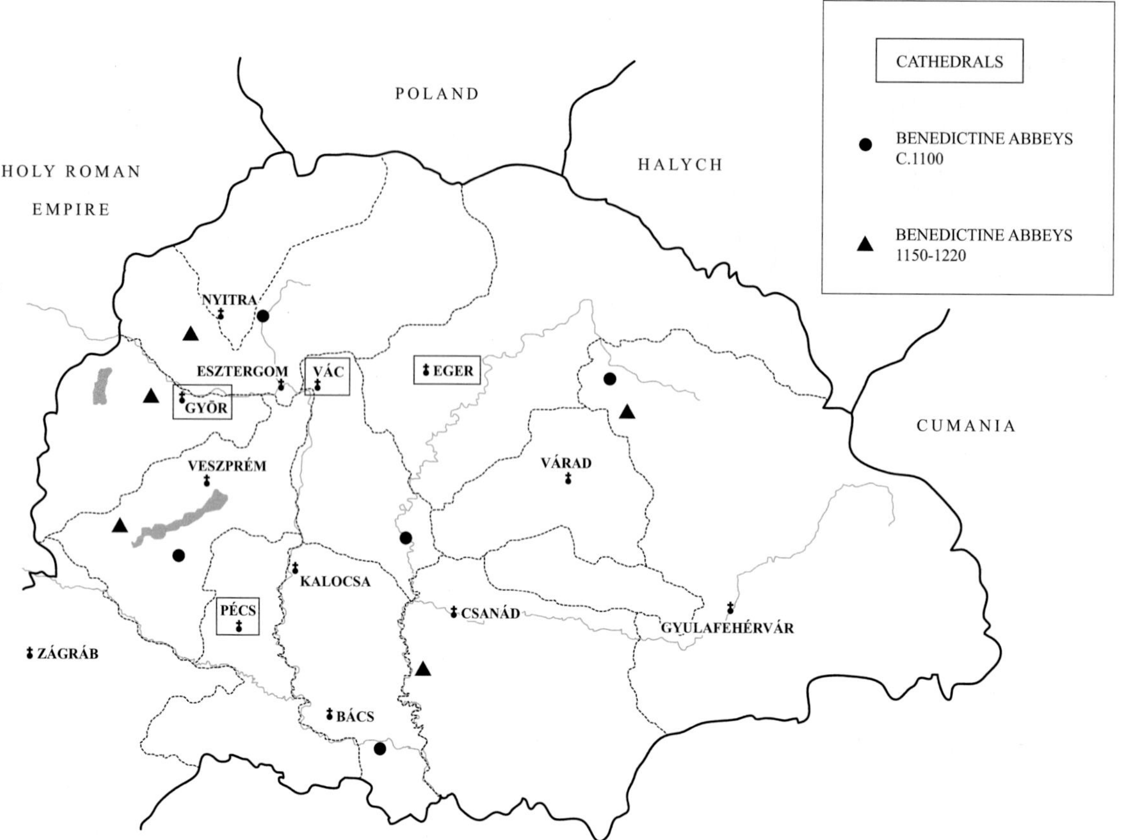

FIGURE 18.2

Geographic distribution of the Benedictine ground plan in medieval Hungary

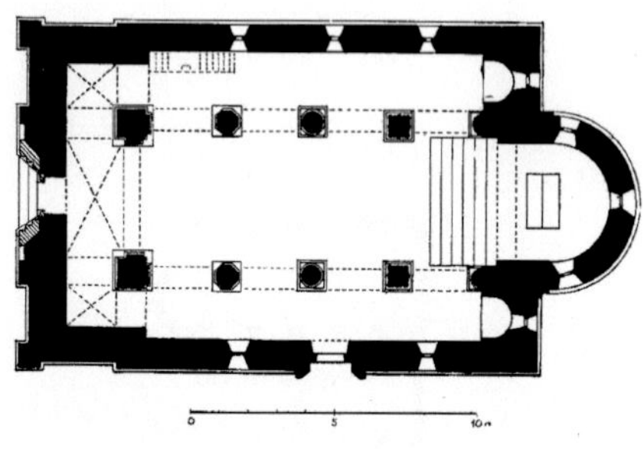

FIGURE 18.3

Harina/Herina: ground plan of the church (After Gerevich 1938)

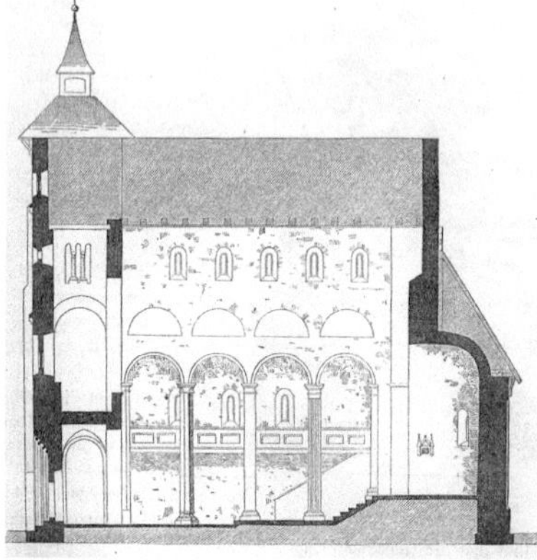

FIGURE 18.4

Harina/Herina: longitudinal section of the church (After Müller 1859)

FIGURE 18.5

Harina/Herina: transverse section of the church (Műemlékvédelmi Dokumentációs Központ, Budapest, Plan Archive, K 2892)

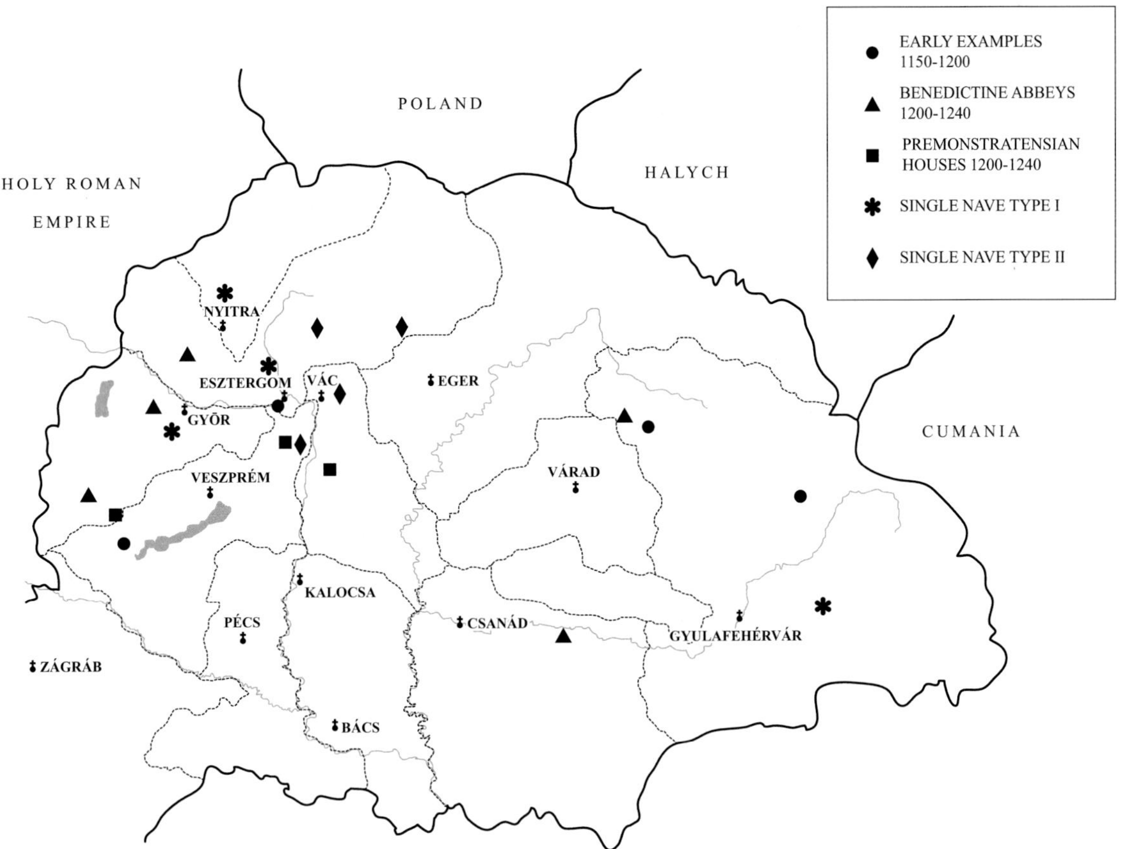

FIGURE 18.6

Geographic distribution of twin-towered churches with an open ground floor. Type 1 churches have aisleless naves and incorporate the west towers into the overall width of the church. Type 2 churches set the western towers outside the width of the aisleless nave.

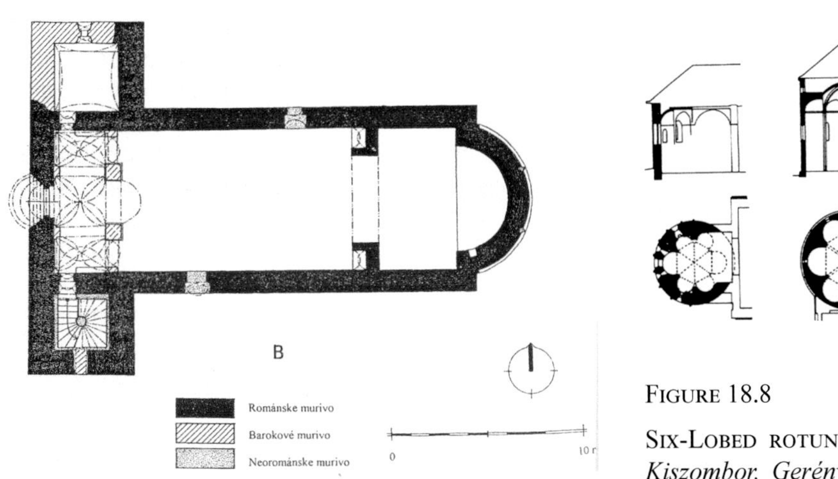

FIGURE 18.7

Jánosi/Janovce: ground plan (After Mencl 1937)

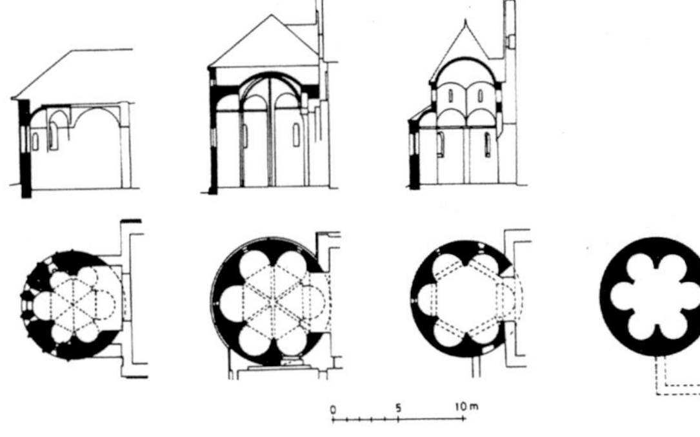

FIGURE 18.8

SIX-LOBED ROTUNDAS IN MEDIEVAL HUNGARY: *Karcsa, Kiszombor, Gerény/Horjani, and Kolozsmonostor/Cluj-Mănăştur (After Dékány 1983)*

Architectural decoration

If architectural plans do not seem to fall into regional patterns in Hungary, we may turn to the architectural decoration. During the 11th century, certain Hungarian churches were decorated in a very special, localised style.[26] One of its most distinctive elements is a frieze of palmette leaves arranged in two registers.[27] The handling is unmistakeable, to the extent that the composition is not found elsewhere in Europe (with just the one exception).[28] The palmette frieze is also usually accompanied by Corinthian-derived capitals decorated with spiny leaves, the so-called *acanthus spinosus*.[29] Early examples include the cathedral of Veszprém, started in the 1030s and finished a few decades

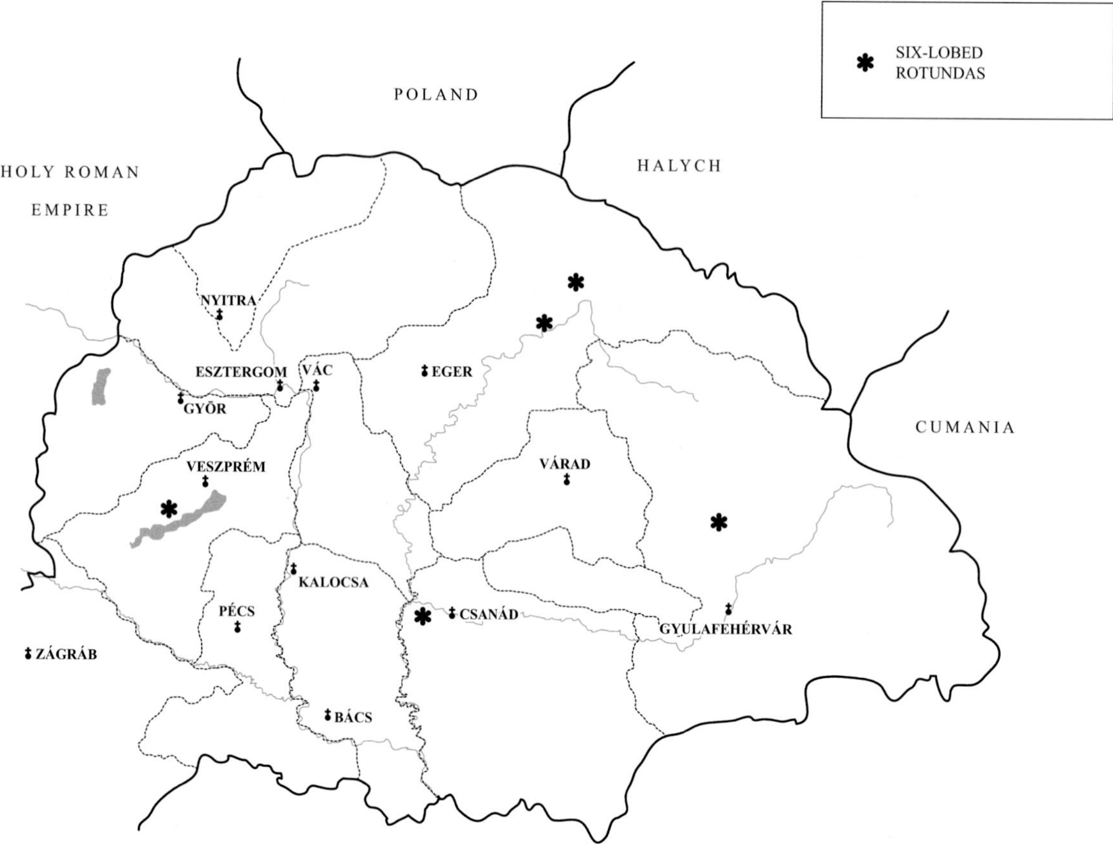

FIGURE 18.9

Geographic distribution of six-lobed rotundas in medieval Hungary

later; the Abbey church of Tihany, founded in 1055; a building of uncertain status and dedication in Pilis (today called Pilisszentkereszt), which preceded the later Cistercian Abbey (Figure 18.10); churches in Visegrád; and the Benedictine Abbey of Szekszárd, founded in 1061. All of these churches are royal foundations.

Later, around 1100, private foundations also took up the style. The aristocratic Hont-Pázmány family founded a relatively large church in Bény, which was embellished with arches decorated with palmette leaves.[30] A Benedictine Abbey with a strangely centralizing ground plan was erected in Feldebrő on the estates of the Aba kindred for which the presence of *acanthus spinosus* combined with a palmette frieze and figural decoration might suggest a date of *c.* 1100.[31] At the same time the tri-apsidal monastic church of Sárvármonostor was founded by the Gutkeled family. The small fragmentary stone carvings found at that site carry spiny acanthus leaves as well as elements of figural decoration.[32] The same combination appears at Dombó, which is one of the richest archaeological sites of the period. Here a large number of capitals and cornices were excavated, decorated by different variations of the palmette frieze as well as the *acanthus spinosus*. Early attempts at rudimentary figural decoration also appear together with vine scrolls and birds. The founder of this Benedictine Abbey is unknown; perhaps it belonged to the archbishop of Kalocsa.[33] A bird eating grapes also appears on a cornice found at the ruins of the monastery of St Peter at Bodrogmonostor which was founded by the Szente-Mágócs family. All of these foundations are usually dated to the end of the 11th century.[34]

It is interesting to note that the early examples of this decorative style are all in western Hungary, in Transdanubia. However, from around 1100, the style seems to have been picked up by private foundations on the periphery: at Bény and Feldebrő to the north, at Sárvármonostor to the East, and at Dombó and many other places in the south. Thus the palmette style originated as a regional style but later diffused across the country (Figure 18.11). Moreover, the difference between the early and later manifestations of the style are more than simply chronological. They can also be connected to different types of patrons.

Another aspect of architectural decoration typical of Hungary is the longevity of a Romanesque repertoire.[35] While Early Gothic architectural elements can be found in Hungary from the late 12th century (as in the royal city of Esztergom), late Romanesque decoration predominates until well into the 13th century.[36] Geometric ornament of a sort associated with Anglo-Norman architecture can be found in the first half of the 13th century at many important sites, such as at the Benedictine Abbey of Lébény or the famous abbey church at Ják (Figure 18.12).[37] While the majority of these buildings are in western Hungary, this same late Romanesque style appears in Transylvania at the cathedral of Gyulafehérvár in the early decades of the 13th century (Figure 18.13).[38] Moreover, a similar late

Romanesque style flourished at the same time in Austria, Silesia, and the Czech lands.

MICRO-REGIONS

All the previously mentioned monuments belong to the top rank of Romanesque architecture in Hungary. Even if we accept that these constitute a national architecture, that is not to say that there are no regional characteristics at a lower level. Clearly there are smaller regions (I describe these as micro-regions) where local architectural traditions dominate. One example is the Saxon Lands (Szászföld or Királyföld in Hungarian; Königsboden in German) in Transylvania. A typical Saxon church is laid out as a three-aisled basilica with a square-shaped choir and semicircular apse to the east and a massive tower incorporating a gallery (and probably a tower-chapel) at the west. Subsequently, the aisles were often demolished, as at Homoróddaróc (Draas; today Drăuşeni in Romania). Here we can also see that above these (now walled-in) arches there are two rows of windows: semicircular openings divided by a column into two parts, and oculi (today also walled in). It is uncertain if the twin windows originally belonged to a gallery above the aisle.[39] (See Figure 18.14 and Colour Plate XXIV (top).)

Another such micro-region can be identified around the monastery of Ják in western Hungary. The south portal of the monastic church was copied in the local parish church (Figures 18.15 and 18.16). The composition proved to be extremely popular and was taken up in the middle of the 13th century in the surrounding area (Figure 18.17). While the main lines of the composition were preserved, the quality deteriorated in the cases of the smaller village churches.[40] There are several examples of such local architectural traditions, though a systematic map of these across the entire medieval kingdom has

FIGURE 18.10

Chamfer with double-palmette frieze from Pilisszentkereszt (Béla Zsolt Szakács)

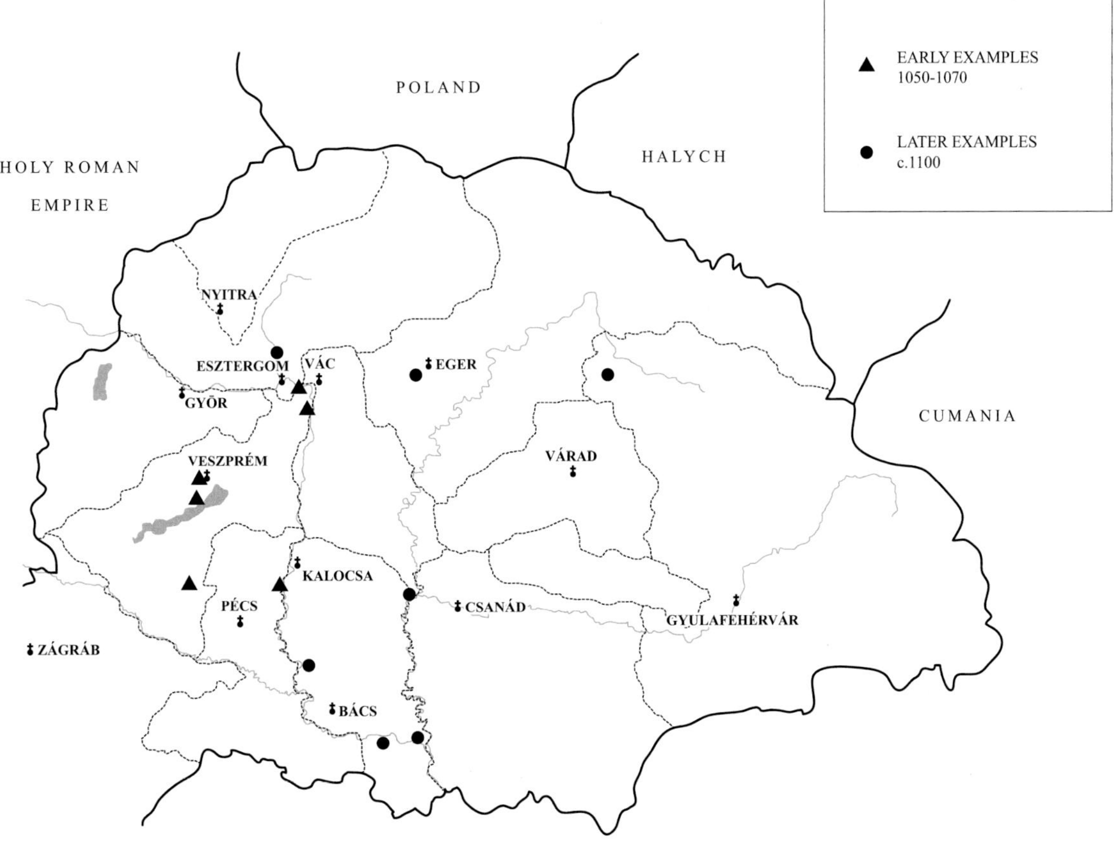

FIGURE 18.11

Geographic distribution of palmette decoration in medieval Hungary

FIGURE 18.12

Ják: abbey, south apse (Béla Zsolt Szakács)

FIGURE 18.13

Gyulafehérvár/Alba Iulia: south apse of the cathedral (Béla Zsolt Szakács)

yet to be created (Figure 18.18). Notwithstanding, these smaller local traditions do not result in a more general regional style.

TWO ILLUMINATING EXAMPLES: LÉBÉNY AND BOLDVA

Can we consequently assert that regional styles did not exist at all? Does it mean that, excepting the preferences of a few micro-regions, Romanesque churches look very similar across the whole of medieval Hungary? In order to better understand the situation, it might be helpful to compare two representative Romanesque abbeys in Hungary. The first example is Lébény in Transdanubia in the west. The second, Boldva, is in the east. The Benedictine Abbey of Lébény mostly dates from the first half of the 13th century and is a high-quality representative of Hungarian Romanesque architecture (Figures 18.1 and 18.19–18.21 and Colour Plate XXIV (bottom)). It is tri-apsidal, has no transept and was built with twin towers with open ground floors at the west. The church is richly decorated with late Romanesque and Early Gothic sculpture, though the overall impression is unquestionably Romanesque. Its compound piers and articulated walls are designed to carry rib vaults.[41]

The abbey church of Boldva is, in certain aspects, the antithesis of Lébény (Figures 18.22 and 18.23). It is more or less the same size and was built at the end of the 12th century for Benedictine monks. However, it is built of brick with an almost total lack of architectural decoration. Only the capitals and the apse semidome are made of stone. The exterior is articulated by pilaster strips, though their consistent deployment is very old-fashioned for the period. The interior is tall and unvaulted with aisles, which are much narrower than the nave.[42] A peculiarity is that a pair of towers frame the east end and were built with chapels on their first floor, looking down into the chancel. Similar tall, unvaulted brick basilicas with evidence of once having had upper chapels can be found in eastern Hungary in the Great Plain (Ákos) and in Transylvania (Harina).[43]

The contrasts between the two examples outlined above might be taken to suggest that there were in fact significant regional differences in the Romanesque architecture of the Hungarian Kingdom. However, these differences are not strictly speaking regional. Rather, they

Figure 18.14

Homoróddaróc/Drăuşeni/Draas: view from north-east (Béla Zsolt Szakács)

Figure 18.15

Ják: abbey, tympanum of the south portal (Béla Zsolt Szakács)

Figure 18.16

Ják: tympanum of the church of St James (Béla Zsolt Szakács)

Figure 18.17

Csempeszkopács: tympanum of the parish church (Béla Zsolt Szakács)

Figure 18.18

Two micro-regions of local Romanesque architectural traditions: Ják and its circle in western Hungary and the Saxon basilicas of Transylvania

FIGURE 18.19

Lébény, Benedictine Abbey: interior (Béla Zsolt Szakács)

FIGURE 18.20

Lébény, Benedictine Abbey: decoration of the south portal (Béla Zsolt Szakács)

FIGURE 18.21

Lébény, Benedictine Abbey: from north-east (Béla Zsolt Szakács)

take to an extreme what is a gradual change from west to east. If the most common types of Romanesque church in Transdanubia differ from what is most representative in the architecture of eastern Hungary, it is probably because Transdanubia is the region closest to western Europe. Stylistic novelties are taken up first here. Moreover, this is the region where the royal residences are situated, where Esztergom, Székesfehérvár, Visegrád, and Buda can be found.[44] The specificities of Transdanubia derive not so much from its regional character but from its geographic situation and may be more chronological than regional.

In sum, it seems that although natural geographic regions can be detected which were identified at least by the late Middle Ages in the vast territory of the medieval kingdom of Hungary, its Romanesque architectural heritage cannot be classified according to regional schools. Those matters of architectural layout and decoration, which seem particular to one part of Hungary, sooner or later can be found all over the country. Special features can appear in smaller areas – micro-regions – but they are not valid for a larger region. The key monuments of Hungarian Romanesque architecture are linked together in different parts of the country, even if this does not exclude the observation that specific elements of decoration are more usual in the western or eastern parts of the kingdom.

HISTORICAL BACKGROUND: ADMINISTRATIVE UNITS

How can we explain the unusual homogeneity of Hungary's architectural traditions? This may be linked to the lack of a powerful regional aristocracy. Aristocratic families had estates throughout Hungary, and in consequence they were unable to develop significant regional authority. Certain parts of the kingdom were assigned to members of the ruling dynasty in the 11th century, but this caused conflict and was soon discontinued.[45] Only two regions were separately administered: Slavonia, which was formally attached to Hungary at the end of the 11th century, and Transylvania, where a separate administration is documented from 1100. These two regions were governed by commissioners (the *ban* and the *voivode*, respectively), who were appointed by the king for short fixed periods to what were non-hereditary positions. Members of the leading families filled different national positions from time to time. Thus, as it owed nothing to a local elite, the buildings patronised by these royal commissioners never acted as a seed from which regional architectural traditions developed.[46]

Most of Hungary was administered in smaller units, the counties (in Hungarian, *vármegye*).[47] Even the leaders of these counties – the counts – were appointed directly by the king and were frequently changed. Local lesser nobility can only be identified from the 13th century. Thus the system of territorial administration did not support the development of local elites. Ecclesiastical administration,

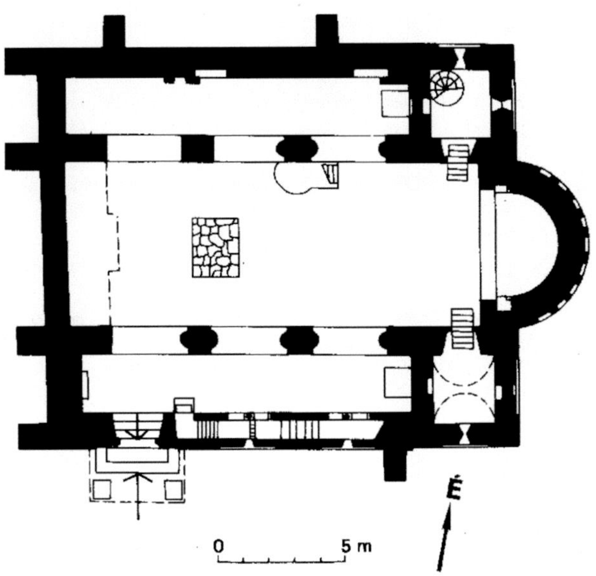

FIGURE 18.22

Boldva, Benedictine Abbey: ground plan (After Valter)

FIGURE 18.23

Boldva, Benedictine Abbey: exterior from south-east (Béla Zsolt Szakács)

as elsewhere in Europe, was centred on relatively large dioceses.[48] Some of these dioceses do seem to have given rise to local liturgical traditions (such as the rites of Esztergom, Kalocsa-Zagreb, and Várad-Transylvania).[49] However, their liturgies do not seem to be specifically and identifiably reflected in the architecture. The bishops and archbishops also moved from one see to another and do not seem anchored to regional interests.

As such, the architecture of the 11th and 12th centuries in the kingdom of Hungary is essentially an interregional architecture. There is a period – the second half of the 13th century – when royal power faltered and oligarchic clans tightened their grip on Hungary's various regions.[50] The major part of Transdanubia was ruled by the Kőszegi family: Transylvania was held by Ladislas Kán, while the western half of Upper Hungary was administered by Matthew Csák. Other smaller polities also came into being. Who knows what would have happened in Hungary if the arrival of a new dynasty, the Franco-Neapolitan House of Anjou under Charles I, had not succeeded in reorganising central government and if the rise of the oligarchic families had not been reversed.[51] By the beginning of the 14th century, the kingdom of Hungary was once more centrally administered and secure within its earlier borders, a situation which then endured more or less into the 16th century. These are the historical circumstances that are most likely the cause for the apparent lack of enduringly regional approaches to Romanesque architecture in Hungary.

NOTES

1 '*Haec enim provincia, eo quod circumquaque sylvis et montibus et praecipue Appennino clauditur, ex antiquo Pannonia dicta, intus planicie campi latissima, decursu fluminum et amnium conspicua, nemoribus diversarum ferarum generibus plenis conserta, tam innata amoenitate faciei laeta, quam agrorum fertilitate locuples esse congoscitur, ut tanquam paradisus Dei vel Aegyptus spectabilis esse videatur*': Otto Frisingensis, *Gesta Friderici*, lib. I, *c*. 31 (MGH Scriptores, vol. 20), ed. G. H. Pertz (Hannover 1869), 368.

2 P. Engel, *The Realm of Saint Stephen* (London 2001), 49–65.

3 For the geography of the medieval Hungarian Kingdom in historical perspective, see B. Bak, *Magyarország történeti topográfiája* (Budapest 1997), 33–40.

4 Nicolaus Olahus, *Hungaria – Athila*, eds. C. Eperjessy and L. Juhász (Budapest 1938), 1–34, esp. 8, 15, 16, 21.

5 B. Zs. Szakács, 'County to Country: Regional Aspects in the Research of Romanesque Art in Hungary', *Acta Historiae Artium*, 49 (2008), 55–62.

6 Á. Mikó and I. Takács, eds., *Pannonia regia. Művészet a Dunántúlon 1000–1541*. Exhibition catalogue (Budapest 1994).

7 T. Kollár, ed., *A középkori Dél-Alföld és Szer* (Szeged 2000).

8 Examples include G. Entz, *Erdély építészete a 11–13. században* (Kolozsvár 1994); P. L. Szőcs et al., eds., *Arhitectura religioasă medievală din Transilvania. Medieval Ecclesiastical Architecture in Transylvania*, 1–6 vols. (Satu Mare 1999–2021); T. Kollár, ed., *Középkori egyházi építészet Szatmárban* (Nyíregyháza 2011); T. ed., *Középkori templomok a Tiszától a Kárpátokig* (Nyíregyháza 2013); T. ed., *Művészet és vallás a Felső-Tisza-vidéken* (Nagyvárad and Nyíregyháza 2014).

9 B. Zs. Szakács, *Árpád-kori építészet a Dunántúlon* (Budapest 2021). This was a, habilitation dissertation defended at the Pázmány Péter Catholic University in 2016 (in print).

10 B. Zs. Szakács, 'Henszlmann and the "Hungarian Provincialism" of Romanesque Architecture', in *Bonum ut Pulchrum. Essays in Art History in Honour of Ernő Marosi on His Seventieth Birthday*, eds. L. Varga et al. (Budapest 2010), 511–18. The theory also appears in T. Gerevich, *Magyarország románkori emlékei* (Budapest 1938).

11 I. Takács, 'Garamszentbenedek temploma és liturgikus felszerelése', in *Paradisum Plantavit*, ed. I. Takács (Pannonhalma 2001), 159–86.

[12] Sz. Papp and T. Koppány, 'Somogyvár', in *Paradisum plantavit* (as n. 11), 350–58; K. Bakay, *Somogyvár. Szent Egyed-monostor* (Budapest 2011).

[13] S. Tóth, 'A 11–12. századi Magyarország Benedek-rendi templomainak maradványai', in *Paradisum plantavit* (as n. 11), 229–66 and 637–50.

[14] B. Zs. Szakács, 'Bencés templomok az Árpád-korban: korszakok és régiók', in *Örökség és küldetés: Bencések Magyarországon*, eds. P. A. Illés and A. Juhász-Laczik (Budapest 2012), 753–63.

[15] B. Zs. Szakács, 'Állandó alaprajzok – változó vélemények? Megjegyzések a "bencés templomtípus" magyarországi pályafutásához', in *Maradandóság és változás*, eds. S. Bodnár et al. (Budapest 2004), 25–37.

[16] B. Zs. Szakács, 'The Place of East Central Europe on the Map of Romanesque Architecture', in *Medieval East Central Europe in a Comparative Perspective*, eds. G. Jaritz and K. Szende (London and New York 2016), 205–24.

[17] D. Dercsényi, 'Zur siebenhundertjährigen Feier der Kirche von Ják', *Acta Historiae Artium*, 4 (1957), 173–202.; B. Zs. Szakács, 'A templomok nyugati térelrendezése és a "nemzetségi monostor" kérdése', in *Arhitectura religioasă medievală din Transilvania. Medieval Ecclesiastical Architecture in Transylvania*, eds. D. Marcu Istrate, A. A. Rusu, and P. L. Szőcs, vol. 3 (Satu Mare 2004), 71–98.

[18] B. Zs. Szakács, 'Toronyaljak és toronyközök a magyarországi romanikában', in *Arhitectura religioasă medievală din Transilvania. Medieval Ecclesiastical Architecture in Transylvania*, vol. 4, eds. P. L. Szőcs and A. A. Rusu (Satu Mare 2007), 7–36.

[19] I. Valter, *Árpád-kori téglatemplomok Nyugat-Dunántúlon* (Budapest 2004), 58–60.

[20] *Középkori egyházi építészet Szatmárban* (as n. 8), 60–91.; P. L. Szőcs, 'Az ákosi monostor és az Ákos nemzetség', *A Szilágyság és a Wesselényi család*, eds. G. Hegyi and A. W. Kovács (Kolozsvár 2012), 7–24.; for the early state of Harina, see F. Müller, 'Die kirchliche Baukunst des romanischen Styles in Siebenbürgen', *Jahrbuch der K. u. K. Central-Commission zur Erforschung und Erhaltung der Baudenkmale*, vol. 3 (1859), 147–94.

[21] K. Ilkó, *Nyitra-vidéki falképfestészet a középkorban* (Budapest 2019), 76–86.

[22] T. Emődi, 'Küküllővár, református templom', in *'... ideje az építésnek...'. A Rómer Flóris Terv műemlék-helyreállításai*, ed. T. Kollár (Budapest 2018), 149–65.

[23] Szakács, 'Bencés templomok' (as n. 14), 759–60. For the latter two see also V. Mencl, *Stredoveká architektúra na Slovensku* (Praha and Prešov 1937), 103–12.

[24] S. Tóth, 'Hatkaréjos rotundáink', *Arhitectura religioasă medievală din Transilvania*, vol. 3 (as n. 17), 7–60. See also T. Dékány, 'A negyedik hatkaréjos rotunda', *Műemlékvédelem*, 27 (1983), 192–200.

[25] The rotunda was excavated by Gergely Buzás in 2014–15. See O. Kovács, 'Almád: rotunda állt az apátságban', *Archeologia – Altum Castrum* (2014), http://archeologia.hu/almad-rotunda-allt-az-apatsagban [accessed 24 October 2019].

[26] S. Tóth, 'A 11. századi magyarországi kőornamentika időrendjéhez', in *Pannonia Regia* (as n. 6), 54–62; cf. M. Takács, *Byzantinische oder byzantinisierende Raumgestaltungen kirchlicher Architektur im frühárpádenzeitlichen Ungarn* (Mainz 2018).

[27] M. Takács, 'Die sogenannte Palmettenornamentik der christlichen Bauten des 11. Jahrhunderts im mittelalterlichen Ungarn', in *Byzanz – das Römerreich im Mittelalter, 3. Teil Peripherie und Nachbarschaft*, eds. F. Daim and J. Drauschke (Mainz 2010), 411–15.

[28] This exception can be found in the north portal of the cathedral of Lund, see S. Tóth, *Román kori kőfaragványok a Magyar Nemzeti Galéria Régi Magyar Gyűjteményében* (Budapest 2010), 37–38.

[29] M. Takács, 'Ornamentale Beziehungen zwischen der Steinmetzkunst von Ungarn und Dalmatien im XI. Jahrhundert', *Hortus Artium Mediaevalium*, 3 (1997), 165–78.

[30] B. Pomfyová, ed., *Stredoveký kostol I. Historické a funkčné premeny architektúry* (Bratislava 2015), 86–89.

[31] E. Marosi, *A romanika Magyarországon* (Budapest 2013), 56–61; B. Zs. Szakács, 'Hungary, Byzantium, Italy: Architectural Connections in the 11th Century', in *Romanesque and the Mediterranean*, eds. R. M. Bacile and J. McNeill (London 2015), 193–204.

[32] K. Havasi, 'Sárvármonostor XI. századi kőfaragványainak katalógusa elé', *Középkori egyházi építészet Szatmárban* (as n. 8), 26–59.

[33] N. Stanojev, *Rakovac. Gradica. Klisa* (Novi Sad 2015).

[34] S. Tóth, 'Az aracsi kő rokonsága', in *A középkori Dél-Alföld* (as n. 7), 429–48.

[35] K. Havasi, 'Romanesque Sculpture in Hungary', in *The Art of Medieval Hungary*, eds. X. Barral i Altet et al. (Rome 2018), 145–63.

[36] E. Marosi, *Die Anfänge der Gotik in Ungarn. Esztergom in der Kunst des 12.–13. Jahrhunderts* (Budapest 1984).

[37] B. Zs. Szakács, 'The Benedictine Abbey Church of Ják', in *The Art of Medieval Hungary* (as n. 33), 393–96.

[38] G. Entz, *A gyulafehérvári székesegyház* (Budapest 1958); I. Takács, 'The First Sanctuary of the Second Cathedral of Gyulafehérvár (Alba Iulia, Ro)', *Acta Historiae Artium*, 53 (2012), 15–43.

[39] The best examples are Nagysink (Cincu), Nádpatak (Rodbav), Földvár (Feldioara), Kaca (Caţa), Morgonda (Merghindeal), Kereszténysziget (Cristian), and Homoróddaróc (Drăuşeni, all in Romania). See W. Horwath, 'Der Emporenbau der romanischen und frühgotischen Kirchen in Siebenbürgen', *Siebenbürgische Vierteljahrsschrift*, 58 (1935), 69–75; H. Fabini, *Atlas der siebenbürgisch-sächsischen Kirchenburgen und Dorfkirchen* (Hermannstadt and Heidelberg 1999).

[40] Churches with portals derived from Ják include Őriszentpéter, Sitke, Dozmat, Magyaszecsőd, Meszlen, Vasalja-Pinkaszentkirály, Domonkosfa (Domanjševci, Slovenia). See I. Valter, *Romanische Sakralbauten Westpannoniens* (Eisenstadt 1985) and Valter, *Árpád-kori* (as n. 19).

[41] B. Zs. Szakács, 'The Benedictine Abbey Church of Lébény', in *The Art of Medieval Hungary* (as n. 33), 389–91.

[42] I. Valter, *Boldva, református templom* (Budapest 1991); and I. Valter, 'A boldvai református templom', in *Myskovszky Viktor és a mai műemlékvédelem Közép-Európában*, ed. A. Balega (Bratislava and Budapest 1999), 162–69–43.

[43] See B. Zs. Szakács, 'Kaplony, római katolikus templom', in *Középkori egyházi építészet Szatmárban* (as n. 8), 238–48.

[44] E. Benkő and K. Orosz, eds., *In medio regni Hungariae. Régészeti, művészettörténeti és történeti kutatások 'az ország közepén'* (Budapest 2015).

[45] A. Zsoldos, ed., *Hercegek és hercegségek a középkori Magyarországon* (Székesfehérvár 2016); D. Bagi, *Divisio regni: Országmegosztás, trónviszály és dinasztikus történetírás az Árpádok, Piastok és Premyslidák birodalmában a 11. és a korai 12. században* (Pécs 2017).

[46] For a similar argument, see T. Rostás, 'Három drávántúli emlék a 13. századból', in *Építészet a középkori Dél-Magyarországon*, ed. T. Kollár (Budapest 2010), 213–93.

[47] Gy. Kristó, *A vármegyék kialakulása Magyarországon* (Budapest 1988); A. Zsoldos, 'Szent István vármegyéi', in *Szent István és az államalapítás*, ed. L. Veszprémy (Budapest 2002), 420–30.

[48] G. Érszegi, 'The Emergence of the Hungarian State, the Adoption and Consolidation of Christianity (970–1095)', in *A Thousand Years of Christianity in Hungary*, eds. P. Cséfalvay and M. A. De Angelis (Budapest 2001), 25–36.

[49] L. Dobszay, *Az esztergomi rítus* (Budapest 2004).

[50] Gy. Kristó, *A feudális széttagolódás Magyarországon* (Budapest 1979); A. Zsoldos, *A Druget-tartomány története 1315–1342* (Budapest 2017).

[51] For the period in general, see Engel, *The Realm* (as n. 2), 124–56; E. Csukovits, *Az Anjouk Magyarországon*, 1–2 vols. (Budapest 2012–19).

The Regional and Transregional in Romanesque Europe (2021), 273–285

REASSESSING THE PROBLEM OF SCANDINAVIAN ROMANESQUE

Benjamin Zweig

Scandinavian Romanesque architecture displays a wide variety of forms and styles. Yet its place in the history of Romanesque art remains peripheral, and it is difficult to define what exactly is Scandinavian about Scandinavian Romanesque. This problem is often viewed from the lens of external influence and geography and told from the perspective of the 'outside in'; Denmark was influenced by Germany, Norway by the British Isles, and Sweden by both, as well as by eastern Europe and Byzantium. While stylistic parallels between continental Europe and Scandinavia situate the region's art in a transregional milieu, such as Lund Cathedral's Rhenish-Lombardic plan and sculpture, this does not explain why certain styles were adopted and leaves the inhabitants of Scandinavia out of the story. But if the problem is instead viewed from the 'inside out,' it becomes clear that 11th- and 12th-century Scandinavian royalty and nobility were instrumental in the foundation and probably in the financing of cathedrals and churches, and they may have consciously adopted certain Romanesque styles as prestige markers to demonstrate their capacities as patrons and associate themselves with current artistic trends.

INTRODUCTION: OUTLINING THE PROBLEM

Scandinavia, the collective regional name for the countries of Denmark, Norway, and Sweden, occupies a difficult place in the history of Romanesque art.[1] The region is replete with a diverse array of forms showing connections with the art and architecture of the wider medieval world, from architectural sculpture indebted to the British Isles, the Rhineland, and Lombardy, to baptismal fonts, processional crucifixes, and wall-paintings indebted to Byzantium, and to local styles and traditions, manifested most strikingly in the form of the stave church.[2] Yet when attempting to locate Scandinavia's place in the broader history of medieval art, this formal diversity presents something of a problem, for it is often very difficult to pinpoint what is distinctly Scandinavian about Scandinavian Romanesque.[3] The region can seem stuck between the proverbial rock and hard place, being too peripheral to be seen to have importance beyond its regionalism, as in localized traditions such as stave churches and rune stones, or, given its geographic expanse and relatively late conversion to Christianity, being seen as the passive recipient of already well-developed artistic trends.

Why has Scandinavia remained so marginal in the study of medieval art? In her 2011 essay 'Would There Have Been Gothic Art Without the Vikings?', Nancy Wicker posits four reasons for the region's peripheralization.[4] The first reason is accessibility: the limitations imposed by distance, the geography of Scandinavia itself, and limited knowledge of and resources for learning the Scandinavian languages. There has been no shortage of excellent scholarship on the region by Scandinavian scholars for over a century, but little of it is known outside Scandinavia, when compared to French and German scholarship, and it is at a particularly disadvantaged position in American scholarship. The second reason is self-imposed: boundaries of discipline and periodization, divisions which have been created between archaeology and art history or between pre-Christian and Christian eras. The third and fourth reasons Wicker calls disparities of scale, media, and function and diversity of subject matter and religion.[5]

While Wicker's analysis focuses primarily on Viking-era art, Scandinavian Romanesque (and later Gothic) art and architecture remains, even for her, 'undoubtedly derivative and connected to the Continent'.[6] Such a connection should not be surprising, for the Romanesque is, as often said, the first 'international' style since antiquity. Thick walls, massive columns and piers, rounded arches, small windows, stone vaulting, sculpted capitals, apsidal east ends, and the clear articulation of parts and their relationships are transregional characteristics of Romanesque architecture.[7] Each of these features is found in abundance in 11th and 12th century buildings throughout Scandinavia. Yet, as Wicker shows, even the region's defenders can fall into the trap of seeing Scandinavia as

  DOI: 10.4324/9781003162827-19

derivative rather than participatory within the history of Romanesque art. What accounts for the persistence of this view? Let me outline three possible and interrelated reasons.

First, there is a tension as to whether the art and architecture of medieval Scandinavia should be treated as that of three distinct modern nations or of a broadly unified cultural region. In his book *Carolingian and Romanesque Architecture*, Kenneth Conant aptly demonstrates this tension when he treats the region as a single entity while nonetheless acknowledging that 'sufficient differences [exist] in the architecture to justify considering the Scandinavian countries respectively'.[8] Both approaches have advantages and drawbacks. Those that consign themselves to national borders are able to show stylistic trends and regional and subregional particularities but can sever historical bonds, as in the case of Lund Cathedral (Figure 19.1 and Colour Plate XXV (top)), now in the Swedish province of Skåne but until 1658 part of Denmark. Those that treat Scandinavia from a unified or surveyors' perspective, such as Armin Tuulse in his comprehensive *Romansk Konst i Norden (Romanesque Art in Scandinavia)* and Aron Andersson in *The Art of Scandinavia*, highlight the region's artistic eclecticism but at the risk of flattening historical distinctions and causations.[9]

Underlying the tension between national and regional approaches is the problem of geography and its relationship to style, often under the rubric of influence. For example, Denmark looks south to German lands, and many of its most ambitious Romanesque buildings show clear parallels to the cathedrals of Speyer and Mainz, whereas a Norwegian building such as Stavanger Cathedral (Figure 19.2 and Colour Plate XXVI (top)) is based upon English models.[10] The case of Sweden is more complex, as its Romanesque architecture displays connections with the art of Saxony, England, and eastern Europe.[11] The preceding links are indisputable and evince real historical relationships – Denmark's with the Holy Roman Empire and Norway's with the British Isles, both of which had grown strong (if not also thoroughly complicated) through the Viking era.[12] But stylistic parallels are often framed as geographically deterministic, which then situates Scandinavia as the passive recipient at the end of a vector of external influence, reaffirming the centre–periphery model that underpins the study of the region.[13]

The third potential reason for the peripheralization of Scandinavia is the coupling of the introduction of Romanesque art and architecture with the region's conversion to Christianity. Because the Romanesque, as a defined style, coincides with the later stages of Scandinavia's conversion and ecclesiastical consolidation, it can be seen as an entity imported from abroad by the Church. While this perspective integrates Scandinavia into the web of European social and cultural networks and institutions, it once again relegates the region to the role of a passive recipient. It further creates an artificial break between the Viking age and the Middle Ages, effectively disregarding cultural and political links forged in previous centuries, in trading towns such as Birka and Hedeby, or the North Sea Empire of King Cnut.[14]

The challenge, therefore, lies in understanding the problem of the Romanesque in Scandinavia as a social and historical phenomenon as much as an exercise in determining stylistic parallels and influences. The problem is very much one of historical *perspective*. In what follows, I would like to, however modestly, shift the perspective on how we might understand Scandinavian Romanesque. I will first explore Romanesque monuments by synthesizing the well-established 'outside in' approach. Second, I will explore what I call an 'inside out' approach that reorients the same problem from a perspective that foregrounds the Scandinavians themselves in the adoption of forms and styles. Third and finally, I will briefly consider how the stave churches, the most distinctive manifestations of Scandinavian Romanesque, might be seen in relation to the 'inside out' point of view. I will focus primarily on architecture, and regrettably have had to leave out the important islands of Gotland and Bornholm, although it is my hope that what I present here might also be applicable to them.

FROM THE OUTSIDE IN: CONVERSION AND STYLE

The conversion of Scandinavia to Christianity is a complex phenomenon.[15] As a matter of course and convenience, the conversion narrative often begins with the ninth-century *Vita Anksarii (Life of Angsar)* by Rimbert, the Archbishop of Hamburg-Bremen (865–88).[16] The *Vita* recounts the history of Angsar (801–65), Rimbert's predecessor at Hamburg-Bremen, who led an important mission to Denmark, where he supposedly built a church at the trading town of Ribe on the west coast of Jutland and went on a mission to the Viking town of Birka in Sweden.[17] Missionary activity continued regularly into the region between the 9th and 11th centuries from Germany as well from the British Isles. The Archbishopric of Hamburg-Bremen had a great interest in converting the Scandinavian lands, in particular the neighbouring Danes, as was famously recounted by Adam of Bremen in his *History of the Archbishops of Hamburg-Bremen* (*c.* 1070).[18] Adam is best known for his fanciful description of the pagan temple at Uppsala, but much of his work details the conversion of Scandinavia and the archbishopric's claims to authority in the region.[19] The missionary stories often exaggerate or even outright invent hostility to Christianity on the part of the Scandinavians, and claim importance for themselves in shepherding its acceptance, such as Adams's dubious claim that King Otto forcibly converted the Danish King Harald Bluetooth, an event repudiated by Harald's own words on the famous Jelling stone.[20]

Narratives such as those of Rimbert and Adam set the predicate for explaining the introduction of church building to the region that continues into the Romanesque period. The assumption is that missionaries, such

FIGURE 19.1

Lund Cathedral: view from north-east (Francois Polito/Wikimedia Commons)

FIGURE 19.2

Stavanger Cathedral: nave looking east (Arkeologisk Museum, Universitetet i Stavanger)

as Angsar, constructed wooden buildings that either took the form of or were replacements for pagan temples and that these wooden churches were then gradually replaced by simple stone structures. The form of these second-wave buildings varied and might have had Anglo-Saxon or German features brought by masons and clergy who settled in the region from abroad. The second-wave buildings were in turn again rebuilt in a building frenzy during the 12th and 13th centuries by a post-conversion-era Church, which brought with it Romanesque forms developed elsewhere.

A primary case study for the introduction of the Romanesque to Scandinavia from the outside in is the Cathedral of Lund (Figure 19.1).[21] The current building was considerably reconstructed in the 19th century but essentially dates to the early to mid-12th century and was a replacement for an earlier stone church dating to the 1080s.[22] Construction of the present building began in the first decade of the 12th century, once Lund had been made the seat of a new archbishopric overseeing the whole of Scandinavia in 1103–04.[23] The crypt altar was consecrated in 1123 followed by the high altar in 1145–46.[24] The cathedral is the example *par excellence* of the so-called Rhenish-Lombardic style in Scandinavia and is closely comparable to contemporary buildings in Lombardy and the Rhineland, in particular the cathedrals of Speyer and Mainz.[25]

Lund is a simple basilica, with a nave divided by a double bay system, aisles, transept, choir, and apse. The three-storied apse has been relatively little changed since its completion around 1160 and displays a special affinity with the east ends of Speyer and Mainz (Figure 19.3). Its exterior arcading, topped by an arched corbel table and blind gallery, employs well-articulated engaged columns with inhabited and classicizing capitals. The 12th-century *Necrologium Lundense* and *Libri memoriales Capituli Lundensis* both record the death of one Donatus, the '*magister operis hujus ecclesie*'.[26] Based on this obit and his name, Donatus has often been interpreted as the presumed Italian master mason who oversaw the opening phases of Lund's construction, probably from shortly after 1104 until the early 1130s, and introduced the Rhenish-Lombardic style to Denmark.

The best-preserved section of the cathedral, as well as among its earliest, is the crypt beneath the choir (Figure 19.4 and Colour Plate XXV (bottom)).[27] The crypt plan echoes that of Speyer, but other parallels have been noted, in particular with that of St Hermes in Ronse (Belgium).[28] The crypt is vaulted and contains very finely worked columns and compound piers, several of which are ornamented with twisted or grooved patterns. Cushion capitals top each column, with the exception of a richly carved capital containing figural and vegetal decoration that tops the column with a large protruding figure known colloquially as 'the giant Finn'.[29]

While Lund's crypt is often compared to continental models, it should be contextualized with several other Scandinavian examples that either predate or are contemporaneous with the cathedral. For example, the vaulted vestibule at the west end of Dalby church in Skåne (begun as early as 1060, vestibule *c.* 1100–60) displays similarly well-worked columns, and one suspects masons who worked there had also worked at Lund.[30] The crypt of Viborg Cathedral, the only medieval section of the building to survive (the rest is 19th-century rebuilding), has granite and porphyry columns dating to around 1130.[31] The crypt at the Church of Our Lady in Århus, uncovered and reconstructed in the 1950s and dating to as early as the 1060s, is vaulted and made up of simple stone pillars.[32] These finds give us some broader indication of the early usage of Romanesque forms in Danish architecture.

As has long been noted, much of Lund's rich corpus of sculpture, particularly the portals and the north and south transept chapels, displays strong relationships with contemporaneous sculpture in Lombardy. The north portal (Figure 19.5) is the richest and most complex: a porch with densely sculpted archivolts, tympanum, and two projecting columns topped by lions, which in its overall form is reminiscent of the west porch of Modena Cathedral.[33] The south portal's archivolts display the same dense mouldings filled with interlocking foliate motifs and animals, especially birds, as is characteristic of 12th-century north Italian sculpture.

After Lund, the cathedral of Ribe (begun *c.* 1150), on the west coast of Jutland, is the best example of the mixture of German and Italian styles found in Danish Romanesque architecture.[34] The fine three-storied apse (Figure 19.6), with blind arcading, once again echoes Lombardic and Rhenish counterparts. The building's interior has retained more of its 12th-century form than Lund, with simple square pillars supporting the nave arcade and galleries defined by an encompassing arch with three subsidiary arches. The cathedral was constructed from tufa imported from the Rhineland. The porch on the south transept, the so-called 'Cat's Head Portal,' is flanked by Lombardic column-bearing lions and a large granite tympanum with a relief depicting the *Deposition*.[35]

Given its status as the seat of Scandinavia's first archbishopric, it is very possible that Lund became a point from which the Rhenish-Lombardic style was disseminated throughout Scandinavia. One pointer in this direction is the small church of St Mary at Vä in north-eastern Skåne (Figure 19.7). As it stands today, part of the nave, most of the choir, and the apse are Romanesque. Its western portal contains ornamented archivolts and capitals that were probably created by masons working at Lund.[36] Indeed, in the 12th century Vä might have resembled something akin to a miniature version of Lund cathedral, with a sculpted southern porch that projected outwards onto two columns, a possible copy of Lund's north portal, and two west towers.[37] The churches of Tveje Merløse (Figure 19.8), its original towers still in place, and Fjenneslev on Sjælland gives a sense of what Vä and many other Romanesque churches throughout the Danish lands were probably like in their 12th-century state.

A final example of German and Italian style in Denmark, and one that is stylistically independent of Lund and Ribe, is the church of St Bendt in Ringsted (Figure 19.9).

FIGURE 19.3

Lund Cathedral: apse (Benjamin Zweig)

FIGURE 19.4

Lund Cathedral: crypt (Benjamin Zweig)

FIGURE 19.5

Lund Cathedral: north portal (Benjamin Zweig)

The building is a three-aisled cruciform basilica with a crossing tower and apsidal chapels off the north and south transepts. Ringsted lacks the sculpture of Lund and Ribe, but its overall design is clearly indebted to North Italian and German examples. Interestingly, when the church was reconstructed in brick around 1170, the builders closely followed the dimensions of the earlier travertine church, completed around 1080, making it one of the finest examples of brick Romanesque in northern Europe.[38]

When turning to Norway, England and the North Sea are seen as the main vector of influence and stylistic unit of measurement. The most prominent surviving Norwegian Romanesque stone building is arguably the Cathedral of Stavanger, perhaps begun as early as *c.* 1100 but certainly in progress by 1125.[39] Its wide aisles and large cylindrical piers recall the cathedrals of Durham and St Magnus, Kirkwall, in the Orkneys (Figure 19.2). Stavanger's south porch is a Norman arch with chevron mouldings (Figure 19.10). Similar mouldings appear on one of the arches in the nave. Anglo-Norman forms are found throughout Norway, as with the 'Norman' arch in the Johannes Chapel in Trondheim Cathedral. However, the picture of a unidirectional influence from the British Isles to Norway is complicated by buildings such as St Mary at Bergen, which contains features related to the German-Lombard tradition found in Denmark or displays an intriguing mix of styles, as in the church's south portal.[40] It has even been suggested that masons trained at Lund constructed the church.[41]

Sweden's Romanesque architecture, much of it concentrated in Östergötland and the Mälar regions, varies even more in the traditions on which it draws. Indeed, one can see various forms and styles in the ruins of some of the earliest surviving examples of stone ecclesiastical architecture in Sweden in the town of Sigtuna, a bishopric from the 1060s until the establishment of a new see at (now Old) Uppsala around 1140–50.[42] The ruins of the church of St Per (*c.* 1100–20) reveal a centralized plan with two axial towers that might have been based on an Anglo-Saxon precedent.[43] The ruins of St Olof (*c.* 1100–40) (Figure 19.11) also display a centralized church, with a crossing tower and short wide nave. Clear

FIGURE 19.6

Ribe Cathedral: eastern end (Ajepbah/Wikimedia Commons)

FIGURE 19.7

Vä, St Mary: view from east (Wikimedia Commons)

FIGURE 19.8

Tveje Merløse: View from south-east (Unknown photographer)

FIGURE 19.9

Ringsted, St Bendt: view from north-east (Benjamin Zweig)

stylistic parallels are difficult to find, however, and it is possible to cite Anglo-Saxon, German, and even Byzantine comparators.[44] The church at Husaby (Figure 19.12) (*c.* 1150) in Östergötland, however, is clearly based upon German models.[45] The west end here is dominated by an imposing westwork, with a rectangular central tower flanked by narrow round towers. The church's westwork is the only fully preserved example of its kind in Sweden, although the feature might have been more widespread as the church of Örberga near Vadstena retains remnants of a 12th-century westwork.[46]

This outside in view of the Romanesque in Scandinavia, as I have briefly summarized it, is based entirely on parallels from continental Europe and the British Isles. This certainly illuminates the internationalism or transregionalism that is a defining feature of Scandinavian Romanesque. But it has a glaring omission: it leaves the Scandinavians themselves out of the picture. It tells us little about the historical conditions within Scandinavia that led to the adoption of Romanesque architecture, about why certain styles and forms were chosen, and what their significance might have been. To do this, we must view these issues from the inside out.

FROM THE INSIDE OUT: AGENTS AND ADOPTION

In his essay 'From Lund or Directly from Speyer,' the Norwegian scholar Hans-Emil Lidén examines the local and international masons and workshops that came to the city of Bergen on behalf of the Norwegian court.[47] Lidén connects the few capital fragments from the now-demolished monastery of Munkeliv to those still *in situ* in Lund and Speyer. But instead of resting on stylistic parallels, he suggests that the Norwegian crusader, King Sigurd I Magnusson (1103–30), who had travelled extensively throughout Europe, or his brother and co-ruler, King

FIGURE 19.10
Stavanger Cathedral: south portal (Arkeologisk Museum, Universitetet i Stavanger)

Øystein (1103–23), of whom there survives a fascinating 'portrait' from Munkeliv, could have been personally involved in bringing masons from abroad to work in Bergen and subsequently train local builders. Lidén admits that his explanation is speculative. Nonetheless, it is important for how it re-centres the perspective of Romanesque art in Norway, highlighting the possible role of the monarchy and nobility as prime movers in the conscious adoption and dissemination of the style. Indeed, the roles that Scandinavian kings, nobility, and high-ranking local clergy might have played in the adoption of Romanesque styles and motifs has often been acknowledged but perhaps has not been as central to the story as it should be. Recently, however, scholars such as Lena Liepe and

FIGURE 19.11

Sigtuna: St Olof (Arlid Vågen/Wikimedia Commons)

Kjartan Hauglid have begun exploring this problem more thoroughly in relation to architecture, while Sandy Heslop has explored it through his recent contribution on the Gunhild Cross (*c.* 1150).[48]

The Scandinavian nobility was, in fact, instrumental in the Christianization of the region.[49] The Norse sagas and local chronicles frequently place so-called missionary kings such as Olaf Tryggvason (*c.* 995–1000) and Olaf Haraldsson (St Olaf) (1015–28) at the centre of the region's conversion.[50] Indeed, claimants to the Norwegian throne had been nominally Christian since the death of Harald Fairhair (d. *c.* 930).[51] In Denmark, Harald Bluetooth's declaration on the Jelling stone that he made all of the Danes Christian is the most famous pronouncement of a top-down conversion process. Even Adam of Bremen praises the Danish king Sven Estridsen (1047–76) for sending out preachers into 'all' of Sweden and Norway.[52] The historian Anders Winroth goes so far as to claim unequivocally that 'Scandinavian kings, not foreign missionaries, converted Scandinavia'.[53] This view should probably be tempered, but there is little doubt that missionaries could not have succeeded without the explicit support of the Scandinavian nobility.

The Scandinavian sources themselves mention how kings, nobility, and wealthy landowners either raised churches themselves or donated lands on which they would be built. For instance, Olaf Tryggvason was credited with building the first church in Norway at Mosterhamn, which would later be the site on which St Olaf held a *thing* during which the earliest Christian laws were introduced to the country and where there is still a small mid-12th-century church.[54] St Olaf was reported to have built churches in Nidaros (Trondheim) and across Norway.[55] Writing in the late 12th century, the Norwegian monk Theodoric describes some of the buildings that King Øystein had erected in Bergen:

> Eysteinn was a paragon of honesty who governed himself no less than his subjects with moderation and wisdom. He was a king who loved peace, an assiduous manager of public affairs, and above all a fosterer of the Christian religion. For this reason he built a monastery in honour of Saint Michael the Archangel beside the city of Bergen, as one can still see to this day. In fact, he built buildings which were of great benefit to the kingdom in very many places – for example, the palace at Bergen, which was a beautiful piece of craftsmanship, though made of wood, and which has now almost collapsed from excessive age.[56]

FIGURE 19.12

Husaby: view from the west (Hans. A. Rosbach/Wikimedia Commons)

Many of the Romanesque buildings described here either were royally sponsored foundations or had direct royal associations. Lund is an important example. Sven Estridsen gave a large land grant to construct a church in Lund, the earliest documented instance of such a gift.[57] Sven also gave a grant to Dalby, which had the earliest known scriptorium in Denmark and that produced the Dalby Book, the earliest known illuminated manuscript produced in Scandinavia.[58] His son St Cnut IV (1080–86) made an even larger grant in 1085 for a church in Lund that was probably the late 11th-century structure incorporated into the north wall of the cathedral in the course of its 12th-century reconstruction.[59] Ultimately Sven's son and St Cnut IV's younger brother, King Erik I (1096–1103), travelled to Rome and met with Pope Paschal II, securing canonisation for his murdered brother and an independent archbishopric at Lund to serve the whole of Scandinavia. Lund thus became a bulwark against the claims of Hamburg-Bremen and reoriented power to the Kingdom of Denmark.[60] The first phase in the construction of Lund Cathedral, during which the crypt was constructed, took place under Archbishop Asser Thorkilson

(d. 1137) and during the reign of King Niels (1104–34), the youngest son of Sven Estridsen. Asser was succeeded by his ambitious and talented nephew Eskil, a friend of Bernard of Clairvaux, who likely oversaw much of the next phase of construction and probably consecrated the high altar in 1145–46.[61]

It is in this context that we might reassess the style of Lund Cathedral. Given its undeniable importance as the first archbishopric in Scandinavia, what happens if, instead of regarding Lund as simply influenced by continental examples, we see Lund foremost as a project with royal and regional support? First, we may surmise that the Rhenish-Lombardic features that define the building's plan and decoration carried prestige value. Adopting forms and plans that echoed imperial buildings like Speyer and Mainz enhanced the value of Lund by association. Indeed, at the time of Lund's planning and initial construction, the cathedrals of Speyer, Mainz, and those in Lombardy represented the most 'modern' or prestigious styles in the Empire. Second, the Danish kings and archbishops who were instrumental in raising Lund must have been well aware of architectural trends in Germany and Italy. They were likely responsible for arranging for foreign master masons such as Donatus to travel to Scandinavia and are the only candidates with the financial and material resources to support the building's construction. If this were the case, then adoption of the Rhenish-Lombardic style at Lund would have shown the Danes' capabilities as builders and patrons to both international and local audiences.

That Scandinavian patrons were instrumental in the construction of important Romanesque buildings and thus contributed to the dissemination of the style is further evidenced by the 12th-century donor portraits in the church of Vä (Figure 19.13 and Colour Plate XXVI (bottom)). As previously discussed, the small church has numerous parallels with Lund, notably its portal sculpture. But it was also a royal foundation and was probably initially patronized by King Niels and his wife Queen Margaret Fredkulla. These are the most likely identities of the figures depicted in the paintings on the chancel arch, although King Valdemar the Great (1154–82) and Queen Sofia have also been suggested.[62] Painted in an Italo-Byzantine style, the queen holds a model of a two-towered church while the king offers a reliquary. Moreover, above the vestibule in the church's west end is a tribune with three arcade openings that would have been reserved for the king and queen. Thus in the 12th century, Vä would have been a private royal church that not only resembled Lund. It would have constituted a visually striking building in the rural landscape and a declaration of royal power on the Danish border with Sweden. Even the Italo-Byzantine painting style was possibly chosen specifically for its prestige value. Vä remained in royal hands until King Valdemar and Queen Sophia confided it to the care of the Premonstratensian Order in the 1160s.[63]

St Bendt, Ringsted, also has well-documented connections to the Danish monarchy. King Valdemar patronized the rebuilding of the church during the 12th century in part to establish a pilgrimage and cult site for his canonized father Cnut Lavard, not to be confused with the other St Cnut, whose burial site is in Odense.[64] Ringsted became a primary site for the burial of Danish nobility along with the cathedral of Roskilde, which was another royal foundation dating as far back as the early 11th century.[65]

But royalty were probably not the only prime movers of Romanesque art in Scandinavia. As alluded to earlier, wealthy landowners and lesser nobility were also influential in the adoption of Romanesque forms. The parish churches at Fjenneslev and Tveje Merløse are fine examples. The church of Fjenneslev was erected by Asser Rig (*c.* 1078–1151) of the powerful Hvide family, whose founder was Asser's father Skjalm and who himself had founded the church of Jørlunde around 1080.[66] As at Vä, there is a 12th-century painting on the chancel arch at Fjenneslev that depicts Asser and his wife Inge together donating the church (Figure 19.14).[67] If the painting dates to the second half of the 12th century as has been proposed, then it was likely commissioned by his son Absalon, who was one of the most powerful churchmen in 12th-century Denmark and was later archbishop of Lund. The church of Tveje Merløse, which is one of the best-preserved Romanesque churches in Denmark with its original travertine western towers, also sits on lands owned by the Hvide family and was built in the mid-12th century.[68] Tveje Merløse, like Vä, contains an arcaded tribune that was reserved for the Hvides. The impact of the Hvides in bringing Romanesque art and architecture to Denmark was probably considerable, and one should note also that they were the initial patrons of Århus Cathedral and founders of Sorø Abbey, one of the most important monastic foundations in Scandinavia.[69]

The Romanesque churches in Husaby and Sigtuna follow the same pattern of royal association that we have seen in Norway and Denmark. Husaby was built on land that was part of the *Uppsala öd*, a network of royal estates that provided the Swedish king with revenues. Moreover, Husaby was reportedly the site of King Olof Skötkonung's (*c.* 995–1022) baptism by St Sigfrid. While probably not itself a royal residence, Sigtuna had enjoyed strong royal connections since the 10th century. A bishopric since the 1060s, the construction of its buildings probably relied on some kind of royal support. Indeed, the church of St Per might have included a royal tribune or gallery at its west end similar to those in the royal and noble edifices in Denmark, for the ruins of the church contain an otherwise unexplained opening that looks out onto the nave.[70]

If, as I have suggested, royalty, nobility, and wealthy landowners were instrumental in the construction of Romanesque architecture in Scandinavia, then greater agency should be given to the Scandinavians themselves in the selection of style and form. Although geographic orientation and established historical relationships probably helped to determine the choice of style to some degree, we should entertain the idea that Scandinavian patrons were adopting styles and motifs as prestige markers, whether Lombardic sculpture, Saxon westworks, Italo-Byzantine painting, or Norman arcades. This would

FIGURE 19.13

Vä, St Mary: chancel arch and wall-paintings of donors (Jonas Dahlin)

FIGURE 19.14

Fjenneslev: donor portraits on chancel arch (Hans A. Rosbach/Wikimedia Commons)

better explain the formal eclecticism of Romanesque art in Scandinavia. It might also give us greater insight into how Scandinavians were looking outwards and attempting to participate in an international style, showing how the local or regional was, in effect, international.

THE STAVE CHURCH AND LOCALIZATION

As noted in the introduction, the stave church is the most distinctive example of regional Scandinavian Romanesque art and architecture. Stave churches today exist almost solely in Norway and are exceptionally complex buildings.[71] Although popularly thought of as representative of a pre-Conversion Nordic architecture, this is not necessarily the case. They are first and foremost churches, mostly dating to between 1150 and 1300 and once numbered in their thousands.[72] Scholars have long noted that many of the surviving stave churches contain motifs ostensibly derived from models outside Scandinavia in combination with older and traditional Scandinavian forms.[73] How might the stave churches and their Romanesque motifs fit within the inside out perspective just outlined?

To make an obvious point, the churches must have had some kind of patronage or community support for their construction and for the selection of the decoration. Whether this was a local landowner or someone of higher rank is unclear. The quality of the portal sculpture in the stave churches at Urnes, Ål, and Borgund (Figure 19.15), among others, makes clear they were the work of highly trained professional carvers.[74] The rounded arches, columns, column-portal combinations, sculpted capitals, and certain ornamental motifs, such as chip-carved bevilled saltire or six- and eight-pointed designs (described by Hauglid as Norman sunken stars), probably derive from stone architecture, although it remains possible that pictorial imagery could be a source as well.[75]

The 'Sogn-Valdres' portal design is perhaps the most commonly cited example of stave church decoration to contain imported forms. In her exhaustive survey, Erla Hohler notes a distinctive subgroup that features

FIGURE 19.15

Borgund: west portal (Micha L. Rieser/Wikimedia Commons)

Rhenish-Lombardic motifs, such as lion capital sculptures, round-headed arches, and vine scroll design, as seen in the west portal at Borgund (see Figure 19.15).[76] One persistent question is where did these motifs come from? An often-proposed answer is that they were transmitted to Norway via regional centres such as Lund.[77] This is certainly plausible, as Lund was the ecclesiastical administrative centre of Norway until 1153. But, like the outside in perspective, it fails to tell us why such forms might have been adopted in the first place.

Unlike the royal foundations, it is difficult to know for certain who might have chosen the stave church portal forms or why, as Hohler notes. Nonetheless, if we accept the suggestion that continental styles had a prestige value throughout Scandinavia, then we can extend this notion and apply it cautiously to the stave portal decoration. That is, the 'imported' elements might have been selected and integrated into preexisting or traditional designs because of the associated prestige value that they held. Part of this value could have been novelty; another part could have been that they were associated with stone structures that themselves were linked to the Norwegian and Scandinavian nobility and were thus fashionable at the time. Another speculative explanation is that local lords or communities hired professional artisans who brought recent styles and techniques with them and implemented these with minimal outside input. It is sadly impossible to know which of these possibilities was the case. But it is not outside the realm of possibility that those who built the stave churches chose Lombardic, Norman, or other non-Scandinavian Romanesque motifs to increase the potential prestige of the building and consequently that of the local community.

What is witnessed in the adoption of Romanesque forms in the stave church portals is different to the way these same forms were used in places such as Lund and Ribe. In the stave churches, what we see might best be described as a process of localization – the adaptation of Romanesque forms, in this case from stone to wood, and merged with pre-existing styles and carving techniques. It is a more synthetic process than what is seen in stone architecture patronized by royalty and nobility. Importantly, it gives us a different picture of the varied usage of a pan-European style in Scandinavia, one that makes the international local.

CONCLUSION

This paper has attempted to shift the perspective from one that most non-Scandinavian scholars of medieval art are perhaps most familiar with – that Scandinavia was a last stop in a vector of artistic influence determined by its neighbours – to one that allows greater agency to Scandinavian patrons themselves in the adoption and development of the Scandinavian Romanesque, or, as I framed it, from the 'outside in' to the 'inside out'. I have attempted to explain the adoption of Romanesque styles by foregrounding the potential value of style. As noted in the introduction, the variety of forms and styles and the geographic expanse of the region presents challenges when trying to determine what, precisely, is Scandinavian about the Scandinavian Romanesque. This essay has touched upon a few of them and does not claim in any way comprehensiveness. In the end, perhaps a better way to understand Romanesque in Scandinavia is to accept its transregionality, its variety, its mix of wholescale internationalism and adaptive localism, as a defining feature of its own regional character, chosen by the people themselves.

ACKNOWLEDGEMENTS

I would like to thank the editors John McNeill and Richard Plant for their work and patience in the production of this paper. I would also like to thank Øystein Ekroll for his hospitality in Trondheim and for discussing with me some of the themes that this paper addresses, and the Center for Advanced Study in the Visual Arts (CASVA) at the National Gallery of Art, Washington, D.C., for their initial support when I was a postdoctoral researcher.

NOTES

1 I use 'Scandinavia' to refer to the countries on the Scandinavian peninsula: Denmark, Norway, and Sweden. Finland and Iceland are

sometimes considered to be part of Scandinavia but are more properly part of the Nordic Countries.

[2] See for example M. Blindheim, 'Scandinavian Art and Its Relation to European Art Around 1200', in *The Year 1200: A Symposium*, eds. François Avril et al. (New York 1975), 429–67; E. Nyborg, 'Byzantizing Crucifixes in Central Medieval Denmark: How, When and Why', in *Denmark and Europe in the Middle Ages, c. 1000–1525: Essays in Honour of Professor Michael H. Gelting*, eds. Kerstin Hundahl et al. (London and New York 2016), 27–42; A. Tuulse, *Romansk Konst i Norden* (Stockholm 1968); A. Andersson, *L'art Scandinave*, vol. 2 (Paris 1968).

[3] See especially *Romanesque Art in Scandinavia*, eds. S. Kaspersen et al. Hafnia 12 (København 2003); also Tuulse, *Romansk Konst* (as n. 2), 9.

[4] N. Wicker, 'Would There Have Been Gothic Art Without the Vikings? The Contribution of Scandinavian Medieval Art', in *Confronting the Borders of Medieval Art*, eds. J. Caskey and A. Cohen (Leiden 2011).

[5] Ibid., 202.

[6] Ibid., 216.

[7] The basic properties of Romanesque as defined by E. Fernie, 'Romanesque Architecture', in *A Companion to Romanesque and Gothic Art in Northern Europe*, ed. Conrad Rudolph (Oxford 2006), 295.

[8] K. J. Conant, *Carolingian and Romanesque Architecture 800 to 1200* (London and New Haven 1993 [1959]), 269.

[9] Tuulse, *Romansk Konst* (as n. 2); Andersson, *L'Art Scandinave* (as n. 2).

[10] Conant, *Carolingian and Romanesque* (as n. 8), 269–75.

[11] Ibid., 271–72.

[12] For a recent exploration of this topic, see A. Winroth, *The Age of the Vikings* (Princeton 2014).

[13] Conant, *Carolingian and Romanesque* (as n. 8), 269.

[14] The most accessible survey of Scandinavia in the Middle Ages in English remains B. Sawyer and P. Sawyer, *Medieval Scandinavia: From Conversion to Reformation, 800–1500* (Minneapolis 1993). For a survey that focuses primarily on medieval Scandinavia politics, see S. Bagge, *Cross and Scepter: The Rise of the Scandinavian Kingdoms from the Vikings to the Reformation* (Princeton 2014).

[15] See A. Winroth, *The Conversion of Scandinavia: Vikings, Merchants, and Missionaries in the Remaking of Northern Europe* (New Haven 2012).

[16] J. Palmer, 'Rimbert's *Vita Anskarii* and Scandinavian Mission in the Ninth Century', *Journal of Ecclesiastical History*, 55 (2004), 235–56.

[17] Ibid.

[18] Adam of Bremen, *History of the Archbishops of Hamburg-Bremen*, trans. Francis J. Tschan (New York 1959), 32, 187.

[19] Winroth, *Conversion of Scandinavia* (as n. 15), 110.

[20] Adam of Bremen, *History* (as n. 18), 56; see also Winroth, *Conversion of Scandinavia* (as n. 15), 113.

[21] E. Cinthio, *Lunds Domkyrka Under Romansk Tid* (Bonn and Lund 1957), 28.

[22] Ibid. For the reconstruction of Lund in the 19th century, see A. Åman, *Helgo Zettervalls Domkyrkorestaureringar* (Uppsala 2015), 23–69.

[23] Cinthio, *Lunds Domkyrka* (as n. 21), 198–203.

[24] Ibid.

[25] Ibid., 145–66.

[26] Ibid., 203, note 1.

[27] Ibid., 49–65.

[28] Ibid., 205.

[29] For this and similar sculptures, see G. Zarnecki, 'A Romanesque Candlestick in Oslo and the Problem of the "Belts of Strength"', in *Kunstindustrimuseet i Oslo. Arbok* (Oslo 1963–64), 45–66.

[30] S. Borgehammar, 'Nordens äldsta bevarade byggnad? Dalby kyrkas värde mellan historia och framtid', in *Kyrkobyggnad och Kyrkorum*, eds. J. von Bonsdorff et al. (Stockholm 2017), 16–17.

[31] J. Vellev, 'Viborg domkirke, krypt og gravplats, et tolkningsforsog', *Museerne i Viborg Amt*, 1 (1971).

[32] V. Michelsen and K. de Fine Licht, *Danmarks Kirker: Århus Amt*, Vol. 16 del 3 (København 1976), 1019–21, 1087.

[33] Cinthio, *Lunds Domkyrka* (as n. 21), 202.

[34] E. Møller, *Danmarks Kirker: Ribe Amt*, 19, Vol. I (København 1979), 61–70.

[35] Ibid.

[36] H. Græbe, *Kyrkorna i Vä* (Stockholm 1971), 43, 128, 136.

[37] Ibid., 21–22.

[38] V. Hermansen and P. Nørlund, *Danmarks Kirker: Sorø Amt*, 5, Vol. I (København 1936), 109.

[39] Conant, *Carolingian and Romanesque Architecture* (as n. 8), 274.

[40] H-E. Lidén, *Mariakirken i Bergen* (Bergen 2000).

[41] Ibid., 6–9.

[42] Winroth, *Conversion of Scandinavia* (as n. 15), 120.

[43] A. Bonnier, 'Medeltidens kyrkor', in *Uppland: Landskapets Kyrkor*, eds. I. Sjöström and U. Sporrong (Stockholm 2004), 32–35.

[44] Wicker, 'Would There Have Been Gothic Art Without the Vikings' (as n. 4), 223.

[45] Conant, *Carolingian and Romanesque Architecture* (as n. 8), 272.

[46] A. Bonnier, 'Sockenkyrkorna under medeltiden', in *Sockenkyrkorna: Kulturarv och Bebyggelsehistoria*, eds. Markus Dahlberg and Kristina Franzén (Stockholm 2002), 144.

[47] H-E. Lidén, 'From Lund or Directly from Speyer: Import of Rhenish-Lombardic Impulses as Manifested in Some 12th Century Churches in Bergen', in *Romanesque Art in Scandinavia* (as n. 3), 19–27. Bergen once contained about eighteen Romanesque religious buildings, including Munkeliv and an imposing cathedral. Both were demolished in the 16th century. Only the church of St. Mary's survives relatively intact.

[48] K. Hauglid, 'A Deliberate Style: The Patronage of Early Romanesque Architecture in Norway', in *Intellectual Culture in Medieval Scandinavia, c. 1100–1350*, ed. S. Georgieva Eriksen (Turnhout 2016), 103–36; L. Liepe, *Medieval Stone Churches of Northern Norway: The Interpretation of Architecture as A Historical Process* (Tromsø 2001); T. A Heslop, 'Gunhild's Cross: Seeing a Romanesque Masterwork Through Denmark', *Art History*, 34 (2020), 433–57.

[49] Bagge, *Cross and Scepter* (as n. 14), 60–70.

[50] Ibid., 63.

[51] Ibid., 67.

[52] Adam of Bremen, *History* (as n. 18), 160.

[53] Winroth, *Conversion of Scandinavia* (as n. 15), 146.

[54] Hauglid, 'Deliberate Style' (as n. 48), 108.

[55] Ibid., 109. Ø. Ekroll, 'The Royal and Christ-Like Martyr: Constructing the Cult of Saint Olav 1030–1220', in *Romanesque Saints, Shrines and Pilgrimage*, eds. J. McNeill and R. Plant (Milton Park 2020), 245–58.

[56] Theodoricus Monachus, *An Account of the Ancient History of the Norwegian Kings*, trans. D. McDougall and I. McDougall, Viking Society for Northern Research Text Series 11 (London 1998), 51.

[57] Sawyer and Sawyer, *Medieval Scandinavia* (as n. 14), 134.

[58] Borgehammar, 'Nordens äldsta' (as n. 30), 11. For the Dalby Book, see M. Andersen, 'The Dalby Book', in *Living Words and Luminous Pictures: Medieval Book Culture in Denmark. Essays*, ed. E. Petersen (Århus 1999), 63–66.

[59] Cinthio, *Lunds Domkyrka* (as n. 21), 13–36.

[60] Hamburg-Bremen attempted to reassert its power in Norway and Sweden after the elevation of Lund, but the creation of the archbishoprics of Trondheim and Uppsala in 1164 effectively voided any further claim to authority in Scandinavia.

[61] Cinthio, *Lunds Domkyrka* (as n. 21), 182.

[62] U. Haastrup, 'Stifterbilleder og deres ikonografi i danske 1100-tals freske', *Iconographisk Post*, 5 (2015), 5–49.

[63] Græbe, *Kyrkorna i Vä* (as n. 36), 10, 129–30.

[64] Hermansen and Nørlund, *Danmarks Kirker: Sorø Amt* (as n. 38), 162; B. Bøggild Johannsen and H. Johannsen, *Danmarks Kirker: Odense Amt*, 9, Vol. I (København 1990), 74.

[65] E. Moltke and E. Møller, *Danmarks Kirke: København Amt*, 3, Vol. III (København 1951), 1267–76; also Hauglid, 'Deliberate Style' (as n. 48), 110.

[66] Hermansen and Nørlund, *Danmarks Kirker: Sorø Amt* (as n. 38), 332.

[67] Haastrup, 'Stifterbilleder' (as n. 62), 26.

[68] M-L. Jørgense and H. Johannsen, *Danmarks Kirker: Holbæk Amt*, 4, Vol. IV (København 1990), 2952–62.

[69] K. Esmark, 'Religious Patronage and Family Consciousness: Sorø Abbey and the "Hvide Family", *c.* 1150–1250', in *Religious and Laity in Western Europe 1000–1400: Interaction, Negotiation, and Power*, eds. J. Burton and E. Jamroziak (Turnhout 2006), 93–110.

[70] Bonnier, 'Medeltidens kyrkor' (as n. 43), 33.

[71] The best general introduction to both the architecture and sculpture is E. Bergendahl Hohler, *Norwegian Stave Church Sculpture*, 2 vols. (Oslo and Boston 1999). See also R. Hauglid, *Norwegian Stave Churches* (Oslo 1990); Tuulse, *Romansk Konst* (as n. 2), 13–20.

[72] Tuulse, *Romansk Konst* (as n. 2), 13–20.

[73] Hohler, *Norwegian Stave Church Sculpture*, 2 (as n. 71), 12.

[74] Ibid., 26.

[75] Hauglid, 'Deliberate Style' (as n. 48), 105.

[76] Hohler, *Norwegian Stave Church Sculpture*, 2 (as n. 71), 85.

[77] Ibid., 19, 29.

The Regional and Transregional in Romanesque Europe (2021), 287–304

THE CREATION OF CASTILIAN IDENTITY UNDER ALFONSO VIII AND LEONOR PLANTAGENET

Elizabeth Valdez del Álamo

The marriage of Leonor Plantagenet to Alfonso VIII of Castile expanded Castilian ties to western France and England and consolidated the identity of newly independent Castile as separate from the kingdom of León. Although few commissions are documented as theirs, the arrival of a Plantagenet queen clearly had an impact. The last quarter of the 12th century saw an influx of English artists working in projects in all media throughout Castile. Spanish and English painters collaborated on manuscripts, while architecture was designed to recall the churches of western France. Wall-paintings, apparently by English artists, are attributable to this time. Artists integrated Islamic motifs and techniques into manuscripts, metalwork, and sculpture for Christian clients. As part of this program for distinctive nationhood, Castile adopted a castle as its heraldic symbol alongside the Plantagenet leopard. With this influx of foreign art, ideas, and artists into their realm, Alfonso and Leonor enriched the visual language of Castile, granting the kingdom a clear, identifiable artistic identity. This paper focuses on works that may be characterized as Romanesque.

In 1170, nine-year-old Leonor Plantagenet wed fourteen-year-old Alfonso VIII of Castile. The marriage resulted in the introduction of new artistic currents into Castile, for it was the first marital tie between England and Spain.[1] Furthermore, the marriage was an important tool in the creation of an identity for Castile as a kingdom distinct from the kingdom of León; the two had been separated when Alfonso VII divided his territory between his sons Sancho III, the father of Alfonso VIII, and Fernando II (Figure 20.1).[2] Alfonso and Leonor enjoyed great good fortune since they came to love each other deeply, to the degree that they later died within weeks of each other, as may happen with devoted couples. The politics of their marriage has been studied by José Manuel Cerda, and its artistic impact has been discussed in studies of Leonor by Dulce Ocón, Rose Walker, Marta Poza, and myself, with emphasis on Leonor's contributions.[3] But there is always more to be said. My intention is to consider transregional and transcultural elements in Romanesque art produced during the reign of Alfonso and Leonor, taking into consideration both their contributions and those of their countrymen. But first a short introduction to our *dramatis personae*.

Alfonso (1155–1214) had a difficult childhood: he was orphaned by the age of three and a pawn in the struggle for power between the magnates of Castile and León during his minority. After Alfonso's father, Sancho III, died in 1157, Alfonso's paternal uncle, Fernando II of León, sought to reunite León and Castile by taking possession of the orphaned boy, but he did not succeed.[4] As part of that effort, Alfonso had been kidnapped, then rescued. His maternal uncle, Sancho VI of Navarre, invaded Castile to reclaim territory lost decades before and remained unfriendly. When Alfonso reached his majority in 1170, there were few eligible candidates for queen to be found in the Iberian Peninsula. This, in part, was due to problems of consanguinity that plagued the royal families of Christian Spain. It may have been Alfonso II, King of Aragón, who suggested a marriage beyond the Pyrenees; he was a nephew of Eleanor of Aquitaine and a friend of her son Richard the Lionheart. An alliance between Castile, Aragón, and Aquitaine would effectively surround unfriendly Navarre and expand Castilian ties beyond south-western France to England.[5] The progeny expected from the marriage would fortify their newly won independence from the Kingdom of León and help prevent further landgrabbing by Alfonso's Leonese uncle, Fernando II.[6] In addition, the marriage to an Angevin princess supported Castilian claims to Gascony.

Leonor (1161–1214) was the daughter of Eleanor, Duchess of Aquitaine and Guyenne, and Countess of Gascony; Henry II Plantagenet was King of England, Duke of Normandy, and Count of Anjou. When she arrived in Castile, Leonor carried with her the aura of two prestigious parents with broad territorial possessions. Her father, Henry II, extended his reach through Europe by marrying his daughters into high-ranking families. According to Robert of Torigni, an initial plan was for Leonor to marry

  DOI: 10.4324/9781003162827-20

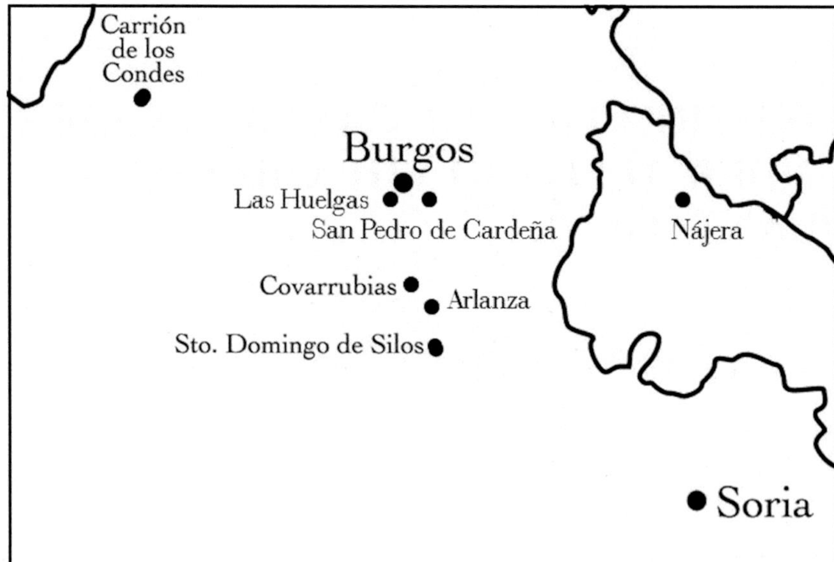

FIGURE 20.1

Burgos and related sites (Map by E. Valdez del Álamo with A. Hill)

a son of the Emperor Frederick Barbarossa, though this was abandoned, and instead she married into the Castilian royal line.[7] For the Plantagenets, an alliance with Castile was a tool in their rivalry with King Louis VII of France, former husband of Eleanor; it also provided an additional ally south of the Pyrenees. For the Aquitanians, marriages into Iberian royal families were frequent, but Eleanor of Aquitaine's marriage to Henry II brought new blood into the Aquitanian line and subsequently into the Castilian line through Leonor.

Together, the Castilian regents patronized and encouraged art that made their realm distinct from its troublesome neighbours. But this is not a paper about patronage; rather, the focus is on how the presence of a Plantagenet queen and others from England modified the choices made for the arts in Castile even where Alfonso and Leonor may not have been directly involved. Although few of the works included here are known to have been commissioned by the royal family of Castile, comparable works are to be found in England, Aquitaine, and Sicily, all with Plantagenet sovereigns. Among the indicators of a shared taste is the phenomenon that the ornamental and iconographic repertoire of English art became widespread.[8] With Leonor in Castile, the last quarter of the 12th century saw an influx of English and western French artists working in projects in all media throughout the kingdom. Burgos, the favoured city of Alfonso and Leonor, and its surrounding area provide a starting point from which the discussion shall turn to other favoured centres, such as Soria and Carrión de los Condes. Spanish and English painters collaborated on a Beatus manuscript produced in the scriptorium of Cardeña, on the outskirts of Burgos, and even on a single miniature for the Bible of Burgos. Since there is no documentary evidence for the commissioning of these volumes, one can only surmise that the presence of an English queen might have something to do with the introduction of English artists into local manuscript production.

The Bible of Burgos serves as an introduction to the collaborations that took place between local and foreign artists in Castile. The manuscript, now in the Biblioteca Provincial of Burgos, seems to be the only surviving volume of what would originally have been a three-volume Bible.[9] That two distinct hands produced the Bible's very appealing Genesis miniature is immediately apparent (Figure 20.2 and Colour Plate XXVII). The Anglo-Iberian collaboration depicts the stories of Adam and Eve in the upper register and Cain and Abel in the lower. Joaquín Yarza Luaces identified the artist of the upper register as English, perhaps trained in Winchester.[10] The frilly borders of the flowers, so characteristic of the scriptorium of Winchester, are similar to the foliage in the Bible, as are the elaborate octopus blossoms with rinceaux inhabited by human figures and animals in the large band at the top.[11] Also characteristic of English manuscripts are the sweetness of the faces and their treatment in profile. Clinging curvilinear drapery, with oval folds separated by parallel S-shaped lines, speak distinctly of the so-called Channel School of painting. The choice of an artist working in the Winchester style may be an example of Plantagenet taste. Henry II chose the Winchester Bible as a gift for a new foundation in Witham (Somerset), and Leonor may have been aware of his preferences.[12] Although we do not know by whom and for whom the Burgos Bible was made, a connection with the royal family, direct or indirect, is apparent.

A Spanish artist painted the lower register of the miniature, the story of Cain and Abel. He was much more active in the production of the manuscript than was the English artist, who seems to have merely passed through Castile. The Spanish artist must have been well regarded in Burgos because he was commissioned to produce the other large miniature depicting the Epiphany (fol. 8v), as well as decorate the rest of this volume of the Bible in addition to the lost volumes, an assumption based upon a fragment that has been discovered sewn into folio 130v

FIGURE 20.2

Bible of Burgos: Story of Adam and Eve (Genesis 2–4), c. *1175–80. (Biblioteca Pública Provincial de Burgos, BP m-173, f. 12r (olim MS 846). By permission of the Biblioteca Pública Provincial de Burgos. See also Colour Plate XXVII.)*

of the *Biblia Antigua* at the Cistercian convent of Las Huelgas. In the Cain and Abel register of the Genesis miniature, the painter reinterprets some characteristics of English art such as the red and blue stripes of the figures' garments, in a manner reminiscent of the English Striped Style. Because the Spanish artist produced additional manuscripts now in the library of Las Huelgas, he may be considered local and most likely formed part of the scriptorium that developed in the Benedictine monastery of San Pedro of Cardeña on the outskirts of Burgos.[13]

This is the same scriptorium in which a new copy of Beatus's *Commentary on the Apocalyse* was soon to be produced (Figures 20.3 and 20.4 and Colour Plate XXVIII (top)).[14] In the Iberian Peninsula, it was customary to read the Apocalypse during Lent, which accounts for the many copies of this text; three were produced during the last decades of the 12th century.[15] One of these was the Cardeña Beatus, dated *c.* 1180 by John Williams on the basis of comparisons to contemporary sculpture such as that at Carrión de los Condes.[16] The revival, in his view, was linked with the Kingdom of Castile and the royal promotion of Cistercian rather than Benedictine monasteries: each new foundation needed its own volume. Rose Walker, on the other hand, proposes that the revival of production may be linked to the recapture of Jerusalem by Saladin in 1187 and the desire on the part of Spanish royalty to defeat the Almohads of the Iberian Peninsula.[17] Certainly, many new Apocalypse manuscripts were produced at that time, but links between the Burgos Bible and the Cardeña Beatus suggest similar and earlier dates for these two manuscripts, of *c.* 1175–80.

An observable relationship exists between the Bible of Burgos and the Beatus, for example, in their depictions of columns with entases.[18] One could add to this the resemblances between certain faces, such as that of Eve in the lower register of the Bible miniature and those of the angels in the Beatus (Figure 20.3). Nevertheless, there are significant differences, such that one wonders whether this painter was a student of the Bible painter or whether the artist was the same, though at a later stage in his career – something that is entirely possible if several years had passed between projects. The Spanish artist of the Beatus was familiar not only with the English Striped Style but also with developments deriving from Byzantine art, for example, the contrast-colour modelling that indicates drapery folds and the distinctive teardrop forms in the clinging damp folds over the body. Several artists were working in the Cardeña scriptorium during the last quarter of the 12th century, and those who were not English sought to emulate the newly imported Byzantinizing styles of their foreign colleagues. By the time the Beatus was being painted, Leonor's sister Joan had married Alfonso's second cousin, William II of Sicily, in 1177, and the decoration of Monreale Cathedral had been in progress from the 1170s to 1186.[19] In that light, stylistic comparisons between the Beatus paintings and the mosaics and sculpture of Monreale are significant, a logical outcome of the long-standing relationship between Spain and Sicily.[20]

An English artist, or one working in an English style, but not the same one as the painter of the Bible, collaborated in the painting of the Cardeña Beatus miniatures (Figure 20.4).[21] The English Apocalypse artist has a greater sense of three-dimensionality, expressed by colourful modelling and active poses, all traits that suggest a later date than the Bible. The damp folds correspond more closely to the body rather than being placed for visual effect, and they evolve into elongated, closely pleated draperies. The figures' long, slender bodies bear slightly enlarged heads with generous mops of hair. Their faces and skin are tinted, and they have rosy cheeks and angular chins. In comparison to the Spanish artist of the Beatus, who works in line, the new English painter uses colour washes and pale highlights to suggest depth. Despite their differences, their shared colour palette unifies the painted decoration of the manuscript.

Leonor, as with Henry II's other children, participated in his penance for Thomas Becket's assassination by promoting the cult of the martyred archbishop, further underlining the transnational nature of the cult. Most significantly, in 1179 she issued the only surviving charter independent of her husband in support of Becket's cult.[22] On this occasion, Leonor took the altar dedicated to Becket in Toledo Cathedral under her protection. The chapel had been founded two years before by Count Nuño Pérez de Lara, Alfonso's childhood tutor, and his wife, Teresa. The chaplain, William, was English and had been Count Nuño's chaplain until the count died in 1177. A copy of the Homilies of Smaragdus at Toledo Cathedral is likely to have been part of that chapel's equipment and is truly multicultural, incorporating as it does, decorative traits of various regions and faiths (Figure 20.5).[23] On folio 74 is a delicate rendition of the Three Marys at the Empty Tomb of Christ; on folio 109, Pentecost and major initials are ornamented with interlace and inhabited octopus scrolls. The artist may have been English, probably working in Toledo itself. Based on the similarities of style, the Homilies may have been produced at about the same time as the Cardeña Beatus, *c.* 1175–80, and, as with the Beatus, the Homilies reflect the mannerisms of scriptoria such as Winchester. The manuscript is clearly identifiable with the English presence in Castile and appropriate for the Becket chapel in Toledo with its English chaplain. Set against a gold background, the figures and architecture are drawn in pen and ink on reserved parchment. The heads of the women and angel are framed by alternating red and green halos, while details of lips and cheeks are highlighted in red wash. The damp-fold drapery that alternately conceals yet clings to their bodies is tinted to suggest shadows along the garments. As each woman gestures to the angel who announces Christ's resurrection, the scene is animated by the shroud swirling against the undulating colours of the marble tomb. Below, the framed band of golden pseudo-Kufic script with entwined white flowers set on a dark background seems just as active.

The prominent band of pseudo-Kufic in the Homilies imitates the bands that frame the surah title in many

FIGURE 20.3

Cardeña Beatus: Christ in Majesty with Angels and the Angel of God Directs Saint John to Write the Book of Revelation (Apocalypse 1[1]), detail, c. 1180. (New York, Metropolitan Museum of Art, 1991.232.3a)

FIGURE 20.4

Cardeña Beatus: Seven Angels Hold the Cups of the Seven Last Plagues; The Hymn of the Lamb (Apocalypse 15[3]), fol. 132r, c. 1180 (New York, Metropolitan Museum of Art, 1991.232.14a. See also Colour Plate XXVIII (top).)

FIGURE 20.5

Book of Homilies of Smaragdus: The Three Women and the Angel at the Tomb of Christ, c. *1175. (Toledo, Biblioteca de la Catedral de Toledo, MS. 44.9, fol. 74r (Archivo y Biblioteca Capitulares, Catedral de Toledo))*

Korans, something a manuscript painter working in Toledo would probably have seen. Its placement below a representation of Christ's tomb is highly symbolic. The use of pseudo-Kufic beneath the image of Christ's triumph over death may refer to Alfonso's wars against the Muslims. His great victory at Cuenca in 1177 is one occasion that might have inspired the prominent placement of the enemy's script in this miniature. Nevertheless, the primary inspiration was most likely Christ's tomb in imperilled Jerusalem, where Christians were also at war with Muslims. Saladin had begun to attack the Crusader State in 1170 and finally took the city in 1187.[24]

The use of Kufic or pseudo-Kufic inscriptions on Christian objects has precedents, but interpretation of the practice is open to debate. In the example provided by the Kufic frame of the silver altar of the Cámara Santa of Oviedo, the script may be variously interpreted as a visualisation of the state of war between Christians and Muslims or as a reference to the Middle Eastern origins of the wooden casket within the altar and its silver encasement.[25] These readings are not necessarily contradictory, and it would be reckless to impose a single approach to the many artworks that bear such inscriptions. In the Homilies miniature, the exotic lettering functions as an evocation of the place in which the pictured events occurred. In a third example, a Kufic frame is also found on an altar frontal in *émail brun* at the monastery of Santo Domingo de Silos (Figure 20.6). Here, a single word is repeated around the frame in opposed pairs. The word, *yumn*, means 'happiness' and probably refers to the joy of seeing the Lamb of God in the central roundel, as do the Apostles who stand at the twelve heavenly portals of a lively, decorative cityscape. The turrets and cupolas crowning the arcade under which the Apostles stand are similar to the elaborate architecture painted in the earlier miniatures of the Cardeña Beatus, especially in the scenes illustrating the second and third chapters of the Apocalypse (Figures 20.7 and 20.8).

Usually dated vaguely to *c.* 1175, perhaps earlier, the panel's chronological range was probably best identified by Peter Lasko: 'the late seventies or even eighties', thus placing it as contemporary with our regents, who generously patronized Silos at that time.[26] The dating is based on the treatment of the slender figures and their clinging curvilinear drapery, and it may have been produced at the monastery of Silos itself, where an enamel workshop had been established around the middle of the 12th century. How the panel was employed has been the subject of some scholarly deliberation. Manuel Gómez Moreno suggested that, sometime after its fabrication, it was combined with the earlier enamel altarpiece of Silos to sheathe the tomb of Santo Domingo, a suggestion accepted by Marie-Madeleine Gauthier.[27] However, as Constancio del Álamo pointed out, none of the extant descriptions of the saint's altar mention the *émail brun* panel, whereas the enamel altarpiece is described as having been there.[28] Furthermore, he determined that the *émail brun* panel is too wide to have fitted into the niche occupied by the tomb. According to Luciano Serrano, the panel was installed on the supports of the high altar before the 18th century when the church was reconstructed.[29] A row of Apostles under an arcade, though more elaborate, is traditional in apse decorations, which is the likely source for the enamel composition and for the *Apostolados* so popular in portal composition of the 12th and 13th centuries.[30]

One *Apostolado* on a grand scale is found in Carrión de los Condes, (Figures 20.9 and 20.10).[31] The parish church of Santiago bears a monumental frieze with figures under an arcade that recalls the friezes of the churches of west France but with the addition of a majestic Christ at the centre, perhaps the first in architectural sculpture.[32] The Apostles on the church façades of western France, for example, Notre Dame la Grande in Poitiers, are arranged in two rows rather than the single line of Carrión and are separated by a stained glass window (Figure 20.11). The figure of Christ appears in a mandorla in the register above them. Similarly, the central tympanum on the west façade of Chartres Cathedral elevates Christ above the apostles. At Charlieu, the arrangement is similar, but all the figures are seated. Although the dating of the Carrión frieze varies greatly, from *c.* 1165 to *c.* 1180, the stylistic qualities suggest it was produced after Leonor had arrived in Spain. Carrión was part of the territory in Leonor's dowry, so the reference to her homeland might be an acknowledgement of that circumstance, even if the queen is not known to be directly associated with this church. In addition, there is a surprisingly close correspondence to the styles of both Cardeña painters. The majestic figure of Christ at the centre of the Carrión frieze shares the characteristic 'organ pipe' drapery folds that are seen in the work of the English artist of the Cardeña Beatus, a similarity most likely due to the mutual interest

FIGURE 20.6

Silos, Monastic Museum of Santo Domingo: altar frontal showing Apostolado, émail brun and cabochons on a wooden core, c. *1180 (52 × 253 × 2.5 cm) (C. and E. V. del Álamo by permission of the Monastery of Silos)*

FIGURE 20.7

Silos, Monastic Museum of Santo Domingo: altar frontal, detail showing Apostle, (C. and E. V. del Álamo by permission of the Monastery of Silos)

FIGURE 20.8

Cardeña Beatus: The Angel of the Church of Sardis with Saint John (Apocalypse 3^{3-6}, fol. 5r, c.1180. New York, Metropolitan Museum of Art, 1991.232.4)

in Classical and Byzantine art. The Apostles, produced by several sculptors, share the clinging curvilinear draperies of the Spanish painter.

Finally, it is interesting to note that the Carrión apostles stand under polylobed arches, an exotic detail ultimately derived from Islamic art. There was a significant Muslim population in the town, so such decorative devices may have been easily available to the designer of the portal.[33] On the other hand, there is a precedent for polylobed arches in Christian architecture in the crossing vault and an interior doorway of San Isidoro in León, where it may refer to Alfonso VI's dominion over Hispanic Muslims.[34] Whether the design at Carrión had the same significance is unlikely, given the very different context and structure. More often, cusped arches frame sacred figures, and, when applied to a portal, they enhance the concept of portal as gateway to heaven, a concept shared by Muslims and Christians alike.[35] In this case, the exotic arches may have reminded viewers that the Apostles' mission of conversion was still active in contemporary Castile.[36]

FIGURE 20.9

Santiago, Carrión de los Condes: façade frieze, c. *1180s (E. A. Lastra)*

FIGURE 20.10

Santiago, Carrión de los Condes: façade frieze, Christ in Majesty with Tetramorph, c. *1180s (J. A. Olañeta)*

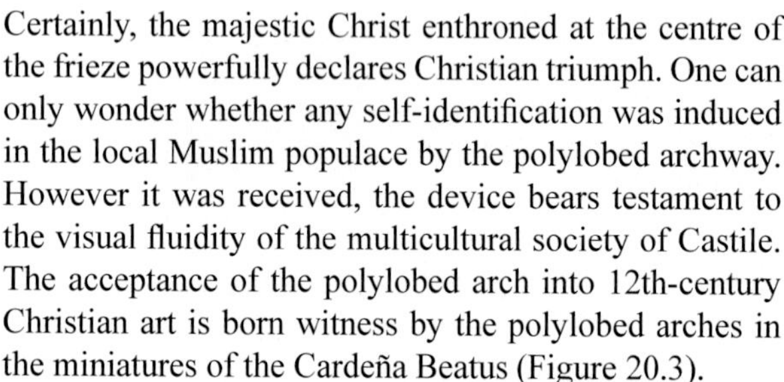

Certainly, the majestic Christ enthroned at the centre of the frieze powerfully declares Christian triumph. One can only wonder whether any self-identification was induced in the local Muslim populace by the polylobed archway. However it was received, the device bears testament to the visual fluidity of the multicultural society of Castile. The acceptance of the polylobed arch into 12th-century Christian art is born witness by the polylobed arches in the miniatures of the Cardeña Beatus (Figure 20.3).

The *Apostolado* is not the only reference to the churches of Poitou in contemporary Castile. The church of Santo Domingo in Soria echoes Poitevin design more closely than does Carrión (Figure 20.12). At Soria, a double arcade is crowned by a rose window, and the strongly slanting sides of the roof evoke Poitiers, yet the whole is much more sober than the Poitevin church. Rather than being filled with figures, the arcades are left blank, providing greater emphasis on the portal and rose. No document links the royal family to this church, as Esther Lozano Lopez has demonstrated.[37] Nevertheless, the ties that link Castile with the Angevin Empire are manifest in the design of Santo Domingo de Soria, built before *c.* 1185.[38] It is apparent that, whoever commissioned it, perhaps the parish itself, wished to evoke this transregional connection. Furthermore, the citizens of Soria must have harboured affection for the king who spent much of his childhood there. The bond between the regents and citizens was marked by Alfonso and Leonor's appearance in Soria shortly after their marriage.

The wall-paintings of the tower at the monastery of San Pedro of Arlanza, apparently by English artists, are also attributable to the era of Alfonso and Leonor, *c.* 1200.[39] Exactly how this tower chamber was employed is a matter of speculation. It may have formed part of the abbot's residence; it may have been a ceremonial hall for visiting dignitaries; or it may have served as a treasury of some sort: the tower is called the Tower of the Treasury (Torre del Tesoro). Arlanza was the burial place of Fernán González, founder of the county of Castile and ancestor of Castilian kings, so there were often royal visits to the monastery. The Castilian allegiance was prominently displayed by placing the emblem of the castle over one of the doorways (Figure 20.13). The introduction of Castilian arms in red and yellow was perhaps Alfonso and Leonor's most enduring contribution to the visualization of a Castilian identity. The Plantagenet arms, featuring leopards on a blue ground, were already established by the time of Leonor's grandfather, Geoffrey Plantagenet, as can be seen on his funerary enamel at Le Mans. Other examples of Alfonso and Leonor's arms may be seen on a column at the Hospital del Rey, the king's hospital in Burgos, founded in 1195 (Figure 20.14), on which both the castle and leopard are carved. Other, more personal examples include a stole and maniple with red and blue castles which Leonor embroidered and sent to the royal treasury of San Isidoro, the first, in 1197, the year that her daughter Berenguela married Alfonso IX of León, and the second, the following year (Figure 20.15 and Colour Plate XXVIII (bottom)). In golden stitches, the queen identified herself:

> ALIENOR REGINA CASTELLE FILIA +
> HENRICI REGIS ANGLIAE ME FECIT+
> SUB ERA MCCXXXV ANNOS+/
> SUB ERA MCCXXXVI ANNOS+
> Eleanor Queen of Castile. daughter
> Of Henry King of England, made me
> In ERA 1235 (1197)/
> In ERA 1236 (1198)

One of the best-known donations of Alfonso and Leonor was made in 1187 to the Cistercian convent they founded in 1180, the site of their future burial, Las Huelgas. The foundation of Las Huelgas was an important element in the royal programme to identify Castile as a site of independent royalty separate from León. Alfonso VIII and Leonor effectively drew on a tradition in both their families: a royal pantheon in León, another in Fontevraud, both convents in which aristocratic nuns cared for the bodies and souls of royal families.[40] The Castilians could, in fact, look back to their own traditional *infantado* at Covarrubias, not far from Burgos. But that seat was empty because the infanta doña Sancha Raimúndez, who

FIGURE 20.11

Poitiers, Notre Dame la Grande: west front, c. *1130 (John McNeill)*

FIGURE 20.12

Soria: Santo Domingo (C. and E. V. del Álamo)

FIGURE 20.13

Barcelona, Museu Nacional d'Art de Catalunya: wall-painting from San Pedro, Arlanza, c. *1200 (Museu Nacional d'Art de Catalunya, Barcelona)*

FIGURE 20.14

Burgos, Hospital del Rey: Plantagenet and Castilian arms. Limestone, c. *1200*

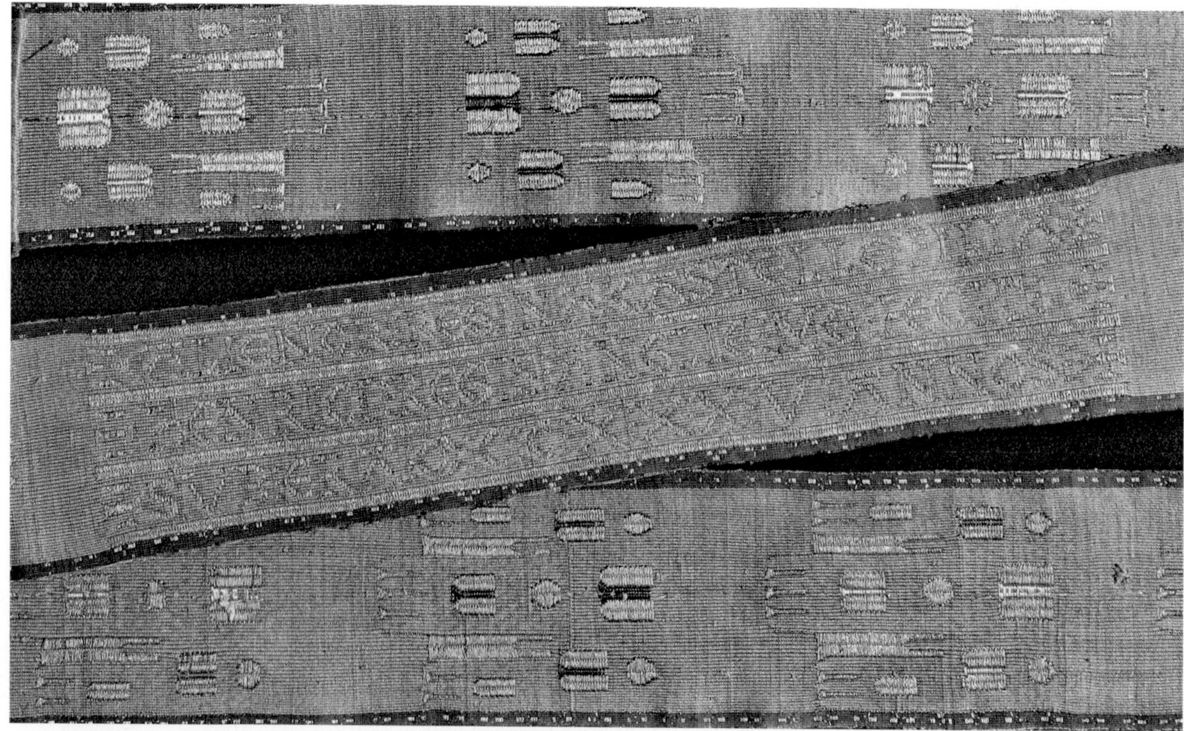

FIGURE 20.15

León, Museo San Isidoro de León: Leonor Plantagenet, embroidered stole and maniple, silk with gold thread (Therese Martin). See also Colour Plate XXVIII (bottom).

last held the *infantado*, was loyal to León and granted Covarrubias to León in her will of 1159.[41] Following tradition, Alfonso and Leonor's daughter Costanza took on the role of *domina*, that is, the lady of the convent, a position distinct from the abbess. The queen very likely was the deciding factor in the decision to commission an English or west French master, Ricardo, to direct the construction of Las Huelgas, for which he was compensated in 1203.[42] One could describe this design as transregional as well. However, as Las Huelgas is clearly early Gothic in style, a discussion of its architecture would stray from my purpose – which is to discuss work that may be deemed Romanesque, and so, I conclude this mention of architecture under Alfonso and Leonor by saying that they seem to have introduced Gothic architecture to Castile. But that is a topic for another paper.

NOTES

1 J. M. Cerda, 'Leonor Plantagenet y la consolidación castellana en el reinado de Alfonso VIII', *Anuario de Estudios Medievales,* 42 (2012), 629–52; J. M. Cerda, 'The Marriage of Alfonso VIII of Castile and Leonor Plantagenet: The First Bond Between Spain and England in the Middle Ages', in *Les stratégies matrimoniales dans l'aristocratie (X^e^–XIIIe Siècles)*, ed. M. Aurell (Turnhout 2013), 143–53. Eleanor, or Leonor, of England is also known as Leonor Plantagenet outside Great Britain.

2 Cerda, 'Leonor Plantagenet y la consolidación' (as n. 1), 631.

3 Cerda, 'Leonor Plantagenet y la consolidación' (as n. 1); D. Ocón Alonso, 'Alfonso VIII, la llegada de las corrientes artísticas de la corte inglesa y el bizantinismo de la escultura hispánica a fines del siglo XII', in *Alfonso VIII y su época, II Curso de Cultura Medieval* (Aguilar de Campóo 1992), 307–20; D. Ocón Alonso, 'El papel artístico de las reinas hispanas a fines del Siglo XII: Leonor de Castilla y Sancha de Aragón', in *La Mujer en el Arte Español* (Madrid 1997); R. Walker, 'Leonor of England, Plantagenet Queen of King Alfonso VIII of Castile and Her Foundation of the Cistercian Abbey of Las Huelgas: In Imitation of Fontevraud?' *Journal of Medieval History,* 31 (2005), 346–68; R. Walker, 'Leonor of England and Eleanor of Castile: Anglo-Iberian Marriage and Cultural Exchange in the Twelfth and Thirteenth Centuries', in *England and Iberia in the Middle Ages*, ed. María Bullón-Fernández (Gordonsville 2007), 67–87; E. Valdez del Álamo, 'Como la reina Leonor de Inglaterra impactó en el románico de Castilla', *Románico,* 20 (2015), 98–105; M. Poza Yagüe, 'Una cum uxore mea: La dimensión artística de un reinado. entre las certezas documentales y las especulaciones iconográficas', in *Alfonso VIII y Leonor de Inglaterra: Confluencias Artísticas en el Entorno de 1200*, eds. M. Poza Yagüe and D. Olivares (Madrid 2017), 71–108; E. Valdez del Álamo, 'Leonor Plantagenet: Reina y Mecenas', in *Alfonso VIII y Leonor de Inglaterra* (as n. 3), 241–60; E. Valdez del Álamo, 'The Marriage of Castile and England as Seen in the Bible of Burgos', in *Manuscripts, Iconography, and the Late Medieval Viewer: Essays in Honor of Adelaide Bennett Hagens*, eds. P. A. Patton and J. K. Golden (Princeton 2017), 85–90.

4 R. Jiménez de Rada, *Historia de Rebus Hispanie Siue Historia Gothica, Corpus Christianorum*, ed. J. Fernández Valverde (Turnhout 1987), lib. 7, cap. 14, line 50; lib. 7, cap. 15; J. González, *El reino de Castilla en la época de Alfonso VIII*, 3 vols. (Madrid 1960), I, 160–66; E. Valdez del Álamo, 'Homage to the Child King: The Adoration of the Magi in Twelfth-Century Castilian Portals', in *Mittelalterliche Bauskulptur in Frankreich und Spanien: Im Spannungsfeld des Chartreser Königsportals und des Pórtico de la Gloria in Santiago de Compostela*, eds. C. Rückert and J. Staebel (Frankfurt am Main 2010), 251–66.

5 González, *El reino* (as n. 4), I, 185.

6 J. M. Cerda, 'La dot gasconne d'Aliénor d'Angleterre: entre royaume de Castille, royaume de France et royaume d'Angleterre', *Cahiers de Civilisation Médiévale,* 54 (2011), 225–42, esp. 228–29.

7 Robert de Torigny, *The Chronicle of Robert de Torigni,* ed. R. Howlett (Rolls Series, Chronicles of the Reigns of Stephen, Henry II, and Richard, I, 4 vols. (London 1882), 224, 234.

8 M.-M. Gauthier, 'Le goût Plantagenet', in *Stil und Uberlieferung in der Kunst des Abendlandes, Epochen Europäischer Kunst*, vol. 1 (Berlin 1967), 139–55.

9 J. Yarza Luaces, 'Biblia de San Pedro de Cardeña', in *Vestiduras ricas: El Real Monasterio de Las Huelgas y su época*, ed. J. Yarza Luaces (Madrid 2007), cat. 1, 140–41; Valdez del Álamo, 'The Marriage of Castile and England' (as n. 3), 85–90.

10 J. Yarza Luaces, 'Las miniaturas de la Biblia de Burgos', *Archivo Español de Arte*, 166 (1969), 185–203, esp. 203; J. Yarza Luaces, 'La miniatura en Galicia, León y Castilla en tiempos de Maestro Mateo', in *Actas, Simposio internacional sobre: O Portico da Gloria e a Arte do seu Tempo* (Santiago de Compostela 1991), 319–35, esp. 321–22; J. Yarza Luaces, *Vestiduras ricas* (as n. 9); J. Williams, 'Bible', *The Art of Medieval Spain a.d. 500–1200* (New York 1993), 299–300.

11 Oxford, Bodl. Lib., MS Auct. D.2.4, fol. 1r; Madrid, Biblioteca Nacional, MS VITR/23/8, fol. 15r; C. M. Kauffmann, *Romanesque Manuscripts 1066–1190* (London 1975), cat. 77, cat. 81, 104–05, 107, Figures 213, 216. A note on fol. 182 makes it clear that the Madrid manuscript was in Spain by the 16th century, although it is not known when it arrived.

12 For a recent account of the extent and limits of Henry II's involvement with the Winchester Bible, see C. Norton, 'Henry of Blois, St Hugh and Henry II: The Winchester Bible Reconsidered', in *Romanesque Patrons and Processes*, eds. J. Camps et al. (Milton Park 2018), 117–41; Gauthier, 'Le goût Plantagenet' (as n. 8), 143, n. 12.

13 S. Herrero González, *Códices miniados en el Monasterio de Las Huelgas* (Madrid and Barcelona 1988), 23–51; eadem, 'Códices iluminados en Burgos y provincia anteriores al siglo XI', in *Estudio e Investigación: Biblioteca*, vol. 16, eds. F. Pérez Rodríguez, Arte antiguo y medieval en la Ribera del Duero (Aranda de Duero 2001), 127–40; Yarza Luaces, *Vestiduras ricas* (as n. 9), 140; Yarza Luaces, 'La Miniatura en Galicia' (as n. 10), 322–23; J. Williams, *The Illustrated Beatus: A Corpus of the Illustrations of the Commentary on the Apocalypse: The Twelfth and Thirteenth Centuries* (London–Turnhout 2003), 26–27.

14 The Beatus manuscript is presently divided between Madrid, Museo Arqueológico Nacional (Ms. 2); New York, The Metropolitan Museum of Art (MMA 1991.232.1–10); Madrid, Coll. Francisco Zabálburu y Basabe; and Girona, Museu d'Art (Inv. 47). Yarza Luaces, 'La Miniatura en Galicia' (as n. 10), 323–24, identifies a Cardeña origin; Williams, *The Twelfth and Thirteenth Centuries* (as n. 13), 26–27, is torn between Cardeña and Toledo.

15 Williams, *The Eleventh and Twelfth Centuries* (as n. 13), 9–10.

16 Ibid. (as n. 13), 9, 25, 27.

17 R. Walker, 'La producción de los Beatos durante el reinado de Alfonso VIII de Castilla y Leonor de Inglaterra ¿una respuesta a la caída de Jerusalén?' in *Alfonso VIII y Leonor de Inglaterra: confluencias artísticas en el entorno de 1200*, eds. M. Poza Yagüe and D. Olivares (Madrid 2017), 357–72.

18 W. Wixom, 'Picturing the Apocalypse: Illustrated Leaves from a Medieval Spanish Manuscript', *The Metropolitan Museum of Art Bulletin*, 59/iii (Winter 2002), 3–46, esp. 23; Williams, *The Twelfth and Thirteenth Centuries* (as in n. 13), 9, 25–26.

19 For a recent summary of the chronology of Monreale, see S. Brodbeck, 'Monreale from Its Origin to the End of the Middle Ages', in *A Companion to Medieval Palermo*, ed. A. Nef (Leiden 2013), 383–412, esp. 400.

20 In 1117, Elvira, a daughter of Alfonso VI, married Roger II of Sicily. Their son William I had wed Margaret of Navarra, aunt of Alfonso VIII, by 1152. The family relationship was extended once again when Alfonso VIII married Leonor Plantagenet, and his second cousin, William II, married her sister Joan. For the impact of these relationships on Spanish art, see Ocón Alonso, 'Alfonso VIII' (as in n. 3), 307–20; eadem, 'El papel artístico' (as in n. 3), 27–39.

[21] John Williams casts doubt on the nationality of the artist, probably unnecessarily. See J. Williams, 'Orientations: Christian Spain and the Art of Its Neighbors', in *The Art of Medieval Spain a.d. 500–1200* (New York 1993), 13–25, esp. 24; Williams, *The Twelfth and Thirteenth Centuries* (as n. 13), 26–27.

[22] González, *El reino* (as n. 4), 191, 373–74; G. Cavero Domínguez, ed., *Tomás Becket y la Península Ibérica (1170–1230)* (León 2013); M. Poza Yagüe, 'Santo Tomás Becket', *Revista Digital de Iconografía Medieval,* 5 (2013), 53–62, esp. 56; J. M. Cerda, 'Leonor Plantagenet and the Cult of Thomas Becket in Castile', in *The Cult of Thomas Becket in the Plantagenet World, c. 1170–c.1220*, eds. P. Webster and M.-P. Gelin (Woodbridge 2016), 133–45, esp. 136–38. Unfortunately, for those interested in Becket, the chapel was transformed when it was appropriated by Count Alvarez de Luna in 1435 and rededicated to Santiago.

[23] Toledo, Cathedral Archive Ms. 44.9 and 44.10. J. Janini, R. Gonzálvez, and A. M. Mundó, *Catálogo de los Manuscritos Litúrgicos de la Catedral de Toledo*, Publicaciones del Instituto Provincial de Investigaciones y Estudios Toledanos. Serie Tercera, Estudios, Catálogos, Repertorios, 11 (Toledo 1977), 183–84, cat. 173; J. Williams, 'Imaginería apocalíptica en el románico tardío español', in *Actas, O Portico da Gloria e a arte do seu tempo* (Santiago de Compostela 1991), 371–82, esp. 375; Williams, *The Art of Medieval Spain* (as in n. 10), 303–04, cat. 55.

[24] J. Riley-Smith, 'The Crusades 1095–1198', in *The New Cambridge Medieval History*, vol. 4, eds. D. Luscombe and J. Riley-Smith (Cambridge 2004), 534–63, esp. 557; Walker, 'La producción de los Beatos' (as in n. 17).

[25] J. D. Dodds, 'Islam, Christianity, and the Problem of Religious Art', in *The Art of Medieval Spain a.d. 500–1200* (New York 1993), 27–37, esp. 34–35; J. Harris, 'Redating the Arca Santa of Oviedo', *The Art Bulletin,* 77 (1995), 82–93, esp. 89.

[26] P. Lasko, *Ars Sacra: 800–1200* (Harmondsworth 1972), 230–31; B. Boehme, 'Panels from Urna of Saint Dominc of Silos', in *The Art of Medieval Spain a.d. 500–1200* (New York 1993), 277–79; M. L. Martín Ansón, 'Los esmaltes silenses: Problematica sobre su orígen', in *De Limoges a Silos* (Madrid, Brussels, and Santo Domingo de Silos 2001), 257–77, esp. 269; C. del Álamo and E. Valdez del Álamo, 'Retablo con esmaltes de Silos', in *De Limoges a Silos* (Madrid, Brussels, and Santo Domingo de Silos 2001), 298–315, esp. 305–6, 310–12.

[27] M. Gómez Moreno, 'La urna de Santo Domingo de Silos', *Archivo Español de Arte,* 14 (1941), 493–502; M.-M. Gauthier, 'L'atelier d'orfèvrerie de Silos à l'époque romane', in *El Románico en Silos* (Santo Domingo de Silos 1990), 377–87, esp. 384–85.

[28] C. del Álamo, 'El sepulcro-altar del cuerpo santo en la antigua iglesia de Silos. Intento de reconstrucción', in *Silos. Un Milenio, 4, Arte, Stvdia Silensia, 28*, ed. A. C. Ibáñez Pérez (Santo Domingo de Silos 2003), 543–66, esp. 563–65.

[29] L. Serrano, *El Real Monasterio de Santo Domingo de Silos* (Burgos 1926), 157; del Álamo, 'El sepulcro-altar' (as n. 28), 565.

[30] Gauthier, 'Le gout Plantagenet' (as n. 8), 150–51.

[31] M. A. García Guinea, *El arte románico en Palencia*, 1961, 4th ed. (Palencia 1990), 126; S. Moralejo Álvarez, 'Esculturas compostelanas del último tercio del siglo doce', *Cuadernos de Estudios Gallegos,* 28 (1974), 294–310; J. D'Emilio, 'Tradición local y aportaciones foráneas en la escultura tardía: Compostela, Lugo y Carrión', in *Actas. O Portico Da Gloria e a arte do seu tempo*, Santiago de Compostela, 3–8 de outubro de 1988 (Santiago de Compostela 1991), 83–101, esp. 89–90; E. A. Lastra, 'Biography of a City: Art, Urbanization, and Shifting Structures of Power in Carrión de los Condes, 1050–1200' (unpublished PhD diss., University of Pennsylvania, 2017), 250–53, 258–61.

[32] Lastra, 'Biography of a City' (as n. 31), 259–60.

[33] *Ibid.*, 39–40, 322–23.

[34] T. Martin, *Queen as King: Politics and Architectural Propaganda in Twelfth-Century Spain* (Leiden and Boston 2006), 106–07.

[35] M. Moreno Alcalde, 'Puertas del Cielo. El Arco Lobulado en el Arte Medieval Español', *Goya,* 295/296 (July 2003), 225–44, esp. 227, 230–32.

[36] Dodds, 'Islam, Christianity' (as n. 25), 36.

[37] E. Lozano López, *Un Mundo en Imágenes: La Portada de Santo Domingo de Soria*, Publicaciones de la Fundación Universitaria Española. Colección Tesis Cum Laude. Serie A, Arte, 25 (Madrid 2006), 26–27, 306, 312.

[38] Ibid., 306.

[39] W. Cahn, 'The Frescoes of San Pedro de Arlanza', in *The Cloisters: Studies in Honor of the Fiftieth Anniversary,* ed. E. C. Parker (New York 1992), 86–109; M. Guardia, 'Pinturas murales de San Pedro de Arlanza (Burgos)', in *Prefiguració del Museu Nacional d'Art de Catalunya* (Barcelona 1992), 174–77; M. Pagès i Paretas, 'Las pinturas de San Pedro de Arlanza en el contexto artístico de su época', in *Alfonso VIII y Leonor de Inglaterra: Confluencias artísticas en el entorno de 1200,* eds. M. Poza Yagüe and D. Olivares (Madrid 2017), 175–200; I. González Hernando, 'Y vivía entre las fieras, pero los ángeles le servían. Poder, saber y representación abacial en el Monasterio de San Pedro de Arlanza', in *En Busca del Saber: Arte y Ciencia en el Mediterráneo Medieval,* eds. A. Uscatescu and I. González Hernando (Madrid 2018), 333–66.

[40] Walker, 'Leonor . . . and Her Foundation' (as n. 3), 359, 362–63.

[41] T. Martin, 'Hacia una clarificación del infantazgo en tiempos de la reina Urraca y su hija la infanta Sancha (ca. 1107–1159)', *E-Spania*, 5 June 2008, 2014, http://e-spania.revues.org/12163.

[42] G. Palomo Fernández and J. C. Ruiz Souza, 'Nuevas hipótesis sobre Las Huelgas de Burgos. Escenografía funeraria de Alfonso X para un proyecto inacabado de Alfonso VIII y Leonor Plantagenêt', *Goya,* 316–17 (2007), 21–44, esp. 24. Cerda, 'Leonor Plantagenet y la consolidación' (as n. 1), 635.

INDEX

(Page references in **bold** refer to illustrations)